STANDARD LESSON COMMENTARY
1997-98

International Sunday School Lessons

published by

STANDARD PUBLISHING

Eugene H. Wigginton, *President*

Mark A. Taylor, *Publisher*

Richard C. McKinley, *Director of Curriculum Development*

Carla Crane, *Assistant Director of Curriculum Development*

Jonathan Underwood, *Senior Editor of Adult Curriculum*

Douglas Redford, *Editor*   Hela M. Campbell, *Office Editor*

Forty-fifth Annual Volume

©1997
The STANDARD PUBLISHING Company
division of STANDEX INTERNATIONAL Corporation
8121 Hamilton Avenue, Cincinnati, Ohio 45231
Printed in U. S. A.

In This Volume

Artists

TITLE PAGES: James E. Seward

Cover design by Listenberger Design Associates

Index of Printed Texts, 1997-98

The printed texts for 1997-98 are arranged here in the order in which they appear in the Bible.
Opposite each reference is the number of the page on which it appears in this volume.

Cumulative Index

A cumulative index for the Scripture passages used in the STANDARD LESSON COMMENTARY *for the years September, 1992—August, 1998, is provided below.*

VI

Fall Quarter, 1997

God Leads a People Home

Special Features

Lessons

Unit 1: Promise to Return

Unit 2: Daniel: Faithful Under Fire

Unit 3: Life After the Return

About these lessons

The focus of these lessons is the captivity of God's people in Babylon, and the fulfillment of His promise to bring them home. The first two lessons highlight the end of the captivity as predicted by Isaiah. Lessons 3 and 4 deal with the contribution of the prophets Haggai and Zechariah to the task of rebuilding the temple. Lessons 5-8 are concerned with the faithfulness of Daniel and his friends while in captivity. The final five lessons emphasize the bold leadership of Ezra and Nehemiah, and the call to repentance by the prophet Malachi.

Sep 7

Sep 14

Sep 21

Sep 28

Oct 5

Oct 12

Oct 19

Oct 26

Nov 2

Nov 9

Nov 16

Nov 23

Nov 30

What a View!

AS YOU CAN SEE FROM the highlighted section of lessons below, this year's studies conclude the six-year cycle of lessons that started in Fall of 1992. If you have been studying these lessons from the beginning of the cycle, now is a good time to reflect on all you have covered. It is similar to scaling a rugged mountain peak, reaching the top, and then surveying the terrain below. What a view!

We trust that if you have participated in this six-year cycle, you have found it to be rich and rewarding. (If you haven't, a new cycle will begin with the 1998-99 lessons.) In either case, the coming year's studies include an instructive blend of Old and New Testament texts.

We begin in the Fall Quarter with the theme "God Leads a People Home," focusing on the return of the Israelite captives from Babylon. Next, we move toward the end of the New Testament for the Winter Quarter, focusing on portions of 1 John, 1 and 2 Peter, and Jude. The theme is "God's People in a Troubled World." The Spring Quarter picks up the tempo with "The Gospel of Action" (Mark). The Summer Quarter rounds out the year with studies from the wisdom literature of the Old Testament.

May the study of God's Word that lies ahead give you a sense of accomplishment, so that when you finish, you can survey where you've been and say, "What a view!"

International Sunday School Lesson Cycle
September, 1992—August, 1998

YEAR	FALL QUARTER (Sept., Oct., Nov.)	WINTER QUARTER (Dec., Jan., Feb.)	SPRING QUARTER (Mar., Apr., May)	SUMMER QUARTER (June, July, Aug.)
1992-1993	Old Testament Personalities (Old Testament Survey)	Good News for All (New Testament Survey)	Believing in Christ (John)	Following God's Purpose (Ephesians, Philippians, Colossians, Philemon)
1993-1994	The Story of Beginnings (Genesis)	The Story of Jesus (Luke)	Good News for God's People (Romans) Set Free by God's Grace (Galatians)	God Redeems a People (Exodus, Leviticus, Numbers, Deuteronomy)
1994-1995	From the Conquest to the Kingdom (Joshua, Judges, 1 and 2 Samuel, 1 Kings)	Jesus the Fulfillment (Matthew)	Christians Living in Community (1 and 2 Corinthians)	A Nation Turns From God (1 and 2 Kings, Amos, Hosea, Micah, Isaiah)
1995-1996	The Story of Christian Beginnings (Acts)	God's Promise of Deliverance (Isaiah) God's Love for All People (Jonah, Ruth)	Teachings of Jesus (Matthew, Mark, Luke)	A Practical Religion (James) God Is With Us (Psalms)
1996-1997	God's People Face Judgment (2 Kings, Jeremiah, Lamentations, Ezekiel, Habakkuk)	New Testament Personalities	Hope for the Future (1 and 2 Thessalonians, Revelation)	Guidance for Ministry (1 and 2 Timothy, Titus) A Call to Faithfulness (Hebrews)
1997-1998	God Leads a People Home (Major Prophets, Minor Prophets, Ezra, Nehemiah)	God's People in a Troubled World (1 and 2 Peter, 1 John, Jude)	The Gospel of Action (Mark)	Wisdom for Living (Job, Proverbs, Ecclesiastes)

Homecoming With Problems

by Orrin Root

NATE IS SO PERSISTENTLY cheerful that friends have dubbed him "The Optimist." They try to trick him into saying something critical or unpleasant, but he refuses. Grudgingly someone commented, "I'll bet you'd have a good word for the devil himself."

"Well," Nate answered with a grin, "he *is* a clever fellow."

How true! We all know how cleverly he manipulated Adam and Eve, and most of us confess that he has manipulated us as well. Still, we are saddened when people respond to God's goodness by turning away from Him. In June of 1995 we studied a lesson series entitled "A Nation Turns From God," and in September of 1996 we followed it up with a series called "God's People Face Judgment."

With this quarter we come to a series of lessons with a more positive theme: "God Leads a People Home." Seventy years of captivity in Babylon are ended. The Lord liberates His people and leads them westward to rebuild their ancient homeland. It is a time of joy; however, we should not be surprised to find that the devil remains as active and clever as always. We shall see people greatly blessed by the Almighty, yet turning away from Him again, as their ancestors had done and as we ourselves have done.

The lessons in this new series are presented in three units, corresponding to the three months of this quarter.

Unit 1. September
Promise to Return

Lesson 1. Here we read of the Jews' return from captivity in Babylon, but we read it from the perspective of a prophecy that Isaiah wrote a hundred years before the captivity began. God had His people's interests in mind, even naming the king who would set the captives free, though that king was not yet born.

Lesson 2. From Isaiah we read about another important element of the Jews' return. They must respond to God's gracious invitation and give Him their trust and obedience.

Lesson 3. Back in their homeland, the Jews promptly began to build God's temple; but in a few years, a combination of circumstances brought this work to a halt. God sent the prophet Haggai to rouse His people out of their indifference and call them back to work.

Lesson 4. God sent the prophet Zechariah to reinforce the call of Haggai. Through a mysterious vision, He said that the Jews would indeed finish the temple; but He added, "Not by might, nor by power, but by my Spirit."

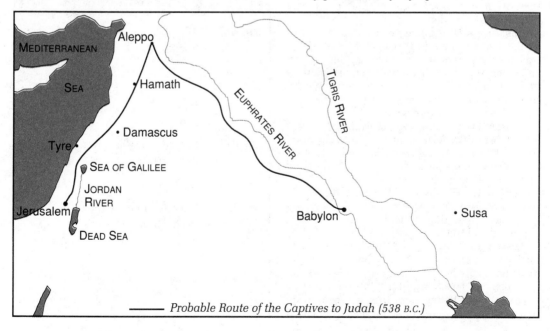

——— *Probable Route of the Captives to Judah (538 B.C.)*

Unit 2. October
Daniel: Faithful Under Fire

Events studied in this unit took place in Babylon during Judah's captivity there. They illustrate the trust and obedience that ought to be seen in God's people today, who are "strangers and pilgrims" in the world (1 Peter 2:11).

Lesson 5. Though Daniel was a captive under orders from a pagan authority, he found a tactful way to decline the rich food of the king's table and eat only what was approved by God's Law.

Lesson 6. Shadrach, Meshach, and Abednego were thrown into a fiery furnace when they refused to worship Nebuchadnezzar's golden image. But the God of Heaven overruled the king and kept His people safe in the flames.

Lesson 7. King Belshazzar's pagan celebration was interrupted by a puzzling message written on the wall. Daniel interpreted the message. It said that Belshazzar's rule was over, and before dawn this prophecy came true.

Lesson 8. Taken captive as young man, Daniel lived in Babylon through all the years of captivity. When he realized that the time of liberation was at hand, he prayed earnestly. He confessed that both he and his people deserved their captivity because of their sins, but he begged for their freedom on the basis of God's mercy.

Unit 3. November
Life After the Return

This unit takes up the story where we left it at the end of Unit 1. Nearly twenty years after the Jews returned to Jerusalem, they completed the Lord's temple there.

Lesson 9. Encouraged by Haggai and Zechariah, the people finished the temple. It was dedicated amidst a great celebration.

Lesson 10. All too soon the liberated captives began to marry heathen women and take up heathen ways. At Ezra's urging, marriages involving heathens were ended.

Lesson 11. For approximately ninety years after the return, Jerusalem was nothing more than a frontier village. Then, encouraged by Nehemiah, the people started to build a wall and make Jerusalem a well-defended city.

Lesson 12. Heathen people near Jerusalem wanted no fortified Jewish city there. They plotted a massacre of the builders, but their plot was frustrated and the wall was completed.

Lesson 13. Cleverly the devil continued to mislead God's people. The last book of the Old Testament tells how they were robbing God and slandering Him. Urged by Malachi, they resolved to do better—and this is a resolution that all of us who serve the Lord ought to make.

From Tragedy to Triumph:
A Time Line of the Captivity and Return

605 B.C.	Few captives, including Daniel and others (Daniel 1:1-7)	Lessons 5—8
597 B.C.	Many captives, including King Jehoiachin and 10,000 others (2 Kings 24:8-16)	
586 B.C.	Jerusalem destroyed, survivors captured, and only "the poor of the land" left behind (2 Kings 25:1-21)	
538 B.C.	Return to Jerusalem, predicted by Isaiah (44:24-28)	Lessons 1, 2
520 B.C.	Rebuilding of temple begins (Haggai 1:1–2:9; Zechariah 4)	Lessons 3, 4
516 B.C.	Temple completed (Ezra 6:14, 15)	Lessons 9—13
458 B.C.	Ezra teaches the Law (Ezra 7:1-10)	
445 B.C.	Nehemiah builds the wall (Nehemiah 2:17, 18)	
430 B.C.	Malachi reproves selfishness (Malachi 3:6-15)	

Be a Leader

by Jeffrey A. Metzger

THE PORTION OF ISRAEL'S history to be studied in the upcoming quarter (the Babylonian captivity and the return homeward) was a crucial time for God's people. Their faith was sorely tested by the troubles and temptations that they faced. During this period, God raised up a succession of strong leaders to confront, correct, and encourage His people, with the goal of leading them home. We will see how the prophet Isaiah, who lived well over a hundred years before the captivity occurred, predicted the captivity and then named the leader (Cyrus) whom God would use to bring His people home. Later prophets (Haggai and Zechariah) addressed the people who had returned home and grown indifferent in the completion of God's house. These were prophets whom God used to stir the people's leaders (Zerubbabel and Joshua) to action.

Other leaders, such as Daniel and his friends, established an example of faithfulness and obedience even in the face of adversity and hostility. Still others (Ezra, Nehemiah, and Malachi) demonstrated courageous and sacrificial leadership in restoring a commitment to God's ways. Their examples illustrate that godly leadership is critical to God's purposes.

Where Is Leadership Learned?

One of the most effective ways to learn leadership is by paying close attention to godly leaders. As you proceed through this quarter's lessons, read and study them with an eye open to leadership lessons. Start the habit of keeping a journal of leadership principles and insights.

Here is an example to get you started: Nehemiah 3. At first glance, this chapter is not one of the most inspiring or captivating portions of Scripture. In fact, one study guide on Nehemiah says of this chapter, "If your time is limited, chapter 3 is a better chapter to skim or skip than others." Don't believe it! There is actually a gold mine of leadership lessons to be gleaned from the contents of Nehemiah 3.

Powerful Principles

Leaders work with people. While some may think of a leader as a rugged, independent sort of person, in reality genuine leaders rarely work alone. Leaders build teams. Seventy-nine names are listed in Nehemiah 3, all of them contributors to the enterprise of rebuilding the walls and gates of Jerusalem. Nehemiah was able to instill within them the vision that he had. Leaders go nowhere without committed followers.

Leaders multiply results. The measure of leadership is not individual achievement, but group achievement. Solomon put it this way: "Two are better than one; because they have a good reward for their labor" (Ecclesiastes 4:9). In the rebuilding of the wall, the "good reward" included additional help, support, and protection, all of which contributed to the success of the project. Because of such teamwork, the monumental task was completed in the remarkable time of fifty-two days (Nehemiah 6:15).

Leaders build bridges of unity. Nehemiah's leadership produced unity from a very diverse collection of people. Consider the different groups mentioned in Nehemiah 3: priests (v. 1), Levites (v. 17), goldsmiths (v. 8), apothecaries (v. 8, a term rendered as "perfume-makers" in the *New International Version*), rulers (vv. 9, 15-19), gatekeepers (v. 29), and merchants (v. 32). Verse 12 tells of one man's daughters who joined him in the endeavor. Such a diverse group became one, because their leader inspired the commitment of all to a common cause.

Leaders persevere in spite of resistance. There will always be some who refuse to cooperate in accomplishing God's work. Nehemiah encountered some men who "put not their necks to the work of their Lord" (Nehemiah 3:5). Why were these men like this? Perhaps they considered rebuilding a wall to be "beneath them." Perhaps they did not approve of Nehemiah's plan, or wanted a bigger voice in decision-making. Sadly, it is still true that many will not participate in worthwhile tasks for God's kingdom for petty, trivial reasons. They refuse to see the "big picture" or to acknowledge that eternal issues are at stake. Nehemiah refused to be deterred by the uncooperative spirit of others.

Such are some of the valuable lessons to be learned from a chapter that some may overlook because it appears to lack excitement. Appearances, however, can be deceiving; a closer look at the chapter has revealed some timely insights into leadership. So it is with leaders: sometimes a person who seems to lack leadership potential simply needs time to be taught and to mature, until he is ready to become a "Daniel" or a "Nehemiah" to his generation.

Learn God's lessons. Be a leader.

Confronting Our Culture

by Jerran D. Jackson

YOUR DOCTOR MAY ASK you if you want to "euthanize" your ailing loved one (physician-assisted suicide is increasingly practiced and promoted). Soon your newspaper will report on debates over nativity scenes on courthouse lawns and over Christmas carols in public school programs. These changes in public life illustrate that Christian beliefs are no longer society's norm. In fact, our culture is becoming increasingly hostile toward Christianity. How should we as Christians respond?

Lessons 5-8 in this quarter offer us some examples of how to serve God amidst a pagan culture. Daniel, Shadrach, Meshach, and Abednego were taken as exiles to Babylon, where the true God was not worshiped. These were dark days for God's people, for Babylonian military superiority was rapidly asserting its control over Judah. Did this mean that Babylonian gods and beliefs were superior to the Hebrew faith? King Nebuchadnezzar seemed to have reality on his side. Nevertheless, in spite of such hostile surroundings, Daniel and his friends remained loyal to their God. Instead of being pulled down by the paganism around them, their faithfulness actually led pagan rulers in Babylon to acknowledge their God! It also resulted in their receiving important positions in the Babylonian government. How did they have such an impact? Let's see what we can learn from these four faithful men.

Integrity

It did not take long for the convictions of Daniel and his friends to be challenged by their pagan environment. Their resolve was tested at their first meal, where the Babylonians served foods not permitted by the Law of Moses. But Daniel "purposed in his heart that he would not defile himself" with the king's delicacies (Daniel 1:8). He was not "a double-minded man," who is "unstable in all his ways" (James 1:8). Daniel was firmly committed to God.

Like Daniel, we will have a positive impact on our culture only if we live with the integrity that comes from obedience to our Lord. Our convictions must not be swayed by the changing winds of political correctness or public favor. Like Joseph with Potiphar's wife, like Shadrach, Meshach and Abednego before angry Nebuchadnezzar, and like Peter and John before the Sanhedrin, we must act upon what God has told us is right. The church has always been weakest when it has sought to adapt to its surroundings. It has been strongest when it has stood firmly for God's unchanging standards and against the tide of public pressure.

Kindness

"You catch more flies with honey than with vinegar," is an often-quoted maxim. Both Joseph and Daniel in the Old Testament prove this to be true. Joseph's trustworthy character led to his being given a position of great responsibility while in prison. The Scripture says that the Lord "gave him favor in the sight of the keeper of the prison" (Genesis 39:21). Similarly, the Lord "brought Daniel into favor and tender love with the prince of the eunuchs" (Daniel 1:9). Daniel's kind and courteous attitude toward his superiors (see Daniel 2:14, 15) was no doubt a key factor contributing to the rise of Daniel and his friends to power, even though they were foreigners.

In confronting our culture with the gospel, we must practice kindness along with our integrity. We often hear the statement, "They won't care how much you know until they know how much you care." In a society where Christians frequently are characterized as "strident fundamentalists," and where rudeness toward authority is accepted, kindness can open doors to a ministry of reconciliation. Genuine kindness has the power to disarm those who are hostile toward Christianity, and to create an interest in our faith. "As we have therefore opportunity, let us do good unto all men" (Galatians 6:10).

Courage

Shadrach, Meshach, and Abednego are prime examples of courage in the face of hostility. Boldly they told Nebuchadnezzar, "Our God whom we serve is able to deliver us from the burning fiery furnace, and he will deliver us out of thine hand, O king. But if not, be it known unto thee, O king, that we will not serve thy gods, nor worship the golden image which thou hast set up" (Daniel 3:17, 18). Courage turns private integrity into public witness.

Christians courageously need to come out of their prayer closet. I am always thrilled to hear believing politicians, businessmen, or sports stars give honor to Jesus for His help in their lives. Similarly, we need to speak kindly but courageously about our faith in Jesus Christ as our Lord and Savior. Our expressions of faith in Him strengthen other Christians and can prompt non-Christians to inquire about the hope that we possess (1 Peter 3:15).

Christians also need to live courageously by their values. This is part of being the salt and the light that Jesus has called His people to be in flavorless, dark surroundings (Matthew 5:13-15). We can point people to God by courageously speaking about and living by our faith.

Action

Edmund Burke observed, "All that is necessary for the triumph of evil is that good men do nothing." Daniel and his friends did not let the evil around them triumph; they acted upon their faith. Their prayer and action spared the lives of all the wise men of Babylon (Daniel 2:12-24). Their courageous actions also led two pagan rulers to acknowledge the true God publicly. Following Shadrach, Meshach, and Abednego's rescue from the furnace, Nebuchadnezzar declared, "There is no other God that can deliver after this sort" (Daniel 3:29). "He is the living God, and steadfast for ever . . . he delivereth and rescueth," added Darius, after Daniel was spared from the lions (Daniel 6:26, 27).

If we want to have a similar impact on unbelievers in our day, we must confront our culture with Christlike actions. We cannot sit on our hands and expect the world to respect or embrace our faith. We must practice what we preach. Speaking to Christians in a hostile environment, Peter wrote, "For so is the will of God, that with well doing ye may put to silence the ignorance of foolish men" (1 Peter 2:15).

Peter counseled "well doing." What can you do? You can speak to your co-worker about joining you for worship. You can write a letter to the editor of your newspaper, commending the Christian servants in your community. You can take an active role in your school Parent Teacher Association. You can become involved in the area hospice organization. You can bless people through personal monthly projects of kindness. You can take a public stand against abortion. You can help a person in your community who is struggling to make ends meet. Daniel Webster, one of America's most respected statesmen, wrote, "Whatever makes men good Christians makes them good citizens." Christlike actions lift up Christ and in turn bless a nation.

Our Aim

Peter wrote to the suffering Christians of his day, "Honor all men. Love the brotherhood. Fear God. Honor the king" (1 Peter 2:17). Paul, who

later would be executed by the Roman government, urged Christians to pray "for kings and all those in authority, that we may live peaceful and quiet lives in all godliness and holiness" (1 Timothy 2:2, *New International Version*). The aim of these men was not to establish a "Christian" government. Their goal was not to have Christian values taught in the Roman schools. Within a pagan setting, Paul and the other apostles evangelized and established churches. Likewise, our aim must be to follow Jesus ourselves and to lead others to follow Him. The impact God wants us to have on our culture must come through our example and our evangelism.

In all our contacts with pagan surroundings, our primary aim must be to transform people by leading them into a personal relationship with Jesus. We will be most effective at confronting our culture with our faith, if we practice integrity, kindness, courage, and Christlike actions. Look at your life. Which of these qualities do you need to develop most as a daily habit? Where do you need to increase in integrity, kindness, courage, or actions? Think specifically; plan practically. You *can* have a greater impact on your corner of the world.

"My kingdom is not of this world," Jesus told Pilate (John 18:36). "Our citizenship is in heaven," Paul echoed (Philippians 3:20, *New International Version*). Jesus did not commission us to take possession of the corridors of power. Jesus did not even call us to "Christianize" our culture. Jesus directed us to make disciples. The Christian transformation of society comes, not through pressure, but through permeation.

Answers to Quarterly Quiz on page 8

Lesson 1—1. Jerusalem. 2. Cyrus. **Lesson 2**—1. wine, milk. 2. David. 3. rain, snow. **Lesson 3**—1. Darius. 2. governor, Zerubbabel; high priest, Joshua. **Lesson 4**—1. an olive tree. 2. might, power, Spirit. **Lesson 5**—1. defile. 2. ten days. **Lesson 6**—1. God, able, deliver. 2. the Son of God. **Lesson 7**—1. numbered. 2. balances, wanting. 3. divided, Persians. **Lesson 8**—1. fasting, sackcloth, ashes. 2. Gabriel. **Lesson 9**—1. Nebuchadnezzar. 2. true. **Lesson 10**—1. true. 2. Judah and Benjamin. **Lesson 11**—1. sepulchres. 2. true. **Lesson 12**—1. mind, work. 2. Sanballat and Tobiah. 3. trumpet. **Lesson 13**—1. tithes, offerings. 2. windows.

Quarterly Quiz

The questions on this page may be used in several ways: as a pretest at the beginning of the quarter; as a review at the end of the quarter; or as a review after each lesson. The questions are based on the Scripture text of each lesson (King James Version). **The answers are on page 7.**

Lesson 1

1. To what place did God say, "Thou shalt be inhabited"? *Isaiah 44:26*
2. What king did Isaiah call the Lord's "anointed"? *Isaiah 45:1*

Lesson 2

1. Through Isaiah, God invited His people to buy ____ and ____ "without money and without price." *Isaiah 55:1*
2. God promised His people the "sure mercies" of (Abraham, Moses, David). *Isaiah 55:3*
3. With what two elements of nature did God compare His Word? *Isaiah 55:10*

Lesson 3

1. Name the Persian king who was ruling when Haggai's prophetic ministry began. *Haggai 1:1*
2. Give the names of both the governor of Judah and the high priest, at the time Haggai prophesied. *Haggai 1:1; 2:2*

Lesson 4

1. In his vision, what did Zechariah see on either side of the candlestick? *Zechariah 4:11*
2. Fill in these blanks: "Not by ____, nor by ____, but by my ____, saith the Lord of hosts." *Zechariah 4:6*

Lesson 5

1. Daniel did not want to ____ himself with the king's food and drink. *Daniel 1:8*
2. For how long did Daniel ask the prince of the eunuchs to test him and his friends? *Daniel 1:12*

Lesson 6

1. "Our ____ whom we serve is ___ to ____ us from the burning fiery furnace." *Daniel 3:17*
2. Whom did Nebuchadnezzar think the fourth man in the fiery furnace resembled? *Daniel 3:25*

Lesson 7

1. *Mene* meant, "God hath ____thy kingdom, and finished it." *Daniel 5:26*
2. *Tekel* meant, "Weighed in the ____, and . . . found ____." *Daniel 5:27*

3. *Peres* meant, "Thy kingdom is ____, and given to the Medes and ___." *Daniel 5:28*

Lesson 8

1. Daniel sought the Lord with "____, and____, and ____." *Daniel 9:3*
2. Who touched Daniel as he was praying? *Daniel 9:21*

Lesson 9

1. Which of these kings is *not* mentioned in connection with the rebuilding of the temple in Jerusalem: Darius, Artaxerxes, Nebuchadnezzar? *Ezra 6:14*
2. As part of the dedication of the new temple, priests and Levites were organized for service. T/F *Ezra 6:18*

Lesson 10

1. Ezra was told that even the priests and Levites were guilty of intermarriage with heathens. T/F *Ezra 9:1*
2. Men from which two tribes gathered to Jerusalem to deal with the problem of intermarriage? *Ezra 10:9*

Lesson 11

1. Nehemiah described Jerusalem as "the city of my fathers' (God, sepulchres, temple)." *Nehemiah 2:5*
2. Nehemiah conducted a survey of Jerusalem by night to view the city wall. T/F *Nehemiah 2:15*

Lesson 12

1. The wall was built, for the people had a ____ to ____. *Nehemiah 4:6*
2. Give the names of the two men who conspired to stop the Jews' efforts to rebuild the wall. *Nehemiah 4:7, 8*
3. Nehemiah arranged for the sound of a ____ to provide a signal to the people. *Nehemiah 4:20*

Lesson 13

1. Through the prophet Malachi, God said that the people had robbed Him in ____ and ____. *Malachi 3:8*
2. God promised to open the (windows, storehouses, treasures) of Heaven. *Malachi 3:10*

God Works for Good

September 7
Lesson 1

DEVOTIONAL READING: Jeremiah 31:1-9.

LESSON SCRIPTURE: Isaiah 44:21—45:8.

PRINTED TEXT: Isaiah 44:24-26; 45:1, 4-7.

Isaiah 44:24-26

24 Thus saith the LORD, thy Redeemer, and he that formed thee from the womb, I am the LORD that maketh all things; that stretcheth forth the heavens alone; that spreadeth abroad the earth by myself;

25 That frustrateth the tokens of the liars, and maketh diviners mad; that turneth wise men backward, and maketh their knowledge foolish;

26 That confirmeth the word of his servant, and performeth the counsel of his messengers; that saith to Jerusalem, Thou shalt be inhabited; and to the cities of Judah, Ye shall be built, and I will raise up the decayed places thereof.

Isaiah 45:1, 4-7

1 Thus saith the LORD to his anointed, to Cyrus, whose right hand I have holden, to subdue nations before him; and I will loose the loins of kings, to open before him the two-leaved gates; and the gates shall not be shut.

. . . .

4 For Jacob my servant's sake, and Israel mine elect, I have even called thee by thy name: I have surnamed thee, though thou hast not known me.

5 I am the LORD, and there is none else, there is no God besides me: I girded thee, though thou hast not known me;

6 That they may know from the rising of the sun, and from the west, that there is none besides me. I am the LORD, and there is none else.

7 I form the light, and create darkness: I make peace, and create evil: I the LORD do all these things.

GOLDEN TEXT: I have blotted out, as a thick cloud, thy transgressions, and, as a cloud, thy sins: return unto me; for I have redeemed thee.—Isaiah 44:22.

> *God Leads a People Home*
> Unit 1: Promise to Return
> (Lessons 1-4)

Lesson Aims

After this lesson a student should be able to:

1. Tell how God was working for Israel's good through the captivity and return.

2. Explain how a nation's moral character can effect God's blessing or His judgment.

3. Suggest ways to disciple others so that they, and their nation, can enjoy God's blessings.

Lesson Outline

INTRODUCTION
   A. Review and Preview
   B. Lesson Background
  I. THE DEPENDABLE CREATOR (Isaiah 44:24-26)
   A. The Lord's Power (v. 24)
   B. The Lord and the Liars (v. 25)
   C. The Lord and His Messengers (v. 26)
 II.THE LORD'S HEATHEN SERVANT (Isaiah 45:1, 4)
   A. The Man (v. 1)
   B. The Mission (v. 4)
    Calendars
III. THE LORD'S MAJESTY (Isaiah 45:5-7)
   A. The Only God (v. 5)
   B. The Famous God (v. 6)
    Chartreuse Fire Trucks
   C. The Almighty God (v. 7)
CONCLUSION
   A. A Way Not Approved
   B. A Way Approved
   C. What to Do Now
   D. Prayer
   E. Thought to Remember

The visual for the first lesson (found in the visuals packet) is a time line that can be displayed throughout the quarter. It is shown on page 13.

Introduction

A. Review and Preview

Because we are Christians, we do most of our Bible study in the New Testament. But the New Testament says that the Old is also for our learning and admonition (Romans 15:4; 1 Corinthians 10:11), so we must study it as well. Over the past five years there have been five series of lessons from the Old Testament:

Autumn, 1993—The Story of Beginnings (Genesis)

Summer, 1994—God Redeems a People (Exodus to Deuteronomy)

Autumn, 1994—From the Conquest to the Kingdom (Joshua, Judges, 1 and 2 Samuel, 1 Kings)

Summer, 1995—A Nation Turns From God (lessons from 1 and 2 Kings and various prophets)

Autumn, 1996—God's People Face Judgment (lessons from 2 Kings and various prophets)

During the next three months we shall see how God's people returned from their captivity in Babylon to live again in the land that God had promised them centuries before. We shall examine both the trials and the triumphs that they experienced. We begin with a text the prophet Isaiah wrote long before the captivity began. Through inspiration from the Holy Spirit, Isaiah was able to tell of future events as accurately as if they had already happened before his eyes.

B. Lesson Background

The prophetic ministry of Isaiah spanned the reigns of four kings of Judah: Uzziah, Jotham, Ahaz, and Hezekiah (Isaiah 1:1). Thus Isaiah witnessed one of the worst kings (Ahaz) and one of the best kings (Hezekiah) to sit on Judah's throne. Much of his preaching exposed the rampant sin that was present in his country. He also told of the judgment that was inescapable if the people did not turn to the Lord in repentance. A sample of this is seen in the opening verses of the book (Isaiah 1:1-9). Later, in the plainest of words, Isaiah prophesied the nation's captivity, and specifically mentioned Babylon as the agent of the captivity (39:5-7). Today's lesson text includes one of Isaiah's prophecies of the end of that captivity.

I. The Dependable Creator (Isaiah 44:24-26)

In the opening verses of our text, the Lord introduces Himself with a description that assures Israel, us, and all the world, that He knows everything and can be trusted to tell the truth.

A. The Lord's Power (v. 24)

24. Thus saith the LORD, thy Redeemer, and he that formed thee from the womb, I am the LORD that maketh all things; that stretcheth forth the heavens alone; that spreadeth abroad the earth by myself.

The Lord describes Himself as *thy Redeemer.* This means the Redeemer of Israel, for this text is addressed to Israel, or Jacob (v. 21). Both names refer to the nation descended from the man Jacob, whose name was changed to Israel (Genesis 32:28). This new name meant "God's soldier" or "God's contender." By the prophet Isaiah's time, however, the nation no longer contended for God; instead, it had become a contender for idols.

Israel's Redeemer is also the Creator: *he that formed thee from the womb*. The phrase *from the womb* suggests the careful, tender forming of an individual rather than a nation. In fact, God did form the individual Jacob, from whom the whole nation descended. He also formed each person in that nation, even as He formed each one of us.

The Lord, Jehovah, not only made us; He made *all things*. Specifically, He made *the heavens* and *the earth*. The sun that warms the whole world, the planets of the solar system, and the countless stars scattered abroad through boundless space—Jehovah made each one and set it in its prescribed path. What power! What wisdom! And all of this God did *alone*: He needed no help or advice from anyone, nor does He today. Shall we set ourselves in opposition to such a Creator? This is what foolish Israel did, and countless foolish people are doing it today.

B. The Lord and the Liars (v. 25)

25. That frustrateth the tokens of the liars, and maketh diviners mad; that turneth wise men backward, and maketh their knowledge foolish.

The Hebrew word rendered *tokens* is the same word used several times in the Old Testament to describe the miraculous acts of God. When doing so, it is usually translated "signs." Examples are found in Exodus 4:17; 2 Kings 20:8-11; and Isaiah 7:14. *The tokens of the liars* probably included magicians' tricks presented as miracles, in order to "prove" that these deceivers were true men of God. Such *tokens* may have also included the signs and omens by which self-appointed prophets or soothsayers pretended to foretell the future and predict success or failure. The Lord declared Himself as the One *that frustrateth* such signs: He showed them to be unreliable by causing events to unfold in a manner different from that predicted by the liars.

Diviners were one group of liars who claimed the ability to discern the future. But events did not match their predictions, and their advice turned out to be bad. Thus the Lord showed that the diviners were *mad*. Here *mad* does not mean "angry"; it means "out of their minds," or "insane." The *New International Version* reads,

"He makes fools of diviners." Divination was one of the occult practices strictly forbidden by God in Deuteronomy 18:10.

Even those known as *wise men* delve into foolish ways when they ignore God. In Isaiah's time these men loved gain rather than God, and found pleasure in the licentious ceremonies of idolatry. Isaiah gave God's warning: their conduct would lead to disaster. About a century later the disaster came. The passing of that century was evidence of God's mercy: He was giving Israel the time and the opportunity to repent. In our day so-called wise men replace the record of creation with theories of evolution and replace God's Word with humanistic reasoning. Then they wonder why disorder and lawlessness grow worse and worse.

C. The Lord and His Messengers (v. 26)

26. That confirmeth the word of his servant, and performeth the counsel of his messengers; that saith to Jerusalem, Thou shalt be inhabited; and to the cities of Judah, Ye shall be built, and I will raise up the decayed places thereof.

As we have seen in verse 25, Jehovah contradicts the words of liars and proves them to be false. In contrast, he *confirmeth the word of his servant*: He does what the true prophet predicts. Future events would confirm the word of Isaiah and establish him as God's servant.

In the next portion of the verse, we read a sample of the *word* to be given by God's *servant* and to be fulfilled at a later time: *that saith to Jerusalem, Thou shalt be inhabited*. Jerusalem was an inhabited city when Isaiah uttered these words, but the Lord had promised that it and other cities would become empty and desolate (Isaiah 6:11, 12). Now the Lord promised a reversal of this: the desolation of Jerusalem would end, and people would live in it once

---

How to Say It

AHAZ. A-haz.
BABYLONIANS. Bab-uh-*low*-nee-unz.
CHALDEANS. Kal-*dee*-unz.
CYRUS. *Sigh*-russ.
HABAKKUK. Huh-*back*-kuk.
HEZEKIAH. Hez-ih-*kye*-uh.
ISAIAH. Eye-*zay*-uh.
JEHU. *Jay*-hew.
JEREMIAH. Jair-uh-*my*-uh.
JOTHAM. *Joe*-thum.
MEDES. Meeds.
SHALOM (Hebrew). shah-*lome*.
UZZIAH. Uh-*zye*-uh.

again. The next line repeats the promise, addressing not only Jerusalem, but also all *the cities of Judah*. They would be demolished by the Babylonians, yet the Lord promised, *Ye shall be built, and I will raise up the decayed places.*

II. The Lord's Heathen Servant (Isaiah 45:1, 4)

Isaiah volunteered to serve Jehovah in spite of the discouraging response he was told he would receive (Isaiah 6:8-12). However, not all of the Lord's servants were this willing. The Lord was also served by people who were not devoted to Him and who did not even believe in Him. He sent the Assyrians to punish the northern kingdom, though they had no intention of serving Him (Isaiah 10:5-7). Likewise Jehovah used Babylon to punish Judah, even though the Babylonians, or Chaldeans, meant to act in their own interest, not Jehovah's (Habakkuk 1:5-7). The next part of our text tells of a king whom Jehovah used to set Israel free—a king who became the Lord's instrument (Ezra 1:1-4), even while he continued to worship false gods.

A. The Man (v. 1)

1. Thus saith the LORD to his anointed, to Cyrus, whose right hand I have holden, to subdue nations before him; and I will loose the loins of kings, to open before him the two-leaved gates; and the gates shall not be shut.

In ancient times a man was *anointed* with oil when he was chosen for a position of power. Kings, priests, and prophets were thus set apart for their work. Calling *Cyrus* the Lord's *anointed* indicates that the Lord had chosen him for a particular task. Cyrus was the Persian king whom God chose to end Babylon's domination and free God's people. We must remember that the entire captivity was still in the future when Isaiah declared this. In this way the marvel of the Lord's prophecy is seen. The Lord not only foretold the captivity and the end of it; He even gave the name of the king who would end it— nearly a century before that king was born!

The Lord promised to hold the *right hand* of Cyrus, indicating the most personal attention.

VISUALS FOR THESE LESSONS

The *Adult Visuals* packet contains classroom-size visuals designed for use with the lessons in the Fall Quarter. The packet is available from your supplier. Order No. 192.

The Lord would *subdue nations before him*, including Babylon. That Jehovah would *loose the loins of kings* is an expression meaning that He would remove the armor that they wore around their waists when going into battle. Thus the Lord would make the kings opposing Cyrus defenseless so that his victory would be easy. *To open before him the two-leaved gates* is another way of saying that God would take away the defenses of Cyrus's enemies. *Two-leaved gates* is more literally rendered from the Hebrew text, "double-doored," and may refer to the strength of Babylon's gates. The phrase *the gates shall not be shut* promises that the enemies would remain defenseless until Cyrus's victory was complete.

B. The Mission (v. 4)

4. For Jacob my servant's sake, and Israel mine elect, I have even called thee by thy name: I have surnamed thee, though thou hast not known me.

Why did the Lord give such special favor to the heathen Cyrus? Why did He give victory, dominion, and glory to a king who did not even worship Him? He did it not for the sake of Cyrus, nor for the great empire that Cyrus built. He did it for the sake of His people. For that purpose He called Cyrus by name a century before Cyrus was born. For that purpose He *surnamed* Cyrus, or gave him an additional name or title. For *surnamed*, the *New International Version* reads, "bestow on you a title of honor." Everything Cyrus was, he was through God's grace. There was no question as to the identity of the real King!

CALENDARS

The 1998 calendars will soon be in the stores. If you dream of expensive sports cars but can only afford a family sedan, you can have Ferraris and Porsches gracing your wall or desk each month. If you grew up with "outdoor plumbing," an Outhouses calendar will remind you of the "good old days." The list goes on and on: there are calendars featuring your favorite breed of dog or cat, various comic strip characters, or famous people, both living and dead.

If the people of God in ancient times had been subject to our modern calendar mania, they would surely have had a "Famous People of Israel" calendar. Monthly pictures might have included Abraham, Moses, Miriam, Joshua, Deborah, David, and Solomon—an impressive array of heroes and heroines who led the Israelites toward their dream of national greatness.

But there could also have been a picture of King Cyrus as a reminder of the lessons God had

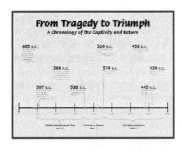

visual for
lesson 1

rising of the sun, and from the west. We may question whether the return of the exiles to their homeland had such an impact. Perhaps, like the prophet, we too should enlarge our vision. Cyrus was raised up so that the Jews could return home and become resettled in their land. In that land, and in the fullness of time, Jesus was born—He who came to provide salvation for all the world and whose kingdom includes many "from the east and west" (Matthew 8:11).

CHARTREUSE FIRE TRUCKS

Who ever heard of a fire truck being anything but red? Well, it seems that red fire trucks are not as visible as chartreuse trucks. When a red fire truck is involved in an accident with another vehicle while on the way to a fire, the other driver's most frequent excuse is, "I didn't see it." For this reason, many fire companies have repainted their red trucks chartreuse. Still, many people want fire trucks to be red simply because they are accustomed to that color.

Centuries before our Scripture text for today, God told Abraham that through him all the families of the earth would be blessed (Genesis 12:3). But Abraham's descendants were comfortable keeping the message of God's love to themselves. They refused to become a "light to the Gentiles." So God did something they did not expect: He sent them, in effect, a chartreuse fire truck. He chose Cyrus—a Gentile—to free Judah from captivity.

Contrary to His people's expectations, God was teaching them that *anyone* can be His servant and know His blessings. Today the world still waits to enjoy God's blessings. He wants His people (the church) to do something that will gain the world's attention and make people aware of the joy they can find in Christ. Is it possible the church needs to repaint its fire truck?   —C. R. B.

to teach His people about the kind of people He uses. God chose Cyrus—a heathen ruler—to overthrow the Babylonians and return the Jews to their homeland, after their long, humbling experience in exile.

God sometimes accomplishes His will through people whom we might consider unlikely agents of His grace. The heroes and heroines He chooses are not always the ones we might choose. Our job, however, is not to give directions to God; it is to trust Him always, no matter whom He may choose to include in the calendars of our lives.   —C. R. B.

III. The Lord's Majesty (Isaiah 45:5-7)

Jehovah chose Cyrus. Jehovah built for Cyrus a mighty empire for the sake of scattered Judah, a nation who was in captivity when Cyrus came to power. Shortly after Cyrus's conquest of Babylon, he set Israel free (Ezra 1:1-4). But this was not done for Israel's sake alone; it was also done for the Lord's sake. The release of the captives from exile demonstrated that the Lord's word was trustworthy. The rest of today's text proclaims the majesty of such a God.

A. The Only God (v. 5)

5. I am the LORD, and there is none else, there is no God besides me: I girded thee, though thou hast not known me.

The Lord is the only true God, and *there is none else.* This one and only God *girded thee* (Cyrus). Thus God wrapped Cyrus in protective armor, while removing the armor from Cyrus's enemies (v. 1).

B. The Famous God (v. 6)

6. That they may know from the rising of the sun, and from the west, that there is none besides me. I am the LORD, and there is none else.

While verse 4 stated that the Lord's calling of Cyrus was done for the sake of "Israel mine elect," here the prophet looks beyond Israel to include peoples throughout the world: *from the*

C. The Almighty God (v. 7)

7. I form the light, and create darkness: I make peace, and create evil: I the Lord do all these things.

God's voice called *light* into existence in the beginning (Genesis 1:3); He then divided the light from the *darkness* (v. 4). Light and darkness are symbols of *peace* and *evil.* In the Hebrew way of thinking, peace is not merely the absence of conflict. Even today, when a Jew greets a friend by saying, "Shalom" (peace), it is a wish for good health and prosperity as well as freedom from strife.

The word *evil* in this verse does not mean anything morally bad. Such acts are man's creation, not God's. The word may be translated "harm"; the *New International Version* uses the word "disaster," while the *New American Standard Bible* reads "calamity." We should be cautious about applying these words to individuals and their circumstances, because the context of this verse is dealing primarily with God's dealings with nations who choose a morally evil path. God raised up the Babylonians to destroy Jerusalem and make captives of its sinful people. This was not an evil act; it was the product of God's justice. But it destroyed the peace of the Israelites along with their city. Later God brought harm to the sinful Babylonians: Cyrus and his army overtook them and their empire. Later still, God brought disaster upon the successors of Cyrus. The swift troops of Alexander the Great swept over the Persian empire and took it away from them. In our own century God has brought evil (harm, disaster, destruction) upon the brutal Nazi regime and upon the vast Soviet empire that once boasted of its godlessness. Any nation dominated by moral evil can expect from God the same kind of evil that He has used to punish empires both ancient and modern.

Conclusion

Not many people today will deny that goodness in America is on the decline. We need not pause to list examples; the evidence is clear. The pressing question is this: What can we do about it?

A. A Way Not Approved

We may think wistfully of how Elijah slew the pagan prophets following his victory at Mount Carmel (1 Kings 18:38-40), or how Jehu overthrew the corrupt government of Queen Jezebel and slaughtered many worshipers of Baal (2 Kings 10:1-28). We may wonder how effective such tactics would be in our time. In fact, some groups are arming themselves and preparing for a day when they believe righteousness will be restored by force. But the teachings of Jesus and the apostles, as well as the example of the early church, contain no indication that God's people should resort to violence.

B. A Way Approved

As seen in the New Testament, the Christian way is to make disciples by telling the good news of Jesus, then to teach those disciples to do all that Jesus commands (Matthew 28:19, 20). Read the book of Acts to see how disciples were made; read the epistles to see how they were taught. In the same ways, we need to win and teach our neighbors, our countrymen, and the people of all the world.

C. What to Do Now

Ask yourself some questions:

Whom do you know who needs to be told about God and His way? Make a short list.

Which of these will you tell first? It may be the one most in need of hearing, the one most likely to respond, or the one you can approach most easily. Choose a name.

When will you tell this person? Set a time. Make an appointment, unless you can talk to him or her without an appointment.

What do you want to tell? List the main points.

How will you begin the conversation? Choose a way that will interest the person with whom you will be talking.

If the last two questions stump you, perhaps you can go along with someone more experienced in visiting people, and see how he tells others about God. Or perhaps you and your friends should form a class and get a skilled evangelist to teach you how he works.

You do know a lot about God and His way. You know people who need to know what you know. If you don't know how to tell them, you need to learn that. The best time to start is now.

D. Prayer

Holy Father, how good it is to have the way of peace and joy set forth plainly in Your Word! Give us wisdom to see Your way through all our problems, and give us courage and grace to help others find the way everlasting. Amen.

E. Thought to Remember

"Blessed is the nation whose God is the Lord" (Psalm 33:12).

Home Daily Bible Readings

Monday, Sept. 1—A Faithful God Deals With Rebellion (Isaiah 63:7-14)

Tuesday, Sept 2—See the Greatness of God (Isaiah 44:1-8)

Wednesday, Sept 3—Return With the Redeemed (Isaiah 44:21-28)

Thursday, Sept. 4—God Defends the Servant People (Isaiah 41:1-10)

Friday, Sept. 5—Water for the Poor (Isaiah 41:14-20)

Saturday, Sept. 6—Cyrus Serves God's People (Isaiah 45:1-8)

Sunday, Sept. 7—River Gladdens the City of God (Psalm 46:1-11)

Learning by Doing

This page contains an alternate lesson plan emphasizing learning activities.
Classes desiring such student involvement will find these suggestions helpful.

NOTE TO TEACHERS: *A student book, Adult Bible Class, is available for class members to use with these lessons. It contains several of the activities referred to on this page. It is also available in Large Print. Order No. 193 (or Large Print Edition, 194).*

Learning Goals

As students participate in today's class session, they should:

1. Tell how God was working for Israel's good through the captivity and return.

2. Explain how a nation's moral character can effect God's blessing or His judgment.

3. Suggest ways to disciple others so that they, and their nation, can enjoy God's blessings.

Into the Lesson

Write each of the following headings on your chalkboard or on poster board (they are also printed in the student book):

•God will eventually punish sin.
•God wants the best for His people.
•God may surprise us with how He does His will.
•God will always win.

Ask each class member to find a partner and to choose one of the sentences. Give them two minutes to discuss with each other how they know the sentence is true. Then allow a few minutes for volunteers to share with the class.

Tell class members that the truth of each of these sentences is illustrated by today's lesson.

Into the Word

Begin with a brief lecture to help the class understand what is happening in today's passage. Use the material under the Introduction in the lesson commentary, and ask a class member to be ready to read Isaiah 1:1-9 and Isaiah 39:5-7 aloud to the class. Explain that today's text was written by Isaiah before Judah's captivity, and that it predicts how the captivity will be ended.

Next, point class members to today's printed text, and distribute the following questions on a handout. (Or refer class members to the student book where they are printed.) Ask a class member to read the text aloud after the questionnaires have been distributed. Class members may jot down answers to the questions after this reading. Or they may work in groups of about five each to study the Scriptures and come up with answers. After five minutes, discuss the questions as a class. Answers given after each question are to help you guide the discussion.

1. How does God affirm His greatness throughout this passage?

He formed us individually, and He is the Creator of all things (44:24). He shows the foolishness of false prophets and the nonsense of human learning separated from God (44:25). He fulfills the prophecies of His own spokesmen. He will be true to His character and to His Word by allowing His people to rebuild and reinhabit Jerusalem (44:26). He shows His glory to all nations by what He will do for His people (45:6). He is the Creator of light and darkness and the controller of both good times and bad (45:7).

2. Whom would God use to accomplish His purposes for the Israelites?

He predicted their restoration through His messengers (44:26) and accomplished this through Cyrus (45:1).

3. What does this passage tell us about Cyrus?

That he would be victorious (45:1) and that he was not a worshiper of the true God (v. 4).

4. Why did God allow the Israelites to be taken into captivity? (See Isaiah 1:1-9.)

Because of their persistent rebellion and disobedience against His will and His word.

5. Why did God have such a plan for the restoration of Judah?

For the good of His people (v. 4) and so that the whole world would acknowledge that God is the only true God (vv. 5, 6).

Into Life

Look again at the sentences used to begin today's session. Ask, "How does today's lesson teach each of these truths?" Use the following questions to add to your discussion:

1. Which of these sentences encourages you most? Why? Which is most frightening? Why?

2. How has God punished our nation for its sin? How has He seemed to delay punishment? What opportunities does His delay give us for discipling others?

3. Have you seen God accomplish His will in ways that were surprising to you? What hope does this give you for the difficult situations facing your nation or your church or your family?

Let's Talk It Over

The questions on this page are designed to encourage review of the lesson Scriptures and to promote discussion of the lesson by the class. The answers provided are only discussion starters. Let your class talk it over from there.

1. How have "wise men" contributed to the moral and spiritual deterioration of our society?

We remember what Paul said about ungodly men in Romans 1: "Professing themselves to be wise, they became fools, and changed the glory of the uncorruptible God into an image made like to corruptible man" (vv. 22, 23). In ages past "wise men" exhibited their foolishness by worshiping idols of metal, stone, and wood. Today they embrace false doctrines such as humanism. Convinced that man has no need of God, the Bible, prayer, or any divine assistance, they exalt human intelligence and ingenuity as the keys to progress. But by removing Biblical influences from government, education, technology, entertainment, and elsewhere, they have opened the door to moral and spiritual chaos. How desperately we need a reemphasis on the true wisdom that is centered in Jesus Christ and His gospel! (See 1 Corinthians 1:18-31.)

2. The Israelites would later see Isaiah's prophecies confirmed in their defeat, captivity, and restoration to their land. This should have strengthened their faith in God's word. God has confirmed many other Old Testament prophecies through the birth, life, death, and resurrection of Jesus. How should this affect the faith of today's ungodly "wise men"?

Open-mindedness is considered a laudable virtue today. If intelligent unbelievers were to undertake in open-minded fashion an investigation of Jesus Christ's fulfillment of various Old Testament prophecies, they would likely be stirred to faith. It is vital that Christians prepare the kinds of books, pamphlets, and other materials that can demonstrate the miracle of fulfilled prophecy. And it is equally vital that we challenge unbelievers to give Jesus Christ their open-minded, unbiased attention.

3. Why is Isaiah's mention of Cyrus such a remarkable prophecy?

Isaiah's prophetic ministry took place during the reigns of Uzziah, Jotham, Ahaz, and Hezekiah (Isaiah 1:1). This means that the last of his prophecies would have been spoken not long after 700 B.C. Cyrus the Great conquered Babylon in 539 B.C. and was then in a position to free the exiled Jews. This mention by name of a ruler who did not appear on the stage of world history until well over a century later must have been a tremendous boost to the exiled Jews' faith. Furthermore, it must have deeply impressed them with its demonstration of God's providential care for them. While they were still awaiting the captivity God promised through Isaiah and other prophets, He was designing both the plan and the man through whom He would restore them to their homeland.

4. "Blessed is the nation whose God is the Lord" (Psalm 33:12). Is it proper for us to apply such a verse to our nation, which has no established religion?

We still exalt God to some extent in our pledge to the flag, in the saying "In God We Trust" on our coins, and in many of our patriotic songs. Increasingly, however, God and His laws are being shoved aside in our secular society. As Christians, we acknowledge the rights of fellow citizens to pursue other religious beliefs or to refrain from any religious practice. But we also affirm our right to promote God and His cause in our society. It is unquestionably true that our nation has experienced tremendous blessings in the past while acknowledging the sovereignty of God. It makes sense for us to insist that a return to God and His principles is the key to future blessings.

5. Our society seems increasingly preoccupied with possessions and pleasures, and apathetic regarding spiritual concerns. How can we possibly influence such a society for Christ?

One way of answering this question is by focusing on the Philippian jailer in Acts 16. He appears to have been a man who had achieved some degree of worldly success. He possessed a measure of authority, a home, and a family. But when he assumed that his prisoners had escaped and was close to ending his own life, only Paul's shout from inside the prison spared him. At that point the jailer was ready to talk about salvation. Most every person has a time of crisis when he or she realizes how empty and futile worldly goals are. We should pray that we will be there, prepared with God's Word, when these modern "Philippian jailers" are open to the discussion of salvation through Jesus Christ.

Return to the Lord

DEVOTIONAL READING: Isaiah 49:8-13.

LESSON SCRIPTURE: Isaiah 55.

PRINTED TEXT: Isaiah 55:1-3, 6-11.

Isaiah 55:1-3, 6-11

1 Ho, every one that thirsteth, come ye to the waters, and he that hath no money; come ye, buy, and eat; yea, come, buy wine and milk without money and without price.

2 Wherefore do ye spend money for that which is not bread? and your labor for that which satisfieth not? hearken diligently unto me, and eat ye that which is good, and let your soul delight itself in fatness.

3 Incline your ear, and come unto me: hear, and your soul shall live; and I will make an everlasting covenant with you, even the sure mercies of David.

. . . .

6 Seek ye the LORD while he may be found, call ye upon him while he is near:

7 Let the wicked forsake his way, and the unrighteous man his thoughts: and let him return unto the LORD, and he will have mercy upon him; and to our God, for he will abundantly pardon.

8 For my thoughts are not your thoughts, neither are your ways my ways, saith the LORD.

9 For as the heavens are higher than the earth, so are my ways higher than your ways, and my thoughts than your thoughts.

10 For as the rain cometh down, and the snow from heaven, and returneth not thither, but watereth the earth, and maketh it bring forth and bud, that it may give seed to the sower, and bread to the eater:

11 So shall my word be that goeth forth out of my mouth: it shall not return unto me void, but it shall accomplish that which I please, and it shall prosper in the thing whereto I sent it.

GOLDEN TEXT: Seek ye the LORD while he may be found, call ye upon him while he is near.—Isaiah 55:6.

God Leads a People Home

Unit 1: Promise to Return

(Lessons 1-4)

Lesson Aims

After this lesson a student should be able to:

1. Summarize God's invitation and what He summoned His people to do.

2. Tell how that invitation applied to Israel and applies to us.

3. Seek to answer God's invitation through obedience to His Word.

Lesson Outline

INTRODUCTION

  A. History Written in Advance

  B. Lesson Background

 I. FREE RICHES OFFERED (Isaiah 55:1-3)

  A. Come and Take (vv. 1, 2)

  B. Obey and Live (v. 3)

    An Invitation to Change

II. SEEK THE LORD (Isaiah 55:6-9)

  A. Seek Him Now (v. 6)

  B. Seek Him on His Terms (vv. 7-9)

    Potemkin Villages of the Soul

III. GOD'S POWERFUL WORD (Isaiah 55:10, 11)

  A. Power of the Rain and Snow (v. 10)

  B. Power of God's Word (v. 11)

CONCLUSION

  A. The Loyal and the Lost

  B. The Larger View

  C. Today

  D. Prayer

  E. Thought to Remember

The visual for Lesson 2 of the visuals packet calls attention to the promise found in Isaiah 55:10, 11. It is shown on page 20.

Introduction

A. History Written in Advance

Last week we turned our thoughts to Israel's release from captivity in Babylon. To learn of that release, we read a passage that the prophet Isaiah wrote approximately one hundred years before the captivity began. Not only did Isaiah announce the deliverance of the captives and the rebuilding of the city of Jerusalem, but he even named the king (Cyrus) whom God would use to accomplish all of this. Thus did the prophet assure God's people that their God

would never abandon them. Isaiah could write so accurately about the future because the Spirit of God gave him the information (2 Peter 1:21). This is one of the wonders of God's Word.

B. Lesson Background

Today we come to a passage from Isaiah that reveals another wonder of God's Word. This single portion of Scripture addresses three different circumstances. Perhaps we could label it a "triple-action prophecy."

First, our text sounded a call to the people of Isaiah's own time. It was a call to repentance and to righteous living similar to what one finds in the opening chapter of Isaiah's prophecies (Isaiah 1:18-20). Second, the text addressed the captives in Babylon, whose future exile Isaiah had already mentioned (Isaiah 39:5-7). The words of our text appealed to them to turn to the Lord that they might be rescued and returned to their own land. Third, our text is one of many striking prophecies of Jesus Christ found within the book of Isaiah. It finds its fulfillment in His call to all the world to receive His salvation.

Our special interest today is in the second of these applications, because this quarter of lessons focuses on Israel's return from Babylon. Whereas last week's lesson focused on God's sovereignty in arranging for the release of His people from exile, this lesson emphasizes the people's responsibility to seek the Lord and answer His gracious invitation.

I. Free Riches Offered (Isaiah 55:1-3)

The blessings of God are not for sale, nor can they be taken by force, by craft, or by human ingenuity. They can be taken only in the way the Giver prescribes.

A. Come and Take (vv. 1, 2)

1. Ho, every one that thirsteth, come ye to the waters, and he that hath no money; come ye, buy, and eat; yea, come, buy wine and milk without money and without price.

Free! In a newspaper ad, on a billboard, or on a placard in a store, this word grabs our attention. Even greater is its appeal to one *that hath no money*. It presents his only opportunity of getting what he needs.

The need for water is obvious. *Wine and milk* are also offered free: *without money and without price*. These two items are often symbolic of an abundance of good things (see Song of Solomon 5:1; Joel 3:18; Amos 9:14). We will see that what Isaiah is talking about is far more precious than food or drink.

2. Wherefore do ye spend money for that which is not bread? and your labor for that which satisfieth not? hearken diligently unto me, and eat ye that which is good, and let your soul delight itself in fatness.

How timely are these words for our materialistic, self-gratifying age! They rebuke us for spending all our *money* and all our *labor* on what fails to satisfy: literal wine and milk, fine clothes and cars and houses, and all the material comforts that we long for, whether we need them or not. God does not ask us to live without material things, but He urgently calls us to *hearken* to Him and to give His words our undivided attention. From His Word we get the spiritual nourishment to satisfy the deeper longings that material wealth leaves unsatisfied. From God's Word and not the grocery store, through the ears and not the mouth, we receive the spiritual food that lets the *soul delight itself in fatness.* From a physical standpoint, we may want to avoid *fatness* and reach for something more healthy, but in Hebrew thinking fatness was a synonym for plenty and luxurious abundance (see Psalm 92:13, 14; Jeremiah 31:14). This is exactly what our spirits find in the Word of God.

B. Obey and Live (v. 3)

3. Incline your ear, and come unto me: hear, and your soul shall live; and I will make an everlasting covenant with you, even the sure mercies of David.

The call of the Lord is *Come unto me: hear.* Hearing means more than simply being aware of the Lord's voice; the call is to come to Him with trust and obedience. Two promises are made to those who hear God's Word and obey it. The first is: *Your soul shall live.* Here God promises to address the real hunger and thirst of the people. Food and drink are essential for physical life to continue, but they fall far short of meeting the needs of the soul.

The second promise given to those who listen to and obey God is this: *I will make an everlasting covenant with you, even the sure mercies of David.* God had made a covenant with Israel at Mount Sinai long before the covenant with David (Exodus 19:5, 6). This covenant was meant to govern the lives of God's people, though frequently it had been disregarded in the past and was treated that way in Isaiah's time. Centuries after this covenant with the nation, God made a covenant with an individual— David, whom God declared to be "a man after his own heart" (1 Samuel 13:14). He promised that David's kingdom would be established forever and that David's house would rule forever (2 Samuel 7:12-29).

How to Say It

BABYLONIANS. Bab-uh-*low*-nee-unz.
CYRUS. *Sigh*-russ.
EZEKIEL. E-*zeek*-e-ul or E-*zeek*-yul.
HEZEKIAH. Hez-ih-*kye-uh*.
ISAIAH. Eye-*zay*-uh.
JEREMIAH. Jair-uh-*my*-uh.
NEHEMIAH. Nee-huh-*my*-uh.
SINAI. *Sigh*-nye or *Sye*-nay-eye.
ZEDEKIAH. Zed-uh-*kye*-uh.

When the kingdom of Judah fell to the Babylonians and King Zedekiah was removed from power, it may have appeared as though the promise to David would be nullified. God's prophets, however, saw the situation differently. Jeremiah, who predicted the downfall of Jerusalem and witnessed his words come to pass, nevertheless preached that God's covenant with David was as unchangeable as the laws of nature (Jeremiah 33:20-22). Ezekiel predicted the day when God's people would be established in their land with David as their king, shepherd, and prince (Ezekiel 37:24-28).

We should keep in mind what God's promise to David stated: his house would rule forever (2 Samuel 7:12-29). This did not necessarily mean that the kings of David's dynasty would rule consecutively without interruption. Zedekiah's overthrow ended that rule, but not permanently. The Son of David, Jesus Christ, came to fulfill the words of the prophets and to receive "the throne of his father David" (Luke 1:32). Isaiah's words in the verse before us are quoted by Paul in Acts 13:34, where the *sure mercies of David* are linked with the resurrection of Jesus. Christians are the beneficiaries of the *everlasting covenant,* by which sins are forgiven and forgotten (Jeremiah 31:31-34).

Verses 4 and 5 are not included in the printed text. They continue the description of the One who would be the source of the "sure mercies of David." The titles of "witness," "leader," and "commander" are all applicable to Jesus. People of all nations continue to answer His call to become subjects of His everlasting kingdom.

AN INVITATION TO CHANGE

The Industrial Revolution was a time of great social turmoil. While it brought many positive changes concerning the way goods were produced, other changes were not so welcome. In the early 1800s, as textile factories in England converted to power looms, machines began to do the work of many men, and thousands of workers lost their jobs. Hand weavers who managed to keep their jobs found their wages decreasing.

In 1811, a group known as the Luddites began sabotaging factories in a vain attempt to force England to return to the old ways. These followers of a legendary general named Ned Ludd smashed the machines that put men out of work and burned to the ground the buildings that housed them. The government responded by making destruction of machinery a capital crime. Before the rebellion quieted a year or two later, more than fifty people had died, either by execution or by violence during the raids.

How different is God's call to return to the old way! In this case, the old way is His original way—the way in which man lived before sin shattered the paradise that God had created. God's blessings will come to rich and poor alike, if they will choose to hear Him and live in covenant with Him. The result of returning to God's "old paths" (Jeremiah 6:16) is always life, not death.

The invitation still stands: listen to God, seek that which is ultimately and eternally satisfying, and find delight in the abundance that only God can provide.   —C. R. B.

visual for
lesson 2

II. Seek the Lord
(Isaiah 55:6-9)

Two parables in Luke 15 picture two sides of what it means to seek the Lord. The parable of the lost sheep (vv. 3-7) pictures God seeking a sinner. How diligently God sought His people through Isaiah and other prophets, and now seeks them through His only begotten Son!

The parable of the prodigal son (vv. 11-24) pictures the sinner seeking God. The lost boy was not found until he said, "I will arise and go to my father." Then he took specific action: "he arose, and came to his father." No sinner is saved against his will; there must be a mutual seeking. The next part of our text encourages us to do our part in seeking the Lord.

A. Seek Him Now (v. 6)

6. Seek ye the LORD while he may be found, call ye upon him while he is near.

"Behold, now is the accepted time; behold, now is the day of salvation" (2 Corinthians 6:2). *While he may be found* implies that the time for seeking the Lord will one day end, but we do not know exactly when. In Isaiah's day, the time was rather long; well over one hundred years passed from the time when he began his ministry to the time when the Babylonians conquered Jerusalem. Then the people who had not

sought the Lord were doomed to captivity, death, or both. Another time to seek the Lord occurred when Cyrus of Persia overtook Babylon and set the Israelites free. About fifty thousand seekers of the Lord went back to Jerusalem to rebuild. No one knows exactly how many people of Israel chose to stay in Babylon, only to be absorbed into the heathen masses.

Today is the time to seek the Lord. *Today* you must make eternal matters a priority. Tomorrow you may be dead, or the Lord may have come to separate His sheep from the goats (Matthew 25:31-46). Seek the Lord—now!

B. Seek Him on His Terms (vv. 7-9)

7. Let the wicked forsake his way, and the unrighteous man his thoughts: and let him return unto the LORD, and he will have mercy upon him; and to our God, for he will abundantly pardon.

The Lord is not to be found in any *wicked* path, nor in any *unrighteous* thought. True seekers of the Lord must *forsake* such ways and such *thoughts*. We must *return unto the Lord* where He is, seeking after His goodness, truth, and holiness. When we meet Him on His terms, not ours, our horrid sins vanish in His abundant *pardon*.

8. For my thoughts are not your thoughts, neither are your ways my ways, saith the LORD.

Our human *thoughts* tend to be selfish thoughts. Our human *ways* may lead to riches, fame, power, or pleasure, but they do not lead to godliness. God's thoughts are unselfish thoughts; His ways lead to sacrifice for the sake of others. This is the high standard that we are called to follow: to live by God's dictates rather than those of the world.

9. For as the heavens are higher than the earth, so are my ways higher than your ways, and my thoughts than your thoughts.

Unselfish *thoughts* are lofty thoughts; *ways* of self-sacrifice and helpfulness are truly "high ways," guiding us to the paths that will satisfy our souls. "Ask for the old paths, where is the good way, and walk therein, and ye shall find rest for your souls" (Jeremiah 6:16).

POTEMKIN VILLAGES OF THE SOUL

Empress Catherine the Great of Russia took an extended tour through the southern part of her empire in 1787. She had entrusted the territory to one of her lovers, Marshal Grigory Potemkin. In order to show Catherine the strength of his authority, he is said to have constructed fake villages all along the route she took through the region. Although historians have come to doubt the legend, the concept of "Potemkin villages" seems so similar to what we see in everyday life that the story has a ring of truth to it.

The plea of Isaiah for the wicked to seek the Lord and forsake their evil ways came because the people of God had long acted as if being known as Israel—God's "chosen people"—was all that mattered. The faith of so many of them was a "false front." There was no substance of morality or godliness beneath it.

Today the evidence of hypocrisy is everywhere, resembling a host of "Potemkin villages" scattered throughout our land. Politicians "talk out of both sides of their mouths," TV commercials claim results that a product cannot deliver, and sometimes we Christians put on a "victorious life" facade, so that others cannot see the dirt on our hands and the hurts in our hearts. God still calls us to enter into covenant relationship with Him and to obey the commands of His Word, so that we may demonstrate a real faith for false times.   —C. R. B.

III. God's Powerful Word (Isaiah 55:10, 11)

The *word* of God (which is the topic of the next two verses) has always been important. It indicates His desire to communicate with those whom He created in His image. God spoke to Adam and Eve in Eden; likewise He spoke to Cain, to Noah, to Abraham, and to Moses. Through His prophets He spoke to people of numerous generations. Some of them listened and obeyed; some of them did not.

Today God is speaking to all of us through His Son (Hebrews 1:1, 2), yet still only a minority are willing to hear and obey. But God's Word remains true, whether it is popular or not. It still has power to accomplish His purposes. We ignore it at our own peril.

A. Power of the Rain and Snow (v. 10)

10. For as the rain cometh down, and the snow from heaven, and returneth not thither, but watereth the earth, and maketh it bring forth and bud, that it may give seed to the sower, and bread to the eater.

Neither the *rain* nor the *snow* is an accident generated by natural forces that function without mind or purpose. Both are gifts from God, designed and given for His purposes. As the Designer intended, they provide moisture to the earth, helping to bring forth a variety of items necessary for life. Not only do these provide our food, but many of them also provide *seed* for sowing, so that we may have food for yet another year. This process has been going on throughout history, and it will go on as long as the world stands, because God wills it.

B. Power of God's Word (v. 11)

11. So shall my word be that goeth forth out of my mouth: it shall not return unto me void, but it shall accomplish that which I please, and it shall prosper in the thing whereto I sent it.

Like the rain and the snow mentioned in the previous verse, the *word* of God is no accident. It is not a random collection of the thoughts of men. It is a gift from God, carefully prepared and given for His specific purposes, and it is designed to *accomplish* those purposes.

This should make us stop and think. What did God send His Word to accomplish? Doesn't God want all of us to come to Him and live? In Christian terms, doesn't He want everyone to be saved? Yet Jesus acknowledged that most of humanity chooses the broad way that leads to destruction (Matthew 7:13, 14). Ancient Hebrews chose that way and went to Babylon; many today are choosing it and going to Hell. Nevertheless, God's Word will accomplish the purpose that its Author has intended. The testimony of history shows that it does indeed *prosper*, even when its critics have sought to eliminate its influence. God's Word from beginning to end encourages us to come to God, to hear and obey. All of Bible history shows that obedience is the way of life for people and for nations. Because all have sinned, God has prepared a way of salvation for sinners through His only begotten Son. Urgently His Word calls us to that way, but it does not force us. The gospel is God's power for salvation, but only for those who believe (Romans 1:16). We have to choose.

Conclusion

We have noted that the text of this lesson can be applied to three specific times: to Isaiah's own time, to the time when the captives in Babylon were set free, and to our time. Currently we have a special interest in the second of these, for we are involved in a series of lessons on the return from Babylon and the rebuilding of Jerusalem.

A. The Loyal and the Lost

Some of the Jews released from Babylon had been there for seventy years; many more had been there for fifty years. Those less than fifty years old had been in Babylon all their lives. Then the power of Babylon was broken, and Cyrus, king of Persia, set the captives free.

About fifty thousand exiles set out for Jerusalem in response to the decree issued by Cyrus. Many of them likely recognized that the prophecies of return spoken years before were being fulfilled. No less loyal and obedient were some who did not return with the fifty thousand. Some, like Ezra, went approximately eighty years later, seeing a great need for the teaching of God's Law. A few years later still, Nehemiah came in response to an urgent need to rebuild Jerusalem's wall. Daniel did not go back to Jerusalem at all, yet no one questions his loyalty to the Lord or his willing obedience.

On the other hand, there must have been some Jews in Babylon who had no interest either in going to Jerusalem or in obeying the Lord. Comfortable where they were, they adjusted to their surroundings and lost their sense of identity as the chosen people of God.

B. The Larger View

In the larger view, our text for today can be applied to all people of all periods of history. First to hear God's word and fail to obey were Adam and Eve. Noah heard and obeyed while most of the rest of the world scoffed. Abraham heard and obeyed when most people were thinking of themselves and ignoring God. The prophets heard and obeyed; most of Israel ignored them or persecuted them until foreign armies overran the land of promise.

Home Daily Bible Readings

Monday, Sept. 8—Salvation Coming Soon (Isaiah 1:18-27)
Tuesday, Sept. 9—Peace Forevermore (Isaiah 54:1-10)
Wednesday, Sept. 10—Streams in the Desert (Isaiah 35:1-10)
Thursday, Sept. 11—Chosen to Be Light (Isaiah 49:1-7)
Friday, Sept. 12—Released From Bondage (Isaiah 49:8-12)
Saturday, Sept. 13—You're Invited! (Jeremiah 31:1-6)
Sunday, Sept. 14—Homecoming (Jeremiah 31:7-13)

Then came Jesus, God's own Son and His supreme spokesman (Hebrews 1:1-4). To all who had failed to obey God, He offered forgiveness— and those in need of forgiveness killed Him. But death was not the end. Jesus lived again and lives forever. "God also hath highly exalted him, and given him a name which is above every name: that at the name of Jesus every knee should bow, of things in heaven, and things in earth, and things under the earth; and that every tongue should confess that Jesus Christ is Lord, to the glory of God the Father" (Philippians 2:9-11). Jesus now reigns in glory, and His reign brings glory to God. That glory will be shared with those who hear His call and obey Him.

C. Today

For you and me, the critical time is *now*. Now we can choose. Do we hear God's Word and obey? Do we worship obediently on the Lord's Day (Hebrews 10:25)? Do we go about our daily tasks, understanding that we are working to bring glory to the Lord (Colossians 3:22-24)? Is Jesus truly the Lord in our homes? Are we daily presenting our bodies as living sacrifices acceptable to God, serving Him in sincerity and truth (Romans 12:1)? Read through the rest of Romans 12 and 13. Use the verses as a checklist to measure your obedience to God's Word. Do you need to improve your obedience in one area or in several?

Of course, God's Word includes more than these two chapters. Do our words reflect a heart in tune with God's aims and desires (Matthew 12:34-37)? Are we obedient in our minds, keeping our thoughts on "whatsoever things are true, whatsoever things are honest, whatsoever things are just, whatsoever things are pure, whatsoever things are lovely, whatsoever things are of good report" (Philippians 4:8)?

Today we are choosing. However, the consequences of those choices affect much more than today. We are also choosing for all eternity, either to live with God forever (Revelation 21:1-7), or to have a part in the lake that burns with fire and brimstone (v. 8).

D. Prayer

How blind we are without You, our Father, and how helpless! How generously You have given Your Word to open our eyes, and Your Spirit to strengthen our minds and muscles! May we today have ears ready to hear and hearts eager to obey, that we may faithfully walk in the way of eternal life. Amen.

E. Thought to Remember

Hear and obey the Lord.

Learning by Doing

This page contains an alternate lesson plan emphasizing learning activities.
Classes desiring such student involvement will find these suggestions helpful.

Learning Goals

As students participate in today's class session, they should:

1. Summarize God's invitation and what He summoned His people to do.

2. Tell how that invitation can apply to three different times in history.

3. Seek to answer God's invitation through obedience to His Word.

Into the Lesson

Have class members divide into pairs, then have each person tell his or her partner a story. The story is to be about one of these themes:

"A time when I was really thirsty."

"I spent money for a meal that wasn't very good."

"I decided that _____ was my favorite food when . . ."

Give them no more than three minutes to share their stories with each other. Then tell them that today's lesson is about satisfaction—the kind that comes from discovering how to obey God.

Into the Word

Remind the class of this quarter's theme: the return of the Jews to Jerusalem from Babylonian captivity. Then use material from the Lesson Background (page 18), emphasizing the idea of a "triple-action prophecy," to give the context for this week's study.

Ask class members to write three headings across a sheet of blank paper: Commands of God, Promises of God, and Descriptions of God. (Or call attention to the student book, where the headings and space to complete this activity are provided.)

Ask a class member to read today's printed text aloud, or, if you're using the student book, ask the class to read the text in unison, alternating the verses between halves of your class. Then ask class members, in groups of three to five, to survey the passage and jot ideas from the verses under each of the headings. Give them several minutes to do this, and then discuss with the entire class. Their answers should look something like this:

Commands of God: Come, buy, and eat (v. 1). Listen to me, and delight in the life I can provide for your soul (vv. 2, 3). Seek the Lord; call on Him (v. 6). Evil persons should forsake their sins and turn to the Lord (v. 7).

Promises of God: Only God brings satisfaction (implied in v. 2). Only God brings life (v. 3). God will make an eternal covenant with you (v. 3). God pardons those who turn from their sin to Him (v. 7). God's Word accomplishes the exact purpose for which He gave it (v. 11).

Descriptions of God: God is the Holy One of Israel (v. 5). God's purposes and methods are distinct from man's (v. 8). God's ways are superior to man's (v. 9). God's Word nourishes what it touches (vv. 10, 11).

After you have agreed with class members on which ideas belong under each heading, give the Bible study groups a second assignment. One-third of the groups should decide how these ideas had *significance to the Jews before the captivity.* One-third should decide how these ideas would come to have *significance to the Jews living in the Babylonian captivity.* The final third of your class should decide how these ideas have *significance to believers today.*

Give groups five minutes to jot down ideas (there is room for this in the student book as well), and then discuss with the class.

Into Life

Class members should look again at the "Commands of God" that they listed earlier and decide, "How can Christians today obey these commands?" Do this in one of two ways:

Circle response. Ask class members, one after the other, to give one answer to the question. No one may respond twice until everyone has responded once. If a member is stumped for an answer, of course, you can let him pass to the next person. If your class is large, do this in groups of six or eight. Then go around the room getting a different response from each group.

Brainstorming. Class members shout out answers as you jot them down on the chalkboard within a ninety-second time limit. After the time has passed, let the class decide which of the suggested ideas are the best ideas. Put a star beside these.

After completing one of these options, challenge class members to review the list of commands and decide which one they need to obey more faithfully. Encourage them to tell the class what they will do to accomplish this.

Let's Talk It Over

*The questions on this page are designed to encourage review of the lesson
Scriptures and to promote discussion of the lesson by the class. The answers
provided are only discussion starters. Let your class talk it over from there.*

1. The invitation to "come . . . to the waters" (Isaiah 55:1) is a very vivid way of pointing to mankind's need for spiritual blessings. How is this so?

Water provides immediate refreshment to a thirsty person, and it also provides long-term benefits for the health of the body. The spiritual blessings that water symbolizes work the same way. A person is immediately refreshed when he experiences the forgiveness of his sins, and when he realizes that he is the recipient of eternal life. But the blessings of the Spirit also work on a long-term basis, guiding the believer into a life of holiness, strengthening him for service, sustaining him in trials, and providing other spiritual benefits. It is interesting to see how this symbolic reference to water appears in other places in Isaiah. See Isaiah 12:2, 3; 35:6, 7; 41:18; 43:19, 20; 44:3, 4.

2. The people of Isaiah's time were urged to listen to God. If they did so, they could go on living as a free people. How did they respond to this message, and why did they respond in the way they did?

The people in general rejected God's message as it was delivered by His prophets. One reason why they responded this way was their hardness of heart. They persisted so long in disobedience to God and rebellion toward His laws that they reached a point at which His message no longer affected them. This is referred to in Isaiah 6:9, 10. Another reason was the fact that false prophets were always preaching a much rosier, more pleasant message. Jeremiah described such leaders as the kind who cry, "Peace, peace; when there is no peace" (Jeremiah 6:14).

3. The Hebrews in captivity in Babylon were urged to listen to God. How did they respond to this message, and why did they respond in the way they did?

Many of the exiles heeded God's message, repented of the sins that had led to their captivity, and were able to return to their homeland. They had learned a painful lesson that God is true to His warnings to the disobedient as well as to His promises to the obedient. The Hebrews in Babylon had tasted of the prophesied punishment, and now they were ready to enjoy the

good things God extends to those who trust and obey Him. We could say that God used destruction and exile to get the attention of the Israelites. They should have returned home prepared to obey; however, as we shall see in future lessons of this quarter, there were still many times when they chose the path of disobedience.

4. People today are urged to listen to God. If they do so, they can enjoy freedom from the guilt of sin and the gift of eternal life. How are they responding to this message, and why are they responding in this manner?

People are responding in the very ways Jesus described in His parable of the sower (Matthew 13:3-9, 18-23). Some in the hardness of their hearts are rejecting God's message altogether; some are accepting it in a superficial manner and then falling away; and others are accepting it while continuing to cling to worldly values.

Thankfully, however, some are accepting the Word of the Lord in simplicity and sincerity, and enjoying its benefits. All too many individuals, however, fall into the first three classes of hearers. Material wealth, an endless parade of amusements, pride in education and worldly wisdom—these are just some of the factors that stand in the way of many who fail to give God's message the hearing it deserves.

5. God's Word was sent to accomplish His will. How can we align ourselves with its power so as to participate in the accomplishment of His will?

Obviously our faith in the Word is a vital factor. We live in an era of widespread skepticism regarding the Bible. But in spite of all the highly publicized doubts expressed by scholars concerning the Bible, we still have a solid basis for confidence in it. We must believe in it, if it is to accomplish its work. Another factor is our personal obedience. We must allow God's revealed will to be fulfilled in our own words and acts if we are to contribute to its accomplishment elsewhere. Still another factor is prayer. It is significant that Jesus taught us to pray, "Thy kingdom come. Thy will be done in earth, as it is in heaven" (Matthew 6:10). We must make it a major emphasis to pray for the accomplishing of God's will everywhere through His Word.

A Time to Rebuild

DEVOTIONAL READING: Psalm 132:1-14.

LESSON SCRIPTURE: Haggai.

PRINTED TEXT: Haggai 1:1-9; 2:1-5.

Haggai 1:1-9

1 In the second year of Darius the king, in the sixth month, in the first day of the month, came the word of the LORD by Haggai the prophet unto Zerubbabel the son of Shealtiel, governor of Judah, and to Joshua the son of Josedech, the high priest, saying,

2 Thus speaketh the LORD of hosts, saying, This people say, The time is not come, the time that the LORD's house should be built.

3 Then came the word of the LORD by Haggai the prophet, saying,

4 Is it time for you, O ye, to dwell in your ceiled houses, and this house lie waste?

5 Now therefore thus saith the LORD of hosts; Consider your ways.

6 Ye have sown much, and bring in little; ye eat, but ye have not enough; ye drink, but ye are not filled with drink; ye clothe you, but there is none warm; and he that earneth wages, earneth wages to put it into a bag with holes.

7 Thus saith the LORD of hosts; Consider your ways.

8 Go up to the mountain, and bring wood, and build the house; and I will take pleasure in it, and I will be glorified, saith the LORD.

9 Ye looked for much, and, lo, it came to little; and when ye brought it home, I did blow upon it. Why? saith the LORD of hosts. Because of mine house that is waste, and ye run every man unto his own house.

Haggai 2:1-5

1 In the seventh month, in the one and twentieth day of the month, came the word of the LORD by the prophet Haggai, saying,

2 Speak now to Zerubbabel the son of Shealtiel, governor of Judah, and to Joshua the son of Josedech, the high priest, and to the residue of the people, saying,

3 Who is left among you that saw this house in her first glory? and how do ye see it now? is it not in your eyes in comparison of it as nothing?

4 Yet now be strong, O Zerubbabel, saith the LORD; and be strong, O Joshua, son of Josedech, the high priest; and be strong, all ye people of the land, saith the LORD, and work: for I am with you, saith the LORD of hosts:

5 According to the word that I covenanted with you when ye came out of Egypt, so my Spirit remaineth among you: fear ye not.

GOLDEN TEXT: Be strong, all ye people of the land, saith the LORD, and work: for I am with you, saith the LORD of hosts.—Haggai 2:4.

God Leads a People Home
Unit 1: Promise to Return
(Lessons 1-4)

Lesson Aims

After this lesson, a student should be able to:

1. Recall the reasons the people stopped rebuilding the temple and why God demanded that they resume.

2. Explain how worldly priorities can divert people from God's purposes, and how God blesses those who put Him first.

3. Suggest at least one area of one's life where God's priorities need to be given more attention.

Lesson Outline

INTRODUCTION
  A. A Hard Message to Believe
  B. Lesson Background
 I. A QUESTION OF TIME (Haggai 1:1-6)
  A. A Prophet Speaks (v. 1)
  B. Popular Opinion (v. 2)
  C. The Lord's Question (vv. 3, 4)
  D. Food for Thought (vv. 5, 6)
    Gold Fever
II. THE LORD'S ANSWER (Haggai 1:7-9)
  A. Think and Build (vv. 7, 8)
  B. Results of Not Building (v. 9)
III. THE GLORY OF GOD'S HOUSE (Haggai 2:1-5)
  A. A New Word From God (vv. 1, 2)
  B. Disappointment (v. 3)
  C. Encouragement (vv. 4, 5)
    An Act of Courage
CONCLUSION
  A. The Priority of Obedience
  B. Greater Glory
  C. Prayer
  D. Thought to Remember

The visual for Lesson 3 (page 28) shows people working on a church building. Use it to highlight Haggai's challenge to build God's house.

Introduction

A. A Hard Message to Believe

In the United States as well as in other "advanced" nations, honest citizens are alarmed by the ever-increasing crime rate. Law enforcement officers plead for more police on the streets—thousands of them. Educators plead for more dollars for schools—millions of them.

Christians plead for a return to God. Still the increase in crime worsens.

Now and then someone arises to suggest that our country cannot survive for long if these conditions continue. In a hundred years or two hundred, this person claims, the United States will be no more. Most respond by saying, "Come on, it's not *that* bad." They do not believe that our country really is headed for destruction.

The people of Israel did not believe Isaiah when he made a similar prediction. But Isaiah was not merely guessing. His information came straight from Heaven. He said that the people would one day be captives in Babylon, and so they were. He also said that a man named Cyrus would set them free, and so he did.

B. Lesson Background

About fifty thousand of the captives traveled as pioneers to their former homeland (Ezra 2:64, 65). Eagerly they built an altar and restored their ancient way of worship (Ezra 3:1-6). Enthusiastically they planned to rebuild the temple (v. 8). Joyously they laid the foundation (vv. 10, 11), although many wept, remembering the magnificence of Solomon's temple (vv. 12, 13). This happened during the second year after the exiles had returned home from Babylon (v. 8).

The enthusiasm that was present when the foundation of the new temple was laid was not easy to maintain. At least three factors helped to make its construction slow and difficult. First, timber had to be brought from faraway Lebanon (Ezra 3:7). This was a time-consuming, costly procedure. Second, the people had to build homes for their families, plant and harvest crops, find pasture for their sheep and cattle, and attend to other necessities. Making a living diverted them from temple building.

A third distraction involved the nearby residents of the territory, referred to as "the people of the land" (Ezra 4:4). These people offered to help, but their offer was refused. They were Samaritans, not pure Jews, although the reasons for refusing their help involved other factors. The Samaritans, who had originated through the mixing of Israelites with Assyrians, had likely been influenced by the Assyrians' pagan beliefs. Since following such beliefs had caused the captivity in the first place, those returning from Babylon were especially sensitive to any such influences. In addition, the Samaritans had not returned to Judah with the captives. The right to rebuild the temple had been given only to the returning Jews.

Angry at such a response, the Samaritans then began to hinder the work in every way they could (Ezra 4:4, 5) For nearly sixteen years, the temple lay partially completed—a sad testimony to the failure of God's people to complete the project they had begun so willingly.

Then, as often happened during critical periods in Old Testament history, God raised up a prophet to challenge His people. Haggai came forward to stir up an indifferent people to resume work on the long-neglected temple.

I. A Question of Time
(Haggai 1:1-6)

A. A Prophet Speaks (v. 1)

1. In the second year of Darius the king, in the sixth month, in the first day of the month, came the word of the LORD by Haggai the prophet unto Zerubbabel the son of Shealtiel, governor of Judah, and to Joshua the son of Josedech, the high priest, saying.

Like other books of the prophets, this one boldly declares that the prophet is speaking for *the Lord*, not for himself. This word was addressed to the two most prominent leaders of the people: *Zerubbabel . . . governor of Judah*, and *Joshua . . . the high priest*. Thus both the political and the spiritual leadership were to be the primary recipients of the divine message.

The other significant person mentioned here is *Darius the king*. His *second year* as ruler of the Persian Empire would have been the year 520 B.C. Just as God had used Cyrus to free the people from captivity, He used Darius to allow them to resume work on their temple.

B. Popular Opinion (v. 2)

2. Thus speaketh the LORD of hosts, saying, This people say, The time is not come, the time that the LORD's house should be built.

At this point, the enthusiasm that had been present when the people laid the foundation of

the temple had been replaced by a stifling indifference to God's work. Perhaps many of the people agreed that there should be a suitable place for worship. They were in favor of seeing the temple completed—but not right now. *The time is not come,* they said. "Crops are not good," they may have reasoned. "Money is scarce; we are busy. A man has to take care of his family first of all. Surely a better time will come." Through such rationalizations as these, they had convinced one another that the completion of the temple was not urgent; it could be postponed.

C. The Lord's Question (vv. 3, 4)

3. Then came the word of the LORD by Haggai the prophet, saying.

Again came the assurance that this was *the word of the Lord*; *Haggai* was only a messenger.

4. Is it time for you, O ye, to dwell in your ceiled houses, and this house lie waste?

While it was not time to build God's *house*, the people had found time to build their own *houses*. These were not ordinary shelters, but *ceiled* (paneled) *houses*—houses lined with precious cedar from Lebanon to cover the rough, unattractive stone and to add beauty and comfort to the dwelling. Why, in contrast, was the Lord's house allowed to lie in *waste*—desolate, incomplete, and useless? Was it really a matter of time, or was it a matter of priorities? The people needed to think about this. Was their comfort more important than their worship? This is an issue we need to address as well.

D. Food for Thought (vv. 5, 6)

5. Now therefore thus saith the LORD of hosts; Consider your ways.

Consider your ways. In other words, think about what you are doing. What does it say about where your priorities lie? Is the cedar paneling in your house dearer to your heart than a roof for God's house? Hardly a man in Israel would actually claim that his house was more important than God's house, but what he was doing said exactly that.

GOLD FEVER

In his whimsical poem, "The Cremation of Sam McGee," Robert Service acknowledged the fact that "there are strange things done in the midnight sun by the men who moil for gold." During the Alaska gold rush of which Service wrote, men endured extreme hardship and risked their lives in hopes of "striking it rich."

In 1896 gold was discovered in Canada's Klondike region. In less than a year, Skagway, Alaska, had become a booming city of twenty

---

How to Say It

ASSYRIANS. Uh-*sear*-e-unz.
CYRUS. *Sigh*-russ.
DARIUS. Duh-*rye*-us.
HAGGAI. *Hag*-a-eye or *Hag*-eye.
JOSEDECH. *Jahss*-uh-dek.
MEDITERRANEAN. *Med*-uh-tuh-*ray*-nee-un (strong accent on *ray*).
NEHEMIAH. Nee-huh-*my*-uh.
PHOENICIANS. Fuh-*nish*-unz.
SAMARITANS. Suh-*mare*-uh-tunz.
SHEALTIEL. She-*al*-tee-el.
SIDON. *Sigh*-dun.
ZERUBBABEL. Zeh-*rub*-uh-bull.

thousand. Prospectors came by boat to Skagway and then climbed the steep Chilkoot Trail over the mountains into Canada, carrying all their possessions on their backs. To prevent food riots, the Canadian "Mounties" required each man to have one ton of food and supplies. It took as many as forty trips up the trail to bring in one's provisions.

Countless men lost all their possessions and even their lives to "gold fever," a disease of the mind and heart, not of the body. Throughout history it has been the same: if not gold, then something else has twisted people's priorities and caused them to divert their attention from what is most important.

For those who resettled Jerusalem, the desire to build fine houses for themselves rather than for God caused their surroundings to decline. Their disease was a disease of the spirit that could not be cured except by turning back to God.   —C. R. B.

6. Ye have sown much, and bring in little; ye eat, but ye have not enough; ye drink, but ye are not filled with drink; ye clothe you, but there is none warm; and he that earneth wages, earneth wages to put it into a bag with holes.

It was true that the crops had not been good. This was a subject that Haggai also wanted the people to "consider": you know who provides rain to assure a good crop, don't you? Could your shameful treatment of His house have something to do with your poor crops?

Most of us can readily identify with Haggai's next observation: *he that earneth wages, earneth wages to put it into a bag with holes.* Where does that paycheck go? It's as if our wallets and purses are full of holes! This was how the wage earners in Israel felt. When crops were poor, prices increased. The wages earned were spent before all needs could be met.

The Lord wanted His people to understand that all of this was connected with their neglect of His house. Certainly the opposition of the Samaritans had been great. But Haggai was calling attention to factors over which the people themselves had control. They needed to quit looking at their surroundings and start looking at themselves.

II. The Lord's Answer
(Haggai 1:7-9)

The question of verse 4 was still unanswered at this point. The people had been summoned to think about their ways (v. 5), and especially about the results of those ways (v. 6). Now the Lord addressed the question He had raised.

visual for lesson 3

A. Think and Build (vv. 7, 8)

7. Thus saith the LORD of hosts; Consider your ways.

Again the people are commanded to *consider your ways.* In verses 5 and 6 this was a challenge to think about the unpleasant results of their ways; in verses 7 and 8 it is a call to think about how to change these ways.

8. Go up to the mountain, and bring wood, and build the house; and I will take pleasure in it, and I will be glorified, saith the LORD.

Neglecting the temple had been the source of many troubles (v. 6). Haggai had asked if it was time to build the Lord's house; obviously it *was* time. He now challenged the people to *bring wood, and build the house.* While there were certain trees available in the vicinity of Jerusalem (see Nehemiah 8:14, 15), it is likely that the heavier timber needed for a house of worship would have to be imported. This is the kind of wood ("cedar trees from Lebanon") that had been used to erect the foundation (Ezra 3:7). Haggai's challenge to *go up to the mountain* may have been a call to secure such wood for completion of the temple.

To obtain this wood, the Jews had earlier used the help of Phoenician lumbermen from Tyre and Sidon. First Kings 5:5-9 gives details of how this was done when Solomon built the first temple. He sent his workmen to the forests of Lebanon, and hired skilled Phoenician lumbermen to direct them. Logs were brought down to the Mediterranean Sea, floated south to Joppa, and then taken overland to Jerusalem. We can easily understand why the people being addressed by Haggai had been content to put off such a formidable task. It required significant time and effort on their part.

But the Lord was not at all content to postpone the rebuilding indefinitely, so through His prophets He provided the prodding that was needed. The primary benefits of completing the temple would be spiritual, not material: it would bring both *pleasure* and glory to the Lord. The builders themselves would honor God with their diligent labor.

B. Results of Not Building (v. 9)

9. Ye looked for much, and, lo, it came to little; and when ye brought it home, I did blow upon it. Why? saith the LORD of hosts. Because of mine house that is waste, and ye run every man unto his own house.

Again the Lord pointed to the disastrous results of the people's neglect of His house, and thus their neglect of their relationship with Him. They had sown their seed with high hopes of a great harvest, but they were sadly disappointed. The harvest was *little*. When they brought it home, it seemed smaller still, as if the breath of God had blown a portion away. *Why* had this happened? Why was the harvest so small? Because the Lord's *house* lay in *waste*. The unfinished temple stood there desolate, abandoned, and useless. Though it could not speak, it testified that God's people were neglecting Him and His house, while *every man* was giving attention to *his own house*.

III. The Glory of God's House (Haggai 2:1-5)

The people had become tired of scant harvests and ongoing poverty. The word Haggai brought from God made sense. Led by their governor Zerubbabel and the high priest Joshua, the people went to work to complete God's house (Haggai 1:12-15). Then God spoke again.

A. A New Word From God (vv. 1, 2)

1. In the seventh month, in the one and twentieth day of the month, came the word of the LORD by the prophet Haggai, saying.

This was nearly a month after the people had resumed work on the temple (Haggai 1:14, 15). Perhaps by this time they realized what a mammoth task they were undertaking, and what obstacles stood in the way. Some of the "old-timers" could also see that this temple would not be as glorious as the one that Solomon had built centuries earlier. If such thoughts were discouraging the workers, God's new message brought encouragement.

It is also important to note the time of year when this *word of the Lord* was given. The twenty-first day of the *seventh month* was the final day of the Feast of Tabernacles, during which the Israelites gave thanks to God for their crops (Leviticus 23:33-43). However, the crops harvested by Haggai's audience had been quite meager, as we have seen. Perhaps there seemed to be little cause for celebration. But the Lord had not forsaken His people, as Haggai's message emphasized.

2. Speak now to Zerubbabel the son of Shealtiel, governor of Judah, and to Joshua the son of Josedech, the high priest, and to the residue of the people, saying.

The message was directed to the political leader, the religious leader, and to all the *residue*, or remainder, *of the people*. All these had gone to work a month before. No doubt many were beginning to lose some of the zeal with which they had begun their work, so God's message was for all of them.

B. Disappointment (v. 3)

3. Who is left among you that saw this house in her first glory? and how do ye see it now? is it not in your eyes in comparison of it as nothing?

This house in her first glory meant the glorious temple that Solomon had built on this site approximately four centuries earlier. Sixty-six years had passed since its destruction by the Babylonians. Not many people in Jerusalem could remember seeing it, but a few of the oldest could. These few could readily see that the new temple would be *in comparison of it as nothing*. This does not necessarily mean that the new one was poorly built, but clearly the residents of Jerusalem could not supply the elaborate ornamentation of the old one. For example, Solomon lined the entire interior of his temple with gold (1 Kings 6:20-35). Such resources were not available to those engaged in the rebuilding effort.

C. Encouragement (vv. 4, 5)

4. Yet now be strong, O Zerubbabel, saith the LORD; and be strong, O Joshua, son of Josedech, the high priest; and be strong, all ye people of the land, saith the LORD, and work: for I am with you, saith the LORD of hosts.

The Lord's message sought to curb the people's discouragement: *be strong . . . and work.* Most encouraging of all was the assurance: *I am with you.* How could they fail?

AN ACT OF COURAGE

Kazul Hiyama (Kah-*zool* High-*yahm*-uh) and his family were farmers near Fresno, California. In the fear and anger that engulfed America after Japan attacked Pearl Harbor in 1941, the Hiyamas and approximately 110,000 other people of Japanese ancestry in the Pacific coastal states were forced into internment camps.

When the Hiyama family was thrust into exile, their neighbor, C. K. Oliver, began farming their land for them. On Christmas Day in 1944, the Hiyamas were finally given permission to come home to their land. Mr. Oliver, the good neighbor, welcomed them back and explained, "We didn't have a lease—I just sent the Hiyamas a check at the end of each year. Yeah, there was some back talk, but . . . it was the decent thing to do. I was raised to treat others as I'd like to be treated. We were friends."

The "decent thing to do" was not the easy thing to do. Oliver and others like him were criticized by some who allowed their wartime anger to overwhelm them. But Oliver knew that living by Jesus' Golden Rule was the right thing to do regardless of what others might say.

The prophet Haggai told both Zerubbabel and Joshua to "be strong" and get on with rebuilding the temple. In the process, their courage would be an example to the nation. Those who do God's will cause others to want to obey Him also.   —C. R. B.

5. According to the word that I covenanted with you when ye came out of Egypt, so my Spirit remaineth among you: fear ye not.

This tells more about the promise of God's presence to those who returned from Babylon. The promise was *according to the word* that God had *covenanted* with their ancestors at Sinai when those ancestors had left *Egypt* to begin their journey to the promised land. The details of this covenant fill much of Exodus, Leviticus, Numbers, and Deuteronomy.

It is noteworthy that this ancient covenant, written some nine hundred years before Haggai's time, included a portion directed specifically to the captives when they returned from the land of their exile (Deuteronomy 30). To those who had returned from Babylon, it reaffirmed the declaration made to their ancestors: obedience would bring blessing; disobedience would bring disaster. As the people resumed work on the temple, they proved once again that God's covenant was dependable. They were obeying Him, and He was blessing them.

Conclusion

A. The Priority of Obedience

The covenant made at Sinai is not for us. We are not subject to its various dietary requirements. We are not asked to bring animals to be sacrificed at an altar. We are not called to Jerusalem three times each year for a special celebration. We worship God in spirit and in truth wherever we are. Ours is the New Covenant foretold in Jeremiah 31:31-34—the covenant by which sins are forgiven and forgotten.

Yet God is still God. Even in the New Testament, there are commandments to be obeyed. Disciples of Jesus are to be taught to obey them (Matthew 28:19, 20). The way to be assured of God's presence and blessing is still *obedience*. Hear the words of Jesus: "If a man love me, he will keep my words: and my Father will love him, and we will come unto him, and make our abode with him" (John 14:23).

B. Greater Glory

The elderly among the returned exiles were sad because the new temple was not as glorious as the old one. But God said, "Just wait." "The glory of this latter house shall be greater than of the former" (Haggai 2:9).

History records how King Herod the Great lavished wealth on the second temple to add to its glory; however, the truly greater glory of this house was manifested when God's Son Jesus stood in its midst. When God's Son taught God's truth in God's house, God's glory was present for all to see.

Approximately forty years after Jesus last stood in that impressive structure, it was destroyed just as the former one had been. By then, however, the greater temple was rising: the true temple in which God lives eternally (Ephesians 2:19-22). Christians comprise this temple—the church. Should we not seek to be obedient day by day, keeping God's true temple holy and without blemish (Ephesians 5:25-27)?

C. Prayer

Thank You, Father, for granting us a place in Your eternal temple. In Jesus' name we ask for wisdom and strength and courage to keep Your temple always holy. Amen.

D. Thought to Remember

"The temple of God is holy, which temple ye are" (1 Corinthians 3:17).

Home Daily Bible Readings

Monday, Sept. 15—Finding a Place for Worship (Psalm 132:1-10)
Tuesday, Sept. 16—God Has Chosen Zion (Psalm 132:11-18)
Wednesday, Sept. 17—Rebuild Now! (Haggai 1:1-8)
Thursday, Sept. 18—Just Say Yes! (Haggai 1:9-15)
Friday, Sept. 19—Vision of a Brighter Future (Haggai 2:1-9)
Saturday, Sept. 20—Blessing for the Obedient (Haggai 2:10-23)
Sunday, Sept. 21—God Builds the House (Psalm 127:1-5)

Learning by Doing

This page contains an alternate lesson plan emphasizing learning activities.
Classes desiring such student involvement will find these suggestions helpful.

Learning Goals

Students in today's class session should:

1. Recall the reasons the people stopped rebuilding the temple and why God demanded that they resume.

2. Explain how worldly priorities can divert people from God's purposes, and how God blesses those who put Him first.

3. Suggest at least one area of one's life where God's priorities need to be given more attention.

Into the Lesson

Distribute paper and ask class members to make a list of numbers from one through seven. As you read the following statements, class members are to decide how each one would or would not be a priority in their lives if it were a real possibility for them this week. They are to rate each possibility as an "A" (top priority), "B" (possible priority), or "C" (not a priority).

1. Tell a Muslim neighbor how to become a Christian.

2. Spend thirty minutes more each day in Bible reading and prayer.

3. Offer to help at a local homeless shelter.

4. Add two hours per week to my service at our church (ushering, teaching, singing, etc.).

5. Read a book by a Christian author to get help with a problem I'm experiencing.

6. Spend ninety minutes per week in a discipling relationship with another Christian.

When students are finished with the exercise, take a poll: How many marked more than one item as an "A" priority? How many marked no "A's"? How many marked all the items "C"?

Ask class members, "Was this exercise difficult or easy? Why?" Point out that you were asking them to choose from a list of equally good items. Theoretically, every choice could be an "A" for someone. Why weren't all of them an "A" for everyone?

Tell the class that today's Bible study looks at the priorities of the Israelites who returned to Jerusalem from captivity in Babylon. Their choices might have seemed clear, but still they had trouble setting the right priorities.

Into the Word

It will be important for you to provide sufficient background with today's lesson, since the book of Haggai may not be familiar to some of your students. Use material from the Introduction to the lesson commentary to prepare a short background lecture. Then call attention to the student book, where the following list of summary statements is printed, out of order and without the chapter and verse references. (If you prefer, you may prepare a handout with these sentences before class to distribute at this point in the lesson.) Class members are to use today's Scripture text to put the statements in the correct order and to tell which section of the text each sentence summarizes.

(1) God spoke through Haggai to address the people's opinion that they need not build the Lord's house now (1:2).

(2) God told the people that looking out for themselves had not brought them the prosperity they were seeking (1:6).

(3) God explained that the people would not prosper until they rebuilt the temple (1:8, 9).

(4) A second time God spoke through Haggai, with a message for the political leader, the religious leader, and the people (2:1, 2).

(5) God used the memory of the first temple to encourage the people to rebuild it (2:3, 4).

(6) God reminded the people of His covenant with them to encourage them (2:5).

Give students about five minutes, in pairs or small groups, to put the sentences in the correct order. Then discuss these questions: How do we know that the Israelites had a priority problem? How did they suffer because their priorities were misaligned? What motives did they have for getting their priorities in order?

Into Life

Have class members discuss the following issues: (1) How are priorities in our culture misaligned? and (2) How are people today suffering because of misplaced priorities? They may do this by looking through newspapers and magazines for ads and articles that answer each question. (Have some of these ready to distribute if you choose to do this.) Or simply ask class members to suggest answers, and write these in two lists on your chalkboard.

Challenge the class to consider how Christians today sometimes suffer from misplaced priorities. What message would God deliver to today's church if He had a spokesman like Haggai? What would He say to your class?

Let's Talk It Over

The questions on this page are designed to encourage review of the lesson Scriptures and to promote discussion of the lesson by the class. The answers provided are only discussion starters. Let your class talk it over from there.

1. Like the people in Jerusalem in Haggai's time, we hear some today who say regarding God's work, "The time is not come," or "The time is not right." What are some specific circumstances in which they say this, and how should we answer such claims?

Some say this in regard to accepting Christ as Savior. Some voice this claim when challenged to tithe or to make a sacrificial commitment of money. Others say it when urged to accept a role of leadership in the church. Still others offer it as an excuse for failing to develop personal Bible study and prayer. We can answer these by pointing out that circumstances will never be ideal for stepping out in faith. The people in Jerusalem could offer some fairly legitimate reasons for delaying construction of the temple. People today will always be able to list some "sensible" reasons for avoiding spiritual challenges. But if God wants us to go forward, we must do so, trusting that He will provide the means.

2. Haggai referred to the "ceiled houses" or "paneled houses" (*New International Version*) that the people had built while neglecting the temple. This should remind us today of the contrast between what people do for God and what they do for themselves. Can you think of examples of this contrast?

Many church leaders are successful businessmen. Do they handle the church's business as diligently as they do their day-to-day obligations? Among those who teach in Sunday school are a great number of public schoolteachers. Do they prepare their Sunday lessons with the same kind of thoroughness and care that they use in their weekday lessons? In many churches are individuals with skills in carpentry, electrical work, plumbing, and other areas. Do they apply these skills as enthusiastically on work done for church facilities as they do on their daily jobs? Certainly the answer should be a resounding "yes" to each of these questions.

3. The citizens of Jerusalem in Haggai's time were allowing their quest for material comforts to draw them away from faithful obedience to God. How does today's quest for material comforts tend to lead many away from God?

Paul's observation that "the love of money is the root of all evil" (1 Timothy 6:10) is accurate in our time. Even Christians sometimes allow this love of money to lure them into unlawful practices and thereby away from God. Outright theft, blackmail, embezzlement, tax fraud, gambling, get-rich-quick schemes that border on illegality—these are some of the fruits that the love of money produces.

4. How does the quest for fun and pleasure tend to lead people away from God?

For the Jews in Jerusalem, it must have seemed much more pleasurable to build their own paneled houses than to labor on the temple for God's "pleasure" (Haggai 1:8). In our time some people seem to neglect worship services because they find these lacking in entertainment and fun. Christians should find enjoyment in worshiping God and in studying His Word together, but the quest for fun must not become the primary aim in these activities. Also, as with money, the desire for pleasure can draw us into idolatry. Certainly some have formed idolatrous attachments to movie and television stars, popular musicians, professional athletes, and other entertainment figures. The more of our time and attention that we focus on fun and pleasure, the less we have to give to God.

5. The lesson writer points out that the greater glory Haggai prophesied regarding the new temple (Haggai 2:9) was fulfilled by Jesus' presence in it. What does this suggest about the kind of "glory" that our church buildings should possess?

There is nothing wrong with constructing large, elaborate houses of worship for growing congregations. However, what is done inside these buildings is the true source of their glory. Is Jesus Christ honored there as Savior and Lord? Is His gospel taught accurately and zealously? Are people being led to confess Him as Savior and to be baptized into Him? Is His spirit of service being demonstrated by leaders and members? Are the believers diligently watching for His promised return? The large church building from which such features are absent enjoys far less glory than the smaller, humbler structure where these characteristics are found.

A Vision of Renewal

DEVOTIONAL READING: Zechariah 7:1-10.

LESSON SCRIPTURE: Zechariah 4.

PRINTED TEXT: Zechariah 4.

Zechariah 4

1 And the angel that talked with me came again, and waked me, as a man that is wakened out of his sleep,

2 And said unto me, What seest thou? And I said, I have looked, and behold a candlestick all of gold, with a bowl upon the top of it, and his seven lamps thereon, and seven pipes to the seven lamps, which are upon the top thereof:

3 And two olive trees by it, one upon the right side of the bowl, and the other upon the left side thereof.

4 So I answered and spake to the angel that talked with me, saying, What are these, my lord?

5 Then the angel that talked with me answered and said unto me, Knowest thou not what these be? And I said, No, my lord.

6 Then he answered and spake unto me, saying, This is the word of the LORD unto Zerubbabel, saying, Not by might, nor by power, but by my Spirit, saith the LORD of hosts.

7 Who art thou, O great mountain? before Zerubbabel thou shalt become a plain: and he shall bring forth the headstone thereof with shoutings, crying, Grace, grace unto it.

8 Moreover the word of the LORD came unto me, saying,

9 The hands of Zerubbabel have laid the foundation of this house; his hands shall also finish it; and thou shalt know that the LORD of hosts hath sent me unto you.

10 For who hath despised the day of small things? for they shall rejoice, and shall see the plummet in the hand of Zerubbabel with those seven; they are the eyes of the LORD, which run to and fro through the whole earth.

11 Then answered I, and said unto him, What are these two olive trees upon the right side of the candlestick and upon the left side thereof?

12 And I answered again, and said unto him, What be these two olive branches, which through the two golden pipes empty the golden oil out of themselves?

13 And he answered me and said, Knowest thou not what these be? And I said, No, my lord.

14 Then said he, These are the two anointed ones, that stand by the Lord of the whole earth.

GOLDEN TEXT: Not by might, nor by power, but by my Spirit, saith the LORD of hosts.—Zechariah 4:6.

God Leads a People Home
Unit 1: Promise to Return
(Lessons 1-4)

Lesson Aims

After this lesson, a student should be able to:

1. Describe and explain Zechariah's vision of the candlestick and the olive trees.

2. Give examples of God's doing great things through small or unlikely instruments.

3. Commit to a specific task for the Lord, "not by might, nor by power, but by God's Spirit."

Lesson Outline

INTRODUCTION
  A. A Prophet's Timing
  B. Lesson Background
I. MYSTERIOUS VISION (Zechariah 4:1-3)
  A. The Interpreter (v. 1)
  B. The Vision (vv. 2, 3)
II. THE EXPLANATION (Zechariah 4:4-10)
  A. Question (vv. 4, 5)
  B. Answer (vv. 6, 7)
    Mountains Into Molehills
  C. Additional Promise (vv. 8-10)
    The Importance of Small Things
III. THE TWO LEADERS (Zechariah 4:11-14)
  A. Repeated Question (vv. 11-13)
  B. Delayed Answer (v. 14)
CONCLUSION
  A. The Power
  B. The Other Side
  C. Prayer
  D. Thought to Remember

Today's visual for Lesson 4 stirs us to accept the challenge of world evangelism, not by our might, but by God's Spirit. It is shown on page 37.

Introduction

A. A Prophet's Timing

Galatians 4:4 tells us, "When the fulness of the time was come, God sent forth his Son." This same statement could apply to how God "sent forth" His prophets at pivotal moments in Old Testament history to challenge His people. Although the prophets often spoke messages of judgment, their coming was the expression of God's great love for His chosen people. His was a love that warned them of the folly of their ways and urged them to change. As we saw in last week's lesson, He sent the prophet Haggai to stir up both the leaders of the returned exiles (Zerubbabel and Joshua) and the people themselves to examine their attitudes and resume construction of the temple.

B. Lesson Background

Two months after Haggai began to sound God's call, God sent another prophet named Zechariah to provide additional encouragement (compare the times given in Haggai 1:1 and Zechariah 1:1). The people responded enthusiastically to the prophets' appeal and resumed work on the long-neglected temple (not many prophets received such an immediate and positive response). The Scriptures also tell us that Haggai and Zechariah did more than just stand on the sidelines and preach; they pitched in and helped with the project (Ezra 5:2)!

Although Haggai and Zechariah were both prophets of God, their messages were delivered in very different styles. Haggai's preaching was bold and direct, challenging the people to give God's house the priority it deserved. Zechariah, on the other hand, used a series of mysterious visions to communicate God's will. His book has been compared to Revelation because of its apocalyptic contents; that is, much of Zechariah's writing describes the struggle between righteousness and evil in highly symbolic terms, portraying God's purposes and God's people triumphant in the end. Someone has likened Haggai's role in the rebuilding program to that of the builder, responsible for the structure of the temple, while Zechariah resembled the artist, adding color and attractive decorations to brighten the interior.

I. Mysterious Vision
(Zechariah 4:1-3)

This passage records the fifth in a series of visions given to Zechariah. By themselves these visions may seem more puzzling than enlightening, but an angel was at hand to help Zechariah understand them. We too are helped by his explanation.

A. The Interpreter (v. 1)

1. And the angel that talked with me came again, and waked me, as a man that is wakened out of his sleep.

This *angel* is mentioned repeatedly in the visions that comprise the first six chapters of the book of Zechariah. His primary purpose seems to be to interpret the visions. We are not given his name or any other information about him. Here he roused Zechariah to get his attention.

B. The Vision (vv. 2, 3)

2. And said unto me, What seest thou? And I said, I have looked, and behold a candlestick all of gold, with a bowl upon the top of it, and his seven lamps thereon, and seven pipes to the seven lamps, which are upon the top thereof.

Don't you wish we could have a photograph or a model to show us just what this was like? The Hebrew word rendered *candlestick* is the word *menorah*. Many today are familiar with this term because of its association with the Jewish holiday of Hanukkah, during which a menorah is lighted each night for a period of eight days. This word literally means "light bearer." Translators of the *King James Version* called it a *candlestick*, for this was the ordinary light bearer of their time. Other versions (such as the *New International Version* and the *New American Standard Bible*) call it a "lampstand," because the lights it bore were *lamps*, not candles. The ordinary lamp of ancient times was a small bowl of olive oil with a wick upon which the oil was burned.

This menorah witnessed by Zechariah had *seven lamps . . . upon the top thereof*. We are not told exactly how these were arranged. The menorah of the Jerusalem temple in the first century offers one possibility. We know what this looked like, because the Arch of Titus in Rome pictures it as a part of the spoil that the Roman general Titus brought back when he conquered Jerusalem in A.D. 70. It had seven lamps in a straight row at the top. Concentric semicircles supported three lamps on each side of the central lamp.

An artist's sketch of the menorah from the Jerusalem temple in the first century A.D. as depicted in a relief on the Arch of Titus in Rome.

In Zechariah's vision there was also a *bowl*, apparently holding a supply of oil for the lamps. Since this also was *upon the top*, we may suppose that it was positioned beside the row of lamps. There were *seven pipes* (the Hebrew reads "lips") to carry oil from the bowl *to the seven lamps*.

3. And two olive trees by it, one upon the right side of the bowl, and the other upon the left side thereof.

We shall read more about these trees in the final part of our printed text.

II. The Explanation
(Zechariah 4:4-10)

A. Question (vv. 4, 5)

4, 5. So I answered and spake to the angel that talked with me, saying, What are these, my lord? Then the angel that talked with me answered and said unto me, Knowest thou not what these be? And I said, No, my lord.

Zechariah was as puzzled as we would have been. He saw the items mentioned above, but what did they mean? It appears that he was specifically concerned with the significance of the two olive trees, about which he repeats his question in verse 11.

B. Answer (vv. 6, 7)

6. Then he answered and spake unto me, saying, This is the word of the LORD unto Zerubbabel, saying, Not by might, nor by power, but by my Spirit, saith the LORD of hosts.

The vision was a message from *the Lord unto Zerubbabel*, the governor of the little colony of returned exiles. Along with Joshua the high priest, the governor carried the burden of leadership. Now that the Lord through His prophets had roused the people to resume work on the temple, the governor may have been wondering whether they would be able to finish the job. The Lord's message was plain: they would indeed finish the job, *not by* their own *might* or *power*, but by God's *Spirit*. How many impossible tasks, both ancient and modern, have been completed by the power of this same Spirit?

With the message of the vision now before us, we can begin to see how Zechariah's vision conveyed this message. The oil flowing into the lamps was a symbol of God's Spirit flowing into the little band of former captives and empowering them to finish the building of God's house. As we saw in last week's lesson, Haggai stated, "The glory of this latter house shall be greater than of the former" (Haggai 2:9). The Son of God, who ministered in the second temple, has enlightened the entire world, giving all its people a knowledge of the glory of God. It is significant that in the New Testament, a candlestick represents the church (Revelation 1:20). Christians are now the channel through which God's Spirit flows, impacting the world for Christ.

7. Who art thou, O great mountain? before Zerubbabel thou shalt become a plain: and he shall bring forth the headstone thereof with shoutings, crying, Grace, grace unto it.

The quality of timber necessary for the temple had to be transported from a *mountain* nearly a hundred miles away in the forests of Lebanon. This had been the source of the wood for the people's houses (Haggai 1:8). However, the term *mountain* may also be a symbol of the formidable difficulties and obstacles that perhaps had discouraged *Zerubbabel* in his leadership. He remembered the indifference of the people. They had worked enthusiastically on the foundation of the temple, then had lapsed into a period of indifference that spanned sixteen years. For now they had resumed work, but would their zeal diminish once again? Zerubbabel also must have been deeply concerned about continued opposition from the surrounding residents of the land, such as that which had earlier frustrated the Jews (Ezra 4:4, 5).

Into the midst of these concerns came the word of God to calm any fears the governor had. He and the people needed only to trust the Lord and proceed with their work. The seemingly overwhelming mountain of adversities would vanish, and the people would move over a level *plain* to victory. The words of this verse are reminiscent of Jesus' teaching about the power of faith to move mountains (Mark 11:23).

As with any attempt to accomplish the Lord's work, the task of rebuilding would not be done by the people's own strength, but neither would it be done without their strength. If Zerubbabel stepped forward and led his people with energy and confidence, he would be able to finish the temple, and to put the *headstone*, or topmost stone, in place. Then what a celebration there would be, including *shoutings* of thankful prayer: *Grace, grace unto it.* This grace would be God's favor, blessing His completed house.

Mountains Into Molehills

Pessimists are said to "make mountains out of molehills." On the other hand, some people turn mountains *into* molehills, succeeding in spite of life's obstacles. For example, Jim Ryun was the world's best mile runner for nearly a decade, in spite of the fact that he had hearing difficulties. He had trouble hearing the starter's pistol go off, and could not hear the footsteps of other runners—both significant handicaps.

He held the world record for the fifteen-hundred-meter run when he ran in that event in the 1968 Olympics at Mexico City. In the first heat he had to place only fourth to go on to the semi-final event, but he was fouled by another run-

How to Say It

APOCALYPTIC. uh-pock-uh-*lip*-tik.
CYRUS. *Sigh*-russ.
HAGGAI. *Hag*-a-eye or *Hag*-eye.
HANUKKAH. *Hahn*-uh-kuh.
MASHIACH. (Hebrew). mah-*she*-ock.
MENORAH. (Hebrew). muh-*nor*-uh.
ZECHARIAH. Zek-uh-*rye*-uh.
ZERUBBABEL. Zeh-*rub*-uh-bull.

ner. The resultant fall cost him the race. Ryun appealed, but it was denied. Although he could have let this defeat turn him against life, this is what Jim Ryun had to say about it:

"I became a Christian. I struggled with hurt and bitterness over the incident . . . I said, 'Lord, you know those Olympic officials know I was fouled!' Then one day I learned forgiveness. God showed me how to become a real winner. I realized I was being tested."

God's message to Zerubbabel was that *real* strength comes from relying on God's Spirit. Even a great mountain will become a plain before Him. This message applies to us as well: mountainous obstacles can be crossed as if they were mere "speed bumps" in the road of life, if we place our trust in God.　　　　—C. R. B.

C. Additional Promise (vv. 8-10)

8, 9. Moreover the word of the Lord came unto me, saying, The hands of Zerubbabel have laid the foundation of this house; his hands shall also finish it; and thou shalt know that the Lord of hosts hath sent me unto you.

The hands of Zerubbabel means the strength and activity of all the people led by Zerubbabel's example of faith in God. The people had *laid the foundation of this house* about sixteen years earlier. Since then the work had been abandoned. Now they were starting again, and in four more years the temple would be completed. Then Zerubbabel and all the people would *know* that the Lord Himself had sent His angel with this assurance of success.

10. For who hath despised the day of small things? for they shall rejoice, and shall see the plummet in the hand of Zerubbabel with those seven; they are the eyes of the Lord, which run to and fro through the whole earth.

Some of the people were disappointed because the new temple did not match the splendor of the one Solomon had built long before (Haggai 2:3). But no one should despise this second temple for being *small* or inferior. Ultimately it would be more glorious than the first one. We saw this point made in last week's lesson (Haggai 2:3-9). It is not the size of the task itself that is important, but the size of the God who is behind it!

A *plummet*, or plumb line, is a weight suspended on a string so that the string will hang straight. Builders use it to be sure that a wall is perfectly vertical. *The plummet in the hand of Zerubbabel* indicated that he was what we might call the inspector of the temple, who would verify that the building was constructed properly. This was a reason to *rejoice*, because Zerubbabel was honest and capable—a man chosen by God (Haggai 2:23).

The second half of this verse, as it appears in our printed text, is difficult to interpret. It seems to say that *those seven*, which refers to *the eyes of the Lord*, were in the *hand of Zerubbabel*. According to the Hebrew text, the phrase *those seven* is actually the subject of this part of the verse. Understood more literally, the verse says, "They shall rejoice and shall see the plumb line in the hand of Zerubbabel—these seven, the eyes of the Lord that run throughout all the earth." It is interesting that, according to Revelation 5:6, the Lamb in the center of the heavenly throne has "seven eyes, which are the seven Spirits of God sent forth into all the earth." The seven Spirits are generally interpreted to mean the Holy Spirit in the fullness of His work. This Spirit already has been declared to be the source of the power by which Zerubbabel and the people would accomplish their task (v. 6). Thus, in the verse before us, the Spirit is described as experiencing great joy from witnessing the success of Zerubbabel.

THE IMPORTANCE OF SMALL THINGS

The Sears Tower is the tallest building in the world. The Boeing 747 is the biggest commercial airliner in the world. Mount Everest is the highest mountain in the world. The *Guinness Book of World Records* lists all of these and thousands of other "ests" in the world. We're impressed with superlatives, aren't we? If something is the biggest, the fastest, or the "mostest," it must be the best, according to the way many people think.

But God is interested in little things. The way our bodies are made demonstrates this. Our sense of touch is one example: scientists tell us that our skin can sense an object as small as 1/25,000th of an inch, and a mother's lips can tell when the temperature of her baby's forehead rises by just six-thousandths of a degree!

So it should not seem strange when the Lord asks Zechariah, "Who hath despised the day of small things?" Although the eyes of God watch over the whole earth, He still takes note of sim-

ple, common items such as a carpenter's plumb line or a lampstand and two olive trees.

Ancient Israel was not a great nation compared with Assyria, Babylon, or Rome. But through this obscure people, the Messiah came to bless the whole world. God can still work wonders through people who are willing to do their small tasks and let Him have the credit.

—C. R. B.

III. The Two Leaders (Zechariah 4:11-14)

A. Repeated Question (vv. 11-13)

11. Then answered I, and said unto him, What are these two olive trees upon the right side of the candlestick and upon the left side thereof?

This question (the same one raised by Zechariah in v. 4) had still not been answered. Perhaps the Lord wanted His prophet to think about it for a while. How often we find something to puzzle us in God's Word! It may be days or even years before we find an explanation, though we both pray for it and search the Bible for it. Meanwhile we are always enriched by our continuing search through the sacred pages. When the explanation finally comes, we treasure it the more because of the wait.

12. And I answered again, and said unto him, What be these two olive branches, which through the two golden pipes empty the golden oil out of themselves?

In asking this question, Zechariah noted three features of the vision not mentioned previously: *two olive branches, two golden pipes, and golden oil* flowing from the branches through the pipes. Perhaps they were partially concealed by foliage; possibly Zechariah had not noticed them until he began to search more carefully for an answer to his question. In searching the Bible for an answer to a puzzling question, we often find unexpected treasures of truth that we have not seen before. Perhaps this is one of God's reasons for letting us wait for an answer.

Usually oil was produced by picking ripe olives, crushing them in a press, and straining

visual for lesson 4

the oil from the pulp. In the vision, the picking, crushing, and straining were bypassed; the branches poured oil directly into the pipes. Having read the rest of the vision, we naturally suppose that the pipes carried the oil to the bowl that supplied the seven lamps.

13. And he answered me and said, Knowest thou not what these be? And I said, No, my lord.

Again the answer to the prophet's question was delayed, and no doubt he grew even more eager to hear it.

B. Delayed Answer (v. 14)

14. Then said he, These are the two anointed ones, that stand by the Lord of the whole earth.

The two anointed ones are most likely the two leaders of the Jewish colony: Zerubbabel and Joshua. From these two the oil was flowing to the bowl and on to the lamps. It should be noted that the Hebrew phrase rendered *anointed ones* is literally "sons of oil." It is not the usual term (*mashiach*) from which we get the word "Messiah." The phrase indicates that God's purpose for Zerubbabel and Joshua was to function as His instruments through which the oil (God's Spirit) flowed. The Spirit directed and encouraged these leaders, who in turn directed and encouraged the workers. Thus by God's Spirit, not by any human power (v. 6), the Lord's house was completed.

Conclusion

The heart of this lesson is seen in the Golden Text from Zechariah 4:6: "Not by might, nor by power, but by my Spirit, saith the Lord of hosts."

A. The Power

No great work for God is done by human might or power alone. Jesus sent His disciples on a mammoth worldwide task, but He said, "I am with you alway, even unto the end of the world" (Matthew 28:20). Previously He had told them, "Without me ye can do nothing" (John 15:5). They were not to begin their task until they were "endued with power from on high" (Luke 24:49). On the Day of Pentecost, God's Spirit came with that power in spectacular fashion, and in one day three thousand repentant sinners came seeking forgiveness (Acts 2:41). The power of the Spirit won them, not the power of the apostles.

When we think about building a lovely church house, starting a church, hiring an additional staff member, or sending a missionary, it is proper to think about our resources. Jesus spoke plainly of counting the cost before

attempting an especially challenging endeavor (Luke 14:25-33), but His intent was not to keep us from undertaking great things. It was rather that we undertake great things with a firm resolution to pay the cost and finish the job. The crucial question is this: Are we sure this is what God wants us to do?

B. The Other Side

The temple was finished by God's Spirit, not by human might or power. That is true. But the other side of this truth is that it was not finished without human might or power. Human hands hewed the stone; human muscle labored mightily to move it into place. In Zechariah's vision, the oil did not produce light without the lamps; in a similar manner, God's Spirit works in human minds, hearts, and bodies to accomplish great things.

If we are thinking of engaging in some worthwhile task for God, it is good to pray for His Spirit to do it. But it is also necessary to dedicate *ourselves* to the task: our minds, our muscle, and our money. It is bad to imagine that we can do anything great for the Lord without His Spirit.

C. Prayer

Lord God of hosts, keep us far from the folly of thinking that we can accomplish any great and good task without You. Help us to be obedient to Your Spirit. May we be bold enough to undertake greater things than we have done before, and may we be faithful to carry them to completion. Amen.

D. Thought to Remember

God's purposes cannot be accomplished apart from God's power.

Home Daily Bible Readings

Monday, Sept. 22—Call to Renewal (Zechariah 1:1-6)
Tuesday, Sept. 23—God Will Live Among Us (Zechariah 2:6-13)
Wednesday, Sept. 24—Empowered by God's Spirit (Zechariah 4:1-7)
Thursday, Sept. 25—"The Day of Small Things" (Zechariah 4:8-14)
Friday, Sept. 26—Time for Kindness and Mercy (Zechariah 7:1-14)
Saturday, Sept. 27—Hearing God's Promise (Zechariah 8:1-13)
Sunday, Sept. 28—The Prince of Peace (Zechariah 9:9-13)

Learning by Doing

This page contains an alternate lesson plan emphasizing learning activities.
Classes desiring such student involvement will find these suggestions helpful.

Learning Goals

As students participate in today's lesson, they should:

1. Describe and explain Zechariah's vision of the candlestick and the olive trees.

2. Give examples of God's doing great things through small or unlikely instruments.

3. Commit to a specific task for the Lord, "not by might, nor by power, but by God's Spirit."

Into the Lesson

Write the following scrambled phrases (without the answers in parentheses) on your chalkboard or on posters that you have prepared before class:

much when Little in is God it is. (Little is much when God is in it.)

by my nor Not Spirit might, by by power, but. (Not by might, nor by power, but by my Spirit.)

with I world even you am alway, unto of the the end. (I am with you alway, even unto the end of the world.)

Challenge class members to unscramble all three sentences. Give a prize to the one who first completes all three correctly. Write the three unscrambled sentences on your chalkboard, and ask, "What do these three sentences have in common?" Point out that each highlights the necessity of God's power to do God's work. Tell the class that today's lesson challenges us to look at how God's Spirit enables His people to do His will.

Into the Word

Note that this week's Scripture records the prophecy of a man who spoke for God about the same time as Haggai. Use the introductory material in the commentary to provide the setting for Zechariah. Note especially the difference in style between his prophecies and those of Haggai.

Next, distribute the following two groups of statements (or refer class members to the student book, where this exercise is printed). Class members are to match the top list of phrases from the Scripture with the proper item from the second list. (Answers are included here for your use.)

List One

2. The golden candlestick with the seven lamps (v. 2)

1. The two olive trees (vv. 3, 11)

3. The great mountain (v. 7)

4. The golden oil flowing through the golden pipes (v. 12)

List Two

1. The two leaders of the Jews: Zerubbabel the governor and Joshua the high priest.

2. Knowledge about God going out from Jerusalem to enlighten the world.

3. The many obstacles that the people faced in rebuilding the temple.

4. God's Spirit.

Next, discuss the following questions with the class:

1. Where would the people get their strength to rebuild the temple?

2. How would they receive this strength? Whom would God use?

3. What do you suppose were some of the obstacles facing the Jews as they approached the task of rebuilding the temple?

4. What were some of the results that would follow the completion of the temple (vv. 7-10)? How would knowing these provide encouragement to Zerubbabel and to the people?

5. How do you suppose Zerubbabel felt when he received this prophecy? How do you suppose the people felt?

Into Life

Distribute the following list of Agree/Disagree statements to the class, or simply read and discuss them, one at a time. The class should decide whether each is true or not, based on the implications of today's Scripture.

1. God's Spirit makes the difference, not my work.

2. God desires His Spirit to work through everyday people who find themselves in places of responsibility.

3. Most great tasks for God are accomplished in spite of a mountain of difficulties.

4. Sometimes the obstacles in our way are too great for us to accomplish a task for God.

5. Great leaders are a source of God's power.

Challenge class members to identify a task that they believe God wants them to accomplish. Do they see great obstacles in the way of their success? Ask them to close with sentence prayers, asking for God's Spirit to flow through them as channels of His power.

Let's Talk It Over

The questions on this page are designed to encourage review of the lesson Scriptures and to promote discussion of the lesson by the class. The answers provided are only discussion starters. Let your class talk it over from there.

1. The phrase, "Not by might, nor by power, but by my Spirit," is of Old Testament origin, but is very much applicable to Christians. How can we fix in our minds the principle found in this phrase?

This would make an excellent slogan for a congregation to feature in its Sunday bulletin or church newsletter. Any worker in the church would do well to print it in a prominent place in his or her Bible. Zerubbabel was given this message in connection with the tremendous challenge of completing the temple. It could also serve as a valuable reminder to the church when undertaking an ambitious new enterprise. A bold evangelistic outreach into the community, an energetic effort to minister to the needy, a faith-stretching building program—these are some examples of challenges the church should tackle only in dependence upon God's Spirit.

2. Zechariah described the difficulties involved in rebuilding the temple as a "great mountain." This should call to mind Jesus' reference to our moving mountains through faith (Matthew 17:20). What are some mountains of difficulty we must move by faith today?

Our commission to evangelize the world seems more of a mountain as time passes. The influence of heathen religions, the lure of political power and financial gain, the highly publicized attacks on the accuracy and authority of the Bible—these are among the factors that challenge us to develop a mountain-moving faith. Another growing mountain of difficulty is our society's rejection of Biblical moral values. Pornography, homosexuality, abortion, divorce, and the like seem to gain in acceptance, in spite of our outcries against them.

3. The lesson writer concludes that the two olive branches in Zechariah's vision were Zerubbabel the governor and Joshua the high priest. As channels through which God's Spirit flowed, these two men were supplying spiritual leadership to the people. How is it appropriate to think of church leaders in this way?

In Bible times, the oil from olive trees served as fuel for light in the temple and in people's homes. Leaders provide spiritual light to guide their people in following God's way. The oil represented the Holy Spirit, who guided and strengthened the people in Zechariah's time, and functions similarly in the church today. Thinking of leaders in this way reminds us of how vital it is that ministers, elders, teachers, and others in influential positions be filled with the Holy Spirit, so that they can provide godly leadership for their congregations.

4. We must work in harmony with God's Spirit, but we must not get in God's way. How can we achieve this kind of balance in our spiritual labor?

Someone has said, "We must pray as if everything depended on God, and we must work as if everything depended on us." This is true, but we often fail to keep the complete picture in perspective. Too many Christians are inclined to pray and then do no more. It may seem like the way of faith to confess, "Lord, it is up to You. There is nothing we can do." But there is something we can do with His guidance and with His power working in us. Other Christians may fall into the trap of believing that God's work can be accomplished through human ingenuity and determined effort. There is nothing wrong with these elements, as long as they are harnessed to God's Spirit. But when these elements are separated from God's Spirit, we can get in God's way and hinder rather than help His cause.

5. What are some prayers we can offer that will help bring us in line with the Holy Spirit's power?

Paul's letter to the Ephesians contains some exciting insights into prayer. In Ephesians 1:15-23 Paul prayed for the Ephesians to receive spiritual enlightenment and divine power. We can apply his prayer to our church. In 3:14-21 he offered a similar prayer, which we can also apply to our own situation. God would surely be pleased if we were to ask Him to "do immeasurably more than all we ask or imagine, according to his power that is at work within us" (3:20, *New International Version*). In 6:10-18 is the familiar listing of the Christian's armor. We need to put on each piece prayerfully. Especially do we need to pray that the Word of God will work mightily as the sword of the Spirit (6:17) in our preaching, teaching, and personal evangelism.

3^φ

Resisting Temptation

October 5
Lesson 5

DEVOTIONAL READING: Psalm 40:1-11.

LESSON SCRIPTURE: Daniel 1.

PRINTED TEXT: Daniel 1:3-5, 8-16.

Oct
5

Daniel 1:3-5, 8-16

3 And the king spake unto Ashpenaz the master of his eunuchs, that he should bring certain of the children of Israel, and of the king's seed, and of the princes;

4 Children in whom was no blemish, but well-favored, and skilful in all wisdom, and cunning in knowledge, and understanding science, and such as had ability in them to stand in the king's palace, and whom they might teach the learning and the tongue of the Chaldeans.

5 And the king appointed them a daily provision of the king's meat, and of the wine which he drank: so nourishing them three years, that at the end thereof they might stand before the king.

. . . .

8 But Daniel purposed in his heart that he would not defile himself with the portion of the king's meat, nor with the wine which he drank: therefore he requested of the prince of the eunuchs that he might not defile himself.

9 Now God had brought Daniel into favor and tender love with the prince of the eunuchs.

10 And the prince of the eunuchs said unto Daniel, I fear my lord the king, who hath appointed your meat and your drink: for why should he see your faces worse liking than the children which are of your sort? then shall ye make me endanger my head to the king.

11 Then said Daniel to Melzar, whom the prince of the eunuchs had set over Daniel, Hananiah, Mishael, and Azariah,

12 Prove thy servants, I beseech thee, ten days; and let them give us pulse to eat, and water to drink.

13 Then let our countenances be looked upon before thee, and the countenance of the children that eat of the portion of the king's meat: and as thou seest, deal with thy servants.

14 So he consented to them in this matter, and proved them ten days.

15 And at the end of ten days their countenances appeared fairer and fatter in flesh than all the children which did eat the portion of the king's meat.

16 Thus Melzar took away the portion of their meat, and the wine that they should drink; and gave them pulse.

GOLDEN TEXT: Daniel purposed in his heart that he would not defile himself with the portion of the king's meat, nor with the wine which he drank.—Daniel 1:8.

God Leads a People Home
Unit 2. Daniel: Faithful Under Fire
(Lessons 5-8)

Lesson Aims

After this lesson, a student should be able to:

1. Tell how Daniel and his companions resisted the temptation to compromise their principles.

2. List some similar temptations that challenge Christians today.

3. Suggest some specific ways to "resist the devil" in those situations.

Lesson Outline

INTRODUCTION
    A. A Brief Review
    B. Lesson Background
  I. CAPTIVE STUDENTS (Daniel 1:3-5)
    A. Cream of the Crop (vv. 3, 4)
    B. Care of the Captives (v. 5)
 II. A TEST AT THE TABLE (Daniel 1:8-14)
    A. Special Request (v. 8)
       Good "Table Manners"
    B. Problem for the Prince (vv. 9, 10)
    C. Daniel's Proposal (vv. 11-14)
       Going by the Book
III. THE RESULTS (Daniel 1:15, 16)
    A. The Ten-Day Result (v. 15)
    B. The Three-Year Result (v. 16)
CONCLUSION
    A. Temptation
    B. Good Voices
    C. Prayer
    D. Thought to Remember

Use the visual for Lesson 5 of the visuals packet to emphasize the importance of resisting temptation, as Daniel did. It is shown on page 44.

Introduction

I know a charming lady who cannot stand to look at mashed potatoes, much less to eat them. Another friend resolutely declines beef and pork, though he likes them as well as I do. He has had a coronary bypass, and does not want to go through that ordeal again. Still another acquaintance is always hungry because she eats little of anything. She claims that is the only way she can control her weight. Then there is a conscientious man who refuses meat of all kinds. He confines himself to a vegetarian diet, because that is what God assigned to man in the beginning (Genesis 1:29).

Truly God has provided edible items in a marvelous variety. Do you know anyone who enjoys all the foods that are available? Most of us restrict our diet in some way. The food offered to Daniel was thought to be the finest in the kingdom, but he turned it down. He knew it would defile him.

A. A Brief Review

In September our four lessons dealt with a promise made and a promise fulfilled. Through the prophet Isaiah, God promised His people's release from captivity in Babylon. Isaiah even named the ruler (Cyrus) who would serve as God's agent to accomplish this, though Cyrus's decree was not issued until nearly one hundred and fifty years after Isaiah's time. When the Medes and Persians overthrew Babylon in 539 B.C., Cyrus took control of Babylon's vast empire. Not long afterward, Cyrus issued the decree that permitted the exiles to return home. Close to fifty thousand people went back to rebuild Jerusalem and the temple, but about twenty more years passed before the temple was actually completed.

B. Lesson Background

In this next unit of lessons, we turn to the book of Daniel for another look at that period of history when Israel was under the rule of Babylon. This domination began when Nebuchadnezzar and his army besieged Jerusalem and forced King Jehoiakim to surrender (Daniel 1:1, 2). This happened in the year 605 B.C. The defeated king was allowed to stay in Jerusalem and rule his people, but he had to pay tribute to Babylon. At that time only a few captives were taken away. Among them were four brave and faithful young men, who, like Joseph in Egypt, found themselves isolated from family and familiar surroundings, and relocated in a distant land that knew little or nothing of the true God.

Despite such an environment, these men made a firm commitment not to isolate themselves from their faith. They realized that, although they were now dwelling in a foreign land, they still had a responsibility to obey God.

I. Captive Students
(Daniel 1:3-5)

The captives taken to Babylon in 605 B.C. may have been used to try to teach King Jehoiakim a lesson. Perhaps he would think twice about rebelling, if some of his sons and his country's prominent young men were held prisoners in Babylon. Their captivity, however, did not mean punishment, menial work, or any kind of mistreatment. They were to be students in a special "honors" program, and were to be treated very well.

A. Cream of the Crop (vv. 3, 4)

3. And the king spake unto Ashpenaz the master of his eunuchs, that he should bring certain of the children of Israel, and of the king's seed, and of the princes.

The officer sent to select from the captives was the manager of the king's household and court. Here he is called *the master of his eunuchs*. Many royal attendants were emasculated, both to make them more submissive and loyal, and to prevent any misconduct with ladies of the court. As used in the Old Testament, however, the particular Hebrew word rendered *eunuchs* can describe any royal official, whether the man was literally a eunuch or not.

The captives chosen were to be young men of the upper class: *of the king's seed, and of the princes*. Here *princes* does not mean the king's sons; it designates men holding high places in government, or what we might call the nobility.

4. Children in whom was no blemish, but well-favored, and skilful in all wisdom, and cunning in knowledge, and understanding science, and such as had ability in them to stand in the king's palace, and whom they might teach the learning and the tongue of the Chaldeans.

How to Say It

ABEDNEGO. Uh-*bed*-nee-go.
ASHPENAZ. *Ash*-pih-naz.
AZARIAH. Az-uh-*rye*-uh.
BABYLONIANS. Bab-uh-*low*-nee-unz.
BELTESHAZZAR. Bel-tih-*shazz*-er.
CHALDEANS. Kal-*dee*-unz.
CYRUS. *Sigh*-russ.
EUNUCHS. *you*-nicks.
HANANIAH. Han-uh-*nye*-uh.
JEHOIAKIM. Jeh-*hoy*-uh-kim.
MEDES. Meeds.
MELZAR. *Mel*-zar.
MESHACH. *Me*-shack.
MISHAEL. *Mish*-a-el.
NEBUCHADNEZZAR. *Neb*-uh-kad-*nezz*-er (strong accent on *nezz*).
SHADRACH. *Shad*-rack.
URIJAH. You-*rye*-juh.

A careful selection process took place for the most attractive, talented, and capable of the captives. They had to be *well-favored*, which means handsome (the Hebrew literally says, "good of appearance"). They had to be highly intelligent, skilled in all varieties of *knowledge*. They needed to possess the natural *ability . . . to stand in the king's palace* as his advisers. They had to be able to learn not only the *tongue*, or language, *of the Chaldeans* (Babylonians), but their entire culture as well.

Obviously, Nebuchadnezzar meant to take the best and brightest young men of Israel and make them into highly trained and loyal Babylonians. Then he would have among his advisers some men who were thoroughly acquainted with Hebrew ways of thinking and acting. Such men would be a valuable asset in dealing with the Jews, whom he intended to keep as a permanent part of his empire.

B. Care of the Captives (v. 5)

5. And the king appointed them a daily provision of the king's meat, and of the wine which he drank: so nourishing them three years, that at the end thereof they might stand before the king.

The best was not too good for these students. Their food and drink came directly from the king's table (the word *meat* means food of all kinds). These young men enjoyed whatever the king ate. Their training period was to last three years. To put their experience in our terms, we might say that they had entered a college-level program of study. At the end of their course of study, the men were to be ready for "entry-level positions" among the king's men.

Verses 6 and 7 (not in our printed text) name four of the Hebrew students. In order to sever their ties with their Hebrew heritage and culture, the prince of the eunuchs gave them Babylonian names that contained references to Babylonian gods. For example, Daniel's new name, Belteshazzar, means, "O Bel, protect the king!" For some reason not explained, the record continues to call Daniel by his Hebrew name; but the others more often are called by their new names: Shadrach, Meshach, and Abednego.

II. A Test at the Table (Daniel 1:8-14)

A. Special Request (v. 8)

8. But Daniel purposed in his heart that he would not defile himself with the portion of the king's meat, nor with the wine which he drank: therefore he requested of the prince of the eunuchs that he might not defile himself.

There were several reasons why *the king's meat* might *defile* a conscientious Hebrew. The Law of Moses did not allow every kind of animal to be used for meat. The king's meat may have included some of the forbidden animals. Second, the Law required that animals be butchered properly, with the blood carefully drained out. This step may have been omitted in preparing food for the king. Third, the king's meat may have been taken from animals offered in sacrifice to pagan gods. Perhaps this applied to the *wine* also, for a part of it was probably poured out in sacrifice to the Babylonian gods.

Daniel's *heart* was set against taking part in pagan worship, and against violating God's Law in any way. He took his request directly to *the prince of the eunuchs*, who was the man primarily responsible for these young captives.

GOOD "TABLE MANNERS"

In 1993 a Kentucky high school student began harassing the teacher in his Spanish class. His calculated approach was to upset the class with cursing and yelling as much and as often as possible. Ultimately he began making veiled threats on her life.

Unfortunately, this is no longer an uncommon phenomenon. Recent surveys of American public school teachers indicate that nearly ten percent have been attacked by students at school, and more than forty percent of them report major discipline problems.

The Spanish teacher in Kentucky filed criminal charges against her "student" and he was fined $33,700 for his actions. But the effect of his actions was so great that her health and mental stability were harmed and she had to ask for early retirement.

We live in an age when "in your face" confrontation—sometimes thoughtless and sometimes exceedingly calculated—is increasingly common. How refreshing was Daniel's approach to his disagreement with the king! Instead of exhibiting rebellious rejection of the king's prescribed diet for him and his friends, he actually *sought permission* to be freed from it!

For the people of God in every age, there will always be both appropriate and inappropriate ways to express their rejection of the world's ways. Daniel's respectful, reasoned stand for his principles endures as an example for us all.

—C. R. B.

B. Problem for the Prince (vv. 9, 10)

9. Now God had brought Daniel into favor and tender love with the prince of the eunuchs.

This does not necessarily mean that God miraculously moved the *prince of the eunuchs* to

visual for lesson 5

favor Daniel. It is more likely that God guided Daniel in acting courteously and cooperatively, and the prince favored him for that reason. If this group of students included captives from a number of heathen nations, probably some of them were quite resentful and hostile toward their superiors.

10. And the prince of the eunuchs said unto Daniel, I fear my lord the king, who hath appointed your meat and your drink: for why should he see your faces worse liking than the children which are of your sort? then shall ye make me endanger my head to the king.

The prince of the eunuchs was told to give the Hebrew captives the same food and drink that *the king* had. This was supposed to be the very best. Now Daniel and his friends were requesting what appeared to be inferior food. If the prince gave it to them and they began to look undernourished, and if the king learned that his order had been disobeyed, then the disobedient officer would probably lose his *head*! King Nebuchadnezzar was not tolerant of people who failed to obey him (see Daniel 2:9-12).

C. Daniel's Proposal (vv. 11-14)

11. Then said Daniel to Melzar, whom the prince of the eunuchs had set over Daniel, Hananiah, Mishael, and Azariah.

Daniel did not embarrass *the prince of the eunuchs* by pressing his request, but neither did he give up. He turned to a lower official who supervised the actual serving of the meals. The Hebrew text reads, "the *melzar*," indicating that this may have been a title rather than a proper name. In this verse we see the Hebrew names of the four students, but later in the book three of them are more often called by their Babylonian names (as in chapter 3).

12. Prove thy servants, I beseech thee, ten days; and let them give us pulse to eat, and water to drink.

Although Daniel proposed this test, clearly he was speaking for his three companions as well as for himself. He said *thy servants,* not *thy servant,* and *give us,* not *give me.* The other three were as faithful to God's Law as Daniel was.

Pulse is a general term including all the foods that might be included in a vegetarian diet. No meat permitted under Hebrew law was available, so the Hebrew youths determined to eat no meat at all. The wine available was likely used in pagan worship, so they chose to drink *water*. Daniel did not ask Melzar to promise a permanent change, but a test for only *ten days*. This would not be long enough to make the Hebrews look seriously undernourished, even if their diet proved to be inadequate.

13, 14. Then let our countenances be looked upon before thee, and the countenance of the children that eat of the portion of the king's meat: and as thou seest, deal with thy servants. So he consented to them in this matter, and proved them ten days.

Melzar himself could check the results after the period of *ten days* had passed. If the *countenances*, or faces, of the Hebrew youths began to look thin and haggard, he could insist that they eat what the king prescribed. But if they continued to look well and strong, why not let them have the food they wanted? The proposal seemed fair enough, so Melzar *consented* to their request and allowed the four youths to be *proved*, or tested.

GOING BY THE BOOK

Prenuptial agreements have been taken to a new extreme by an Albuquerque, New Mexico, couple. Their penchant for "going by the book" is seen in the terms of the agreement they signed before getting married.

Among the terms agreed to by this "happy couple" are these: go to bed at 11:30 P.M. and rise at 6:30 A.M.; pay cash for everything, including a future home; leave nothing on the floor at night; never follow another car closer than one car length per ten miles per hour; and always do their grocery shopping from a list.

The "prince of the eunuchs" who was in charge of Daniel and his friends was another "go by the book" fellow, but with far more reason than the couple from Albuquerque. If his young Hebrew charges were not kept in good condition, he could lose his head for not following his orders. Fortunately, he was willing to test the proposal Daniel made to him.

Daniel and his friends were going by a different book from that of the prince of the eunuchs. They were following the Law of God. To blindly follow some other authority's command or slavishly observe a code that allows no spontaneity or personal growth (as in the case of the Albuquerque couple) may bring us only frustration. But to live by godly principles will always bear positive results.   —C. R. B.

III. The Results
(Daniel 1:15, 16)

A. The Ten-Day Result (v. 15)

15. And at the end of ten days their countenances appeared fairer and fatter in flesh than all the children which did eat the portion of the king's meat.

The results were decisive and irrefutable. The four Hebrew students obviously were in better condition than the others. It is interesting to note how the vocabulary of the *King James Version* is different from that of today's English, for today we reserve the term *fairer* for ladies rather than men (actually it is the same Hebrew phrase translated "well-favored" in v. 4). While *fatter* is a condition most want to avoid today, in Biblical times fatness symbolized prosperity and health for both animals and people (see Genesis 41:2; Habakkuk 1:16). The *New International Version* renders this passage in terms that we might use today: the Hebrew students "looked healthier and better nourished than any of the young men who ate the royal food."

B. The Three-Year Result (v. 16)

16. Thus Melzar took away the portion of their meat, and the wine that they should drink; and gave them pulse.

Since the Hebrew students showed no ill effects from their ten-day test, there seemed to be no reason not to let them have what they wanted on a regular basis. The long-term result of their commitment to obey God is recorded in the verses following our text (17-20). When the three-year course of study was finished, the final examination was held in the presence of the king. Which students graduated "with honors"? The four Hebrews, of course. The king "found them ten times better than all the magicians and astrologers that were in all his realm" (v. 20). The four served so wisely and so well that they were given prominent places in the government of Babylon (Daniel 2:49). All of today's students, whether in elementary school, high school, or college, would do well to put God first in their lives as these young men did.

Conclusion

Daniel, Hananiah, Mishael, Azariah—these young fellows are amazing! Remember where they came from and when they lived. They came from Jerusalem, from upper-class Jerusalem, from the ruling families (Daniel 1:3). They lived during a time when Israel's king, Jehoiakim, was doing "that which was evil in the sight of the Lord" (2 Kings 23:37). It was a time when the sin of Jerusalem had become intolerable before God, so much so that He sent the armies of Babylon to punish it.

One might expect young men from such a background to be somewhat spoiled, and therefore totally unprepared for survival as captives in a foreign land. Instead, we find four young Hebrews thoroughly, almost fanatically devoted to God and His way. It's wonderful!

A. Temptation

Our lesson title directs our thoughts to temptation, so let's consider the temptations that these young men faced in Jerusalem before they were taken to Babylon. They lived in a society where evil was the rule, not the exception. How easily they could have gone with the flow, and become as evil as the rest! They could have robbed in broad daylight. The corrupt courts would not have convicted them; their fathers were rich and powerful men. How easily they could have given themselves to drunken brawling and revelry! Yet these fellows remained clean, sober, upright young men. It's wonderful!

Also consider the temptation they confronted when they were taken far from home. They could have said, "We're in Babylon. God's Law is not the law here." They could have said, "We're captives. We have no choice." How natural it would have been to ignore the Law of God and enjoy the privileges of tuition-free students in the University of Babylon! But they did have a choice, and they knew it.

From this example and many others in Scripture, it is clear that we too have a choice. "The devil made me do it" is a lie. The devil entices me; he does not compel me. He cannot make me do anything unless I consent. God says, "Resist the devil, and he will flee from you" (James 4:7). God promises that no temptation will be too powerful for us to overcome (1 Corinthians 10:13). If we give in to temptation, it is because we fail to do our best and to use the resources God has provided.

B. Good Voices

King Jehoiakim must have hated God's Word. He murdered the prophet Urijah, even dragging him back from Egypt to kill him (Jeremiah 26:20-23). Evil voices were many and loud in Jerusalem during Jehoiakim's reign.

But there must have been good voices, too. Otherwise, how did Daniel and his friends know anything about God's Law? Somehow they knew what it said, and they were determined to obey it. Who was speaking for the Lord amid all the evil voices?

Some men in King Jehoiakim's presence dared to protest when the king burned the book containing Jeremiah's messages (Jeremiah 36:25). Perhaps some parents in Jerusalem were still teaching God's Word to their children, as the Law commanded them to do (Deuteronomy 6:6, 7). Perhaps some sons in rich families were tutored by better men than their fathers. Perhaps some godly priests still served as teachers for growing children. There may have been many quiet voices speaking for good, even in that dark and evil time.

There were also some public voices speaking loud and clear for the Lord. Such was the voice of Urijah the prophet before the king killed him. Jeremiah was neither killed nor silenced. He kept on speaking for God while most of the people ignored him and went their merry way, until the Babylonians came and demolished Jerusalem.

Has there ever been a time so bad that no good voice was heard? Will there ever be such a time? We need to have our ears attuned to the good. We need to have our "senses exercised to discern both good and evil" (Hebrews 5:14). We need to choose the good. In choosing, we have an unfailing guide in God's written Word, if we use it well. It is capable of equipping God's man for every good work (2 Timothy 3:16, 17).

C. Prayer

Thank You for the Bible, Father—the one book whose message is always good and true. As we study it, give us wisdom to understand it, strength to follow it, and grace and forgiveness when we turn aside from it. Amen.

D. Thought to Remember

Resist the devil; draw near to God.

Home Daily Bible Readings

Monday, Sept. 29—Tempted to Taste (Daniel 1:1-7)

Tuesday, Sept. 30—Refusing to Compromise (Daniel 1:8-13)

Wednesday, Oct. 1—Wisdom Comes From God (Daniel 1:14-21)

Thursday, Oct. 2—God Rewarded Right Action (2 Samuel 22:21-25)

Friday, Oct. 3—Amid a Cloud of Witnesses (Hebrews 12:1-10)

Saturday, Oct. 4—God's Law Is a Lamp (Psalm 119:105-112)

Sunday, Oct. 5—Partake of the Bread and Cup (1 Corinthians 11:23-32)

Learning by Doing

This page contains an alternate lesson plan emphasizing learning activities.
Classes desiring such student involvement will find these suggestions helpful.

Learning Goals

As students participate in today's class session, they should:

1. Tell how Daniel and his companions resisted the temptation to compromise their principles.

2. List some similar temptations that challenge Christians today.

3. Suggest some specific ways to "resist the devil" in those situations.

Into the Lesson

Ask class members to find a partner with whom each can complete the following sentence: "The last time I went on a diet . . . " Give them three minutes to finish the sentence for each other; then ask a few volunteers to share responses with the class.

Ask the class, "Why go on a diet? Are diets good or bad? Do you have any convictions about food or drink that relate to your religion? Have you ever known anyone whose religion forbade them to eat or drink anything?"

Option. Ask the class to make a list of times when peer pressure is a factor in human behavior. They can do this first in pairs; then you can conduct this as a brainstorming activity with the entire class. After you have made a long list on your chalkboard, ask the class to determine which of those items represent temptations or challenges for the Christian. Ask class members to decide which of these items is the biggest problem to the most Christians, in their opinion.

After either (or both) of the above activities, tell the class that today's lesson will look at four followers of God who determined to obey Him with their diet, even though everyone surrounding them was living by a different standard.

Into the Word

Point class members to the student book, where the following lists of names and quotes is printed. They are to match the quotes with the names of the speakers after reading Daniel 1:1-16. The quotes, of course, are not found in the Bible, but they are reasonable quotes for the characters in the story, based on what the Scripture says. (The quotes follow the correct names here, but they are mixed up in the student book. If you prefer to make your own handout, mix the names and quotes in that.)

Nebuchadnezzar—"I want to educate some of my captives in the ways of my country. That way I'll be better able to rule their people."

Jehoiakim—"Even though I was king of God's people in Judah, the pagan Babylonian king conquered us after besieging our capital city."

Ashpenaz—"I screened captives from many lands to find young men to serve in the king's palace. They needed to be in excellent physical shape and of a superior intellect. They were to learn the language and culture of my people."

Daniel—"The king's food was not prepared according to the standards prescribed by God for my people. And so I asked the chief official for permission to eat something else."

Hananiah—"Even though the Babylonians changed my name to Shadrach, I did not want them to interfere with my obedience to God."

Mishael—"We feared that the king's wine had been offered to his gods, and so we refused to drink it. But I did not refuse the Babylonian name, Meshach, which was given to me."

Azariah—"It did not matter what they called me. I liked Abednego as well as any name. God did not give me my name. But He did set the standards for what His people should eat and drink, and I would not violate those."

Melzar—"Daniel's proposition seemed fair to me. What could go wrong during a ten-day test? But I never expected those four Hebrews to look healthier after a diet of vegetables."

Encourage class members to work in pairs to match the names and quotes. Give them eight to ten minutes to do this. Then discuss the statements with the class, explaining background information and filling in details as you do so.

Into Life

If you did the activity about peer pressure at the beginning of class, look again at your list. If you did not do this activity, do it now.

Ask the class to decide whether it is harder for Christians today to resist temptation than it must have been for the four Hebrews (see the Conclusion to the lesson commentary).

Ask a volunteer to read James 4:7. Ask, "What are some practical ways that Christians can 'resist the devil' today when surrounded by pressures to disobey God?"

End with sentence prayers for strength to obey God this week.

Let's Talk It Over

The questions on this page are designed to encourage review of the lesson Scriptures and to promote discussion of the lesson by the class. The answers provided are only discussion starters. Let your class talk it over from there.

1. Daniel "purposed in his heart" (Daniel 1:8), or "resolved" (*New International Version*) to avoid defiling himself. How can we help Christian young people and adults to follow Daniel's example?

It is important to establish our purposes and resolutions before specific temptations come our way. The Christian who commits himself to keeping his body strong and healthy for God's use will be prepared to withstand the temptation to experiment with drugs or use alcoholic beverages. The believer who has resolved to maintain sexual purity will be more likely to reject the pressure to indulge in illicit relations. In our preaching and teaching in the church and at home, we must urge young people and ourselves as adults, "Make up your mind now to follow God's ways. Settle it now in your heart that you will refuse to yield to temptation."

2. Daniel's godly character made a favorable impression on the prince of the eunuchs. What are some of the positive effects our Christian character can exert on non-Christian people?

One benefit is that it helps to restore a little of the lost sense of trust in one's fellowman. Another possible benefit is that people may follow our example. We can imagine an observer saying, "Those Christians are evidence that even in today's world, some people can be kind and fair and forgiving. I want to be like that." Certainly the best possible benefit is gaining an opportunity to share our faith. Peter discusses the Christian's need for exemplary behavior in 1 Peter 3:8-17, and he relates it to our opportunity for witnessing: "Be ready always to give an answer to every man that asketh you a reason of the hope that is in you" (1 Peter 3:15).

3. Daniel suggested an alternative to eating the king's unacceptable food. What are some alternatives we can suggest when invited to engage in morally questionable practices?

A friend may invite us to see a movie containing objectionable material. We can simply suggest viewing a more wholesome film instead, or attending a ball game or going bowling or skating. Another friend may want us to go to a party at which there will be liquor and/or drugs. Rather than merely saying no, we could suggest

going to a Christian gathering, where genuine fun is not marred by unhealthy practices. Another example lies in the question of how to celebrate a day such as Halloween. Some Christians feel that this holiday, with its disturbing emphasis on the occult, is best to avoid. But some churches have arranged parties and fellowships at this time of the year, challenging those who come to dress like Bible characters, while omitting references to witches and goblins.

4. Daniel and his three friends could have justified participation in heathen worship on the basis of their being captives in a foreign land. Today people justify sins on the basis of being discriminated against because of race, national origin, economic status, or religious preference. What shall we say to this?

Almost any person can claim to have been discriminated against or deprived in some way. People have suffered from having too much or too little education, from being too attractive physically or not attractive enough, from having vision, hearing, or speech problems, and from various other limitations. Without doubt, racial prejudice, sex discrimination, and oppression of the poor are serious problems that our society must labor to overcome. Even so, everyone must face his or her personal responsibility to live an honest, law-abiding, and productive life.

5. What are some important principles to keep in mind in resisting the devil?

First, we should recognize that the devil is not invincible. Various books and films in recent years have made him appear to be the strongest force on earth. We remember John's assuring statement: "Greater is he that is in you, than he that is in the world" (1 John 4:4). Second, we must keep in mind that the devil does not believe in a "fair fight." He uses lies and deceptions. It is vital that we be discerning and "not ignorant of his devices" (2 Corinthians 2:11). Finally, we can take confidence in the fact that the devil is doomed to ultimate defeat. "For this purpose the Son of God was manifested, that he might destroy the works of the devil" (1 John 3:8). If we keep ourselves firmly on the side of our conquering Savior, we can enjoy the fruits of His triumph over the devil.

Unwavering Faith

DEVOTIONAL READING: Psalm 27:7-14.

LESSON SCRIPTURE: Daniel 3.

PRINTED TEXT: Daniel 3:14-25.

Daniel 3:14-25

14 Nebuchadnezzar spake and said unto them, Is it true, O Shadrach, Meshach, and Abednego? do not ye serve my gods, nor worship the golden image which I have set up?

15 Now if ye be ready that at what time ye hear the sound of the cornet, flute, harp, sackbut, psaltery, and dulcimer, and all kinds of music, ye fall down and worship the image which I have made; well: but if ye worship not, ye shall be cast the same hour into the midst of a burning fiery furnace; and who is that God that shall deliver you out of my hands?

16 Shadrach, Meshach, and Abednego, answered and said to the king, O Nebuchadnezzar, we are not careful to answer thee in this matter.

17 If it be so, our God whom we serve is able to deliver us from the burning fiery furnace, and he will deliver us out of thine hand, O king.

18 But if not, be it known unto thee, O king, that we will not serve thy gods, nor worship the golden image which thou hast set up.

19 Then was Nebuchadnezzar full of fury, and the form of his visage was changed

against Shadrach, Meshach, and Abednego: therefore he spake, and commanded that they should heat the furnace one seven times more than it was wont to be heated.

20 And he commanded the most mighty men that were in his army to bind Shadrach, Meshach, and Abednego, and to cast them into the burning fiery furnace.

21 Then these men were bound in their coats, their hose, and their hats, and their other garments, and were cast into the midst of the burning fiery furnace.

22 Therefore because the king's commandment was urgent, and the furnace exceeding hot, the flame of the fire slew those men that took up Shadrach, Meshach, and Abednego.

23 And these three men, Shadrach, Meshach, and Abednego, fell down bound into the midst of the burning fiery furnace.

24 Then Nebuchadnezzar the king was astonished, and rose up in haste, and spake, and said unto his counselors, Did not we cast three men bound into the midst of the fire? They answered and said unto the king, True, O king.

25 He answered and said, Lo, I see four men loose, walking in the midst of the fire, and they have no hurt; and the form of the fourth is like the Son of God.

Oct
12

GOLDEN TEXT: Be it known unto thee, O king, that we will not serve thy gods, nor worship the golden image which thou hast set up.—Daniel 3:18.

> ## God Leads a People Home
> Unit 2. Daniel: Faithful Under Fire
> (Lessons 5-8)

Lesson Aims

After this lesson, a student should be able to:

1. Recall the events surrounding Shadrach, Meshach, and Abednego's stand for God, the consequences they faced, and the result.

2. Describe a circumstance that Christians face today, where a stand for their faith may have significant consequences.

3. Make a commitment to stand for God, whether He rescues the believer from the temporal consequences or "if not."

Lesson Outline

INTRODUCTION
  A. Rookies of the Year
  B. Lesson Background
  I. DETERMINATION (Daniel 3:14-18)
  A. Second Chance (vv. 14, 15)
  B. Trust in the Greater King (vv. 16-18)
    Walking Backward
 II. FIRE! (Daniel 3:19-23)
  A. Feed the Fire! (v. 19)
  B. Tie the Victims! (v. 20)
  C. Throw Them In! (vv. 21-23)
III. SURPRISE! (Daniel 3:24, 25)
  A. Astonished King (v. 24)
  B. Astonishing Sight (v. 25)
    Alive!
CONCLUSION
  A. Faith
  B. Obeying the Law
  C. Obeying God
  D. Prayer
  E. Thought to Remember

The words on the visual for Lesson 6 focus on God's presence with us when we face challenging circumstances. It is shown on page 53.

Introduction

A. Rookies of the Year

Last week we read how four Hebrew youths became honor students in Babylon and became "rookies" on the king's team of wise men (Daniel 1:17-20). These young men not only had brilliant minds; they also had help from the Lord. With the aid of a revelation from God, Daniel was able to answer a question that had stumped all the senior wise men of the realm. He told Nebuchadnezzar about the contents of a dream the king had (and which he had forgotten) and then interpreted it in detail. As a reward, Nebuchadnezzar appointed Daniel chief of the wise men and ruler of the province of Babylon (Daniel 2:48). His three friends also became important officials in the province (v. 49).

Naturally, some native Babylonians and older wise men were not pleased to have these foreign youngsters in authority over them. No doubt they watched eagerly for the young men to commit some serious error, that they might report this to the king.

B. Lesson Background

Opportunity for such criticism came at a great celebration planned by Nebuchadnezzar (Daniel 3:1, 2). The centerpiece of this occasion was a huge image set up in the plain of Dura. Apparently this was located somewhere near the city of Babylon (though its exact location has not been determined). The image is not described in detail. Some students think that it may have been a statue of Nebuchadnezzar. It is interesting to recall the dream that Daniel interpreted in chapter 2, in which Nebuchadnezzar was represented by a "head of gold" (vv. 37, 38). Some believe that the king reacted in sinful pride to this interpretation, and decided to erect a golden image in his honor. He may have desired to be treated as a god—something that was true of various rulers of the ancient Near East. Whatever the specific nature of the image, it was in some way linked with the worship of the Babylonian gods, and Shadrach, Meshach, and Abednego recognized this (3:18). Bowing to it was clearly a test of one's loyalty to Nebuchadnezzar, his empire, and the Babylonian gods.

The simple description given tells us only the material used to construct the image and its size. It was made of gold. Considering its great size, most commentators suppose that this means it was gold plated, not made of solid gold. The image was sixty cubits high and six cubits wide (3:1), or, ninety feet tall and nine feet wide.

To this celebration officials were invited from all the provinces of the far-flung Babylonian empire. A vast crowd gathered on the plain before the image. Then a herald shouted an announcement. At the sound of the instruments, everyone was to fall down and worship the golden image. Anyone who did not do so would be thrown immediately into a "burning fiery furnace" (Daniel 3:6).

Upon hearing the instruments, instantly everyone in the vast throng dropped to his knees and bent forward with his face to the ground—that is, nearly everyone. Shadrach, Meshach, and Abednego remained standing. Jews worshiped Jehovah and no one else.

We may wonder where Daniel was on this occasion. Most certainly he was not bowing down with the heathens. We can hardly believe he was away on business when rulers of all the provinces were summoned to Babylon. Perhaps he and a few others of the king's "inner circle" were seated with the king and were not required to bow down, but the record does not say so. We simply have no definite information about where Daniel was or what he was doing.

Some of those who were envious of the success of the young Hebrews were not too engrossed in worship to raise their heads and see them still standing. This was clearly an act of rebellion. At the earliest opportunity, these watchful Chaldeans reported what they had seen to the king, and the king sent for the disobedient men. Our text takes up the story at this point.

I. Determination
(Daniel 3:14-18)

The king was furious, not only because he had been disobeyed, but because the disobedient ones were his favorites. These young Hebrews had proved themselves honest and capable men—the best officials in the province. Nebuchadnezzar could not afford to lose men like that; he had too many of the other kind. But neither could he afford to retract his sentence of death. That would make him appear to be a weak, indecisive ruler, who did not have enough backbone to enforce his own decree. He decided to bend just a bit at this point and give the offenders a second chance.

A. Second Chance (vv. 14, 15)

14. Nebuchadnezzar spake and said unto them, Is it true, O Shadrach, Meshach, and Abednego? do not ye serve my gods, nor worship the golden image which I have set up?

First, the king wanted to verify the accusation. Was it really *true* that these fine young men had disobeyed their king? Apparently they had gained a reputation for being men of integrity, not given to rebellious behavior.

15. Now if ye be ready that at what time ye hear the sound of the cornet, flute, harp, sackbut, psaltery, and dulcimer, and all kinds of music, ye fall down and worship the image which I have made; well: but if ye worship not, ye shall be cast the same hour into the midst of a burning fiery furnace; and who is that God that shall deliver you out of my hands?

How to Say It
ABEDNEGO. Uh-*bed*-nee-go.
ARAMAIC. Air-uh-*may*-ick.
BABYLONIAN. Bab-uh-*low*-nee-un.
CHALDEANS. Kal-*dee*-unz.
DURA. *Dur*-uh.
MESHACH. *Me*-shack.
NEBUCHADNEZZAR. *Neb*-uh-kad-*nezz*-er (strong accent on *nezz*).
SHADRACH. *Shad*-rack.

Even if they had disobeyed the king's command earlier, Shadrach, Meshach, and Abednego still could save their lives by prompt obedience. The choice before them was clear. If, upon hearing the *sound* of the instruments listed, they would *fall down and worship the image*, their earlier failure to obey would be overlooked, and they would continue in their offices and in the king's favor. However, if they would not worship the image, neither their official position nor the king's favor would save them from being thrown into the *fiery furnace* like common traitors. Nebuchadnezzar knew that these men trusted Jehovah, the God of the Jews; but he felt certain that no deity could rescue them he decided to kill them. His question, with which this verse concludes, constituted a direct challenge to the faith that the young men had chosen to exercise: *who is that God that shall deliver you out of my hands?*

Some of the names of the instruments mentioned in this verse may be unfamiliar to many of us. A *cornet* was a type of horn. The Aramaic word (keep in mind that this portion of Daniel is written in Aramaic, not Hebrew) translated *sackbut* apparently refers to some kind of harp. The *psaltery* was a stringed instrument. The word for *dulcimer* is one that many see as describing an instrument resembling the bagpipe.

B. Trust in the Greater King
(vv. 16-18)

16. Shadrach, Meshach, and Abednego, answered and said to the king, O Nebuchadnezzar, we are not careful to answer thee in this matter.

Here the word *careful* means that the three Hebrews saw no need to be cautious in framing a response to the king's demand. They knew exactly where they stood; there was no need to deny or evade the facts, and no need to offer an excuse for what they were doing (or refusing to do). They would simply tell the truth, regardless of the consequences. Christians ought to be characterized by such strength of conviction.

17. If it be so, our God whom we serve is able to deliver us from the burning fiery furnace, and he will deliver us out of thine hand, O king.

First came the answer to the king's question at the end of verse 15. Shadrach, Meshach, and Abednego were sure that the God they served was *able to deliver* them from the hottest *furnace* and from the wrath of this powerful *king*. He would deliver them now, if that was His will.

18. But if not, be it known unto thee, O king, that we will not serve thy gods, nor worship the golden image which thou hast set up.

Here is the second statement of which the three men were quite sure. Even if their God did not choose to rescue them from the furnace and the king, this would not affect their devotion to Him. They still would not *worship* Nebuchadnezzar's pagan gods nor his *golden image*. Their faith in God did not depend on circumstances.

WALKING BACKWARD

What would life be like if we were all alike: if everyone had blond hair, or were exactly six feet tall, or spoke with a British accent? The church (and society) would be poorer by far if this were the case. Yet we tend to look with suspicion on people who live their lives without regard for what others think about their peculiarities. They may be creative, idealistic, intelligent, and otherwise normal, but we still think of them as eccentrics. In a book about eccentrics, Scottish psychologist David Weeks tells of a man named Marvin Staples, who is an example of this. Staples walks backward everywhere in the belief that it does not aggravate the arthritis in his knees and back. He also claims that walking backward is more spiritual!

Shadrach, Meshach, and Abednego were certainly backward fellows in the eyes of the Babylonians. How strange to say to King Nebuchadnezzar, "We will not bow to your idols *even if* God doesn't save us from the fiery furnace"! But for them, "walking backward" actually *was* more spiritual. Their faith in God's power—whether or not He exercised it in their behalf—distinguished them from the ordinary brand of mortals. They truly were God's eccentrics! Would our faith ever cause anyone to say that about us? —C. R. B.

II. Fire!
(Daniel 3:19-23)

We can understand how the king must have felt at this point. He was being forced to give an order that he did not want to give, and forced to destroy three fine young officials whom he

would rather keep. He had tried to save them because they were useful in his government. He had offered them a second chance. But they had spurned his offer, defied his authority, and continued stubbornly in their disobedience. Furious, the king did what he felt he had to do.

A. Feed the Fire! (v. 19)

19. Then was Nebuchadnezzar full of fury, and the form of his visage was changed against Shadrach, Meshach, and Abednego: therefore he spake, and commanded that they should heat the furnace one seven times more than it was wont to be heated.

Fed by frustration, the king's *fury* flamed. His *visage*, or facial expression, which had been friendly toward the three Hebrews, now *changed* drastically and noticeably. He wanted the fire to be as furious as he was. Men heaped fuel on it until it roared as never before, and grew *seven times* hotter than *it was wont*, or accustomed, *to be heated*. The phrase *one seven times* reflects the way numbers are sometimes stated in the Bible (similar to the familiar "seventy times seven").

We are not told anything about the usual purpose of this furnace. Perhaps it was a smelter for iron or copper. Intense heat was normal for it, but now this heat was multiplied. There had to be an opening at the top for smoke, and apparently there was a door in the side. Thus fuel, ore, or men could be thrown inside; through the door, the king or anyone else could see the fire.

B. Tie the Victims! (v. 20)

20. And he commanded the most mighty men that were in his army to bind Shadrach, Meshach, and Abednego, and to cast them into the burning fiery furnace.

The king was in no mood to be gentle with any who defied his authority. He called his strongest soldiers to *bind Shadrach, Meshach, and Abednego*. Probably the soldiers handled them more roughly than necessary.

C. Throw Them In! (vv. 21-23)

21. Then these men were bound in their coats, their hose, and their hats, and their other garments, and were cast into the midst of the burning fiery furnace.

Fully clothed, the victims were *bound* securely and *cast into . . . the furnace*. The word *hose* has changed in meaning since the time of the *King James Version*; some versions render the Aramaic word as "trousers." Perhaps what we think of as "breeches" may be closer to the meaning.

22. Therefore because the king's command-ment was urgent, and the furnace exceeding hot, the flame of the fire slew those men that took up Shadrach, Meshach, and Abednego.

We can imagine two strong soldiers carrying a bound man between them, running swiftly toward the scorching heat of the *furnace*, hurl-ing their victim inside, then reeling back to fall and die—their lungs seared by the pitiless heat. Thus, in seconds, six stalwart soldiers lay dead, their grim duty completed.

23. And these three men, Shadrach, Meshach, and Abednego, fell down bound into the midst of the burning fiery furnace.

In flames that could melt iron, the victims were expected to be reduced swiftly to nothing.

III. Surprise!
(Daniel 3:24, 25)

A. Astonished King (v. 24)

24. Then Nebuchadnezzar the king was astonished, and rose up in haste, and spake, and said unto his counselors, Did not we cast three men bound into the midst of the fire? They answered and said unto the king, True, O king.

Apparently *Nebuchadnezzar* had been seated calmly throughout the proceedings, but what he now saw brought him to his feet *in haste*. He was sure he had seen *three men* thrown *into the midst of the fire*; he was sure they had been securely *bound*. He consulted his *counselors* to confirm those facts. Yes, they said, it was *true*.

B. Astonishing Sight (v. 25)

25. He answered and said, Lo, I see four men loose, walking in the midst of the fire, and they have no hurt; and the form of the fourth is like the Son of God.

The king had one more reason to be "aston-ished" (v. 24). Three men had been thrown into the fire; now *four* were there. The three had been securely bound; now they were *loose*. They "fell down" as they entered the furnace (v. 23); now they were on their feet, even *walking in the midst of the fire*. They should have been inciner-ated, but the king looked and said, *They have no hurt*. In a fire that could melt iron, the three Hebrews were not even scorched!

Shadrach, Meshach, and Abednego were eas-ily identified in the blazing light. The *fourth* man, however, was a stranger, and he looked *like the Son of God*. Other versions translate this phrase, "a son of the gods." Probably this is what Nebuchadnezzar meant. His pagan mind had no idea that there was only one God; much less was he aware of only one Son of God. We are not told how this fourth man was different. The king

was not certain just what or whom he was see-ing, and thus it is difficult for us to be certain. What *is* certain is that God had not abandoned His devoted servants.

ALIVE!

Eighty-six-year-old Mildred Clarke of Albany, New York, lay unconscious in her apartment. The man who found her said that she was cold and rigid, and he could find no pulse. Emergency medical technicians pronounced her dead. A police officer, the coroner, and two morgue attendants all agreed on the diagnosis.

Shortly after Mildred was taken to the morgue, the funeral home that was to hold her memorial service called for her body. However, as the body bag was taken from the forty-degree refrigerator, the morgue employee thought he heard Mildred breathing inside the bag. He found her to be alive, and she was rushed to the hospital for treatment.

At the opposite end of the thermal spectrum, King Nebuchadnezzar was shocked to find that the men he had tried to incinerate were very much alive, walking freely in the fiery furnace that he had intended to be their crematorium. Even more surprising, he saw a fourth figure that he likened to the Son of God.

The three Hebrews and Mildred Clarke all had to die again, of course, even after the amazing brush with death they each experi-enced. But the presence of the fourth person with Shadrach, Meshach, and Abednego gives hope to all who are faithful to God. Those who live by faith in God will never be forsaken by Him—even in the midst of extreme testing.

—C. R. B.

Conclusion

A. Faith

The three Hebrews' statement of faith had two dimensions: they stated what they believed and what they would do because of their belief. First,

visual for
lesson 6

they believed that God was able to deliver them from the fiery furnace and would deliver them if He chose to do so. Second, they would obey God whether He chose to deliver them or not.

B. Obeying the Law

Obeying God does not always mean that we break the civil law or defy the government and its authority. Clearly Jesus tells us to give Caesar what belongs to him (Mark 12:17). Clearly Paul tells us that the government is God's servant, and resistance to it is resistance to Him (Romans 13:1-7). The apostle also instructs us to pray "for all that are in authority" (1 Timothy 2:1, 2). Christians should be law-abiding citizens—with rare exceptions.

C. Obeying God

Christians obey God first of all. They do not disobey Him even if the law requires it. The heroes of today's lesson were ordered to do what God had forbidden. They refused. Later the early Christians were forbidden to do what God commanded. They said, "We ought to obey God rather than men" (Acts 5:29).

Following such examples, we too must obey the law unless it commands us to do what God forbids or forbids us to do what God commands. And when we must disobey the law, we take the consequences. The three Hebrews accepted the fire; the apostles accepted imprisonment and beating (Acts 5:17, 18, 40). Stephen was killed, as was James the apostle (Acts 7:59; 12:1, 2). According to tradition, Peter and Paul also were put to death because of their Christian faith. So were many other Christians during the brutal Roman persecutions. In all the record of such injustices, there is no hint of any violent resistance toward the persecutors. We should follow the example of the apostles: "being reviled, we bless; being persecuted, we suffer it" (1 Corinthians 4:12). There is also the example of Jesus, "who, when he was reviled, reviled not again; when he suffered, he threatened not; but committed himself to him that judgeth righteously" (1 Peter 2:23).

We may have laws we should not have; we may lack laws we should have. We may have some corrupt officials. We may see injustice done. But in the Bible we see no command or example that encourages us, for example, to bomb an abortion clinic or shoot an abortion doctor. Neither command nor example suggests a riot in response to an unpopular decision in the courts. Neither command nor example indicates that we should stockpile weapons and practice military maneuvers to be ready to take part in an armed rebellion. Neither command nor example encourages us to damage public or private property, assassinate an official, or evade taxes. Christians are to be good citizens with a reputation for integrity.

Envious Chaldeans were eager to have the three Hebrews put to death, but the three showed no hostility toward those enemies. Being public officials, they took care to be the best public officials. Thus they brought honor to the God who cared for them. And they were not silent about His care and their trust in Him. Their testimony brought honor to the God they served.

Christians are taught to honor God in the same ways. They are taught to be so good in what they do and what they say that their enemies can find nothing bad to say about them (1 Peter 2:11-17). In addition, they are taught to be "holding forth the word of life" (Philippians 2:14-16). This was what the first Christians did. Their exemplary way of life and sound teaching won "favor with all the people" (Acts 2:47). When jealous officials drove them out of town, they "went every where preaching the word" (Acts 8:4).

Shall we not also honor Jesus by our faithful living and true teaching throughout our lives, even unto death? For that we can expect far more than we can ever earn: we can expect "a crown of life" (Revelation 2:10).

D. Prayer

Heavenly Father, we know that You are able to do whatever You wish, and that what You do is always right. As we put our trust in You, help us to do right and to teach truth in every time of trouble and every time of joy. Amen.

E. Thought to Remember

Trust and obey.

Home Daily Bible Readings

Monday, Oct. 6—Bow Before the Golden Statue (Daniel 3:1-7)
Tuesday, Oct. 7—Stand Your Ground (Daniel 3:8-15)
Wednesday, Oct. 8—Into the Furnace of Fire (Daniel 3:16-23)
Thursday, Oct. 9—Four Unbound in the Fire (Daniel 3:24-30)
Friday, Oct. 10—Rescued From the Lions (Psalm 35:17-28)
Saturday, Oct. 11—Saved From My Foes (Psalm 27:1-6)
Sunday, Oct. 12—Christ's Messengers Endure (Matthew 10:16-23)

Learning by Doing

This page contains an alternate lesson plan emphasizing learning activities.
Classes desiring such student involvement will find these suggestions helpful.

Learning Goals

As students participate in today's class session, they should:

1. Recall the events surrounding Shadrach, Meshach, and Abednego's stand for God, the consequences they faced, and the result.

2. Describe a circumstance that Christians face today, where a stand for their faith may have significant consequences.

3. Make a commitment to stand for God, whether He rescues the believer from the temporal consequences or "if not."

Into the Lesson

To begin today's session, prepare a handout with the following agree/disagree statements. Or, read the statements slowly to your group and ask them to raise their hands after each statement to indicate whether they agree or disagree with it.

1. The right decision usually brings the best result.

2. If we obey God, He will rescue us from our enemies.

3. The older I get, the more I'm faced with opportunities to stand alone for God.

4. The older I get, the easier it is for me to stand alone for God.

If you have time, ask the class members to explain why they agree or disagree with each statement. Have them discuss challenges to faith that Christians today are facing.

Into the Word

Remind class members of the historical setting of this week's lesson. You may want to tell them a few facts about Nebuchadnezzar, or ask a class member to prepare a brief report about him and present it at this time.

Divide your class into several groups, with about five in each group. The groups will be asked to listen carefully to the story in Daniel 3 as it is read, and to react to the story at several stopping points.

Group One: Decide how they think Shadrach, Meshach, and Abednego are feeling at this place in the story.

Group Two: Decide who is right, who is wrong, and what God is doing about it.

Group Three: Decide on a contemporary parallel to the action in the story. Can they think of a circumstance just like this that happens or has happened in our world?

(If you have more than three groups, you may repeat the assignments among the groups.)

Ask three class members to read Daniel 3:1-13 aloud to your group. One reader should serve as the narrator, another should read the words of the herald (vv. 4-6), and the third should read the words of the Chaldeans.

After verses 1-13 have been read, tell class members that this is the first stopping point. Send them to their groups to discuss their assignments. Allow representatives from Group One and Group Two to report to the class; tell Group Three members that their report will come later.

Next, have Daniel 3:14-18 read aloud. Use the narrator from the first reading, and add two more readers: one to read the words of Nebuchadnezzar (vv. 14, 15), and the other, the words of Shadrach, Meshach, and Abednego (vv. 16-18). Ask the groups to complete their assignments at this next stopping point, and, once again, allow only the first two groups to report.

Complete this procedure with verses 19-23, 24-27, and 28-30.

Into Life

Now let representatives from Group Three share their insights for each of the sections in Daniel 3. After the report on each passage, write a phrase or two on your chalkboard to summarize what the group suggested.

Next, send class members back into their groups. Ask them to share times that they have faced (or someone they know has faced) peer pressure to disobey God. Does God always reward obedience as He did for Shadrach, Meshach, and Abednego? Ask members if they think it would be possible for them to obey God if their situation seemed as hopeless as the situation of these three. Does someone in the group have a testimony that shows how God honored his or her obedience as He did for the three Hebrews?

In closing, ask class members to think of a situation in their lives where obeying God seems most difficult. Have them pray in their groups about these situations, asking God for the courage to obey Him as did Shadrach, Meshach, and Abednego.

Let's Talk It Over

The questions on this page are designed to encourage review of the lesson Scriptures and to promote discussion of the lesson by the class. The answers provided are only discussion starters. Let your class talk it over from there.

1. Nebuchadnezzar was obviously prone to fierce anger. But the three Hebrews were unaffected by this. How can we respond to the person who is angry with us over our faith or our moral stand?

In Proverbs 16:14 we read, "The wrath of a king is as messengers of death: but a wise man will pacify it." Certainly we would not want to go out of our way to make a civil authority angry with us. But if any such official oversteps his bounds and interferes with our right to worship and serve God, we must speak up and risk his wrath. We should also avoid unnecessarily offending ordinary citizens. But if they challenge our right to proclaim our faith and to take our stand for Biblical moral values, we must meet their challenge boldly and risk their anger. Jesus urged us, "Fear not them which kill the body . . . but rather fear him which is able to destroy both soul and body in hell" (Matthew 10:28).

2. "Our God . . . is able to deliver us" (Daniel 3:17). How can we fix this truth in our minds?

The unswerving faith and boldness of the three Hebrews should impress us deeply. The king's sense of wonder at their deliverance from the flames should reverberate in our minds. This story should inspire us to step out and speak out for the Lord. We should imitate the Hebrews' determination to be true to God whatever the consequences. Then we may well be able to declare out of our own experience, "God is indeed able to deliver those who trust Him!"

3. Because of God's deliverance of His three servants, Nebuchadnezzar was led to acknowledge the greatness of the true God (Daniel 3:28, 29). How can we more effectively use our occasions of deliverance as testimonies to non-Christian acquaintances?

If God has delivered us in a mighty way, let us say so. Perhaps He has rescued us from bondage to alcohol or drugs; possibly He has preserved our marriage and home in a time of terrible crisis; or He has given us a remarkable victory over illness or injury. Whatever the circumstance, we must testify to His mercy and power. There is always a danger that we will fall into the trap of sounding as though we are saying, "Listen to what happened to me." Also, we may need to allow our account of God's deliverance to work its own powerful effects. Our hearers may "tune us out" if we use the occasion for an overly aggressive evangelistic appeal.

4. When we consider disobeying man's regulations, should they conflict with God's laws, we must be careful. Can you think of some examples of such disobedience that may be questionable?

We would be justified in protesting a public school's attempt to ban any student-initiated use of the Bible from its building, as long as such use is in accordance with school regulations. Thus, if a student takes a Bible to school to read during a break period or to use in connection with an assignment, this would be legitimate. But if a student is reading a Bible when he is supposed to be reading his textbook or listening to his teacher, the school has a right to restrict Bible reading (as long as it restricts any other activity that interferes with classroom work). Another example involves evangelism in the workplace. If an employee engages in some low-pressure personal evangelism during his lunch hour or at break time, few of the other employees may object. But if he does it when he is supposed to be working, his employer may rightfully warn him to stop. It is not persecution for a person or organization to prohibit us from religious activity when that person or organization has a legitimate claim on our time.

5. The lesson writer lists several unacceptable responses that believers could make to laws with which they disagree. What should we do about unjust laws or about public officials with whom we take issue?

In 1 Timothy 2:1, 2 we are exhorted to pray "for kings, and for all that are in authority." We should be persistent in praying for those who rule over us and for the enacting and enforcing of just laws. In addition we can take some definite actions, such as informing ourselves about candidates and issues, voting carefully, writing to leaders, circulating petitions, organizing community meetings, and the like. We may even want to run for public office ourselves and serve under God's guidelines for His glory.

Weighed and Found Wanting

DEVOTIONAL READING: Daniel 7:1-3, 15-18.

LESSON SCRIPTURE: Daniel 5.

PRINTED TEXT: Daniel 5:1-7, 25-28.

Daniel 5:1-7, 25-28

1 Belshazzar the king made a great feast to a thousand of his lords, and drank wine before the thousand.

2 Belshazzar, while he tasted the wine, commanded to bring the golden and silver vessels which his father Nebuchadnezzar had taken out of the temple which was in Jerusalem; that the king and his princes, his wives and his concubines, might drink therein.

3 Then they brought the golden vessels that were taken out of the temple of the house of God which was at Jerusalem; and the king and his princes, his wives and his concubines, drank in them.

4 They drank wine, and praised the gods of gold, and of silver, of brass, of iron, of wood, and of stone.

5 In the same hour came forth fingers of a man's hand, and wrote over against the candlestick upon the plaster of the wall of the king's palace: and the king saw the part of the hand that wrote.

6 Then the king's countenance was changed, and his thoughts troubled him, so that the joints of his loins were loosed, and his knees smote one against another.

7 The king cried aloud to bring in the astrologers, the Chaldeans, and the soothsayers. And the king spake, and said to the wise men of Babylon, Whosoever shall read this writing, and show me the interpretation thereof, shall be clothed with scarlet, and have a chain of gold about his neck, and shall be the third ruler in the kingdom.

. . . .

25 And this is the writing that was written, MENE, MENE, TEKEL, UPHARSIN.

26 This is the interpretation of the thing: MENE; God hath numbered thy kingdom, and finished it.

27 TEKEL; Thou art weighed in the balances, and art found wanting.

28 PERES; Thy kingdom is divided, and given to the Medes and Persians.

GOLDEN TEXT: Thou art weighed in the balances, and art found wanting.—Daniel 5:27.

God Leads a People Home
Unit 2. Daniel: Faithful Under Fire
(Lessons 5-8)

Lesson Aims

After this lesson, students should be able to:
1. Tell how God humbled the arrogant Belshazzar and why.
2. Describe why pride is destructive to one's relationship with God.
3. Renew a commitment to humble themselves in the sight of the Lord (James 4:10).

Lesson Outline

INTRODUCTION
    A. Famous Phrases
    B. Lesson Background
  I. PAGAN BANQUET (Daniel 5:1-4)
    A. Flaunting Royal Power (vv. 1-3)
    B. Praising Lifeless Idols (v. 4)
      "Pride Goeth Before Destruction"
  II. MYSTERIOUS MESSAGE (Daniel 5:5-7)
    A. Shocking Sight (v. 5)
    B. Frightened King (v. 6)
    C. Call for Help (v. 7)
  III. THE INTERPRETATION (Daniel 5:25-28)
    A. The Words (v. 25)
    B. The Meaning (vv. 26-28)
    A Kingdom Made of Dominoes
CONCLUSION
    A. Jehovah Rules Nations
    B. Jehovah Rules People
    C. Prayer
    D. Thought to Remember

Use the visual for Lesson 7 of the visuals packet to highlight today's golden text from Daniel 5:27. It is shown on page 60.

Introduction

A. Famous Phrases

It is interesting how certain Biblical terms and phrases have become a part of our daily speech and writing. For example, a person speaks of "washing his hands" of some terrible deed—a reference to Pontius Pilate's cowardly way of dealing with Jesus. The person who uses the phrase may not even be aware of its origin, or may be staunchly opposed to the Bible's message. But in this case, he most certainly has been influenced by the Bible.

Another often-used phrase is "the handwriting on the wall." This means that someone has reached a point in a particular situation where his outlook is rather grim. The person involved can detect no way out of his dilemma. He can see clearly "the handwriting on the wall," whether there is actually any writing or not.

Today's lesson text from Daniel tells of the incident that is the source of this phrase. King Belshazzar did not just see "the handwriting on the wall"; he actually saw a hand writing on the wall of his palace! The message conveyed to him by Daniel, who interpreted the writing, is summarized by our lesson title: "Weighed and Found Wanting."

B. Lesson Background

Today's lesson brings us to the time when the Babylonian empire, once thought to be virtually invincible, was about to collapse. By this time the mighty Nebuchadnezzar was no longer living; Nabonidus was emperor of the vast realm that Nebuchadnezzar had amassed. Nabonidus's son Belshazzar is called "king" in our text, a designation that may indicate that he and his father served for a time as co-regents (or "dual kings"). It is also possible that Nabonidus put Belshazzar in charge of the entire empire, while Nabonidus was engaged in military campaigns or in pursuits that took him away from the kingdom for an extended period of time.

Daniel had ruled the province of Babylon in the days of Nebuchadnezzar (Daniel 2:48), but apparently one of the king's successors had given Daniel's position to someone else. Daniel was still in Babylon, perhaps serving among the scholars rather than the rulers. It seems that Belshazzar was scarcely aware of his presence or his reputation.

I. Pagan Banquet
(Daniel 5:1-4)

Appearing only briefly in the Biblical record, Belshazzar seems to have been a vain and ostentatious ruler. This was the disposition of many ancient kings. Perhaps he was influenced by the demeanor of Nebuchadnezzar. We considered the grand celebration revolving around Nebuchadnezzar's golden image in last week's lesson (Daniel 3:1-7). A verbal expression of Nebuchadnezzar's excessive pride is found in Daniel 4:29, 30.

A. Flaunting Royal Power (vv. 1-3)

1. Belshazzar the king made a great feast to a thousand of his lords, and drank wine before the thousand.

How to Say It

ARAMAIC. Air-uh-*may*-ick.
BABYLONIANS. Bab-uh-*low*-nee-unz.
BELSHAZZAR. Bel-*shazz*-er.
CHALDEANS. Kal-*dee*-unz.
DARIUS. Duh-*rye*-us.
EUPHRATES. You-*fray*-teez.
MEDES. Meeds.
MENE (Aramaic). *Me*-nay.
NABONIDUS. Nab-uh-*nye*-dus.
NEBUCHADNEZZAR. *Neb*-uh-kad-*nezz*-er
  (strong accent on *nezz*).
PARAS (Aramaic). *par*-ahss.
PERES (Aramaic). *pair*-ess.
TEKEL (Aramaic). *Tee*-kel.
TIGRIS. *Tie*-griss.
UPHARSIN (Aramaic). Oo-*far*-sin.

The number of guests (*a thousand*) attending this *feast* is impressive. The king's wives and concubines also were there (v. 2). If the guests brought their wives and concubines, the size of the crowd was multiplied. No doubt the menu included a variety of delicacies, but special mention is made of the *wine*. From the record that follows, it is apparent that the king drank enough to become a bit reckless. The excessive use of such beverages has always been accompanied by negative consequences.

2. Belshazzar, while he tasted the wine, commanded to bring the golden and silver vessels which his father Nebuchadnezzar had taken out of the temple which was in Jerusalem; that the king and his princes, his wives and his concubines, might drink therein.

Nebuchadnezzar had destroyed the *temple* in *Jerusalem* many years earlier, but first he had robbed it of its *golden and silver vessels*. These vessels had been sacred, by virtue of being dedicated to Jehovah; but now the drunken king ordered them to be brought to the banquet hall and used as ordinary drinking cups.

In this verse Nebuchadnezzar is called the *father* of *Belshazzar*. This disturbs some Bible students, because Babylonian records seem to make it plain that Belshazzar's father was Nabonidus. But the words *father* and *son* are not always used in the Bible with their literal meanings. Joseph was made a "father" to Pharaoh (Genesis 45:8), meaning that he instructed Pharaoh, and guided and cared for him as a father guides and cares for his son. A later Joseph is called a "son of David" (Matthew 1:20), meaning a descendant of David. Thus in our text the word *father* may mean no more than a pre-

decessor in the government of Babylon, although some students think that Nebuchadnezzar was also Belshazzar's maternal grandfather, that is, the father of Belshazzar's mother.

3. Then they brought the golden vessels that were taken out of the temple of the house of God which was at Jerusalem; and the king and his princes, his wives and his concubines, drank in them.

The command was obeyed: the sacred *vessels* were *brought* and used for common, profane purposes. Obviously this was meant to flaunt the power of Babylon as conqueror of Jerusalem, and the power of Belshazzar who held the people of *Jerusalem* as his captives.

B. Praising Lifeless Idols (v. 4)

4. They drank wine, and praised the gods of gold, and of silver, of brass, of iron, of wood, and of stone.

Now the blasphemy grew worse. With the vessels of the living God in their hands, the reckless revelers gave their praise to lifeless idols. The implication was plain. Not only were the people of Babylon boasting of their triumph over the people of Jerusalem; they were declaring the gods of Babylon as triumphant over Jehovah, the God of Jerusalem. So thought the proud Babylonians. The lifeless idols heard and knew nothing of this "praise"; but the living God knew, and He judged that the time had come to call a halt to such irreverence.

"PRIDE GOETH BEFORE DESTRUCTION"

From the very beginning, humanity has devised ways to boast of its greatness. In Genesis 11 we read of the tower of Babel, a tower that was supposed to "reach unto heaven" (v. 4). "Let us make us a name" is what the builders said.

Recently this urge went high-tech. In 1993, a group named Space Marketing, Inc., concocted an outrageous attention-getting scheme: they planned to put mile-long billboards into orbit in space. The advertisements on them would be visible from anywhere on earth with the naked eye! Fortunately, sanity prevailed and we have heard no more of the scheme.

Belshazzar's banquet was a testimony to his ego. It was a feast for "a thousand of his lords" and for the king's wives and concubines. To show how great he was, Belshazzar called for the vessels of the temple of God in Jerusalem to be brought out, so he and his guests could drink their wine from these precious vessels that had been dedicated to the God of Heaven. Although not a tower reaching to the heavens or a billboard orbiting through space, this ill-advised act was still a monument to Belshazzar's pride.

Any scheme that places our self-esteem above our regard for God will surely lead us into trouble, as Belshazzar discovered to his regret.

—C. R. B.

II. Mysterious Message (Daniel 5:5-7)

A. Shocking Sight (v. 5)

5. In the same hour came forth fingers of a man's hand, and wrote over against the candlestick upon the plaster of the wall of the king's palace: and the king saw the part of the hand that wrote.

Imagine the sheer terror at witnessing such an eerie sight as this! Not a whole hand, but just the *fingers of a man's hand* were seen. Perhaps holding a piece of charcoal or a writing instrument of some kind, they *wrote . . . upon the plaster of the wall.* This did not happen in a dark corner, but *over against the candlestick* (more likely a lampstand). Excavations of ancient Babylon have shown that the palace wall did have a thin coating of white plaster. Against such a background, the light allowed Belshazzar to view clearly what was happening: *the king saw the part of the hand that wrote.*

B. Frightened King (v. 6)

6. Then the king's countenance was changed, and his thoughts troubled him, so that the joints of his loins were loosed, and his knees smote one against another.

Probably the king's *countenance*, or appearance, had been quite merry to this point, as he participated in the praise of Babylon's phony gods (v. 4). Suddenly it was *changed*; all laughter and revelry ceased at once. For *the joints of his loins* to be *loosed* means that Belshazzar's legs became weak—perhaps "like jelly," as we would say. *His knees* literally *smote*, or knocked, against each other. Besides being thus affected physically, Belshazzar's *thoughts troubled him.* He knew that what he was seeing was not the result of his excessive drinking; it was real and it was terrifying.

C. Call for Help (v. 7)

7. The king cried aloud to bring in the astrologers, the Chaldeans, and the soothsayers. And the king spake, and said to the wise men of Babylon, Whosoever shall read this writing, and show me the interpretation thereof, shall be clothed with scarlet, and have a chain of gold about his neck, and shall be the third ruler in the kingdom.

The frightened king wanted to consult all *the wise men of Babylon.* Among them were genuine scholars such as astronomers, philosophers, and historians. There were also various kinds of phony magicians, fortunetellers, and psychics. It should be noted that while the term *Chaldeans* often refers to all Babylonians (as in Daniel 5:30), it is also used in the book of Daniel to describe (as here) a particular group of wise men from whom the king sought counsel as needed. Once Daniel had been the "chief of the governors" over this group (Daniel 2:48), but now he was not even considered as one of them. Likely he was quite old at this point; perhaps he was enjoying an honorable retirement.

Belshazzar could not even read the *writing*, much less explain it. We do not have any indication what the language might have been, only what the writing meant, according to Daniel's interpretation. The king promised an extravagant reward to anyone who would *read* the writing and provide an *interpretation.* Such a person would not only have fine clothing and jewelry; he would also be made *the third ruler in the kingdom.* Belshazzar himself was the second ruler; his father (Nabonidus) was the first.

Verses 8-24 are not included in our printed text, but they present several important facts worth noting. First, in dealing with this crisis, the wise men were no smarter than the king. They could not read and explain the writing, and Belshazzar's fear increased (vv. 8, 9).

Second, the queen came to Belshazzar's aid. Most Bible students agree that this was the king's mother, not his wife, and perhaps a daughter of Nebuchadnezzar. Belshazzar's wives were already with him at the banquet (vv. 2, 3), but the queen was not. When she heard of her son's distress, she came to advise the king. She recalled that Daniel had once been regarded as the wisest of the wise men, and recommended that Belshazzar call for him (vv. 10-12).

Third, Daniel was summoned, and was given the same offer that had been given to the wise men (vv. 13-16). He declined the reward, but agreed to explain the writing.

visual for
lesson 7

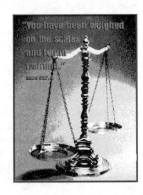

III. The Interpretation
(Daniel 5:25-28)

A. The Words (v. 25)

25. And this is the writing that was written, MENE, MENE, TEKEL, UPHARSIN.

Confidently Daniel read *the writing*. These words are Aramaic (the language in which this portion of the book of Daniel is written) and may be translated, "Numbered, numbered, weighed, and divided." Without further explanation, however, Belshazzar was not much wiser than he had been before, and neither are we.

B. The Meaning (vv. 26-28)

26. This is the interpretation of the thing: MENE; God hath numbered thy kingdom, and finished it.

The first word, *Mene*, means *numbered or* "counted." It meant that God had been counting the days of Belshazzar's reign, and had come to the end. That He had *finished it* may refer either to His counting or to Belshazzar's reign. The word *Mene* was repeated, probably for additional emphasis.

27. TEKEL; Thou art weighed in the balances, and art found wanting.

The second word, *Tekel*, means *weighed.* It is akin to the Hebrew word *shekel*, which came to refer to a unit of money. It meant that God had weighed Belshazzar on His own scales, and had determined his worth according to divine standards. Thus weighed, he was *found wanting*, or lacking, what was required in a man to be king of Babylon.

28. PERES; Thy kingdom is divided, and given to the Medes and Persians.

Peres in this verse may look very different from *Upharsin* in verse 25, but the difference is only minor. The letter *U* in *Upharsin* represents "and" in Aramaic; after the *u*, the *p* is generally rendered *ph*. The final *in* is a plural ending in Aramaic: "divisions" instead of "division." Belshazzar was about to lose his kingdom. It would not be given to a single nation, but to two peoples—*the Medes and Persians*. It is noteworthy that another Aramaic word, *paras*, which is closely related to *peres*, means *Persians*. Thus we have a play on words, through which the idea of the kingdom being divided is linked with the people who will bring about the division.

Unwelcome as this message was, Belshazzar kept his promise. Fine clothing and a golden chain were brought to Daniel, and the king proclaimed him third ruler in the kingdom (v. 29). The prophecy on the wall was fulfilled "in that night" (v. 30): when the citizens of Babylon awoke in the morning, they soon learned that Belshazzar was dead, and a Mede by the name of Darius was now in power (v. 31). It should be noted that this is not the same man as the Darius during whose reign the temple was rebuilt (Ezra 6:15).

Other historical records outside the Bible help us understand how this conquest of Babylon may have happened. Long before Belshazzar's feast, an alliance of Medes and Persians had invaded the Babylonian Empire from the northeast. These invaders had taken possession of a large area between the Tigris and Euphrates Rivers, and were very close to the city of Babylon. Perhaps they or their sympathizers had infiltrated the city and had some influence there. Many Babylonians must have been dissatisfied with Belshazzar's rule and by his father's frequent absence from the government, because resistance to the Medes and Persians does not seem to have been very strong. Perhaps some of the guests at the banquet were secretly hoping that the invaders would seize control of the empire.

The Euphrates River flowed through the middle of Babylon. A Greek historian later wrote that the invaders dug a huge depression in the plain outside the city, and diverted the flow of the river into it to make a lake. Then they slipped into the city by way of the empty riverbed. Perhaps security was lax during the feast, and the city gates were carelessly left unlocked. Perhaps the invaders had friends inside to open the gates for them. However this was done, the invaders entered quietly, took the city with little or no fighting, and killed Belshazzar.

The new king must have had an active and capable intelligence department. Learning that Daniel had predicted his victory, he may have concluded that Daniel was on his side. Probably he also learned of his reputation as the wisest of the wise men. Promptly Daniel was given a high place in the new administration (Daniel 6:1-3). Once again the wisdom of being on God's side and remaining true to Him in every circumstance was illustrated.

A KINGDOM MADE OF DOMINOES

In every generation, college students around the world have sought ways to avoid studying. In the mid-1980s one of these study-avoidance activities was the "domino-pushover scheme." In October of 1985, a group of Japanese students worked for a solid month setting up 710,899 dominoes in such a way that by touching one, all of them would go down in order. You may have seen it on television. It took only two minutes for that whole month's efforts to be obliterated, but it was a treat to see, nevertheless.

Belshazzar followed his father Nebuchadnezzar as ruler of the Babylonian empire. Decades of effort had gone into the making of this great empire, but in our text for today we see it all come crashing down in a few hours' time. Because it had been built on human power and human pride, it could not last forever.

The students set up their dominoes to fall down, but the Babylonians tried to set up a kingdom that would never topple. Nevertheless, the seeds of ungodliness had been sown and the harvest came with brutal speed.   —C. R. B.

Conclusion

A. Jehovah Rules Nations

"Blessed is the nation whose God is the Lord" (Psalm 33:12). The history of Israel recorded in the Old Testament illustrates the truth of this statement time and again. Obedient Israel was blessed with victory and peace; disobedient Israel experienced defeat and national turmoil.

Vividly the book of Daniel reminds us that Jehovah is God of the whole world, not of Israel alone. Among the heathen He raises up great empires, uses them for His purposes, and then removes them from the stage of history because their own purposes are evil.

B. Jehovah Rules People

Jehovah also rules people. He empowers them as He empowers nations; He uses them as He uses nations; He removes them as He removes nations.

Jehovah gave Nebuchadnezzar his power (Daniel 2:37, 38), and used him to punish wicked Judah. But Nebuchadnezzar became intolerably arrogant, and chapter 4 of Daniel tells how God humbled him. Some strange affliction made the king think that he was one of the beasts of the field (see Daniel 4:28-33). After Nebuchadnezzar was returned to sanity and power, he wrote, "Now I Nebuchadnezzar praise and extol and honor the King of heaven, all whose works are truth, and his ways judgment: and those that walk in pride he is able to abase" (v. 37).

Belshazzar also became arrogant, but God did not humble him and send him back to finish his job. By then it was time to end the captivity of God's people in Babylon. God simply removed Belshazzar from power and gave his kingdom to the Medes and Persians. It was a Persian ruler, Cyrus, who set the captives free.

Other examples of arrogant individuals may come to mind. We may think of Napoleon in exile on the island of St. Helena, of Hitler committing suicide in his bunker, or of Mussolini dead and dishonored in the streets of Rome. However, not all the arrogant ones are leaders of nations. Whom do you know that talks or acts proudly?

Who looks at all the intricate complexity of living things and still says, "We see no reason to think there is any supernatural Creator"? Who teaches children that there is no God, and then wonders why increasing numbers of them shoot one another?

Who is elected to govern with justice and wisdom, and then enriches himself and his friends with graft and corruption? Who is employed to enforce the law, and then takes bribes and lets criminals continue in their lawlessness?

Who says, "If God wants me to listen, He's got to talk to me directly"? Who says, "God talks to me directly all the time. I don't need the Bible"?

Who violates his marriage vow by divorce, adultery, mistreatment, or neglect? Who says, "Don't tell me what to do. This is *my* life"?

Who takes pride in evading taxes? Who overcharges customers for his own gain? Who demands more pay than he earns?

Who says, "I know what I'm doing. Don't expect *me* to stay within that silly speed limit"?

How do *you* talk or act arrogantly?

C. Prayer

Lord God Almighty, we do want to subdue our selfish pride and do Your will. Please help us to die to self that we might truly live for You. In Jesus' name. Amen.

D. Thought to Remember

"God resisteth the proud, and giveth grace to the humble" (1 Peter 5:5).

Home Daily Bible Readings

Monday, Oct. 13—Handwriting on the Wall (Daniel 5:1-9)

Tuesday, Oct. 14—Daniel Can Read the Writing (Daniel 5:10-17)

Wednesday, Oct. 15—Weighed and Found Wanting (Daniel 5:18-31)

Thursday, Oct. 16—A New Kingdom Coming (Daniel 7:1-3, 15-18)

Friday, Oct. 17—Day of Judgment Fixed (Acts 17:22-31)

Saturday, Oct. 18—Judged by Careless Words Spoken (Matthew 12:33-37)

Sunday, Oct. 19—Be Patient Until the Lord's Coming (James 5:1-11)

Learning by Doing

This page contains an alternate lesson plan emphasizing learning activities.
Classes desiring such student involvement will find these suggestions helpful.

Learning Goals

As students participate in today's class session, they should:

1. Tell how God humbled the arrogant Belshazzar and why.

2. Describe why pride is destructive to one's relationship with God.

3. Renew a commitment to humble themselves in the sight of the Lord (James 4:10).

Into the Lesson

Display the following Scripture verses on a bulletin board or on a chalkboard under the heading, "Proverbs About Pride":

"When pride cometh, then cometh shame: but with the lowly is wisdom" (Proverbs 11:2).

"Pride goeth before destruction, and a haughty spirit before a fall" (Proverbs 16:18).

"He that is of a proud heart stirreth up strife: but he that putteth his trust in the Lord shall be made fat" (Proverbs 28:25).

"Seest thou a man wise in his own conceit? There is more hope of a fool than of him" (Proverbs 26:12).

"Boast not thyself of tomorrow; for thou knowest not what a day may bring forth" (Proverbs 27:1).

Use these proverbs in one or several of the following ways as an introductory activity for today's lesson. You may either choose one of these projects for the entire class, or suggest all of them, divide the class into groups, and let each group choose one of the activities.

Newspaper search. Distribute newspapers and magazines to class members. In groups, they should find advertisements or articles to illustrate the truths of these proverbs.

"I once knew a person . . ." In groups or pairs, class members should tell each other stories from history or from their own personal experience to illustrate the truth of at least one of these proverbs.

Create a picture. Class members should use some medium, such as crayons and paper, modeling clay, or felt-tip pens and construction paper, to portray the truth of one or more of these proverbs. They may do this alone, in pairs, or in groups.

Give groups at least ten minutes to finish their activities. Then let groups share their work with the class.

Tell the class that today's Bible story provides another illustration of the destructive nature of pride.

Into the Word

Use the Lesson Background in the commentary to connect this week's study with last week's. Explain the relationship of Belshazzar to Nebuchadnezzar, and tell when this story took place during the Babylonian captivity.

Read Daniel 5:1-4 aloud to the class. Ask, "What kind of a party did Belshazzar throw? Why do you suppose he used the gold and silver vessels from the Jerusalem temple for drinking wine? What indication do you find in these verses that Belshazzar was a proud man?"

Read verses 5-9 aloud. Ask, "Why did Belshazzar become pale and weak? Why was the message on the wall so hard to discern?"

Read verses 10-16 aloud. Ask, "Why do you suppose it hadn't occurred to Belshazzar to summon Daniel? How serious was Belshazzar about finding the meaning of his vision?"

Read verses 17-24 aloud. Ask, "How did Daniel respond to Belshazzar's promise of reward? Why do you think he responded this way? What lesson should Belshazzar have learned from Nebuchadnezzar? Why do you suppose he didn't learn it?"

Read verses 25-31 aloud. Use information from the commentary to explain the meaning of the message and how Belshazzar's reign ended.

Into Life

Ask the class to look again at the proverbs that you considered earlier. Ask class members, in the same groups that worked earlier, to decide how the story of Belshazzar illustrates any or all of these Scriptures.

Write the following incomplete sentence on your chalkboard: "Pride is a problem for me when . . ." Ask class members to complete the sentence in their small groups. (Anyone who doesn't want to do so may pass, of course.)

After several minutes, ask the class, "Do you see any trends here? That is, what do your answers seem to have in common?"

Ask class members to have a closing prayer session in their small groups. Encourage them to mention specific issues raised in the course of today's lesson.

Let's Talk It Over

The questions on this page are designed to encourage review of the lesson Scriptures and to promote discussion of the lesson by the class. The answers provided are only discussion starters. Let your class talk it over from there.

1. Belshazzar's act of ungodly arrogance occurred while he was drinking heavily. How does drunkenness sometimes affect the drinker's self-assurance and pride?

Belshazzar's drinking may have inflated his pride in his kingdom and in his gods. So he used the temple vessels as a sign of contempt toward both God's people and their God. He experienced what Solomon had warned about in Proverbs 20:1: "Wine is a mocker, strong drink is raging: and whosoever is deceived thereby is not wise." Today alcohol deceives people in the same way. Some believe that while under its influence, they are physically stronger or mentally sharper than they would be otherwise. The results are frequent fights and tragic automobile accidents. Other drinkers tend to think that they are more attractive and sexually appealing than they would be otherwise. The result is that they make fools of themselves.

2. What are some present-day counterparts to Belshazzar's act of using sacred things in a thoughtless and profane way?

The use of God's name in vulgar oaths is a prominent example. We hear this especially in the workplace, out on the streets, and on television. Individuals who would deny believing in God or Jesus Christ nevertheless resort to their names when wanting to express displeasure. Another profane use of what is sacred shows up in movies and television programs, whenever Biblical statements, or phrases or lines from Christian hymns are irreverently quoted for laughs. Some programs have also mocked Biblical doctrines, the practice of prayer, the Christian's call to holiness, and the gospel ministry. There are also many highly publicized "works of art" that ridicule Christ and His cross and make light of fundamental Christian doctrines. Finally, modern music includes many lyrics mocking God, Christ, and the Bible.

3. To know that our days are "numbered," as Belshazzar's were, would be very frightening. But how might it be helpful to think of our days in this fashion?

It is interesting to consider how the word "number" is used in the prayer found in Psalm 90:12: "Teach us to number our days, that we may apply our hearts unto wisdom." This tells us that *we* are to number our days, using the time we have in the most judicious manner. This thought speaks to non-Christians, reminding them that they do not have unlimited time to make their decision about salvation. For those already Christians, the challenge should be clear. If we are going to achieve such goals as win our neighbors to Christ, read through the entire Bible, or establish a powerful prayer life, then we should get busy working on them *now*.

4. Pride causes some people to dictate to God the terms of their relationship with Him. What are some examples of this?

Some people make a career change, get married, or move to another community without praying for God's guidance in the matter. Once the change is made, they may ask God to bless it. If problems then arise in connection with the change, the people are inclined to question God for His failure to bless them. To go a step further, there are people who indulge in actual sin, then plead for God to bail them out of the painful consequences. If He does not do so, they become bitter toward Him. The lesson writer mentions the person who says, "If God wants me to listen, He's got to talk to me directly." This sentiment is expressed in other ways; for example, some people challenge God to do something special for them before they will commit themselves to trusting and obeying Him. God is God, and we must yield to Him on His terms and conditions, if we are to be blessed.

5. What are some steps we can take to develop a proper humility before God?

It is important that we keep in mind how small and how weak we are. The psalmist surveyed the heavens and asked, "What is man, that thou art mindful of him?" (Psalm 8:4). Perhaps it would help us to do the same. It is also important to keep in mind how prone to sin we are. In another place the psalmist said, "There is none that doeth good, no, not one" (Psalm 53:3). We must also take the opposite perspective and contemplate how great and wise and holy God is. Our weakness and God's power—if that combination does not stir us to humility, perhaps nothing else will.

Daniel's Prayer of Confession

DEVOTIONAL READING: **Daniel 7:7-14.**

LESSON SCRIPTURE: **Daniel 9.**

PRINTED TEXT: **Daniel 9:3-6, 18-23.**

Daniel 9:3-6, 18-23

3 And I set my face unto the Lord God, to seek by prayer and supplications, with fasting, and sackcloth, and ashes:

4 And I prayed unto the LORD my God, and made my confession, and said, O Lord, the great and dreadful God, keeping the covenant and mercy to them that love him, and to them that keep his commandments;

5 We have sinned, and have committed iniquity, and have done wickedly, and have rebelled, even by departing from thy precepts and from thy judgments:

6 Neither have we hearkened unto thy servants the prophets, which spake in thy name to our kings, our princes, and our fathers, and to all the people of the land.

· · · · · · · · · · · · · ·

18 O my God, incline thine ear, and hear; open thine eyes, and behold our desolations, and the city which is called by thy name: for we do not present our supplications before thee for our righteousnesses, but for thy great mercies.

19 O Lord, hear; O Lord, forgive; O Lord, hearken and do; defer not, for thine own sake, O my God: for thy city and thy people are called by thy name.

20 And while I was speaking, and praying, and confessing my sin and the sin of my people Israel, and presenting my supplication before the LORD my God for the holy mountain of my God;

21 Yea, while I was speaking in prayer, even the man Gabriel, whom I had seen in the vision at the beginning, being caused to fly swiftly, touched me about the time of the evening oblation.

22 And he informed me, and talked with me, and said, O Daniel, I am now come forth to give thee skill and understanding.

23 At the beginning of thy supplications the commandment came forth, and I am come to show thee; for thou art greatly beloved: therefore understand the matter, and consider the vision.

Oct 26

GOLDEN TEXT: At the beginning of thy supplications the commandment came forth, and I am come to show thee; for thou art greatly beloved.—Daniel 9:23.

Lesson Aims

After this lesson, students should be able to:

1. Summarize Daniel's prayer in Daniel 9 and God's response.

2. Explain the importance of confessing personal and national sin to God.

3. Resolve to be completely honest with God in acknowledging sin, and seek His help in overcoming it daily.

Lesson Outline

INTRODUCTION
    A. A Confused Prophet
    B. Lesson Background
 I. CONFESSION (Daniel 9:3-6)
    A. Daniel's Grief (v. 3)
    B. Daniel's God (v. 4)
    C. Sin (v. 5)
    D. Stubbornness (v. 6)
        A "Sad" Condition
 II. PLEA (Daniel 9:18, 19)
    A. Hear and See (v. 18)
    B. Hear and Do (v. 19)
III. ANSWER (Daniel 9:20-23)
    A. Quick Response (v. 20)
    B. Messenger From Heaven (v. 21)
    C. Purpose of the Message (vv. 22, 23)
        "Telephone Tag"
CONCLUSION
    A. We Can Choose
    B. Confessing Our Sins
    C. Prayer
    D. Thought to Remember

The urgent need to pray for our nation is the theme of the visual for Lesson 8 of the visuals packet. It is shown on page 69.

Introduction

A. A Confused Prophet

My parents and their friends were amused when a self-appointed prophet made headlines by announcing that Jesus would appear and that the world would end in 1914. Some people were not so amused; they sold their property and moved to a hilltop community to meet the Lord. My folks, however, stayed on their farm. "If the Lord does come," Dad commented, "probably He will be looking for us here where we live."

When 1915 arrived and the Lord had not returned, the "prophet" had some explaining to do. He was right about the year, he said, and only half wrong about the event. The conflict that came to be called World War I began in 1914, and he thought that it would conclude with the battle of Armageddon and the end of the world.

B. Lesson Background

There was no such uncertainty in Daniel's understanding of events in his time (Daniel 9:1, 2). Very plainly Jeremiah had preached and written that Judah and the nearby nations would serve the king of Babylon for seventy years (Jeremiah 25:1, 11). Daniel himself had been taken from Jerusalem to Babylon when that service began (Daniel 1:1-7). At the time that the Medes and Persians took control of Babylon (which happened in last week's lesson), the seventy years were almost completed. How thrilled Daniel must have been to realize that the time of captivity in a foreign land was nearly over!

What was the right action for Daniel to take? Should he spread the good news that liberty was at hand? Should he start choosing leaders and raising funds? Should he first approach the new rulers, asking permission for the Jews to leave? All of these needed to be done, but Daniel gave top priority to none of them. He went first to Jehovah, the King of Heaven.

I. Confession
(Daniel 9:3-6)

Daniel chose to pray. How should his prayer begin? With a shout of praise, or a happy psalm of thanksgiving for his people's freedom? With a plea for wisdom to organize the people for their trip, or a plea for adequate funding? With a request that God would move the new rulers to support a return of the Jews to Jerusalem? Daniel began his prayer with a confession of both his and the nation's sin.

A. Daniel's Grief (v. 3)

3. And I set my face unto the Lord God, to seek by prayer and supplications, with fasting, and sackcloth, and ashes.

Doesn't freedom call for rejoicing and celebration? Yes, but sin calls for sorrow, mourning, and repentance. The ancient symbols of these were going without food (*fasting*), wearing rough and unattractive *sackcloth*, and putting *ashes* on one's head. A similar expression of repentance took place in the time of Ezra (Ezra 9:3).

B. Daniel's God (v. 4)

4. And I prayed unto the LORD my God, and made my confession, and said, O Lord, the great and dreadful God, keeping the covenant and mercy to them that love him, and to them that keep his commandments.

Daniel acknowledged the nature of the God who heard his prayer. Jehovah is not like one of the powerless pagan idols; He is *great*. He is big enough to fill earth and Heaven, and mighty enough to do anything He wants to do. Jehovah is also *dreadful*. Today this word has mostly negative connotations. Here it simply means that Jehovah is a God to be feared.

The people of Israel should have known all of this by now. God had placed them in subjection to Babylon for seventy years because they had disobeyed Him. No other God deserved their allegiance and obedience. He alone is dependable, *keeping the covenant*. He provides every good He promises, and He provides every punishment He promises. How good it is to know that He supplies mercy to them that love him, and to them that keep *his commandments*! *Mercy* represents the Hebrew word *hesed*—a word that, according to many students, means far more than mercy. In other versions it is translated "kindness," "steadfast love," or "lovingkindness." Perhaps it is best understood to mean love in action—a love that always seeks what is best for the person who is loved.

C. Sin (v. 5)

5. We have sinned, and have committed iniquity, and have done wickedly, and have rebelled, even by departing from thy precepts and from thy judgments.

It should be noted that Daniel did not consider himself as more righteous than his countrymen, though it seems that he certainly could have. He included himself (we) among the sinners. In his confession, Daniel used four different words to confess what he and his people had done. Any of them may be translated "sin," but

---

How to Say It

BABYLONIANS. Bab-uh-*low*-nee-unz.
DARIUS. Duh-*rye*-us.
ENOCH. *E*-nock.
GABRIEL. *Gay*-bree-ul.
HESED (Hebrew). *hess*-ed.
MEDES. Meeds.
OBLATION. uh-*blay*-shun.
ZECHARIAH. Zek-uh-*rye*-uh.

---

they seem to be arranged to move from bad to worse. To show this progression in English, we may translate as follows: "We have missed the mark; we have been crooked; we have acted wickedly; we have openly rebelled." Daniel knew that he could not excuse himself and his people by claiming that they had no way of knowing what was wrong. They had been given God's precepts and judgments; they had sinned by departing from them instead of obeying them.

D. Stubbornness (v. 6)

6. Neither have we hearkened unto thy servants the prophets, which spake in thy name to our kings, our princes, and our fathers, and to all the people of the land.

Most of the people of Israel did not have God's Law in their living rooms for daily reading, as we now have the Bible. However, that did not provide any excuse for their disobedience. God had constantly sent His *prophets* to remind His people of His Law, to point out their violation of it, and to urge them to be obedient. The prophets presented their messages *to all the people of the land*, from the king in his palace to the humblest peasant. God's actions should have produced a sincere and nationwide repentance among His people.

Daniel's prayer continued as recorded in verses 7-17. Repeatedly he acknowledged the goodness of God and the badness of His people. He noted that God had done nothing to provoke such despicable behavior as that which His people had shown toward Him. They had brazenly turned from Him and had chosen to follow other gods. Even when the captivity began, the people had not ceased their disobedience to God. "All this evil is come upon us: yet made we not our prayer before the Lord our God, that we might turn from our iniquities, and understand thy truth" (v. 13). Daniel also confessed that he and the people were characterized by "confusion of faces" (v. 7). The Hebrew text reads, "shamefaced." Such was the judgment upon a people who were "not at all ashamed, neither could they blush" (Jeremiah 6:15).

The next part of our printed text continues Daniel's plea for God's mercy upon himself and the people.

A "SAD" CONDITION

When most people go to bed at night, they expect the sun to come over the horizon the next morning. Even we Christians who wish for the imminent return of Christ live our lives in the expectation that the sun will rise on schedule if the Son does not return before morning.

However, for some people the sun does not come up in the morning, and this makes them "SAD." Seasonal Affective Disorder is the name given to an ailment that affects a multitude of people who live in far northern territories such as Alaska and Sweden. During the winter in Barrow, Alaska, for example, the sun does not rise for sixty-five days. As the darkness settles in, it brings with it a darkness of the spirit as well. Depression, irritability, increased consumption of alcoholic beverages, listlessness, and eating disorders are all symptoms of SAD.

The people of God for whom Daniel prayed were also in a sad condition. This had happened, not because they had no light, but for a more serious reason: they had willfully rejected the light that God had given them. As Daniel said, "Neither have we hearkened unto thy servants the prophets" (Daniel 9:6).

When we reject the light of God's Word, and Jesus, "the Light of the world," we bring the darkness of sin upon our souls. We have only ourselves to blame for our sad condition.

—C. R. B.

II. Plea
(Daniel 9:18, 19)

Daniel could not make a case that the captive people deserved to be set free. He pleaded that the Lord would look with favor on the temple that now was desolate, but he asked this favor "for the Lord's sake," not Israel's (v. 17).

A. Hear and See (v. 18)

18. O my God, incline thine ear, and hear; open thine eyes, and behold our desolations, and the city which is called by thy name: for we do not present our supplications before thee for our righteousnesses, but for thy great mercies.

Daniel asked the Lord to both listen and look. This does not mean that he thought God did not know about the circumstances of His people. Daniel was asking that God would now give those circumstances His attention and do something to change them. This is apparent from the next verse.

Daniel asked God to give attention to *our desolations*: the desolation of the people in captivity, and the desolation of the homeland they had left behind. In Babylon the captives felt abandoned, ruined, and worthless. Their despair is reflected in the words of Psalm 137, particularly verse 4: "How shall we sing the Lord's song in a strange land?" Jerusalem also was abandoned. The Babylonians had burned everything in it that could be burned, and they had battered

down the walls of stone. Half a century had passed since the destruction. The tragedy was that this had happened to *the city which is called by thy name*—the city that was known as the Lord's, and as the site of a glorious temple dedicated to Him. Now both city and temple were in ruins. This damaged the Lord's reputation in the eyes of heathen people, who would conclude that He was powerless to preserve His own city.

Daniel could not plead that his people had become so good that they deserved to be restored to their homeland; only on the basis of God's *great mercies* could he make such an appeal. We are saved today on this same basis. Were it not for the fact that God is "rich in mercy" (Ephesians 2:4), we would be eternally lost in our sins.

B. Hear and Do (v. 19)

19. O Lord, hear; O Lord, forgive; O Lord, hearken and do; defer not, for thine own sake, O my God: for thy city and thy people are called by thy name.

The captives were not good enough to deserve any favor from the Lord. Daniel asked the Lord to *forgive* them and to restore them to their homeland for the Lord's *own sake*. The Lord had said that He would break the power of Babylon after seventy years (Jeremiah 25:11, 12). He had promised to restore the people of Israel to their own land after that time (Jeremiah 29:10). Now the seventy years were almost over. The power of Babylon was broken: Darius the Mede had seized its kingdom (Daniel 5:31). Now God's people must be returned to their homeland to fulfill His promise. Daniel prayed that it would be so, even though the people were not worthy of such forgiveness and favor.

III. Answer
(Daniel 9:20-23)

A response came from Heaven even before Daniel finished his prayer: a surprising response that looked far beyond the Jews' return to their homeland. It was a response both reassuring and disturbing. Parts of it still remain puzzling to us. The rest of our printed text, however, is concerned with the fact that a response did come.

A. Quick Response (v. 20)

20. And while I was speaking, and praying, and confessing my sin and the sin of my people Israel, and presenting my supplication before the LORD my God for the holy mountain of my God.

Briefly this describes the contents of Daniel's prayer. He was *confessing* his sin and the sin of his *people*, admitting that they did not deserve any special favor from God. At the same time, he was *presenting* his *supplication*, not so much for the unworthy people as *for the holy mountain of my God*. This referred to the hill in Jerusalem where God's temple had stood before the Babylonians destroyed it. Daniel was asking that this hill might again be graced with the presence of a holy temple of the Lord.

visual for
lesson 8

B. Messenger From Heaven (v. 21)

21. Yea, while I was speaking in prayer, even the man Gabriel, whom I had seen in the vision at the beginning, being caused to fly swiftly, touched me about the time of the evening oblation.

Gabriel had come to Daniel at an earlier time to explain the meaning of a *vision* (Daniel 8:15-26). Now he came again while Daniel *was speaking in prayer*. To Daniel he appeared as a *man* (the name *Gabriel* means "man of God"), but no doubt he was the same angel who was sent centuries later with messages for Zechariah (Luke 1:8-20) and for Mary (Luke 1:26-38). With a message he came to Daniel *about the time of the evening oblation*, or sacrifice, which was also a time of prayer for the Jews.

C. Purpose of the Message (vv. 22, 23)

22. And he informed me, and talked with me, and said, O Daniel, I am now come forth to give thee skill and understanding.

The *New International Version* reads "insight" instead of *skill*. Daniel had been praying about the restoration of Jerusalem according to God's promise. Gabriel came to give him information not only about that, but also about what would happen in future centuries.

"TELEPHONE TAG"

"Telephone tag" is a name given to a game many of us are forced to play nowadays. We try to talk to someone by phone, but get his phone-answering machine. Then he calls us back and leaves a message on our machine. And then we call him back—and so it goes. At times we wonder if those machines are really any help.

However, answering machines do have their uses. One bashful man who couldn't work up the courage to propose marriage to the woman he loved waited until he knew she would be away from home. Then he left a message on her answering machine. She replied, "Yes!" with a poem that she left on his answering machine!

Fortunately for Daniel (as well as for us), God is not in the business of playing telephone tag. When Daniel offered his prayer of intercession for his people, God heard his prayer and replied

to him through the angel Gabriel. The answer to Daniel's prayer was that he would receive "skill and understanding" (Daniel 9:22). Then came a message of how God was going to deal with His people.

Our God has not left us without means by which we can know Him. Most of this knowledge comes through our reading of Scripture, but some also comes through the person-to-person communication that takes place when we open our hearts to God in prayer.   —C. R. B.

23. At the beginning of thy supplications the commandment came forth, and I am come to show thee; for thou art greatly beloved: therefore understand the matter, and consider the vision.

At the beginning of Daniel's plea, God had given the response to Gabriel. Gabriel had come swiftly (v. 21) and had arrived before the prayer was finished, in order to *show* Daniel what would happen. Daniel was granted the opportunity to receive this revelation, because he was *greatly beloved*. All through the seventy years of captivity, he had faithfully interpreted God's messages given through dreams and even through a hand writing on a wall. Now Gabriel said that he should give attention to another *matter*.

The angel's message concerning this matter is recorded in verses 24-27, which follow our printed text. These verses tell of a period of "seventy weeks" that were still in the future when the angel spoke. Most students agree that *weeks* here refers to periods of seven years, not seven days. In other words, the seventy weeks were seven times seventy years, or a total of 490 years. These seventy weeks were then divided into groups of sixty-two weeks, seven weeks, and one week.

Careful students of the Bible have come to differing conclusions about the meaning of these four verses. Without trying to go into too many details, we suggest the following summary of Gabriel's prophecy.

Jerusalem would be rebuilt and fortified, though not without difficulty and trouble (v.

25). Unfortunately its people would not obey God much better than they had done before the city was destroyed. Nevertheless, the nation would be allowed to continue until the Messiah would come (v. 25). He would "make reconciliation for iniquity" (v. 24) by taking the sins of His people upon Himself and being slain in the place of sinners. He would make a covenant with many (v. 27), but officially the nation would reject Him. He would be "cut off" (v. 26) by crucifixion, and His followers would be persecuted. Thus the transgression of His enemies would become complete within the seventy weeks (v. 24), resulting in the eventual destruction of Jerusalem (v. 26). This happened in A.D. 70 when the Romans ravaged the city.

Conclusion

Daniel prayed that Jerusalem would be restored (Daniel 9:16-19). It was gratifying to be assured that the city would indeed be rebuilt, but it must have been discouraging to learn that it would be destroyed again later. In a way, this is but a reflection of the rather discouraging record of humanity.

A. We Can Choose

However, through all the dark centuries of discouraging history, this encouraging truth shines like a beacon from a lighthouse: We can choose. You can choose. I can choose. Every person on earth can choose. Enoch chose to walk with God when everyone else was taking another way. So did Noah. Abraham chose obedience, though it meant starting on a long trip without knowing where he was going (Hebrews 11:8). Moses chose affliction with God's people rather than the pleasures of sin (Hebrews 11:24, 25). Daniel chose the lions' den rather than a life without prayer (Daniel 6:10). Jesus chose death rather than disobedience to God's will (Luke 22:42).

Too easily we excuse ourselves by saying, "Everybody sins. We're going to do it too; we can't help it." But we can help it, and we must. Daily we must resist the devil. God will not let any temptation be so strong that we can't defeat it (1 Corinthians 10:13). He provides a way of escape, but we must provide the will and the determination to use it.

B. Confessing Our Sins

Daniel's reaction to the sins of his countrymen provides a powerful example for us. When Daniel prayed his prayer of confession, he spoke just as much about his own sins as he did about the sins of others (Daniel 9:20).

We think of Daniel as a righteous man—a man who remained loyal to God in the midst of very trying circumstances. Although exiled in a foreign land, he refused to compromise his principles. He served with integrity and wisdom, displaying an "excellent spirit" (Daniel 6:3). But Daniel also realized that he was not perfect, and that he had no right to speak only of "their sins." He too had to depend upon God's mercy.

We live in a world where sin is rampant. "Evil men" truly seem to "wax worse and worse" (2 Timothy 3:13). Just when we think the standards can go no lower, we read or hear of an incident that leaves us shaking our heads in disbelief.

As Christians, however, we must realize that we have not always been faithful to the task Jesus has given us to do. If we were really the salt of the earth and the light of the world, would our surroundings be as corrupt as they are? In a day when many Christians react to social ills by protests, boycotts, and campaigns, have we forgotten the priority of prayer?

Daniel's response to the sins of his nation should remind us that we cannot fight our spiritual battles victoriously with carnal weapons. Our primary source of power to change our world is still *prayer.*

C. Prayer

We confess that we are sinners, Father—sinners unworthy of Your grace and unworthy of eternal life. Yet we do believe in Jesus, Father, and we do want to do His will. Forgive us our sins, we pray, and help us on to joy forever with You. Amen.

D. Thought to Remember

"God be merciful to me a sinner" (Luke 18:13).

Home Daily Bible Readings

Monday, Oct. 20—No Fault Found in Daniel (Daniel 6:1-9)
Tuesday, Oct. 21—His Prayers Broke the King's Law (Daniel 6:10-18)
Wednesday, Oct. 22—Protected From the Lions (Daniel 6:19-28)
Thursday, Oct. 23—Open Shame for Disobedience (Daniel 9:1-10)
Friday, Oct. 24—Claiming the Mercies of God (Daniel 9:11-19)
Saturday, Oct. 25—Wisdom and Mystery in Reply (Daniel 9:20-27)
Sunday, Oct. 26—The Lord Is Our Saving God (Habakkuk 3:13-19a)

Learning by Doing

This page contains an alternate lesson plan emphasizing learning activities.
Classes desiring such student involvement will find these suggestions helpful.

Learning Goals

After this lesson, students should be able to:

1. Summarize Daniel's prayer in Daniel 9 and God's response.

2. Explain the importance of confessing personal and national sin to God.

3. Resolve to be completely honest with God in acknowledging sin, and seek His help in overcoming it daily.

Into the Lesson

Before class begins, type or print each of the following situations on a slip of paper:

1. A new monitoring system detects the more than ninety minutes in personal long distance phone calls that you have made in one month from your office telephone. Your supervisor asks you about these calls.

2. Your neighbor's hamster escapes from its cage onto your patio, and your dog catches and kills the pet. You find the dead animal.

3. Your car slips out of gear and rolls down your driveway, across the street, and into a new red sports car parked in front of your neighbor's house. Your neighbor runs from his house screaming, "What happened?"

To begin today's session, divide the class into four groups. (If you have more than thirty class members, use more than four groups, giving the same assignment to more than one group.) Distribute the above four situations to the groups. Ask them to choose two volunteers who will present a ninety-second role play and act out how the characters in the situations react. Or each group can just discuss the situation and suggest reactions.

After the role plays or the discussion, raise these issues with the class:

1. How do people often first react when confronted with their wrongdoing?

2. Why is it sometimes easier to make excuses than to admit a mistake?

3. Why is saying "I'm sorry" sometimes so difficult?

Tell the class that today's study will consider the issue of why and how to confess sin.

Into the Word

Ask someone to read Daniel 9:1, 2 aloud. Discuss the historical background of this text, using the Lesson Background in the commen-

tary. Next, give listening assignments to the four groups that met earlier. As you read Daniel 9:3-19, have each group listen for one of the following in the passage: (1) descriptions of God; (2) sins of the people; (3) punishments of God; and (4) pleas for mercy.

Read the text slowly (saying verse numbers aloud as you come to them), encouraging class members to jot down phrases or verse numbers that apply to their assignments. Give the groups four or five minutes to examine their lists. Invite each group to share its responses briefly with the class.

Next, discuss these questions with the class:

1. Considering that Daniel's prayer comes at the end of the captivity, and not the beginning of it, what seems surprising about it?

2. Upon what basis does Daniel ask God to forgive the people? Have you ever heard or prayed this kind of prayer? Why don't we pray this way more often today?

3. According to Daniel 9:20, whose sin did Daniel confess? What does this tell us about Daniel? Why do you think Daniel believed it was necessary to confess *his* sin? Should confession of national sins today be accompanied by confession of personal sins and of the failures of the church? Why is this an important connection to make?

Into Life

To conclude, give each of your groups one of the following assignments:

1. In a topical Bible or concordance, find a list of passages about confessing sin. Choose a few verses to read to the entire class.

2. List national sins that Christians in our country should confess to God.

3. List congregational sins that our church or our church leaders should confess to God.

4. In hymnals or chorus books, look for songs that express either confession of sin or sorrow for it.

Give the groups several minutes, then let each one report, in the order above. After the last group has reported, ask its members to choose one song for all the class to sing. Afterward, lead in a time of sentence prayers, in which class members ask God's forgiveness for the sins that the small groups listed. If you wish, you may end the session by singing the song again.

Let's Talk It Over

The questions on this page are designed to encourage review of the lesson Scriptures and to promote discussion of the lesson by the class. The answers provided are only discussion starters. Let your class talk it over from there.

1. Do we give enough attention in the church and in our personal lives to confession of sin? Why is it important that we give this careful attention?

Perhaps we acknowledge regularly in our public and private prayers that we are sinners, unworthy of God's favor. But a more detailed confession is needed. In 1 John 1:9 we are told, "If we confess our sins, he is faithful and just to forgive us our sins, and to cleanse us from all unrighteousness." The forgiveness and cleansing come as we bring before God our daily blunders, failures, and transgressions. Have we lied? Have we entertained lust in our hearts? Have we acted selfishly? Have we spoken harshly? Let us confess these, and with God's help let us forsake them. If we fail to do this, we hamper God's power at work in us.

2. Daniel confessed Israel's rebellion against God. In what ways can we say that our nation has rebelled against God?

All we need to do to answer this is to examine the Ten Commandments in Exodus 20:1-17. We have made idols out of possessions, recreation, sex, and personal power. We have not only used God's name and Jesus' name in idle cursing; we have also been guilty of mocking the sacred truths of God's Word. We use the day designated for the worship of God primarily as a day for the fulfillment of personal wants and desires. Instead of honoring parents we have often insulted them, abused them, and neglected them when they have grown old. We have become a violent nation, murdering children in their mother's wombs and slaughtering one another on our city streets. Adultery and general sexual license are rampant in our society. We are lovers and makers of lies (see Revelation 22:15), from the highest levels of government on down. We are filled with illicit desires for material things and immoral pleasures.

3. Why do we need to cultivate the practice of praying for God to be honored and glorified?

This was a significant aspect of Daniel's prayer in our lesson text (Daniel 9:18, 19). We must recognize that this is the ultimate purpose of prayer. Prayer enables us to obtain God's help, to find peace in the midst of turmoil, to gain victory over temptation, and to minister to other people who are in need. All of these aims, however, must be seen as subordinate to the loftiest aim of bringing glory to God. It can also be noted that emphasizing prayer for God's glory is one way of combating the temptation to seek our own glory.

4. What are some reasons why we can find encouragement for the future in spite of this world's darkness?

The Bible shows how throughout the centuries God has caused light to shine in the midst of human darkness. Old Testament Israel experienced many periods in which evil reigned, but God sent His prophets to bring repentance, healing, and light. Violence and oppression were rampant when Jesus came as "the light of the world" (John 8:12). As dark as our present era often seems, we have many reasons for hope. There are still multitudes of people reading, studying, obeying, and teaching the Bible. Great numbers of people are also praying for God's will to be done on earth. Men and women of faith are still going forth as evangelists and missionaries to proclaim the gospel. Most important of all, God is in control of the course of human history.

5. Why is it wise for us to choose to be honest before God?

We are constantly tempted to believe that we can hide from God some of what we think and do. But the Bible reminds us in many places of the truth spelled out in Hebrews 4:13: "Neither is there any creature that is not manifest in his sight: but all things are naked and opened unto the eyes of him with whom we have to do." We need to be honest before God, because He already knows all about us. Furthermore, the Bible points out that a day is coming "when God shall judge the secrets of men by Jesus Christ" (Romans 2:16). We need to be honest before God, because He will someday reveal all our secrets. Finally, honesty before God is appropriate to our relationship with Him as child to Father. "Your Father knoweth what things ye have need of, before ye ask him" (Matthew 6:8). But He also desires that we share with Him all our concerns, temptations, and failures.

Completing the Temple

DEVOTIONAL READING: Psalm 126.

LESSON SCRIPTURE: Ezra 6.

PRINTED TEXT: Ezra 6:14-22.

Ezra 6:14-22

14 And the elders of the Jews builded, and they prospered through the prophesying of Haggai the prophet and Zechariah the son of Iddo. And they builded, and finished it, according to the commandment of the God of Israel, and according to the commandment of Cyrus, and Darius, and Artaxerxes king of Persia.

15 And this house was finished on the third day of the month Adar, which was in the sixth year of the reign of Darius the king.

16 And the children of Israel, the priests, and the Levites, and the rest of the children of the captivity, kept the dedication of this house of God with joy,

17 And offered at the dedication of this house of God a hundred bullocks, two hundred rams, four hundred lambs; and for a sin offering for all Israel, twelve he goats, according to the number of the tribes of Israel.

18 And they set the priests in their divisions, and the Levites in their courses, for the service of God, which is at Jerusalem; as it is written in the book of Moses.

19 And the children of the captivity kept the passover upon the fourteenth day of the first month.

20 For the priests and the Levites were purified together, all of them were pure, and killed the passover for all the children of the captivity, and for their brethren the priests, and for themselves.

21 And the children of Israel, which were come again out of captivity, and all such as had separated themselves unto them from the filthiness of the heathen of the land, to seek the LORD God of Israel, did eat,

22 And kept the feast of unleavened bread seven days with joy: for the LORD had made them joyful, and turned the heart of the king of Assyria unto them, to strengthen their hands in the work of the house of God, the God of Israel.

GOLDEN TEXT: The children of Israel, the priests, and the Levites, and the rest of the children of the captivity, kept the dedication of this house of God with joy.—Ezra 6:16.

God Leads a People Home
Unit 3: Life After the Return
(Lessons 9-13)

Lesson Aims

After this lesson, a student should be able to:

1. Summarize the events connected with the rebuilding of the temple after the exiles returned from captivity.

2. Compare the obstacles faced by the exiles rebuilding the temple with obstacles faced by Christians trying to do God's will today.

3. Commit to God's work in an area where obstacles have been especially challenging.

Lesson Outline

INTRODUCTION
    A. Barriers to Building
    B. Lesson Background
  I. THE TEMPLE (Ezra 6:14, 15)
    A. The Completion (v. 14)
    B. The Date (v. 15)
 II. THE DEDICATION (Ezra 6:16-18)
    A. Joyous Gathering (v. 16)
       Celebration
    B. Joyous Offerings (v. 17)
    C. Joyous Service (v. 18)
III. THE PASSOVER (Ezra 6:19-22)
    A. The Proper Time (v. 19)
    B. The Proper Officials (v. 20)
    C. The Proper Participants (v. 21)
    D. The Week of Celebration (v. 22)
       A Symbol of Freedom
CONCLUSION
    A. The Message to Us
    B. What Comes First?
    C. Prayer
    D. Thought to Remember

The visual for Lesson 9 is an artist's design of how the temple rebuilt by the Jews may have looked in the first century. It is shown on page 75.

Introduction

A. Barriers to Building

After World War I ended in 1918, the post-war boom in the economy lasted through most of the "roaring twenties." In the midwestern part of the United States, a growing church sold its overcrowded building and started to build a structure big enough to meet its needs.

Then came 1929. The stock market crashed, and the Great Depression began. Some church members lost their businesses; others lost their jobs. Plans to complete the proposed church building had to be put on hold.

At the time the "crash" occurred, the basement of the new building had already been dug and walled. The congregation proceeded to build a roof over the basement, and it soon became another overcrowded meeting place. It served that purpose all through the Depression and another world war. Then came another post-war boom, and the building that had been planned and needed for so long was finally completed about twenty years after it was begun.

The temple that the returning exiles built in Jerusalem had no basement, but it did have a foundation, which was laid amidst great celebration (Ezra 3:11). Before long, however, a spiritual "Great Depression" set in, caused by opposition from "the people of the land," who "weakened the hands of the people of Judah, and troubled them in building" (4:4). It would be sixteen years before this "crash" ended and work on the temple resumed.

B. Lesson Background

Let us review briefly the lessons we studied in September. We read of Israel's freedom after seventy years of captivity in Babylon, and of the rebuilding of the nation of Judah. In the first two lessons, we looked at this from the perspective of the prophet Isaiah, who wrote of these events long before they happened. He even named Cyrus, the king who would set Israel free, long before the king was born.

The people of Israel came home from Babylon just as Isaiah had predicted. Eagerly they began to rebuild the temple, but the difficulties were many and discouraging. The work was slow, and for a time it stopped altogether. Then God sent two prophets, Haggai and Zechariah, to challenge the people to finish the temple. We read about that in our last two lessons in September. At the urging of these prophets, the difficulties were overcome and the temple was finished about twenty years after it was begun.

In October our four lessons from Daniel told of events that occurred in Babylon during the years when the people of Israel were captives there. We read of four young men who stood for God's principles even in a heathen land. Three of them obeyed God's Law even at the risk of being thrown into a fiery furnace. We also read of the hand that wrote on the wall, and of the end of Babylon's power. Finally, we studied Daniel's prayer for his people when they were on the verge of being set free to go back home.

With this final unit of the quarter, we take up the story where we left it at the end of September. The captivity is over; the people of Israel have been home for a little more than twenty years. At last the temple is completed.

I. The Temple
(Ezra 6:14, 15)

A. The Completion (v. 14)

14. And the elders of the Jews builded, and they prospered through the prophesying of Haggai the prophet and Zechariah the son of Iddo. And they builded, and finished it, according to the commandment of the God of Israel, and according to the commandment of Cyrus, and Darius, and Artaxerxes king of Persia.

The reference to *the elders* does not mean that younger men had no part in the work. Probably they did most of the heavier work, but the elders are given credit because they supervised the endeavor. In a similar way it is said that Solomon built the first temple (1 Kings 6:14). Perhaps his own hands lifted no stone and placed no timber, but Solomon authorized, directed, and financed the construction.

Our lessons for September 21 and 28 focused on *the prophesying of Haggai . . . and Zechariah.* When work on the temple had stopped completely and the people's priorities had become misplaced, these two prophets stirred up the elders and the people to resume the task. The people kept building until *they finished it, according to the commandment of the God of Israel:* the commandment given through His prophets (Haggai 1:8; Zechariah 4:9). The completion of the temple was also *according to the commandment* of those rulers of the Medes and Persians who had taken control of Babylon's empire. Three rulers are named.

Cyrus was king of the Medes and Persians when they overtook Babylon. In the first year of his reign, he issued a decree that any among the people of Israel who desired should "go up to Jerusalem, . . . and build the house of the Lord God of Israel" (Ezra 1:3).

The *Darius* whose name appears in our text was not the Mede who "took the kingdom" on the night Belshazzar was slain (Daniel 5:31). Apparently that Darius served as a governor under the authority of Cyrus. This Darius was another man, who ruled the Persian empire from 521 to 486 B.C. Thus he was ruling when the temple in Jerusalem was completed. In fact, when progress on the temple had been threatened again by the enemies of God's people, Darius had the official records searched. The original decree of Cyrus was found, certifying that he

had indeed granted permission to the Jews to rebuild their temple. Darius then told those who opposed the project, "Let the work of this house of God alone" (Ezra 6:7). He even authorized the use of royal funds to cover any expenses (v. 8)!

Artaxerxes ruled the Persian empire from 465 to 424 B.C. It seems surprising to see his name here, since his reign occurred so long after the temple had been completed (Ezra 4:7-24). He may have been added to the list here, because he also contributed to efforts "to beautify the house of the Lord" (Ezra 7:27; see also vv. 21-24). The point seems to be that although opposition to rebuilding occurred during the reigns of these Persian rulers (see 4:5-7), God overruled those efforts and blessed His people with success. Certainly it is noteworthy that the commandment of the God of Israel is mentioned ahead of the commandment of earthly rulers.

B. The Date (v. 15)

15. And this house was finished on the third day of the month Adar, which was in the sixth year of the reign of Darius the king.

This was the year 516 B.C., slightly more than twenty years after the first group of captives had returned from Babylon. *Adar* is the Babylonian name for the twelfth *month* of the year (the Jews often used the Babylonian names of months following the exile). It did not come at the beginning of winter as our twelfth month of December does, but at the end of winter— around the last part of February and the first part of March.

II. The Dedication
(Ezra 6:16-18)

Can you imagine how the people felt at this moment? For twenty years the temple had stood incomplete—a constant reminder of a duty left undone. Now, at last, the job was finished. There was a suitable place in which to honor the God of Heaven and to worship Him according to His ancient Law. What a sense of satisfaction and relief must have been present! It was a time to celebrate!

visual for
lesson 9

How to Say It

ADAR. *A*-dar.
ARTAXERXES. Are-tuh-*zerk*-sees.
ASSYRIA. Uh-*sear*-e-uh.
BABYLONIAN. Bab-uh-*low*-nee-un.
BELSHAZZAR. Bel-*shazz*-er.
CYRUS. *Sigh*-russ.
DARIUS. Duh-*rye*-us.
HAGGAI. *Hag*-a-eye or *Hag*-eye.
IDDO. *Id*-doe.
MEDES. Meeds.
ZECHARIAH. Zek-uh-*rye*-uh.

A. Joyous Gathering (v. 16)

16. And the children of Israel, the priests, and the Levites, and the rest of the children of the captivity, kept the dedication of this house of God with joy.

Many of those gathered on this occasion were *children of the captivity,* because they had been born during the captivity in Babylon. But now they assembled as *children of Israel,* rejoicing in their identity as God's people. *The priests, and the Levites* were leaders in the religious ceremonies of *dedication,* but the entire nation experienced the *joy* of the occasion.

CELEBRATION

"White House Santa" lives in Glendale, California, not Washington, D.C. His real name is Robert George, and a few years ago he was engaged in a running battle with City Hall. The "problem" was that George was keeping his Christmas lights on year-round—all fifty-two thousand of them! He also had his house and yard decorated with fake snow on the roof, approximately one hundred Christmas trees and ten thousand ornaments, and a styrofoam reindeer that stood fourteen feet tall.

The reason for George's efforts was that he liked to invite groups of poor, disabled, and terminally ill children to his house to let them celebrate the spirit of Christmas throughout the year. He knew that many of them might not live to see another Christmas. But the city council decided that all of this celebration was a nuisance, and told George to limit his visitors to two terminally ill children per month.

The city council was probably dealing with neighbors' complaints about noise and traffic, but don't you suppose there were some real evil-doers in town whom they could have picked on? Why make life difficult for someone who was trying to bring some joy into the lives of unfortunate children?

The Jews who sought to rebuild the temple encountered considerable opposition. Their "neighbors" considered their efforts a nuisance. Not only did these critics complain; they did all they could to limit progress on the temple. With God's help, however, the people completed the task, and dedicated the house of God with a great celebration. Eventually, those who rejoice in what God has done will win, in spite of the opposition they face.   —C. R. B.

B. Joyous Offerings (v. 17)

17. And offered at the dedication of this house of God a hundred bullocks, two hundred rams, four hundred lambs; and for a sin offering for all Israel, twelve he goats, according to the number of the tribes of Israel.

The joy and gratitude of the people were reflected in the large numbers of animals offered in sacrifice. Big as these numbers may appear, they represent only a fraction of the number of sacrifices offered at the dedication of Solomon's temple some four and a half centuries earlier (1 Kings 8:63). This is another indication that the second temple did not possess the splendor of Solomon's. Still, the completion of it was a notable achievement.

The presentation of a *sin offering for all Israel* was significant. It called attention to the fact that the people were aware of their personal guilt in failing to give God and His work priority. Just as important as building a new temple was the commitment of a renewed people.

The offering of *twelve he goats* to represent *the number of the tribes of Israel* is also noteworthy. It is difficult to know whether people from every tribe would have been present for this dedication. More important was the fact that this represented an attempt to go back to Israel's "roots"—to acknowledge God's original plan of setting aside the twelve tribes to serve Him, even though these tribes had experienced much turmoil through the years.

C. Joyous Service (v. 18)

18. And they set the priests in their divisions, and the Levites in their courses, for the service of God, which is at Jerusalem; as it is written in the book of Moses.

The book of Moses ordered that *the Levites* should assist *the priests* and take care of the tabernacle (Numbers 3:5-10). Naturally they later took care of the temple. Moses' book also ordered that one family of Levites, Aaron's family, should be the source of Israel's priests (Exodus 28:1). In David's time there were so many priests and Levites that they could not all serve at once. David therefore organized them in *divisions* and *courses*, each of which served in its turn. This organization is described in 1 Chronicles 23-26. The same system was reestablished when the second temple was completed.

III. The Passover
(Ezra 6:19-22)

The Passover looked back more than nine hundred years before the time of our lesson, to the time when the people of Israel were about to become an independent nation. For many years before that time they had been slaves in Egypt. Then God sent Moses and Aaron to proclaim that it was time for them to leave their bondage and move to a land He had promised them. However, the pharaoh of Egypt was not willing to release such a large number of slaves.

God then sent ten plagues to compel the cruel Egyptian taskmasters to let His people go. In the last plague, God destroyed the firstborn in every Egyptian home. Israelite homes, however, were marked with the blood of a lamb on the doorposts. God promised to "pass over" those homes without harming those inside (see Exodus 12:1-14); thus the name "Passover."

A. The Proper Time (v. 19)

19. And the children of the captivity kept the passover upon the fourteenth day of the first month.

The Israelites who had come back from *captivity* in Babylon *kept the passover* on the anniversary of the day when the Lord "passed over" the Israelite homes. This was *the fourteenth day of the first month* (Leviticus 23:5). The temple had been completed a few weeks earlier, on the third day of the last month of the year (v. 15).

B. The Proper Officials (v. 20)

20. For the priests and the Levites were purified together, all of them were pure, and killed the passover for all the children of the captivity, and for their brethren the priests, and for themselves.

According to the Law of Moses, there were many ways in which a person might become impure or unclean. One might be defiled by contact with an unclean person or animal, or with a dead person or animal (Leviticus 22:4-8). In most cases the Law did not imply that the unclean person had done anything wrong; it was simply a matter of sanitation and health. An unclean person could be purified by washing himself and his clothing, and by waiting a specified time—a day, a week, or a longer period. In some cases a sacrifice also was required.

A priest or a Levite who was unclean could not take his usual part in the ceremonies of worship. *The priests and the Levites* who were to officiate at this dedication of the temple had done whatever was necessary to purify themselves. It appears that the Levites were primarily responsible for slaying the Passover lambs, since they performed this act for all the people, *for their brethren the priests, and for themselves.* The priests were to officiate at the altar itself (Numbers 18:1-7). Priests and Levites were *brethren*, because all of them were descendants of Jacob's son Levi.

C. The Proper Participants (v. 21)

21. And the children of Israel, which were come again out of captivity, and all such as had separated themselves unto them from the filthiness of the heathen of the land, to seek the LORD God of Israel, did eat.

The Israelites who had returned from Babylon had been in their homeland now for close to twenty years. Apparently during that time they had converted some of *the heathen of the land* who lived near them. These converted ones now joined in the celebration of the Passover. Possibly some of these people had Jewish ancestors and therefore possessed a certain amount of knowledge of Jewish laws and traditions.

D. The Week of Celebration (v. 22)

22. And kept the feast of unleavened bread seven days with joy: for the LORD had made them joyful, and turned the heart of the king of Assyria unto them, to strengthen their hands in the work of the house of God, the God of Israel.

The feast of unleavened bread was celebrated during the seven days immediately following the eating of the Passover meal. The absence of leaven was a reminder of Israel's deliverance from slavery in Egypt. Leaving in haste, the people had taken their bread dough in the kneading troughs before leaven could be added to it. Thus, unleavened bread had been their food during the first days of their journey out of Egypt. Exodus 12:39 tells us, "And they baked unleavened cakes of the dough which they brought forth out of Egypt, for it was not leavened; because they were thrust out of Egypt, and could not tarry, neither had they prepared for themselves any victuals."

The Passover feast was always celebrated *with joy*, because it was a part of Israel's annual celebration of its freedom. This year, however, there was an added reason for joy: *the Lord had made them joyful* by moving *the king of Assyria* to be favorable toward them and to *strengthen their hands* in the rebuilding of the temple. We may question why Darius, who was the Persian ruler at this time, is designated the king of Assyria, since the empire of Assyria had passed from the stage of history by now. However, even after the Assyrian empire collapsed, the term *Assyria* continued to be used in historical records to describe territories the Assyrians had once occupied. The title may have also served to convey the message that Assyria, which had once been used of God to punish His people, was now being used to strengthen them through the assistance that Darius had provided the people in completing the temple.

A SYMBOL OF FREEDOM

The Eiffel Tower was the tallest structure in the world at the time it was built. When the tower was proposed, French writers, artists, and intellectuals denounced the project, predicting it would collapse within twenty years. But the common people were captivated by the idea, and the tower was completed in 1889, commemorating the one hundredth anniversary of the French Revolution. When the tower opened to the public on May 15 of that year, there was a great celebration that included everyone from common French peasants to potentates from around the world.

The project to rebuild the temple in Jerusalem had its critics also. But when it was completed, the celebration included both local Jews and those who had returned from far-off Babylon. The temple was dedicated with a great sacrifice, and then everyone joined in a joyful feast, giving thanks to God.

Sacrifice and rejoicing are the appropriate responses of Christians everywhere to the fact that we have gained our freedom through Jesus Christ. Sin has been conquered, we have been "brought back home," and the temple of God has been rebuilt (through the presence of His Spirit) in the lives of all who follow Jesus. In every land, Christians from all walks of life—from peasants to potentates—can celebrate and rejoice in what God has done.   —C. R. B.

Conclusion

A. The Message to Us

This lesson's message to us should be clear. Let's put it in the words of Paul: "Let us not be weary in well doing: for in due season we shall reap, if we faint not" (Galatians 6:9).

What is proving to be difficult for your congregation? Building a new house of worship or adding to the one you have? Winning new people to Christ? Employing a youth minister to brighten your hope for the church of tomorrow? Recruiting and training teachers and leaders? Supporting a missionary, a Christian college, or a new church in a poor neighborhood? Whatever your challenge may be, today's lesson presents an example that tells us, "Hang in there!"

B. What Comes First?

A bulletin board in front of a church building once posted this timely suggestion as a challenge to passersby:

Give God what is right
Not what is left.

Haggai rebuked the people of Israel because they put their own houses ahead of God's house. They were not content with simple shelters; they needed "ceiled houses" (Haggai 1:4), paneled with costly cedar from Lebanon. Do you really need all those comforts that end up taking more time and attention than God's work?

When God gave His laws to His people, He required a tenth of each person's income, along with other offerings. Now that we are under grace and not under the Law, can we be content to give any less than was required under the Law? Is God getting the best from us, or merely the leftovers?

Will we give God what is right, not what is left?

C. Prayer

Father, we do want to give You what is right. As the priests and Levites of old purified themselves for the Passover, may we with Your help cleanse ourselves from selfishness, and present to You our time, talent, and treasure. Amen.

D. Thought to Remember

When doing God's work, never give up!

Home Daily Bible Readings

Monday, Oct. 27—Altar Set in Its Place (Ezra 3:1-7)

Tuesday, Oct. 28—Cheers and Tears at the Start (Ezra 3:8-13)

Wednesday, Oct. 29—Darius Backs the Temple Project (Ezra 6:1-12)

Thursday, Oct. 30—They Built and They Prospered (Ezra 6:13-22)

Friday, Oct. 31—God Dwells With the Contrite (Isaiah 57:15-21)

Saturday, Nov. 1—No Earthly Temple Large Enough (Isaiah 66:1-5)

Sunday, Nov. 2—Zion Restored Once More (Psalm 126:1-6)

Learning by Doing

This page contains an alternate lesson plan emphasizing learning activities.
Classes desiring such student involvement will find these suggestions helpful.

Learning Goals

After completing this lesson, students should be able to:

1. Summarize the events connected with the rebuilding of the temple after the exiles returned from captivity.

2. Compare the obstacles faced by the exiles rebuilding the temple with obstacles faced by Christians trying to do God's will today.

3. Commit to God's work in an area where obstacles have been especially challenging.

Into the Lesson

Give all students a sheet of paper and have them turn it horizontally. They should draw three lines across the paper: one across the middle, a parallel line along the top, and a third parallel line along the bottom. Tell the class to label the middle line as "Normal," the top line as "Ecstasy," and the bottom line as "Despair." They are to use this paper to chart their lives, beginning whenever they wish until the present year. They should divide the page into years, or periods of years. For each year or period, they should put a dot to indicate how they would rate their lives during that time. How close were they to "Normal," "Ecstasy," or "Despair"?

After they have rated each year or period, they should connect the dots. The resulting line is a pattern of their lives. Let class members compare their charts with each other and tell each other about the variances in their lives. What made some times happier than others?

Tell the class that today's lesson looks at a time when God's people were very happy. This happiness followed a time of great difficulty. We will look at what brought the people happiness, what caused their difficulties, and what we can learn from their experience.

Into the Word

Briefly explain how this week's lesson fits into the current quarter of study. Review the previous lessons from Daniel, and tell how the history in this week's lesson fits with Lesson 3 (from Haggai) and Lesson 4 (from Zechariah). (It would be helpful to include with this an overview of the captivity, the return to Israel, and the years that went by before the temple was finally completed.) Use the commentary to prepare a short lecture highlighting these items.

Next, ask class members if they can recall from previous lessons some of the obstacles that kept the people from completing the temple. List these on the chalkboard. Possible responses should include: misplaced priorities, apathy, unhappiness with the inferior quality of the new temple when compared with Solomon's, and the opposition from surrounding peoples.

Then read today's printed text, Ezra 6:14-22, aloud. As the text is being read, class members should jot down words to describe the emotions of the Israelites during the events recounted here. After the reading, ask class members to shout out these words as you list them (beside the list of obstacles) on your chalkboard.

Ask the class, "Why did the Israelites feel such joy? What had happened to them to enhance their joy? Would their celebration have been so intense if it had not been preceded by so many hardships?"

Into Life

Have class members look again at their life charts. Can they see comparisons between their experiences and those of the Israelites? Did any of them experience intense joy only after times of severe difficulty?

Ask them to reflect on the causes of their hardships. Were their "down" times caused by obedience to God? Disobedience? The sin of others? Who in the class can share a testimony of how trying to follow God brought disappointment or sadness? Ask the class to consider what lessons we can learn from these testimonies and from the experiences of the Israelites.

Before class, write each of the words of Galatians 6:9 on a separate sheet of paper. Distribute the sheets, in random order, to members of your class at this point in the lesson. Ask the students to stand before the class and to arrange themselves in the correct order. Tell class members that the message of this verse summarizes the lesson we can learn from the experiences of the returning Israelites.

Ask class members to relate any obstacles they are facing now because of their efforts to serve God. You may do this with the entire class, or by encouraging class members to share with each other in groups. If they meet in groups, end with prayers in the groups for both perseverance and joy.

Let's Talk It Over

The questions on this page are designed to encourage review of the lesson Scriptures and to promote discussion of the lesson by the class. The answers provided are only discussion starters. Let your class talk it over from there.

1. The rebuilding of the temple must surely have included the efforts of young and old working together. What are some factors to keep in mind in encouraging young and old to work together harmoniously in the church?

Mutual respect is vital. Younger members must respect the wisdom that comes with maturity and experience. Older members must respect the enthusiasm and desire for change that characterize the young. It is important that older members remain active in the work of the church, even when their physical strength and mental prowess have diminished somewhat. Like the elders who directed the work of rebuilding the temple, they may still be able to give some valuable direction and guidance. Younger members must accept the possibility that the major share of the actual work may fall on their shoulders. Every person in the church should appreciate the fact that there is valuable work to be done by all.

2. The unfinished temple stood for twenty years as a reminder of work that needed to be completed. Do we have similar reminders in our church of such work?

Empty pews on Sunday morning may be a clear reminder of evangelistic work left undone. If some of them represent new converts who have begun to drift away, that may warn us of the importance of a better effort at follow-up teaching and discipling. Crowded Sunday school classrooms may speak to us of the need for establishing new classes or constructing larger facilities. If we see young people from our congregation attending youth programs at other churches, it should stir us to improve our own programs. Perhaps there are repairs to be made on our building that have been put off, but now should be completed. Like the people of Jerusalem, we may be guilty of procrastination.

3. Why was it appropriate that one of the first events to be held in connection with the completed temple was a Passover celebration?

The original Passover signaled the beginning of Israel as a nation. While enslaved in Egypt, the Israelites were a distinct race of people, but they could hardly be called a nation. When they left Egypt after the first Passover, they were unit-ed under Moses' leadership. After crossing the Jordan River under the leadership of Joshua, they again celebrated a significant Passover (Joshua 5:10). Following this they began the conquest of Canaan. Another significant Passover was celebrated following the reforms effected by King Josiah, described in 2 Kings 23:21-23. With these earlier Passovers having been observed at particularly significant times, it was quite appropriate that another Passover should follow the rebuilding of the temple.

4. The Jews found joy in the fact that God had made it possible for them to complete the temple. Why do we need to emphasize such joy in the Lord when our church completes a successful program or project?

It is easy to forget the truth expressed in Psalm 127:1: "Except the Lord build the house, they labor in vain that build it." If our planning proves fruitful, let us be joyful that the Lord guided it. If we acknowledge the contributions various members made, let us rejoice that the Lord inspired and guided those members. Let us make certain that we do not pay the Lord only "lip service" for our achievements. Let us instead give Him all the glory, and rejoice in the way He works in and through His people.

5. We can easily become discouraged when our church faces difficulties in achieving its goals. How can we view such difficulties as opportunities?

It is unrealistic to expect our church to avoid difficulties and problems. We must keep in mind that the devil is waging war against the church. We must also remember that churches are made up of fallible human beings. But God specializes in turning difficulties into dramatic victories. If we have friction in the church, He can use it to call attention to our need for better communication. If we are facing some serious financial problems, He can challenge us to greater sacrificial giving. If we are not winning the lost, He can stir within us a fresh evangelistic fervor. If we are hindered from growing by inadequate facilities, He can give us the vision to build. It is important that we refuse to be preoccupied with problems and that we resolve instead to be energized by opportunities.

Preserving the Faith

DEVOTIONAL READING: Deuteronomy 6:1-9.

LESSON SCRIPTURE: Ezra 9:1—10:17.

PRINTED TEXT: Ezra 9:1-3; 10:9-14.

Ezra 9:1-3

1 Now when these things were done, the princes came to me, saying, The people of Israel, and the priests, and the Levites, have not separated themselves from the people of the lands, doing according to their abominations, even of the Canaanites, the Hittites, the Perizzites, the Jebusites, the Ammonites, the Moabites, the Egyptians, and the Amorites.

2 For they have taken of their daughters for themselves, and for their sons: so that the holy seed have mingled themselves with the people of those lands: yea, the hand of the princes and rulers hath been chief in this trespass.

3 And when I heard this thing, I rent my garment and my mantle, and plucked off the hair of my head and of my beard, and sat down astonished.

Ezra 10:9-14

9 Then all the men of Judah and Benjamin gathered themselves together unto Jerusalem within three days. It was the ninth month, on the twentieth day of the month; and all the people sat in the street of the house of God,

trembling because of this matter, and for the great rain.

10 And Ezra the priest stood up, and said unto them, Ye have transgressed, and have taken strange wives, to increase the trespass of Israel.

11 Now therefore make confession unto the LORD God of your fathers, and do his pleasure: and separate yourselves from the people of the land, and from the strange wives.

12 Then all the congregation answered and said with a loud voice, As thou hast said, so must we do.

13 But the people are many, and it is a time of much rain, and we are not able to stand without, neither is this a work of one day or two: for we are many that have transgressed in this thing.

14 Let now our rulers of all the congregation stand, and let all them which have taken strange wives in our cities come at appointed times, and with them the elders of every city, and the judges thereof, until the fierce wrath of our God for this matter be turned from us.

GOLDEN TEXT: Now therefore make confession unto the LORD God of your fathers, and do his pleasure.—Ezra 10:11.

God Leads a People Home
Unit 3: Life After the Return
(Lessons 9-13)

Lesson Aims

After this lesson a student should be able to:

1. Tell how Ezra and his people dealt with a situation where God's Law had been ignored.

2. Express some principles, based on this passage, that can be applied in dealing with problems faced by Christians and/or the church today.

3. Suggest one or two ways to apply those principles in dealing with a specific situation.

Lesson Outline

INTRODUCTION
  A. A Perilous Pattern
  B. Lesson Background
  I. HEARING BAD NEWS (Ezra 9:1-3)
  A. Israel's Sin (vv. 1, 2)
    A Spiritual Biosphere?
  B. Ezra's Grief (v. 3)
  II. DEALING WITH SIN (Ezra 10:9-11)
  A. Meeting in the Rain (v. 9)
  B. Facing the Facts (v. 10)
  C. Calling for Confession (v. 11)
  III. MAKING A CHANGE (Ezra 10:12-14)
  A. Confessing the Sin (v. 12)
  B. Facing the Difficulties (v. 13)
  C. Forming a Plan (v. 14)
CONCLUSION
  A. Attention
  B. Wrong
  C. Authority
  D. Mixing With Unbelievers
  E. Prayer
  F. Thought to Remember

The visual for Lesson 10 calls attention to our Golden Text for today, found in Ezra 10:11. It is shown on page 84.

Introduction

A. A Perilous Pattern

Often we hear people complain that our world is becoming worse. Boys now shoot real bullets as casually as their grandfathers played cops and robbers with sticks for their guns. Language once banned from "polite society" is now broadcast from coast to coast. Illicit sex is so common among teenagers that many teachers and government officials think it is better to recommend "safe sex" than to advise abstinence.

The Bible provides different examples of how later generations became more corrupt than previous ones. One is found in the first few chapters of Genesis. "God saw every thing that he had made, and, behold, it was very good" (Genesis 1:31). But only nine generations later, "God saw that the wickedness of man was great in the earth, and that every imagination of the thoughts of his heart was only evil continually" (Genesis 6:5).

Our recent lessons have reminded us that God's people became so ungodly that they were punished with captivity in Babylon. When they were released, many went to Jerusalem to rebuild God's house. But because of opposition from nearby residents, and the failure to give the temple the priority it deserved, approximately twenty years passed before the temple was completed.

With today's lesson we turn to a time close to eighty years after the exiles returned. The children of those who had completed the temple had lapsed into serious disobedience. They were in danger of bringing God's judgment upon themselves, as their forefathers had done.

B. Lesson Background

As we have observed, not all of the Jews went home to Jerusalem when Cyrus's decree permitted them to go. Ezra belonged to a family that chose to stay in Babylon. He was a priest and a scholar, well versed in the Law and eager to go to Jerusalem to teach it there (Ezra 7:6, 10).

The Persian ruler at the time of Ezra's return was Artaxerxes (Ezra 7:1). Not only did he allow Ezra to travel to Jerusalem, but he even provided generous financial support (vv. 11-26).

How to Say It

AMMONITES. *Am*-uh-nites.
AMORITES. *Am*-uh-rites.
ARTAXERXES. Are-tuh-*zerk*-sees.
BOAZ. *Boe*-az.
CANAANITES. *Kay*-nuh-nites.
EGYPTIANS. E-*jip*-shuns.
HITTITES. *Hit*-tites.
JEBUSITES. *Jeb*-you-sites.
MOABITES. *Moe*-ub-ites.
MOABITESS. *Moe*-ub-*ite*-ess. (strong accent on *Moe*).
PERIZZITES. *Pair*-ih-zites.
SHECHANIAH. Shek-uh-*nye*-uh.

He authorized Ezra both to teach God's Law and to appoint "magistrates and judges" to enforce it (v. 25). Chapter 8 of Ezra records that more than seventeen hundred men of Israel gathered to accompany Ezra from Babylon to Jerusalem (they are counted in vv. 1-20). This occurred in the seventh year of Artaxerxes, which would have been 458 B.C.

I. Hearing Bad News
(Ezra 9:1-3)

Ezra likely did not know exactly what to expect when he arrived in Jerusalem to begin his teaching ministry. Perhaps he was anticipating some neglect of the Law, but it seems that he found the situation much worse than he thought it would be.

A. Israel's Sin (vv. 1, 2)

1. Now when these things were done, the princes came to me, saying, The people of Israel, and the priests, and the Levites, have not separated themselves from the people of the lands, doing according to their abominations, even of the Canaanites, the Hittites, the Perizzites, the Jebusites, the Ammonites, the Moabites, the Egyptians, and the Amorites.

These things were the matters of business that demanded attention when Ezra arrived in Jerusalem (Ezra 8:32-36). When these were taken care of, certain *princes*, or leaders of the people, approached him with a new issue of concern. *The people of Israel* were no longer a people *separated*, or set apart, from the heathen. Even *the priests, and the Levites* (the religious leaders) had violated God's Law in this matter. *Their abominations* could have included wickedness of many kinds. One is singled out in the next verse.

Eight heathen nations are named in the princes' indictment. Most are among those that Israel was commanded to destroy almost a thousand years earlier (Deuteronomy 7:1, 2). Had Israel faithfully followed God's instructions back then, the problem now being confronted would have been less likely to surface.

2. For they have taken of their daughters for themselves, and for their sons: so that the holy seed have mingled themselves with the people of those lands: yea, the hand of the princes and rulers hath been chief in this trespass.

Marrying heathens was strictly forbidden in God's Law. Why? Because God knew that heathen spouses would turn His holy people away from Him and lead them to worship other gods (Deuteronomy 7:3-5). Not only had *the princes and rulers* failed to enforce the Law; they were

the *chief* offenders! Here the word *rulers* seems to refer to a class of leaders somewhat less influential than the princes. Not all of the leaders were involved in these violations, for some of the princes brought the bad news to Ezra (v. 1), obviously hoping he would do something about this disturbing problem.

A pioneer community usually has more men than women. Probably this was true of the pioneer community of Jews trying to restore their ancient homeland. One who took a foreign wife could defend himself by saying that no one else was available. But this was unacceptable in light of how God wanted His people to live. His Law made no exceptions. It would be better to live and die a bachelor than to become entangled in the abominations of the heathen.

It is noteworthy to consider the reference to the *Moabites* in verse 1. We know that Ruth was a Moabitess whom Boaz, an Israelite, married. She went on to play an instrumental part in the plan of God for His people and for the world (Ruth 4:13, 17; Matthew 1:1, 5). Ruth, however, gave every indication of "converting" to faith in the true God (Ruth 1:16). In addition, the Law of Moses did not specifically prohibit marriage to Moabites. Perhaps by the time of Ezra, they had become especially corrupted through pagan influences.

A SPIRITUAL BIOSPHERE?

Biosphere II was an unprecedented scientific experiment. For two years in the Arizona desert near Tucson, eight humans and nearly four thousand species of plants and animals were locked inside a sealed structure designed to be a totally self-sufficient world. For the experiment to be successful, there was to be no contamination from the outside world.

However, not all went precisely as planned. New oxygen had to be pumped in twice, and the system was opened numerous times: once for surgery on a crew member, and on other occasions to bring in seeds, sleeping pills, mousetraps, and makeup! The crew found that they could grow only about eighty percent of the food they needed; as a result, they lost an average of fourteen percent of their body weight during the experiment. Given the complexity and sophistication of the project, perhaps even more could have gone wrong.

Ancient Israel was also an "experiment" in human isolation—an isolation of the spirit, not of the body. God wanted Israel to separate itself from its neighbors so that the people could maintain a pure faith in God. But the people failed to maintain their separation. Even the leaders succumbed to the temptation to mingle with the pagan people who surrounded the nation.

God did not ask the Israelites for a Biosphere experience, just a commitment to keep themselves untainted by idolatry and sin. It is what He asks of us as well.   —C. R. B.

B. Ezra's Grief (v. 3)

3. And when I heard this thing, I rent my garment and my mantle, and plucked off the hair of my head and of my beard, and sat down astonished.

Ezra reacted immediately and intensely to the distressing news; he *rent*, or tore, his clothing. This was a traditional way of expressing shock, distress, and grief. Ezra's sorrow was so great that one act of tearing was not enough to express it. He tore both his *garment* and his *mantle* (both the tunic worn next to the body and the outer robe), and then tore out bits of his *hair* and *beard*. He was horrified and speechless with dismay.

Word of Ezra's reaction spread. Others who deplored this blatant violation of the Law came to sit and grieve with him (v. 4). Silently they assembled until the time of the evening sacrifice and prayer. Then Ezra knelt and prayed (v. 5), and poured out his anguish over what had happened (vv. 6-15).

As time passed, more and more people gathered to weep with Ezra. One of them, a man named Shechaniah, suggested that the situation was not beyond repair. Why not send away all those wives that had been taken illegally? Shechaniah said that this was a matter for Ezra to handle, and pledged his and others' support for whatever Ezra chose to do (10:1-4).

Ezra accepted this suggestion. He issued a proclamation: all Israel must gather at Jerusalem within three days. If any man refused to come, his property would be confiscated and he would be banished from Israel (10:6-8).

II. Dealing With Sin (Ezra 10:9-11)

Israel's regular times of meeting (such as for the various feasts) were conveniently spaced and generally occurred during good weather; however, Ezra was calling an emergency meeting. Delay was out of the question. Everyone must be in Jerusalem within three days.

A. Meeting in the Rain (v. 9)

9. Then all the men of Judah and Benjamin gathered themselves together unto Jerusalem within three days. It was the ninth month, on the twentieth day of the month; and all the peo-

ple sat in the street of the house of God, trembling because of this matter, and for the great rain.

Most of the people who had been captives in Babylon were from the southern tribes of *Judah and Benjamin*. People of the other tribes had been scattered abroad long before the Babylonian captivity (2 Kings 17:1-6). Now *all the men* of Judah and Benjamin came *unto Jerusalem*. This assembly was held in *the ninth month*, which was (in terms of our calendar) the month of December. Thus it was the middle of winter; the air was chilly, and the rain was heavy.

All the people sat in the street. Street is a term describing the open square in front of *the house of God* (the temple). It was an area large enough to accommodate all the individuals who were present. They were likely forbidden to enter the temple itself until they had dealt with their sin. Those assembled were *trembling because of this matter*—trembling with apprehension because they did not know what would be done in the matter of their unholy marriages. Certainly another reason for their trembling was *the great rain* and cold.

B. Facing the Facts (v. 10)

10. And Ezra the priest stood up, and said unto them, Ye have transgressed, and have taken strange wives, to increase the trespass of Israel.

Plainly Ezra stated the facts. Some of the men before him had broken God's Law by taking *strange*, or foreign, *wives*, who were not women of Israel. The nation had been guilty of many transgressions before this, but now they had added one more *trespass* to the already lengthy list.

C. Calling for Confession (v. 11)

11. Now therefore make confession unto the LORD God of your fathers, and do his pleasure: and separate yourselves from the people of the land, and from the strange wives.

visual for
lesson 10

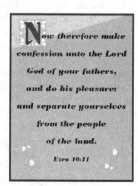

Now therefore make confession unto the Lord God of your fathers, and do his pleasure: and separate yourselves from the people of the land.

Ezra 10:11

Ezra asked the husbands of the pagan wives to *make confession* that they were violating God's Law, and, more important, to stop this. They must *separate* themselves *from* their foreign *wives*. Continuing the transgression would only make matters worse.

III. Making a Change
(Ezra 10:12-14)

Verses 12-14 tell how the crowd responded to Ezra. Perhaps some discussion took place, or some suggestions were made, abandoned, or amended. The remainder of our printed text states the conclusion of the discussion.

A. Confessing the Sin (v. 12)

12. Then all the congregation answered and said with a loud voice, As thou hast said, so must we do.

The *congregation* agreed in principle. Ezra was right. The men had been doing wrong; they must stop it. They must get rid of their heathen wives.

B. Facing the Difficulties (v. 13)

13. But the people are many, and it is a time of much rain, and we are not able to stand without, neither is this a work of one day or two: for we are many that have transgressed in this thing.

The men agreed upon what they must do; but as they thought about translating it into action, other considerations became plain. It was not possible to resolve this matter on that day or the next, it was not practical to involve all the men in doing it, and it was not necessary to stand in the *rain* until it was done. Ezra 10:18-44 lists one hundred and fourteen men who had taken foreign wives. They needed some orderly way of handling all the separations, in surroundings that were not so adverse.

C. Forming a Plan (v. 14)

14. Let now our rulers of all the congregation stand, and let all them which have taken strange wives in our cities come at appointed times, and with them the elders of every city, and the judges thereof, until the fierce wrath of our God for this matter be turned from us.

Here are the main features of the plan that was formed. First, the *rulers* were to *stand* and take charge in handling this matter for the entire *congregation*. Second, each man with a foreign wife was to make an appointment and have his case dealt with apart from the others. Third, *elders* and *judges* of every city were to be involved, making sure that the men of that city would be treated fairly. They could also make sure that no offender would fail to make an appointment. Fourth, this orderly and reasonable process was to continue until there were no heathen wives in Israel. Thus would *the fierce wrath of our God* be *turned* away.

As might be expected, there was some opposition to the suggested plan, as we see from verse 15. That the men named there were "employed against this matter" means that they "worked against it." The Hebrew text literally reads, "They stood against this."

Verses 16 and 17 tell briefly how this plan was carried out. Ezra and certain other chief men served as a kind of "divorce court." In three months they handled all the cases of intermarriage, and Israel was free of the influence of heathen foreigners.

At the same time, ending the marriages was not a simple matter of deporting the entire group. The husbands came at appointed times to have each case considered individually. This suggests that an effort was made to make separation as fair as possible. Perhaps alimony and child care were arranged, for it would not be fair to send a wife away with small children and no means of support.

Conclusion

In Israel the Law God gave to Moses was the law of the land. Ezra came with authority from the king to enforce this Law, and he did enforce it; but he was also wise enough to rally popular support as well as royal authority.

God's people today are in a different situation. An elaborate system of courts is in place to deal with those who violate the law of the land. Christians often have a part in the administration of justice, but usually the church as the church does not.

Within the church are many problems to which the law of the land does not apply. Does our lesson provide any suggestions for dealing with such problems?

A. Attention

Ezra knew that the problem of intermarriage required immediate attention. It could not wait for good weather. He called for a mass meeting, though it had to be held in the open and in the cold rain of winter.

In the church we sometimes ignore some misbehavior, dispute, or resentment, hoping it will go away by itself. Sometimes it does; but sometimes dissatisfied people go around voicing their complaints and lining up support for themselves until a little problem becomes a big one.

Usually a problem in the church does not require a mass meeting in the rain or anywhere else. Matthew 18:15-17 outlines steps to be taken before a personal matter is called to the attention of the whole church. If a Christian is doing something wrong, can't one or two of his best friends call it to his attention? Yet we hesitate; we prefer not to say anything, because we don't want to get involved. After all, we don't want to seem critical, and who are we to judge others? Thus do we miss our chance to save a soul from death (James 5:19, 20).

Our friend who is doing wrong may be highly sensitive about his behavior, and may resent our efforts to help him. We need to speak gently, and to watch our own attitude carefully (Galatians 6:1). But if we say nothing, how can we justify our silence?

B. Wrong

Our lesson has to do with a plain case of wrongdoing. Those who were breaking the Law of God could not deny it. When a Christian's wrongdoing is equally clear, there is a special need to speak to him with care. The one most obviously in the wrong may be most furiously angry at a rebuke, but does that excuse us from letting the wrong go unrebuked?

In other disputes among Christians, the wrong is not so obvious. Shall we have the sermon before the Lord's Supper, or after it? How long should the sermon be? Should it get more laughs, or not so many? Shall we sing hymns from the hymnal, or choruses printed in the bulletin? What shall we do in our midweek meeting? What kind of social gathering is appropriate?

All these matters can be and are disputed. Surely any Christian is entitled to have his own opinion and to express it. But beware of thinking that your opinion represents the will of God.

C. Authority

In the case studied today, the authority was not Ezra, but God. God said His people should not marry heathens, and that settled it. When New Testament teaching is plain, there should be no argument among Christians. We do believe God and His Word, don't we?

In a general way, the law of the land tends to agree with God's Word that stealing, murder, and mayhem are wrong. But when it comes to sexual sins, our lawmakers seem to have gone along with the heathen opinion that "sexual relations between consenting adults are nobody's business but their own." God is unmoved by popular opinion. He still bars adulterers and fornicators from His kingdom, along with other unrighteous people (1 Corinthians 6:9, 10). Even homosexuals—"abusers of themselves with mankind"—are barred. Some modern churches have voted that homosexuals may actually hold positions of leadership in the kingdom. Can God's people outvote God? Can people who try to do so be God's people?

D. Mixing With Unbelievers

While we are not under the Law that God gave to Moses, the New Testament seems to assume that a Christian will marry no one but a Christian. A widow "is at liberty to be married to whom she will; only in the Lord" (1 Corinthians 7:39). Paul was likely single, but he claimed a right to have a wife who was a "sister," that is, a Christian (1 Corinthians 9:5). But if a Christian is already married to an unbeliever, the recommended remedy is not a quick divorce. It is to live so admirably that the unbeliever will be moved to become a Christian too (1 Corinthians 7:12-16; 1 Peter 3:1, 2).

This illustrates what our relationship with the world at large should be. We are separate from the world in that we carefully avoid the world's wrongdoing. Yet we are in the world, in order to stay in constant and cordial contact with people who are not Christians. Otherwise how can we "preach the gospel to every creature" (Mark 16:15)?

E. Prayer

Heavenly Father, with sorrow we confess that we ourselves have been guilty of many sins; with joy we thank You for Your gracious forgiveness in Christ; with earnestness we promise to try to keep ourselves pure. Amen.

F. Thought to Remember

What God says is final.

Home Daily Bible Readings

Monday, Nov. 3—A Scribe Skilled in the Law (Ezra 7:6-10)
Tuesday, Nov. 4—Hand of God Gave Courage (Ezra 7:21-28)
Wednesday, Nov. 5—Guilt Mounting Up to Heaven (Ezra 9:1-9)
Thursday, Nov. 6—Fear a Just God's Anger (Ezra 9:10-15)
Friday, Nov. 7—Hope for the Returned Exiles (Ezra 10:1-8)
Saturday, Nov. 8—Confess and Separate Yourselves (Ezra 10:9-17)
Sunday, Nov. 9—House of Prayer for All Peoples (Isaiah 56:1-8)

Learning by Doing

This page contains an alternate lesson plan emphasizing learning activities.
Classes desiring such student involvement will find these suggestions helpful.

Learning Goals

As students participate in today's class session, they should:

1. Tell how Ezra and his people dealt with a situation where God's Law had been ignored.

2. Express some principles, based on this passage, that can be applied in dealing with problems faced by Christians and/or the church today.

3. Suggest one or two ways to apply those principles in dealing with a specific situation.

Into the Lesson

Write the following sentence on your chalkboard for class members to see as they arrive:

People today take sin for granted. We see it:

> in the work place
> in the schools
> in advertising
> in entertainment
> in our friends
> in the church

Divide your class into groups of about five to seven members each. Your goal is to have each group discuss two of the areas listed above, and to have each area discussed by at least one group. Here's one way to accomplish this:

Ask each group to choose the three areas they would most like to discuss, and to rate them in terms of their first, second, and third choices. In random order, call on the groups and ask them to give you their choices. Appoint a "secretary" to keep track, so that every topic is discussed by at least one group.

Give the groups five or six minutes to do their assignments, then ask for a sentence or two to summarize the discussion of each of the six topics. Ask, "How is taking sin for granted in this area affecting our society?"

Tell your group that today's Bible study looks at the negative effects that taking sin for granted had on God's people many centuries ago. We will seek to discover some principles for dealing with sin in our own time.

Into the Word

Set the stage for today's Bible study by summarizing the material under the Lesson Background in the commentary. Conduct today's study through the series of questions printed here (they are also found in the student book). You may discuss these questions as a large group, or ask the small groups formed earlier to consider them. If you think you will be pressed for time, you may want to provide a brief summary of the sections that are not included in today's printed text, rather than taking time to read and discuss these sections.

Ezra 9:1-4—What problem was brought to Ezra's attention? How serious was it? Was it a violation of man's tradition or God's truth?

Ezra 9:5-15—Had Ezra committed the sin for which he sought God's forgiveness? What strikes you as remarkable about his prayer?

Ezra 10:1-8—Why did the people gather around the place were Ezra prayed? What solution was proposed, and how did Ezra respond to this suggestion?

Ezra 10:9-11—Try to picture this scene. If you did not know how the story turned out, what outcome might you predict to Ezra's rigid command?

Ezra 10:12-17—Why do you suppose the people reacted as they did?

Into Life

Give one of the following sentences, written on a slip of paper before class, to each of your small groups:

Sin is no laughing matter.

A little compromise can lead to a lot of regret.

The time to deal with sin is now, not later.

The remedy for sin is sometimes very painful.

True, heartfelt sorrow for sin can lead to a solution for sin.

Ask class members, in their groups, to follow this procedure: (1) Decide how today's Bible study illustrates the truth of the principle. (2) Share contemporary examples to illustrate the principle. These can come from their own lives, the lives of people they know, or from current events. (3) Consider how understanding this principle could solve a problem or lend insight to an issue currently faced by someone they know. This "someone" could be themselves, a friend, or a relative. Perhaps it applies to some situation in the church (although such a subject should be handled cautiously).

Give the groups six or eight minutes to complete this activity, then discuss it with the entire class. End with a time of prayer, either with all the class or in the study groups.

Let's Talk It Over

The questions on this page are designed to encourage review of the lesson Scriptures and to promote discussion of the lesson by the class. The answers provided are only discussion starters. Let your class talk it over from there.

1. Marital unions between believers and unbelievers represent a continuing danger. What can the church do to combat such a practice?

In both the church and the Christian home, the peril of the unequal yoke (2 Corinthians 6:14) should be stressed early and often with young children. It is important to encourage Christian teenagers and young adults to date others within their faith. Other answers include: making literature available in the church dealing with dating and marriage, showing films and videos in which these topics are addressed, and encouraging young people to attend conventions and other special gatherings where these matters are discussed.

2. The people felt that the rainy day was not the time to deal with the problem of their intermarriage with the heathen. Can you think of examples of problems in the church that should be dealt with only at the right time and in the right place?

Some problems are best dealt with privately. If a church member or leader has been guilty of sexual sin, other leaders will want to approach this person in a quiet, discreet way. Other problems may need to be handled publicly. If there is disagreement within the church over a building project, it is well to get the congregation together to discuss the pros and cons. It may be best for leaders to go to members' homes to deal with certain situations. The problem of a teacher's introducing unsound doctrine, a member's spreading damaging gossip, or a leader's tendency to undermine the efforts of other leaders could be examples. Of course, there are certain doctrinal misunderstandings or questions that the preacher may treat from the pulpit.

3. The lesson writer suggests that a fair and merciful settlement was arranged with the wives and children of the men involved in the heathen marriages. What are some Biblical principles that might have influenced Ezra in these arrangements?

The lesson writer points to the fact that each case was handled individually (Ezra 10:14) as an indication that some kind of financial settlement was probably made. One broad principle that bears on this matter is that found in Leviticus

19:18: "Thou shalt love thy neighbor as thyself." These family members were closer than neighbors and surely deserving of loving provision. The Law also made special provisions for husbandless wives and fatherless children (see Exodus 22:22; Deuteronomy 24:17; 26:12).

4. All too often matters of opinion become a focus of dissension in the church. What can we do to prevent this from happening?

A first step is to educate members on what are matters of faith and matters of opinion. Some may not realize, for example, that the New Testament does not authorize a particular order of worship, or that it does not specify who is to preside at the Lord's table or who is to distribute the emblems. Perhaps a second step is to acknowledge that every member has a legitimate prerogative to express his or her opinion. Without doubt problems sometimes arise because certain members feel that their viewpoints are not regarded as important. Another step is for leaders to act promptly when any member begins to make his or her opinions an occasion for dissension. A firm but loving discussion at the outset of the matter could prevent it from becoming a more serious problem.

5. Immoral sexual relationships involving church members can do tremendous damage to a congregation. What are some principles to remember in dealing with these situations?

We dare not follow the world's lead and take such situations lightly. At the same time we must follow Jesus' example of mercy toward penitent sinners. His "Neither do I condemn thee: go, and sin no more" (John 8:11) offers a perfect balance of mercy and caution against repeating sin. An important point to keep in mind is that, as damaging as sexual sins are, they are as forgivable as sins of lying, losing our temper, and other "lesser" offenses. Another principle is that of restoring the sinner "in the spirit of meekness" (Galatians 6:1). The person who has received forgiveness for sexual sin needs to be restored to active discipleship. The church can help him or her to get back into worship, Bible study, prayer, and service for Christ. The church can also contribute to restoring harmony to the families affected by the sin.

A Leader Appears

DEVOTIONAL READING: Psalm 146.

LESSON SCRIPTURE: Nehemiah 1, 2.

PRINTED TEXT: Nehemiah 2:4-8, 15-18.

Nehemiah 2:4-8, 15-18

4 Then the king said unto me, For what dost thou make request? So I prayed to the God of heaven.

5 And I said unto the king, If it please the king, and if thy servant have found favor in thy sight, that thou wouldest send me unto Judah, unto the city of my fathers' sepulchres, that I may build it.

6 And the king said unto me, (the queen also sitting by him,) For how long shall thy journey be? and when wilt thou return? So it pleased the king to send me; and I set him a time.

7 Moreover I said unto the king, If it please the king, let letters be given me to the governors beyond the river, that they may convey me over till I come into Judah;

8 And a letter unto Asaph the keeper of the king's forest, that he may give me timber to make beams for the gates of the palace which appertained to the house, and for the wall of the city, and for the house that I shall enter into. And the king granted me, according to the good hand of my God upon me.

· · · · · · · · · · · · · ·

15 Then went I up in the night by the brook, and viewed the wall, and turned back, and entered by the gate of the valley, and so returned.

16 And the rulers knew not whither I went, or what I did; neither had I as yet told it to the Jews, nor to the priests, nor to the nobles, nor to the rulers, nor to the rest that did the work.

17 Then said I unto them, Ye see the distress that we are in, how Jerusalem lieth waste, and the gates thereof are burned with fire: come, and let us build up the wall of Jerusalem, that we be no more a reproach.

18 Then I told them of the hand of my God which was good upon me; as also the king's words that he had spoken unto me. And they said, Let us rise up and build. So they strengthened their hands for this good work.

Nov 16

GOLDEN TEXT: Come, and let us build up the wall of Jerusalem, that we be no more a reproach.—Nehemiah 2:17.

> ## God Leads a People Home
> Unit 3: Life After the Return
> (Lessons 9-13)

Lesson Aims

After this lesson, a student should be able to:

1. Describe how Nehemiah got the work of rebuilding the walls of Jerusalem started.

2. Tell how Nehemiah's example can be a model for Christian leadership today.

3. Develop a plan for addressing a specific area of church life that is being neglected.

Lesson Outline

INTRODUCTION
    A. Builders and Breakers
    B. Lesson Background
 I. ROYAL HELP (Nehemiah 2:4-8)
    A. Request (vv. 4, 5)
    B. Approval (v. 6)
    C. Details (vv. 7, 8)
 II. SECRET SURVEY (Nehemiah 2:15, 16)
    A. Finishing the Survey (v. 15)
    B. Keeping the Secret (v. 16)
    Out for a Walk in the Evening
III. PUBLIC ANNOUNCEMENT (Nehemiah 2:17, 18)
    A. Call to Action (v. 17)
    B. Encouragement (v. 18a)
    C. Response (v. 18b)
    Inspiring the People to Rebuild
CONCLUSION
    A. Complacency
    B. Selfishness
    C. Leadership
    D. Prayer
    E. Thought to Remember

The visual for Lesson 11 highlights what archaeologists have found regarding the wall of Jerusalem. It is shown on page 91.

Introduction

A. Builders and Breakers

Have you ever watched a wrecking crew tear down a building? In some cases, depending on the importance of the size of the building, a large crowd will gather to witness the demolition. In a fairly short time, a once-useful structure is turned into a pile of rubble. The crowd then disperses, and everyone returns to his or her daily routine.

On the other hand, erecting a building is a process that involves far less drama and excitement. No crowds gather to watch it happen. Construction is a laborious, often painfully slow effort. Progress may come only in bits and pieces. Patience is required on the part of the builders and the people who are waiting for the job to be completed.

Consider by way of comparison the Biblical walls of Jericho and Jerusalem. With one trumpet blast Jericho's wall was demolished. On the other hand, when Jerusalem's wall was rebuilt, a much more time-consuming effort was required. The people who participated in the endeavor had to commit themselves to hard work, from sunrise to sunset.

It is much easier to destroy something than to build something. A beautiful home that took months to complete can turn to ashes in minutes. Think of how quickly the walls of Jerusalem were turned to rubble by the Babylonians!

Today's lesson text tells of the leadership provided by Nehemiah in rebuilding the wall of Jerusalem. We are reminded that builders will always reap an abundance of rewards, if they have the faith and perseverance to stay their course.

B. Lesson Background

Today's lesson brings us to a time about thirteen years after Ezra came to Jerusalem and the heathen marriages (which were the subject of last week's lesson) had been ended. Our story begins in the Persian capital of Shushan (also called Susa), far from Jerusalem.

Like Ezra, Nehemiah belonged to a Jewish family that did not go back to Jerusalem when the captivity ended. When we first meet Nehemiah, he is serving as cupbearer to the Persian king Artaxerxes, in the capital city of Shushan. (There were actually four capital cities in the Persian empire; the Persian kings often went to Shushan to reside during the winter because of the milder climate there.) The cupbearer's job was a rather risky one. He had to taste any wine brought before the king. Thus, if it had been secretly poisoned by an enemy of the king, the king would know it before actually drinking the wine himself.

For Nehemiah to have held the position of cupbearer means that he was trusted and highly regarded by the king, and it appears that he was a good friend as well. It also seems that Nehemiah was quite happy with his position. Apparently he assumed that the Jews who had returned to Jerusalem had restored the city to much of what it was before the captivity.

Then Nehemiah's brother and some other men came from Jerusalem with disturbing news. The holy city of Jerusalem was not a city at all. It resembled a frontier village. The walls and gates were in ruins, just as Nebuchadnezzar's men had left them more than a hundred years before (Nehemiah 1:1-3). Nehemiah sat down and cried, and then he prayed (vv. 4-11). His parents probably had taught him to love Jerusalem, the city of God. Now its once mighty walls were only heaps of rubble. Nehemiah could not bear the thought. Something had to be done!

I. Royal Help
(Nehemiah 2:4-8)

Nehemiah did not act impulsively. He must have thought and planned and prayed for a long time. In fact, four months passed before he took his problem to the king (this is the length of time between the month Chisleu, mentioned in 1:1, and Nisan, mentioned in 2:1). As Nehemiah was serving the king his wine, the king noticed the sad expression on his face—a look he had not seen before. Recognizing that Nehemiah's appearance reflected "sorrow of heart" (2:2), the king asked why he was so upset. Nehemiah explained that he was mourning for "the city, the place of my fathers' sepulchres" (v. 3).

A. Request (vv. 4, 5)

4. Then the king said unto me, For what dost thou make request? So I prayed to the God of heaven.

Artaxerxes knew that something was troubling his cupbearer. He could also tell that Nehemiah wanted to make a *request* of him. So *the king* asked what Nehemiah needed.

Before answering, Nehemiah offered a quick prayer to his true King. He had a rather sizable request to make, and verse 2 says that he was "very sore afraid." If his petition displeased the king, Nehemiah might be demoted, fired, jailed, or even executed. So he *prayed* just before voicing his request. Throughout this book, Nehemiah is pictured as a man of prayer (1:4; 4:4, 9; 5:19; 6:9, 14; 13:14, 22, 29, 31).

5. And I said unto the king, If it please the king, and if thy servant have found favor in thy sight, that thou wouldest send me unto Judah, unto the city of my fathers' sepulchres, that I may build it.

Here was the bare outline of Nehemiah's request. He not only wanted time off; he also wanted the king to send him to build Jerusalem. This meant that the Persian government would assume the cost of the trip and the cost of rebuilding the ruined walls and gates.

B. Approval (v. 6)

6. And the king said unto me, (the queen also sitting by him,) For how long shall thy journey be? and when wilt thou return? So it pleased the king to send me; and I set him a time.

The king's reaction was favorable. There were some sound reasons for him to grant Nehemiah's request. First, it would be good for the Persian empire to have a well-fortified city in Judah. Second, the king knew that Nehemiah was capable and loyal—the kind of man who could administer this project. Third, he knew that Nehemiah's heart was in this particular job. So the king was *pleased* to send Nehemiah. He then asked a very practical, businesslike question: How long would it take to do the job?

In response Nehemiah *set him a time.* This is another indication that Nehemiah had thought much about this project. He had never seen Jerusalem himself, but his brother had (Nehemiah 1:1-3). From his brother, Nehemiah had learned about the conditions in the city: stone was at hand; timber had to be transported from Lebanon; some of the people were dissatisfied with Jerusalem as it was; a good leader could enlist them to work with enthusiasm. Nehemiah was thus able to estimate how long it would take to do what he wanted to do. Perhaps he asked to be away for a certain amount of time, and then had that time extended, since he apparently was in Judah for a twelve-year period (Nehemiah 5:14).

C. Details (vv. 7, 8)

7. Moreover I said unto the king, If it please the king, let letters be given me to the governors beyond the river, that they may convey me over till I come into Judah.

Again we see that Nehemiah had been thinking and planning. All the *governors beyond the* (Euphrates) *river* were subject to the king. Nehemiah needed letters ordering them to conduct him safely through their territories until he came *into Judah,* where Jerusalem was located. It should be noted that here, *beyond the river* refers to Palestine, because the phrase is being used by someone speaking in Mesopotamia. But

visual for
lesson 11

when someone in Palestine speaks of a place *beyond the river*, he is referring to Mesopotamia (as in 1 Kings 14:15 and Isaiah 7:20).

8. And a letter unto Asaph the keeper of the king's forest, that he may give me timber to make beams for the gates of the palace which appertained to the house, and for the wall of the city, and for the house that I shall enter into. And the king granted me, according to the good hand of my God upon me.

Nehemiah then asked for a more costly favor. He needed *timber* from *the king's forest.* Earlier rebuilders of Jerusalem had brought timber from Lebanon, far to the north (Ezra 3:7). It seems probable that Nehemiah would do the same. Stone for the walls was available at Jerusalem, but several gates would need to be inserted at various points. Probably each gate would be enclosed in a tower, where men could be stationed in case of attack. Heavy timber would be needed for the upper floor of a tower and for the large doors. *The palace which appertained to the house* may have been a citadel or fort that overlooked the temple. It too would need timber for upper floors and for doors. In addition, Nehemiah planned a *house* for himself. This probably would include not only his residence, but also offices for himself and other officials of Jerusalem.

All told, this was no small amount of timber for which Nehemiah was asking, but the king promptly *granted* it. Nehemiah had been praying for just such a response, and now he gave credit to *the good hand of my God.* Clearly the real king in this situation was not Artaxerxes, but the Almighty.

II. Secret Survey
(Nehemiah 2:15, 16)

Nehemiah's arrival in Jerusalem was far from secret. It was seen by friends and foes alike, for the king sent a detachment of cavalry to escort him (v. 9). The enemies of the Jews were especially unhappy about Nehemiah's intentions, because "there was come a man to seek the welfare of the children of Israel" (v. 10).

Three days after Nehemiah arrived, he and a few of his men went out secretly by night to survey the ruined walls. Verses 12-14 tell how they conducted the survey. It seems that they went out to the southwest side of the city, then turned eastward after they reached the south side. When they turned north on the east side, they found the way so filled with rubble that Nehemiah's horse could go no farther. The wall was in ruins, just as Nehemiah had heard from his brother.

How to Say It

ARTAXERXES. Ar-tuh-*zerk*-sees.
ASAPH. *A*-saff.
BABYLONIANS. Bab-uh-*low*-nee-unz.
CHISLEU. *Kiss*-loo.
EUPHRATES. You-*fray*-teez.
HAGGAI. *Hag*-a-eye or *Hag*-eye.
KIDRON. *Kid*-ron.
MESOPOTAMIA. *Mess*-uh-puh-*tay*-me-uh (strong accent on *tay*).
NEBUCHADNEZZAR. *Neb*-uh-kad-*nezz*-er (strong accent on *nezz*).
NEHEMIAH. Nee-huh-*my*-uh.
NISAN. *Nye*-san.
SHUSHAN. *Shoe*-shan.
SUSA. *Soo*-suh.

A. Finishing the Survey (v. 15)

15. Then went I up in the night by the brook, and viewed the wall, and turned back, and entered by the gate of the valley, and so returned.

This statement is not very clear. Perhaps it means that Nehemiah left his horse with one of his men and proceeded on foot to where the horse could not go. Thus he completed his survey of the *wall.* He may have gone north *by the brook* (Kidron) to look at the fallen wall from the east side of the city. Then at the northeast corner of the city he *turned back.* Possibly this means that Nehemiah went back by the same way he had come; but it seems more probable that from the northeast corner he *turned back* toward his starting point by going west on the north side of the city and south on the west side. Thus he made a complete circuit of Jerusalem. He then entered once more through the *gate of the valley* by which he had left (v. 13), and so *returned* to his lodging. Having thus obtained a general idea of the size of the job he had come to do, Nehemiah could lay plans for organizing the workers and accomplishing the task.

B. Keeping the Secret (v. 16)

16. And the rulers knew not whither I went, or what I did; neither had I as yet told it to the Jews, nor to the priests, nor to the nobles, nor to the rulers, nor to the rest that did the work.

No one knew about Nehemiah's excursion except the few men who had gone with him to conduct it. It seems that Nehemiah was keeping his plans secret until he understood the situation well enough to talk about it intelligently and present some definite plans to the groups mentioned in this verse. Their cooperation was essential to the success of Nehemiah's efforts.

OUT FOR A WALK IN THE EVENING

Eleven-year-old Michael Dixon had a habit of sleepwalking, but his mother was not overly concerned about it until the police awakened her one night. Her sleepwalking son had outdone himself. The police in a city one hundred miles from Michael's home had found him at 2:45 A.M., walking in his sleep by a railroad track in their community. He was barefoot and dirty, but otherwise fine.

All Michael could say for himself was that he had dreamed he was being chased by someone and ran into a closet to hide. Apparently he had hitched a ride on a freight train. No one could say how he got on and off the train without seriously injuring himself.

Nehemiah also went for a "midnight stroll," but he was not walking in his sleep. His purpose was to examine the state of Jerusalem's walls so he could challenge his people to rebuild them. Certain enemies of the Jews were opposed to the project, so it seemed best to make this inspection under cover of darkness.

We can hardly recommend such secrecy as a normal means of getting our work done, even when doing good, but on this occasion God was directing Nehemiah in his actions. The question for us is: Is it ever right for us to do secretly what we believe God is calling us to do? A related question to consider is this: Under what circumstances may this be the right action? Nehemiah's example shows us that there are situations where not only our praying but also our planning should be conducted in our "closet" (Matthew 6:6). —C. R. B.

III. Public Announcement (Nehemiah 2:17, 18)

A. Call to Action (v. 17)

17. Then said I unto them, Ye see the distress that we are in, how Jerusalem lieth waste, and the gates thereof are burned with fire: come, and let us build up the wall of Jerusalem, that we be no more a reproach.

Then does not necessarily mean the day after Nehemiah's survey of the city. Nehemiah and his men may have consulted and planned for several days before deciding that the time was right to make their plans known. Perhaps Nehemiah spoke first with some of the leaders, and then met with all the people.

The ruined walls were likely as distressing to the people of Jerusalem as they were to Nehemiah. Nearly ninety years had passed since the first group of captives had come back from Babylon. Nehemiah tried to kindle within his

hearers a passion for the lovely city they had never seen. To them he called, *Come, and let us build up the wall of Jerusalem, that we be no more a reproach.* Nehemiah felt reproached, disgraced, and distressed by the condition of the holy city. He longed for Jerusalem to be "the joy of the whole earth" (Psalm 48:2) once again.

B. Encouragement (v. 18a)

18a. Then I told them of the hand of my God which was good upon me; as also the king's words that he had spoken unto me.

Nehemiah could point to three sources of encouragement in his rebuilding efforts. First, he was sure that God's *hand* was helping him. Evidence of this was seen in the success of his project thus far. Second, *the king's words* had been thoroughly supportive of his plans. Third, before Nehemiah stood the people whose strong hands could use the stone and timber to build a city as glorious as the one that once stood—if only their hearts were as strong as their hands.

C. Response (v. 18b)

18b. And they said, Let us rise up and build. So they strengthened their hands for this good work.

We need not suppose that this response came instantly or unanimously. There may have been questions, discussion, or even some opposition. But the final answer of the majority was clear: *Let us rise up and build!* So the willing hearts of the people *strengthened their hands*, and they prepared for *this good work*.

The enemies of the Jews thought that their project was a huge joke (Nehemiah 2:19, 20; 4:1-3). But the Jews took it seriously. Quickly they began the task, assigning different portions of the wall to different groups (Nehemiah 3). With enthusiasm and energy they built the wall to half its intended height, "for the people had a mind to work" (Nehemiah 4:6).

INSPIRING THE PEOPLE TO REBUILD

Ann Kendall may seem like an unlikely leader. She is a small, middle-aged, British archaeologist. Since the late 1970s, however, she has been leading the people of the Andes (*An*-deez) Mountains in rebuilding the architectural remnants of an ancient civilization.

In pre-Hispanic times, the Inca people developed an advanced form of agriculture high in the Andes. They terraced the mountains and invented an elaborate system of irrigation canals that turned the arid landscape into the site of abundant harvests.

As Kendall has led the people and labored along with them, many of the thousand-year-old terraces and canals have been restored. She has demonstrated that the ancient ways are far better than modern technology for the poor and primitive people living in that rugged mountain setting. A new prosperity has come to the people whom she has motivated to rebuild the ancient works of their distant ancestors.

Nehemiah proved himself to be a great leader also. His vision for restoring the city of Jerusalem struck a spark in his disheartened people. After listening to Nehemiah's encouraging words, they said, "Let us rise up and build." With renewed commitment, they rebuilt the walls and gates of the city of Jerusalem. Good leaders inspire their people and also involve themselves in the work. —C. R. B.

Conclusion

A. Complacency

Are we too easily content, and satisfied to do less than we ought to do for the Lord? I knew a congregation where the weekly offering was nearly always a little less than the weekly budget. Expenses were cut. For seven years there was no pay raise for the two ministers, the secretary, or the custodian. Leaders pleaded for increased offerings, but the members were unmoved. "We're getting by," they said. "Things are fine as they are."

Then the roof began to leak, and badly. On rainy Sundays, worshipers found themselves moving to other pews. Someone suggested a special offering, and the sum of twenty thousand dollars was given in a week. This congregation could have been paying fair wages to its employees long before this, could have been expanding its work, could have been giving more to missions, and could have been laying up an emergency fund so that no special offering would have been needed for a new roof. But it had been too easily content just to "get by."

B. Selfishness

Selfish is one of the adjectives that critics apply to the Jews who returned to rebuild Jerusalem. Other negative terms are *racist*, *narrow*, and *bigoted*. They rejected their neighbors' help with the temple, they divorced heathen wives, and they wanted a strong and well-defended city for themselves.

But their separation from heathen influences was not a matter of race or nation; it was a matter of religion and morality. A pagan became acceptable when he or she forsook paganism, believed in Jehovah, and obeyed Him. A shining example is Ruth (Ruth 1:16). Likewise we Christians have an obligation to keep ourselves

and the church pure, but we also have an obligation to help unbelievers become Christians.

In one congregation where I served, a charter member thought I was working too hard. "You don't have to get everybody in town to come to church," she said. "We have lovely meetings with our kinfolk and friends, and we manage to pay your salary. We don't need those people from the south side."

What about those people from the south side? Didn't Jesus die for them?

C. Leadership

God's people can do better than they are doing. If some leader stirs them up with a vision and with power, they will do better. Haggai roused the people who were satisfied with their nice homes, and they built God's house. Ezra roused the men who were content with their heathen wives, and they took steps to rid themselves of that influence. Nehemiah roused the people who had become comfortable amid the ruins of Jerusalem, and a well-fortified city began to rise.

What if there is no such leader among us? Then all of us will have to work harder and encourage each other to keep working.

D. Prayer

Father, we pray that we will not become smug and self-satisfied in our relationship with You and in our work for You. Help us to be more aware of the tasks in our church that we can do. Like those in Nehemiah's day, may we respond to these tasks with "a mind to work." Amen.

E. Thought to Remember

In doing God's work, only our best is good enough.

Home Daily Bible Readings

Monday, Nov. 10—Jerusalem Is Destroyed (2 Chronicles 36:1-9)
Tuesday, Nov. 11—Claiming God's Promise (Nehemiah 1:1-11)
Wednesday, Nov. 12—Enlisting Help From the King (Nehemiah 2:1-8)
Thursday, Nov. 13—Let's Work Together (Nehemiah 2:11-18)
Friday, Nov. 14—Peace Within the Walls (Psalm 122:1-9)
Saturday, Nov. 15—Happy Are Those Who Trust God (Psalm 146:1-10)
Sunday, Nov. 16—Peace for Lovers of God's Law (Psalm 119:162-176)

Learning by Doing

This page contains an alternate lesson plan emphasizing learning activities.
Classes desiring such student involvement will find these suggestions helpful.

Learning Goals

After this lesson, a student should be able to:

1. Describe how Nehemiah got the work of rebuilding the walls of Jerusalem started.

2. Tell how Nehemiah's example can be a model for Christian leadership today.

3. Develop a plan for addressing a specific area of church life that is being neglected.

Into the Lesson

Use one of the following ideas as an opening activity for this week's lesson:

"Picture this." Go to a school supply store, and get a set of pictures of famous leaders. Mount these on your wall before class members arrive. Beside each picture mount a large sheet of paper. Make sure plenty of felt-tip markers or crayons are available.

To begin your session, ask class members to walk around the room, look at the pictures, and write beside each picture phrases that describe that leader. When they have finished, read what they have written to the entire class. Then discuss this question: "What makes a great leader?"

Acrostic. Write L-E-A-D-E-R vertically down your chalkboard. Ask, "What makes a great leader?" Class members should respond with words that begin with each of the letters in the word *leader*. Then ask, "Can you think of anything significant that has been accomplished without a leader? Can you think of important projects that have failed because of poor leadership?"

Tell your class that today's Bible study will look at how God used a leader to begin an important project for Him.

Into the Word

Before class, write the following list of characteristics on your chalkboard or on a poster. Make sure to cover the list before students enter the room.

- He prays.
- He plans.
- He takes risks.
- He sees possibilities.
- He needs followers.

Use the Lesson Background in the commentary to explain the setting for today's Bible study. Tell class members that Nehemiah is one of the most outstanding and well-known leaders in the Bible. This week we will discover why he is often examined as a model of leadership.

Have the class listen for characteristics of a leader that are seen in Nehemiah, as one or two volunteers read today's printed text. After the reading, ask class members to suggest these characteristics as you write them on the chalkboard. Then show your list and compare it with the list class members have compiled.

Next, ask class members to form themselves quickly into groups of two or three and to discuss how Nehemiah demonstrated each of the characteristics from both lists.

Into Life

Ask the class, "Which of our characteristics is the most important one for a leader to demonstrate?" If you have time, ask the small groups to rank the characteristics in order, from most important to least important.

Ask the class to compile a list of "situations where we need leadership today." Ask them to think of as many as they can in sixty or ninety seconds. They may suggest general areas (home, school, church, nation) or specific situations ("our church's building campaign," "our youth program," "the pornography problem in our city"). Discuss which characteristic from among those listed is most needed to provide the leadership each situation requires.

Next, ask the class to consider how and where each of them may have a potential leadership role. Although not all of us can be a Nehemiah, each of us will have the opportunity to lead in some way at some time. Where could your class members lead? With a committee at the church or in the school system? On the job? At home? In the neighborhood? After several minutes, allow time for class members to share with the entire group where they think they may be called to be a leader. You may also encourage them to consider how they can support a leader by serving as an effective follower.

In closing, point to the list of "situations where we need a leader." Ask for volunteers to choose one of the situations as a prayer request. Challenge class members to decide how they could be either an effective leader or follower in at least one of these situations. Let volunteers tell which they have chosen, then conclude with sentence prayers from the class.

Let's Talk It Over

The questions on this page are designed to encourage review of the lesson Scriptures and to promote discussion of the lesson by the class. The answers provided are only discussion starters. Let your class talk it over from there.

1. Nehemiah combined praying and planning. Why is this a good example for the church?

It may seem that extensive planning for the church's future is contrary to the principle of walking by faith. But Paul certainly was not hesitant to plan ahead (see Romans 15:23-29). We could say that praying followed by planning followed by more praying is an excellent pattern. We should pray for God's guidance before we plan. Then, once we have formed plans under His guidance, we should pray again for His power in executing the plans. To pray without planning is pointless. To plan without praying is powerless. If our plans are not in line with God's will, we are likely to waste a great deal of time, effort, and perhaps money.

2. "And the king granted me, according to the good hand of my God upon me" (Nehemiah 2:8). How may we be encouraged by this beautiful statement of Nehemiah?

It is helpful to think of God's invisible hand nudging us and gently prodding us in the way we should go. He nudged Nehemiah and led him to ask the king boldly for what was needed for his mission. When we need to speak a word of witness to an unsaved acquaintance, or a word of reproof to a straying brother or sister in Christ, God's hand can administer that gentle prodding. God's invisible hand is also present to guide us through difficulties. Nehemiah knew he was taking a risk by approaching the king about rebuilding Jerusalem. We may also be hesitant to take risks in our Christian discipleship. But if we will accept a challenge placed before us, God's hand will guide us through whatever difficulties we encounter.

3. Nehemiah kept his plans secret until he was prepared to announce them and put them into motion. Are there any circumstances in which church leaders might want to keep a matter temporarily secret from the congregation?

This question requires some careful thought. Failure by leaders to communicate plans and decisions to the members is a frequent cause of misunderstanding in churches. And yet there are times when leaders may feel it wise to delay the announcement of certain plans. For example, they may delay presenting a construction or remodeling project until they know how much it will cost, how long it will take, and similar details. In the calling of a minister, leaders may not want to publicize the name of a specific candidate until they are sure the man is available and interested. Of course, what we are talking about here is not a secret agenda on the part of leaders, but their examining plans carefully so that they can do the most effective job of informing the people. This was also what Nehemiah's "secret" involved.

4. The lesson writer observes that after close to ninety years back in Jerusalem, the majority of the Jews probably regarded the city's ruinous condition as normal. What are some negative situations in the church that we may come to regard as normal?

Empty pews on a Sunday morning may seem normal. However, we know that potential visitors from among the unsaved and from backsliding members should be filling those pews. In some churches it may seem normal to have offerings that barely cover the congregation's regular expenses. Other churches may consider it normal when few young people are present for services. Such a church's days are numbered, unless it makes a conscientious effort to minister to the youth in its community.

5. Every church must address the question, "In our determination to maintain spiritual purity and separation from the world, have we insulated ourselves from people who need our witness?" If our answer is yes, what can we do about it?

We probably carry on a full range of programs and ministries within our church. But what kinds of ministries do we have outside the church? Is there a neighboring community without a church? Could we establish a congregation there? We probably hold a Vacation Bible School for our church's children. Could we hold one in another area where a great many children live without contact with any church? Are there prisons, children's homes, nursing homes, and the like nearby in which we could be ministering? Could members be helping staff a pregnancy crisis center? These are a few possibilities.

The Courage to Continue

DEVOTIONAL READING: Nehemiah 9:6-15.

LESSON SCRIPTURE: Nehemiah 4.

PRINTED TEXT: Nehemiah 4:6-9, 15-23.

Nehemiah 4:6-9, 15-23

6 So built we the wall; and all the wall was joined together unto the half thereof: for the people had a mind to work.

7 But it came to pass, that when Sanballat, and Tobiah, and the Arabians, and the Ammonites, and the Ashdodites, heard that the walls of Jerusalem were made up, and that the breaches began to be stopped, then they were very wroth,

8 And conspired all of them together to come and to fight against Jerusalem, and to hinder it.

9 Nevertheless we made our prayer unto our God, and set a watch against them day and night, because of them.

· · · · · · · · · · · · ·

15 And it came to pass, when our enemies heard that it was known unto us, and God had brought their counsel to nought, that we returned all of us to the wall, every one unto his work.

16 And it came to pass from that time forth, that the half of my servants wrought in the work, and the other half of them held both the spears, the shields, and the bows, and the habergeons; and the rulers were behind all the house of Judah.

17 They which builded on the wall, and they that bare burdens, with those that laded, every one with one of his hands wrought in the work, and with the other hand held a weapon.

18 For the builders, every one had his sword girded by his side, and so builded. And he that sounded the trumpet was by me.

19 And I said unto the nobles, and to the rulers, and to the rest of the people, The work is great and large, and we are separated upon the wall, one far from another.

20 In what place therefore ye hear the sound of the trumpet, resort ye thither unto us: our God shall fight for us.

21 So we labored in the work: and half of them held the spears from the rising of the morning till the stars appeared.

22 Likewise at the same time said I unto the people, Let every one with his servant lodge within Jerusalem, that in the night they may be a guard to us, and labor on the day.

23 So neither I, nor my brethren, nor my servants, nor the men of the guard which followed me, none of us put off our clothes, saving that every one put them off for washing.

GOLDEN TEXT: Our God shall fight for us.—Nehemiah 4:20.

> ## God Leads a People Home
> Unit 3: Life After the Return
> (Lessons 9-13)

Lesson Aims

After this lesson, a student should be able to:

1. Tell how the wall of Jerusalem was built in spite of angry opposition.

2. Describe how the same courage and commitment that overcame opposition and rebuilt the walls of Jerusalem can help the church defeat opposition today.

3. Make a courageous commitment to deal with some specific hindrance to the church or to one's own service for the Lord.

Lesson Outline

INTRODUCTION
   A. Divine Providence and Human Effort
   B. Lesson Background
 I. DEADLY DANGER (Nehemiah 4:6-9)
   A. Progress (v. 6)
   B. Rising Anger (v. 7)
   C. Conspiracy (v. 8)
   D. Prayerful Defense (v. 9)
 II. WATCHFUL WORKERS (Nehemiah 4:15-18a)
   A. Back to Work (v. 15)
   B. Protection (v. 16)
   C. One-Handed Workers (v. 17)
   D. Builders Ready for Battle (v. 18a)
III. BATTLE PLAN (Nehemiah 4:18b-23)
   A. Communication (v. 18b)
   B. Mobilization (vv. 19, 20)
     A Warning on the Wall
   C. Toiling On (v. 21)
   D. Diligence (vv. 22, 23)
     The Necessity of Vigilance
CONCLUSION
   A. Triumphant Finish
   B. Leadership
   C. Elders
   D. Followers
   E. Prayer
   F. Thought to Remember

Introduction

A. Divine Providence and Human Effort

From beginning to end, the Bible shows God and man working together for good results. In the second chapter of Genesis, we read that "the Lord God planted a garden eastward in Eden" and furnished it with "every tree that is pleasant to the sight, and good for food." Then "the Lord God took the man, and put him into the garden of Eden to dress it and to keep it" (Genesis 2:8, 9, 15). In the last chapter of Revelation, we read of the "river of water of life" flowing from God's throne. On either side of it is the "tree of life." Coupled with such provisions for the redeemed is this additional promise: "his servants shall serve him" (Revelation 22:1-3). God and man will still be in partnership.

B. Lesson Background

Last week we read of Nehemiah's journey to Jerusalem and of his preparations to rebuild the city walls. Vigorously he roused the people to turn their frontier village into a beautiful, well-defended city. The people responded to Nehemiah's plea with enthusiasm: "Let us rise up and build" (Nehemiah 2:18).

We should recall that the temple in Jerusalem was not rebuilt without having to overcome strong opposition from nearby residents. The same was true of the project to reconstruct the city walls. Enemies living nearby saw what was going on, and they jeered at the Jews' efforts. A fox could break down any wall those "feeble Jews" could build, they claimed (Nehemiah 4:1-3). But the people were unmoved by the taunting and diligently worked on.

I. Deadly Danger
(Nehemiah 4:6-9)

"Sticks and stones may break my bones, but words can never hurt me." Probably all of us have either heard or used these lines. The truth, however, is that words sometimes do hurt, and we all know that. Usually it is best if we can ignore hostile or critical words and go on with what we are doing. Likewise, Nehemiah and his fellow Jews were sensible to ignore the ridicule of their enemies and keep building the wall.

A. Progress (v. 6)

6. So built we the wall; and all the wall was joined together unto the half thereof: for the people had a mind to work.

In a remarkably short time there were no serious gaps in the new wall. All around the city it was built up to *half* of its intended height. Of course the lower part was easiest to build; no ramps were needed, by which workers carried heavy stones to the top of the wall. But the most important reason for the rapid progress is stated at the end of this verse: *the people had a mind to work.* They possessed an attitude that refused to be intimidated or defeated.

B. Rising Anger (v. 7)

7. But it came to pass, that when Sanballat, and Tobiah, and the Arabians, and the Ammonites, and the Ashdodites, heard that the walls of Jerusalem were made up, and that the breaches began to be stopped, then they were very wroth.

As progress was made and the *breaches*, or gaps, began to be filled, suddenly rebuilding the *walls* no longer looked like such a foolish idea. Instead, the enemies who had predicted failure were beginning to look foolish. In particular, *Sanballat* and *Tobiah* were annoyed with anything that promoted the welfare of the Jews (Nehemiah 2:10), and this project certainly did that. These men and other enemies *were very wroth*, or angry, and they decided to do more than just talk against the Jews.

Three national groups are named among the enemies. *The Ashdodites* were Philistines from the coastal plain west of Jerusalem. *The Arabians, and the Ammonites* came from the East. Apparently people from these groups had moved into the area around Jerusalem while the Jews were captives in Babylon.

C. Conspiracy (v. 8)

8. And conspired all of them together to come and to fight against Jerusalem, and to hinder it.

Secretly the three groups plotted *to fight against Jerusalem. Hinder* is a very mild word for what they meant to do. The Hebrew text literally means, "to make confusion." From verse 11, we see that they actually intended to kill the workers on the wall. We have no estimate of how many men these three groups could bring to their attack. If they took time to summon reinforcements from fellow tribesmen living farther away, probably they greatly outnumbered the Jews.

D. Prayerful Defense (v. 9)

9. Nevertheless we made our prayer unto our God, and set a watch against them day and night, because of them.

News of the hostile plot leaked out and reached the Jews who were working in Jerusalem. Their response was an ideal combination of divine providence with human effort. They offered *prayer*, asking God for help, and they also *set a watch* (an armed guard) to be ready for an attack at any time, day or night.

Verses 10-14 add some important details. We note that the builders seemed to be getting discouraged. They were tired, and the rubbish on the site made the work difficult (v. 10). Then we see that the enemies were planning a surprise attack (v. 11). Jerusalem had a number of open gates in the half-built wall. If an invading force of tough guerrilla fighters came swiftly through each gate, they could quickly overpower the unarmed workers. But the plotters were not as secretive as they thought. We are told that the Jews living near them learned of their plot and warned those in Jerusalem (v. 12). So Nehemiah armed many of the workers (v. 13) and urged his people to trust the Lord and fight bravely (v. 14).

II. Watchful Workers (Nehemiah 4:15-18a)

It appears that word of how the Jews had armed themselves was carried back to the enemies. These foes had been ready to slaughter unarmed workers, but they were not so ready to attack men armed for battle. They decided to call off the assault, or at least to postpone it.

A. Back to Work (v. 15)

15. And it came to pass, when our enemies heard that it was known unto us, and God had brought their counsel to nought, that we returned all of us to the wall, every one unto his work.

The enemies' *counsel* refers to their plot to murder the unarmed workers. *God had brought their counsel to nought* by seeing that a warning reached the workers. It is noteworthy that the Hebrew word translated *brought . . . to nought* is the same word rendered *frustrateth* in Isaiah 44:25 (see Lesson 1). There God frustrated the efforts of the "diviners"; here He thwarted the efforts of the Jews' enemies, forcing them to abandon their plot for the time being. The Jews resumed work on the wall, but with the precautions described in the following verses.

B. Protection (v. 16)

16. And it came to pass from that time forth, that the half of my servants wrought in the work, and the other half of them held both the spears, the shields, and the bows, and the habergeons; and the rulers were behind all the house of Judah.

As governor of the province, Nehemiah had an unknown number of servants on his staff, perhaps to assist him in various administrative matters. Now, as a precautionary measure, *half of them* continued in the work on the wall while the *other half* formed an armed guard. The men were well supplied, having *spears* and *bows* as well as *shields* and the coats of armor referred to here as *habergeons*. The other Jews at work on the wall are called *the house of Judah*. They were working in family groups and occupational groups as described in Nehemiah 3. Rulers of each group were *behind* the people; apparently they acted as foremen, and were prepared to become commanders in case of battle.

C. One-Handed Workers (v. 17)

17. They which builded on the wall, and they that bare burdens, with those that laded, every one with one of his hands wrought in the work, and with the other hand held a weapon.

Some of the men were doing work that could be done with one hand. For example, some must have been clearing away all the rubbish that had accumulated (v.10). A man could pick up trash with *one of his hands* and put it in a basket. Then two men could carry the basket between them, each holding a side of it with one hand while his *other hand* held a sword or spear or bow. Some of the stones for the wall could be carried in the same way.

D. Builders Ready for Battle (v. 18a)

18a. For the builders, every one had his sword girded by his side, and so builded.

On the other hand, some of the work could not be done by workmen with only one hand available. If a man needed both hands to do his job, he had a *sword* fastened to his belt, so that he could "change hats" and become a soldier at a moment's notice.

III. Battle Plan
(Nehemiah 4:18b-23)

A. Communication (v. 18b)

18b. And he that sounded the trumpet was by me.

As supervisor of the entire project, Nehemiah was constantly moving about to keep in touch with all that was going on. Workers at the other end of the city might be half a mile away. Sounding a *trumpet* (perhaps through a series of prearranged signals) was the best way to communicate any sudden developments to the other workers. Thus the trumpeter stayed beside Nehemiah continually.

B. Mobilization (vv. 19, 20)

19. And I said unto the nobles, and to the rulers, and to the rest of the people, The work is great and large, and we are separated upon the wall, one far from another.

Alone on its section of the wall, a small group of workers would be easy prey for a band of guerrilla fighters that might charge through a nearby space where a gate had not yet been built. Nehemiah did not want any group to face such an assault alone.

20. In what place therefore ye hear the sound of the trumpet, resort ye thither unto us: our God shall fight for us.

At this point the wall was only half as high as it was going to be (v. 6), but it was high enough so that someone on top of it would have a clear view of the surrounding territory. Nehemiah could not be everywhere at once, but armed men could be spaced around the city to keep watch in all directions. If one of them saw a hostile party coming, he could wave across town to Nehemiah. The trumpeter could then run swiftly to the threatened point, and the trumpet call would bring other armed men to that point.

Explaining this plan, Nehemiah added that the men would not be alone in battle: *Our God shall fight for us.* As practical a person as Nehemiah was, he never forgot God's part in any undertaking. He knew that only with God's help was success in this endeavor possible.

A WARNING ON THE WALL

In many large metropolitan areas these days, it seems the *Theftus interruptus* is the official city bird. That's what one comic has designated as the Latin name for the ever-present (and sometimes maddening) car alarm. Alarms that merely beep, sound a siren, and flash the lights are now out-of-date. So is the alarm that speaks in a semi-human voice as you get near the car, warning, "*Step back*! In three seconds an alarm will sound if you do not!"

Thieves have figured out how to bypass many alarms; the rest just brazenly ignore the devices while they steal the car. The fact that honest people hear the alarms so often—and thus pay no attention to what is happening—works to the thieves' advantage. Today the state-of-the-art protective device is an active alarm that broadcasts an electronic signal. Cars equipped this way have a ninety percent recovery rate.

To thwart his enemies as they tried to interfere with the work on the wall, Nehemiah stationed a trumpeter so that a warning could be

---

How to Say It

 AMMONITES. *Am*-uh-nites.
ARABIANS. Uh-*ray*-bee-unz.
ASHDODITES. *Ash*-duh-dites.
ELUL. *E*-lool.
HABERGEONS. *hab*-er-junz.
NEHEMIAH. Nee-huh-*my*-uh.
PHILISTINES. Fuh-*liss*-teens or *Fill*-us-teens.
SANBALLAT. San-*bal*-ut.
TOBIAH. Toe-*by*-uh.

sounded if his workers were threatened. He said, "When you hear the trumpet sound the alarm, rush to our side so we can defend ourselves." The people of God in every age must watch out for the enemy, but we must never let that become our primary focus. We should not let the enemy's threats deter us from the work God has called us to do.   —C. R. B.

C. Toiling On (v. 21)

21. So we labored in the work: and half of them held the spears from the rising of the morning till the stars appeared.

The work went on in spite of the threat of violence. It proceeded more slowly, of course, for half the workers were now standing guard. The others tried to make up for this by working longer days: *from the rising of the morning till the stars appeared.*

D. Diligence (vv. 22, 23)

22. Likewise at the same time said I unto the people, Let every one with his servant lodge within Jerusalem, that in the night they may be a guard to us, and labor on the day.

Many of the builders lived in villages outside *Jerusalem.* Nehemiah asked them to sleep in town instead of going home for the night. This would protect them from personal harm during the journey to and from their homes. They would also be on hand to fight if a sudden attack occurred at *night.*

23. So neither I, nor my brethren, nor my servants, nor the men of the guard which followed me, none of us put off our clothes, saving that every one put them off for washing.

Nehemiah and his *brethren* (a term most likely referring to those officials closest to him) set the example of diligence. They slept with their *clothes* on so that they would be ready for instant action in case of attack by night.

The last clause of this verse is so puzzling that we can hardly find two versions that translate it alike. The Hebrew literally reads, "each one his weapon water." It is difficult for us to tell exactly what this is saying. The *King James Version* takes it to mean that a man took off his clothes only for washing—either washing the clothes or washing the man. Certainly both men and clothing needed frequent washing. But several versions take the phrase to mean that a man did not put down his weapon even when he went for water, either for a drink or for washing. This is the sense in which the *New International Version* understands the verse: "Each had his weapon, even when he went for water." From any translation we can see that everyone was on full alert.

THE NECESSITY OF VIGILANCE

In 1790 John Philpot Curran said, "The condition upon which God hath given liberty to man is eternal vigilance; which condition if he break, servitude is at once the consequence of his crime and the punishment of his guilt." Curran's abbreviated version of this thought is more familiar to most people: "Eternal vigilance is the price of liberty."

We see the wisdom of this advice in many areas of our lives. Careful, regular maintenance of the family car can help to insure our family's freedom from possible injury or death. In earthquake-prone regions of the world, building codes are reviewed after each major quake to see what changes are needed to protect people from future disasters. When an airliner crashes, that model of plane may be grounded until the cause of the crash is determined and any suspect parts are replaced on similar aircraft. Only by attending to such matters with "vigilance" now do we lessen the possibility of encountering future problems.

Years before Nehemiah and the Jews returned to Jerusalem, their ancestors had failed to be vigilant against the threats of idolatry and other forms of ungodliness. They eventually paid the price through their captivity in a foreign land. Now, to retain their newly gained freedom, they had to do their work with vigilance, always being ready to fight off an attack from their enemies. The same vigilance is needed by the people of God today: "Your adversary the devil, as a roaring lion, walketh about, seeking whom he may devour" (1 Peter 5:8).   —C. R. B.

Conclusion

A. Triumphant Finish

"So the wall was finished in the twenty and fifth day of the month Elul, in fifty and two days" (Nehemiah 6:15).

The wall was completed early in October (this is our equivalent of the month of Elul). This offers another illustration of how skillfully and carefully Nehemiah made his plans and carried them out. He called the people to work on the wall after they were through with the harvest of barley and wheat. The weather was hot, but there was little or no rain. Nehemiah organized the workers so well that they finished the job early in autumn. There was still a little time to gather the autumn harvest before the Feast of Tabernacles.

The Jews' remarkable success dealt a severe blow to their enemies' schemes. Nehemiah 6:16 tells us, "When all our enemies heard thereof, and all the heathen that were about us saw these things, they were much cast down in their own eyes: for they perceived that this work was wrought of our God." God's people and God's purposes had triumphed mightily.

B. Leadership

Nehemiah's success seems to indicate that he was an exemplary leader. Can we glean from him some suggestions for leadership in the church?

1. Nehemiah trusted in God and prayed earnestly (Nehemiah 1:4-11; 2:4; 4:9).

2. Nehemiah was unselfishly devoted to the task at hand (Nehemiah 5:14-18).

3. Nehemiah was persuasive rather than demanding. He convinced the people that an improved city would be good for them, good for the nation, and good for the glory of God (Nehemiah 2:17, 18).

4. Nehemiah was practical in thought and action. He made workable plans, and he carried them out (Nehemiah 4:13-22).

5. Nehemiah was continually among the workers, encouraging them so well that they willingly worked from early in the morning until well into the night (Nehemiah 4:19-21).

6. Nehemiah took sensible precautions when danger threatened, but he did not stop the work (Nehemiah 4:7-9, 17-20).

7. Nehemiah kept on until the job was done, thus encouraging the people to persevere (Nehemiah 4:14, 15; 6:15, 16).

C. Elders

Elders are called to be leaders in the Lord's church (Acts 14:23; 20:17; 1 Timothy 5:17; Titus 1:5; 1 Peter 5:1-3). They are to be mature men. It is hoped that through years of experience they not only have gained the ability to lead well, but also have shown this ability so clearly that church members have confidence in them.

In choosing elders we should give close attention to Scriptures such as 1 Timothy 3:1-7 and Titus 1:5-9. There we find descriptions of the kind of men who ought to lead in Christian work. We should also give thought to the other name given to elders: they are called *bishops* (Philippians 1:1; 1 Timothy 3:1, 2; Titus 1:7), which means "overseers." This implies the ability to manage and organize tasks effectively. How wonderful it is when a church's leaders not only are godly men, but also are gifted with leadership ability like Nehemiah's!

D. Followers

Can you imagine what would have happened if the people of Jerusalem had answered Nehemiah's appeal by saying, "Forget it! Who needs a wall?"

How many once-great churches are living unhappily amid the ruins of their former greatness? Is it because they lack leaders, or is it because the people are not exerting themselves to bring the saving gospel to their neighbors?

How many now-great churches are content with their greatness, and do not care for the lost souls in their own cities and on the other side of the world? Is it because their leaders have no vision, or is it because the people are not willing to sacrifice to send the light?

Nehemiah was a magnificent leader, but the wall was built by thousands of eager followers who traded their comfort for hard work and danger until the job was done.

Jesus said, "I will build my church; and the gates of hell shall not prevail against it" (Matthew 16:18). The church will be preserved until He comes again, but this very day it needs countless thousands of eager members working and sacrificing for the Savior to make it "a glorious church, not having spot, or wrinkle, or any such thing; but . . . holy and without blemish" (Ephesians 5:27).

E. Prayer

God of our fathers, and our God, we thank You for preserving Your ancient people in spite of their faults, until the Savior came. And now we thank You for preserving Your church in spite of its faults, until He comes again. As we confess all our faults, we thank You for the gracious forgiveness we have in our Savior, and we pledge ourselves to be more like Him. Amen.

F. Thought to Remember

We can do better.

Home Daily Bible Readings

Monday, Nov. 17—They Had a Mind to Work (Nehemiah 4:1-9)
Tuesday, Nov. 18—"Our God Shall Fight for Us" (Nehemiah 4:10-20)
Wednesday, Nov. 19—God's Sentinels on the Wall (Isaiah 62:6-12)
Thursday, Nov. 20—The Prophet As Sentinel (Ezekiel 33:1-9)
Friday, Nov. 21—God As Refuge and Fortress (Psalm 91:1-16)
Saturday, Nov. 22—All Nations Worship in Jerusalem (Zechariah 14:16-21)
Sunday, Nov. 23—Heaven's Bread for Their Hunger (Nehemiah 9:6-15)

Learning by Doing

This page contains an alternate lesson plan emphasizing learning activities.
Classes desiring such student involvement will find these suggestions helpful.

Learning Goals

As students participate in today's class session, they should:

1. Tell how the wall of Jerusalem was built in spite of angry opposition.

2. Describe how the same courage and commitment that overcame opposition and rebuilt the walls of Jerusalem can help the church defeat opposition today.

3. Make a courageous commitment to deal with some specific hindrance to the church or to one's own service for the Lord.

Into the Lesson

Use one or more of the following ideas to begin today's session:

Building blocks. Bring a pile of wooden building blocks, toy wooden logs, or some other toy building set to your classroom. Perhaps you can bring several sets and arrange them at different places in the room. Have class members try to build something with them as they arrive. When your session begins, ask class members to think about the kind of building toys they played with when they were young. What kind of building toys do their children or grandchildren use now? Is building with toys always fun? Is it ever difficult? What makes it difficult? Do the children ever need an adult to help them? (A better question might be, "Do the adults ever need the children to help them?")

Guest speaker. Invite someone from one of the building professions to speak for five minutes to your class. Maybe a member of your church is a carpenter, electrician, plumber, or general contractor. Ask your guest to focus on "problems that can arise when you're building something." He may want to tell funny stories about building projects that went awry.

Share a story. Instead of a building professional, maybe you could invite a class member who has built a house to tell your group why the project turned out to be harder than he thought it would be. Or you could invite several to tell stories about a building or remodeling project that tried their patience.

The point of any of these activities is to lead class members to think about the challenges and difficulties that may arise whenever anyone attempts to build anything. Tell the class that today's Bible study will show them the special challenges that God's people faced when they undertook to rebuild the walls of Jerusalem.

Into the Word

Ask the class to make two lists as they read today's text from Nehemiah 4: "Obstacles to Building the Wall," and "How the Obstacles Were Overcome." Class members may make the lists in small groups or as a class. If they work in small groups, write the two lists on your chalkboard as the groups report.

Next, discuss the following questions with your class:

1. How important was Nehemiah's role in overcoming the obstacles? How would the people have progressed without such a leader?

2. What was God's role in the people's overcoming the obstacles? How much credit did they give to God?

3. What did the people do to overcome the obstacles? What kind of energy and creativity did they expend to make sure that their plans were not frustrated?

Into Life

Ask the class to make two more lists (again, either in groups or as a class) covering the following topics: "What God Wants Our Church to Accomplish," and "Obstacles to Accomplishing These Goals." (If you prefer, you may discuss "our class" instead of "our church.")

Have the class consider how the example of Nehemiah and his people can help them overcome the obstacles that they have listed. Do they need to depend more on God? Do they need to be more strategic and resourceful? Are they waiting for a leader like Nehemiah to provide the necessary direction and initiative?

Next, with this second set of lists in mind, have the class work on one more list. This one should state prayer requests that relate to the challenges and obstacles that your church (or your class) is facing. Use these prayer requests in one of several ways:

(1) Class members can pray in the small groups that were formed earlier.

(2) Individuals in the class can volunteer to pray aloud for one of the requests.

(3) Duplicate the list of prayer requests and mail it to class members during the week following your class session.

Let's Talk It Over

The questions on this page are designed to encourage review of the lesson Scriptures and to promote discussion of the lesson by the class. The answers provided are only discussion starters. Let your class talk it over from there.

1. "The people had a mind to work" (Nehemiah 4:6). Is this statement descriptive of our church? If not, how can we make it so?

Perhaps the ridicule from the Jews' enemies, recorded in Nehemiah 4:1-3, spurred them to such devotion. That is something we should use to our advantage today. Critics of the church regard it as ignorant, misguided, and irrelevant. Such charges should stir us to demonstrate a zeal for the truth centered in Jesus. Perhaps an even better reason why the Jews had a mind to work was the thorough planning Nehemiah had done. The people knew what needed to be done; they had access to the materials they required; and they enjoyed official approval—all thanks to Nehemiah. When church leaders plan in a similarly thorough way, the members will be much more likely to put their minds and their hearts into the work.

2. The men who worked on Jerusalem's walls combined prayer with a careful watch for their enemies. What are some circumstances in which we need to combine our prayers with positive actions?

In some religious groups, the use of physicians and medicines to combat sickness is viewed as contrary to faith. Simply praying for the sick is supposed to be a sufficient response. However, the New Testament in no place forbids us to combine prayer with the treatment provided by doctors. Also, in regard to our evangelistic labors in the church, it is vital that we pray *and* witness, pray *and* call, pray *and* actively seek the lost. Similarly, we need to do more for needy people than to pray that they will be "warmed and filled" (James 2:16).

3. Nehemiah set up a plan in which, if an enemy attacked, a trumpeter would summon armed workers to the place of the attack. There are occasions in which Christians must rally around a church or fellow believer under attack. What are examples of this?

It is unfortunate that Christians sometimes are guilty of sexual sin. On occasion, however, ministers and other workers in the church are wrongfully accused of such sin. We must rally around these fellow believers and support them as they endeavor to prove their innocence.

Another example that we may note is the case of Christians who lose their jobs because they refuse to compromise their faith. A part of our support for them will be prayer for a new and better job. There is also the matter of fellow believers suffering as a result of serious illnesses or accidents. Satan can use such circumstances to attack a believer's faith. But our loving support and our prayers can thwart the enemy.

4. The Jews' enemies tried several different tactics to hinder the rebuilding of Jerusalem's wall. What are some of the tactics Satan uses to try and destroy the church? How can we overcome these tactics?

One of Satan's strategies is to divide and conquer. If he can sow division and conflict within the church, he can destroy fellowship and brotherly love. Whenever division threatens, we should recognize it as Satan's work, whatever human factors may be involved. Satan is also clever at employing lies and half-truths. We must combat the "father of lies" (John 8:44, *New International Version*) by "speaking the truth in love" (Ephesians 4:15). Another Satanic tactic is that of lulling us into indifference and self-satisfaction. When this happens, we must heed Christ's call to "be zealous . . . and repent" (Revelation 3:19).

5. "There are too many chiefs and not enough Indians." Occasionally one hears such a complaint about the church. How can we cultivate the spirit of "followship" in our congregation?

It is well to keep in mind that we are all followers in the church. Jesus Christ is ultimately the only leader. Those who would lead as ministers, elders, or teachers must demonstrate first of all that they follow Christ. In line with that, it is important that leaders make it their aim to lead where Christ would lead. Their own visions of what the church should be and their own opinions as to what is best for the congregation, must be subordinate to what Christ wants. To go a step further, leaders must demonstrate that they rely on God's Word and prayer as their primary tools in fulfilling their responsibilities. Members will be more likely to follow a leader who humbly relies on these resources.

Reward of the Faithful

DEVOTIONAL READING: Malachi 2:17—3:5.

LESSON SCRIPTURE: Malachi 2:17—3:18.

PRINTED TEXT: Malachi 3:6-18.

Malachi 3:6-18

6 For I am the LORD, I change not; therefore ye sons of Jacob are not consumed.

7 Even from the days of your fathers ye are gone away from mine ordinances, and have not kept them. Return unto me, and I will return unto you, saith the LORD of hosts. But ye said, Wherein shall we return?

8 Will a man rob God? Yet ye have robbed me. But ye say, Wherein have we robbed thee? In tithes and offerings.

9 Ye are cursed with a curse: for ye have robbed me, even this whole nation.

10 Bring ye all the tithes into the storehouse, that there may be meat in mine house, and prove me now herewith, saith the LORD of hosts, if I will not open you the windows of heaven, and pour you out a blessing, that there shall not be room enough to receive it.

11 And I will rebuke the devourer for your sakes, and he shall not destroy the fruits of your ground; neither shall your vine cast her fruit before the time in the field, saith the LORD of hosts.

12 And all nations shall call you blessed: for ye shall be a delightsome land, saith the LORD of hosts.

13 Your words have been stout against me, saith the LORD. Yet ye say, What have we spoken so much against thee?

14 Ye have said, It is vain to serve God: and what profit is it that we have kept his ordinance, and that we have walked mournfully before the LORD of hosts?

15 And now we call the proud happy; yea, they that work wickedness are set up; yea, they that tempt God are even delivered.

16 Then they that feared the LORD spake often one to another: and the LORD hearkened, and heard it, and a book of remembrance was written before him for them that feared the LORD, and that thought upon his name.

17 And they shall be mine, saith the LORD of hosts, in that day when I make up my jewels; and I will spare them, as a man spareth his own son that serveth him.

18 Then shall ye return, and discern between the righteous and the wicked, between him that serveth God and him that serveth him not.

GOLDEN TEXT: Return unto me, and I will return unto you, saith the LORD of hosts.—Malachi 3:7.

God Leads a People Home

Unit 3: Life After the Return

(Lessons 9-13)

Lesson Aims

After this lesson, a student should be able to:

1. Describe the charges that the Lord brought against His rebellious people, and His promise of reward to those who followed Him faithfully.

2. Relate some of the blessings promised to those who do not compromise in their commitment to the Lord.

3. Repent of any compromise in one's commitment to the Lord and resolve to honor God as sovereign Lord of his or her life.

Lesson Outline

INTRODUCTION
    A. Looking Back
    B. Lesson Background
  I. THE LORD AND THE ROBBERS (Malachi 3:6-9)
    A. The Changeless Lord (v. 6)
    B. The Changeable People (v. 7)
    C. The Charge of Robbery (v. 8)
    D. The Result of Robbery (v. 9)
    The Art of Generous Giving
  II. THE LORD AND THE GIVERS (Malachi 3:10-12)
    A. The Action of Honesty (v. 10a)
    B. The Result of Honesty (vv. 10b-12)
  III. THE LORD AND THE TALKERS (Malachi 3:13-18)
    A. Slanderers of God (vv. 13-15)
    B. God-Fearing Talkers (vv. 16-18)
CONCLUSION
    A. Christian Giving
    B. Speaking for God
    C. Prayer
    D. Thought to Remember

The visual for Lesson 13 highlights God's loving invitation. It is shown on page 109.

Introduction

A. Looking Back

In September we began a lesson series entitled, "God Leads a People Home." Knowing that going home is often an occasion for joy, perhaps we thought, "These will be happy lessons." And for the most part they have been. After seventy years of captivity in Babylon, God's people were set free. Assisted by the king of Persia, but most of all by the King of Heaven, they went home.

We have seen, however, that the process of going back home and rebuilding was not an easy one. The joy of coming home was mingled with repeated disappointments. For every step forward that God's people took, something occurred to push them two steps back. It was thrilling to read of captives being released, but it was sad to see the people so engrossed in their own business that it took over twenty years to build God's house. It was exciting to see them take possession of the land they had lost, but it was disheartening to read of the marriages to heathen women. We were glad to read of reclaimed farms and rebuilt homes, but sad to find that after many years Jerusalem was still only a frontier village, not the great city it once had been.

On the other hand, each disappointment was followed by an occasion for joy. The people were slow to build God's temple, but at Haggai and Zechariah's urging they completed it in triumph. The men did take heathen wives, but they responded to Ezra's plea by ending the unlawful marriages. They had been content for too long with a village, but Nehemiah's challenge roused them to make Jerusalem a strong, well-defended city.

B. Lesson Background

With today's lesson (the final one in this quarter), we come to a time about fifteen years after Nehemiah had led his people in building the city wall and making Jerusalem a respectable city. Again we find disappointment reflected in our text, but when we read on to the end, there is a sense of joy and hope.

A word is in order concerning the prophet Malachi, whose book is the last one in the Old Testament. Little is known about Malachi himself; his name means "my messenger." Malachi addresses many of the issues that are of great concern in the book of Nehemiah, such as intermarriage (Malachi 2:11-16) and the bringing of acceptable tithes and offerings (Nehemiah 10:37-39 and Malachi 3:8-10). Malachi also refers to a "governor" (1:8), which was Nehemiah's title (Nehemiah 5:14). All of this indicates that Malachi probably

---

How to Say It

HAGGAI. *Hag*-a-eye or *Hag*-eye.
MALACHI. *Mal*-uh-kye.
MELCHIZEDEK. Mel-*kizz*-ih-dek.
NEHEMIAH. Nee-huh-*my*-uh.
ZECHARIAH. Zek-uh-*rye*-uh.

prophesied during the time of Nehemiah and perhaps provided additional support for Nehemiah's efforts. Having just concluded a series of lessons from the book of Nehemiah, it is appropriate to consider the message of Malachi.

I. The Lord and the Robbers (Malachi 3:6-9)

A. The Changeless Lord (v. 6)

6. For I am the LORD, I change not; therefore ye sons of Jacob are not consumed.

What a comfort it is to know that *the Lord* is changeless in the midst of *change!* When everything around us seems to be in a state of utter chaos and out of control, He remains the same. We can depend on Him. If He were as changeable as we are, He might have wiped out His chosen people when they continued to turn away from Him. But He chose those people to bring the Redeemer into the world. Unworthy as they were, they still were not *consumed.* God had a purpose for them, and He preserved them until the Redeemer appeared.

B. The Changeable People (v. 7)

7. Even from the days of your fathers ye are gone away from mine ordinances, and have not kept them. Return unto me, and I will return unto you, saith the LORD of hosts. But ye said, Wherein shall we return?

Ye are gone away from mine ordinances, and have not kept them. The changeless Lord brought His indictment against a changing people, given to constant disobedience. After the strenuous work of building the wall of Jerusalem, the people had gathered to hear God's Law read under the leadership of Ezra (Nehemiah 8:1-8). They had promised to obey it; Nehemiah 10:28, 29 tells how "every one having knowledge, and having understanding" took an oath "to walk in God's law." But now they were breaking their promise and thus breaking God's Law. This was not a new thing in Israel. It had been going on, God said, *even from the days of your fathers.* This is quite an indictment, when one considers that Malachi lived close to a thousand years after Israel's deliverance from bondage in Egypt.

Return unto me. This was God's call to His disobedient people. Changeable as they were, they could change for the better, by pledging to serve God faithfully and then fulfilling that promise. *And I will return unto you.* This does not mean that God was as changeable as His people. He had not turned away from them; they had turned away from Him. If they would turn back, they would find that He was with them as He had been before.

Trying to put on innocent faces, the people asked, *Wherein shall we return?* "What do You mean? Just what do You want us to do?" But they knew—or if they did not know, they should have known. They had heard the Law read (Nehemiah 8:1-8), and perhaps it had been read to them at other times as well (Deuteronomy 31:10, 11). There were plenty of opportunities for the people to know what they had to do; their question was simply an attempt to dodge their responsibility. In the next verse we see God's answer to the people's question. He told them exactly what He meant.

C. The Charge of Robbery (v. 8)

8. Will a man rob God? Yet ye have robbed me. But ye say, Wherein have we robbed thee? In tithes and offerings.

Will a man rob God? The very idea seems unthinkable. God provides "every good gift and every perfect gift" (James 1:17). He "giveth us richly all things to enjoy" (1 Timothy 6:17). From Him we have "life, and breath, and all things" (Acts 17:25). Simple gratitude should keep us from taking anything from the great Giver who has bestowed so much upon us. And if we lack a sense of gratitude, then fear should keep us from robbing God, for no robbery can be hidden from Him (Jeremiah 16:17, 18). Robbing God is utterly foolish. Still, this has been man's way from the beginning. Gifted with the fruit of every tree in Eden except one, Adam and Eve stole from the forbidden tree and suffered the bitter consequence (Genesis 2:17).

Again the people tried to pretend that they were innocent: *Wherein have we robbed thee?* "What do You mean? Tell us how we have robbed You." And the Lord answered in the plainest of terms: *In tithes and offerings.* Clearly the Law declared that a tithe, or a tenth, of the produce of the land belonged to the Lord (Leviticus 27:30), and was to be used to support both priests and Levites. *Offerings* may refer to the portions of sacrifices set aside for the priests (Exodus 29:27, 28; Leviticus 7:32), or to gifts received for special projects such as the tabernacle (Exodus 25:1-7). If a man used any of the tithes or offerings for himself, he was robbing God by taking that which He had designated to be used in a particular way.

D. The Result of Robbery (v. 9)

9. Ye are cursed with a curse: for ye have robbed me, even this whole nation.

The robbers were not just a few people who were insensitive, ungrateful, and foolish. *This whole nation* was guilty, and was therefore *cursed with a curse*. The nature of this curse is indicated in verse 11, which tells what punishments would cease if the robbery ceased.

THE ART OF GENEROUS GIVING

Just about a century ago, Andrew Carnegie announced that he would build a library in any city or town that would tax itself each year in the amount of ten percent of the value of his gift—a tithe, if you will—in order to run the library. Carnegie's generous offer was accepted by 1,679 communities across America.

Someone has observed that a modern comparison would be Bill Gates of Microsoft offering to give computers to the poor people of the nation. Such an act would be equally revolutionary in concept and in results. The Carnegie libraries made the tools for learning available free of charge to a vast number of Americans who otherwise would not have had a chance to better their lives through education.

Perhaps the most unusual part of Carnegie's generosity was that it seems to have been an act of true generosity rather than a deed to bring personal recognition to him. Carnegie gave not just money, but an illustration of the meaning of giving. The Jews of Malachi's day had lost, not only the art of generous giving, but the art of giving itself. They were not giving God His due. It showed in their selfish and shameless treatment of their fellow citizens, and it showed in the way they dealt with God who had blessed them materially. To this present day, our contribution to God's work is an indication of the strength of our faith and spirituality.   —C. R. B.

II. The Lord and the Givers
(Malachi 3:10-12)

By reason of God's curse, the robbers in Israel lost more than they gained by their robbery. How could they escape this devastating curse? Simply by changing their selfish ways: by putting an end to their robbery and practicing honesty with God. This was what the Lord now asked them to do.

A. The Action of Honesty (v. 10a)

10a. Bring ye all the tithes into the storehouse, that there may be meat in mine house.

The *tithes* belonged to the Lord. *The storehouse* was a granary or warehouse where wheat, barley, or dried fruits could be kept until they were needed. This area is referred to as the "treasuries" in Nehemiah 13:12. In the *King James Version*, *meat* means foods of all kinds, including grain and fruit. The tithes thus brought

to God's house were meant to support the Levites (Numbers 18:24, 30, 31), whose work included teaching, leading in worship, and taking care of the temple. The Levites in turn gave a tithe of what they received to the priests (Numbers 18:25-28).

Originally the Levites lived in cities scattered throughout the land of Israel, so it was not too hard to deliver the tithes to them (Numbers 35:1-3). In this time after the captivity, however, the Israelites occupied only a small portion of the territory that had been theirs previously. Probably the Levites had no more than one town at this point, and perhaps none at all. Of course they still needed food.

B. The Result of Honesty (vv. 10b-12)

10b. And prove me now herewith, saith the LORD of hosts, if I will not open you the windows of heaven, and pour you out a blessing, that there shall not be room enough to receive it.

God invited the people to *prove*, or test Him, to see if His promise was true. Usually it is not wise to conduct such a test of God (the same Hebrew word rendered *proved* is used in Psalm 95:9 of the Israelites in the wilderness). Here, however, God sets the terms, and challenges His people to break out of their spiritual apathy. His promise to them could easily be tested. If the people acted honestly with God, the next harvest would provide the proof. The *windows of heaven* would pour forth enough rain to mature the grapes and other fruits. From Heaven would also come the control of various pests, such as locusts, and any plant diseases. The harvest would be abundant, and the nine-tenths kept by honest men would prove to be much more than the ten-tenths kept by robbers. The shortage of food would be ended; there would be no shortage except a shortage of space to store the huge harvest.

11. And I will rebuke the devourer for your sakes, and he shall not destroy the fruits of your ground; neither shall your vine cast her fruit before the time in the field, saith the LORD of hosts.

Locusts were the most frequent *devourer* of crops in Israel. Millions of them swarmed over the land, ravaging and ruining Israel's crops. But at God's *rebuke* they would trouble Israel no more. The fruit of the *vine* would ripen fully, instead of falling to the ground *before the time* when it was ready to be picked. There was no cause of crop failure that the Lord could not control, and He would control them all for the sake of honest men in Israel—if only honest men could be found.

12. And all nations shall call you blessed: for ye shall be a delightsome land, saith the LORD of hosts.

If God's people acted honestly, the beauty and productivity of their land would not be hidden. All the heathen people of the surrounding *nations* would know that the Lord's people were more *blessed* than any other people. The abundance of the crops would make Israel *a delightsome land.*

III. The Lord and the Talkers (Malachi 3:13-18)

Those who had been robbing God had been slandering Him as well. Apparently they were deceived by their own lies. If they had known the truth about the Lord, how could they have been foolish enough to rob and slander Him?

A. Slanderers of God (vv. 13-15)

13. Your words have been stout against me, saith the LORD. Yet ye say, What have we spoken so much against thee?

The talk against the Lord had not been trivial. The slanderers' *words* had been *stout.* The Hebrew word means "strong" or "hard." The *New International Version* reads, "You have said harsh things against me." Once more the people tried to pretend they were innocent: "Who, us? What did we say against You?"

14. Ye have said, It is vain to serve God: and what profit is it that we have kept his ordinance, and that we have walked mournfully before the LORD of hosts?

The slanderers had been saying that it was *vain*, or useless, to serve God. They claimed there was no *profit* in keeping His commands. This contradicted a clear promise of God. Deuteronomy 28, for example, lists many blessings that God promised to obedient Israel (vv. 1-14); a larger section elaborates on disastrous curses that God would bring upon a disobedient people (vv. 15-68).

What God had been doing should have been plain to the slanderers, but they did not acknowledge this. When crops were good, they gave credit to their own efforts, or to the good earth and ample rainfall. When crops failed, perhaps they spoke of bad luck, a long dry spell, or a plague of locusts. They did not see God at work in these situations. So they asked what profit could be gained from serving God. Their attitude was similar to those today who ask, "What's in it for me?" The simple truth was that every shekel of profit on their bottom line was from God, and so was all the red ink of a bad year.

15. And now we call the proud happy; yea, they that work wickedness are set up; yea, they that tempt God are even delivered.

Around them the slanderers saw circumstances that seemed to contradict the Lord's promises. People who paid no attention to God and His promises remained proud and prosperous and happy. We could point to similar situations today. Each year millions of dollars go to entertainers and athletes who make no effort to obey God. Other millions go to crooked politicians and dishonest lawyers. Such individuals do not prove that God's promise is false; they show that God is patient. He is waiting for wrongdoers to repent—to stop doing wrong and start doing right (2 Peter 3:9).

We need to remember that God's action is not limited to this earth. He does not settle all of His accounts in this life. Very instructive is Jesus' story of the rich man and Lazarus (Luke 16:19-31). The rich man wore fine clothes and lived in luxury until he died, then he found himself begging vainly for a drop of water. Lazarus lay helpless, feeding on the crumbs from the rich man's table, until he died. From then on, however, Lazarus was never in want again. Even though wrong may seem to dominate our world, God in His justice will make all things right.

B. God-Fearing Talkers (vv. 16-18)

16. Then they that feared the LORD spake often one to another: and the LORD hearkened, and heard it, and a book of remembrance was written before him for them that feared the LORD, and that thought upon his name.

How good it is for God-fearing people to talk together often! We do it when we meet on Sunday morning, and again on Sunday evening. Some of us love to talk together so much that we have a midweek meeting, a class meeting, a women's fellowship meeting, a neighborhood meeting, or some other group meeting. We share our blessings and our disasters; we build up our faith in God and His promises.

visual for
lesson 13

RETURN UNTO ME, AND I WILL RETURN UNTO YOU, SAITH THE LORD OF HOSTS.
— Malachi 3:7 —

While God is listening when we talk with Him in prayer, He is also listening when we talk with one another, and what He hears is not forgotten. It is recorded in *a book of remembrance*, a record of *them that feared the Lord, and that thought upon his name*. That God keeps such a book is also evident from Exodus 32:32, 33; Psalm 69:28; 87:6; and Daniel 12:1. The New Testament equivalent is the "book of life" (Revelation 20:12, 15).

17. And they shall be mine, saith the LORD of hosts, in that day when I make up my jewels; and I will spare them, as a man spareth his own son that serveth him.

On a *day* of God's choosing, the Lord Jesus will come to earth in heavenly power and glory (Matthew 25:31). His people from all places and all times will be gathered to be with Him forever (1 Thessalonians 4:14-17). These are His *jewels*, His precious possessions. An old song says, "Little children, little children, Who love their Redeemer, Are the jewels, precious jewels, His loved and His own." But our text indicates that adults are also the Lord's jewels—adults who fear the Lord and think upon His name (v. 16). During their lives on earth, these jewels are not flawless, but divine grace and forgiveness will take away every flaw and make each of them a perfected treasure in the eternal kingdom.

18. Then shall ye return, and discern between the righteous and the wicked, between him that serveth God and him that serveth him not.

The slanderers were saying that it made no difference whether they did right or wrong (vv. 14, 15). On that day when the Lord will gather His jewels, all mankind will recognize the clear distinction between *the righteous and the wicked*—but then it will be too late to change sides. Good and bad will be separated—forever.

Conclusion

Malachi's challenging words remind us that it does pay to serve God; it does pay to obey His Word; it does pay to do right. The "pleasures of sin" last only "for a season" (Hebrews 11:25). In the long run, it pays to serve God.

A. Christian Giving

The tithe was an essential part of Israelite giving. Actually it has its Biblical roots before the establishment of the nation of Israel and the giving of the Law of Moses. Abram gave a tenth of the spoil from his battle with a coalition of Near Eastern kings to Melchizedek (Genesis 14:18-20). Jacob made a vow at Bethel to give a tenth to God of whatever he received (Genesis 28:22).

Just as there are no regulations on how long to pray or to read the Bible, there are no laws to specify how much a Christian must give. Still, the principle of not robbing God is a valid one for Christians to keep in mind. Grateful for His gifts, we should gladly bring *at least* the whole tithe into the "storehouse" of the church. If we would do any less, conscience should accuse us of robbing God. In so doing, we are actually robbing ourselves of the joy and blessing that comes from recognizing that God is the owner of all we have. We are only stewards.

B. Speaking for God

As Christians we seldom speak against God. But how often do we say a word *for* Him? Do we mention Him in casual conversation, giving Him credit for a pleasant day, a needed rain, or a blooming flower? When others speak against Him, are we content to be neutral? Careless talkers often imply that it is useless to serve God, as did the slanderers in Malachi's day. "Why go to church?" they ask. "What does it do for you? What do you get for the money you give?" Do we take time to explain that God gives us all the blessings we have, and that we would feel small and selfish if we used them only for ourselves? How ungrateful it would be not to give Him our worship, our time, and our money!

C. Prayer

We do believe You, Father. Again we promise to obey You, because we know not only that it is best for us, but also that it is right. Forgive our sins, we pray, in Jesus' name, and keep us safe among Your jewels. Amen.

D. Thought to Remember

It pays to serve God.

Home Daily Bible Readings

Learning by Doing

This page contains an alternate lesson plan emphasizing learning activities.
Classes desiring such student involvement will find these suggestions helpful.

Learning Goals

As students participate in today's class session, they should:

1. Describe the charges that the Lord brought against His rebellious people, and His promise of reward to those who followed Him faithfully.

2. Relate some of the blessings promised to those who do not compromise in their commitment to the Lord.

3. Repent of any compromise in one's commitment to the Lord, and resolve to honor God as sovereign Lord of his or her life.

Into the Lesson

Use one of the following ideas to begin today's class session:

Write a sentence. Write the following words on your chalkboard: *faithful, God, disobedience, judgment.* Ask class members to write a sentence that uses at least three of the four words. After several minutes, ask volunteers to read their sentences. Then tell the class that today's Bible study gives us a picture of God's faithfulness and how He responds to the unfaithfulness of His followers.

Word reactions. Ask class members, alone or in groups, to jot down a word or to create a simple drawing that expresses their first reaction to each of these words: *tithe, statute, blessing, faithful, God-fearing.* After they have shared their responses, tell them that each of these words or ideas is central to today's Bible study.

Into the Word

Explain to the class that today's text was written by the prophet Malachi about fifteen years after Nehemiah led the Israelites in rebuilding the wall of Jerusalem.

Next, use one or more of the following Bible study activities with your class. If you wish, you can divide the class into groups of between five and seven. Then describe all the activities and let the groups decide which one they wish to do.

Marked Bibles. Duplicate Malachi 3:6-18 (or use the printed text found in the student book), and ask class members to mark it in this way:

Underline every phrase that speaks of the faithfulness of God.

Circle every phrase that describes the sins of the people.

Put a star beside every command of God.

Put an exclamation point beside every promise of God.

At the bottom or on the back of their paper (or of the page in their book), they should paraphrase their favorite verse from this passage.

What Is God Like? Give students paper and crayons or whatever kind of art material you would like to use. Tell them that this chapter gives us a clear picture of God. Ask them to draw a picture that highlights one of the characteristics of God found in this chapter. After a few minutes, each student should explain how his picture illustrates what this chapter says about God.

Wanted: Faithful Christians. Class members should write a "want ad," directed by God to the church today. The want ad should express God's desire for faithful Christians, and should also express God's message as found in this passage from Malachi.

"Great Is Thy Faithfulness." Ask class members to write a new stanza to this familiar hymn. The new stanza should praise the faithfulness of God as it is described in today's passage.

Allow time for students to share their work with the entire class. During this feedback time, correct any misunderstandings of the text, or explain ideas using the lesson commentary.

Into Life

Write the following phrases on slips of paper (a different phrase on each slip). Prepare enough slips for everyone in your class to have one.

God is faithful.

God is just.

God blesses obedience.

Distribute the slips randomly among class members. Ask them to find two other people who have the same phrase that they have, and, as a group, to decide: (1) how today's text teaches this truth, (2) how I've seen this truth in my own life, and (3) how this truth should affect the way I live.

After five minutes, ask class members to share responses with everyone in the class. If class members wish, they may express particular prayer requests or commitments based on this discussion. Close the class session by leading the group in singing "Great Is Thy Faithfulness," or by listening to a recording of it before your closing prayer.

Let's Talk It Over

The questions on this page are designed to encourage review of the lesson Scriptures and to promote discussion of the lesson by the class. The answers provided are only discussion starters. Let your class talk it over from there.

1. The Jews asked, "Wherein shall we return?" (Malachi 3:7). People today ask, "What's wrong with the way I live? Why shouldn't I go to Heaven?" How should we answer them?

Nearly two thousand years after the gospel of grace was first proclaimed, people are still inclined to think that their good works will gain them a place in Heaven. The non-Christian who is honest, hard-working, fair, and generous finds it difficult to understand why these traits are not enough to earn eternal life. We must show such persons that God's holy nature makes it impossible for Him to overlook any sin. Only moral perfection could earn any person a place in Heaven, and even the most upstanding individual must admit to falling short of such perfection. So the answer to, "What's wrong with the way I live?" is, "You are not good enough for Heaven." But Jesus Christ *is* good enough, and His perfect sacrifice opens a way for us—a way of grace.

2. What are some ways in which people today are guilty of robbing God?

Since all that we possess belongs to God, we rob Him whenever we use anything in a selfish, evil way, rather than employing it for His glory. For example, we rob God by the way we use our bodies. When we abuse them with drugs, alcohol, gluttony, or overwork, or when we dedicate them to the pursuit of unbridled pleasure, we fail to glorify Him with our bodies (see 1 Corinthians 6:19, 20). We also rob God by misusing our time. Every second we live belongs to Him, and we should acknowledge His ownership by prayerful use of our time (see Psalm 90:12). And of course, we rob God when we use our money carelessly. It is important that we keep in mind that all of our financial resources—not merely what we put into the offering plate at church—belong to God and must be used in a way that will please Him.

3. God has promised His faithful stewards that He will open the windows of Heaven and pour out a blessing on them. Why is this an especially appealing promise?

When it was originally given, this promise spoke of abundant rain that would contribute to a bountiful harvest. We can all appreciate what rain can do to a parched field, garden, or lawn. It quickly transforms brown, withering plants into green, growing ones. We are reminded that if we are faithful to God, He will refresh the dryness of our souls and make us grow again if we have been stagnant. Also, the idea that God *pours* out His blessings is encouraging. It has often been stated that no one can outgive God. He responds to our small sacrifices of money, time, and effort by pouring out good things upon us.

4. Farmers in Bible times had little control over the success or failure of their crops. They should have recognized that they were dependent on God for an abundant harvest. How does this apply to modern farmers?

Today's farmers have access to improved seed, a vast array of pesticides and herbicides, and many labor-saving machines. But they are still very much at the mercy of the weather conditions. Drought remains a danger in this twentieth century, as it was in Bible times. Floods and destructive winds exist today, as they did then. Farmers and those who depend on the labors of farmers (and that includes us all) should be inclined to look heavenward for God's blessings on the agricultural enterprise. Does a successful harvest mean that God is pleased with us? Does crop failure signify that God is punishing us? The answer is "not necessarily" in either case. But we should be alert when droughts and floods do occur and see if God is trying to get our attention.

5. Like those described in Malachi 3:16 who "feared the Lord [and] spake often one to another," we Christians often speak with one another. What can we do to make our talk more spiritually helpful?

Perhaps it will help if we make it a practice to ask certain questions: "How is your faith doing?" "Have you been having a good personal devotional time?" "Are there any temptations with which you have been struggling?" "What kind of prayers may I offer on your behalf?" Such questions may seem a bit personal. However, if we are to fulfill our duty of edifying one another (Romans 14:19; 15:2), we must be more open with one another about our struggles.

Winter Quarter, 1997-98

God's People in a Troubled World

Special Features

Lessons

Unit 1: God's Love in a Troubled World

Unit 2: Hope for God's People

Unit 3: Endurance of God's People

The Gospel of Action (Mark)

Unit 1: Early Ministry of Jesus

About these lessons

These studies are based on passages from the letters of 1 John, 1 and 2 Peter, and Jude. They focus on the struggles faced by first-century Christians, but they also highlight the God-given resources that are still available to followers of Jesus today, no matter how troubled our world may be.

Dec 7

Dec 14

Dec 21

Dec 28

Jan 4

Jan 11

Jan 18

Jan 25

Feb 1

Feb 8

Feb 15

Feb 22

Mar 1

Quarterly Quiz

The questions on this page may be used in several ways: as a pretest at the beginning of the quarter; as a review at the end of the quarter; or as a review after each lesson. The questions are based on the Scripture text of each lesson (King James Version). ***The answers are on page 119.***

Lesson 1

1. "If we say that we have _____ with him, and walk in _____, we lie, and do not the truth." *1 John 1:6*
2. John says that we can know that we know the Lord, if we (read His Word, keep His commandments, live by faith). *1 John 2:3*

Lesson 2

1. What does John say is the message that "ye heard from the beginning"? *1 John 3:11*
2. What Old Testament character does John use as an illustration of *not* loving others? *1 John 3:12*
3. What is the evidence that we have passed from death to life? *1 John 3:14*

Lesson 3

1. Who said these words: "Joseph . . . fear not to take unto thee Mary thy wife"? *Matthew 1:20*
2. John says that if our love is made perfect, we will have boldness in the day of _____. *1 John 4:17*

Lesson 4

1. "This is the victory that overcometh the world, even our _____." *1 John 5:4*
2. John says that Jesus came by ____ and _____. *1 John 5:6*

Lesson 5

1. Peter tells Christians to rejoice that they no longer have to face trials. T/F *1 Peter 1:6, 7*
2. Peter says that (prophets, priests, kings) "inquired and searched diligently" concerning the subject of salvation. *1 Peter 1:10*

Lesson 6

1. "As newborn _____, desire the sincere _____ of the word, that ye may _____ thereby." *1 Peter 2:2*
2. Peter calls Christians a _____ generation, a ____ priesthood, a ____ nation, and a _____ people. *1 Peter 2:9*

Lesson 7

1. How many were "saved by water" in the ark? *1 Peter 3:20*
2. Baptism involves the answer of a ___ ___ toward God. *1 Peter 3:21*

3. Peter told his readers not to be surprised at the trial they would undergo. T/F *1 Peter 4:12*

Lesson 8

1. What two words does Peter use to describe himself: teacher and apostle, elder and witness, or laborer and servant? *1 Peter 5:1*
2. What kind of person does God resist? *1 Peter 5:5*
3. What figure does Peter use to describe the devil? *1 Peter 5:8*

Lesson 9

1. God's power has given us "all things that pertain unto ____ and ____." *2 Peter 1:3*.
2. Name the eight qualities that Peter desires Christians to add to their lives. *2 Peter 1:5-7*
3. Peter's writings consisted of truths never before heard by his readers. T/F *2 Peter 1:12*

Lesson 10

1. Whom does Peter call a "preacher of righteousness"? *2 Peter 2:5*
2. What two cities are used as an example of God's judgment upon sin? *2 Peter 2:6*
3. Peter describes the false teachers as "wells without ____." *2 Peter 2:17*.

Lesson 11

1. In the last days, writes Peter, (dreamers, prophets, scoffers) will come. *2 Peter 3:3*
2. God is not willing that any should _____. *2 Peter 3:9*
3. What did Peter say will come as a "thief in the night"? *2 Peter 3:10*

Lesson 12

1. Jude exhorts his readers to (lay down their lives, contend for the faith, be of one mind). *Jude 3*
2. We are to keep ourselves in the ___ of ___. *Jude 21*

Lesson 13

1. From what town did Jesus travel to be baptized? *Mark 1:9*
2. Where did the Spirit lead Jesus to be tempted? *Mark 1:12*
3. Name the four disciples whom Jesus called by the Sea of Galilee. *Mark 1:16-20*

Standing Strong in Troubled Times

by Johnny Pressley

WHY DO BAD THINGS HAPPEN to good people?" This is one of the most perplexing questions of human existence. For ages people have faced all manner of suffering and hardship, and the common response has often been, "Why?" However, the focus of Scripture is not upon why bad things happen to good people, but upon how people should live in a world that is filled with trouble.

The theme for this quarter's study is "God's People in a Troubled World." Each lesson is designed to show students how God wants them to deal with situations in life that are undesirable or difficult. The texts selected for study are drawn from the latter portion of the New Testament—1 John, 1 and 2 Peter, and Jude. These books are commonly referred to as part of the "general epistles" (in contrast to the "prison epistles" or the "pastoral epistles" of 1 and 2 Timothy and Titus). The greatest value of this study will not be found in the accurate portrayal of our troubled world, but in the Biblical guidelines for how to live peacefully in the midst of life's storms.

Standing Strong in God's Love

The first unit of four lessons will use the epistle of 1 John to develop the theme of "God's Love in a Troubled World." The three epistles known as 1, 2, and 3 John were written by the apostle John, who also wrote the Gospel bearing his name and the book of Revelation. The apostle John was well qualified to write about trouble, especially that which is unique to the church. As one of the original twelve apostles, John witnessed the opposition that Jesus faced at the hands of the Jewish religious leaders. Of all the twelve, only John stood at the foot of the cross and watched Jesus die. As the longest surviving apostle (dying somewhere near the end of the first century), John was acquainted with the martyr's death of his apostolic partners. For over sixty years, he guided the church as it struggled with mounting persecution from without and destructive heresies from within.

For the apostle John, the key to standing strong in one's faith in the midst of hardships is to meditate upon the love of God. John speaks of the love of God from the perspective of one who has explored it to the fullest. In the Gospel of

John he is the disciple "whom Jesus loved" (John 13:23; 19:26; 21:7, 20). There was apparently a bond of friendship between them that surpassed what the other disciples had come to experience. John knew the benefits of having a loving relationship with Christ. Herein lies the strength Christians need to deal with the troubled situations they will face in life.

Our four lessons from 1 John will demonstrate practical ways to live within the love of God. **Lesson 1** ("Living in God's Light") will use 1 John 1 and 2 to show that to develop a loving relationship with God, we must "walk in the light" rather than in the darkness. We cannot expect to get close to a God of light and holiness until we become a holy people who honestly confess that we have sinned, and then work aggressively to change our conduct.

Lesson 2 ("Living in God's Love") will show from 1 John 3 that to maintain a loving relationship with God, we must share the love that we have received from God with others around us. The genuineness of our words of love for the invisible God can be tested by the way we treat the human image of God that we see on a daily basis.

The point of **Lesson 3** ("Celebrating God's Love"), taken from 1 John 4, is that to truly understand and appreciate the love of God, we must observe how it was manifested to us through Jesus Christ, particularly in His death at Calvary. **Lesson 4** ("Conquering Through Faith in Christ") will complete this unit with a lesson from 1 John 5. It emphasizes that a victorious Christian life must be firmly grounded upon faith in Jesus Christ as the Son of God.

Standing Strong in Christian Hope

"Hope for God's People" is the theme of the second unit of four lessons, all taken from the epistle of 1 Peter. The two epistles known as 1 and 2 Peter were written by the apostle Peter— the man who was generally the "spokesman" among the apostles. With John, Peter shared an insider's view of the troubles faced by Jesus throughout His ministry as well as those experienced by the early church. Peter himself faced perilous times throughout the early chapters of the book of Acts, being arrested and imprisoned on more than one occasion (Acts 4:1-22; 5:17-

42). According to early church tradition, Peter eventually died a martyr's death by being crucified upside down.

Peter's purpose for writing 1 Peter was to warn his readers of a growing wave of persecution against the church, which eventually manifested itself in imperial edicts from Rome as well as a general hostility against the church within various communities. The emphasis in 1 Peter is twofold: how to live in such a way that your ungodly neighbors will have no solid basis on which to criticize you, and how to deal with persecution should it happen. Thus the epistle is more than just a doctrinal treatise; it is filled with practical guidelines that possess just as much relevance today as they did in Peter's day.

For Peter, the key to enduring troubled times is to focus upon our hope for the future through Jesus Christ. Peter understood that in a sinful world that is hostile to God and His will, Christians are "strangers and pilgrims" (1 Peter 2:11). The "treasures" that are valued by the world no longer have any appeal to Christians, for such riches cannot compare to the eternal inheritance awaiting the followers of Jesus (1 Peter 1:3, 4). We can remain strong and victorious, even when property and life are taken from us, as long as we maintain our "lively hope" (1 Peter 1:3).

The nature of our hope according to 1 Peter 1 will be developed in **Lesson 5** ("Living in Hope"). Here we will consider what makes our hope in Christ such a precious possession. **Lesson 6** ("Becoming God's People") will use 1 Peter 2 to challenge the church to live up to its divine calling. Peter uses several Old Testament descriptions of the people of God (Israel) to illustrate in a very practical way what our daily lifestyle and mission should be as today's people of God (the church).

Lesson 7 ("Hope in Suffering With Christ") will be drawn from portions of 1 Peter 3 and 4, and will call attention to the primary purpose of Peter's epistle. Peter offers counsel on how to confront the upcoming "fiery trial" (1 Peter 4:12), and points those who suffer to the example set by Jesus when He also suffered.

Lesson 8 ("Living in Humility") will focus upon 1 Peter 5, which concludes Peter's letter. It is a glowing testimony to the transforming power of Christ that this beautiful chapter on humble service was written by a man who was at one time outspoken, strong-willed, and often misguided. After three and a half years of observing Jesus and some thirty years of ministry in the church, Peter well understood that the spirit of humility is the Christian's source of power in the midst of troubled times.

Standing Strong on Biblical Truth

While our hearts are to be filled with God's love and hope, our minds are to be grounded in God's truth. The necessity of sound doctrine within the church is the theme that will be developed in our final unit of four lessons, "Endurance of God's People." Our lesson texts will be taken from the apostle Peter's second epistle and from the little epistle of Jude.

The Biblical writer Jude was one of four half-brothers of Jesus (Matthew 13:55). He is mentioned as one of those who joined in prayer in Jerusalem following Jesus' ascension (Acts 1:14). We can only speculate regarding Jude's years of ministry in the church. However, we know for certain that he was strongly committed to the inspired teachings established by the apostles (Jude 3, 17)—a sentiment also expressed by Peter (2 Peter 1:16-21; 3:2). It should become readily evident why 2 Peter and Jude have been linked together in this unit of study. Not only do these writings share a common interest in certain key doctrinal issues (such as the problem of false teachers and the second coming of Christ), but both epistles affirm that the key to standing strong in troubled times is a firm commitment to the truth found in Jesus.

Lesson 9 ("Confirming Our Calling") will use 2 Peter 1 to develop a theme that is prominent throughout both of Peter's epistles—godliness. God expects His people to practice at all times a holy lifestyle appropriate for their claim to serve a holy God. Such godly living is learned by giving careful attention to godly truth.

The issue of false teachers and their influence is raised in **Lesson 10** ("Rejecting False Teachings"). Here our study from 2 Peter 2 will show why false teachers constitute such a serious threat to Christians and to the church. **Lesson 11** ("Believing in the Promise") will use 2 Peter 3 to illustrate how easily an essential doctrine like the second coming of Christ can be mishandled and ridiculed by "scoffers," and why it is important that we regularly go back and review what the Bible actually says.

The final lesson of this unit of study ("Keeping the Faith") will bring this series of lessons to a fitting conclusion. Our text from Jude will remind us of our duty to take a bold stand for the faith that was "once delivered unto the saints" (Jude 3) by the apostles.

God's people are not exempt from the troubles of this life. But we have an advantage that the world does not possess or acknowledge. We can endure whatever hardships come our way without being defeated, when we stand strong in the love, hope, and truth that God provides.

Flip That Switch!

by Terry A. Clark

THE GUIDE SAID THAT WE were more than a quarter of a mile underground, in a part of the cave called the "cathedral room." Our tour group was awed by the grandeur of that which our eyes beheld. Then the guide turned out the lights!

The utter darkness was fascinating for a moment. Before long, however, it became smothering and claustrophobic. I heard the woman behind me whisper something about a panic attack. The guide said, "And now folks, here's the best part of my day." With that, he flipped the switch and the room was again engulfed in light.

It is impossible to measure God's experiences the way we normally do, but the first Christmas must have been one of His greatest days. Man's sin had sentenced him to live in utter darkness. When God sent His own Son to be the Light of the world, He scattered the darkness, forever destroying its power. In the first unit of this quarter's study, you will see God at work dispelling the darkness. Through Jesus He has placed us in the spotlight of His wonderful love.

Light and Love

Is there any doubt that we live in troubled times? Listening to the evening news or reading the newspaper is discouraging. The headlines are usually enough to nauseate us. But we who are God's children have a different perspective. We have the grand privilege of telling the world that in God there "is no darkness at all" (1 John 1:5). The blood of Jesus His Son "cleanseth us from all sin" (1 John 1:7). His forgiveness purifies us "from all unrighteousness" (1 John 1:9). Notice how many times that little word *all* appears. God deals with our sin completely. That must cause something of a panic attack in Hell!

God calls us to live in His light, and to proclaim that light to those who live in darkness. My greatest joys in the ministry have not centered on building buildings or speaking before vast audiences. The greatest joy has been seeing people lifted out of the depths of sin's darkness and delivered to God's radiant light.

Love has brought us into the light. "How great is the love the Father has lavished on us" (1 John 3:1, *New International Version*). The Father's love placed Jesus in the manger and on the cross. He did that to "destroy the works of the devil" (1 John 3:8). We often think of that from a broad, sweeping perspective. I prefer to think of it on a personal level.

Do you remember the serial murderer Jeffrey Dahmer? Shortly before his death he professed faith in Christ and was baptized into Him in a prison whirlpool. After his murder I wrote an article for my local newspaper expressing my confidence in Dahmer's presence in Heaven, providing that his conversion had been genuine. I thought my article was a great statement of faith and hope for even the worst of sinners. Instead, my phone rang off the wall with protests! People asked if I had lost my mind. I explained countless times: God loved Jeffrey Dahmer. Jesus died for Jeffrey Dahmer. At his baptism the old Jeffrey Dahmer was buried, and a new Jeffrey Dahmer arose from the watery grave, alive in Christ—sins gone "as far as the east is from the west" (Psalm 103:12).

I thanked God that one courageous man walked into prison to tell Jeffrey Dahmer that God loved him, wanted him to be saved, and had given His own Son to accomplish that. Living in God's love demands that we love even the unlovely. Jeffrey Dahmer was hard to love and easy to hate. But God gives us no choice about loving. To fail to love is to be a "murderer" (1 John 3:15).

God calls His people to put their love to work, not just speak the words (1 John 3:17, 18). God did not merely tell us that He loved us. He acted on our behalf, giving the most sacrificial of all gifts—His Son (John 3:16; 1 John 3:16). The lesson immediately preceding Christmas focuses on God's intentional act of giving Jesus to save us from our sins (Matthew 1:21). Because He did that, we must "love one another" (1 John 4:7).

Faith and Obedience

The final lesson of the first unit may seem out of place with the others, yet there is a natural connection. This lesson provides the simple test of a person's relationship with God: "He that hath the Son hath life; and he that hath not the Son of God hath not life" (1 John 5:12).

Do you know people who don't know Jesus? I'm sure you do. They are your friends, neighbors, relatives, and co-workers. Will your faith in Christ manifest itself in obedience to Him in the area of evangelism? Sharing your faith is love in action. Flip the switch! Change a life! Proclaim God's love to a troubled world!

An Inside Look at Hope

by J. Michael Shannon

DANTE, IN HIS EPIC *INFERNO*, imagines that over the gates of Hell is this inscription: "Abandon hope, all ye who enter here." It does not surprise us that Hell is a place without hope, but we must also consider that for people who have no hope, this life can be a hell. There is no success in this life without hope. More important, there is not even survival without hope.

Hope is much more than just a wish thrown into the air. It is more than simple optimism or positive thinking. A little child was once asked his definition of hope. He said, "It's wishing for something you know ain't gonna happen." That is not hope at all, much less genuine hope. Genuine hope is a Biblical conviction founded on the promises of God. Hope depends on having something to look forward to. With Christ we always have that.

The Barriers to Genuine Hope

Why do so many people lose hope? There are many reasons but two stand out. One is misplaced priorities. People are disappointed because life does not turn out the way they wanted. They desire items that they never should have desired in the first place. They pursue values that are contradictory to the values of the gospel. If we continue to nurture ideas or actions that do not produce hope, then we should not be surprised if hope eludes us.

Another reason people lose hope is misplaced confidence. People often assume that the Bible promises a trouble-free life. Nowhere does the Bible make such an offer; in fact, it promises precisely the opposite. Peter warns us not to be "surprised at the painful trial you are suffering, as though something strange were happening to you" (1 Peter 4:12, *New International Version*). We might be prone to ask, as did the late humorist Erma Bombeck, "If life is a bowl of cherries, why am I always in the pits?" The Bible never promises the bowl of cherries.

There are several different types of suffering. First, there is what we might call natural suffering. These are the troubles that come our way simply because we live on planet earth. Earth is not Heaven. It suffers the effects of the fall, just as man does (Romans 8:20, 21); therefore many "dangers, toils and snares" exist. Christians do not escape these, but they have access to the resources for enduring them.

Second, there is self-inflicted suffering. This is the trouble that comes our way because we have been foolish and have made poor choices. None of us is all-wise, so all of us will undergo this kind of suffering. If we obeyed God's wisdom, we would have less of this type of suffering. Yet, even when we have chosen foolishly, God's grace will forgive us and provide strength to choose correctly in future circumstances.

Third, there is Christian suffering. This is the suffering that many have willingly endured for the cause of Christ. They are suffering not because they are outside of God's will, but because they are in it. Here is where Christians "are partakers of Christ's sufferings" (1 Peter 4:13).

We live in times that often seem hopeless and disheartening. It is hard to have hope after reading the newspaper or watching a television news program. Many, desperate for some glimmer of hope, place their trust in the wrong person or wrong philosophy of life. They turn to any number of "experts" who claim to have the answers, yet none can deliver. Some even deliver the opposite of what they promise.

In the play *Zorba the Greek*, the main character reveals his philosophy of life to a young friend. He says, "I fear nothing, I hope for nothing, I am free." Does a lack of hope free us? Does genuine hope enslave us? A person with no hope is imprisoned by his cynicism. Genuine hope liberates.

The Source of Genuine Hope

How do we find genuine hope? We find it only through Jesus. No doubt you expected to see that in this essay. The statement is true enough, but we must go further. Exactly how does Jesus give us hope?

Jesus' teachings give hope. Look at His many timeless and practical teachings that are recorded in the New Testament. From the Sermon on the Mount to His words at His ascension, Jesus gave His hearers hope for this life and the life to come.

Jesus' example gives hope. Look at how he approached life with a spiritual optimism. "For the joy that was set before him" (Hebrews 12:2), He could endure suffering and ridicule. He faced death, aware of His Father's purpose for Him (John 10:17, 18), and committed His spirit to the Father's care (Luke 23:46).

Jesus' sacrifice gives hope. By solving our sin problem, Jesus removed the biggest negative influence in our lives. The old gospel song reminds us, "My hope is built on nothing less than Jesus' blood and righteousness." Those who have never committed themselves to the Christ of the cross could retitle that song, "My hope is built on nothing."

Jesus' resurrection gives hope. What is the most fearsome thing we can imagine? It is death. From our perspective it seems so final. But Jesus shows us that even death can be defeated. Alexander Campbell was hosting the skeptic Robert Owen as they prepared for their upcoming debate. Campbell gave Owen a tour of his farm and asked the skeptic, "Do you have any fear in death?" Owen replied that he did not. Campbell then asked, "Then do you have any hope in death?" Owen admitted that he did not. Campbell pointed to an ox passively munching on hay and swishing flies and said, "Then you are no better off than that ox, for he neither fears nor hopes in death."

Jesus' promise gives hope. Think about the promise that He will prepare a place for us and return to take us home (John 14:2, 3). It is a great comfort to know that Jesus is taking our eternal destiny personally. He is handling all the arrangements, and He will be in charge of our homecoming.

If you were watching a video replay of your favorite football team winning a championship game, you would not mind seeing all the team's missed plays and fumbles. Why? Because you already know the score! We can be confident in this life, because we already know its outcome. Read the Scriptures and you will see the "grand finale." "The kingdoms of this world are become the kingdoms of our Lord and of his Christ; and he shall reign for ever and ever" (Revelation 11:15). Peter says that God "has given us new birth into a living hope through the resurrection of Jesus Christ from the dead" (1 Peter 1:3, *New International Version*). It is a living hope because our Savior is living. The Bible is a book of hope from beginning to end.

The Power of Genuine Hope

Hope will not drop into our lives unexpectedly. Hope, like other great virtues, is developed. Hope grows as we grow in knowledge and wisdom. With patience we will find that hope has indeed become a part of the very fabric of our lives.

Some people take their greatest trial and transform it into victory by letting God use it. A former drug addict uses his experience to help others. A person like Charles Colson takes his prison sentence and turns it into a ministry. This should not surprise us, because God has worked this way in the past time and again. God took the shame and outrage of the cross of Christ, and turned it into an instrument of salvation for the world.

There is something special about those who maintain hope in the midst of difficult circumstances. Such hope is a marvelous witness to the world of the power of the Christian message. Think of how impressed the Philippian jailer was when Paul and Silas sang in prison!

Of course, we do not want to take this too far. We should not become spiritual masochists who invite suffering. The truth is that we do not have to invite it, for it will come anyway. What we want to do is to keep the "big picture" in mind. If we can look forward to the positive, powerful results of suffering, then we can endure the process. The birth of a baby brings much pain to the mother. Sometimes, immediately following the birth, a mother will vow never to go through it again; however, usually she changes her mind and has another child. The pain passes, the beauty remains. The joys of eternity put the pain of this life into proper perspective.

Perhaps you have heard the story of the little boy at the pet store, deciding which dog he would buy. He pointed to the pup furiously wagging his tail and said, "I want him—the one with the happy ending." We all want a happy ending. Thanks to Jesus, we know that one is waiting. Thanks to Jesus, there is hope.

Answers to Quarterly Quiz on page 114

Lesson 1—1. fellowship, darkness. 2. keep His commandments. **Lesson 2**—1. love one another. 2. Cain. 3. loving the brethren. **Lesson 3**—1. the angel of the Lord. 2. judgment. **Lesson 4**—1. faith. 2. water, blood. **Lesson 5**—1. false. 2. prophets. **Lesson 6**—1. babes, milk, grow. 2. chosen, royal, holy, peculiar. **Lesson 7**—1. eight. 2. good conscience. 3. true. **Lesson 8**—1. elder and witness. 2. proud. 3. a roaring lion. **Lesson 9**—1. life, godliness. 2. faith, virtue, knowledge, temperance, patience, godliness, brotherly kindness, charity. 3. false. **Lesson 10**—1. Noah. 2. Sodom and Gomorrah. 3. water. **Lesson 11**—1. scoffers. 2. perish. 3. the day of the Lord. **Lesson 12**—1. contend for the faith. 2. love, God. **Lesson 13**—1. Nazareth of Galilee. 2. into the wilderness. 3. Peter, Andrew, James, John.

Drawing From the Well of Truth

by Mark B. Reed

WHY IS IT THAT WHEN OUR WORLD talks about religious truth, the meaning of the word *truth* suddenly changes?

We examine a historical record and credit it as right or wrong. No one says that a historical fact like the assassination of John F. Kennedy is both true and false. The details of the case might be disputed, but everyone agrees that a chain of historical events led to his death—events that actually happened.

In the courtroom judges and juries do not hand down ambiguous verdicts saying, "We feel that the defendant is guilty in the eyes of his accusers, but innocent in the eyes of his friends. So we suggest that each person make up his own mind, as his heart leads. And the defendant will be guilty to him or her, or innocent to him or her, as each chooses to believe." How absurd! The defendant is guilty or not guilty, based on the evidence—the truth.

However, when it comes to moral and religious truth, our society takes the relativity route: whatever seems good to you—no hard facts—no absolutes. The word *truth* suddenly changes into some mystical abstraction that cannot be defined or relied upon.

The Bible rejects the notion that religious truth is relative. It declares that truth by definition is absolute and available through the one true God.

A Thirsty World

Never has the world been so desperate for truth and yet so blind to its presence—except perhaps the day Christ died. People are thirsty, yet they walk by the well of truth and head for the saloon, looking for something that will kill the pain, something that will make them happy. Instead they come away drunk, their mouths bitter, their spirits still dissatisfied.

In his two letters Peter warns against false teachers who exploit students, doctoring up the truth until it tastes more palatable—the "new and improved" truth with more zest and better taste! They offer synthetic truth, and people throng around them for a sip. Our culture's fascination with the spirit world, eastern mysticism, the "health and wealth" gospel, and many cults attests to this thirst for truth. People want a code by which to live, a standard in which to trust. Yet without a core of absolute truth, they are left with no foundation.

Daily Nourishment

Truth is more than a courtroom verdict or a historical statistic. It is a life-giving force. It sustains mental and spiritual life. The ability to think on truth is in itself a refreshing truth.

Peter reminds us to cling tightly to the truth Christ has given. If we fail to review it and remind one another of it, we will drift from truth into near truths and from near truths to half-truths and from half-truths to lies. And the whole process will seem logical.

Peter says that through God's promises, which are truth, we commune with God and take on His nature (2 Peter 1:4). Those who build on the truth of God's promises grow in the qualities listed in 2 Peter 1:5-7—faith, virtue, knowledge, temperance, patience, godliness, brotherly kindness, and charity (love). Those who doubt God's truth (Peter calls them scoffers) rely on their own judgment, experience, and natural instincts. They forget that God's truth is unchanging, while their version of truth changes as their experience, feelings, and instincts change.

Drawing Others to the Well of Truth

The best way to confront a lie is to teach the truth. Every time we state a truth of God, we nourish ourselves and those who hear it. No matter how simple the truth, we must keep on speaking it to ourselves, to our children, to the woman at the coffee shop, to the other fathers at the soccer game, to every available ear.

We can also help others by demonstrating the truth of truth—not with arrogance, but with humble and consistent obedience to the principles of God's Word, especially when it would be much easier to doubt or deny the Word. For example, one of my co-workers, a Christian, told me about his financial problems, but affirmed his faith in God's provision. He said that his family had agreed that even during this financial crisis, they would continue giving fifteen percent of their income to Christ's kingdom work. What a testimony to the truth!

Both Peter and Jude predicted that an age of falsehood and scoffing would come. It has, but the situation is not hopeless. The Bible declares that God's truth will continue and that lies will fade away. And in the end, His truth will be known and vindicated before every eye and ear.

Living in God's Light

December 7
Lesson 1

DEVOTIONAL READING: John 1:1-14.

LESSON SCRIPTURE: 1 John 1:1—2:11.

PRINTED TEXT: 1 John 1:5-10; 2:3-11.

1 John 1:5-10

5 This then is the message which we have heard of him, and declare unto you, that God is light, and in him is no darkness at all.

6 If we say that we have fellowship with him, and walk in darkness, we lie, and do not the truth:

7 But if we walk in the light, as he is in the light, we have fellowship one with another, and the blood of Jesus Christ his Son cleanseth us from all sin.

8 If we say that we have no sin, we deceive ourselves, and the truth is not in us.

9 If we confess our sins, he is faithful and just to forgive us our sins, and to cleanse us from all unrighteousness.

10 If we say that we have not sinned, we make him a liar, and his word is not in us.

1 John 2:3-11

3 And hereby we do know that we know him, if we keep his commandments.

4 He that saith, I know him, and keepeth not his commandments, is a liar, and the truth is not in him.

5 But whoso keepeth his word, in him verily is the love of God perfected: hereby know we that we are in him.

6 He that saith he abideth in him ought himself also so to walk, even as he walked.

7 Brethren, I write no new commandment unto you, but an old commandment which ye had from the beginning. The old commandment is the word which ye have heard from the beginning.

8 Again, a new commandment I write unto you, which thing is true in him and in you: because the darkness is past, and the true light now shineth.

9 He that saith he is in the light, and hateth his brother, is in darkness even until now.

10 He that loveth his brother abideth in the light, and there is none occasion of stumbling in him.

11 But he that hateth his brother is in darkness, and walketh in darkness, and knoweth not whither he goeth, because that darkness hath blinded his eyes.

GOLDEN TEXT: If we walk in the light, as he is in the light, we have fellowship one with another, and the blood of Jesus Christ his Son cleanseth us from all sin.—1 John 1:7.

God's People in a Troubled World
Unit 1: God's Love in a Troubled World
(Lessons 1-4)

Lesson Aims

After this lesson, a student should be able to:
1. Explain what it means to walk in the light in terms of our relationship with both God and others.
2. List some conditions that oppose the light.
3. Suggest one specific step to take to shine God's light in the world.

Lesson Outline

INTRODUCTION
    A. Guided by the Light
    B. Rejecting the Light
    C. Lesson Background
  I. SOURCE OF LIGHT (1 John 1:5-7)
    A. Message Heard (v. 5)
    B. Fellowship With Christ (vv. 6, 7)
      Light That Endures
 II. SUBSTANCE OF LIGHT (1 John 1:8-10)
    A. Sin Extinguishes Light (v. 8)
    B. Sin Erased by Jesus (vv. 9, 10)
III. SERVING THE LIGHT (1 John 2:3-11)
    A. Keeping Christ's Word (vv. 3-6)
    B. A New Commandment (vv. 7, 8)
    C. Light Shines Through Love (vv. 9-11)
      Blinded by Darkness
CONCLUSION
    A. Letting Your Light Shine
    B. Prayer
    C. Thought To Remember

The visual for Lesson 1 found in the visuals packet challenges us to "walk in the light." It is shown on page 125.

Introduction

A. Guided by the Light

Several years ago a biologist spent several months doing research to discover why tiny sea turtles, once they are hatched, invariably make their way to the sea where they can live, rather than toward land where they will perish. His research indicated that the newly hatched turtles cannot hear and have no sense of taste, and that their eyesight is very poor. He finally concluded that they were drawn to the sea by light, which they were able to discern in spite of their poor vision. Light directed the turtles in their journey to their natural home.

When Jesus called Himself the "light of the world" (John 8:12), He used a metaphor that offers several possibilities of application. Certainly one would be that He provides direction to guide us to abundant and eternal life.

B. Rejecting the Light

Another illustration suggests a different application. It is said that hundreds of birds die nightly by beating their wings against the light in the upraised hand of the Statue of Liberty in New York harbor. Nevertheless, the light continues to shine. Many foolish critics destroy themselves by hurling their lives against Jesus, the light of the world, and His Word. These critics die and fade into oblivion, but the light of Christ continues to shine.

C. Lesson Background

It is generally agreed that John, the "beloved apostle," wrote the three epistles that bear his name. John was probably one of the two disciples of John the Baptist who listened to the Baptist's testimony and "followed Jesus" (John 1:37). First John was probably written between A.D. 90 and 95, after John wrote his Gospel and before he wrote the book of Revelation.

In this epistle John was writing against a false teaching or philosophy known as Gnosticism. Gnostics claimed to have special esoteric (or secret) knowledge given by God (and given only to them). A major tenet of this group was that all matter is evil—a perspective that led to two different outgrowths of doctrine and practice. One group said that since all matter is evil, one ought to practice asceticism and isolate himself from the world. This often led to punishing the body, avoiding any physical pleasure, and practicing monasticism (living in isolation from others). A second group claimed that if all matter were evil, it was useless even to try to resist. One could indulge in any manner of evil as long as his spirit was right with God. It was against such teaching that John leveled the denunciations against continual sin that we see in this letter.

VISUALS FOR THESE LESSONS

The *Adult Visuals* packet contains classroom-size visuals designed for use with the lessons in the Winter Quarter. The packet is available from your supplier. Order No. 292.

This lesson will also reveal a tendency in John's writings to present spiritual lessons through the use of antithetical pairs (opposites). In 1 John 1:5-7 we read of light and darkness, which also appear in 2:8, 9. In 2:4 is the contrast between lying and truth, and in 2:10, 11, love and hatred are mentioned (see also 4:19, 20).

In the first four verses of 1 John (not in our printed text) are found three great Christian concepts to which John will turn repeatedly throughout his letter: eternal life, fellowship, and joy. All come through the light of the gospel of Christ, and all are interrelated. The fullness of Christian joy comes through the assurance of eternal life, and through fellowship with Jesus and with others of "like precious faith."

I. Source of Light
(1 John 1:5-7)

A. Message Heard (v. 5)

5. This then is the message which we have heard of him, and declare unto you, that God is light, and in him is no darkness at all.

The *message* John is talking about is one that *we have heard of him.* The *him* refers to Jesus, who was introduced in the previous verses as the "Word of life" that was "from the beginning" and was "manifested unto us" (vv. 1, 2). Christ was in the beginning with God and cooperated with the Father in the creation of everything (John 1:1-3; Colossians 1:16; Hebrews 1:1, 2), including *light* (Genesis 1:3). Thus Jesus is rightfully the source of the truth that *God is light,* both natural and spiritual. The antithesis between *light* and *darkness* is a favorite concept of John, used frequently in his Gospel (1:5; 3:19; 8:12; 11:9, 10; 12:35, 46).

B. Fellowship With Christ (vv. 6, 7)

6. If we say that we have fellowship with him, and walk in darkness, we lie, and do not the truth.

Fellowship involves sharing. When we follow what John and the other actual witnesses of the life of Christ have declared to us about Jesus and His will, we share Christ's love, joy, and salvation with these early Christian saints and also with people around us today who serve Jesus.

The Greek word translated *fellowship* is *koinonia,* meaning "to have in common." (The style of Greek in which the New Testament was written is called *koine* Greek, indicating that it was the common language of the populace.) The early church continued in fellowship (Acts 2:42) in many ways. They held their material goods in common and shared with others in need (Acts 2:44, 45; 4:32, 34-37). They shared the message

of salvation with others (Acts 8:4). They shared in the worship of prayer and praise with fellow Christians around the Lord's table; in fact, the Greek word rendered "communion" in 1 Corinthians 10:16 is the word *koinonia.* Paul also speaks of sharing in Christ's sufferings as a way to know Him (Philippians 3:10).

Walking in *darkness* refers to much more than just committing heinous sins such as adultery, robbery, and murder. It also means both not knowing what is right and not doing what is right in our daily lives. So we must study the Word of God to know the truth, and then live by it. To have fellowship with Christ we must saturate our minds with the account of Jesus' life in the Gospels. By doing so, we will know what He would have us to do in the situations that we confront. We need to consult Christ, rather than the delusions of this world, to help us with our daily problems and to provide the counsel that we need. We do this through the disciplined study of His Word and through prayer.

LIGHT THAT ENDURES

No one knows how long a lightbulb will last. Many of us have had the experience of installing several at the same time, and discovering that some burn out before others. The average lightbulb lasts from 750 to a 1000 hours. A notable exception to this is a lightbulb in the fire department at Livermore, California, that is said to have burned continuously since 1901!

Certainly it is frustrating when a lightbulb burns out, forcing us to walk in darkness until it can be replaced. In the spiritual world, the light from God never stops showing us the way. If we walk in darkness, it is because we choose to walk in darkness. When one thinks how easy it is to stumble in the dark, and how dangerous it is in the dark, one wonders that anyone would choose darkness over light. The light of God's wisdom and holiness shines brightly, and when we walk in that light we walk safely and with a real sense of security. No one can ever turn out

---

How to Say It

ASCETICISM. Uh-*set*-uh-sizz-um.
ESOTERIC. ess-oh-*tare*-ick.
GNOSTICISM. *Nahss*-tih-sizz-um.
GNOSTICS. *Nahss*-ticks.
KOINE (Greek). *koy*-nay.
KOINONIA (Greek). koy-no-*nee*-uh.
MONASTICISM. muh-*nass*-tuh-sizz-um.
PHOS (Greek). fohss.
SOCRATES. *Sock*-ruh-teez.

His light, but anyone can choose to ignore it and stumble through life. To do so is more than foolish; it is sin. —R. C. S.

7. But if we walk in the light, as he is in the light, we have fellowship one with another, and the blood of Jesus Christ his Son cleanseth us from all sin.

John acknowledges in this verse that even though we *walk in the light*, in fellowship with Christ, we may *sin*. In such an instance there is a way of forgiveness through the *blood of Jesus Christ*. This calls to mind the Biblical doctrine of atonement. This word, also found in Romans 5:11, is elsewhere translated by some form of the word "reconciliation." It is a term that looks at man as an enemy of God because of sin, but as reconciled to God through the blood of Christ shed on the cross for us.

The renowned Greek philosopher Socrates once said, "There may be a God who can be both just and merciful and still forgive man's sin, but I do not see how He can do it." In the wonderful plan of atonement called the gospel, God in His wisdom has accomplished that seeming impossibility. He has been just in justifying sinful man (Romans 3:26). He has reconciled us to Himself through Jesus (2 Corinthians 5:18). Only Jesus could do this, for He alone is the only begotten, sinless Son of God.

II. Substance of Light (1 John 1:8-10)

A. Sin Extinguishes Light (v. 8)

8. If we say that we have no sin, we deceive ourselves, and the truth is not in us.

We should keep in mind the Gnostic heresy that John was seeking to expose in this letter. As we saw under the Lesson Background, some of the Gnostics claimed that, if all matter is evil, there was no need to follow any kind of moral restraints. In their thinking, breaking God's Law did not matter. *Sin* was an irrelevant term.

It is obvious that such a teaching constituted a direct attack on the gospel message. We must recognize our sin before we can be saved. We are not in a position to receive good news until we understand the bad news of our spiritual condition. As Jesus put it, only the sick need the services of a physician (Matthew 9:12). A missionary to Japan once said that the most difficult task in converting people there was to explain the meaning of sin, because there was no word for the New Testament concept of sin in their language. Yet many so-called "good moral people" everywhere refuse to accept the fact of their guilt before God.

While one of the effects of light is to dispel darkness, it is also possible for the darkness of sin to extinguish light. When we sin, we separate ourselves from God. If we do not repent and confess our sin but continue in it, we not only extinguish the light of Christ from our lives, but we cease to be lights shining for Him. If we deny the seriousness of our condition, we will *deceive* no one but *ourselves*. It will be clear that *the truth is not in us*.

B. Sin Erased by Jesus (vv. 9, 10)

9. If we confess our sins, he is faithful and just to forgive us our sins, and to cleanse us from all unrighteousness.

We must understand and remember that John is writing to Christians as to how their *sins* may be forgiven—not to the unsaved. To truly *confess* we must be repentant of the evil we have done. Thus Peter told Simon the sorcerer to repent and pray if he was to have any hope of being forgiven of his covetousness for money and power (Acts 8:22).

10. If we say that we have not sinned, we make him a liar, and his word is not in us.

Again John emphasizes the blatant hypocrisy involved in attempting to live the Christian life while remaining on friendly terms with sin. Not only do we "deceive ourselves" (v. 8), but in regard to God, we *make him a liar*, since His Word is very clear that we have sinned (Romans 3:23). Christians do not boast of sinless perfection; they "glory" in the cross of Christ (Galatians 6:14), by whose power they are able to "sin less" as they mature.

III. Serving the Light (1 John 2:3-11)

A. Keeping Christ's Word (vv. 3-6)

3. And hereby we do know that we know him, if we keep his commandments.

Jesus had said, "If ye love me, keep my commandments" (John 14:15). *Commandments* is a plural noun both there and in this verse. Any imperative uttered by Jesus or by His apostles would be considered a commandment. However, Jesus taught that the greatest commandments are to love God and to love one another (Matthew 22:36-39).

4. He that saith, I know him, and keepeth not his commandments, is a liar, and the truth is not in him.

Once again John attacks the kind of hypocrisy against which he wrote so adamantly in chapter one. It is similar to the hypocrisy that James denounces of faith without works (James 2:14-17).

5, 6. But whoso keepeth his word, in him verily is the love of God perfected: hereby know we that we are in him. He that saith he abideth in him ought himself also so to walk, even as he walked.

The *love of God* is much more than mere feeling or emotionalism; it is an active, giving love, as John 3:16 makes plain. For that love to become mature or *perfected* in someone requires a life of active, faithful obedience to Christ. This is what the term *walk* implies. It covers all our activities at home, at work, and at leisure. It challenges us to ask whether people see our everyday conduct as a witness to Christ's message of salvation and His power to change lives. It is a favorite expression of both Paul, who uses it thirty-one times in his writings, and John, who uses it nine times in his epistles.

Verses 3-6 also address the question that is one of the main issues of 1 John: "How can one be sure of his salvation?" The phrase *hereby know we that we are in him* could apply either to what John has just written in verse 5 or to what he is about to write in verse 6. In either case, John emphasizes obedience (as he does in verse 3) as the means by which we can *know . . . that we are in him.*

B. A New Commandment
(vv. 7, 8)

7. Brethren, I write no new commandment unto you, but an old commandment which ye had from the beginning. The old commandment is the word which ye have heard from the beginning.

The word *beginning* probably refers to the beginning of the gospel with the life, death, and resurrection of Christ (although it could also refer to the beginning of a believer's walk with Christ). Over a half century had passed between Jesus' ministry and John's present exhortation, yet the commandments of Jesus were still valid. Though it is not spelled out here, the *old commandment* apparently was Christ's command to love one another. Jesus had said that by our love, all men will know that we are His disciples (John 13:35).

8. Again, a new commandment I write unto you, which thing is true in him and in you: because the darkness is past, and the true light now shineth.

John returns to the light-versus-darkness theme of 1:5-7. Jesus is the light of the world, but His followers must shine for Him in the darkness of a corrupt world. The Greek word for light, *phos*, is seen in the name of the chemical element *phosphorus*, which means "light-bearing." Christians are called to be "light-bearers"

for Christ, radiating His light in our daily lives. Light illuminates, so we should dispel error. Light guides, thus we should lead people to righteousness. Light attracts, therefore our lives should cause others to take a closer look at Jesus. If we are true reflections of Him, people will say of us:

> To me, 'twas not the truth you taught,
>   To you so plain, to me so dim,
> But when you came to me you brought
>   A sense of Him.
> And from your eyes He beckons me;
>   And from your life His love is shed
> 'Till I lose sight of you and see
>   The Christ instead.
>
> —Anonymous

C. Light Shines Through Love
(vv. 9-11)

9-11. He that saith he is in the light, and hateth his brother, is in darkness even until now. He that loveth his brother abideth in the light, and there is none occasion of stumbling in him. But he that hateth his brother is in darkness, and walketh in darkness, and knoweth not whither he goeth, because that darkness hath blinded his eyes.

To John, love manifested in kindness toward others is the main criterion of the Christian's walk *in the light.* In chapter 3 (vv. 11, 12) he illustrates this point by referring to Cain and Abel, and then challenges Christians to show compassion, not hatred, to needy brethren (vv. 16-18). If our expression of love is limited to words, it is not real love.

BLINDED BY DARKNESS

Years ago mules were used in the mines deep beneath the earth to transport the ore that was discovered. It was thought unkind to bring these animals to the surface to see the light in which they would never live nor work. So they were kept underground; they were fed there, worked there, and they died there. In the process, their handlers noticed an interesting thing. Eventually those mules, living in darkness, went blind.

visual for
lesson 1

John says that walking in spiritual darkness makes men spiritually blind. Someone has said, "Sin cuts the optic nerve of the soul." In our text one specific sin is named—hatred (1 John 2:9-11). Certainly other sins blind us as well. When we become blinded to the seriousness of sin, we eventually stop thinking of it as sin at all. We become blinded to the harm we do to others and blinded to the harm we do to ourselves. The longer we are kept from the light, the more serious is our spiritual blindness.

Physical blindness is a condition that likely no one would deliberately choose. Incredible as it seems, some choose to be blind spiritually. It is a tragic choice, for walking in spiritual darkness here leads to a place of eternal darkness.

—R. C. S.

Conclusion

The message of this lesson can be summarized in John's emphasis on the concept of light versus darkness. Christ is the light of the world, bringing truth, hope, love, and salvation to mankind. His followers are to radiate this light to others. We must not hide our light under a bushel. We must not let it go out, smothered by sin, or by lack of faith, dedication, or zeal. We must practice Christian charity to the needy, give generously to the church, and live honestly and morally before others. The only hope of the world is Christ, and we are His only help in taking the message of redemption to others throughout the world by means of personal evangelism.

A. Letting Your Light Shine

In Philippians 2:15 Paul urges his readers to "shine as lights" in the midst of a "crooked and perverse nation." The word for *lights* refers to heavenly luminaries. The *New International Version* translates it as "stars." Instead of being "movie" stars, Christians ought to be "moving" stars, beautifying the world by deeds of justice, mercy, and love wherever they go.

Most everyone is familiar with the story of how Henry Stanley, the British newspaper reporter, found the Christian missionary David Livingstone in darkest Africa, far removed from civilization. When he found him, he reportedly said, "Dr. Livingstone, I presume." But there was more to the story. On his return to London, the worldly Stanley told his colleagues that if he had stayed with Livingstone one day longer, he would have been compelled to become a Christian, though Livingstone had said nothing about Christianity to him. Livingstone's light was truly shining.

Some of the most dramatic moments in any courtroom trial occur when the witnesses are called to the stand to testify. They take an oath to tell "the truth, the whole truth, and nothing but the truth," and the reliability of their evidence determines the outcome of the case. Firsthand evidence carries the most weight. We possess the direct evidence of the witness of the apostles to the story and message of Christ. We must "take the stand" and witness for our Lord.

In 1891 a train company was being sued because a person had been killed at a train crossing. The plaintiff's lawyer interrogated the night watchman at the crossing. When asked if he was on duty, he responded with, "Yes, sir." "Did you have a lantern?" "Yes, sir." "Did you wave the lantern?" "Yes, sir." His testimony was so convincing that the plaintiff lost the case. Afterward, the president of the company congratulated the watchman on his testimony, telling him that it saved the company money and that he would be rewarded.

He then asked, "Weren't you nervous on the stand?" "Well, sir, I was a little afraid they would ask if my lantern was lit." Christians are just as hypocritical if their lights are not shining for the Lord.

B. Prayer

Father, thank You for sending Jesus to take away our sins. Help us to live for Him in our daily lives. We now confess our failures and surrender to You. May we walk in the light of Your Word. Amen.

C. Thought to Remember

"Let your light so shine before men, that they may see your good works, and glorify your Father which is in heaven" (Matthew 5:16).

Home Daily Bible Readings

Monday, Dec. 1—Living in the Light (1 John 1:1-10)
Tuesday, Dec. 2—To Obey Is to Love God (John 14:15-21)
Wednesday, Dec. 3—True Light Already Shining (1 John 2:7-11)
Thursday, Dec. 4—Be Merciful As God Is Merciful (Luke 6:32-38)
Friday, Dec. 5—Child to Be Called God's Son (Luke 1:26-38)
Saturday, Dec. 6—Christ Shines in the Darkness (John 1:1-13)
Sunday, Dec. 7—See the Salvation of God (Luke 3:1-6)

Learning by Doing

This page contains an alternate lesson plan emphasizing learning activities.
Classes desiring such student involvement will find these suggestions helpful.

Learning Goals

After the completion of this lesson, a student should be able to:

1. Explain what it means to walk in the light in terms of our relationship with both God and others.

2. List some conditions that oppose the light.

3. Suggest one specific step to take to shine God's light in the world.

Into the Lesson

In preparation for today's class, bring a flashlight, a candle, a match for lighting the candle, and a small bowl. Begin the lesson by holding up the flashlight. Ask, "What is the purpose of a flashlight? Why do we use a flashlight?"

Most students probably will say that we use a flashlight to show the way in the dark. However, a flashlight also can be used to warn others of danger, to signal for help, and to point others to a specific object or location.

Point out that we need a light only when it is dark. Our need for spiritual light emphasizes that we have limited understanding and also that we live in a sin-darkened world. In today's lesson we will see that God has provided the spiritual light we need so that we can live in a way that pleases Him.

Into the Word

Note that today's lesson is the first of four lessons based on 1 John. These lessons show how we should conduct ourselves as followers of Jesus while living in a troubled world. See the Lesson Background in the commentary for information on John's epistles.

John was fond of using contrasts to emphasize certain truths. In 1 John 1:5 we see his first contrast: light and darkness. Write "light" on the left side of a sheet of poster board or newsprint and "darkness" on the right side. Then ask your students to call out various contrasts that this pair symbolizes (this activity appears in the student book). Some suggested contrasts: God/Satan; right/wrong; life/death; joy/sorrow; righteousness/sin; build up/tear down. Note that positive benefits and blessings are associated with light, while all that is negative and destructive is associated with darkness.

As we "have fellowship" with God (1 John 1:6), we live in the light. Ask, "What does it

mean to have fellowship with God? How do we do this?" The key word is "walk" (v. 7). To have fellowship with God means to walk with Him. As we walk with Him, He gives us the light we need for each step. The lesson commentary on verse 6 gives some ideas on how we can have fellowship with God.

People of the light are to live (walk) in a certain way. In contrast, people of darkness also walk in a certain way. Direct your students to 1 John 1:5-10. Tell them to read the passage and to look for everything it says about what it means to walk in the light and to walk in darkness (this activity is also in the student book). Here are some ideas to get you started:

People of the light:
- walk in the light (v. 7).
- have fellowship with other believers (v. 7).
- are cleansed of their sins (vv. 7, 9).
- are not ashamed to confess their sins (v. 9).

People of the darkness:
- do not "do" the truth (v. 6).
- deceive themselves (v. 8).
- do not live by the Word (v. 10).

Now, direct students to the second passage in today's lesson (1 John 2:3-11), and ask them to do the same activity.

People of the light:
- keep Christ's commandments (v. 3).
- live in the love of God (v. 5).
- are Christlike (v. 6).
- love their brothers (v. 10).

People of the darkness:
- live a lie (v. 4).
- hate their brothers (vv. 9, 11).
- are spiritually blind (v. 11).

Into Life

Light is meant to dispel darkness, but sometimes this works the other way around. Display the candle you brought to class and light it. Just as the candle sends out light, we also, as we walk with Christ, send out a witness to those who see our lives (Matthew 5:14-16). But if we fail to walk with Christ and fail to walk in the light, the world's darkness can actually suffocate our light. Demonstrate this by putting a small bowl over the candle until it goes out.

In conclusion, challenge students to think of one specific action they can take this week to shine forth God's light in their world.

Let's Talk It Over

The questions on this page are designed to encourage review of the lesson Scriptures and to promote discussion of the lesson by the class. The answers provided are only discussion starters. Let your class talk it over from there.

1. With so much to lose, why does anyone choose to "walk in darkness" (1 John 1:6)? What is the appeal?

It would be dishonest or hypocritical of us to pretend that sin has no appeal. If that were true, it would be no problem to live a sin-free life. Even the Bible makes reference to "the pleasures of sin for a season" (Hebrews 11:25). The deeds of darkness may indeed satisfy a base desire momentarily, but the final result is devastating. "Whatsoever a man soweth, that shall he also reap. For he that soweth to his flesh shall of the flesh reap corruption; but he that soweth to the Spirit shall of the Spirit reap life everlasting" (Galatians 6:7, 8).

2. How is fellowship created by walking in the light?

The foundation for fellowship is having something in common. If we have received the forgiveness of sins through Jesus as our Savior and Lord, we have that in common with all other Christians. If we are making every effort to "walk in the light" (1 John 1:7), we have joined the company of those on the straight and narrow path that leads to life (Matthew 7:14). Our fellowship is cultivated as we encourage one another, and as we carry out the many other "one another" commands directed to believers. If someone is inconsistent in his walk, or abandons truth and righteousness in favor of sin, he has broken true fellowship with those in the light, and their relationship with that person should then be focused on restoration.

3. If "light" refers to truth and righteousness, is it possible to always "walk in the light"?

In today's text John certainly makes a strong argument for Christians to "walk in the light," but if that requires perfect obedience, then none of us qualifies. In God there is no darkness at all, yet we know that we sometimes revert to the ways of darkness, in spite of our best intentions. Thankfully, God has made provision for our forgiveness in Jesus Christ. Because His blood cleanses us from all sin, we can be restored to the fellowship of the light as long as we are repentant and trusting in Jesus. Therefore, it is by the grace of God that we are able to "walk in the light."

4. Why is confession so important to being forgiven? Is there any need for or value in the public confession of sins?

Some of those to whom John was writing had the attitude that the flesh is evil, and that evil deeds should be expected. They believed that their behavior in the flesh had no impact on their relationship with God, which is a matter of the spirit. John clearly states that there is a direct connection between one's behavior and his claim to know God. Confession of sins demonstrates a recognition of evil willfully chosen, and it accepts responsibility for one's acts. Confession from a repentant and contrite heart is the opposite of pride and self-approval. Generally speaking, confession of sins has become a private matter. Seldom do we hear someone confess a sin to the congregation or even a smaller group. However, "Confess your sins to each other" (James 5:16, *New International Version*) is one of the "one another" commands of Scripture. Without such confession to a caring and trusted Christian friend, we miss the kind of accountability that can help us overcome temptation, and we miss the reassuring words of encouragement and affirmation (whether we receive them or speak them) as we perform this role for one another.

5. If love directed to others is the chief measure of walking in the light, what evidence of that love is in your life?

Too often what we would consider love is really closer to passive goodwill. If we have to define our regard for others in terms of what we have refrained from doing—not hating, not slandering, not being mean to or purposely hurting others—we have described a vacuum. We are similar to the Pharisee who thanked God for what he was not (Luke 18:11). What are the positive acts of love that we render, or believe we should render? No, we cannot do everything, but we can do something. Are there any hungry whom we can feed, naked whom we can clothe, imprisoned whom we can visit, sick whom we can help, ignorant whom we can teach, or confused to whom we can give a word of truth and hope? Walking in the light means walking in the steps of Jesus and doing what He would do (1 John 2:6).

Living in God's Love

DEVOTIONAL READING: Micah 4:1-7; 5:2-4.

LESSON SCRIPTURE: 1 John 3.

PRINTED TEXT: 1 John 3:1-18.

1 John 3:1-18

1 Behold, what manner of love the Father hath bestowed upon us, that we should be called the sons of God: therefore the world knoweth us not, because it knew him not.

2 Beloved, now are we the sons of God, and it doth not yet appear what we shall be: but we know that, when he shall appear, we shall be like him; for we shall see him as he is.

3 And every man that hath this hope in him purifieth himself, even as he is pure.

4 Whosoever committeth sin transgresseth also the law: for sin is the transgression of the law.

5 And ye know that he was manifested to take away our sins; and in him is no sin.

6 Whosoever abideth in him sinneth not: whosoever sinneth hath not seen him, neither known him.

7 Little children, let no man deceive you: he that doeth righteousness is righteous, even as he is righteous.

8 He that committeth sin is of the devil; for the devil sinneth from the beginning. For this purpose the Son of God was manifested, that he might destroy the works of the devil.

9 Whosoever is born of God doth not commit sin; for his seed remaineth in him: and he cannot sin, because he is born of God.

10 In this the children of God are manifest, and the children of the devil: whosoever doeth not righteousness is not of God, neither he that loveth not his brother.

11 For this is the message that ye heard from the beginning, that we should love one another.

12 Not as Cain, who was of that wicked one, and slew his brother. And wherefore slew he him? Because his own works were evil, and his brother's righteous.

13 Marvel not, my brethren, if the world hate you.

14 We know that we have passed from death unto life, because we love the brethren. He that loveth not his brother abideth in death.

15 Whosoever hateth his brother is a murderer: and ye know that no murderer hath eternal life abiding in him.

16 Hereby perceive we the love of God, because he laid down his life for us: and we ought to lay down our lives for the brethren.

17 But whoso hath this world's good, and seeth his brother have need, and shutteth up his bowels of compassion from him, how dwelleth the love of God in him?

18 My little children, let us not love in word, neither in tongue; but in deed and truth.

GOLDEN TEXT: This is the message that ye heard from the beginning, that we should love one another.—1 John 3:11.

God's People in a Troubled World
Unit 1: God's Love in a Troubled World
(Lessons 1-4)

Lesson Aims

After completing this lesson, the student should:

1. Define love as God has expressed it to us and as we are to express it to others.

2. Explain why living in God's love often results in being hated by the world.

3. Suggest one new way to "love . . . in deed and in truth" this week.

Lesson Outline

INTRODUCTION
    A. Lost Love Letter
    B. Lesson Background
 I. POSSESSED BY GOD'S LOVE (1 John 3:1, 2)
    A. Present Blessing (v. 1)
    B. Future Reality (v. 2)
 II. PURITY IN GOD'S LOVE (1 John 3:3-9)
    A. Avoiding Sin (vv. 3-6)
    B. Pursuing Righteousness (vv. 7-9)
III. PRACTICE OF GOD'S LOVE (1 John 3:10-18)
    A. Love and Life (vv. 10-15)
      Love and Hate
    B. Love in Action (vv. 16-18)
      Matching the Numbers
CONCLUSION
    A. Two Great Words
    B. Prayer
    C. Thought to Remember

The visual for Lesson 2 in the visuals packet calls attention to various New Testament passages on the subject of love. It is shown on page 133.

Introduction

A. Lost Love Letter

A nineteenth-century Australian author, a certain Miss Manning, was in love with a handsome British gentleman, and he was seriously interested in her. One day he wrote to her declaring his love for her and his desire to marry her. But he was being transferred to India, and asked her to write immediately. If he did not hear from her by a given date, he would conclude that she had rejected him.

Quickly Miss Manning wrote her eager acceptance of the man's proposal. Since it was a rainy day, her brother offered to take her love letter to the local post office. But her suitor never responded. The disappointed young woman still loved this man—so deeply in fact that she never married. She went on to become a very successful writer.

Twenty-five years later the Manning family moved to a new house. Cleaning out the attic, Miss Manning found her brother's old raincoat, and as she went through its pockets she discovered the letter she had written in acceptance of the British gentleman's proposal. Her brother had forgotten to mail it.

Today we want to consider God's love letter to the world. This letter has been "mailed" to us through the greatest gift of all: God's only begotten Son. God wants everyone to be saved (1 Timothy 2:3, 4). We must not allow His letter of love to be lost; we must share it with a world lost in sin.

B. Lesson Background

We noted last week that the author of 1 John is most likely John, the "beloved apostle." He is given this title, probably because of the passage in John 19:26, which tells of how Jesus, as He was dying on the cross, delivered His mother into John's care. There he is called "the disciple . . . whom he [Jesus] loved." This phrase is also found in John's Gospel in 13:23; 20:2; 21:7; and 21:20, and is usually considered as a reference to John in each instance.

John was the brother of James. His father's name was Zebedee (Matthew 4:21), and his mother was called Salome (compare Matthew 27:55, 56 with Mark 15:40, 41). James and John were a very volatile pair, so much so that Jesus designated them *Boanerges*, meaning "sons of thunder." They certainly lived up to this title when they urged Jesus to call down fire on the Samaritan village whose residents had refused hospitality to Jesus and His followers (Luke 9:51-56). In another incident, John complained to Jesus, "Master, we saw one casting out devils in thy name, and he followeth not us; and we forbade him, because he followeth not us" (Mark 9:38). Jesus told John not to stand in the way of such a miracle worker, "for there is no man which shall do a miracle in my name, that can lightly speak evil of me" (v. 39). Later, through their mother, James and John selfishly asked Jesus to let them sit on His right and His left in His kingdom (Matthew 20:20, 21).

However, the powerful demonstration of Jesus' sacrificial love on the cross changed these men from "sons of thunder" to "sons of sunlight." James became the first apostolic martyr (Acts 12:2). In our text for today we see how

John, now aged, became the apostle of love, advocating the practice of the kind of love that was demonstrated by his Master.

I. Possessed by God's Love
(1 John 3:1, 2)
A. Present Blessing (v. 1)

1. Behold, what manner of love the Father hath bestowed upon us, that we should be called the sons of God: therefore the world knoweth us not, because it knew him not.

To be a child of God is the greatest blessing a person can have in this life. We are all God's children physically, through creation, but only those who have been born again by accepting Jesus as Savior are God's spiritual children. John affirms this in his Gospel (John 1:12, 13).

Jesus brought to the Jews of His day a revolutionary concept of the fatherhood of God. Their religious leaders worshiped God, but they had no concept of Him as a personal, intimate Father, who is deeply concerned for each and every individual. To them, God cared more about proper ritualistic observance than He did for sinners who had gone astray. Jesus, particularly in the parable of the prodigal son, taught otherwise.

There is a persistent cry in the world today for recognition of the brotherhood of man, but there can be no brotherhood of man without the fatherhood of God. The problem, as this verse indicates, is that *the world* does not accept or believe the fact that we can become *sons of God* only through Jesus. The sinful world rejected Jesus and continues for the most part to do so. They therefore reject our witness to Him as this verse states, and as Jesus Himself predicted (John 15:18-20).

B. Future Reality (v. 2)

2. Beloved, now are we the sons of God, and it doth not yet appear what we shall be: but we know that, when he shall appear, we shall be like him; for we shall see him as he is.

This verse contains one of the most precious promises of God's Word: that we shall someday *see* Jesus *as he is*. We will also *be like him*, in

that we will have a resurrected, spiritual body that is fitted for eternal life in Heaven. Paul explains the doctrine of the resurrected body in 1 Corinthians 15:35-57.

In this verse John says that this will happen *when he shall appear*, referring to the blessed hope of the second coming of our Lord. It has been estimated that the doctrine of Christ's return appears 318 times in the New Testament, which means that it is mentioned, on the average, every twenty verses.

II. Purity in God's Love
(1 John 3:3-9)
A. Avoiding Sin (vv. 3-6)

3. And every man that hath this hope in him purifieth himself, even as he is pure.

The *hope* mentioned here is that of verse two: that someday we will see Jesus as He is and that we shall be like Him. We are striving in this life to be like Him in Christian character, but we sometimes fail. That is why we confess our sins and ask for forgiveness, a point we saw in last week's lesson text (1 John 1:9).

To possess such a hope, John tells us that we must purify ourselves as Jesus was *pure*. While on earth, though tempted as we are by the sinful conditions around Him, Jesus remained pure of any sin. We who bear His name should seek this same purity. Paul urged Timothy to "flee also youthful lusts" (2 Timothy 2:22).

The exhortation to purify ourselves is similar to the phrase found in Acts 2:40, where Peter told the multitude on the Day of Pentecost to "save yourselves." Actually they could not save themselves without Christ's cleansing power, nor can we purify ourselves without Him. On the other hand, we do save ourselves when we decide to come to Christ. Jesus will purify us from our past sins, but we must then make the effort to remain pure through surrender to His will and to the guidance of the Holy Spirit.

4. Whosoever committeth sin transgresseth also the law: for sin is the transgression of the law.

The Greek phrase translated *transgresseth also the law* literally means "does the lawlessness." John is not referring to the Law of Moses; he is defining sin as a rejection of all law—of any absolute standards of conduct.

5. And ye know that he was manifested to take away our sins; and in him is no sin.

Here we see an essential element of God's plan to save lost mankind: only someone with *no sin* could *take away our sins*. God had made a law that in His righteousness He had to keep: "The soul that sinneth, it shall die"

How to Say It

BOANERGES. Bo-uh-*nur*-geez.
GNOSTICS. *Nahss*-ticks.
SALOME. Suh-*lo*-me.
SAMARITAN. Suh-*mare*-uh-tun.
ZEBEDEE. *Zeb*-uh-dee.

(Ezekiel 18:4). This law is repeated in the New Testament in Romans 6:23 where Paul writes, "The wages of sin is death." Being holy and righteous, God had to make such a law in order to condemn sin; He could not condone it. Yet in His grace, He did not want mankind to die eternally. How could the penalty of death for sin be paid? Animal sacrifices could not do this, for animals have no concept of sin or guilt. No human could pay it, for all humans have sinned. A perfect, sinless sacrifice was required, and Jesus provided it. Thus God is just in justifying sinners (Romans 3:26).

6. Whosoever abideth in him sinneth not: whosoever sinneth hath not seen him, neither known him.

This may seem to contradict John's earlier statement in 1 John 2:1: "If any man sin, we have an advocate with the Father, Jesus Christ the righteous." However, the tense of the Greek verb rendered *sin* in 1 John 2:1 describes sinning at a particular point, or stumbling. Here in 1 John 3:6, the tense of the verb translated *sinneth* indicates continuing in sin as a way of life. Many of the Gnostic teachers were advocating doing this.

B. Pursuing Righteousness (vv. 7-9)

7. Little children, let no man deceive you: he that doeth righteousness is righteous, even as he is righteous.

John was an old man at the writing of this letter, so he considered all his fellow Christians as his *little children*. He remained concerned that some may be deceived by false doctrine, most likely that of the Gnostics. We too must constantly be on guard for any unscriptural teaching, lest we are drawn into error.

True *righteousness* means acting according to the will of God as revealed in the Scriptures. Jesus is our example to follow in this regard. When we face any decision, trial, or temptation, we should ask ourselves the question, "What would Jesus have me do?" Then we should follow His teachings, being inspired by the examples of mercy and justice demonstrated in His life.

8. He that committeth sin is of the devil; for the devil sinneth from the beginning. For this purpose the Son of God was manifested, that he might destroy the works of the devil.

Here the *beginning* probably refers to Satan's influence in the Garden of Eden, where he tempted Adam and Eve into sin. Jesus used the same language when He described the devil as a "murderer from the beginning" (John 8:44).

Another purpose of Jesus' death is given here: *that he might destroy the works of the devil.* The

book of Hebrews also says that Jesus destroyed the devil, who "had the power of death" (Hebrews 2:14).

9. Whosoever is born of God doth not commit sin; for his seed remaineth in him: and he cannot sin, because he is born of God.

As in verse 6, the tense of the Greek verb rendered *commit sin* indicates continuing in sin. The Holy Spirit is most likely the *seed* dwelling in the Christian, since one is born of the Spirit (John 3:5) and is given power over sin through the Spirit's presence. As long as the Christian remains under the control of the Spirit, sin will not be the controlling force in his life.

The difference between a sinner and a saint might be illustrated in this way: A drunk staggers in the gutter toward an apartment in the slums. Perhaps once in a while his foot touches the sidewalk. This would represent the sinner headed toward Hell, who may occasionally do a good deed. On the other hand, a well-dressed, clean-cut man walks on the sidewalk toward a mansion in the suburbs. His foot may slip occasionally into the gutter, but when it does he removes his shoe, wipes it off, and proceeds. This represents the saint striving for Heaven. Sometimes he may be "overtaken in a fault" (Galatians 6:1), but he asks for forgiveness and continues toward Heaven.

II. Practice of God's Love (1 John 3:10-18)

A. Love and Life (vv. 10-15)

10, 11. In this the children of God are manifest, and the children of the devil: whosoever doeth not righteousness is not of God, neither he that loveth not his brother. For this is the message that ye heard from the beginning, that we should love one another.

John returns to his emphasis upon *love* of others. Here he considers it to be the main evidence of *righteousness*. Is not every sin somehow related to a lack of love? The adulterer does not love his wife. The thief or murderer does not love his victim. The idolater does not love God. The liar does not love the truth.

The word *beginning* most likely refers to the beginning of the gospel through the life, death, and resurrection of Jesus. It could also mean the beginning of a Christian's knowledge of Jesus, whose love moves him to *love one another*.

12. Not as Cain, who was of that wicked one, and slew his brother. And wherefore slew he him? Because his own works were evil, and his brother's righteous.

An *evil* person such as Cain will usually feel hostility toward someone who is *righteous*, such as Abel. Abel's offering had been deemed "more excellent" by God (Hebrews 11:4), while Cain's had met with rejection. Motives for murder may include envy, greed, lust, hatred, or anger over some trivial argument, but it is always wrong. Jesus said that anger and vicious name-calling are in themselves worthy of eternal punishment (Matthew 5:21, 22).

13. Marvel not, my brethren, if the world hate you.

Cain hated Abel because Abel's righteousness served to condemn Cain's lack of righteousness. The same is true of Christians today, whose righteousness exposes the evil of wicked people. So they respond with *hate.*

LOVE AND HATE

Before the fall of Communism, a Christian missionary was detained at the border of a Communist country. He was carrying a script for a filmstrip. When the border guards searched him, they found the script. They could not read very much English, but they knew the word Jesus, and that word was on every page. They fined the missionary, canceled his visa, and would not let him enter the country (even though it was not illegal to transport such a document).

The missionary said that a strange feeling came over him as he drove back over the road he had just traveled. At first he could not identify the feeling. Then he realized that he had been face to face with real hatred for the first time. As with all who serve Christ and the church, he had encountered rejection before, but this was different. These people genuinely hated him. He thought of a Scripture verse: "They hated me without a cause" (John 15:25). There was no reason for the guards to hate him, for he would have done no harm in their country. Later he remembered 1 John 3:13: "Marvel not, my brethren, if the world hate you." And he recalled the words of John 15:18, where Jesus said, "If the world hate you, ye know that it hated me before it hated you." Suddenly he realized that these guards hated him because they hated Jesus.

In recalling this incident, the missionary later stated that over his lifetime of service to Christ he had received several honors. But the greatest honor he ever received came that day on the border of a Communist country, when men hated him because they hated Jesus.   —R. C. S.

14, 15. We know that we have passed from death unto life, because we love the brethren. He that loveth not his brother abideth in death. Whosoever hateth his brother is a murderer:

and ye know that no murderer hath eternal life abiding in him.

John is again setting forth the principle, stated by Jesus throughout the Sermon on the Mount, that sin is defined not only by the outward acts, but by the thoughts and intents of the heart. In Matthew 15:18-20, Jesus taught that "out of the heart" come those acts of murder, adultery, theft, and violence that truly "defile" a man.

John's statement that *no murderer hath eternal life abiding in him* is in harmony with Jesus' teaching that eternal life is a present reality of fellowship with God (see John 17:3). Such a relationship is incompatible with hatred as well as with all manner of sin.

B. Love in Action (vv. 16-18)

16. Hereby perceive we the love of God, because he laid down his life for us: and we ought to lay down our lives for the brethren.

Some may claim to see God's love in a baby's smile, a child's laughter, a beautiful sunset, or a neighbor's kind deed. While all of these should indeed be considered as gifts of love from God, the strongest evidence of His love remains the fact that *he laid down his life for us.* He has given us the best gift of all: His only Son.

A Sunday school teacher read the passage of Scripture where Jesus says, "My yoke is easy." "What is a yoke?" she asked the class of children. One replied, "Something they put on the necks of animals." "So, what is the meaning of God's yoke?" the teacher asked. After a time of silence, one child replied, "That's when God puts His arms around our neck."

John also says that the depth of God's love should motivate us to be willing to *lay down our lives for the brethren.* Jesus once said that there was no greater demonstration of love than to lay down one's life for a friend (John 15:13). But Jesus went the second mile and laid down His life for His enemies (Romans 5:7-10).

MATCHING THE NUMBERS

It is only a coincidence when the numbers that identify one Biblical text also identify a related text. No one believes that the numbering

visual for lesson 2

"For this is the message that ye heard from the beginning, that we should love one another."
1 John 3:11

of chapters and verses in our Bible was inspired. But when they match, it is an interesting and helpful coincidence. For example, the question of Job 14 (v. 14) is answered in John 14 (vv. 6, 19). When discussing baptism we need to understand John 3:5 in the light of Titus 3:5.

In today's lesson we can see that John 3:16 and 1 John 3:16 are closely related. Most every Christian knows and can quote John 3:16, for it is the most familiar verse in the New Testament. It is appropriately called the golden text of the Bible. But we must also see that God's love for us is not only a great gift; it also places on us a great obligation. 1 John 3:16 challenges us to respond to God's love by laying down our lives for others. In other times and places, that has meant a sacrificial death. In all times and places, it means a sacrificial life. The apostle Paul calls it a living sacrifice (Romans 12:1).

We should remember that there is more than one way to lay down our lives. We must keep our eyes open each day to opportunities to do this and thus to bear witness to Christ's love in us. He who gave His life for us desires that we give ours to Him and on behalf of others.   —R. C. S.

17. But whoso hath this world's good, and seeth his brother have need, and shutteth up his bowels of compassion from him, how dwelleth the love of God in him?

John now turns from sins of commission that are not in harmony with God's love, to sins of omission: the failure to do good and to demonstrate *compassion* to others. The necessity of such kindness was the lesson of Jesus' parable of the good Samaritan.

The word *bowels*, referring to the lower viscera of the body, is a literal translation of the Greek term. In the culture of that day, emotions were associated with this part of the body. Today we usually refer to emotions as coming from the heart (although we still speak of having a "gut feeling").

18. My little children, let us not love in word, neither in tongue; but in deed and in truth.

Essentially John is saying, "Put your money where your mouth is." It is hypocritical to talk about what is right and not do it. This is similar to the teaching of James concerning faith and works in James 2:14-17, where he also encourages helping the needy.

Conclusion

A. Two Great Words

There are two great words in this lesson: hope and love. They make up two-thirds of Paul's wonderful trilogy in 1 Corinthians 13:13: faith, hope, and charity, or love.

In the Christian vocabulary, love is not romantic affection based only on emotion. It is based upon the value of the object loved; and every person is valuable in God's sight since He gave His Son to save everyone. We should therefore respect the value of every person. This is increasingly important in a world where life is often cheap, and where an individual's worth is measured by external or material criteria.

Hope in the Christian vocabulary is more than wishful thinking. It is an assurance based on the reasonableness of our faith and the reliability of God's promises. It is a combination of desire and expectation. Hope keeps us from despair, anguish, loneliness, fear, and all the cares of life related to the future. It keeps the soul calm and secure in days of adversity. Hope does not remove troubles, but sustains the soul in time of troubles. Like an anchor, it does not dispel the storm, quiet the roaring waves, avert the rolling thunder, or bid the winds be still; but it enables the vessel to ride out the fury of the gale and keeps it from being driven on the rocks.

Thank God for our abiding hope in Christ—a hope that serves as "an anchor of the soul" (Hebrews 6:19).

B. Prayer

Lord, grant us a full portion of Your Holy Spirit, that we may live lives of purity in Your presence. Help us to show the spirit of Christ's love toward all mankind so that others may know the hope and joy of salvation. Amen.

C. Thought to Remember

There can be no brotherhood of man without the fatherhood of God.

Home Daily Bible Readings

Monday, Dec. 8—Living in God's Love (1 John 2:18-28)

Tuesday, Dec. 9—We Are God's Children Now (1 John 2:29—3:8)

Wednesday, Dec. 10—Give Our Lives for One Another (1 John 3:9-17)

Thursday, Dec. 11—Love in Truth and Action (1 John 3:18-24)

Friday, Dec. 12—God Teaches the Way of Peace (Micah 4:1-7; 5:2-5a)

Saturday, Dec. 13—Fruits Worthy of Repentance (Luke 3:7-18)

Sunday, Dec. 14—God of Peace Goes With Us (Philippians 4:4-9)

Learning by Doing

This page contains an alternate lesson plan emphasizing learning activities.
Classes desiring such student involvement will find these suggestions helpful.

Learning Goals

After this lesson, your students should be able to:

1. Define love as God has expressed it to us and as we are to express it to others.

2. Explain why living in God's love often results in being hated by the world.

3. Suggest one new way to "love . . . in deed and in truth" this week.

Into the Lesson

The theme of this lesson is God's love. Begin the lesson by asking your students to suggest evidences of God's love. Urge them to use evidences that they have experienced personally during the past week.

You can also introduce this lesson on God's love by writing the following fill-in-the-blank/open-ended statement on the chalkboard or on a sheet of newsprint: "I love _____ because . . ." Then ask the students to take turns filling in the blank and saying why they love the object of their affection. This can be a person, place, or thing. For example: "I love ice cream because . . ." "I love (name of wife/husband/child) because . . ."

Now ask students to imagine that God is completing that statement: "I love (each fills in his or her own name) because . . ." How would God complete it? What reason would He give for loving each one of them individually?

The truth is that God would not even complete that statement. He loves us simply because it is His nature to love.

Into the Word

Bring to class several colorful photos of beautiful flowers along with photos of unattractive weeds (you may need to go to your local public library for this). Show the photos and ask, "Why are some gardens filled with beautiful flowers, while others become overrun with weeds?" Usually the difference lies in the attention the garden receives. Emphasize that if we do not attend to cultivating God's love in our hearts, our lives will produce weeds, not flowers.

Last week we contrasted light and darkness. This week the contrast is between *love* and *hatred*. Write those two words on the chalkboard or on newsprint, and then ask the students to see what 1 John 3:11-18 says about the

person who loves and the person who hates (this activity is in the student book).

The person who loves: loves others (vv. 11, 14); produces hatred on the part of the world (v. 13); is willing to make personal sacrifices for the sake of others (v. 16); backs up his words with his actions (v. 18).

The person who hates: is capable of violent actions (v. 12); is jealous of those who are righteous (v. 12); hates Christ and followers of Christ (v. 13); is spiritually dead (v. 15); is selfish and uncaring (v. 17).

Discuss the story of Cain and Abel, which is mentioned in verse 12 (you may want to read Genesis 4:3-8). Ask, "How does this story illustrate both love and hatred?" (See the lesson commentary on 1 John 3:12, 13.)

Into Life

Divide the class into groups of three, and give a hymnal to each group. Ask the members of each group to select a favorite hymn that extols the love of God. Then instruct them to choose one stanza of their hymn and read it aloud to the rest of the class. (If your class does not work well in groups, or if it is not convenient to divide them into groups, each student can do this activity alone. Or you may instead select several hymns about God's love in advance, and read your favorite stanzas aloud to the class.)

Living for Christ often results in being hated by the world (1 John 3:13). Ask if any of your students can give examples of this from their personal experiences. Have any of them been harassed by co-workers, neighbors, or family members because of their stand for Christ or for Biblical truth? Suggest that opposition from the world often is inspired by guilt. People who are living in sin may feel condemned or judged by the life of a righteous and godly person, and they take their anger out on that person.

First John 3:17, 18 challenges us to put love in action. Ask if anyone has ever told someone in need, "I'm praying for you," instead of giving that person the help he or she really needed. Why is this an inadequate response?

Conclude the lesson by asking each student to think of one person who needs some kind of practical help or assistance. Offer this challenge: "What specifically will you do this week to express Christian love to that person?"

Let's Talk It Over

The questions on this page are designed to encourage review of the lesson Scriptures and to promote discussion of the lesson by the class. The answers provided are only discussion starters. Let your class talk it over from there.

1. Parents who adopt assume significant responsibilities and obligations. Which of these apply to God in His adoption of us, and what does that tell about His love for us?

The decision to adopt in our society can never be taken casually. It is a lengthy and costly process. The commitment of the prospective parents is tested repeatedly. Adopting a child means assuming responsibility for physical care, emotional nurture, discipline, moral training, and education. It is assumed that a parent will invest much of himself or herself in the children, whether they are naturally born or adopted. It helps us know the depth of God's love to understand that He desires to make us His children—not His slaves or His pets. To accomplish our adoption required a huge "investment" on God's part. It is an amazing love that moved Him to assume the responsibilities of an adoptive parent toward us.

2. Do you know someone whom you consider pure? What is most appealing about his or her purity? Is personal purity something you desire for yourself? Why or why not?

In our culture there is an increasing desire for purity in food, water, and the environment. As a personal quality, however, purity may be associated with prudishness, rigidity about rules, and intolerance. We have been conditioned to believe that excitement and stimulation come from that which is naughty or contrary to approved behavior. For those reasons, the call to personal and moral purity may not seem very appealing. Perhaps we need to be reminded of the attractiveness of purity in Jesus. Jesus could be trusted to do the right thing, not out of self-interest, but with regard to the will of His Father and the needs of others. He was pure in character, pure in motive, and pure in purpose. God desires that we become single-minded (pure) in our devotion to Him and His will.

3. If sin is a matter of crossing moral boundaries established by God, how close to those boundaries do you walk? What safeguards have you established to protect yourself from moral failure?

There have always been believers who like to live just as close to the edge of sin as possible.

For instance, they know that adultery is sin, but they allow themselves to flirt with someone they find attractive. They know that holding a grudge or seeking revenge is a sin, but they secretly celebrate the misfortune of someone they dislike. To harbor such thoughts is to dance on the edge of disaster morally and spiritually. As followers of Jesus, we should be building positive traits in our character, and keeping as far from sin as possible. Moral laws mark the edge of the chasm of destruction, and our degree of attention to them serves as the barrier that keeps us away from the edge. How close to the edge are you erecting your barrier?

4. Habitual, repeated sin is evidence that we do not know God (1 John 3:6). Are there sins that have been rationalized and are part of our culture? What about your life? What are the sinful habits that need to be corrected?

Our culture is guilty of a number of sins and idolatries that have become part of the moral landscape. The pursuit of material possessions or wealth competes with devotion to God, even in the lives of many professed believers. An alarming number of people excuse cheating or other dishonest conduct when it seems in their own best interest. Modesty and self-control have been largely cast aside in favor of flamboyance and self-indulgence. Sacrifice is a concept seldom found today. Have you allowed any of these attitudes to control your thinking? Do changes need to be made? When believers in Jesus truly repent and turn from sin, there will always be a marked difference between them and others in the society.

5. Has your church (or class or small group) established a reputation for caring for those in need? How? What more can you do?

As followers of Jesus, we are to be experts in love (John 15:12-17). This love should be especially evident in how we treat those among us who are in need. Do you have an established response system for needs in your group? Is it working? Are there those who gladly testify to the love that they have received through deeds done for them? If we claim to have the love of God inside us, there will be practical evidence in how we treat others around us.

Celebrating God's Love

DEVOTIONAL READING: Isaiah 9:2-7.

LESSON SCRIPTURE: Matthew 1:18-25; 1 John 4.

PRINTED TEXT: Matthew 1:20, 21; 1 John 4:7-17.

Matthew 1:20, 21

20 But while he thought on these things, behold, the angel of the Lord appeared unto him in a dream, saying, Joseph, thou son of David, fear not to take unto thee Mary thy wife: for that which is conceived in her is of the Holy Ghost.

21 And she shall bring forth a son, and thou shalt call his name JESUS: for he shall save his people from their sins.

1 John 4:7-17

7 Beloved, let us love one another: for love is of God; and every one that loveth is born of God, and knoweth God.

8 He that loveth not knoweth not God; for God is love.

9 In this was manifested the love of God toward us, because that God sent his only begotten Son into the world, that we might live through him.

10 Herein is love, not that we loved God, but that he loved us, and sent his Son to be the propitiation for our sins.

11 Beloved, if God so loved us, we ought also to love one another.

12 No man hath seen God at any time. If we love one another, God dwelleth in us, and his love is perfected in us.

13 Hereby know we that we dwell in him, and he in us, because he hath given us of his Spirit.

14 And we have seen and do testify that the Father sent the Son to be the Saviour of the world.

15 Whosoever shall confess that Jesus is the Son of God, God dwelleth in him, and he in God.

16 And we have known and believed the love that God hath to us. God is love; and he that dwelleth in love dwelleth in God, and God in him.

17 Herein is our love made perfect, that we may have boldness in the day of judgment: because as he is, so are we in this world.

GOLDEN TEXT: In this was manifested the love of God toward us,
because that God sent his only begotten Son into the world,
that we might live through him.—1 John 4:9.

God's People in a Troubled World
Unit 1: God's Love in a Troubled World
(Lessons 1-4)

Lesson Aims

After a study of this lesson, the student ought to be able to:

1. Tell how the life of Jesus demonstrates God's love to us.

2. Explain how the Christian's life can also be a demonstration of God's love.

3. Plan some deliberate expression of God's love to be added to one's traditional celebration of Christmas.

Lesson Outline

INTRODUCTION
  A. The Message of Christmas
  B. Jesus Is Real
  C. Lesson Background
 I. SAVIOR PROMISED (Matthew 1:20, 21)
  A. Angel Explains (v. 20)
  B. Name Defined (v. 21)
 II. LOVE PERFECTED (1 John 4:7-13)
  A. From God to Us (vv. 7-10)
    Begotten or Forgotten?
  B. From Us to Others (vv. 11-13)
III. SON GIVEN (1 John 4:14-17)
  A. Testimony Sure (vv. 14, 15)
  B. Love Perfected (vv. 16, 17)
CONCLUSION
  A. The Love of God
  B. Prayer
  C. Thought to Remember

Use the visual for Lesson 3 to highlight today's Golden Text from 1 John 4:9. The visual is shown on page 140.

Introduction

A. The Message of Christmas

Someone has said, "The message of Easter is 'Think of Heaven,' the message of the Fourth of July is 'Think of our nation,' the message of Thanksgiving is 'Think of your blessings,' the message of New Year's Day is 'Think of the passing of time,' but the message of Christmas is 'Think of others.'" God was thinking of all of us when He sent Jesus into our world, and all who have the true spirit of Christmas—and of the Christ of Christmas—think of others.

B. Jesus Is Real

Most of us have heard the story of the newspaper editor in New York City who answered a little girl's letter about Santa Claus. George Alder once wrote a paraphrase of it, which appeared in *The Lookout* (December 22, 1974). Here are some excerpts:

Dear Virginia:

Yes, there really is a Jesus. I know that it's not fashionable with a lot of people to talk about Him or write about Him in schoolbooks, or to let children sing about Him in school Christmas programs, or even to respect Him or remember Him on Christmas Day, but He is real.

I know that you've known some adults who say that they believe there was a Jesus and who make a lot of fuss about Christmas cards, decorations, and presents, yet who just don't act as if they really know Him. But this doesn't mean that He isn't real. Just because I don't know your friends doesn't mean that your friends aren't real. Just because we don't know anything much about people in far off lands doesn't mean that they don't exist. And just because we never saw George Washington or Abraham Lincoln doesn't prove that they were never presidents of our country.

So, Virginia, it happens now that a lot of people don't know Jesus in a personal way, so they're inclined to treat Him as if He were not real. Maybe some of them are afraid that if they accepted Him as real, then they'd feel responsible to honor, obey, and follow Him. They're missing what Christmas is all about when they think that Jesus isn't real.

For Christians, Virginia, Christmas is a wonderful time, because not only do we have all the fun of decorations, carols, presents, and greeting cards, but we also know the One whose birthday we celebrate. After all, it is a little strange, don't you think, to send cards, buy gifts, and do all those Christmas things to celebrate a birthday for someone who isn't real?

You see, Virginia, we don't generally keep on giving birthday presents for people who have died. Christmas is a birthday party for someone who's alive. Jesus is real, all right. Open your heart to Him and you'll know that. Millions of others have opened their hearts to Him, and that's why we still have Christmas.

C. Lesson Background

Mary and Joseph were residents of the village of Nazareth in Galilee. Both of them were descendants of David. Joseph's genealogy is found in Matthew 1:2-16, while Mary's is believed to be recorded in Luke 3:23-38. The angel Gabriel had announced to Mary that she, although a virgin, would be the mother of the Son of God (Luke 1:26-38). He also told her of the miraculous pregnancy of her relative, Elisabeth, whose son became John the Baptist. At some time after this, Mary went to visit Elisabeth, who lived in the "hill country" of Judah (Luke 1:39), approximately eighty miles away. She may have done this to avoid the talk surrounding her own pregnancy.

Joseph and Mary had been betrothed (or "espoused," as Matthew 1:18 reads in the *King James Version*), which describes an agreement to marry that was made possibly a year before the wedding. It was considered as binding as the actual vows. Unfaithfulness during this period constituted grounds for a legal divorce.

We do not know exactly how Joseph became aware of Mary's condition. Perhaps it became evident upon her return from Elisabeth's home. Perhaps Mary told him of the angel's visit. In either case, it appears that Joseph was skeptical of Mary's explanation. We can imagine some of his feelings at this time: shock, disappointment in Mary, and sorrow at the loss of his planned happiness. Yet he loved Mary and did not want to see her made into a "public example" (Matthew 1:19). To save her the embarrassment and punishment of a public trial, he determined to make their separation as private as possible. It was at this point that an angel appeared to assure Joseph of Mary's innocence. This is where our printed text begins.

I. Savior Promised (Matthew 1:20, 21)

A. Angel Explains (v. 20)

20. But while he thought on these things, behold, the angel of the Lord appeared unto him in a dream, saying, Joseph, thou son of David, fear not to take unto thee Mary thy wife: for that which is conceived in her is of the Holy Ghost.

Matthew records three times in his nativity account that God revealed His message *in a dream*: here, to the wise men (2:12), and again to Joseph (2:19, 20). On this occasion, *the angel of the Lord* (probably Gabriel, who had spoken to Mary) explained to *Joseph* that Mary's baby was divinely *conceived*. This, as verses 22 and 23 further explain, fulfilled the prophecy of Isaiah 7:14. Thus Joseph's fear as to Mary's virtue and purity was allayed.

Some skeptics have denied the doctrine of the virgin birth on the grounds that it is not taught anywhere in the New Testament except here and in Luke's Gospel (1:26-32). These two pas-

---

How to Say It

GABRIEL. *Gay*-bree-ul.
PATMOS. *Pat*-muss.
PROPITIATION. pro-*pih*-she-*a*-shun (strong accent on *a*).

---

sages ought to be sufficient. However, what Paul states in Romans 1:1-4 and Galatians 4:4 is in harmony with the doctrine. The virgin birth was a necessary part of Jesus' coming to our world as God's Son, so that He could prove to us the love of God (John 3:16).

Others deny the virgin birth on the basis that it was impossible. But Jesus said that with God all things are possible (Matthew 19:26; see also Luke 1:37). Dr. Howard A. Kelly, past professor at Johns Hopkins University, once stated, "To deny the virgin birth is to deny the power of God. To those who say it is biologically impossible, I reply that with God all things are possible."

Following the account of Jesus' birth, Joseph appears only once more in the Gospels, when he and Mary took Jesus to the temple at the age of twelve (Luke 2:41-52). He may have died before Jesus began His ministry.

B. Name Defined (v. 21)

21. And she shall bring forth a son, and thou shalt call his name JESUS: for he shall save his people from their sins.

The name *Jesus* means "Jehovah is the Savior" or "Salvation is of Jehovah." During His ministry, Jesus emphasized that the salvation of mankind was His mission. He once said, "The Son of man is come to seek and to save that which was lost" (Luke 19:10).

In commenting on this verse, J. W. McGarvey observes that Jesus came to save from the guilt, power, and punishment of sin (*Fourfold Gospel*, p. 25). He saves from the guilt (penalty) of sin by having shed His blood so that our sins may be forgiven when we meet the terms of pardon. He saves from the power of sin by bestowing the gift of the Holy Spirit, who enables us to serve righteousness rather than sin. He saves from the punishment of sin by His resurrection from the grave, which assures us of eternal life rather than eternal death.

II. Love Perfected (1 John 4:7-13)

A. From God to Us (vv. 7-10)

7. Beloved, let us love one another: for love is of God; and every one that loveth is born of God, and knoweth God.

When we celebrate Jesus' birth as Christians, we can also celebrate our second birth, which is spiritual. This verse says that *every one that loveth is born of God*. However, when we compare it with John 3:5, we realize that there is more to being born again than just love. This illustrates an important principle of Bible study: All verses on a given subject must be taken into consideration.

Our knowledge of God comes first from a study of His Word, where we learn of His love, mercy, kindness, justice, and His plan of salvation for our souls. We then draw closer to Him through experiencing daily His forgiveness, patience, goodness, and providence in our lives, and through seeking Him by continued study and prayer.

Some claim that a sufficient knowledge of God can be gained from nature. Certainly it is true that we can know something of God through the beauty of the natural world. But we cannot know His love (and thus know Him) without Jesus our Savior.

8. He that loveth not, knoweth not God; for God is love.

This verse gives us the greatest description of God: *God is love*. The wording of the Greek text forbids this to be translated, "Love is God." Some think that simply because they possess a deep love for someone, they are right with God. Others believe that God is not a real personality, but that wherever any type of love is present, one finds God. Both of these approaches reverse the correct order: only when we turn to God can we find love both defined and demonstrated.

During one of Admiral Richard Byrd's explorations in the Antarctic, he thought he was nearing land. He called to his sailors to let down the anchor to measure the depth of the water. From the helm he asked, "How deep is the water?" The cry came back, "Ninety fathoms and deeper yet." Later he cried out again, "How deep is the water?" The answer came back, "One hundred fathoms and deeper yet." A third time he called, and the answer was, "One hundred ten fathoms and deeper yet." So it is with God's love; the more we experience it, the more we find it is "deeper yet."

The strongest proof that we know God is our love for others. Jesus said, "By this shall all men know that ye are my disciples, if ye have love one to another" (John 13:35). Love is the trademark by which all followers of Jesus are to be identified.

9. In this was manifested the love of God toward us, because that God sent his only begotten Son into the world, that we might live through him.

visual for
lesson 3

Whenever we begin to doubt God's love, we need only to turn to the story of the birth and death of Christ to be assured that He still loves us. How better could He show His love than to give His only Son. If He had written "I love you" across the sky two thousand years ago, only those who saw it could have believed the message, and even then it would not have proved His love. If He had given everyone a million dollars then, such a gift would mean nothing to us now. But the gift of His Son is timeless—a gift that everyone can understand. It is a gift that truly "keeps on giving."

A man in the post office told the clerk that he wanted his package to arrive at its destination by Christmas. The package contained a birthday present for his father, who was born on Christmas Day. Another person in line said, "I'm glad I wasn't born on Christmas. Pity the person who is: he gets only one celebration instead of two." A third person said, "I'm glad I don't know anyone born on Christmas Day." A woman silenced the talk when she said, "I'm glad I do."

Consider God's Christmas Gift:
> The Wrapping: Luke 2:12
> The Trimming: Luke 2:13, 14
> The Contents: Galatians 4:4, 5
> The Tag: Luke 2:11
> The Purpose: John 3:16

"Thanks be unto God for his unspeakable gift" (2 Corinthians 9:15).

10. Herein is love, not that we loved God, but that he loved us, and sent his Son to be the propitiation for our sins.

The word *propitiation* also appears in 1 John 2:2. It means a "mercy covering," and refers to the atoning sacrifice of Christ that covers *our sins*, and thus satisfies the righteous wrath of God. At the cross, the sinless Christ took upon Himself the wrath of God that we, though sinful, might be forgiven. As Isaiah prophesied, "The Lord hath laid on him the iniquity of us all" (Isaiah 53:6).

No act of *love* by us can come close to equaling what God did in giving Jesus for our salvation, and what Jesus did in willingly giving His life to die in our place. Such love should motivate us to love both God and others.

BEGOTTEN OR FORGOTTEN?

A young father was holding his young son (his only child) on his lap. It was Sunday afternoon and the father was thinking about the Scripture he'd heard in church that morning. He said to his little boy, "You're my only begotten son." The little boy replied, "Daddy, don't say that. Don't call me your only forgotten son!" It does seem sometimes that God's only *begotten* Son is also His only *forgotten* Son. Christ is either neglected or ignored by a large segment of the world's population. Even Christians sometimes forget His claim on their lives. That claim is based primarily on who Jesus is. If Jesus Christ is not uniquely God's Son, His only begotten, then we do not have to take seriously His demands of us. But if He is God's only begotten Son, then we must take Him seriously. If we fail to do this, we do so at our own eternal peril.

The great issue of Scripture is, "What think ye of Christ? whose son is he?" (Matthew 22:42). As a little chorus says, "Everybody ought to know who Jesus is."   —R. C. S.

B. From Us to Others (vv. 11-13)

11. Beloved, if God so loved us, we ought also to love one another.

Someone has said that a religion that consists only of an injunction to love one's neighbor could not be sufficient to lead one to do so. The point is that we need motivation to lead us to act in love toward others. Christianity gives us the spiritual power to be loving in our relationships with others. Our inspiration is the love of God toward us in Christ, which was the focus of verse 10. No other religion offers such motivation; only in the gospel do we have both the statement and the manifestation of God's love for mankind. It is obviously hypocritical if we claim His love for ourselves and do not demonstrate a similar love for *one another*.

12. No man hath seen God at any time. If we love one another, God dwelleth in us, and his love is perfected in us.

Although we cannot see God physically, we can experience His presence by His love, both as it is manifested to us in Christ and as it is manifested to us in others. The word for *perfected* conveys the idea of becoming mature. The more love we practice, the more mature we become; thus do we come to know God better each day.

One family has a little game they play at the dinner table. "What is salt?" asks one child. "Salt is what spoils the beans if you leave it out," another will reply. "What is milk?" asks another. Someone answers, "Milk is what spoils the cereal if you leave it out." Finally the father asks, "What is love?" When no reply comes, he says, "Love is what spoils Christian living when you leave it out."

13. Hereby know we that we dwell in him, and he in us, because he hath given us of his Spirit.

Since we are born of the *Spirit* (John 3:5), we have the Spirit *in us*. Peter promised the people gathered on the Day of Pentecost that if they would repent and be baptized, they would receive the gift of the Holy Spirit (Acts 2:38). Acts 5:32 tells us that God has given His Spirit "to them that obey him." Paul says that we are the temple of God's Spirit (1 Corinthians 3:16). He also says that if we have not the Spirit of Christ, we are none of His (Romans 8:9). The Spirit will bear "witness with our spirit, that we are the children of God" (Romans 8: 16).

God's Spirit is seen in us when we manifest the fruit of the Spirit as described by Paul in Galatians 5:22, 23. These qualities all spring from God's love for us and our response to that love. Joy is the exuberance that comes from having found real love. Peace is love having surrendered. Long-suffering is love on the anvil, bearing blow after blow of adversity. Gentleness is love caring for others. Goodness is love serving. Faith is love trusting others. Meekness is love bowing at the feet of the Master. Temperance is love under control.

A group of college students toured the slums of a city. One of the girls, seeing a little girl playing in the dirt, asked the guide, "Why doesn't her mother clean her up?" He replied, "That girl's mother probably loves her, but she doesn't hate dirt. You hate the dirt, but you don't love the girl enough to come down here and clean her up. Until hate for the dirt and love for the child are in the same person, that little girl will probably remain as she is." When we have the Spirit of God, we will hate sin and love sinners enough to do something to save the lost. We will see people as Jesus saw them.

III. Son Given
(1 John 4:14-17)

A. Testimony Sure (vv. 14, 15)

14. And we have seen and do testify that the Father sent the Son to be the Saviour of the world.

John was sure of his message, for he had *seen*, heard, and touched the living and resurrected

Lord (1 John 1:1, 2). The Greek word translated *testify* is the source of the word "martyr." The apostles testified with their lives for the truth of the gospel message. Tradition has it that all the original twelve who knew Jesus personally (except Judas) died a martyr's death, except possibly John himself—and his faith in the truth led to his exile on the island of Patmos. These men would not have sacrificed their lives as they did for a fraud.

Sir James Simpson, the discoverer of chloroform, was a scientist of great reputation. Once he was asked what his greatest discovery was. Without any hesitation and with firm conviction he replied, "That I am a sinner and that I have a Savior in Jesus Christ." Such testimony by Simpson and by millions more through the years affirms what John states in this verse.

15. Whosoever shall confess that Jesus is the Son of God, God dwelleth in him, and he in God.

Paul speaks of such confession as leading to salvation (Romans 10:9, 10). He urged Timothy to be faithful to the confession (or "profession") that he had made (1 Timothy 6:12).

B. Love Perfected (vv. 16, 17)

16. And we have known and believed the love that God hath to us. God is love; and he that dwelleth in love dwelleth in God, and God in him.

John repeats one of the great themes of his letter: *God is love.* Once a person grasps this marvelous truth, he will surely turn to God to find the power and glory of salvation. To think on this truth, and to understand and live by it, is to understand the message and meaning of the Christmas story.

17. Herein is our love made perfect, that we may have boldness in the day of judgment: because as he is, so are we in this world.

Again, the word translated *perfect* means "mature." We will never be absolutely blameless in our expression of love to others within the complex relationships of life. But we can conduct ourselves toward others in a mature way. We can have a Christlike spirit of love in our hearts, even though at times, because of lack of understanding or knowledge, we fail to express it correctly in our acts toward others.

A *day of judgment* is certain (Hebrews 9:27). Jesus said that His Word will judge us in that day (John 12:48). If we accept Him as Savior, strive to carry out His teachings, and live as His ambassadors *in this world*, we can face the judgment with *boldness*. Jesus will say, "Well done, thou good and faithful servant . . . enter thou into the joy of thy lord."

Conclusion

A. The Love of God

The love of God is an ocean whose depth no line can sound.

It is a sky of unknown dimensions; no telescope or spacecraft can reach its heights.

It dwells within an immeasurable country; no survey can find its boundary.

It is a mine of such wealth that man's engineering skill cannot begin to exhaust its riches.

It is a pole of attraction that no explorer can accurately discover.

It is a forest of such beauty that no botanist can completely analyze and describe its variety.

It is a truth that no philosopher can deny or adequately explain.

In the Pacific Ocean there is a cavity in the ocean floor that is so deep that the highest mountain peak in the world could be turned upside down and plunged into it, and the water would still flow over it. So it is with the depth of God's love. We can pour into His great heart of love all the sin, sorrow, and suffering of humanity, and it is overwhelmed by His redeeming grace.

B. Prayer

Thank You, heavenly Father, for Your love as demonstrated in the gift of salvation through the sacrifice of Christ our Savior. May we truly honor Him in this Christmas season by making Him Lord of our lives. Amen.

C. Thought to Remember

"For God so loved the world, that he gave his only begotten Son, that whosoever believeth in him should not perish, but have everlasting life" (John 3:16).

Home Daily Bible Readings

Learning by Doing

This page contains an alternate lesson plan emphasizing learning activities.
Classes desiring such student involvement will find these suggestions helpful.

Learning Goals

After this lesson, a student should be able to:

1. Tell how the life of Jesus demonstrates God's love to us.

2. Explain how the Christian's life can also be a demonstration of God's love.

3. Plan some deliberate expression of God's love to be added to one's traditional celebration of Christmas.

Into the Lesson

Before your class enters the room, write the word *celebration* on the chalkboard or a sheet of newsprint. Then introduce this Christmas lesson on celebrating God's love by asking students how they celebrate Christmas. Do some have special family traditions that enhance their celebration of Christmas?

Into the Word

Joseph is sometimes the forgotten man of the Christmas story. He is mentioned only briefly and with little detail. The "innkeeper" (who does not even appear in the Bible) sometimes gets more attention in Christmas plays and dramas than does Joseph. But Joseph was a man of remarkable character, and he played a significant role in the birth of Jesus. Your students can begin to appreciate the kind of man Joseph was by considering the following scenarios (these are listed in the student book):

• Joseph's espoused wife became pregnant before they were married—and he knew he wasn't the father. What would most men do in a situation like that? What did Joseph do?

• An angelic visitor told Joseph in a dream that the Holy Spirit had made Mary pregnant. How would most men react to a message like that? What did Joseph do?

• In a dream, the angel told Joseph that the promised child would be a very special person—a Savior. How would most men react to a dream like that? What did Joseph do?

After considering these scenarios, ask the students to suggest words that describe Joseph's character. What kind of man was he?

Next, shift the focus to the Savior who was promised. How did this promise demonstrate God's love? (It showed that He was concerned for the spiritual condition of His people, and was committed to doing something about it.)

Building on the idea of a demonstration of God's love, now move to the 1 John passage in today's lesson. 1 John 4:8 says, "God is love." Ask, "What does that mean? In what sense can we say that 'God is love'? If 'God is love,' why do bad things happen to good people?" (Have the class consider that the very essence of God is love. It is His nature to love. When He is being most "natural," He is reaching out in love. As for "bad things," they should not be blamed on God. They result from sin, and from the fact that we live in a sin-polluted and sin-corrupted world that God will make new one day, as promised in 2 Peter 3:13. Tragedies or difficult circumstances do not negate the fact that God loves us and wants only what is best for us.) Emphasize that the ultimate demonstration of God's love is the sending of His Son (1 John 4:10). This is what Christmas is all about. Jesus is truly "the reason for the season."

Into Life

Hold up a small mirror. Then pass it around the class and let everyone look in the mirror. What do they see? What they see is a reflection of their image. When God looks at us, He wants to see a reflection of His love. But He also wants to see us reflecting His love to others.

Earlier you raised the issue of celebrations at Christmas. Now go back to this topic, and ask the students to evaluate their celebrations. How many of these actually exalt Christ and demonstrate the real meaning of Christmas? (Don't scold or criticize; just challenge the students to make their own personal evaluations.)

Ask if some students would like to talk about how their celebrations exalt Christ. Others may want to say what they plan to do differently this year to add an expression of God's love to their celebration of Christmas. (Some suggestions: invite a single person with no family to spend Christmas Day with them; read the Christmas story on Christmas morning; visit a nursing home over the holidays, and plan to do so on a regular basis in the future; make a personal commitment or recommitment to Christ.)

In closing, challenge each student to be more aware of the fact that Christmas is primarily a demonstration of God's love for us; therefore, our celebrations of Christmas should express His love to others.

Let's Talk It Over

The questions on this page are designed to encourage review of the lesson Scriptures and to promote discussion of the lesson by the class. The answers provided are only discussion starters. Let your class talk it over from there.

1. Since the conception of Jesus was the direct work of God, what specific physical advantages might the Father have given to the Son? What was God's purpose in sending Jesus as He did?

God could have made Jesus tall, muscular, and handsome. He could have chosen fair skin or dark skin, straight hair or curly hair, any blood type, and any level of intelligence. The historical record, however, does not highlight any of these characteristics of Jesus, with the possible exception of intelligence. In fact, the prophecy of Isaiah 53:2 stated that "he had no beauty or majesty to attract us to him, nothing in his appearance that we should desire him" (*New International Version*). It seems that Jesus was no more than ordinary in all of His physical features, and undoubtedly that was part of God's design. The intention was that the Son humble Himself and take the form of a servant (Philippians 2:5-8).

2. Do you believe that people today appreciate God's gift of a Savior? What would cause people to have a greater appreciation?

For many people, the celebration of Christmas has little to do with the receiving of a Savior. Even though they may talk about what Christmas really means, their level of appreciation is relative to their sense of need. If I receive a bowling ball as a gift, I will not be nearly as appreciative as someone who likes to bowl. I do not need a bowling ball, since I have no desire to go bowling. So long as people do not understand that they are sinners, that they are actually under the tyranny of sin, and that they stand condemned before God for their sin, they cannot fully appreciate the Christmas message.

3. If God had chosen not to send Jesus, what would the result be for us? Other than love, was there anything that made sending His Son necessary?

If God sent His Son "that we might live through him" (1 John 4:9), then without His coming we could look forward to only condemnation and death. It is important to understand that God had no other motive than love in providing for our salvation. He was not compelled to rescue us out of pride or the need to prove

anything. He was not infatuated with us because we are so attractive. Neither was sending His Son a casual decision. It was an intentional choice motivated purely by love.

4. What are some of the qualities of God's love that we should copy in our love for others?

God's love was a choice of the will and not a response based upon attraction or natural affinity. We tend to operate on emotion when it comes to love. We sometimes discriminate, choosing to love those whom we find appealing, or who may be able to benefit us in some way. Also, God's love took the initiative. God's love gave (John 3:16); His love sent (1 John 4:9). Our love for one another should be evidenced in action, not just in what we say.

5. What deeds of love in the lives of others have persuaded you that God is present in them (1 John 4:12)?

Jesus made love the hallmark of discipleship (John 13:34, 35). If you have been involved in regular fellowship with other Christians, hopefully you can point to acts of love that you have observed in them. Some of those acts of love perhaps have been directed your way. Was there an encouraging word, an offer to pray, an invitation to have coffee or share a meal, a hospital visit, a card, a letter, a pie, help with a task, an offer to watch your children, a ride when your car broke down, a listening ear, a broad shoulder? One person simply taking a genuine, unselfish interest in another can be a powerful expression of God-inspired love.

6. How will your observance of Christmas testify that Jesus is Savior?

For years I resisted putting lights on our house and shrubs at Christmas. Then one year I read that the display of lights was actually initiated as a means of honoring the One who came as the Light of the world. Now I display our lights annually. You can sing in a choir, go caroling in a nursing home, volunteer to serve Christmas dinner at a Christian benevolence mission, participate in a "live nativity," or lead your family in a special reading of the Christmas story. There are many ways to exalt Christ at Christmas.

Conquering Through Faith in Christ

DEVOTIONAL READING: Romans 8:31-39.

LESSON SCRIPTURE: 1 John 5:1-12.

PRINTED TEXT: 1 John 5:1-12.

1 John 5:1-12

1 Whosoever believeth that Jesus is the Christ is born of God: and every one that loveth him that begat loveth him also that is begotten of him.

2 By this we know that we love the children of God, when we love God, and keep his commandments.

3 For this is the love of God, that we keep his commandments: and his commandments are not grievous.

4 For whatsoever is born of God overcometh the world: and this is the victory that overcometh the world, even our faith.

5 Who is he that overcometh the world, but he that believeth that Jesus is the Son of God?

6 This is he that came by water and blood, even Jesus Christ; not by water only, but by water and blood. And it is the Spirit that beareth witness, because the Spirit is truth.

7 For there are three that bear record in heaven, the Father, the Word, and the Holy Ghost: and these three are one.

8 And there are three that bear witness in earth, the spirit, and the water, and the blood: and these three agree in one.

9 If we receive the witness of men, the witness of God is greater: for this is the witness of God which he hath testified of his Son.

10 He that believeth on the Son of God hath the witness in himself: he that believeth not God hath made him a liar; because he believeth not the record that God gave of his Son.

11 And this is the record, that God hath given to us eternal life, and this life is in his Son.

12 He that hath the Son hath life; and he that hath not the Son of God hath not life.

GOLDEN TEXT: This is the victory that overcometh the world, even our faith.
Who is he that overcometh the world, but he that believeth
that Jesus is the Son of God?—1 John 5:4, 5.

God's People in a Troubled World
Unit 1: God's Love in a Troubled World
(Lessons 1-4)

Lesson Aims

After this lesson, students should be able to:

1. List some of the blessings we receive through faith in Jesus Christ.

2. Describe how faith is concerned with what we do as well as what we believe.

3. Determine to make a specific stand of faith this week.

Lesson Outline

INTRODUCTION
    A. Exalting Christ
    B. Seeing Christ
    C. Lesson Background
 I. PLACED IN GOD'S FAMILY (1 John 5:1-3)
    A. Love Begets (v. 1)
    B. Love Obeys (vv. 2, 3)
 II. POSITION IN GOD'S FAMILY (1 John 5:4-10)
    A. Faith Conquers (v. 4)
      Victory in Jesus
    B. Object of Faith (vv. 5, 6a)
    C. Witness for Faith (vv. 6b-10)
      Misplaced Faith
III. PURPOSE IN GOD'S FAMILY (1 John 5:11, 12)
    A. Source of Life (v. 11)
    B. Seal of Life (v. 12)
CONCLUSION
    A. Three Essentials
    B. Prayer
    C. Thought to Remember

The visual for Lesson 4 in the visuals packet focuses on the importance of faith in obtaining spiritual victory. It is shown on page 148.

Introduction

A. Exalting Christ

A number of prominent literary men were assembled in London many years ago. The conversation veered to a discussion of the illustrious figures of the past. Someone in the group suddenly asked, "Gentlemen, what would you do if Beethoven were to enter this room?" Another replied, "We would give him the ovation that he rightly deserves."

This started a series of nostalgic reflections, as another asked, "What if Shakespeare would enter the room?" The answer was given: "We would arise and toast him as the greatest dramatist of history." "What if Queen Victoria would enter?" A quick response was, "We would stand at attention and salute with honor Her Majesty."

Finally, the most important question was raised: "What if Jesus Christ would appear?" The unanimous response was, "We would fall on our knees in humble adoration and worship Him."

The object of John's writing was to give his readers such a clear view of Christ that they would acknowledge His lordship, demonstrate His love to others, and obey His commands. As today's lesson proceeds, we need to keep the greatness, glory, and grandeur of Christ before our minds, so that we too will worship and follow Him.

B. Seeing Christ

In a certain museum there is a painting that seems to be nothing more than a crazy patchwork of colors, with paint scattered randomly across the canvas. One would think that only a connoisseur of modern art could appreciate it. But when viewed through a specially colored filter, something remarkable happens. Emerging from the maze, the words "Jesus Saves" appear clearly and distinctly.

For many people, life is a meaningless maze of random incidents. Nothing seems to make sense. Then Christ comes into that life, and an amazing transformation takes place. Suddenly, situations and circumstances begin to make sense. Just as the colored filter allowed one to make sense out of a picture, so Christ can give meaning to life.

To carry our comparison a step further, we need the New Testament account of Christ's life, written under the influence of the Holy Spirit, as the lens through which to see Him. Here we find what John calls "the record that God gave of his Son" (1 John 5:10). We are reminded of the purpose of John's Gospel: "that ye might believe that Jesus is the Christ, the Son of God; and that believing ye might have life through his name" (John 20:31).

C. Lesson Background

Thus far in our studies from 1 John, we have focused on the most prominent themes in the book, including light, love, and life. With today's lesson (the final one in this unit), we come to a passage that highlights another purpose behind John's letter: to give his readers assurance of their salvation and their eternal life in Christ. John addresses a question that many Christians through the years have posed: "How can I know with certainty that I am saved?"

I. Placed in God's Family
(1 John 5:1-3)

A. Love Begets (v. 1)

1. Whosoever believeth that Jesus is the Christ is born of God: and every one that loveth him that begat loveth him also that is begotten of him.

The word *Christ* is the Greek term for the Hebrew word *Messiah*. Both mean "the Anointed One." In the Old Testament, three types of people were anointed: prophets, priests, and kings. Jesus perfectly fulfills all three of these offices. He has prophesied of His return (Matthew 24:44), of the eternal home that He has gone to prepare for us (John 14:1-4), and of the eternal punishment of the wicked (Matthew 25:46). As our High Priest, He made the only sacrifice that can cover our sins by His death on the cross (Hebrews 7:26, 27). He now makes intercession for us (Hebrews 7:25). As our King, He rules over the church, His kingdom on earth (Colossians 1:13).

To believe that *Jesus is the Christ* can be mere mental acceptance, such as that which the demons possess (Mark 1:23, 24). Here, however, John is talking about a saving faith in which one commits his life to Christ (Romans 5:1). "Belief" and "faith" are both translations of the same Greek word, so we must decide by context the extent of the meaning of the word.

John also states that belief is essential to being *born of God*. Earlier he indicated that love is essential (4:7). This illustrates the principle, stated in last week's lesson, that all Scripture on a given subject must be taken into consideration, and harmonized into a complete picture of God's plan of salvation.

Those *begotten of him*, whom we should love, are all Christians, for they too are in God's family. How can we manifest this love? Here are some suggestions based on selected passages from the New Testament:

1. Rejoice with those who rejoice, and weep with those who weep (Romans 12:15).

2. Seek the good of others (Romans 12:10; 1 Corinthians 10:33).

3. Forgive one another (Colossians 3:13).

4. Bear one another's burdens (Galatians 6:2).

5. Take care not to offend (Romans 14:21; 1 Corinthians 8:12, 13).

6. Show compassion (1 John 3:17, 18).

7. Do not engage in harsh judgments of others (Matthew 7:1, 2).

8. Avoid envy (1 Corinthians 13:4).

9. Be kind and tenderhearted (Ephesians 4:32).

10. Do not speak evil of others (James 4:11).

B. Love Obeys (vv. 2, 3)

2. By this we know that we love the children of God, when we love God, and keep his commandments.

Jesus taught that *love* is the motivation to *keep* God's *commandments* (John 14:15). Love and law are not mutually exclusive. J. W. McGarvey wrote, "Love without law is power without direction, and law without love is machinery without a motor" (*Fourfold Gospel*, p. 604).

3. For this is the love of God, that we keep his commandments: and his commandments are not grievous.

God in His *love* wants us to *keep his commandments*, because He knows that it is best for us to do so. Through keeping them we find the abundant life. The Greek word *grievous* was used to describe a heavy bar that might be burdensome to someone. This is not true of God's commandments. They are reasonable, just, and designed to provide a life of joy and freedom for Christ's disciples.

II. Position in God's Family
(1 John 5:4-10)

A. Faith Conquers (v. 4)

4. For whatsoever is born of God overcometh the world: and this is the victory that overcometh the world, even our faith.

The term *world* renders the Greek word *kosmos*. This word possesses a number of meanings in the New Testament. Quite often it means far more than just the physical world. Earlier John exhorted Christians to "love not the world, neither the things that are in the world" (1 John 2:15). This may appear to contradict the declaration of John 3:16 that "God so loved the world." But John 3:16 is describing the world of humanity, whereas in 1 John 2:15 *world* means, as one writer puts it, "human society in so far as it is organized on wrong principles, and characterized by base desires, false values, and egoism."

How to Say It

CERINTHIANS. Suh-*rin*-thee-unz.
CERINTHUS. Suh-*rin*-thus.
CYPRIAN. *Sip*-ree-un.
DOCETISM. Doe-*set*-iz-um.
DONATUS. *Don*-uh-tuss.
GNOSTICS. *Nahss*-ticks.
KOSMOS (Greek). *kahss*-moss.

Still another observes, "'The world' is not made up of so many outward objects that can be specified; it is the sum of those influences emanating from men and things around us, which draw us away from God." This is the *world* that Christians are commanded not to love but to overcome, even while loving those who have been corrupted by the world. It is similar to the idea of hating the sin but loving the sinner.

Whereas the *world* is characterized by a fascination with sight (the "lust of the eyes," says 1 John 2:16), Christians are to overcome the world by *faith*. Our faith in Christ and His promises will enable us to conquer the worldly temptations all around us. Materialism and secularism are subtle influences to which we sometimes yield without realizing it. We are tempted to put our trust in money, possessions, technology, and philosophy, instead of in God as revealed in the Scriptures. By *faith* we can conquer these enemies of the soul.

In the third century, Cyprian of Carthage wrote a letter to a friend in which he said, "It is a bad world Donatus, an exceedingly bad world. But I have discovered in the midst of it a great and holy people who have learned a great secret. They have found a joy that is a thousand times better than any of the pleasures of our sinful life. They are despised and persecuted, but they care not. They are masters of their souls. They have overcome the world."

In John 16:33 Jesus assured His disciples that although they would suffer tribulation in the world, they could still "be of good cheer," for He had "overcome the world." These words were meant for disciples both then and now, for Jesus triumphed over him who rules "the darkness of this world" (Ephesians 6:12). Through Jesus there is victory over sin and its consequences.

VICTORY IN JESUS

There once was a lady who attended church regularly, but who refused to sing the hymn, "Onward Christian Soldiers." Deeply concerned about world peace, she felt that a militaristic song was incompatible with Christian faith. What she failed to understand was that speaking of spiritual warfare or singing of victory in Jesus has nothing to do with wars among nations. It is only taking a picture familiar to all and using it to explain a spiritual principle. Faith in Christ does give us victory over sin, loneliness, weakness, temptation, and discouragement. Perhaps this is the reason for the popularity of the old song, "Victory in Jesus."

At the same time, it is not completely accurate to say that faith brings victory. Faith is itself the victory. Overcoming the world may seem impossible at times. But when we read the book of Revelation, we know that future victory is not in doubt. When we read John's words in 1 John 4:4 ("Greater is he that is in you, than he that is in the world"), we know that present victory is attainable. We are always overcomers—as long as our faith is in the Great Overcomer: Christ Jesus.   —R. C. S.

B. Object of Faith (vv. 5, 6a)

5. Who is he that overcometh the world, but he that believeth that Jesus is the Son of God?

John claims that only the true believer in *Jesus* as *the Son of God* can overcome *the world*. John also wrote of this victory in the book of Revelation, as he recorded these triumphant words spoken by a voice from Heaven: "Now is come salvation, and strength, and the kingdom of our God, and the power of his Christ: for the accuser of our brethren is cast down" (Revelation 12:10).

This victory over the world applies to more than an individual's triumph. It also speaks to the church in its efforts to counter the influence of Satan in society. If people would truly believe in Jesus as God's Son and be fully committed to Him, civilization would experience a victory over the social problems that have developed primarily because man's soul is not right with God.

6a. This is he that came by water and blood, even Jesus Christ; not by water only, but by water and blood.

Having identified the One in whom our faith is placed, John elaborates on this point by describing Jesus as *he that came by water and blood*. Several suggestions have been made as to the meaning of this phrase. Among the most common are the following. First, some believe that the two terms emphasized the humanity of Jesus, thus countering the heretical teaching, held by some of the Gnostics, that Jesus was not human, but only seemed to be. This viewpoint was referred to as *Docetism*, a term that comes

visual for
lesson 4

F amily of God

A dherence to His Commands

I rrefutable Testimony

T ruth from God

H ope for Eternal Life

IS THE VICTORY

from a Greek word meaning "to seem." Second, others take *water* to refer to Jesus' baptism and *blood* to signify His death. A third view understands the two terms to describe the water and the blood that flowed from Jesus' side at His crucifixion, when a Roman soldier pierced His side with a spear (John 19:32-35). According to this position, John would again be challenging the Gnostic denial of the humanity of Jesus.

Most Bible students and commentators prefer the second of these interpretations; that is, *water* refers to Jesus' baptism and *blood* to His death. This would have been a crucial point for John to establish, because of the existence of a branch of Gnostics known as the Cerinthians (not to be confused with the Corinthians!). Their leader, Cerinthus, taught that the divine Christ descended on the human Jesus at His baptism, but left Him before His death. Such teaching was an effort to keep deity from suffering, which was abhorrent to Cerinthus.

John's strong emphasis on *water and blood* was most likely a response to these false teachers. He declared that Jesus' baptism (*water*) and His death (*blood*) were the focal points of His ministry (in a sense, the beginning and the end). Jesus' death did not nullify or contradict His baptism; rather, both His baptism and His death were essential to the fulfillment of His mission.

C. Witness for Faith (vv. 6b-10)

6b. And it is the Spirit that beareth witness, because the Spirit is truth.

The *Spirit* testified to Jesus' position and authority throughout His ministry. Peter declared, "God anointed Jesus of Nazareth with the Holy Ghost and with power: who went about doing good, and healing all that were oppressed of the devil; for God was with him" (Acts 10:38). Jesus also promised the apostles that they would receive the Holy Spirit, who would guide them into all truth and glorify Jesus (John 16:13, 14).

7. For there are three that bear record in heaven, the Father, the Word, and the Holy Ghost: and these three are one.

The words of this verse and the first part of verse 8 ("in heaven, the Father, the Word, and the Holy Ghost: and these three are one. And there are three that bear witness in earth") are left out of most recent versions of the New Testament, because they do not appear in the best of the ancient Greek manuscripts (only in two rather late ones). They do not appear in any manuscript or translation from before the sixteenth century.

This does not mean that the doctrine of the Trinity is not a Biblical teaching. The *Father*, the Son (*the Word*), and the *Holy Ghost* appear together in Matthew 28:19 and 2 Corinthians 13:14. The use of *Word* to refer to Jesus calls to mind the opening verses of John's Gospel (John 1:1-3, 14).

8. And there are three that bear witness in earth, the spirit, and the water, and the blood: and these three agree in one.

John was interested in establishing the truth about who Jesus was, in order to respond to the false teachers of his day. In the Old Testament two or three witnesses were necessary to confirm a testimony (Deuteronomy 19:15). So John appealed to three divine witnesses. The *spirit* is the Holy Spirit, although for some reason the word is not capitalized in the *King James Version*. Jesus' submission to baptism in *water* by John the Baptist established His relationship to God the Father as announced at that time (Matthew 3:16, 17). By shedding His *blood*, He accomplished His Father's plan for the salvation of mankind. The apostle John had been associated with these events and knew that they were true.

9. If we receive the witness of men, the witness of God is greater: for this is the witness of God which he hath testified of his Son.

Three times God had given *witness* audibly to the eternal sonship of Jesus. The first was at His baptism, as already noted. The second time occurred when God declared His pleasure in His Son Jesus on the mount of transfiguration (Matthew 17:5), during which John was present. Finally, God spoke from Heaven in response to Jesus' prayer (John 12:27, 28).

10. He that believeth on the Son of God hath the witness in himself: he that believeth not God hath made him a liar; because he believeth not the record that God gave of his Son.

The *witness* that we have within us is the Holy Spirit promised to us by Jesus (John 7:37-39) and in Peter's sermon to the crowd at Pentecost (Acts 2:38). Paul teaches that Christians are the temple of the Holy Spirit (1 Corinthians 3:16; 6:19). He says that the Spirit "beareth witness with our spirit, that we are the children of God" (Romans 8:16).

The *record that God gave of his Son* is found in the New Testament Scriptures, given to us by the apostles under the inspiration of the Holy Spirit. As noted earlier, Jesus promised that the Spirit would guide His apostles into all truth (John 16:13), and when we follow their word we can claim that promise as ours.

MISPLACED FAITH

When Communism fell in Poland, and a free economy was introduced, American dollars appeared all over the country. For years Poles had saved their money in American dollars, often sent to them by relatives in America. They refused to save money in Polish currency, for they had no faith in it.

Of course, faith in the economic sense is not the same as faith in the spiritual sense. Spiritually, we can never put our faith in money, no matter what country issues the currency. While Christians in Poland saved dollars as everyone else tried to do, they, like us, recognized that ultimately faith must be in Christ, never in material things. Money can be stolen. Currencies can lose their value through inflation. As a gospel song says, "Some build their hopes on the ever-drifting sand; Some on their fame, or their treasure or their land; Mine's on the Rock that forever shall stand, Jesus the 'Rock of Ages.'" Faith in Christ possesses a worth that does not diminish over the years. In fact, it grows more valuable with every passing year.

A well-known insurance company once advertised using the slogan, "Get a piece of the rock." In Christ we have not merely a piece of the rock; we have the Rock of Ages Himself—firm and unmovable.   —R. C. S.

III. Purpose in God's Family (1 John 5:11, 12)

A. Source of Life (v. 11)

11. And this is the record, that God hath given to us eternal life, and this life is in his Son.

The purpose of the *record* of all that God has done is to bring to mankind *eternal life*. He gave us physical life at birth. He can give us spiritual life through a rebirth, made possible through Jesus Christ *his Son*. As we are told in Acts 4:12, there is salvation in no other name under Heaven. God wants all humanity to find this life

Home Daily Bible Readings

Monday, Dec. 22—Living Victoriously (1 John 5:1-12)

Tuesday, Dec. 23—Love Poured Into Our Hearts (Romans 5:1-11)

Wednesday, Dec. 24—Peace Among Those God Favors (Luke 2:1-15)

Thursday, Dec. 25—Ruler for the People of God (Matthew 2:1-12)

Friday, Dec. 26—God Has Spoken by the Son (Hebrews 1:1-6)

Saturday, Dec. 27—See the Salvation of Our God (Isaiah 52:7-10)

Sunday, Dec. 28—Victory Through Jesus Christ (1 Corinthians 15:50-58)

(1 Timothy 2:4). He wants no one to perish in their sins (2 Peter 3:9).

Many think of eternal life in terms of endless ages spent in the bliss of Heaven, where there is no more sin, sorrow, or suffering. Certainly that is part of it (Revelation 21:4). However, the only definition of this term is found in John 17:3, where Jesus says that eternal life is to "know thee the only true God, and Jesus Christ, whom thou hast sent." Thus eternal life is a relationship with God, not with time.

B. Seal of Life (v.12)

12. He that hath the Son hath life; and he that hath not the Son of God hath not life.

Nothing can be simpler and at the same time more profound than this. What one does with *the Son* is not a "trivial pursuit"; it is a matter of *life* and death.

Conclusion

A. Three Essentials

We are all familiar with Paul's beautiful trilogy at the end of 1 Corinthians 13: faith, hope, and charity, or love. Notice that in this epistle of 1 John that we have been studying over the past month, John also uses these terms as qualities of the children of God. In this lesson he exalts *faith* as the source of victory in life. In our last lesson he emphasized *love* as the expression of our family relationship in Christ. In our lesson from 1 John 3, we were challenged by the blessed *hope* of seeing Jesus as He is and of being like Him someday.

We should also note how often one or more of these three essentials appear near the beginning of Paul's letters to churches. See Ephesians 1:15; Philippians 1:9; Colossians 1:3-5; 1 Thessalonians 1:3; and 2 Thessalonians 1:3. More than any other standard of growth, the three essentials seemed to serve as a kind of "measuring stick" by which Paul determined the level of maturity that a congregation had reached.

Remember: faith, hope, and love are the three essentials, not the three electives!

B. Prayer

Father, may we in faith trust Your Word, in hope wait expectantly for our everlasting home in glory, and in love care for others and show that we belong to Jesus. In His name we pray, amen.

C. Thought to Remember

Eternal life is a relationship with God, not with time.

Learning by Doing

This page contains an alternate lesson plan emphasizing learning activities.
Classes desiring such student involvement will find these suggestions helpful.

Learning Goals

After completing this lesson, your students should be able to:

1. List some of the blessings we receive through faith in Jesus Christ.

2. Describe how faith is concerned with what we do as well as what we believe.

3. Determine to make a specific stand of faith this week.

Into the Lesson

Begin by relating the anecdote that appears in the lesson Introduction ("Exalting Christ"). Then ask, "What would you do if Christ were to enter this classroom? How would you respond to Him?"

Likely, most students will say that they would bow down and worship Him. If He were to make a dramatic appearance such as that, they probably would. However, the challenge of living the Christian life is to exalt and worship Christ daily, in situations that may not appear to possess a great deal of "drama."

Today's lesson is about conquering the daily adversities, disappointments, and temptations of life through faith in Christ.

Into the Word

This lesson begins at the right place: spiritual birth (1 John 5:1). When we first believe in and accept Christ as our Savior, we are spiritual infants. Tell your students to think back to the time when they first accepted Christ and to think about how they felt at that time (this activity is also found in the student book). Then ask, "What's good about the new birth and about being a spiritual infant?" They may suggest some of these ideas:

• A fresh start (2 Corinthians 5:17)
• Excitement and enthusiasm
• Forgiveness of sins
• A relationship with our heavenly Father
• Fellowship with others in God's family

Also ask, "What do we expect to happen to infants?" (We expect them to grow, develop, and mature.)

In this passage John identifies three specific evidences of spiritual growth and maturity: loving other believers (v. 1), keeping God's commandments (vv. 2, 3), and overcoming the world by faith (vv. 4, 5).

One evidence of spiritual growth and maturity is loving other believers. The lesson commentary (under 1 John 5:1) lists ten ways this love can be demonstrated in the Christian community. Write the list on the chalkboard or a sheet of newsprint, and challenge your students to give a specific example of each in operation (this activity is also included in the student book). Here is an example to go with "Avoid harsh judgments": While driving home one night, you see a member of your church leave a bar and walk to his car. Your first thought is, "He was in there drinking," but you realize that there could be legitimate reasons why he was in the bar. So you keep an open mind.

Another evidence of spiritual growth is keeping God's commandments. Some Christians believe that accepting Christ as Savior liberates them from all rules and regulations, but this simply is not true. Ask the students to suggest some of the laws that believers must follow. For example:

• The teachings of Jesus (John 14:15)
• The law of love (Romans 13:8-10)
• The laws of the government (Romans 13:1)
• The disciplines of a local church
• The rules of the family

A third evidence of spiritual growth is overcoming the world by faith. Use these questions to help your students think about how to be overcomers:

• What is your greatest and most persistent temptation?

• What happened the last time you were tempted in this area?

• If you overcame and resisted, how were you able to be an overcomer? If you gave in, why did you fail?

• What role did faith play in your overcoming or your failure?

(If your class works well in small groups, divide students into groups of three to discuss these questions.)

Into Life

As you bring the lesson to a close, challenge your students to determine to be overcomers during the coming week. Urge them to focus on one bad habit or attitude. Encourage them to put their full faith in Christ to help them be an overcomer in that specific area.

Let's Talk It Over

The questions on this page are designed to encourage review of the lesson Scriptures and to promote discussion of the lesson by the class. The answers provided are only discussion starters. Let your class talk it over from there.

1. First John 5:1 implies that anyone who loves God loves the children of God. Why is it important to keep this link in mind?

Evidently some of those who received this letter from the apostle John held the opinion that their relationship with God was a separate matter from their relationship with other believers. Not only here, but in the rest of the letter, John calls into question the sincerity of faith and the depth of commitment of anyone who does not show concern for other believers. Love is not an option; it is integral to the character of the Christian. John is directly linking what one professes to believe with what one does. His argument is that if there is no correspondence between the two, the profession is suspect.

2. How do we know what love demands in terms of behavior? Can we trust our instincts? What is the standard?

About thirty years ago we began to hear a lot about "situation ethics." Those who promoted situation ethics rejected the possibility of any absolute standard of right and wrong behavior, insisting that judgments about what is right must be made with the particular situation in view. They concocted preposterous circumstances to try to demonstrate that the loving thing to do may, at times, be exactly the opposite of generally accepted norms. The Bible teaches that love is expressed when we love God and keep His commandments. The definition of loving behavior has been established by the laws of God, and by the example of Jesus in perfect obedience. We do not have to wonder what love would do. We certainly cannot trust the instincts of our sinful nature.

3. Do you agree with the statement that God's commandments are "not grievous" (1 John 5:3)? Why or why not? How does one come to that conclusion?

Anyone who agrees with John's statement is probably one who has made a sincere effort to know God's commands and to live by them. The person who suspects that God is a cosmic killjoy, out to ruin all our fun by a burdensome list of difficult rules, neither knows God nor His commands very well. Making the effort to become familiar with God's commands and to obey them proves to us that they are not arbitrary, nor are they given just to test our resolve. God's laws have a practical purpose and are meant to preserve, protect, and enrich our lives. Like any parent who establishes standards for his or her children, God issues commands that are an expression of His love, and "in keeping them there is great reward" (Psalm 19:11).

4. The words "victory" and "overcometh" (1 John 5:4) depict a struggle. What does it mean to overcome the world? What would it mean to be overcome by the world?

The "world" in this context refers to the perspectives and attitudes arrayed against the will of God. Such temporal values as money, fame, power, and lust appeal to our base nature and can easily distract us from eternal, spiritual values. To overcome the world means maintaining faith and trust in God and in Jesus as the Savior—so much so that we resist the enticements of this world when they conflict with God's will and His values. To be overcome would mean sacrificing our faith and character in favor of this world's rewards. Christians must take this struggle seriously, realizing that we cannot remain passive and hope to overcome.

5. What evidence or testimony that Jesus is the divine Son of God carries the most weight for you? Why?

The forms of evidence and testimony will vary in their impact from person to person. Concerning the issue of the identity of Jesus as the Son of God, John's point is that we have the benefit of multiple witnesses. You may be most influenced by the testimony of the prophecies that were fulfilled in Jesus. The eyewitness accounts of His life and ministry, or His effect upon those who knew Him best may impress you most. John argues that beyond the human witnesses, we have the witness of God, and it is greater (1 John 5:9). The Father confirmed the identity of the Son through the visits by angels at the time of Jesus' birth, through the voice heard from Heaven on three occasions, and through Jesus' miracle-working power. Finally, the Holy Spirit gives persuasive testimony, not only as manifested in the life of Jesus, but as demonstrated in the lives of His followers.

Living in Hope

DEVOTIONAL READING: Hebrews 11:1-12.

LESSON SCRIPTURE: 1 Peter 1:3-22.

PRINTED TEXT: 1 Peter 1:3-12.

1 Peter 1:3-12

3 Blessed be the God and Father of our Lord Jesus Christ, which according to his abundant mercy hath begotten us again unto a lively hope by the resurrection of Jesus Christ from the dead,

4 To an inheritance incorruptible, and undefiled, and that fadeth not away, reserved in heaven for you,

5 Who are kept by the power of God through faith unto salvation ready to be revealed in the last time.

6 Wherein ye greatly rejoice, though now for a season, if need be, ye are in heaviness through manifold temptations:

7 That the trial of your faith, being much more precious than of gold that perisheth, though it be tried with fire, might be found unto praise and honor and glory at the appearing of Jesus Christ:

8 Whom having not seen, ye love; in whom, though now ye see him not, yet believing, ye rejoice with joy unspeakable and full of glory:

9 Receiving the end of your faith, even the salvation of your souls.

10 Of which salvation the prophets have inquired and searched diligently, who prophesied of the grace that should come unto you:

11 Searching what, or what manner of time the Spirit of Christ which was in them did signify, when it testified beforehand the sufferings of Christ, and the glory that should follow.

12 Unto whom it was revealed, that not unto themselves, but unto us they did minister the things, which are now reported unto you by them that have preached the gospel unto you with the Holy Ghost sent down from heaven; which things the angels desire to look into.

GOLDEN TEXT: God . . . hath begotten us again unto a lively hope by the resurrection of Jesus Christ from the dead.—1 Peter 1:3.

God's People in a Troubled World
Unit 2: Hope for God's People
(Lessons 5-8)

Lesson Aims

The study of this lesson is designed to help students:

1. Describe the source, demonstration, and object of the hope to which Christians have been "begotten."

2. Tell how such hope can help Christians face the pressures of modern life.

3. State their confidence of Christian hope in terms of overcoming a specific trial.

Lesson Outline

INTRODUCTION
  A. Checking Our Mail
  B. Lesson Background
 I. A THANKSGIVING PRAYER (1 Peter 1:3-5)
  A. A New Birth (v. 3)
    Doctor Hope
  B. An Inheritance Unfading (v. 4)
  C. A Completed Salvation (v. 5)
II. OUR PRECIOUS FAITH (1 Peter 1:6-9)
  A. Not Without Trials (v. 6)
  B. More Precious Than Gold (v. 7)
    Gold and Paper
  C. Triumphant Love and Joy (v. 8)
  D. The Goal of Faith (v. 9)
III. THE ROOTS OF OUR FAITH (1 Peter 1:10-12)
  A. Foretold by the Prophets (v. 10)
  B. Indebted to the Prophets (v. 11)
  C. Revealed Through the Prophets (v. 12)
CONCLUSION
  A. The Other Side of Suffering
  B. Prayer
  C. Thought to Remember

Use the visual for Lesson 5 as an illustration of individuals who praise God despite their trials. It is shown on page 156.

Introduction

A. Checking Our Mail

Consider a familiar scene. Before entering the house at the end of the day, you go to your mailbox to get the mail. The last few weeks have been demanding. You are under fire from colleagues in the office because of your stand on some controversial issues. Even some members of your own family refuse to have anything to do with you because of your commitment to Christ. You are accused of being a troublemaker, of being old-fashioned and rigid. There have been days you have not felt like praying, let alone praising God.

You begin shuffling through the advertisements and bills, when suddenly your eye falls upon some handwriting that looks vaguely familiar. You look in the upper left-hand corner of the envelope, and notice that you have received a letter from a friend whom you have not seen for over thirty years. He is the one who led you to Christ. Because of his encouragement, you have been faithful, witnessing for Christ over the years and serving in spite of doubts and rejection by others. Running into the house and dropping all the other mail, you sit down in the chair and rip open the letter. The first few words make your heart jump: "Blessed be the God and Father of our Lord Jesus Christ . . ." Tears of thanksgiving begin to well up. Clearly this letter is not a piece of third-class junk mail, addressed to "Occupant." It is a letter addressed to a friend by a friend.

So it is with the letters, or epistles, in the New Testament. On one level they are letters sent from a friend(s) to a friend(s). On a higher level, however, they are letters sent from our heavenly Father to all of His children, including us. We need to ponder over every word, earnestly desiring to hear God—His encouragements, warnings, and exhortations.

B. Lesson Background

Some of the readers of 1 Peter would likely have heard Peter's sermon on the Day of Pentecost, ten days after Christ's ascension. Other readers would not have been in Jerusalem on that climactic day, but no doubt they had heard the story many times from the first generation of believers. There had been much celebration when the church was born. Many people were drawn to the faith because of the truths of the gospel, and because of the fellowship among Christians that confirmed that those truths had indeed changed their lives.

But life had grown tougher for Peter and for many of the Christians during the decades that followed. Many had been rejected by family members, others had lost their jobs, some had been imprisoned, and others had even given their lives for Christ's sake. By the time Peter wrote the letter we know as 1 Peter, the government-sanctioned persecution of Christians was beginning to intensify. Peter himself was probably living in Rome when he wrote the letter; the mention of "Babylon" in 1 Peter 5:13 is generally recognized as a cryptic, or hidden, reference to the capital of the empire that rivaled ancient Babylon in both splendor and oppression. Since the persecution of believers does not seem to have yet broken out in full force, the most probable time of writing is sometime before the end of A.D. 64, just prior to the outbreak of persecution under Emperor Nero. The storm clouds were gathering, and Christians throughout the empire, including Peter, would be affected.

In this letter, Peter encourages fellow Christians to remain steadfast and hopeful in the midst of the approaching severe hardships. He assures them that such difficulties are not a sign that their faith is weak or misdirected; rather, their faith in Christ is more than adequate to sustain them through whatever trials may come. In clarifying the nature of and reasons for suffering, Peter ultimately provides a basis for Christians to better understand the purpose of suffering from an eternal perspective, which then provides comfort and hope. Specifically, 1 Peter contains six passages that deal with the issue of suffering (1:6, 7; 2:19-25; 3:13-22; 4:1-6; 4:12-19; 5:6-10). Most of these passages will be covered during the next four Sundays.

The recipients of 1 Peter are described in the opening verse as "strangers scattered throughout Pontus, Galatia, Cappadocia, Asia, and Bithynia." These areas cover the northern, central, and western provinces of Asia Minor (modern Turkey). Residents from those areas had listened to and responded to Peter's preaching on the Day of Pentecost (see Acts 2:9-11). Now, more than thirty years after that first gospel sermon, some of those same residents (as well as another generation of Christians) were "hearing" a sermon from Peter by means of this letter.

I. A Thanksgiving Prayer (1 Peter 1:3-5)

A. A New Birth (v. 3)

3. Blessed be the God and Father of our Lord Jesus Christ, which according to his abundant mercy hath begotten us again unto a lively hope by the resurrection of Jesus Christ from the dead.

When a baby is born, there is much rejoicing. If the baby survives a life-threatening disease following his birth, the joy will likely be multiplied. Similarly, when a person becomes a Christian, there is rejoicing, both in Heaven and on earth. One's conversion, however, may quickly be followed by faith-threatening situations. How should a Christian respond when his faith is challenged by events beyond his control?

How to Say It

BITHYNIA. Bih-*thin*-e-uh.
CAPPADOCIA. Cap-uh-*doe*-shuh.
GALATIA. Guh-*lay*-shuh.
PONTUS. *Pon*-tuss.
TELOS (Greek). *tell*-awss.

What should he do when subjected to the hostile actions of neighbors or even family? Peter's doxology challenges us to rejoice and to praise God for what He has done for us. *God . . . according to his abundant mercy hath begotten us.* What beautiful words! God as merciful and loving *Father* is the divine initiator of our salvation. New life comes, not through what we do, but through what He has done in Christ. It is both Christ's death and *resurrection* and our death to sin and our resurrection (in baptism) that allow us to share in this new life. "Old things are passed away; behold, all things are become new" (2 Corinthians 5:17).

God's actions result in what Peter calls a *lively hope*, a term rendered "living hope" in the *New International Version* and the *New American Standard Bible*. How can Peter begin a letter about suffering on such a positive note? Because of the confidence and the solid certainty found only in Christ!

DOCTOR HOPE

It seemed to Polish linguist Ludwig Zamenhof (*Lood*-vig *Zah*-men-hoff) that many of the problems among nations were caused by simple misunderstandings. He believed that a universal language would be a big step in easing world tensions. A man who understood nine languages, he developed what he hoped would become a universal language. It was easy to learn and easy to pronounce. There were very few rules. He did not publish it under his own name, but chose the name Doctor "Esperanto" (Ess-pair-*ahn*-toe), a word that means *hope*. The language became known as Esperanto and is understood by several million people all over the world. However, despite Dr. Zamenhof's good intentions, it never caught on to the extent that he wished, and has not replaced English as the international language.

For Christians, the word *hope* is a lovely word that captures what Christ can give to people of all languages. Regardless of the vast differences between cultures, all human beings will die. All human beings need hope. The only sure hope is the Christian hope. Christ alone merits the title of "Doctor Hope." —R. C. S.

B. An Inheritance Unfading (v. 4)

4. To an inheritance incorruptible, and undefiled, and that fadeth not away, reserved in heaven for you.

This verse continues the emphasis on the hope and certainty of the Christian faith by describing the *inheritance* awaiting all believers. Often the confiscation and loss of material possessions accompanied the persecution of Christians in the first century (see Hebrews 10:34). Peter reminds his readers of their true riches in Christ. The three adjectives (*incorruptible, and undefiled, and that fadeth not away*) clearly contrast the differences between an earthly and a heavenly inheritance.

The nature of a person's hope is totally dependent upon the nature of that which is hoped for and its value. The Christian's hope is imperishable; it cannot be destroyed by war, defaced by enemies, or damaged by the passing of time. A Christian's death does not mean leaving his inheritance behind, for death is the time at which he gains his inheritance. The riches of Christ, *reserved in heaven*, are far more valuable than anything we can inherit from anyone in this life.

C. A Completed Salvation (v. 5)

5. Who are kept by the power of God through faith unto salvation ready to be revealed in the last time.

Here we are presented with a statement of how divine and human factors are involved in living the Christian life. On the one hand, the life of the Christian is one that is continually sustained by *the power of God*. The Greek word rendered *kept* is a military term, used in New Testament times to describe the responsibility of a sentry or guard. On the other hand, this keeping hinges on the believer's *faith*. Note that, although *salvation* means being forgiven of the past, it has a future dimension as well. The fulfillment or completion of the Christian's salvation, which will occur at the return of Jesus, should motivate him toward perseverance in his pilgrimage.

visual for
lesson 5

II. Our Precious Faith
(1 Peter 1:6-9)

In this section Peter turns to the major theme of his epistle: how Christians are to confront their hardships. He has laid the groundwork for dealing with this by his bold declaration of Christian hope in verses 3-5.

A. Not Without Trials (v. 6)

6. Wherein ye greatly rejoice, though now for a season, if need be, ye are in heaviness through manifold temptations.

The Christian life is not often an easy life. While the followers of Jesus have every reason to *rejoice*, they also know what it is like to experience the pain of rejection and slander by those dearest to them, as well as by those who are complete strangers. How thrilling is one's conversion to Christ! But how troubling are the trials and difficulties that can accompany it! The word *temptations* is perhaps better understood in this context as referring to the trials that beset the Christian from without rather than the temptations that entice him from within.

The word translated *heaviness* carries the idea of being "grieved." Such times may cause a believer to question his life in Christ. But these periods of grief last only *for a season*, in contrast to the eternal rewards awaiting those whose faith does not waver. In the remaining verses of this section, Peter presents reasons why Christians should remain faithful to the end.

B. More Precious Than Gold (v. 7)

7. That the trial of your faith, being much more precious than of gold that perisheth, though it be tried with fire, might be found unto praise and honor and glory at the appearing of Jesus Christ.

The Christian's *faith* is more *precious* than *gold*, and, like gold, it is placed in a furnace and proven true only after much testing. Such a comparison offers a most reassuring perspective on the sufferings of believers, and encourages them not to lose heart. To be more specific, when gold is submitted to the destructive agent of *fire*, the eventual result is an element of far greater value than before the heat is applied. Various kinds of trials may appear to be destructive, but in the end they pave the way for Christians to demonstrate true faith (1 Peter 4:12-14 and James 1:3, 12). Trials do not negate a Christian's testimony; they are designed to be part of his testimony to the world.

Taken together, verses 6 and 7 remind us that our trials, though they may seem to work against us, result in faithful Christians praising God *at the appearing of Jesus Christ* (1 Peter 1:13; 4:13; 5:1). The emphasis is not upon the "fiery trial" itself (4:12), but upon the outcome: Christians are to give glory to God by living faithfully, obediently, and confidently, and He will reward them for their steadfastness.

GOLD AND PAPER

Can you imagine what gold would say if it could talk to the jeweler? "Don't put me in the fire! It's hot in there. I don't want to go through the fire." And the jeweler would reply, "You must go through the fire. Now you are just a lump of ore. When I get through with you, you will have the potential to become a beautiful ornament—something that is admired by everyone. Don't you understand that I'm trying to make something out of you?"

Or can you imagine what the paper would say to the poet if paper could talk? "Don't write on me. That pen scratches and hurts. I am clean and white, and you are making marks all over me." But the poet would respond, "Right now you are only a worthless piece of paper. When I get through with you, you will be a masterpiece. The pain is but for a moment. I must do this, for I am trying to make something out of you."

Of course, these imaginary incidents are not perfect illustrations of God's dealings with us. God does not put us through the fire. He does *permit* us to pass through the fire. God does not bring us pain, but He may *allow* us to suffer pain. And if we complain, God may say to us, "I permit this to happen because I want to make something out of you. Now you are just a lump of clay, but when you are all finished, you will be something beautiful and useful. You will be a masterpiece."   —R. C. S.

C. Triumphant Love and Joy (v. 8)

8. Whom having not seen, ye love; in whom, though now ye see him not, yet believing, ye rejoice with joy unspeakable and full of glory.

Unlike Peter, many of his readers have *not seen* the Lord; yet they *love* Him, and they *rejoice* exceedingly because their faith is strong enough to convince them of that which they do not see. May we follow their example as people who walk by faith, not by sight!

D. The Goal of Faith (v. 9)

9. Receiving the end of your faith, even the salvation of your souls.

Peter now calls attention to the ultimate victory that belongs to Christians alone. The Greek word translated *end* is *telos*. It refers to the goal or the fulfillment of our faith. Although we do not see the Lord now, the promise is that we

will "see his face" (Revelation 22:4). Faith will one day be rewarded with sight. For now, however, this promise should influence our daily perspective. We must move away from dependency upon sight to dependency upon the insight that comes by faith. This will enable us to cope with existing conditions, though admittedly trying, in an attitude of victory.

We can summarize verses 3-9 under the topic of salvation in Christ. Peter makes three points about this salvation. First, it begins with a new birth into a living hope. Second, its value is demonstrated through the trials that we experience. Finally, its completion will occur at the end of this age, when Christ returns.

It is in light of their promised *salvation* that Christians should evaluate every circumstance and decision. Because Christ has come and because Christ is coming, there ought to be a difference in how we live.

III. The Roots of Our Faith (1 Peter 1:10-12)

A. Foretold by the Prophets (v. 10)

10. Of which salvation the prophets have inquired and searched diligently, who prophesied of the grace that should come unto you.

Christian faith is not a recent invention, or a fad that is here today and gone tomorrow. It is grounded in God's activity in the past, using the Old Testament *prophets . . . who prophesied of the grace that should come unto you*. The inquiries by the prophets were concerned with the circumstances of *salvation* that involved the sufferings and glories of the Christ. Perhaps the most striking of these prophecies of *grace* is found in Isaiah 53, which vividly pictures the sufferings of Christ for the sins of others. No wonder the prophets *inquired and searched diligently* into such a wondrous salvation!

B. Indebted to the Prophets (v. 11)

11. Searching what, or what manner of time the Spirit of Christ which was in them did signify, when it testified beforehand the sufferings of Christ, and the glory that should follow.

For the apostle's readers, to be reminded that the message of salvation they had heard and embraced had been foretold ages before through the *Spirit of Christ* to the prophets was a glorious reassurance. The enemies of the faith were destined to fail miserably if they believed that their efforts could somehow silence the Christian message. God's plan had been, was now, and surely would be accomplished, no matter what circumstances Christians may be facing. *Sufferings* had been a part of God's plan for the

Founder of the Christian faith, followed by an entrance into glory (Hebrews 12:2). His disciples should not be surprised if they are called upon to travel the same path.

C. Revealed Through the Prophets (v. 12)

12. Unto whom it was revealed, that not unto themselves, but unto us they did minister the things, which are now reported unto you by them that have preached the gospel unto you with the Holy Ghost sent down from heaven; which things the angels desire to look into.

The prophets were men who served God and ministered to others rather than *themselves*. They preached a challenging, often unpopular, message to their contemporaries. Their glimpses into the future were directed at *us*, who through *the gospel* have believed in the Christ whose coming they foretold.

If Christians need still more assurance of the glory of their faith, they should recognize that, in addition to the prophets, even *angels* have eagerly desired to penetrate the mysteries of the gospel. The Greek word rendered *look into* means "to look intently or with great interest."

This is part of what makes our faith more precious than gold: it is the product of a divinely guided plan—so wonderful that even the angels stand in awe of it. What a privilege to possess such a spiritual treasure!

Conclusion

A. The Other Side of Suffering

As we noted in the Introduction to today's lesson, Peter wrote the epistle we know as 1 Peter to warn his readers of the very real possibility of being martyred for their faith in Christ. They should not be taken aback by the "fiery trial" that is fast approaching (1 Peter 4:12).

In the verses that we have studied today, Peter has explained the "other side" of suffering to people who are undergoing or facing severe trials and temptations. He presents a perspective that is grounded in eternal values. He helps us see that the Christian life is one of living between a glorious event of the past (the resurrection of Christ) and an equally glorious event of the future (the return of Christ). When people lose sense of the importance of the past and have no positive outlook on the future, they will eventually see no meaning in the present. It is in light of what God has done for us and will do for us that Christians commit themselves in the present to living lives that reflect God's grace, joy, and love.

Even as it offered hope in the middle of the first century, Peter's letter continues to do the same at the end of the twentieth century. It instills courage and assurance within Christ's flock, whether we face some devastating crisis or whether we prepare to meet the ordinary changes and challenges of everyday life.

I loved buying toys for our children when they were little. Some of my favorite toys (if not theirs!) were called "weebles." Weebles were egg-shaped toys that looked like popular cartoon characters or had the features of humans. In the bottom of each weeble was a lead weight, so that no matter how the weeble was placed on the floor, it would always bounce back up. The slogan used in advertisements for these toys was: "Weebles wobble but they don't fall down!"

Over the years I have often thought of the Christian life as similar to the "life" of a weeble. No matter what knocks us down, we are able to get back up. Why? Because of our living hope in God the Father and in Jesus our Lord!

Peter's letter places considerable emphasis upon the unsurpassed power and grace of God in caring for His people even in the midst of suffering and persecution. Regardless of our circumstances, we are never forsaken. Is it any wonder that 1 Peter has been called "the epistle of hope"?

B. Prayer

Father, we praise You that we are a part of Your family. For the hope that is ours because of Christ we praise You. When He comes again, may we be found faithful and holy. In Jesus' name. Amen.

C. Thought to Remember

Living in hope means living confidently, expectantly, and faithfully.

Home Daily Bible Readings

Monday, Dec. 29—News Angels Want to Know (1 Peter 1:10-16)
Tuesday, Dec. 30—Faith and Hope Set on God (1 Peter 1:17-21)
Wednesday, Dec. 31—Hope Overcomes Death (1 Corinthians 15:12-20)
Thursday, Jan. 1—Faith Makes Hope Sure (Hebrews 10:39—11:7)
Friday, Jan. 2—Holy Spirit Gives Power (Acts 1:6-11)
Saturday, Jan. 3—Filled With the Holy Spirit (Acts 2:1-4, 14-21)
Sunday, Jan. 4—God Gives Us Hope (Acts 2:37-47)

Learning by Doing

This page contains an alternate lesson plan emphasizing learning activities.
Classes desiring such student involvement will find these suggestions helpful.

Learning Goals

After this lesson, students should be able to:

1. Describe the source, demonstration, and object of the hope to which Christians have been "begotten."

2. Tell how such hope can help Christians face the pressures of modern life.

3. State their confidence of Christian hope in terms of overcoming a specific trial.

Into the Lesson

Before class, write the word *hope* on the chalkboard. As the students gather, ask them to be thinking about what hope means to them. What role does hope play in their lives?

Next, have your students imagine that they have been shipwrecked and marooned on an uninhabited island. In a situation like that, what would give them hope? What would happen if they lost all hope of ever being rescued?

Every day we are confronted with adversities, disappointments, distresses, heartaches, tragedies, and sorrows, either personally or through the modern media. These situations have the potential of draining us of hope and filling our hearts with despair.

In today's lesson Peter gives some positive instructions for those in danger of being overwhelmed by life's adversities.

Into the Word

Comment on the background of 1 Peter. It was written to Christians who were on the brink of facing severe persecution. Peter wanted to arm them in advance, so they would be prepared when adversity entered their lives.

Ask your students to suggest some possible responses to adversity. This may be easier for them if you name a specific adversity, such as the loss of a job or the unfaithfulness of a spouse (this activity appears in the student book). In responding, perhaps they can draw on their own experiences. Some may even be willing to share their experiences. Here are a few suggested responses: despair; hopelessness; anger (especially at God); emotional outbursts (even violent episodes); depression; revenge (against the person causing or perceived as causing their distress); withdrawal; denial; giving up.

Now direct the students to today's Scripture, and ask them to look for the responses in the midst of adversity, which Peter describes in 1 Peter 1:3-9. You may want to divide the class into groups of three for this Bible study activity (it is found in the student book). These positive responses should be identified:

- Praise (v. 3)
- Hope for the future in spite of the current hardships (vv. 3, 9)
- Rejoicing (v. 6). Note: we don't rejoice because of adversity, but in spite of it.
- Faith (vv. 7, 8)
- Love (v. 8)

Many people in the church talk about "Christian hope." Ask students to put that phrase in their own words. What does Christian hope mean to them? How much of it relates to what happens in this life? How much relates to the life to come?

Point out to your students that Christian hope is based on:

- the Scriptures,
- the promises of God found therein, and
- the resurrection of Jesus.

Into Life

There may come a time when, like the believers to whom Peter wrote his letter, we will face outright persecution for our faith in Christ. How do your students feel about this possibility? Do they believe they will ever face persecution for their faith? If that day ever comes, how do they think they will respond?

We all have been in situations in which it seemed like there was no hope: a serious illness, a broken relationship, a troubled marriage, a financial crisis. Maybe some of your students would be willing to tell about a time when they felt like giving up hope—and then tell how they were able to hold on to hope (this activity is found in the student book). Be sure your students know that being in distress and being tempted to give up hope does not mean that they have lost their faith or that they have betrayed Christ.

As you bring the lesson to a close, ask your students to think about a problem that is currently troubling them. Perhaps it is a problem at work, a problem with their children, a problem with their spouse, or a problem with a neighbor. Assure them that there is hope for their difficulty—hope found in Christ.

Let's Talk It Over

The questions on this page are designed to encourage review of the lesson Scriptures and to promote discussion of the lesson by the class. The answers provided are only discussion starters. Let your class talk it over from there.

1. What are some of the high hopes that new parents have for their child? What is the measure of how realistic these hopes are? What are the limits to the hopes of those who are children of God?

New parents love to fantasize about their child becoming famous in some way—as an intellectual genius, a musician, an athlete, an artist, or the like. There are many factors, however, that place limits upon the realization of such dreams, including genetic influences, opportunities for development, available wealth for paying teachers and coaches, illness or injury, and personal motivation. In some cases the parents cannot control these potentially limiting factors, and they are forced to temper their hopes to make them more realistic. With God, however, much more is possible. God can alter circumstances and He can re-create people. His power is proven in the resurrection of Jesus from the dead. As our adoptive parent, He has the right and the power to raise our hopes of eternal life and the triumph of righteousness.

2. What risks threaten any potential inheritance you may receive on earth? Which of those risks apply to the inheritance promised by God? Why?

Treasures in this world are not secure. Theft, illness, accident, family disputes, changing markets, natural disasters, economic recession, or inflation may destroy part of or all of any inheritance you hope to receive. The inheritance promised to the children of God, however, is not subject to any of these contingencies. God does not get sick, nor does He have accidents. No higher authority can confiscate His wealth, and His treasures do not decay as time passes. His family members may dispute with one another, but He is the perfect Judge who treats His children impartially. The destructive forces of this world cannot touch the world to come. The security of our inheritance is dependent upon the grace of our heavenly Father, "who does not change like shifting shadows" (James 1:17, *New International Version*).

3. What are some modern trials of faith that Christians experience? How can these trials result in greater praise and glory to Christ?

The athletes who will compete in the Olympic games this winter have undergone many trials. Through rigorous competition they have demonstrated the depth of their commitment, the level of their ability, and the effectiveness of their training. Through those trials they have perfected their performance, so that what we see at the Olympics will be the best they have to give. Circumstances that put our faith to the test can be seen as trials. Any time that our integrity is challenged by temptation, it is a trial of our faith. Will we do what is honest? Will we do what is moral? Will we do what is generous? Will we be true to our commitments? Will we live like the Christian we profess to be, even when the immediate cost is great? Whenever we choose what is right, even though it is also costly or difficult, this glorifies Christ because we are surrendering to His lordship over our lives.

4. How do thoughts of Jesus' "appearing" (1 Peter 1:7) help you endure trials of faith?

The way that you evaluate the relative cost of doing what is right in any set of circumstances depends largely upon your perspective. If your motto of life is, "You only go around once, so grab all the gusto you can," you may be likely to surrender personal integrity in exchange for immediate wealth, pleasure, power, or fame. If, however, you consider that Jesus may appear at any time to judge the world and to reign with His saints, the temporal enticements of this world suddenly seem less important.

5. What advantage do Christians have over the prophets and over angels with regard to the gospel?

Parts of God's plan were revealed to the prophets, but they were always couched in future tense. Thus the "big picture" remained somewhat of a puzzle to them. For us, the role of Jesus as the fulfillment of what the prophets said is a matter of record. We can examine what God has done and gain a high degree of understanding. Angels, it seems, are intensely interested in God's saving work, but the fact remains that it was not for them. Jesus took human form in order to accomplish redemption for humans. Nowhere does Scripture indicate that angels are included in God's redemption plan.

Becoming God's People

DEVOTIONAL READING: 2 Corinthians 1:3-14.

LESSON SCRIPTURE: 1 Peter 2:1-10.

PRINTED TEXT: 1 Peter 2:1-10.

1 Peter 2:1-10

1 Wherefore laying aside all malice, and all guile, and hypocrisies, and envies, and all evil speakings,

2 As newborn babes, desire the sincere milk of the word, that ye may grow thereby:

3 If so be ye have tasted that the Lord is gracious.

4 To whom coming, as unto a living stone, disallowed indeed of men, but chosen of God, and precious,

5 Ye also, as lively stones, are built up a spiritual house, a holy priesthood, to offer up spiritual sacrifices, acceptable to God by Jesus Christ.

6 Wherefore also it is contained in the Scripture, Behold, I lay in Zion a chief corner stone, elect, precious: and he that believeth on him shall not be confounded.

7 Unto you therefore which believe he is precious: but unto them which be disobedient, the stone which the builders disallowed, the same is made the head of the corner,

8 And a stone of stumbling, and a rock of offense, even to them which stumble at the word, being disobedient: whereunto also they were appointed.

9 But ye are a chosen generation, a royal priesthood, a holy nation, a peculiar people; that ye should show forth the praises of him who hath called you out of darkness into his marvelous light:

10 Which in time past were not a people, but are now the people of God: which had not obtained mercy, but now have obtained mercy.

GOLDEN TEXT: Which in time past were not a people, but are now the people of God: which had not obtained mercy, but now have obtained mercy.—1 Peter 2:10.

God's People in a Troubled World
Unit 2: Hope for God's People
(Lessons 5-8)

Lesson Aims

The study of this lesson is designed to help students:

1. List the word pictures Peter uses to describe the privileges and responsibilities of being God's people.

2. Explain how these privileges and responsibilities should be demonstrated by God's people today.

3. Make a commitment to live as God's people by both shunning evil and pursuing holiness.

Lesson Outline

INTRODUCTION
  A. On Being and Doing
  B. Lesson Background
 I. THE CALL TO HOLINESS (1 Peter 2:1-3)
  A. Rejecting the Bad (v. 1)
  B. Seeking the Pure (vv. 2, 3)
II. OUR IDENTITY AS GOD'S PEOPLE (1 Peter 2:4-10)
  A. Christ, the Living Stone (v. 4)
  B. Christians as Living Stones (v. 5)
  C. A Prophecy Fulfilled (v. 6)
  D. Christ, the Stone of Stumbling (vv. 7, 8)
    The Rejected Stone
  E. Our Privilege and Purpose (vv. 9, 10)
    The People of God
CONCLUSION
  A. Pilgrims With Purpose
  B. Prayer
  C. Thought to Remember

The visual for Lesson 6 in the visuals packet highlights the difference that becoming part of God's people makes. It is shown on page 165.

Introduction

A. On Being and Doing

"Before you can know what you want to do, you have to know who you want to be." I cannot recall how many times I heard my mother say this to my sister, my brothers, and me. And over the years, I do not know how many times I have said this to my own son and daughter, as my wife and I have tried to prepare them to be responsible Christian adults, doing the things that God wants them to do.

A person who aspires to be someone else or who tries to look or act like someone else is often called a "wanna-be." Eager youngsters may say, "I wanna-be a doctor . . . a teacher . . . a rich person . . . a famous singer . . . a sports star."

What do you "wanna-be"? Or perhaps more important, *who* do you "wanna-be"? Our text today challenges us to be a people growing in God's grace so that we may proclaim that grace to others.

B. Lesson Background

We saw in last week's lesson that Peter was writing to Christians who were living in trying times. In the opening verses, he reminds them of their new birth in Christ and of the hope that can sustain them in the midst of their trials "with fire" (1 Peter 1:7). Their salvation is not endangered by whatever trials may come, for it is firmly grounded in the words of the prophets (vv. 10, 11). It declares something so remarkable that even the angels desire to investigate it further (v. 12).

In the remaining verses of chapter 1, Peter challenges his readers to renounce their former pagan practices and imitate Him who said, "Be ye holy; for I am holy" (v. 16). They are to reflect on the price that was paid to redeem them from their former purposeless existence: the blood of Christ, who was "foreordained before the foundation of the world" (vv. 18-21). Verses 22-25 continue the exhortation, emphasizing that because Christians have accepted the gospel, their lives must reflect the "unfeigned," or sincere, love that should characterize the entire Christian family.

In today's text, taken from chapter 2, Peter continues to challenge Christians to rid themselves of what is destructive to their growth, and to develop a craving for the "milk of the word." It is not enough to be born again; so great a faith as this demands an uncompromising commitment to maturity. Peter also reminds Christians of their identity as God's people—an identity that at one time was not theirs to enjoy. Within these verses are some of the most important teachings in Scripture about what the church is meant to be and to do.

I. The Call to Holiness
(1 Peter 2:1-3)

A. Rejecting the Bad (v. 1)

1. Wherefore laying aside all malice, and all guile, and hypocrisies, and envies, and all evil speakings.

In more recent translations, the word *wherefore* is translated "therefore." A good rule of thumb is that whenever you see this word, you should ask what it is "there for." Here it links the upcoming exhortations to maturity with the need to love others (1:22) and with having been born again (1:23).

Some of the most negative words in 1 Peter appear in this verse. They describe sins that have often wrought havoc within congregations, preventing them from being effective witnesses for Christ. Such characteristics should never be found within God's holy people. The idea of *laying aside* literally means taking off one's clothes; here the figurative meaning is casting off wrong or harmful practices. The same kind of language is used in Ephesians 4:22-24, where Paul urges Christians to "put off" the old man and "put on" the new man.

Even though Christians were victims of slander from outsiders (see 1 Peter 2:12 and 3:16), it apparently did not prevent them from practicing it toward one another. Perhaps bickering and division arose among the believers because of the persecution that was being directed toward them. However, this was a time for Christians to be united, not divided.

B. Seeking the Pure (vv. 2, 3)

2. As newborn babes, desire the sincere milk of the word, that ye may grow thereby.

Peter's description of his readers as *newborn babes* should not be considered an insult that rebukes them for their immaturity. It is a description arising from their new birth described in 1 Peter 1:3, 23. The fact that they are babies in a spiritual sense demonstrates that they have been delivered from sin and its consequences, but also highlights their need to *grow* in their salvation. Just as a nursing baby naturally craves his mother's milk, so should Christians naturally *desire* spiritual *milk*.

The word *sincere* may seem odd as a description of milk. The Greek word is actually the opposite of the word rendered "guile" in verse 1. Thus the term is often rendered "pure spiritual milk," as in the *New International Version* and *Today's English Version*.

One of the most horrible tastes is that of bad milk. Christians are to seek the pure milk of God's Word which gave them new life, and will also provide what they need to grow in that life. The faithful preaching and teaching of this "milk" is a necessity for a strong and healthy body of Christ.

3. If so be ye have tasted that the Lord is gracious.

To have such a craving for good milk should not be difficult, since these Christians have already *tasted that the Lord is gracious*. This

How to Say It

ASSYRIA. Uh-*sear*-e-uh.

verse calls to mind Psalm 34:8, the context of which stresses that God delivers from affliction those who persevere in faith to the end. It was an appropriate message for believers who were facing their own afflictions from an increasingly hostile society.

II. Our Identity as God's People (1 Peter 2:4-10)

In this section, Peter draws heavily upon the Old Testament to show that the church is what Israel was at one time: God's people, with all the accompanying privileges and responsibilities. Three of the passages refer to a "stone." Peter uses all the texts to show what God has done through Jesus to establish the new community that was prophesied in the Old Testament.

A. Christ, the Living Stone (v. 4)

4. To whom coming, as unto a living stone, disallowed indeed of men, but chosen of God, and precious.

In the Old Testament, only a priest could draw near to God in worship. Now, under the New Covenant, all believers enjoy the privilege of *coming* to God (Hebrews 10:19-22). All are priests, as Peter states in the next verse.

Jesus is the cornerstone of the Christian faith, and He is a *living stone*, for He has triumphed over death. Sadly, this stone was *disallowed*, or rejected, when He was on earth, and He continues to be rejected. The verb used implies examination of the stone by builders, who then cast it aside as unfit for further use. Such calloused treatment does not and cannot affect who Jesus is. He remains *chosen of God, and precious*.

B. Christians as Living Stones (v. 5)

5. Ye also, as lively stones, are built up a spiritual house, a holy priesthood, to offer up spiritual sacrifices, acceptable to God by Jesus Christ.

By their union with the life-giving cornerstone, Christians become *lively stones*. As noted last week under the discussion of the "lively hope" in 1 Peter 1:3, more recent translations use "living" instead of *lively*, and the same is true in this verse. These are not individual stones lying scattered about in isolation from each other; they are a group of stones being *built up*. The church is the house of God—not a building, however, but a *spiritual house*, where His Holy Spirit dwells. Paul uses similar language in Ephesians 2:20-22.

Because of Christ there is now no "official" priesthood with special privileges and responsibilities. Together with Christ and in union with one another, Christians form a *holy priesthood*. As priests, they offer to God the *spiritual sacrifices* of consecrated lives (Romans 12:1), words of praise (Hebrews 13:15), and good works (Hebrews 13:16). Since these are offered in union with Christ, they are most *acceptable to God*.

C. A Prophecy Fulfilled (v. 6)

6. Wherefore also it is contained in the Scripture, Behold, I lay in Zion a chief corner stone, elect, precious: and he that believeth on him shall not be confounded.

The first quotation from the Old Testament in this section of 1 Peter comes from Isaiah 28:16. In the context, the prophet addresses the rulers of Jerusalem who have rejected his advice and entered into a political alliance with Assyria. He stresses the need for these leaders to put their confidence in God (Israel's true leader), because He is their sure foundation.

Jesus is the *chief corner stone* that God has laid *in Zion*. The term *elect* calls attention to Jesus' distinctive mission and to God's special delight in Him (Isaiah 42:1; Matthew 17:5). We are to recognize this by treating the cornerstone as *precious*. The writer of Hebrews tells Christians that they have come to "mount Zion" by having come to Jesus and His church (Hebrews 12:22-24).

The fact that a cornerstone has been laid indicates the construction of a new building. In the same way, Christians are now a new community, whose existence is possible only because of what God has done through Christ. Faith, not the privilege of birth or background, effects the union. To those who believe in Christ as the cornerstone, He becomes a source of honor. They will never be *confounded* (disappointed or disillusioned) by Him. To those who reject Jesus, He is the source of shame and scandal. Those in this latter group stumble over the stone to their eternal ruin.

D. Christ, the Stone of Stumbling (vv. 7, 8)

7. Unto you therefore which believe he is precious: but unto them which be disobedient, the stone which the builders disallowed, the same is made the head of the corner.

In this verse Peter contrasts those who believe and those who do not. Jesus is the cornerstone

for those who *believe* in Him, but a stumbling stone for the *disobedient*. Each person chooses what kind of stone Jesus will be to him or her.

Here Peter quotes another Old Testament text (Psalm 118:22). The psalm describes a person who, like those in Peter's day, was violently opposed by his enemies, but in time witnessed a heartening display of the power and goodness of God. The psalm also tells how a *stone* would be *disallowed*, or rejected, by the *builders*—a term that calls to mind those leaders and men of influence in Jesus' time (such as the scribes and Pharisees) who rejected His message and sought to kill Him. Although the stone was judged as unfit by these builders, God examined it and deemed it worthy to be used as the *head of the corner*.

Such a reminder as this was especially appropriate for those reading this letter, for Peter was writing at a time when the *builders* (the Roman authorities) were exhibiting a growing hostility to Christians. It is noteworthy that in today's society, many of those who are considered *builders*, or people of great influence ("movers and shakers"), possess a highly negative attitude toward the Christian message and toward the church. Christians should remember, as verse 5 points out, that they are being "built up" as God's new community—a kingdom "not of this world" (John 18:36).

8. And a stone of stumbling, and a rock of offense, even to them which stumble at the word, being disobedient: whereunto also they were appointed.

Here Peter quotes Isaiah 8:14, where the prophet is being encouraged to trust in God as his "sanctuary." Those within "both the houses of Israel" who refuse to do so will find God to be *a stone of stumbling, and a rock of offense*. In applying to Jesus the verses that he has quoted, Peter is saying that if one does not choose to build his life on Jesus, the cornerstone will become a "stumbling block." Everyone who hears of Jesus must make the decision to obey or disobey—to build or to stumble.

The word *appointed* may appear to imply that God designates certain individuals to be obedient and some to be disobedient. But what is *appointed* is not the choice that individuals make; it is the stumbling that occurs whenever they reject the stone. For those who reject Jesus and His salvation, the only course available to them is a path of stumbling.

THE REJECTED STONE

The idea of a "disallowed," or rejected, stone is illustrated in the life of the great sculptor, Michelangelo. One of his most famous works is his magnificent sculpture of King David, which stands in the courtyard of the University of Florence. The stone from which this sculpture was carved had lain unused in the work yard in Florence for fifty years. Another sculptor had tried to make something out of it and had given up, leaving a great gash in the middle of the stone. But Michelangelo saw in that rejected stone a young David going out to meet Goliath with only his sling. It took someone of his genius to see the possibilities in a stone that others had rejected.

In the same way it took great faith to see in the crucified (rejected) Christ the Savior of the world and the Lord of life. Perhaps it took more faith for those in the first century than for those of us living now. We are accustomed to talking about a cross and a crucified man. But in those early days, both Jews and Greeks were repelled by such "foolishness" (1 Corinthians 1:22-24). Though many of them rejected Christ, sincere seekers after truth accepted Him, and they still do. It is sobering to think that those who reject Christ will be rejected by Christ; those who receive Christ will be received by Christ; and those who confess Christ will be confessed by Christ.   —R. C. S.

E. Our Privilege and Purpose
(vv. 9, 10)

9. But ye are a chosen generation, a royal priesthood, a holy nation, a peculiar people; that ye should show forth the praises of him who hath called you out of darkness into his marvelous light.

In the first verse of this letter, Peter addresses his fellow Christians as "strangers," and in 2:11 he calls them "strangers and pilgrims." These followers of Jesus were living in a world into which they did not fit. Because of their faith, they were being ostracized, ridiculed, and persecuted by their government, their masters, their neighbors, and even their spouses. Peter reminds them of the benefits and privileges of their salvation in Christ. One of these is that, although they are living in communities that reject them, they are part of a worldwide community of believers in Jesus Christ that loves and accepts them. This is why Peter could write the same message to a variety of congregations in Asia Minor (1:1); although they were "scattered," they were united by their belief in Jesus Christ, the living stone.

Here Peter continues his use of the Old Testament to highlight the privileges and responsibilities that Christians possess. In contrast to those who reject Jesus and therefore are destined to destruction (v. 8), Christians have

visual for lesson 6

been given a unique identity. In fact, we have received all the titles that once applied to ancient Israel (see Exodus 19:3-6). Born anew through God's love, we are now the *chosen generation*. Our security is not rooted in what we have done, but because of who we are through God's grace.

Moreover, Christians constitute a *royal priesthood*, which offers spiritual sacrifices to the King of kings (v. 5). Our lives are to be lives of service (Romans 12:1), manifesting to the world that we belong to Jesus. The label of *holy nation* was applied to Israel as one of the nations of its time; now it is the church's task to transcend all national barriers and incorporate those from all lands into one grand nation of believers in Jesus.

The phrase *peculiar people* does not mean that Christians are called to be "weird." It is better rendered as "a people for God's own possession" (*New American Standard Bible*; see also Exodus 19:5; Deuteronomy 14:2). Just as an individual's "peculiarities" are those qualities unique to him, so God desires to have a people that are uniquely His. *Peculiar* thus describes our relationship to God, not to the world.

The identity we possess as the people of God is not something to be kept to ourselves. We have received this high standing for a purpose: *to show forth the praises* of God, who is the source of our standing. How do we do this? By giving verbal witness of the truth of the gospel (1 Peter 1:25; 3:15) and by holy living (1:16; 2:12, 15; 3:1, 16).

What this verse declares is still a revolutionary statement of the church's nature and mission. The spread of the gospel is not dependent upon a few; rather, all Christians are expected to be serving as God's priests, providing a witness to a watching world. The new Israel, brought from darkness to light, has an evangelistic responsibility to bring others to the light. A reminder of the change that our conversion has effected in us should move us to share the message of conversion with others.

10. Which in time past were not a people, but are now the people of God: which had not obtained mercy, but now have obtained mercy.

Again Peter refers to the Old Testament, using Hosea 2:23 to establish the identity of his readers as God's people. The reference to God's *mercy* links this verse with the preceding one, for by God's mercy we are called to leave sin's darkness and come into His light. Some see this verse as providing evidence that Peter's readership consisted primarily of Gentile Christians, since Gentiles *in time past were not . . . the people of God*, as the Jews were.

Multitudes of people in our world have an identity crisis; they do not know who they are because they do not know God. Such is not the case with Christians; we know who we are, and we know what we should do. Now let's do it.

THE PEOPLE OF GOD

Gerald Kennedy tells a story about a church picnic held by a river. Some of the members set out in boats to go down the river. As they traveled they passed two girls on the bank. One asked the other who those people in the boats were. The other replied, "I can't imagine who they can be. They're all such different types."

What an apt description of the church! Christians have different levels of education and different levels of income. They enjoy different hobbies and interests, come from different races, and live in different parts of town—or in different lands. Often they do not speak the same language. But they are one people because of one thing they have in common: their faith in the Lord Jesus Christ. And this that they have in common is far more significant than all the areas in which they differ. Without Christ they would not be a distinct people at all. Because of Christ they *are* a distinct people, easily distinguished by their faith, love, and character. Differences in culture and language cannot separate them. Social, economic, and educational differences cannot separate them. When they were joined to Christ, they were joined to one another. They are a distinct and identifiable people—the people of God.   —R. C. S.

Conclusion

A. Pilgrims With Purpose

"This world is not my home, I'm just a passin' through . . ." Perhaps you have heard or sung these words of an old gospel song. Peter reminds us not to be too comfortable on earth. We are "strangers and pilgrims" (1 Peter 2:11), marching to Zion. As "strangers" we live here, but never really become citizens. As "pilgrims" we are here for only a short time. What matters is how we live until we die or until Christ returns.

This perspective places us in conflict with the surrounding society and its values. As Christians we live in a culture that makes every effort to seduce us and to ridicule our faith. Peter does not deny the pressures to give up the faith, but he does stress the need for continued perseverance through the resources that are available for victorious living, even in the midst of trials. Throughout his letter there is evidence of a robust faith that takes both sin and salvation with the utmost seriousness, and proclaims the possibility of victory through divine grace.

We must beware of adopting a selfish model of the church, viewing it as a mother caring only for the faithful. The church is directed to go into the world, not to isolate itself from the world. All edification within the church should be undertaken for the essential purpose of becoming a more effective instrument through which the saved are united in Christ and the lost are won to Christ.

A church is either a missionary church, sent out into the world, or it is no church at all. The Christian is not a member of the church simply to share its comforts. He is to share in taking its message to a lost world.

B. Prayer

O God, may we be grateful for Your steadfast mercy; may we be bold in proclaiming the gospel; and may we lead others to join us in our pilgrimage to our heavenly home. In Jesus' name, amen.

C. Thought to Remember

The purpose of becoming God's people is not personal well-being, but public witness.

Home Daily Bible Readings

Monday, Jan. 5—Now We Are God's People (Psalm 100:1-5)
Tuesday, Jan. 6—Glory of the Lord Appears (Isaiah 60:1-6)
Wednesday, Jan. 7—Firstfruits of the Spirit (Romans 8:18-27)
Thursday, Jan. 8—Comfort in Time of Suffering (2 Corinthians 1:3-14)
Friday, Jan. 9—Teach Your Children (Deuteronomy 6:1-9)
Saturday, Jan. 10—Proclaim God's Mighty Acts (Psalm 145:8-13)
Sunday, Jan. 11—Love God and Your Neighbor (Matthew 22:34-40)

Learning by Doing

This page contains an alternate lesson plan emphasizing learning activities. Classes desiring such student involvement will find these suggestions helpful.

Learning Goals

After they have completed this lesson, your students should be able to:

1. List the word pictures Peter uses to describe the privileges and responsibilities of being God's people.

2. Explain how these privileges and responsibilities should be demonstrated by God's people today.

3. Make a commitment to live as God's people by both shunning evil and pursuing holiness.

Into the Lesson

Introduce this lesson on becoming God's people by asking your students to list some of the benefits and blessings of being members of a local church. As they call out ideas, write their suggestions on the chalkboard. Responses will probably include: acceptance by other believers; a sense of belonging to a group; fellowship; a sense of community; worship; opportunities for Christian service.

Of course, we should remember that we are not only members of a local church; we are also members of the people of God. This includes Christians from all times and all places. When Peter wrote in our text about becoming God's people, he meant joining a fellowship that has a very special place in God's plan.

Into the Word

Direct the students to 1 Peter 2:1. In this verse Peter mentions how his readers once lived. Paul also does this in some of his letters (see Ephesians 2:1-3, 12; Colossians 3:5-7). Ask, "What is the benefit of thinking about the kind of people we were before we accepted Jesus Christ as Savior and became members of the body of Christ?"

From today's lesson text, ask your students to help you compile a "before" picture (before we became God's people) and an "after" picture (now that we have become God's people). Write the information that results from this exercise on the chalkboard or a sheet of newsprint (this activity is found in the student book).

The "before" picture should include such items as are mentioned in verse 1: hateful, deceitful, two-faced (hypocritical), envious, slanderous. Also, tell the students to look at verse 10, where "before" characteristics include:

having no identity as God's people, and having no claim on God's mercy.

Next, ask the students to look through the rest of the passage in search of terms that describe Christians "after" they have become part of God's people. The passage includes these ideas:

• spiritual babies (v. 2), implying a second birth, or being born again.

• living stones (v. 5), implying that members of the church are dynamic, and also that they work together to form a larger whole.

• chosen by God (v. 9), emphasizing that we are now what Israel once was during the Old Testament period.

• priests (v. 9), emphasizing that we have direct access to God.

• holy (v. 9), emphasizing that there are moral and ethical demands for us to keep.

• God's "peculiar" people (vv. 9, 10), emphasizing that we are fully and completely God's. (You may want to consult the lesson commentary on the meaning of "peculiar" in verse 9.)

• objects of God's mercy (v. 10), emphasizing that we are recipients of the best that God has.

Into Life

In 1 Peter 2:1, Peter exhorts us to rid ourselves of certain negative qualities and bad habits. Ask students if any of these apply to them. Perhaps some would be willing to talk about such applications. Just talking about bad habits won't get rid of them, but it can be a first step.

The "sincere milk of the word" (v. 2) suggests the importance of the Bible to spiritual growth. Ask your students to suggest how they can make Scripture a more regular part of their daily lives. Suggestions may include: Scripture memory; reading devotional classics; listening to Scripture on tape; listening to Bible-based sermons and Sunday school lessons.

Next, ask the students to suggest some things that inhibit and stunt spiritual growth. For examples: movies and TV programs that glorify greed and promote lust; worldly entertainment; dwelling on impure thoughts (see Philippians 4:8); bad habits; resisting the correction and discipline of the Holy Spirit.

In closing, challenge your students to live as faithful members of the body of Christ by avoiding evil and pursuing holiness in the daily choices that they make.

Let's Talk It Over

The questions on this page are designed to encourage review of the lesson Scriptures and to promote discussion of the lesson by the class. The answers provided are only discussion starters. Let your class talk it over from there.

1. What are the opposites of malice, guile, hypocrisy, envy, and evil speaking? How do you cultivate these opposites in your character?

The act of "laying aside" the negative qualities of 1 Peter 2:1 is more easily done by focusing on the positive opposites. If malice includes spite, ill will, or contempt, we should work on developing kindness instead. Guile implies deception and fraud. A positive opposite would be candor, fairness, and complete honesty. If we do not want to be guilty of hypocrisy, we must be genuine and sincere. When the rivalry and covetousness that spring from envy are overcome, in their place will be affirmation of others and generosity. We may replace evil speaking with silence, but a more positive alternative would be encouragement, blessing, and praise. Knowing what we want to empty out of our character is only the beginning. We must also have a clear idea of what we desire to build into our character. These positive qualities all require some intentional action on our part. We cannot wait passively and merely hope that they appear.

2. Is the desire for the "milk of the word" (1 Peter 2:2) natural to new Christians, or is it an acquired taste? How may we increase our desire for the Word of God?

We may wish that Christians were instilled with an insatiable hunger for the Word of God, but this is not the case. Since Peter makes this an imperative command, we may assume that it is a matter of obedience and not nature. Peter wanted his readers to cultivate this desire out of recognition of their need. By understanding that we enter Christianity like helpless infants, and that the Word of God is the food that can cause us to grow, our desire for the Word will increase. It is also a desire that increases with experience. The more we learn and apply from God's Word, the more practical we find it to be, and the more we desire to know.

3. In order to form a "spiritual house" (1 Peter 2:5), Christians must be connected to one another. What is gained by Christians working together in community rather than remaining detached?

There are many people today who believe that they can "go it alone" in terms of faith and be solitary Christians. The New Testament, however, everywhere assumes that believers will be living in community with other believers. The many "one another" commands found in the New Testament can be obeyed only in relationship to other believers. We gain strength, encouragement, and direction from the ministry of fellow believers, and we have the opportunity to exercise our gifts and fulfill our personal ministry. No one believer is the body of Christ. As we cooperate together, each one contributing according to his or her gifts and strengths, we truly function as the body of Christ and we accomplish His will.

4. How can Jesus be both a cornerstone and a stumbling stone? What are the objections some raise concerning Jesus?

For those who believe in Jesus and accept His lordship, He is a precious cornerstone. Some, however, stumble over the claims Jesus made about Himself. When you understand the scope of these claims, it is impossible to remain neutral. Jesus was a lunatic or a liar, or else he was the divine Son of God. There have always been those who object to the idea that the Son of God should come from such humble and obscure beginnings, that He would surround Himself with such ignoble followers, that He would not establish His rule by might, and, finally, that He would die such a hideous death. If these facts about Jesus prevent anyone from accepting His true identity, then He has become a stumbling stone to them. As Peter points out, however, the problem lies with the fact that such individuals are "disobedient" (1 Peter 2:8).

5. With privilege comes responsibility. What are the responsibilities attached to Christians being a "chosen people"?

Peter identifies Christians as filling a role that once belonged to the Jews. We are called to this special status ("a chosen generation, a royal priesthood, a holy nation, a peculiar people") not as a matter of private privilege, but with the intention that God should be praised. The Jews seldom understood the missionary aspect of God's calling them as His people. Our relationship with God should result in directing those around us to Him and to His praise.

Hope in Suffering With Christ

DEVOTIONAL READING: 1 Peter 2:18-25.

LESSON SCRIPTURE: 1 Peter 3:8-21; 4:12-16.

PRINTED TEXT: 1 Peter 3:13-21; 4:12-16.

1 Peter 3:13-21

13 And who is he that will harm you, if ye be followers of that which is good?

14 But and if ye suffer for righteousness' sake, happy are ye: and be not afraid of their terror, neither be troubled;

15 But sanctify the Lord God in your hearts: and be ready always to give an answer to every man that asketh you a reason of the hope that is in you, with meekness and fear:

16 Having a good conscience; that, whereas they speak evil of you, as of evildoers, they may be ashamed that falsely accuse your good conversation in Christ.

17 For it is better, if the will of God be so, that ye suffer for well doing, than for evil doing.

18 For Christ also hath once suffered for sins, the just for the unjust, that he might bring us to God, being put to death in the flesh, but quickened by the Spirit:

19 By which also he went and preached unto the spirits in prison;

20 Which sometime were disobedient, when once the long-suffering of God waited in the days of Noah, while the ark was a preparing, wherein few, that is, eight souls were saved by water.

21 The like figure whereunto even baptism doth also now save us, (not the putting away of the filth of the flesh, but the answer of a good conscience toward God,) by the resurrection of Jesus Christ.

1 Peter 4:12-16

12 Beloved, think it not strange concerning the fiery trial which is to try you, as though some strange thing happened unto you:

13 But rejoice, inasmuch as ye are partakers of Christ's sufferings; that, when his glory shall be revealed, ye may be glad also with exceeding joy.

14 If ye be reproached for the name of Christ, happy are ye; for the Spirit of glory and of God resteth upon you: on their part he is evil spoken of, but on your part he is glorified.

15 But let none of you suffer as a murderer, or as a thief, or as an evildoer, or as a busybody in other men's matters.

16 Yet if any man suffer as a Christian, let him not be ashamed; but let him glorify God on this behalf.

Jan 18

GOLDEN TEXT: If any man suffer as a Christian, let him not be ashamed; but let him glorify God on this behalf.—1 Peter 4:16.

God's People in a Troubled World
Unit 2: Hope for God's People
(Lessons 5-8)

Lesson Aims

After this lesson, students should be able to:

1. Tell how Peter says Christians should prepare for and respond to suffering.

2. Explain how Christian hope equips the modern believer to cope with opposition and suffering.

3. Prepare a statement of the "reason of the hope" that one has as a Christian, in order to be ready with an answer when asked.

Lesson Outline

INTRODUCTION
    A. What Matters Most
    B. Lesson Background
I. LIVING UNDER UNJUST PERSECUTION (1 Peter 3:13-17)
    A. Happy Witnesses (vv. 13, 14)
    B. Ready Witnesses (v. 15)
    C. Convincing Witnesses (vv. 16, 17)
II. LIVING BY CHRIST'S EXAMPLE (1 Peter 3:18-21)
    A. Christ's Proclamation of Victory (vv. 18-20)
    B. The Importance of Baptism (v. 21)
III. LIVING THROUGH TRIALS (1 Peter 4:12-16)
    A. Don't Be Surprised (v. 12)
    B. Participate in Christ's Sufferings (v. 13)
      A Peculiar Honor
    C. Rejoice! (v. 14)
    D. Invalid Reasons for Suffering (v. 15)
    E. A Valid Reason for Suffering (v. 16)
      Not a Thing of the Past
CONCLUSION
    A. The Eternal Perspective
    B. Prayer
    C. Thought to Remember

Today's visual for Lesson 7 focuses on Scriptures addressed to persecuted Christians. It is shown on page 172.

Introduction

A. What Matters Most

Years ago our family lived in Scotland where I was taking additional schooling. One weekend I took my wife and two young children to see the Queen of England and the rest of her family, who were attending some special events near our home. After the royal procession passed by, I asked my five-year-old son what he thought of the Queen. He talked about the beautiful carriages, and seemed especially impressed by the soldiers who rode atop them, the splendid white horses, and the golden wheels. I was somewhat disappointed by his response. I had taken my son to see the Queen of England, and all he saw were carriages, soldiers, and horses! He had missed what mattered the most.

Sometimes when we read the Bible, we encounter puzzling passages, such as the one in today's text (1 Peter 3:18-20). We are frustrated, because certain details in the passage seem to leave us with more questions than answers. But these difficulties should not deter us from the primary purpose of Bible study: to help us "grow in grace, and in the knowledge of our Lord and Saviour Jesus Christ" (2 Peter 3:18). This is what matters the most; we dare not miss it.

B. Lesson Background

In last week's lesson from 1 Peter 2:1-10, we were challenged to be growing and witnessing Christians. Christians are not permanent citizens of the earth, so we should not live as if we are. Indeed, we are only "strangers and pilgrims" (1 Peter 2:11), and our true home is Heaven (Philippians 3:20). The kingdom to which we belong is not of this world (John 18:36). Our foe does not consist of "flesh and blood," but of spiritual forces (Ephesians 6:12). Our conduct should reflect these convictions.

The verses leading up to our Scripture for today include various teachings that focus on how Christians are to live as citizens of a foreign country. Peter highlights how our loyalty to Christ should affect our relationships with civil authorities (1 Peter 2:13, 14, 17), people on the job (v. 18), our spouses (3:1-7), and our brothers and sisters in the church (3:8, 9). The primary motivation and example of our conduct is Christ Himself.

In today's lesson text, Peter addresses the issue of how Christians are to conduct themselves when their status as "foreigners" brings them face to face with suffering and persecution. Our study is especially relevant to the theme of this quarter: "God's People in a Troubled World." In good times it is easy to make Christ our Lord; in good times it is easy to declare that our hope is firm. But what about bad times? How do we respond when bad things happen to God's children? What attitudes should we have? What actions should we take? These are the concerns Peter addresses in today's Scripture.

I. Living Under Unjust Persecution (1 Peter 3:13-17)

A. Happy Witnesses (vv. 13, 14)

13. And who is he that will harm you, if ye be followers of that which is good?

In 1 Peter 3:8-12, Peter summarizes the qualities that should characterize members of the Christian community. In quoting Psalm 34:12-16, Peter reminds his readers that the person who wishes to live a happy life is admonished not only to avoid evil, but to help overcome evil by doing good and pursuing peace. Such a person will usually not face *harm* from others, which seems to be the point of Peter's question. His words may also mean that if Christians are enthusiastic for what is *good*, no one can cause them any real harm. Even death is not a tragedy, but a triumph.

14. But and if ye suffer for righteousness' sake, happy are ye: and be not afraid of their terror, neither be troubled.

Even if our lives of *righteousness* should at some time require us to *suffer* physical harm, we should count it a blessing. Such suffering is a mark of God's approval of who we are and what we are doing. The Greek word rendered *happy* is the same word translated "blessed" in the Beatitudes. The specific Beatitude about suffering (Matthew 5:11) should come to mind.

Although following Jesus carries a costly price, there is no reason for fear of or preoccupation with what the enemies of Christians may do. We are not to be *troubled* by such matters (see also John 14:1, 27).

B. Ready Witnesses (v. 15)

15. But sanctify the Lord God in your hearts: and be ready always to give an answer to every man that asketh you a reason of the hope that is in you, with meekness and fear.

While verse 14 focuses primarily on what we should not do in the face of unjust suffering, this verse emphasizes what we should do. Rather than yielding to fear when faced with the possibility of persecution, Christians are to *sanctify the Lord God* in their *hearts*. The presence of God with His people, even in the throes of the most severe trials, is reaffirmed.

The Greek word translated *answer* is one from which our word "apology" comes. While to us an apology usually implies being sorry for something one has said or done, this word means a "defense" of one's faith in Christ. When questioned or accused, believers were to witness unashamedly to the truth and proclaim their faith, trusting the Holy Spirit to provide the

necessary words (Matthew 10:16-20; Mark 13:9, 11).

The hope that is in you refers not just to Christians' conviction about the future, but to the attitude of peace and serenity that they possessed even though threatened by their foes. Such a spirit would invite questions from curious observers. Each of us should ask, "Is my faith the kind that causes others to ask the reason for my hope?"

Meekness and fear describes the attitude with which we should defend our faith. We are not to browbeat others or become arrogant and obnoxious. We should always respect those whom we address, seeking in compassion to lead them from darkness to light. Paul encouraged Timothy to "be gentle unto all men, apt to teach, patient; in meekness instructing those that oppose themselves" (2 Timothy 2:24, 25). Our mission is not to win arguments, but to win the lost.

C. Convincing Witnesses (vv. 16, 17)

16. Having a good conscience; that, whereas they speak evil of you, as of evildoers, they may be ashamed that falsely accuse your good conversation in Christ.

The word *conversation* refers to Christian character in general, not only to our speech. This verse teaches that it is the quality of our conduct and behavior (more than our eloquence or logical explanations) that will convince questioners of the truth of our convictions. Many times nonbelievers will resort to unfounded attacks on the Christian's character. We need to maintain a *good*, or clear, *conscience*, which in time will show that the accusations against us have no basis in fact.

17. For it is better, if the will of God be so, that ye suffer for well doing, than for evildoing.

The best Christian witness is an honest life that refutes the defamation and slander of skeptics through its visible and consistent goodness (1 Peter 2:12; 3:1, 2). Peter calls Christians to suffer for their good deeds, as Jesus did (2:19-23), and not for their sins. Those who do are within *the will of God* and should "commit the keeping of their souls to him in well doing" (4:19).

II. Living by Christ's Example (1 Peter 3:18-21)

Even though these verses may raise many questions, we must keep in mind their context. They include an exhortation to those who "suffer for well doing" (v. 17), based on the example of Christ Himself and on the consequences of Christian baptism.

A. Christ's Proclamation of Victory

(vv. 18-20)

18. For Christ also hath once suffered for sins, the just for the unjust, that he might bring us to God, being put to death in the flesh, but quickened by the Spirit.

Recalling the example of suffering given by Jesus, Peter sets forth the redemptive purpose of His death and resurrection. Three beautiful truths in this verse need to be highlighted. First, we have Christ's example as a motive to endure in hard times. If Christians think that their suffering is unjust, they should reflect upon Jesus' suffering *for sins*, which was totally undeserved (*the just for the unjust*). Second, the phrase *that he might bring us to God* stresses that Christ's death for our sins has given us access to God (Romans 5:1, 2). Third, the apparent defeat of Jesus' death was turned into a glorious victory when He was *quickened*, or made alive. Death thus becomes a moment of triumph for the Christian, because he shares in the fruits of Jesus' victory.

19, 20. By which also he went and preached unto the spirits in prison; which sometime were disobedient, when once the long-suffering of God waited in the days of Noah, while the ark was a preparing, wherein few, that is, eight souls were saved by water.

The interpretation of this very difficult passage must take into account the preceding verse. The phrase "quickened by the Spirit" in verse 18 could refer to the Holy Spirit. Others, however, take it to mean that Jesus was "made alive in the spirit," a translation that is followed in the *New American Standard Bible*. In this state He *went and preached unto the spirits in prison*. Four questions must be addressed concerning this statement.

First, who are these *spirits*, described in verse 20 as *disobedient*? The word *spirits*, unless accompanied by language that would have to refer to human beings (as in "spirits of just men"

visual for
lesson 7

If you are not suffering for Christ,
WHY AREN'T YOU?

in Hebrews 12:23), tends to describe supernatural beings, whether good or evil (as in Luke 10:20 and Hebrews 1:14). (It is possible, however, that departed human spirits may be included in this group as well.) Second Peter 2:4 speaks of "angels that sinned"; apparently their disobedience was part of the general wickedness that filled the earth *in the days of Noah*. Some say that Genesis 6:1-4, which mentions the "sons of God" who sinned prior to the flood, is referring to these angels who were *disobedient*.

Second, what is the *prison*? Obviously some kind of confinement is described. Some believe that this is the place known as Hades (the realm of the dead). The Greek word used in 2 Peter 2:4 to describe the punishment of fallen angels is rendered as "cast them down to hell" in the *King James Version* and as "sent them to hell" in the *New International Version*. The fallen angels' prison is described in this verse and in Jude 6 as a place of darkness, where they are in "chains" awaiting judgment.

Third, what did Jesus say when He preached to these spirits? It is important to note that the Greek word rendered *preached* simply means "to announce" or "proclaim." Jesus went to these spirits to announce, not good news, but bad news: their doom was certain because of His victory over evil. This verse says nothing about a second chance for the dead to hear the gospel and be saved.

Fourth, when did all of this occur? This seems to be describing something that happened between Jesus' death and resurrection. In the *spirit* (that is, *before* He received His resurrection body that allowed Him to move among people and eat with them), Jesus went to other *spirits* and declared that their judgment was certain.

While complete understanding of what these verses mean may elude us, it is clear that the message of these verses is closely linked with the theme of Christ's triumph through the cross over Satan, death, and all powers of evil (see John 12:31; Ephesians 1:20-22; Colossians 2:15). This truth was meant to encourage those believers in Peter's day who were suffering for their faith. The spiritual powers of evil that stand behind those earthly powers hostile to Christians have been soundly defeated.

Concerning the days of Noah, Peter adds that *few, that is, eight souls were saved by water*. The phrase *saved by water* is literally "saved through, or by means of, water." The water that was the instrument of judgment upon the world in Noah's time was the instrument by which he and his family found deliverance in the *ark*. This leads to the reference to Christian baptism in verse 21.

The message of consolation that these words conveyed to suffering believers should not be overlooked. Even though Christians are outnumbered by hostile forces (as Noah and the few with him were outnumbered), those forces are doomed to eternal destruction. Noah and his family must have been very aware that they constituted a minority. So did the Christians in Peter's day. But in the end Noah and his family were saved. Eight with God are a majority! Indeed, one with God is a majority!

B. The Importance of Baptism (v. 21)

21. The like figure whereunto even baptism doth also now save us, (not the putting away of the filth of the flesh, but the answer of a good conscience toward God,) by the resurrection of Jesus Christ.

Peter uses the salvation of Noah and his family in the flood as a type, or model, of the Christian's salvation through *baptism*. On our part, baptism demonstrates *the answer of a good conscience*, one that is fully assured that what God requires is being done. Baptism is both an act of commitment to Christ as well as the act in which God unites us with the risen Christ, giving us the power to live up to our commitment (Romans 6:1-11). It also looks forward to the resurrection of our bodies (Romans 8:11).

Even though we may not be able to answer all of our questions about verses 18-21, let us not miss their primary emphasis: the victory achieved by means of Jesus' death and resurrection. Our response to these verses ought not to be perplexity but praise for the victory we find in Him. Praise God that it is a victory in which all of Jesus' followers can share!

III. Living Through Trials
(1 Peter 4:12-16)

A. Don't Be Surprised (v. 12)

12. Beloved, think it not strange concerning the fiery trial which is to try you, as though some strange thing happened unto you.

Severe trials should not seem *strange*, or surprising, to us (see 2 Timothy 3:12). Faith in Christ does not mean immunity from hard times; it sustains us in the midst of them.

B. Participate in Christ's Sufferings
(v. 13)

13. But rejoice, inasmuch as ye are partakers of Christ's sufferings; that, when his glory shall be revealed, ye may be glad also with exceeding joy.

As Christians we partake not only of Christ's life but also of His *sufferings* (Romans 8:17). But

---

How to Say It

HADES. *Hay*-deez.

---

we endure these sufferings, because we have the "big picture" in view. Paul writes, "The sufferings of this present time are not worthy to be compared with the glory which shall be revealed in us" (Romans 8:18).

A PECULIAR HONOR

During the worst days of Communist oppression in Europe, a preacher in Eastern Europe was taken to police headquarters. The officers tried to get him to confess to working against the state, but he would not. They tried to get him to implicate other believers, but he would not. After a lengthy interrogation, they beat him and threw him into a cell. He lay on the floor, wept, and prayed. He wondered how God could have allowed him to be treated so. Then he realized that it was the week before Easter. Suddenly he saw his suffering in a different light. The next day he was again interrogated. He said to the man who had beaten him the day before, "I want to thank you for something. You have done me a great honor. You have beaten me on the very same week that my Savior was beaten and crucified. You could not have given me any greater honor than that."

The Communist official was taken aback. In a few days he released the preacher. When he did he said to him, "I have interrogated many people, but you are the only one who has not reacted with hatred. You reacted with love. I respect you."

For the first readers of this letter from the apostle Peter, persecution was a very real possibility. Peter encouraged them to view their experience as a way to identify with Christ. They would be like Him in their suffering. What an honor!   —R. C. S.

C. Rejoice! (v. 14)

14. If ye be reproached for the name of Christ, happy are ye; for the Spirit of glory and of God resteth upon you: on their part he is evil spoken of, but on your part he is glorified.

Again, as in 1 Peter 3:14, Peter encourages *reproached* Christians to be *happy*, or "blessed," as the word is rendered in the Beatitudes. Suffering does not mean that God is displeased with us or has abandoned us; rather, we are assured that the sustaining presence of His *Spirit* will abide with us. Through our faithfulness, Jesus will be *glorified*.

D. Invalid Reasons for Suffering
(v. 15)

15. But let none of you suffer as a murderer, or as a thief, or as an evildoer, or as a busybody in other men's matters.

As noted in 1 Peter 2:19, 20, a Christian's suffering must take place for the right reason. No Christian should derive any satisfaction whatsoever from suffering for sins he has committed. Such suffering is deserved; it carries no honor.

E. A Valid Reason for Suffering
(v. 16)

16. Yet if any man suffer as a Christian, let him not be ashamed; but let him glorify God on this behalf.

Besides this verse, the name *Christian* is found only in Acts 11:26 and 26:28. To *suffer* because one bears the name of *Christian* does carry honor, for such suffering gives the believer the opportunity to "give an answer" for his hope (1 Peter 3:15). Thus are we to *glorify God*, showing to others who have no hope that our hope is living and real.

NOT A THING OF THE PAST

In May of 1996, missionaries in Ghana, West Africa, reported the conversion of an old African woman who had been a worshiper of idols. Upon her conversion to Christianity, she had all her idols burned. This brought threats of retaliation, not only to this lady, but to the entire church. The lady, however, stood firm, as did the church. The threats were not carried out. Eventually the church grew and began meeting in a larger house of worship.

While the threats against Christians were not carried out in this case, they sometimes have

been. And certainly this experience must have caused some fear in the hearts of the Christians in Ghana. But the impact was also positive. Persecution brought growth, as it so often has. On many continents, the church has thrived under persecution. Such was the experience of the early church, for following the martyrdom of Stephen, the Christians "were all scattered abroad" (Acts 8:1). Three verses later we read that "they that were scattered abroad went every where preaching the word" (v. 4).

Of course, we who live without the threat of persecution do not long for it. But we must never forget how real it is for numerous brothers and sisters around the globe. Let us pray for them to be courageous witnesses, and let us pray that we will be the same, should we ever face real persecution.   —R. C. S.

Conclusion

A. The Eternal Perspective

For the Christian, hope is not "wishful thinking." It is a solid certainty, a confident expectation because of what God has done, is doing, and will do in Christ. Baptism indicates first and foremost our identification with Christ in His death, burial, and resurrection. We rise from the baptismal waters to "walk in newness of life" (Romans 6:4), and live daily in view of the "blessed hope" of Christ's return (Titus 2:13).

Every year tens of thousands of Christians around the world die as martyrs for their faith. Others suffer ridicule, social rejection, and financial loss because they have chosen to stand for Christ and His principles. Regardless of what kind of suffering we may experience, we must live lives that honor Jesus and that reflect the eternal perspective. We must refuse to compromise so that we can merely "get along." We must daily renew our "pledge of allegiance," first made at our conversion, to be faithful to Christ whatever the cost.

B. Prayer

Our Father, may we never forget that the way to the crown is the way of the cross. As Your Son suffered for righteousness' sake, so have countless of His followers suffered through the centuries. May we be found faithful in all we say and do, regardless of the cost to be paid. We ask for boldness in taking the gospel to a lost world. In Jesus' name. Amen.

C. Thought to Remember

May we be found confident at Christ's coming because we have been faithful in spite of the evil around us.

Home Daily Bible Readings

Monday, Jan. 12—Living With Persecution (1 Peter 2:18-25)

Tuesday, Jan. 13—Following the Example of Christ (1 Peter 3:8-22)

Wednesday, Jan. 14—Sufferers for Christ Are Blessed (1 Peter 4:12-19)

Thursday, Jan. 15—Peter Defends the Gospel (Acts 4:1-13)

Friday, Jan. 16—Be Glorified With Christ (Romans 8:6-17)

Saturday, Jan. 17—Crown of Life for Enduring (Revelation 2:8-11)

Sunday, Jan. 18—Privilege to Suffer for Christ (Philippians 1:25-30)

Learning by Doing

This page contains an alternate lesson plan emphasizing learning activities.
Classes desiring such student involvement will find these suggestions helpful.

Learning Goals

After the completion of this lesson, students should be able to:

1. Tell how Peter says Christians should prepare for and respond to suffering.

2. Explain how Christian hope equips the modern believer to cope with opposition and suffering.

3. Prepare a statement of the "reason of the hope" that one has as a Christian, in order to be ready with an answer when asked.

Into the Lesson

Before the class begins, write this statement on the chalkboard: "If you are not suffering some kind of persecution, you are not really a Christian." Then introduce this lesson on suffering for doing right by relating this anecdote:

A young army recruit was home on leave after completing basic training. A friend from his church said to him, "It must really be tough being a Christian in the army. Don't the guys get on you and make fun of you?" The recruit replied, "It's no trouble at all. The other guys don't even know I'm a Christian."

Now direct your students' attention to the statement you wrote on the chalkboard. What do they think about it? Do they agree or disagree? What reasons do they have for their answers?

Into the Word

Jesus said, "In the world ye shall have tribulation" (John 16:33). He also said, "Ye are not of the world, but I have chosen you out of the world, therefore the world hateth you" (John 15:19). As Christians we are to expect opposition and hostility from the world. However, we must be sure the opposition and hostility are responses to our Christian lifestyle, and not to something else about us and the way we live.

One of the primary themes in this lesson is that we should rejoice when we suffer for doing good. Ask the students to read through today's lesson texts (1 Peter 3:13-21; 4:12-16), and look for all the places where this theme is mentioned. It can be found in these verses: 3:13, 14, 16, 17, 18; 4:13, 14, 16.

Next, ask the students to look at these passages again and search for what Peter says about our resources for dealing with opposition and suffering when they do come. Also, ask them to explain how each resource can help them deal with such circumstances (this activity is in the student book).

These are the resources Peter lists:

• A prepared witness (3:15; 4:12). We should not be surprised when opposition surfaces. We are to "be ready" for whenever we are questioned about our faith.

• A humble witness (3:15). We should not come across as proud or "showy" in our witness; "meekness and fear" are the keys.

• A clear conscience (3:16). Knowing that the opposition has arisen because of our faith in Christ (and not because of some offense that we have done) can encourage us.

• The example of Christ (3:18). Christ shows us how to act under pressure.

• Baptism (3:21). We can point to baptism as our spiritual "landmark." This can give us assurance when we are tempted to doubt or give up our faith in the face of adversity and the tempter's assaults.

• Co-sufferers with Christ (4:13): Knowing that we are suffering with Christ inspires a more fervent commitment.

• Anticipation of Christ's return (4:13). All of life should be lived in view of the hope of being with Christ for eternity.

• The Holy Spirit (4:14). The Spirit gives us guidance and support in speaking up for Christ (see Matthew 10:17-20).

Into Life

Point out that as Christians we need to be ready to witness for Christ, explain what we believe and why, and answer those who criticize and accuse us. Tell your students to think about what they believe about Jesus Christ. If someone were to ask them, could they give an answer?

Urge your students to spend the coming week thinking and talking about their beliefs. It would be most helpful if they could get together with a mature Christian, or with a Christian who has been successful in maintaining a faithful witness for Christ in a hostile setting at work, school, or some other location.

As a follow-up to this class, some may want to consider conducting an elective class for one quarter, dealing with the subject of personal evangelism or "witnessing in the workplace." Be sure to pursue such interest if it is present.

Let's Talk It Over

The questions on this page are designed to encourage review of the lesson Scriptures and to promote discussion of the lesson by the class. The answers provided are only discussion starters. Let your class talk it over from there.

1. In what ways are Christians in this culture most likely to suffer for their faith? Is it possible to experience that suffering and still be happy? How?

Thankfully, Christians in this culture are generally free to worship and practice their faith without fear of arrest or imprisonment. The suffering we sometimes endure is more subtle. It occurs when Christian convictions or values come into conflict with those of others around us. You may have an employer who does not agree with your commitment to worship on Sunday, or your commitment to family. Christian faith and conviction may put you at odds with school officials and teachers over curriculum choices or behavior standards. Christian scruples may cause those who disagree with you to belittle, scorn, or ostracize you. In order to remain happy in such circumstances, you must be convinced that it is better to obey and please God than to please people (Acts 4:19). If you compromise your convictions, your greatest persecution may come from your own conscience. It is a happier circumstance to suffer persecution, yet with a clear conscience.

2. Have you ever prepared an answer to explain your hope as a Christian? What are some things you would say?

Since we are to "be ready always" to give an intelligent answer to someone who inquires about our hope (1 Peter 3:15), it is a good idea to give some advance thought to our answer. We may want to share some of the classic arguments for the identity of Christ as God's Son: the miracles He performed, His inspired teaching, His death and resurrection, and the commitment of His first-century followers. Another approach is to make your answer very personal, testifying to the difference that knowing Jesus has made in your life. You will discover that the reasons you find most compelling for believing in Jesus will have the greatest impact upon others.

3. What is the best defense against the slander and ridicule that you receive because of your faith?

If we establish a reputation for a character that is consistent, sincere, and devoted to Christian principles, this is the best protection we possess against the wounds of slander and ridicule. It does not mean that we will not be slandered or ridiculed; it simply means that the number of people who believe the slander will likely be few. A life lived in consistent obedience to noble principles will generally be admired, even by those who do not agree with the principles. This seems to be the point of the question Peter asks in 1 Peter 3:13: "And who is he that will harm you, if ye be followers of that which is good?"

4. The convictions that Christians hold often put us in the minority. How do you deal with having to stand against the crowd?

It is not easy to stand alone. We marvel at how Noah and his family could do it for more than one hundred years. First, you must keep your relationship with God fresh and dynamic. You do that through regular worship, prayer, and meditation in the Word. If God is a very present reality in your life, it makes the pressure of the crowd easier to withstand. It is also a lot easier if you are not entirely alone. To have a prayer partner, a small group, or a Bible class who agrees with you, prays for you, encourages you, and holds you accountable can give you great courage and spiritual power.

5. What spiritual realities are proclaimed through baptism? How does baptism bring comfort to the believer?

The same flood waters that meant destruction for everyone else caused the ark to float, thus distinguishing Noah and his family as belonging to God. Baptism is a physical act that distinguishes us as one of God's children. By baptism we identify with Christ in His burial and resurrection. Through repentance we die to sin and then, having been buried with Christ by baptism, we rise to "walk in newness of life" (Romans 6:4). The past is forgiven; "all things are become new" (2 Corinthians 5:17). Baptism is comforting to believers as an unforgettable assurance of God's acceptance and forgiveness, just as it was for the Ethiopian eunuch (Acts 8:36-39) and for Saul (Acts 22:16). Later, Saul (as Paul) used baptism to challenge Christians to maintain a consistent walk with Christ (Romans 6:4; Galatians 3:27; Colossians 2:8-12).

Living in Humility

DEVOTIONAL READING: Romans 12:9-21.

LESSON SCRIPTURE: 1 Peter 5:1-11.

PRINTED TEXT: 1 Peter 5:1-11.

1 Peter 5:1-11

1 The elders which are among you I exhort, who am also an elder, and a witness of the sufferings of Christ, and also a partaker of the glory that shall be revealed:

2 Feed the flock of God which is among you, taking the oversight thereof, not by constraint, but willingly; not for filthy lucre, but of a ready mind;

3 Neither as being lords over God's heritage, but being ensamples to the flock.

4 And when the chief Shepherd shall appear, ye shall receive a crown of glory that fadeth not away.

5 Likewise, ye younger, submit yourselves unto the elder. Yea, all of you be subject one to another, and be clothed with humility: for God resisteth the proud, and giveth grace to the humble.

6 Humble yourselves therefore under the mighty hand of God, that he may exalt you in due time:

7 Casting all your care upon him; for he careth for you.

8 Be sober, be vigilant; because your adversary the devil, as a roaring lion, walketh about, seeking whom he may devour:

9 Whom resist steadfast in the faith, knowing that the same afflictions are accomplished in your brethren that are in the world.

10 But the God of all grace, who hath called us unto his eternal glory by Christ Jesus, after that ye have suffered a while, make you perfect, stablish, strengthen, settle you.

11 To him be glory and dominion for ever and ever. Amen.

Jan 25

GOLDEN TEXT: All of you be subject one to another, and be clothed with humility: for God resisteth the proud, and giveth grace to the humble.—1 Peter 5:5.

God's People in a Troubled World
Unit 2: Hope for God's People
(Lessons 5-8)

Lesson Aims

After completing this lesson, students should be able to:

1. Tell what Peter says about the need for Christian leaders and followers to practice humility.

2. Explain how the practice of humility toward God and one another helps Christians to glorify God and resist Satan.

3. Prayerfully cultivate a spirit of humility toward God and toward fellow believers.

Lesson Outline

INTRODUCTION
 A. No Room for Pride
 B. Lesson Background
 I. HUMILITY IN THE CHURCH (1 Peter 5:1-5a)
 A. From One Elder to Other Elders (v. 1)
 B. The Elder's Calling (vv. 2, 3)
 C. The Elder's Crown (v. 4)
  A Crown of Glory
 D. Respecting One Another (v. 5a)
 II. HUMILITY BEFORE GOD (1 Peter 5:5b-11)
 A. An Important Principle (v. 5b)
 B. The Blessings of Humility (vv. 6, 7)
 C. The Enemy of Humility (vv. 8, 9)
  Deadly but Defeated
 D. The Reward of Humility (vv. 10, 11)
CONCLUSION
 A. Knowing Our Place
 B. Prayer
 C. Thought to Remember

First Peter 5:5 tells younger Christians to submit to older ones. Use the visual for Lesson 8 to illustrate this point. It is shown on page 181.

Introduction

A. No Room for Pride

There are many words that can describe our country: beautiful, free, blessed, wealthy, to list just a few. Unfortunately, another that could be suggested is "haughty," a term that means "blatantly and disdainfully proud." Solomon reminds us, "Pride goeth before destruction, and a haughty spirit before a fall" (Proverbs 16:18). Consider these words of Abraham Lincoln as he

challenged Americans of his day not to forget the source of their blessings: "Intoxicated with unbroken success, we have become too self-sufficient to feel the necessity of redeeming and preserving grace, too proud to pray to the God who made us. We have grown in numbers, wealth, and power as no other nation has grown, but we have forgotten God." How appropriate are his words for our time!

In the passage we are studying today, Peter reminds us that there is no room for haughtiness or pride in the life of a Christian or in the Christian community. Such an attitude will render both the congregation and the individual believer powerless.

William Gladstone, a nineteenth-century British prime minister, observed, "Humility as a sovereign grace is a creation of Christianity." Jesus made humility a virtue by His complete reversal of human values. It is the meek, not the mighty, who will be victorious (Matthew 5:5). He who pushes himself forward will be humiliated; he who humbles himself will be elevated (Matthew 23:12; Luke 14:11). The necessity of humility is clearly stated in Matthew 18:3, where Jesus said, "Except ye be converted, and become as little children, ye shall not enter into the kingdom of heaven." The person who brings himself down to such an utterly dependent state is the one who will be greatest in the kingdom (v. 4), because he has learned to be dependent on God's power and not on his own intelligence or cunning.

In the passage we are studying today, Peter draws our attention to the need for humility in our relationships with God and with one another. Both of these are critical areas. On the one hand, one of the reasons we often fail in our fight against Satan is that we fail to humble ourselves before God and His Word. On the other hand, one of the reasons there is so much turmoil within some congregations is that Christians do not live humbly with one another. For example, leaders who exhibit arrogance often produce arrogant followers. Followers who are haughty may well encourage their leaders to assert their influence in negative ways. The command of Scripture is clear: "All of you be subject one to another, and be clothed with humility: for God resisteth the proud, and giveth grace to the humble" (1 Peter 5:5). In the Christian life, victory comes through *submission*.

B. Lesson Background

In 1 Peter 4:1-6 Peter reminds his readers that Christianity means a death to the pagan way of life—a radical break with the past. In 4:7-11 he offers more general advice, focusing on relations within the church. We are to show love toward one another and respect one another's gifts. In 4:12-19 the trials of Christians are kept in perspective by reminding them of their glorious future. In verse 17 Peter makes this sobering observation: "The time is come that judgment must begin at the house of God." It is therefore important for the "house of God" (the church) to get its house in order and to do whatever "cleaning" is necessary. The words in today's text, taken from 1 Peter 5, deal with attitudes that must be present for this to happen.

I. Humility in the Church
(1 Peter 5:1-5a)

This passage is one of the most important in the Bible on the duties of those men who accept the responsibility to serve as elders of a congregation. The verses indicate that, rather than merely filling an office or a position, the task of shepherding the flock ought to be uppermost in the mind of an elder.

A. From One Elder to Other Elders
(v. 1)

1. The elders which are among you I exhort, who am also an elder, and a witness of the sufferings of Christ, and also a partaker of the glory that shall be revealed.

The designations of *elders*, "bishops" (also rendered as "overseers"), and "shepherds" are used interchangeably in the New Testament to describe the functions of those individuals who are ultimately accountable for the welfare of a congregation and its members. Paul's words to the Ephesian elders include exhortations both about being "overseers" and shepherding the flock (Acts 20:28). We should keep in mind Peter's earlier warning about judgment falling upon the house of God (1 Peter 4:17); perhaps elders are now addressed as the ones most responsible for putting God's house in order.

It is important to note the presence of the plural form *elders*. The New Testament knows of no one being called "the elder" or "the bishop" of a congregation. The emphasis is on a plurality of leaders. More insight and wisdom are available when two or more men are responsible for the ultimate care of a congregation, than if just one is serving as an elder. There is also less room for mistakes or hasty, careless actions.

Another point of interest is the fact that Peter considered himself *also an elder*. In the Greek text only one word is used, perhaps best rendered as "fellow elder." Yet Peter was justified in speaking with some authority to other elders, because he had both seen and testified to the

sufferings of Christ. In addition he was *a partaker of the glory that shall be revealed*. Here Peter may have had in mind the transfiguration of Christ (Matthew 17:1-9; 2 Peter 1:16-18), where His glory was revealed as a foretaste of the glory to be shared one day by His followers (Romans 8:17, 18).

B. The Elder's Calling (vv. 2, 3)

2. Feed the flock of God which is among you, taking the oversight thereof, not by constraint, but willingly; not for filthy lucre, but of a ready mind.

This verse includes both positives and negatives in describing the ministry of the elders. First, elders are to *feed the flock*—a command reminiscent of Jesus' words to Peter in John 21:15-17, and of Paul's words to the elders of the church in Ephesus (Acts 20:28). The verb *feed* literally means "to shepherd." It refers to providing the needed nourishment for God's people, especially through the "milk of the word" (1 Peter 2:2). The phrase *flock of God* reminds us of two truths: (1) like sheep, Christians need guidance and care, and (2) elders must always remember that Christians belong to God first and foremost. Elders are not owners or bosses; they are stewards, or caretakers, of God's people.

How do elders fulfill this command? Two qualities are mentioned in this verse. First, elders must serve as those who are freely and *willingly* doing God's work, not as persons under compulsion. Their ministry should be done with eager service; they should "desire the office" (1 Timothy 3:1). Second, elders must serve, not for the sake of the financial compensation they may receive (1 Timothy 5:17, 18), but with a generous heart. Their motives should be noble, not mercenary.

3. Neither as being lords over God's heritage, but being ensamples to the flock.

Peter continues his description of the responsibilities of elders, again using both a negative and a positive statement. Their attitude must not be that of *lords* over slaves. The exercise of Biblical leadership should be affirming, not authoritarian. God does not want elders who desire to build sheep pens to control people! The term *God's heritage* emphasizes the elders' task as a ministry given to them by God; it is not a position that they have "taken over." The *New International Version* reads, "not lording it over those entrusted to you."

On the positive side, the elders are to lead by being *ensamples*, or examples, of Christlike character. Paul tells the Corinthians, "Be ye followers of me, even as I also am of Christ" (1 Corinthians 11:1).

Taken together, verses 2 and 3 remind us that the primary responsibility of elders is to care for people. They should not view their task in terms of making decisions or transacting business. They are the ones responsible for the doctrinal well-being of a congregation by teaching and rebuking (1 Timothy 3:2; 5:17; Titus 1:9), equipping the saints for ministry (Ephesians 4:11-16), and caring for the physical and spiritual needs of the flock (Acts 20:28; James 5:14).

Elders are examples, equippers, and encouragers, not enforcers. They are caretakers and counselors, not commanders and controllers.

C. The Elder's Crown (v. 4)

4. And when the chief Shepherd shall appear, ye shall receive a crown of glory that fadeth not away.

Rather than talking about any one man being "the shepherd" or "the chief elder" of a congregation, it is proper to speak only of Christ in such terms (Hebrews 13:20; 1 Peter 2:25). Peter appeals to the elders based on the certainty of Christ's return—an important theme in this letter (1:7, 13; 2:12; 4:7, 13).

Money and the praises of people are rewards that all too quickly will lose their luster; thus they are not worth seeking. Instead, elders are to keep before them the promise of the reward that *fadeth not away* (see also 1 Peter 1:4).

A CROWN OF GLORY

Crowns are normally kept under lock and key. The British crown is kept in the Tower of London, the Austrian crown in the Hofburg Palace. Both are closely guarded. History records that the Hungarian crown was taken twice; in fact, in the fourteenth century, Charles of Anjou could not be crowned with it, because it had been stolen and taken out of the country. At the end of World War II, the Allies took the crown to America, and later returned it to Hungary after democracy replaced a Communist dictatorship.

Crowns are precious. However, all the crowns of the world are mere trinkets compared with the crown of glory that God will give to every faithful servant of His. This crown is not made of gold or silver, and thus will never tarnish. It is not made of precious stones, and thus cannot be robbed of its treasure. It is not kept locked away to be displayed on special occasions. It is a crown of unfading glory—the reward of those who lead lovingly and serve diligently. How appropriate that we should receive a crown, for Christ has made us kings (Revelation 1:6), and we shall reign with Him (2 Timothy 2:12). God will not forget to reward royally those who do not forget to serve Him faithfully.   —R. C. S.

D. Respecting One Another (v. 5a)

5a. Likewise, ye younger, submit yourselves unto the elder. Yea, all of you be subject to one another, and be clothed with humility.

Here Peter seems to be using the term *elder* in the general sense of "the elderly" (similar to when we say "respect your elders"). These terms may possess, however, a more "spiritual" sense; in other words, the spiritually *younger* (babes in Christ, who are more vulnerable to straying from the faith) should *submit* to the more mature Christians and learn from their example.

To submit or *be subject to one another* is not a negative concept in Scripture. It is an attitude modeled by Jesus and to be exhibited by *all* His followers. The verb *be clothed* literally means "tie about yourselves." It expresses the effort required to cultivate the true *humility* expected of the Christian. Perhaps Peter was thinking about Jesus' washing the disciples' feet in the upper room, when He "took a towel, and girded himself" (John 13:4).

II. Humility Before God
(1 Peter 5:5b-11)

A. An Important Principle (v. 5b)

5b. For God resisteth the proud, and giveth grace to the humble.

In their relations with one another, all Christians must practice humility, spurred on by the knowledge of God's manner of dealing with the *proud* and the *humble*. The principle stated by Peter is taken from Proverbs 3:34. C. S. Lewis stated the danger of pride in these words: "A proud man is always looking down on things and people: and, of course, as long as you are looking down, you cannot see something that is above you."

The word *grace* is used eight times in 1 Peter (1:2, 10, 13; 3:7; 4:10; 5:5, 10, 12). It is the source of all blessings for the believer. Grace is identified with the salvation that has come through Jesus (1:10; 3:7), the faithful exercising of God's gifts (4:10), the sustaining power of God (5:5, 12), and the completed salvation that will be received at Christ's second coming (1:13). All of this is rooted in the God of all grace (5:10).

B. The Blessings of Humility (vv. 6, 7)

6. Humble yourselves therefore under the mighty hand of God, that he may exalt you in due time.

Humility is needed not only toward "one another" (v. 5), but also toward God Himself. The phrase *under the mighty hand of God* comes from the Old Testament (for examples, see

visual for
lesson 8

Deuteronomy 3:24; 9:26; Joshua 4:24; Daniel 9:15), and refers to those mighty acts by which God raised up a people for Himself and brought them out of Egyptian bondage. In addition, this verse suggests that Christians are to accept their present sufferings as being under the control of a sovereign God. *In due time* He will *exalt* His people, and work through their circumstances for good (Romans 8:28).

7. Casting all your care upon him; for he careth for you.

Peter invites us to place our total trust in God. We can do this in full assurance, because *he careth for you.* While our twentieth-century world is quite different from Peter's, his words remain true. Whatever the burdens of daily living, we can bring them to the Lord (Psalm 55:22).

The words translated *care* and *careth* are two different words in the Greek text. The word for *careth* speaks of God's concern for us. The word rendered *care* comes from a word meaning "to divide." Cares and anxieties have the potential to make us "go to pieces," keeping us from a wholehearted commitment to Christ. By bringing our cares to God, we do not necessarily eliminate the circumstances that cause our cares, but we find our anxieties replaced by His peace.

C. The Enemy of Humility (vv. 8, 9)

8. Be sober, be vigilant; because your adversary the devil, as a roaring lion, walketh about, seeking whom he may devour.

Trusting God does not mean that we are freed from the need for constant vigilance. Even though Jesus, the Lion of the tribe of Judah (Revelation 5:5), has defeated the lion-devil (Hebrews 2:14, 15; 1 John 3:8), we must not let down our defenses. Satan never rests in his attempts to destroy Christians. The word *sober* conveys the idea of self-control. The person who through God's Spirit has cultivated this quality will not be as likely to fall under the control of Satan.

The descriptions of Satan in this verse are significant. The word *devil* means "accuser" or "slanderer"; he is the father of lies (John 8:44). In New Testament times, the term *adversary* described an opponent in a lawsuit—an appropriate term in light of the many false charges Christians were facing. Some see in the phrase *roaring lion* a reference to the means by which Christians were often put to death under Emperor Nero's persecution.

DEADLY BUT DEFEATED

His name is Criswell, and he has been a teacher, a mortician, and a newsman. He claims to be able to predict the future, and he claims eighty-six percent accuracy. But some of his failures are quite notable. For example, he predicted that Cuban dictator Fidel Castro would be assassinated in 1970 by a woman. It didn't happen. He predicted that there would be an underwater volcano that would erupt in the Pacific Ocean in 1971, creating new islands. It didn't happen.

Criswell also predicted that the devil would rule the earth, beginning in 1975. Again, it didn't happen, because he got the date wrong. The devil began to rule the earth long, long ago. If the lion is the king of the jungle, then the lion is a suitable image to describe the devil. The lion is dangerous and deadly. The devil is as dangerous to us as he was to Adam and Eve. According to Jesus, he is the prince of this world (John 12:31). We must remember, however, that the devil rules as a usurper. The old song is still true: "This is my Father's world." He who sought to thwart God's purposes in Eden has been destroyed through the cross and the empty tomb (Hebrews 2:14, 15; 1 John 3:8). His eventual eternal doom is sure.

In the meantime, we need to be on our guard constantly. While we are to avoid temptation as much as possible, we will always be tempted in some way until the Lord's final victory, when Satan and his cohorts will be "cast into the lake of fire and brimstone . . . for ever and ever" (Revelation 20:10). Now is the time to get on the winning side.   —R. C. S.

9. Whom resist steadfast in the faith, knowing that the same afflictions are accomplished in your brethren that are in the world.

The best way to resist the devil is by remaining *steadfast in the faith.* An additional source of encouragement to sufferers is provided by the knowledge that *the same afflictions are accomplished in your brethren.* Persecution is the common lot of Christians everywhere (2 Timothy 3:12); no one should feel alone or deserted when he suffers for Jesus' sake.

D. The Reward of Humility

(vv. 10, 11)

10. But the God of all grace, who hath called us unto his eternal glory by Christ Jesus, after that ye have suffered a while, make you perfect, stablish, strengthen, settle you.

As Peter's letter nears its end, he assures his readers with a promise that is meant to highlight the contrast between the readers' present trials and the blessings that will come *after* their hardships. Suffering Christians have not been rejected nor forsaken by God. They are recipients of His sustaining *grace*. Suffering is only for *a while*, a point Peter emphasized in 1 Peter 1:6, 7. On the other hand, the *glory* that awaits the faithful servants of Jesus is *eternal* (2 Corinthians 4:17, 18).

In the meantime, God's grace is sufficient to meet all our spiritual needs. He will make us *perfect*—a word that is used in the New Testament to describe the mending of nets (Mark 1:19). The word *stablish* is an older form of "establish"; it means that God will make us "stable" in the midst of our hardships.

Our God is loving, powerful, and faithful. Having obtained our salvation at such a great price and having called us through the preaching of the gospel, He will never abandon us, no matter how dark our surroundings may seem.

11. To him be glory and dominion for ever and ever. Amen.

In light of God's faithfulness, how else can we respond but with praise! Even though our new life in Christ does not render us immune to the attacks of Satan, we still trust God because of who He is. Let us praise Him that we are "more than conquerors" (Romans 8:37).

Conclusion

A. Knowing Our Place

Several years ago I talked to a shepherd. He told me that sheep are not at all the clean and cuddly creatures that they may appear to be. He said that they are dirty, and often need to be dipped in strong chemicals to rid them of lice, ticks, and other pests. They are frequently wayward and obstinate. What a humbling reminder of what we, God's flock, can be like!

It is good for leaders to remember such a description. Elders need to be concerned about the condition of their flock. They need to be caring, patient, and loving. Elders are shepherds feeding the flock, not cowboys driving a herd. They also need to be concerned with their own spiritual condition, for they are to be examples in all areas of life.

It is also good for followers to remember this description. It will help them understand and appreciate more fully the ministry of elders. Elders are gifted by God, in order to help all Christians in moving toward maturity in Christ (Ephesians 4:11-16).

Far too often there is strife between elders and other brothers and sisters in Christ. As God's people we must never forget who the real enemy is—Satan. One of the greatest embarrassments a church can experience occurs when division surfaces between leaders and followers. When Christians do not get along with one another, they do nothing but harm their witness and hinder the impact of the gospel.

The focus of today's lesson, humility, brings us to the root of the problem. True followers of Christ have no right to insist upon their rights. If there is a lack of humility in our relationships with one another, it probably indicates a failure to humble ourselves before God. A Christian follows Jesus, who freely gave up His rights, and lives in dependence on Him alone.

Elders should say to the flock, "Come, follow us, because we follow Jesus, the chief Shepherd. Together, let's help each other get home safely." All of us must be alert to the tactics of the enemy, but most important, we must be sure that we are firmly grounded in the grace and power of the One whose kingdom is forever!

B. Prayer

Gracious God, we thank You for Jesus who humbled Himself for our sakes. May we be willing to humble ourselves in service for Your praise and glory. Amen.

C. Thought to Remember

Only the humble will be honored by God.

Home Daily Bible Readings

Learning by Doing

This page contains an alternate lesson plan emphasizing learning activities.
Classes desiring such student involvement will find these suggestions helpful.

Learning Goals

After completing this lesson, your students should be able to:

1. Tell what Peter says about the need for Christian leaders and followers to practice humility.

2. Explain how the practice of humility toward God and one another helps Christians to glorify God and resist Satan.

3. Prayerfully cultivate a spirit of humility toward God and toward fellow believers.

Into the Lesson

Introduce this lesson on humility by writing the word *haughty* on the chalkboard. Then ask, "What do you think of when you see this word?" (You may want to use the quotation from Abraham Lincoln found in the first paragraph of the lesson Introduction.)

All of us are guilty of pride. But when we come to Christ, He introduces us to an "upside down" outlook. In today's lesson the focus is on living a life of humility as explained by Peter.

Into the Word

Peter's instructions in 1 Peter 5:1-5a were primarily for elders in the church. He draws a series of contrasts between what elders are to do and what they are not to do. Lead your students in the following activity (which also appears in the student book). First, tell them to search 1 Peter 5:1-5a for what elders are to do. Call attention to the following:

• Teach God's Word to those in the church ("feed the flock," v. 2).

• Be an overseer, providing leadership (v. 2).

• Serve willingly (v. 2).

• Serve with a noble purpose rather than simply to earn money (v. 2).

• Be an example to the believers (v. 3).

• Be aware of who the real Shepherd of the church is (v. 4).

• Serve in the light of eternity (v. 4).

• Submit to others. Note that the command in verse 5 to be "clothed with humility" is for all Christians, including elders.

Now go back to the same passage and ask the students to look for what elders should not do. Note the following:

• Do not serve with a feeling of being forced to do so (v. 2).

• Do not serve only for what you get out of it (v. 2).

• Do not "lord it over" those you are to serve (v. 3).

In the rest of this passage (vv. 5b-11), Peter addresses relationships among believers. According to Peter, why should we be humble? Consider the following:

• Because God opposes the proud but helps the humble (v. 5).

• Because ultimately, God will exalt the humble (v. 6). (We are talking about genuine humility here, not the phony humility of someone who pretends to be humble because he thinks others expect it of him.)

• Because God genuinely cares for us (v. 7).

• Because Satan wants to devour us (v. 8).

• Because God will reward humility (v. 10).

Into Life

Humility is so foreign to our nature that sometimes we actually do not know what a humble response is. Use the situations below to help your students evaluate how to be humble. In each case they should answer this question: "What is the humble thing to do?" (These situations are printed in the student book.)

• You sang a solo in the morning worship service and believe that you did a good job. After the service, someone compliments you on your song. What do you say?

• You are the chairman of a committee that organized an effective and successful community ministry project. However, since you are so tied up at your job, most of the planning and the actual work was done by other members of your committee. On Sunday morning, the minister calls you up front and praises you in glowing terms. What do you say?

• On your way home, you stop at the grocery store to pick up a few items. All the checkouts are busy but one, so you head for it. But just before you get there, an elderly lady with an overloaded shopping cart pushes in front of you. What do you say?

Bring the lesson to a close by telling your students to think of one person toward whom they tend to have a less-than-humble attitude. Challenge students to make a commitment to treat that person with humility during the coming week.

Let's Talk It Over

The questions on this page are designed to encourage review of the lesson Scriptures and to promote discussion of the lesson by the class. The answers provided are only discussion starters. Let your class talk it over from there.

1. Elders are cast in the role of shepherds. How does the work of a shepherd relate to the work of an elder?

The image of a shepherd is an instructive one, even for those of us who are only remotely familiar with all that is involved. We know, for instance, that shepherds are responsible for seeing that their flock is fed. In the case of an elder, their "flock" of believers must be fed on the true Word of God. The shepherd cares for the sick and injured sheep. The elder should minister to those in his charge who are suffering illness or personal difficulty by offering prayer, counsel, and encouragement. The shepherd must protect the sheep from predators. The elder must be vigilant in protecting the integrity of the church from false teachings and from sinful behavior. The shepherd must also rescue the lost and endangered sheep. The elder must seek to restore believers who may be falling away or becoming entrapped in sin.

2. How is it out of character for elders to be bossy or controlling?

The leadership of the elder is not to be one of dogmatic rule, but one of example. In the case of shepherds, the welfare and needs of the flock must take priority. So, too, in the church the welfare and needs of believers should be uppermost in the minds of elders. The sheep cannot be commanded from afar; they must be gently led by their shepherds. Jesus, the "chief Shepherd" (1 Peter 5:4), called others to follow Him, and then He led the way by example. This is the ideal for those who would serve well as elders.

3. What are some examples of the humility called for between Christians?

The quality of humility has to do with how we regard ourselves relative to how we regard others. Peter writes, "All of you be subject one to another, and be clothed with humility" (1 Peter 5:5). What would the clothing of humility look like? The most recent designer fashion? No, more likely it would look like the apron of service, the coveralls of the worker, or the gloves of the one who labors on behalf of others. In our churches, the clothing of humility may be the usher's badge or the nursery worker's smock. It would apply to the one who teaches the Sunday

school class, the one who provides transportation for another, the one who parks in the far corner of the parking lot on purpose, the one who hosted the youth social last week, or the one who took a meal to a bereaved family.

4. Can you tell about a time when you cast your cares upon the Lord? Explain what happened. How do we know that God cares?

Even though we are invited by Scripture to cast all our cares upon the Lord (1 Peter 5:7), many of us find that difficult to do. We believe that there must be something more we can do about our circumstances. We hate the feeling of being out of control. In such times, it will bring a sense of peace if we can trust God. Peter learned something about this kind of trust when he stepped out of the boat to walk to Jesus on the water (Matthew 14:28-31). Hopefully you have had the wonderful experience of God's comfort and peace in the face of overwhelming circumstances that were beyond your control. We can know that God cares for us because of His revelation of Himself throughout history, but most of all because He sent His only Son to be our Savior. He has gone to great lengths to demonstrate how much He cares for us.

5. Have you ever known anyone whom Satan "devoured"? What was the outcome for them? How has that influenced the way you regard Satan?

The Bible certainly treats the existence of Satan with all seriousness. He has made himself the adversary of God and of all who would pursue the will of God. Whatever power Satan possesses is arrayed against God and against Christians. Peter pictures him as a "roaring lion" (1 Peter 5:8). As such, he hopes to scare the lame or otherwise vulnerable prey. Unfortunately, nearly all of us can name someone who made a good start with Jesus, but who turned back to the ways of this world and to the temptations of Satan. The outcome is usually sad for that individual, but also for those close to him. The selfishness and sin that accompany Satan's way bring a harvest of heartache. Observing that pain in another's life should make us all the more vigilant against the work of Satan, and all the more faithful to Christ.

Confirming Our Calling

DEVOTIONAL READING: 2 Peter 1:16-21.

LESSON SCRIPTURE: 2 Peter 1.

PRINTED TEXT: 2 Peter 1:3-15.

2 Peter 1:3-15

3 According as his divine power hath given unto us all things that pertain unto life and godliness, through the knowledge of him that hath called us to glory and virtue:

4 Whereby are given unto us exceeding great and precious promises; that by these ye might be partakers of the divine nature, having escaped the corruption that is in the world through lust.

5 And besides this, giving all diligence, add to your faith virtue; and to virtue, knowledge;

6 And to knowledge, temperance; and to temperance, patience; and to patience, godliness;

7 And to godliness, brotherly kindness; and to brotherly kindness, charity.

8 For if these things be in you, and abound, they make you that ye shall neither be barren nor unfruitful in the knowledge of our Lord Jesus Christ.

9 But he that lacketh these things is blind, and cannot see afar off, and hath forgotten that he was purged from his old sins.

10 Wherefore the rather, brethren, give diligence to make your calling and election sure: for if ye do these things, ye shall never fall:

11 For so an entrance shall be ministered unto you abundantly into the everlasting kingdom of our Lord and Saviour Jesus Christ.

12 Wherefore I will not be negligent to put you always in remembrance of these things, though ye know them, and be established in the present truth.

13 Yea, I think it meet, as long as I am in this tabernacle, to stir you up by putting you in remembrance;

14 Knowing that shortly I must put off this my tabernacle, even as our Lord Jesus Christ hath showed me.

15 Moreover I will endeavor that ye may be able after my decease to have these things always in remembrance.

**Feb
1**

GOLDEN TEXT: Brethren, give diligence to make your calling and election sure:
for if ye do these things, ye shall never fall.—2 Peter 1:10.

God's People in a Troubled World
Unit 3: Endurance of God's People
(Lessons 9-12)

Lesson Aims

After completing this lesson, each student should be able to:

1. Describe how God's call and our response are foundational to our relationship with Christ.

2. List the qualities that Peter says should be present and increasing in the life of a believer.

3. Suggest a specific way to "give diligence" to developing one of these qualities in his or her life.

Lesson Outline

INTRODUCTION
    A. Worthy of Our Calling
    B. Lesson Background
  I. A CALL TO GODLINESS (2 Peter 1:3-7)
    A. By Divine Power (vv. 3, 4)
       A Little Off Center
    B. In Specific Areas (vv. 5-7)
  II. A CALL TO GROWTH (2 Peter 1:8-11)
    A. Toward a Heavenly View (vv. 8, 9)
       Lest We Forget
    B. On a Solid Foundation (vv. 10, 11)
  III. A CALL TO REMEMBRANCE (2 Peter 1:12-15)
    A. Of the Truths We Have Been Taught
      (v. 12)
    B. Of the Teachers Who Have Taught Us
      (vv. 13-15)
CONCLUSION
    A. Seeing the Need for Change
    B. Prayer
    C. Thought to Remember

The visual for Lesson 9 in the visuals packet encourages us to give "diligence" to our Christian growth. It is shown on page 189.

Introduction

A. Worthy of Our Calling

During the old days of black-and-white TV, there was a popular television show called "Branded." Set back in the days of the American cavalry, the plot revolved around a man who had been accused of "conduct unbecoming" a military officer. Each week the opening scene replayed the officer's court martial, during which his commander broke the man's sword in half and ripped his military insignias from his coat. He was declared to be "unworthy of wearing the uniform" of the United States Cavalry.

The apostle Peter is concerned that his readers not be found "unworthy of wearing the uniform" of a Christian, because they are still hanging on to the habits of their sinful past. In today's lesson text he urges all of us to genuinely pursue a holy lifestyle that is appropriate for people who have been called into fellowship with a holy God.

B. Lesson Background

The epistle of 2 Peter focuses upon the theme of defending the truths that God has revealed to us. For example, chapter 2 calls attention to false teachers within the church who are contradicting sound doctrine, while chapter 3 speaks of scoffers outside the church who malign the belief of Christians in the return of Christ and the end of the world. Chapter 1 reminds us that before we can deal effectively with those around us who undermine God's truth, we must first make sure that we ourselves are living according to the truth. This is a theme that is developed in the opening chapter of both 1 Peter and 2 Peter: the defense of doctrinal truth must be grounded upon the application of that truth in the lives of those who would defend it. In other words, we must practice what we preach.

I. A Call to Godliness
(2 Peter 1:3-7)

A. By Divine Power (vv. 3, 4)

3. According as his divine power hath given unto us all things that pertain unto life and godliness, through the knowledge of him that hath called us to glory and virtue.

God *hath called us to glory and virtue.* It is God's desire that we as Christians cease operating according to the sinful attitudes and desires of the world. We are no longer to practice sin, but to display righteous deeds. We are no longer to yield to the desires of our flesh, but to follow the leading of the Holy Spirit. We are no longer to live for self, but for the will of God.

God has called us to practice *godliness,* that is, the imitation of the moral and righteous qualities of God. However, He has done more than simply issue a challenge to godliness. He *hath given unto us all things that pertain unto life and godliness.* In other words, God has also provided the resources by which we can attain a measure of godliness in this life. We have the guidance of His Word to show us what to do (2 Timothy 3:16, 17). We have the indwelling gift of the Holy Spirit to strengthen our will power (Romans

8:12-14). We have the fellowship of the church to provide mutual encouragement as we grow together (Hebrews 10:24, 25).

Perhaps the greatest aid to our pursuit of godliness is that we have been given *the knowledge of him that hath called us*. One of the grand implications of the incarnation of the Son of God into human form is that we now have a visible example of what divine godliness looks like in the flesh. We sinners do not have to imagine a godly life in theory; we can see it in operation. In the accounts of Jesus' life provided by eyewitnesses such as Peter and the other apostles (2 Peter 1:16), we are given a realistic model of how God wants us to conduct ourselves.

4. Whereby are given unto us exceeding great and precious promises; that by these ye might be partakers of the divine nature, having escaped the corruption that is in the world through lust.

Some have drawn unwarranted ideas from the phrase *partakers of the divine nature*. Many cults use this passage to teach the idea that mankind will eventually become gods (or at least those from among mankind who join these cults). This heretical idea has a long history among groups on the fringe of orthodox Christianity. It is clearly contradicted by the general teaching of Scripture, which makes a sharp distinction between the Creator and His creatures (as in Romans 1:22-25). As the context of 2 Peter 1:4 reveals, to "participate in the divine nature" (*New International Version*) is to practice the moral qualities of God as demonstrated in the life of Jesus.

A LITTLE OFF CENTER

As a young man entered the church building one Sunday morning, a lady who knew him approached and said, "Let me straighten your tie. It's a little bit off center." He replied, "That's a pretty good description of my entire life."

We'd like to think that the sin in our lives means that we are only "a little bit off center." But the apostle Peter describes it more accurately: *corruption* (2 Peter 1:4). That is exactly the right word. Sin is not just a small defect in our lives. The apostle Peter knew, from his own bitter experience, that God takes sin seriously. So must we. It corrodes our souls as rust corrodes metal. It corrupts our lives as decay destroys living tissue. When we understand that, we do not take sin lightly, nor do we take our forgiveness for granted. One man observed, "I love to sin. God loves to forgive. The world is admirably arranged." We must not view our sins in such a flippant way.

Often we sing the chorus, "Because He lives, I can face tomorrow." For those who understand the true nature of sin, the problem is not so much in facing tomorrow as it is in facing yesterday. Peter deals with both: forgiveness for yesterday and strength for tomorrow. Once we are forgiven for the past, we can live in such a way that we will not have to face again the agony of repentance, nor shed its bitter tears. God would spare us this by a call to a better way: the way of holiness.   —R. C. S.

B. In Specific Areas (vv. 5-7)

5. And besides this, giving all diligence, add to your faith virtue; and to virtue, knowledge.

God's call to godly living has been moved from the theoretical to the actual in the example of Jesus Christ. Now Peter continues to give his message a practical relevance by listing a series of godly qualities. Some see the total number of these qualities as eight; others believe that *faith* is meant to serve as the foundation for the other qualities. This would make the number seven, which is a Biblical symbol of completeness. Either way, one should not suppose that these are the only characteristics of a godly life. Rather, they should be viewed as a comprehensive list that should be compared to similar passages (such as Galatians 5:22, 23 and Colossians 3:12-14).

The quality of *virtue* refers to a Greek word that is difficult to translate into English. Some have suggested "goodness," "moral strength," or "moral excellence." It seems to refer to the inner strength to do what one knows is right and thus to put one's faith into action.

There are several possibilities of what Peter has in mind when he speaks of *knowledge* as a godly attribute. It could refer to the knowledge obtained from a serious study of the Scriptures. But in this case it probably refers to the maturing of the way a person thinks rather than to the factual contents of his mind. With the accumulation of Biblical data, we also need to develop an attitude that knows how to put this data to work before a decision is made or an action is taken.

6. And to knowledge, temperance; and to temperance, patience; and to patience, godliness.

Temperance is self-control over every aspect of one's life, including the desires for food and drink, the desires for sexual pleasure, and the balance between work, recreation, and sleep. Temperate people do not allow themselves to be directed by their inner feelings; instead, they maintain control of the flesh (1 Corinthians 6:12).

Patience is not a passive acceptance of whatever happens to us. It is a determination not to allow adversity to move us from our convictions. It is a willful decision to endure situations that we could resist, yet choose not to for the sake of a higher good. It is a quality of strength, not weakness.

The concept of *godliness* pervades this entire passage. In general it refers to our attempt to follow the pattern of God's righteous conduct. In this listing of "godly" qualities, it probably refers specifically to the attitude of reverence and piety toward God at all times, even during our "secular" activities. Everything we do is to be done with a consideration as to what would be appropriate in the presence of God. Everything is to be done for His glory (1 Corinthians 10:31).

7. And to godliness, brotherly kindness; and to brotherly kindness, charity.

Brotherly kindness refers to the kind of unconditional love that can be found within strong, healthy families. Christians should seek this quality by determining to treat their brothers and sisters in Christ in a considerate manner always, regardless of how they are treated in return. This is unconditional love.

Many will readily associate the word *charity* with the classic *King James* rendering of 1 Corinthians 13. In this chapter Paul provides a masterful and timeless definition of the Biblical meaning of *charity*, or love. Such love is a willful choice, not a capricious emotion.

II. A Call to Growth
(2 Peter 1:8-11)

A. Toward a Heavenly View (vv. 8, 9)

8. For if these things be in you, and abound, they make you that ye shall neither be barren nor unfruitful in the knowledge of our Lord Jesus Christ.

Before we become Christians, we have within us some good qualities. No one is completely evil. Our conversion to Christ, however, brings a new perspective on reality, and the realization that we have many weaknesses that are the result of the influence of sin. While we experience a "new birth," this does not instantly transform us into godly people. Godliness involves a lifelong process of growth (Philippians 3:12-14).

So it is that a Christian must never be content with the level of spiritual maturity he has attained in this life. Whatever godly qualities we can now claim must be made to *abound* and grow to a greater depth and a wider manifestation. The *New International Version* emphasizes the growth process with its translation, "if you possess these qualities in increasing measure."

A Christian who does not actively pursue spiritual growth will ultimately be judged by God as *barren and unfruitful.*

9. But he that lacketh these things is blind, and cannot see afar off, and hath forgotten that he was purged from his old sins.

Peter offers a somewhat humorous illustration of a Christian who does not actively pursue spiritual growth. He is like a nearsighted person who *cannot see afar off.* Objects close to him are easy to see. In other words, this type of Christian is doing some things right. But he is missing the bigger picture. He does not see that Christ's holy lifestyle does more than just save us from our past; it also challenges us to strive for holiness in our daily conduct.

The Christian who ignores his spiritual growth is *blind* to a key aspect of the Christian life. He has *forgotten that he was purged from his old sins*, and thus should be aggressively moving away from his old manner of life. It is wrong for a person to celebrate freedom from sin through Christ, while continuing to cling to his old sinful habits.

LEST WE FORGET

When the British made plans to celebrate the jubilee of the reign of Queen Victoria, they turned to the nation's poet laureate and asked him to write something suitable for such a significant occasion. The man who received this formidable assignment was Rudyard Kipling. Within the poem that he composed is this haunting refrain:

> Lord God of Hosts, be with us yet.
> Lest we forget—lest we forget!

How easily we forget! Sometimes we forget intentionally and sometimes unintentionally. Something we must never forget is the fact that we were "purged," or cleansed, from our sins (2 Peter 1:9). We must constantly keep in mind what we were before Christ redeemed us and what we have become by His grace. In today's lesson the measure of our ability to remember is the cultivation of the eight virtues listed in 2 Peter 1:5-7.

We often see carved on a Communion table the words, "In Remembrance of Me." Of course, these were the words of Jesus when He instituted the Lord's Supper in the upper room. The table is always a time to remember Him, but it should also be a time to remember what we were—and what we have become by God's grace. Wise was the man who said, "I'm not yet what I ought to be and not yet what I am going to be, but by the grace of God I'm not what I was."

—R. C. S.

B. On a Solid Foundation
(vv. 10, 11)

10. Wherefore the rather, brethren, give diligence to make your calling and election sure: for if ye do these things, ye shall never fall.

The words *your calling and election* bring to the minds of many the popular idea of a predestination in which God has already chosen whom He will save, regardless of our desires. Once the will of God has consigned people to either Heaven or Hell, there is nothing we can do, so we are told, to change our eternal destiny. This "unconditional election," as it is called, operates outside the bounds of our free will.

There is, however, a better way to understand the Biblical references to election and predestination. God does choose whom He will bless with the eternal joys of Heaven. But His choice is based upon His foreknowledge of our choices (Romans 8:29; 1 Peter 1:1, 2). That is, God chooses those individuals who choose to accept His offer of salvation. This concept is well illustrated in Christ's parable of the marriage feast, found in Matthew 22:1-14. Many who were originally invited to the feast later refused to come. Of those who did choose to come, one was cast out because he was not wearing the wedding clothes expected by the host. The parable closes with this lesson: "Many are called, but few are chosen" (Matthew 22:14). In other words, to be "chosen" for the heavenly feast, one must come when invited, and he must come on God's terms.

This view of election corresponds well with the Biblical emphasis upon salvation being available to all people, not to just a select few (Mark 16:15, 16; 1 Timothy 2:3-6). It is also consistent with Peter's admonition that we *give diligence to make* our *calling and election sure.* Being part of God's elect is not something arbitrarily determined by God in which our fate has already been sealed, but it is something that we can this day choose and *make sure.* In the context of our Scripture, one way in which we make our election sure is to seek after a godly life that is consistent with the faith that we claim to have within. But note: Peter is not teaching a salvation by works. He understands that the kind of faith that saves is one that naturally manifests itself in bearing the fruit of good works (John 14:23, 24; James 2:14-26).

The phrase *ye shall never fall* must also be understood in the same "conditional" manner; as long as we *do these things* and give proper attention to our growth in Christ, we will not fall. To become careless and indifferent about *these things* is to invite spiritual disaster.

visual for
lesson 9

11. For so an entrance shall be ministered unto you abundantly into the everlasting kingdom of our Lord and Saviour Jesus Christ.

The great hope of the Christian faith is to move from this life to *the everlasting kingdom of our Lord and Saviour Jesus Christ.* This heavenly hope guides all we do in our Christian walk. Herein lies a fundamental reason why the doctrine of election is mentioned in Scripture. The truth that "God chooses those who choose Him" is so firmly established that our eternal blessings can be spoken of as already being predetermined or "predestined." You see, one need never fear that after a lifetime of faithful service to God, all his efforts will be for naught. God will always be faithful to His Word, and He will fulfill His salvation promises to us.

III. A Call to Remembrance
(2 Peter 1:12-15)
A. Of the Truths We Have Been Taught
(v. 12)

12. Wherefore I will not be negligent to put you always in remembrance of these things, though ye know them, and be established in the present truth.

As a preacher of the gospel, Peter does not see himself as one proclaiming new truths. Rather, his task is to encourage Christians to practice what they already *know* to be true. This is an accurate picture of what the preaching and teaching ministry within the church involves. A good teacher will try to introduce his students to new concepts and unfamiliar passages of Scripture, but much of this will be new dressing on familiar themes.

Peter also reminds us that an important part of preaching and teaching is repetition. Good messages and solid ideas should not be spoken only once, as if those who hear will instantly be changed. Periodically people need to be reminded of great truths, and encouraged once again to do what they know they should do. If a student preparing for the ministry were to ask, "What do I do when I have preached everything I know?" Peter's answer would be, "Preach it all again until they get it right."

B. Of the Teachers Who Have Taught Us (vv. 13-15)

13, 14. Yea, I think it meet, as long as I am in this tabernacle, to stir you up by putting you in remembrance; knowing that shortly I must put off this my tabernacle, even as our Lord Jesus Christ hath showed me.

Peter's description of his body as a *tabernacle* or tent brings to mind the temporary nature of our earthly existence. Peter knew that he was nearing the time when he would "break camp," take down his tent, and go to his heavenly home. When he wrote these words in approximately A.D. 64, Peter was advanced in age. He likely recalled Christ's prophecy that he would die as an old man, who would be taken where he did not want to go (John 21:18, 19). With the persecution of the church intensifying at this time, Peter knew that his death was near.

15. Moreover I will endeavor that ye may be able after my decease to have these things always in remembrance.

Peter's preaching and teaching ministry would not end on the day he died. His words would remain in the hearts of those whom he had instructed. This is a matter of great joy and encouragement for all who are involved in a ministry of preaching or teaching the Scriptures, because we know the legacy that we leave with those who have heard our message.

Let us also look at this matter from the perspective of the readers. Fond memories of the apostle Peter would naturally bring to mind the messages he had preached. We would do well as Christians to recall from time to time those men and women who in the past nurtured us in the faith. A few moments of reflection upon such persons should bring to mind the good lessons we learned from them, and inspire us to pass those lessons on to others. The writer of Hebrews says, "Remember those who led you, who spoke the word of God to you; and considering the outcome of their way of life, imitate their faith" (Hebrews 13:7, *New American Standard Bible*).

Conclusion

A. Seeing the Need for Change

A country-western song from several years ago included this refrain: "O Lord, it's hard to be humble when you're perfect in every way." We assume that the songwriter was just being humorous, for reasonable people do not really think that they are perfect. Then again, we realize that there is an element of truth in these words, in the fact that people tainted by sin often do not see the need to change. They may regret what they are doing. They may acknowledge that they are not perfect. But they do not see the urgency in changing. We could rewrite the song to say, "It's hard to change when you do not see the need to change."

The same could be said for many within the church. Christians generally have a desire to be Christlike and holy. We know what we ought to be doing. But sometimes we become comfortable in being "saved by grace and not by works," and take a relaxed approach to Christian service and to holy living. After all, we reason, our salvation could not be jeopardized by what we do or do not do.

We would do well to remember that the gospel message that reveals to the lost God's plan of salvation also reveals to the saints God's further instructions. The attitude of faith that initially saves us is expected to grow within us. The pursuit of godliness should not be treated like an elective course in a college curriculum. Consider it one of the core requirements for graduation.

B. Prayer

Father, we thank You for having called us through Your Word to be in a saved relationship with You. Now help us each day to live lives that express our gratitude for the privileges You have given to us. In Jesus' name we pray, amen.

C. Thought to Remember

"Grow in grace, and in the knowledge of our Lord and Saviour Jesus Christ" (2 Peter 3:18).

Home Daily Bible Readings

Monday, Jan. 26—Support Your Faith With Goodness (2 Peter 1:1-11)
Tuesday, Jan. 27—Make the Good Confession (1 Timothy 6:12-16)
Wednesday, Jan. 28—Transformed by a Renewed Mind (Romans 12:1-8)
Thursday, Jan. 29—Living by Christ's Teaching (Matthew 5:1-12)
Friday, Jan. 30—Share Bread With the Hungry (Isaiah 58:6-12)
Saturday, Jan. 31—Seek Peace and Pursue It (Psalm 34:4-14)
Sunday, Feb. 1—Doing the Works of God (John 14:8-17)

Learning by Doing

This page contains an alternate lesson plan emphasizing learning activities.
Classes desiring such student involvement will find these suggestions helpful.

Learning Goals

After this lesson, a student should be able to:

1. Describe how God's call and our response are foundational to our relationship with Christ.

2. List the qualities that Peter says should be present and increasing in the life of a believer.

3. Suggest a specific way to "give diligence" to developing one of these qualities in his or her life.

Into the Lesson

Introduce today's lesson by asking your students what they do when the phone rings. (If you have a phone that you can "hook up" so that it will ring at just this moment, this would be an effective visual aid. If you don't have one, there may be a toy phone in your church's nursery.)

When the phone rings, we answer it to find out who is calling and to learn what that person wants. According to today's lesson, all Christians have been called by God to practical godly living (2 Peter 1:3). Remind your students that it is up to us to answer that call and then to respond to the Caller's instructions. This lesson tells us some ways to respond.

Into the Word

Not only has God called us to godliness, but He has also provided all that we need to live righteously (2 Peter 1:3). What are some of these resources for godly living that God provides? Ask your students to "brainstorm" ideas. Among the suggestions probably will be these: the new birth; the Holy Spirit; the Scriptures; the church; other believers; Christian parents and a Christian home; a godly heritage, including the examples of godly men and women of the past; Christian music and literature.

Along with resources for godly living, God also gives us His promises (v. 4). As we take advantage of these promises, we become "partakers of the divine nature." The Bible is full of promises, and every Christian has his or her favorite. Ask your students to read their favorite promises from the Bible, and to testify of times when God fulfilled His promises in their lives. How did God's fulfillment of His promises enable them to grow spiritually?

Speaking of spiritual growth, Peter gives us the building blocks of spiritual growth in verses 5-7. Reproduce the drawing of building blocks (found in the student book) on the chalkboard or a sheet of newsprint. Then ask your students to help you fill in the blocks with the qualities mentioned by Peter. The qualities (in order) are: faith, virtue, knowledge, temperance, patience, godliness, brotherly kindness, and charity. You may want to compare the list of the fruit of the Spirit in Galatians 5:22, 23 to this list of building blocks (see also Colossians 3:12-14).

Next, ask the students to put these qualities in their own words, so that they can have a clearer understanding of what they mean (for help, see the lesson commentary). For examples:

• Faith: a belief in Jesus as Savior and Lord.

• Virtue: right action.

• Knowledge: a growing and maturing way of thinking.

• Temperance: self-control.

• Patience: a determination to wait because of the value of what is being waited for (see Isaiah 40:31).

• Godliness: an attitude of reverence.

• Brotherly kindness: love for other believers.

• Charity: unconditional love—the kind of love that God has for us, and that He demonstrated through the cross.

Into Life

The building blocks of spiritual growth are not optional. If we are to fulfill our spiritual calling, they are essential (2 Peter 1:8). Ask your students, "What is the opposite of growth?" Point out that in a farmer's field or in a garden, the opposite of growth is death (there may be a farmer or gardener in your class who can provide an illustration of this). A plant is either growing or it is dying. If it is growing, it is producing fruit—or has the potential to produce fruit. If it is dying, it is barren.

The same principle applies to the Christian life. Remind your students that their choice is not simply between whether to grow or not to grow. Their choice is between spiritual growth and spiritual death.

As you bring the lesson to a close, call attention to the building blocks of spiritual growth discussed earlier. Then tell students to focus on one of these building blocks during the coming week. What specifically can they do during the week to develop this quality and thus to encourage their spiritual growth?

Let's Talk It Over

The questions on this page are designed to encourage review of the lesson Scriptures and to promote discussion of the lesson by the class. The answers provided are only discussion starters. Let your class talk it over from there.

1. How does being in Christ remove excuses for not living godly lives? What are some of the blessings included in "all things that pertain unto life and godliness" (2 Peter 1:3)?

God has called us to Himself through Jesus Christ, and He has provided for the forgiveness of our sins. The call to a restored relationship with God is a call to glory, but it is also a call to virtue. We honor our heavenly Father by adopting His values and obeying His moral commands. These objectives are possible because of the blessings that God provides. In Christ we have the benefits of experiencing a new birth (John 3:5-8), being a new creation (2 Corinthians 5:17), having the indwelling Holy Spirit (Acts 2:38; Romans 8:13-16), possessing the armor of God (Ephesians 6:13-17), and enjoying the privilege of prayer (Ephesians 6:18). We are responsible for our moral choices. We cannot excuse ourselves as unable to withstand temptation. God has done His part in furnishing what we need to conquer sin.

2. Could you say that you are "giving all diligence" to add to your faith the qualities listed by Peter (2 Peter 1:5-7)? What measures have you taken? What more could you do?

Sadly, many new believers have never been involved in a deliberate and organized effort to develop Christian character or to gain in Bible knowledge. In some cases the efforts made have simply not been effective. Recognizing that need, many churches now are offering systematic, intentional discipling opportunities for believers. Many churches are attempting to see to it that every member will be involved in a Bible study and in an accountability relationship appropriate for the maturity of the individual. While methods may differ from place to place, the common desire should be to make development of Christian character a priority. Whatever "giving all diligence" means, it probably requires more than most of us have given.

3. In an age of self-indulgence, how can we grow in "temperance" (self-control)?

Our society promotes self-indulgence. Everywhere we turn we find encouragement to buy products or services to accommodate every whim and desire. Utility and practicality is no longer the measure of value. We look for image and style. We are impressed with power, size, and novelty. Entire industries cater to our desire for amusement and pleasure. If we are to learn temperance in such a culture, we must learn to move against the tide. The practice of fasting on a recurring basis can build self-control. In addition to the common fast from food, try fasting from other self-indulgences. For example, can you go without watching television for a week? Could you give up desserts for a month? Do you really need to go to that sporting event next week? What are other self-indulgences that are detracting from time and resources that should be invested in other ways? Will you put some limits upon yourself?

4. What are the things "afar off" (2 Peter 1:9) that should remain in view for the godly Christian?

It seems that there were nearsighted believers in Peter's day just as there are today. These are believers whose sight is impaired, both when looking to the past and when looking to the future. They are blind to the cleansing that they received when Jesus forgave their sins; thus they have lost their appreciation of God's grace and their motivation to remain pure. They cannot see far enough ahead to realize the destiny to which they have been called, and to begin behaving like children of the King. For such individuals, the things that are near—possessions, pleasures, positions of power—distract them from pursuing spiritual goals.

5. If godly character is evidence of our "calling and election" (2 Peter 1:10), what does lack of such character signify?

No matter what our understanding of "calling" and "election," Peter is affirming that the formation of godly character is sure evidence that we are among the elect and the called. To lack godly character, or to have no interest in maintaining such character, casts doubt upon the genuineness of one's call and election. Since Peter has commanded that we give "all diligence" to the formation of godly character (2 Peter 1:5), we know that accomplishing this is not automatic. We must exert our utmost effort in pursuing this goal.

Rejecting False Teachings

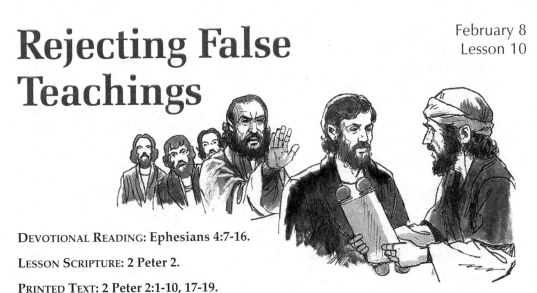

DEVOTIONAL READING: Ephesians 4:7-16.

LESSON SCRIPTURE: 2 Peter 2.

PRINTED TEXT: 2 Peter 2:1-10, 17-19.

2 Peter 2:1-10, 17-19

1 But there were false prophets also among the people, even as there shall be false teachers among you, who privily shall bring in damnable heresies, even denying the Lord that bought them, and bring upon themselves swift destruction.

2 And many shall follow their pernicious ways; by reason of whom the way of truth shall be evil spoken of.

3 And through covetousness shall they with feigned words make merchandise of you: whose judgment now of a long time lingereth not, and their damnation slumbereth not.

4 For if God spared not the angels that sinned, but cast them down to hell, and delivered them into chains of darkness, to be reserved unto judgment;

5 And spared not the old world, but saved Noah the eighth person, a preacher of righteousness, bringing in the flood upon the world of the ungodly;

6 And turning the cities of Sodom and Gomorrah into ashes condemned them with an overthrow, making them an ensample unto those that after should live ungodly;

7 And delivered just Lot, vexed with the filthy conversation of the wicked:

8 (For that righteous man dwelling among them, in seeing and hearing, vexed his righteous soul from day to day with their unlawful deeds:)

9 The Lord knoweth how to deliver the godly out of temptation, and to reserve the unjust unto the day of judgment to be punished:

10 But chiefly them that walk after the flesh in the lust of uncleanness, and despise government. Presumptuous are they, self-willed, they are not afraid to speak evil of dignities.

. . . .

17 These are wells without water, clouds that are carried with a tempest; to whom the mist of darkness is reserved for ever.

18 For when they speak great swelling words of vanity, they allure through the lusts of the flesh, through much wantonness, those that were clean escaped from them who live in error.

19 While they promise them liberty, they themselves are the servants of corruption: for of whom a man is overcome, of the same is he brought in bondage.

Feb 8

GOLDEN TEXT: There shall be false teachers among you, who privily shall bring in damnable heresies.—2 Peter 2:1.

God's People in a Troubled World
Unit 3: Endurance of God's People
(Lessons 9-12)

Lesson Aims

After completing this lesson, each student should be able to:

1. Recall what Peter says about the character, behavior, and destiny of false teachers.

2. Identify some false teachings that challenge the church and her mission today.

3. Suggest some measures the church can take to protect its members from being led astray by false teachings.

Lesson Outline

Introduction

A. They're All Around Us

"I am God," Jim Jones is reported to have said to the members of his People's Temple "church" nearly twenty years ago. This was one of many strange statements spoken by the unstable leader of this obscure little cult. We might never have heard of Jones and his heretical teaching if not for that infamous day when he ordered his followers to drink Kool-Aid laced with cyanide. The resulting mass suicide of over nine hundred men, women, and children shocked the entire world, and brought to our attention once again the existence of cults and the dangers that accompany involvement with them.

We may wonder how seemingly rational people can be drawn to such irrational and unorthodox ideas. None of this, however, would have come as a surprise to the apostle Peter. He warned his readers that teachers who pervert the truths of Scripture should be viewed as a deadly danger.

For most people in the church today, the most immediate and serious threat is not the extremist cults. It is those cults who have become established and respectable neighbors. It is also the many mainstream churches and preachers who have abandoned Biblical authority in favor of the religious and philosophical ideas of men. This lesson should serve as a good reminder that we are constantly surrounded by false teaching in a variety of forms. We cannot afford to let down our guard.

B. Lesson Background

From the historical records available to us, we understand that the church of the first three centuries faced two major problems. The first was persecution by outsiders, notably by the Roman government. Many Christians died during several waves of persecution, but in God's design the end results were often positive. Persecution served as a time of testing for the church, separating the fainthearted from those who had a genuine commitment to Christ. The latter were strengthened and emboldened by their difficulties. Furthermore, the courageous testimony of Christian martyrs actually attracted new people to Christ. As the second-century preacher and theologian Tertullian observed, "The blood of the martyrs is the seed of the church."

The second major problem for the early church was a more insidious threat that rarely yielded positive results. Many leaders within the church used their positions of prominence and respect to teach a variety of new doctrines that contradicted the faith established by the apostles. For Christians who wanted to do what was right, this was an enemy that was often difficult to detect. The resulting controversies brought charges of heresy, and produced division within the church. Twenty centuries later we still struggle with this subtle, yet formidable foe.

The epistle of 1 Peter focuses primarily upon the first of these enemies: the threat of persecution to the church. Peter wrote this letter to assist Christians in facing the coming hardships. The epistle of 2 Peter calls attention to the second enemy: false teaching. While chapter 3 deals with erroneous ideas that creep into the

How to Say It

GOMORRAH. Guh-*more*-uh.
LUCIFER. *Loo*-sih-fur.
SODOM. *Sod*-um.
TARTARUS. *Tar*-tuh-rus.
TERTULLIAN. Tur-*tull*-yun.

church from the secular world, chapter 2 exposes the problem of false teachers within the body of Christ. Peter strongly emphasizes the very real threat that these teachers pose, but he also affirms their certain condemnation.

I. Reality of False Teachers (2 Peter 2:1, 2)

A. Present in the Church (v. 1)

1. But there were false prophets also among the people, even as there shall be false teachers among you, who privily shall bring in damnable heresies, even denying the Lord that bought them, and bring upon themselves swift destruction.

Peter begins his discussion of false teachers within the church with a reminder from Old Testament history: *there were false prophets also among the people*. Old Testament Israel was constantly plagued by false prophets who tried to pervert the faith and practice of God's people (see, for example, Jeremiah 23:16-32). Given this pervasive phenomenon among God's people in the Old Testament age, it should come as no surprise, writes Peter, that *there shall be false teachers among you*.

The false teachers that Peter envisions within the church are said to deny *the Lord that bought them*. This does not necessarily mean that false teachers will say bad things about Jesus. As a general rule, today many false teachers speak of themselves as "Christians." But they betray their claim of loyalty by teaching doctrines contrary to the words of Christ and His chosen apostles. They teach what *their* wisdom says should be right, subtly setting themselves up as a competing authority with the Head of the church. This is no way to treat the One whose death bought them redemption from sin.

Note the strong language of Peter. False doctrine includes *damnable heresies*. We should distinguish these from the mistaken ideas we often get that generally have no serious implications on our faith, and are readily corrected with good Bible study. What Peter seems to have in mind are ideas that pervert Biblical teaching to the point that God is defamed, Jesus is denied,

faith is undermined, and the church is divided. The Greek word for *heresies* literally refers to teachings so strange that they divide people. Such teachings must not be tolerated or viewed lightly, for they *privily*, or subtly, influence unwary Christians with ideas that are *damnable*, or deserving of God's punishment.

B. Poisoning the Church (v. 2)

2. And many shall follow their pernicious ways; by reason of whom the way of truth shall be evil spoken of.

The *King James Version* speaks of false teaching as being *pernicious*, meaning something dangerous or deadly. This is a good description of false teaching, but not the best rendering of the Greek word used here by Peter. The *Revised Standard Version* captures the idea with the word "licentious," which means "acting without moral restraint." Apparently Peter was familiar with people whose moral lifestyle degenerated as they moved farther away from doctrinal soundness.

This is certainly not an uncommon pattern today. Churches that weaken their commitment to Biblical authority in matters of theology also tend to be more accommodating to the moral values of modern society. For example, they will reinterpret the Biblical condemnation of practices such as homosexuality, and view them as concessions to a "less enlightened" culture. By so doing they can then justify homosexual marriages and ordinations in the church, and charge those who hold to the traditional teaching of Scripture with bigotry. As Peter puts it, they speak *evil* of *the way of truth*.

TRUE OR FALSE?

In 1965 "Father Divine" died. He claimed to be God. In fact, his real name was George Baker, and he was born on Hutchinson's Island, Georgia, some time between 1864 and 1877. He began his movement in Georgia, where he was put on trial as "John Doe, alias God." To avoid being put in a mental hospital, he went to New York where he founded his "Heaven." He claimed that no one who believed in him would ever die. That was true—only because when anyone got sick, he put them out of the communal dwelling so that he could claim, "Nobody ever dies in my house." But he himself died, his organization having amassed ten million dollars.

It seems obvious that any man who claims to be God is a false teacher. Usually, however, false teachers are not so obvious. Their teaching sounds logical and clear, until you realize that there is a gap somewhere in the process by which they got from A and B to X, Y, and Z.

Then you begin to search the Scriptures. You begin to see that merely quoting a Bible verse out of context does not make a teaching true.

There have always been false teachers, and there will be until the end of time. But there is no false teaching in the Bible. It is true and wholly reliable. We must continually compare the teachings of men with its standards. We must not be swayed by eloquence, educational attainments, prestige, or wealth. Every teaching must be true to God's Word.   —R. C. S.

II. Condemnation of False Teachers (2 Peter 2:3-10)

A. Their Mixed Motives (v. 3)

3. And through covetousness shall they with feigned words make merchandise of you: whose judgment now of a long time lingereth not, and their damnation slumbereth not.

One of Peter's concerns about false teachers is that they often *make merchandise* of the church. That is, they exploit people for gain. This harmful practice is all too common among modern cults, who not only exploit the money and possessions of their followers, but often exercise a control that compromises sexual purity and damages self-esteem. They win over their followers with *feigned words*, meaning false statements designed to trick the unsuspecting. The motivation for such evil is *covetousness*, or greed, perhaps for material gain, but just as likely for power, control, and prestige.

It is tempting to think that *judgment* may never actually come upon these false teachers, since so many practice their wickedness for years (even a lifetime) without ever suffering for the harm they do. But Peter affirms that God's wrath against false teachers *lingereth not*, and *slumbereth not*. God has not forgotten them. He still intends to bring upon all who pervert the truth an eternal *damnation*, just as He promised of old. To build his readers' confidence in this promise, Peter reminds them of three powerful examples from the Old Testament of the judgment of God against sin.

B. Their Evil Forerunners (vv. 4-8)

4. For if God spared not the angels that sinned, but cast them down to hell, and delivered them into chains of darkness, to be reserved unto judgment.

Peter's first example of God's judgment is the condemnation of the *angels that sinned*. There are two incidents to which this most likely refers. One is the rebellion of the angels near the beginning of creation—an episode for which the Bible provides few details. It seems to be reflected in Isaiah 14:12-15, which suggests that a chief angel ("Lucifer" in v. 12 of the *King James Version*) led some kind of rebellion against God's authority.

The other possibility is that Peter is alluding to the disobedience recorded in 1 Peter 3:19, 20. This passage mentions "the spirits . . . which sometime were disobedient, when once the long-suffering of God waited in the days of Noah." (See the discussion of this Scripture in Lesson 7.) The Greek word rendered *cast . . . into hell* means "to confine or imprison." It is the word from which we get the term *Tartarus,* which some believe to be the place where these rebellious angels are *reserved unto judgment.* Regardless of the nature of the sin of these angels, the emphasis here is on the certainty of their condemnation. God did not tolerate their disobedience. Their sentence is irreversible.

5. And spared not the old world, but saved Noah the eighth person, a preacher of righteousness, bringing in the flood upon the world of the ungodly.

Peter's second example of divine judgment is God's destruction of an *ungodly* generation by means of the *flood* in the days of *Noah* (Genesis 6-9). This event stands as one of the most compelling examples of God's judgment in history, and firmly supports Peter's argument that we should not doubt that God can and will deal aggressively with sin.

Peter's description to Noah as *the eighth person* may indicate that Noah was the last person to enter the ark (perhaps after making one final appeal to the scoffers of his day). Another possibility is that the verse is simply restating what 1 Peter 3:20 tells us: Noah and seven members of his family were protected by God during the flood.

6. And turning the cities of Sodom and Gomorrah into ashes condemned them with an overthrow, making them an ensample unto those that after should live ungodly.

The third example offered by Peter of the reality of God's judgment against sinners is the destruction of *Sodom and Gomorrah* by fire and brimstone from Heaven (Genesis 19:24-28). The story is familiar, and the outpouring of God's wrath is unmistakable. In this verse Peter reminds his readers why the study of an incident such as this from the Old Testament is so important. It serves as an *ensample*, or example, for our benefit (Romans 15:4; 1 Corinthians 10:11). God's judgment against Sodom and Gomorrah illustrates what false teachers within the church can expect.

7, 8. And delivered just Lot, vexed with the filthy conversation of the wicked: (for that righteous man dwelling among them, in seeing and hearing, vexed his righteous soul from day to day with their unlawful deeds:).

Again (as with Noah) a contrast is presented between God's deliverance of a *just* person and His condemnation of the *wicked*. *Lot* may seem a strange choice to serve as a model of a *righteous man*. The Old Testament account of Lot emphasizes his weaknesses: how he chose what he thought was the best land for pasture and left the inferior land for his uncle Abram (Genesis 13:10, 11), and how he eventually moved into the wicked city of Sodom and hesitated to leave it before its destruction (Genesis 19:15, 16), losing in the process his wife and two sons-in-law. Peter prefers to focus upon Lot's redeeming strength: he was *vexed*, or distressed, by the ungodly practices of those in Sodom. The Old Testament account supports this description of Lot, for there was apparently enough moral conviction within him that God saw fit to rescue him from the deadly fire and brimstone.

The references to Noah and Lot are not out of place in this message of divine judgment. Peter wants his readers to understand that the God who is sure to judge sin will be just as sure to protect the righteous.

THE SINS OF SODOM

No one can be absolutely certain of the site of Sodom, but many Bible students believe it to be at the bottom of the Dead Sea. The Dead Sea is approximately thirteen hundred feet below sea level—the lowest place below sea level on earth! Some see this as coincidental. Others see it as the work of God. They claim that it shows how much God hates sexual sin. He pounded Sodom down into the face of the ground until today it is the lowest spot on earth.

Today sexual sins are seen as little more than misdemeanors. We are asked to accept homosexuality as natural. God did not. In Romans 1:24-27 Paul states plainly what we see demonstrated in the Old Testament story of Sodom. We do not have to wonder what God thinks of such acts. To the apostle Peter, the fiery destruction of Sodom is a vivid example of what awaits the ungodly. Notice that Lot was "vexed" (distressed) by the lives that the men of Sodom led (2 Peter 2:7). The righteous today share that distress. We can neither dismiss nor take lightly what God takes so seriously. The current of evil that sweeps across our world may seem to have popular support behind it, but followers of God and of His truth can never condone it nor be content in the midst of it.   —R. C. S.

C. Their Certain Destiny (v. 9)

9. The Lord knoweth how to deliver the godly out of temptation, and to reserve the unjust unto the day of judgment to be punished.

The first part of verse 9 states the secondary lesson learned from the examples of Noah and Lot—*the Lord knoweth how to deliver the godly*. The latter part returns to the primary theme of this passage and brings it to a fitting conclusion. The lesson cannot be missed: All who practice sin and ungodliness will most certainly face a day of divine *judgment* and punishment. In contrast, the godly do not have to succumb to the pressures and lies of false teachers. The Lord will give them strength to stand firm in His truth.

D. Their Rebellious Attitude (v. 10)

10. But chiefly them that walk after the flesh in the lust of uncleanness, and despise government. Presumptuous are they, self-willed, they are not afraid to speak evil of dignities.

Sometimes we who are committed to Biblical authority wonder how a person could reject the truth clearly expressed in God's Word and teach a lie. Peter explains that such people are motivated by *the lust of uncleanness*. They are governed by the sinful desires of *the flesh*. They want to do things from which God's people have traditionally refrained. Whereas faithful Christians learn to say "no" to their inner lusts, those who are drawn to falsehood have decided to yield to the sinful longings within. They *despise government*, rejecting all rules imposed on them from without and determining that they will do exactly what they feel like doing. The struggle with the flesh is common to us all, but their "solution" is unacceptable.

A second motivation of those who teach false doctrine is that they are *presumptuous*, or arrogant. They have too high a view of themselves and of the need to fulfill their will and desires. They dare to say things that contradict the very words of God. They speak when they should be listening to Him. They put their thoughts and desires ahead of His Word. They can be called *self-willed*, for they have more commitment to their own will than to the will of God.

Peter calls attention to a particular false teaching that illustrates the presumptuous attitude of all false teachers. It apparently has something to do with slander against *dignities*, better translated as "celestial beings" (*New International Version*), or angels. Perhaps Peter had in mind some of the "fables" about which others were warned (1 Timothy 1:4; Titus 1:14). Whatever the heresy, he is critical of those who would suggest any impropriety among God's angels and would dare to *speak evil* of them. Verse 11, along with Jude 8 and 9, remind us that angels themselves do not speak ill of other creatures, even of the devil. It is truly presumptuous for a fallible human teacher to do what the holy angels consider to be improper.

III. Futility of False Teachers (2 Peter 2:17-19)

A. Shallow and Unstable (v. 17)

17. These are wells without water, clouds that are carried with a tempest; to whom the mist of darkness is reserved for ever.

One of the noticeable characteristics of false teachers is that they tend to keep picking up new heresies. Part of the reason for this is that once one has opened the door to reinterpreting Scripture, he has placed before himself unlimited possibilities for reworking his theology. However, no matter how sophisticated his new ideas or explanations, they can never have the ring of truth found in doctrine that is clearly expressed in God's Word. Those who abandon solid Biblical teaching will eventually find themselves with a shallow theology, like *wells without water*. They will be inclined to follow any convincing wind of doctrine, and will become as unstable as *clouds that are carried with a tempest*. They can never enjoy the satisfaction found in knowing God's truth.

B. Making Empty Promises (vv. 18, 19)

18. For when they speak great swelling words of vanity, they allure through the lusts of the flesh, through much wantonness, those that were clean escaped from them who live in error.

It should come as no surprise that those who have been motivated by sinful lusts to move away from Biblical truth would then try to *allure*, or seduce, others to join them by appealing to their *lusts of the flesh*. Peter seems to suggest that the most susceptible victims for this false teaching are those who are *clean escaped*, that is, those who are recent converts to Christ. Not only do they lack the maturity to recognize and resist false teachers, but they are still close enough to their former ungodly lifestyles to be tempted by a "Christian" teacher who can show them how to justify resuming their former practices in the name of Christ.

19. While they promise them liberty, they themselves are the servants of corruption: for of whom a man is overcome, of the same is he brought in bondage.

False teachers who compromise with sinful lusts and desires attract a following because they promise *liberty* from the traditional interpretations of Scripture. What actually develops, however, is a slavery far more dangerous than that of one's pre-Christian life, for it involves a false assurance that all is now right with God. Those who teach false doctrines and immoral practices ultimately bring *bondage* and ruin to those who heed their words.

Conclusion

A. Let the Student Beware

One of the ancient Latin phrases that has carried over into English usage is *caveat emptor* (*cav*-ee-aht *emp*-tor): "let the buyer beware." This phrase is typically used of a business deal or purchase in which no special warranty or guarantee is given. The buyer is forewarned that he enters into this transaction at his own risk.

Perhaps we need a similar warning within the church: "let the student beware." It is important that Christians learn that listening to a teacher who has rejected Biblical authority is a risky proposition. It has the potential of taking away all that they have gained spiritually, and placing them back under the judgment of God.

B. Prayer

Heavenly Father, help us as we strive to maintain a commitment to Your Word and Your Word alone. In Jesus' name we pray. Amen.

C. Thought to Remember

"As newborn babes, desire the sincere milk of the word, that ye may grow thereby" (1 Peter 2:2).

Home Daily Bible Readings

Monday, Feb. 2—God Can Rescue the Godly (2 Peter 2:1-10a)
Tuesday, Feb. 3—Teachers Gone Astray (2 Peter 2:10b-16)
Wednesday, Feb. 4—Slaves of Corruption (2 Peter 2:17-22)
Thursday, Feb. 5—Grow Up Into Christ (Ephesians 4:7-16)
Friday, Feb. 6—See No One but Jesus (Matthew 17:1-8)
Saturday, Feb. 7—Be Guileless in What Is Evil (Romans 16:17-20)
Sunday, Feb. 8—To Love and Obey Means Life (Deuteronomy 30:15-20)

Learning by Doing

This page contains an alternate lesson plan emphasizing learning activities.
Classes desiring such student involvement will find these suggestions helpful.

Learning Goals

After this lesson, students should be able to:

1. Recall what Peter says about the character, behavior, and destiny of false teachers.

2. Identify some false teachings that challenge the church and her mission today.

3. Suggest some measures the church can take to protect its members from being led astray by false teachings.

Into the Lesson

Begin by writing the word *cults* on the chalkboard. Then ask, "When you think of *cults*, what images come to your mind?" Names such as David Koresh and Jim Jones may be mentioned, for they are prime examples of false teachers. However, as pointed out in the Introduction to the lesson commentary, extremist cult leaders do not represent the most serious threat to the church. The most serious threat comes from teachers within the church who corrupt and distort the gospel. In today's lesson we will look at some of the characteristics of such teachers.

Into the Word

The first part of our lesson text (2 Peter 2:1-3) raises three significant issues. These issues can be stated in terms of a series of tensions between two seemingly similar but very different ideas. Use the questions below to examine each of these three tensions.

Tension 1: False teaching vs. mistaken or misleading teaching (v. 1).

• What is the difference between a teacher who intentionally distorts the gospel and a teacher who misleads his listeners because of ignorance? Aren't both promoting wrong and misleading teachings?

Tension 2: Permissiveness vs. tolerance (v. 2).

• How can we tell if we are being tolerant (allowing for differences of opinion) or are being permissive (that is, condoning and approving of practices contrary to the Scriptures)? What are some false teachings that false teachers want us to accept? (Examples: God loves us too much to punish us for our sins. Homosexuality is a legitimate "alternative" lifestyle.)

Tension 3: Exploitation vs. legitimate compensation (v. 3).

• While preaching and teaching the gospel are legitimate occupations, some are in it only for what they can get out of it. At what point does "legitimate compensation" become "exploitation"? How much profit or gain is too much? Is the real issue here amount or motivation?

The second part of the lesson (2 Peter 2:4-9) deals with the theme: "Have no fear; God will judge false teachers." To prove his point, Peter cites three examples from Old Testament history. Tell your students to look through these verses and find the examples. Then ask them to summarize the lesson that each example teaches (this activity appears in the student book).

1. Fallen angels (v. 4). Just because false teachers have not been judged yet, does not mean that they won't be judged.

2. The flood (v. 5). God is patient, but eventually judgment will come.

3. Sodom and Gomorrah (v. 6). God's sure judgment on the wickedness in these cities is an example to the ungodly and a source of assurance to the righteous.

The third part of the lesson (2 Peter 2:10, 17-19) gives us a profile of false teachers. Divide the class into groups of three, and tell the students to look for the characteristics of false teachers that appear in these verses (or refer to the student book, where this activity is found). Write the responses on the chalkboard or a sheet of newsprint, creating a profile of false teachers.

• Motivated by allegiance to the flesh (v. 10)
• Rejecting legitimate authority (v. 10)
• Arrogant (v. 10)
• Selfish and self-centered (v. 10)
• Irreverent (v. 10)
• Shallow and superficial (v. 17)
• Unstable (v. 17)
• Candidates for divine judgment (v. 17)
• Using empty and meaningless words (v. 18)
• Preying on the weak (v. 18)
• Making promises they cannot fulfill (v. 19)
• Slaves of corruption (v. 19)

Into Life

In closing, point out that the reason false teachers in the church are so dangerous is that they claim the authority of the Word of God. Emphasize that the church has a right and a responsibility to protect itself from false teachers. Also, as individual Christians we must protect ourselves. The primary way we can do this is by knowing the Word of God.

Let's Talk It Over

The questions on this page are designed to encourage review of the lesson Scriptures and to promote discussion of the lesson by the class. The answers provided are only discussion starters. Let your class talk it over from there.

1. Why have there been so many false teachers over the centuries? What makes Christians vulnerable to them?

Peter's statement that "there shall be false teachers among you" (2 Peter 2:1) might be considered a "safe" prediction, based upon the past experience of God's people. It seems that there is something seductive about the role of the prophet or teacher. Some desire the sense of power that comes when others look up to them as an authority. They desire it so much that they are willing to fabricate teaching that will gain an audience. Christians are vulnerable to such false teachers when they are not able to distinguish truth from error, or when they are enticed by some seductive teaching. God's truth calls us to a way that is "straight and narrow" (Matthew 7:13, 14), so if a teacher comes along and promotes an easier, more popular way of living, it is hard for some to resist him.

2. How is it that false teachers speak evil of "the way of truth" (2 Peter 2:2)?

As false teachers gain a following, they also gain in credibility. It is human nature to accept something as more plausible when others profess to believe it. As false teachings begin to add adherents, they become competing belief systems to Christianity. In order to establish an identity, false teachers may attack Christianity at those points in which they differ, bringing disrepute upon the truth and promoting their own ideas. On the other hand, those who are not able to distinguish error from truth may associate the false and sometimes extravagant ideas of the false teachers with true Christianity, and dismiss both as not worthy of acceptance.

3. What effect do you believe the threat of impending judgment has upon the ungodly? Explain.

News of impending judgment has no effect upon the ungodly if they do not believe it, and clearly many do not. While (according to one poll) over 90% of Americans believe in God, and over 75% believe in Jesus as the Son of God, the number who believe in Hell is just a little over 50%. Just as the people of Noah's day ignored his preaching about a coming flood, the ungodly today nonchalantly ignore teaching about God's judgment and the condemnation of sinners. The more immediate prospects of lost opportunities, damaged relationships, ruined health, wasted resources, and an uncertain future are perhaps more compelling reasons in this culture for turning away from sin. Those threats are real, obvious, and frightening enough to be persuasive in many cases. There will certainly be a day of judgment, but we may find it easier to reach the ungodly if we concentrate on the immediate advantages of turning to and following Jesus.

4. Can you give an example of false teaching that is an accommodation to the "lust of uncleanness" (2 Peter 2:10)? Explain.

The false teachers that Peter had in mind are described as arrogant, brutish, enslaved to base instincts, shameless, adulterous, and greedy. It seems that their teachings were concocted to approve their lifestyles. Today there are still those who want to modify God's truth to excuse, or even endorse, one particular immorality or another. Perhaps the most obvious example are those who argue for acceptance of homosexuality and same-sex marriage. Can you think of other spiritual or moral compromises that some are willing to make in order to indulge themselves in personal pleasures? For example, have we adopted a form of Christianity that approves idolatry of possessions or food, with little mention of fasting, self-control, or sacrifice?

5. Peter calls false teachers "wells without water" (2 Peter 2:17). In contrast, Jesus is the source of "living water" (John 4:10-14). Have you found your Christian faith to be a consistent source of personal refreshment and satisfaction? Talk about it.

This calls for some very personal reflection, but if you have placed your faith in Jesus, hopefully you can testify to how dependable and reassuring God's truth is. Unlike the false teachers, who will be discredited in time or whose teaching proves impractical or even destructive, we can meditate for a lifetime upon the truth of God, apply it in increasing measure every day, and discover further evidence of its value in the process. Personally I have never regretted obedience to God's truth. My only regrets concern those times I have chosen another way.

Believing in the Promise

DEVOTIONAL READING: Jeremiah 17:5-10.

LESSON SCRIPTURE: 2 Peter 3.

PRINTED TEXT: 2 Peter 3:1-13.

2 Peter 3:1-13

1 This second epistle, beloved, I now write unto you; in both which I stir up your pure minds by way of remembrance:

2 That ye may be mindful of the words which were spoken before by the holy prophets, and of the commandment of us the apostles of the Lord and Saviour:

3 Knowing this first, that there shall come in the last days scoffers, walking after their own lusts,

4 And saying, Where is the promise of his coming? for since the fathers fell asleep, all things continue as they were from the beginning of the creation.

5 For this they willingly are ignorant of, that by the word of God the heavens were of old, and the earth standing out of the water and in the water:

6 Whereby the world that then was, being overflowed with water, perished:

7 But the heavens and the earth, which are now, by the same word are kept in store, reserved unto fire against the day of judgment and perdition of ungodly men.

8 But, beloved, be not ignorant of this one thing, that one day is with the Lord as a thousand years, and a thousand years as one day.

9 The Lord is not slack concerning his promise, as some men count slackness; but is long-suffering to us-ward, not willing that any should perish, but that all should come to repentance.

10 But the day of the Lord will come as a thief in the night; in the which the heavens shall pass away with a great noise, and the elements shall melt with fervent heat, the earth also and the works that are therein shall be burned up.

11 Seeing then that all these things shall be dissolved, what manner of persons ought ye to be in all holy conversation and godliness,

12 Looking for and hasting unto the coming of the day of God, wherein the heavens being on fire shall be dissolved, and the elements shall melt with fervent heat?

13 Nevertheless we, according to his promise, look for new heavens and a new earth, wherein dwelleth righteousness.

Feb
15

GOLDEN TEXT: We, according to his promise, look for new heavens and a new earth, wherein dwelleth righteousness.—2 Peter 3:13.

God's People in a Troubled World
Unit 3: Endurance of God's People
(Lessons 9-12)

Lesson Aims

After this lesson, students should be able to:

1. Tell what Peter says will happen when the Lord returns and what the scoffers say about His coming.

2. Tell how the Lord's patience is an opportunity for believers to serve Christ and for unbelievers to accept Him, though the scoffers see it as a delay.

3. Suggest some specific ways to pursue holiness and to answer modern scoffers as one looks forward to the Lord's return.

Lesson Outline

INTRODUCTION
    A. Help My Unbelief
    B. Lesson Background
  I. WHAT WE ARE HEARING (2 Peter 3:1-4)
    A. Sound Advice (vv. 1, 2)
    B. Foolish Talk (vv. 3, 4)
       He Will Return
 II. WHAT WE SHOULD REMEMBER (2 Peter 3:5-9)
    A. God's Powerful Word (vv. 5-7)
    B. God's Amazing Grace (vv. 8, 9)
III. WHAT WE MUST DO (2 Peter 3:10-13)
    A. Our Present Challenge (vv. 10, 11)
       A Thief in the Night
    B. Our Future Hope (vv. 12, 13)
CONCLUSION
    A. "Ready or Not, Here I Come!"
    B. Prayer
    C. Thought to Remember

Use the visual for Lesson 11 to call attention to Peter's teaching concerning the return of Jesus. It is shown on page 203.

Introduction

A. Help My Unbelief

On one occasion when Jesus healed a demon-possessed boy, he first asked the father if the man believed that Jesus could cast out demons. The father replied, "Lord, I believe; help thou mine unbelief" (Mark 9:24). This is one of the great statements of faith in the New Testament. On the one hand it acknowledges the presence of faith, but at the same time it admits to a gen-

uine struggle with doubt and fear. Such an honest statement bares one's soul to God and humbly seeks His help. In this case, Jesus responded by granting the man's request and casting the demon from his son.

In the third chapter of 2 Peter, the question is not, "Do you believe that Jesus can heal?" but, "Do you believe that Jesus is coming again?" The words of the father in Mark 9 are appropriate here. It has been nearly two thousand years since Christ promised to return, and even sincere believers sometimes question His delay. Peter offers his readers good reasons to continue believing in the promise of Christ's return, no matter how long it takes. As we study this lesson, let our attitude also be, "I believe; help thou mine unbelief."

B. Lesson Background

A discussion of the second coming of Christ was an appropriate way for Peter to end his two epistles. Peter was an excellent authority to speak on this subject. He was present on the Mount of Olives when Christ gave His extended lesson on the second coming, recorded in Matthew 24 and 25. This is not to say that Peter understood Christ's words at that time. It is apparent from Acts 1:6-8 that the apostles were unclear regarding Christ's real mission, even as He prepared to return to Heaven. They still envisioned a political kingdom on earth. They were curious about the timing of its arrival. But Christ's response told them to leave matters of timing to God, and to think not in terms of earthly kingdoms but of a Spirit-led ministry to the world. The closing chapter of 2 Peter reflects this more mature understanding of Christ's return. Peter's focus will not be upon kingdoms and timetables, but upon our responsibilities as Christians as we eagerly await the return of our Lord.

I. What We Are Hearing
(2 Peter 3:1-4)

A. Sound Advice (vv. 1, 2)

1. This second epistle, beloved, I now write unto you; in both which I stir up your pure minds by way of remembrance.

This verse establishes a clear link between 1 and 2 Peter. It tells us the order of the two books, and that both epistles were written to the same group of churches (identified in 1 Peter 1:1). It also indicates that Peter had a key theme that he was trying to develop within both epistles. One might assume that this common theme would be the second coming of Christ, since that is the immediate subject of this chapter. But

1 Peter does not deal with this topic. The theme that both epistles share in common is godliness. The first chapter of each epistle begins with a call for an active pursuit of godly living, and then the idea is interspersed throughout the remaining chapters. Second Peter 3 is a good example of how this works. While the focus of chapter 3 is upon the second coming of Christ, godliness is shown to be a natural consequence of this vital doctrine (vv. 11-14).

2. That ye may be mindful of the words which were spoken before by the holy prophets, and of the commandment of us the apostles of the Lord and Saviour.

Peter does not tell us the specific *command-ment* of the Lord that he wants his readers to remember at this time. If we assume that this command is one associated with the second coming of Christ, the one that naturally comes to mind is that we always watch and stay ready (the theme of Matthew 24:42—25:30, the largest portion of Jesus' discourse on His second coming). Jesus' advice on how to prepare for His return is to practice daily a godly lifestyle in service to others. This kind of readiness through godly living is often mentioned in the writings of the apostles as well as in the Old Testament prophets. Both groups of inspired teachers have much more to say about godly living than about the details of future events.

B. Foolish Talk (vv. 3, 4)

3. Knowing this first, that there shall come in the last days scoffers, walking after their own lusts.

Peter warns the church to expect *scoffers* to attack and ridicule the beliefs of the church concerning the return of Christ. These will be people more devoted to their ideas and interests than to the Word and will of God, for they will give priority to satisfying *their own lusts.*

Many people today assume that the phrase *the last days* refers to a brief period of time immediately preceding the return of Christ. However, the Biblical use of this phrase refers to the entire age following Christ's death and resurrection. For example, Peter told the crowd on the Day of Pentecost that Joel's prophecy of the Holy Spirit being poured out "in the last days" was now being fulfilled (Acts 2:16, 17). The Biblical idea seems to be that all of history after Calvary is "the last days" or "the latter days" in reference to Christ's completed mission of redemption, while the Old Testament age that preceded Calvary is "the former days." Thus the church has been living in "the last days" since its beginning and has always been subject to the threat of scoffers.

visual for lesson 11

4. And saying, Where is the promise of his coming? for since the fathers fell asleep, all things continue as they were from the beginning of the creation.

The scoffers are pointing to the delay in Christ's *coming,* and suggesting from this that a Christian's hope is unwarranted. They base their skepticism on a belief that the Christian concept of the end of the world is simply impossible. The Biblical view of the future is that history and creation will one day come to a cataclysmic end with fire. This scenario is improbable, the scoffers argue, because there is no precedent for such a spectacular event on a universal scale: *All things continue as they were from the beginning of the creation.* The idea that nature follows a uniform pattern and has no room for exceptional, miraculous events is a belief that challenges not only the doctrine of the second coming, but all doctrines that speak of supernatural activity (such as the divine inspiration of Scripture and the miracles of Christ).

HE WILL RETURN

Many years ago a young lady in Savannah, Georgia, fell in love with a sailor, and he declared his love for her. When he and his ship-mates left Savannah on duty, he promised to return to her someday. From that point on, the young lady met every ship that came into the harbor. She waved a handkerchief by day and a lantern by night as a signal to the sailor. She trained her dog to wake her if a ship came in the night. She greeted every ship for forty-four years—but the sailor never returned. Visitors to Savannah today can see a statue that commemo-rates the faithfulness of this woman. She waited in vain, yet people pay tribute to her faith and devotion.

Christians do not wait in vain for the return of their Lord. Every other promise He made came true, and we have no doubt that He will keep this promise as well. Skeptics may scoff at our loyalty and say that we wait in vain. But we do not. We have the word of Christ, the word of angels (Acts 1:10, 11), and the word of the apos-tles. Christ will return. Waiting, however, does not mean idleness. If we really believe in the return of Christ, we will make every minute count. We will overlook no opportunity to serve. We will warn others. If there is a delay in His return, we know the reason (2 Peter 3:9). In fact, we are torn between a desire for His soon return and a desire to have more time to reach others with the gospel of Christ. But we will remain ready, night or day, to meet our Lord. —R. C. S.

II. What We Should Remember (2 Peter 3:5-9)

The arguments of the scoffers may seem overwhelming at times, but Peter offers a bold response to their claims.

A. God's Powerful Word (vv. 5-7)

5. For this they willingly are ignorant of, that by the word of God the heavens were of old, and the earth standing out of the water and in the water.

In response to the scoffers' argument that nothing radical ever occurs in nature, Peter reminds his readers of God's creation of the universe. He highlights two of God's acts. The first is the creation of the heavens. This may refer either to the creation of the firmament on the second day (Genesis 1:6-8) or to the creation of the heavenly bodies on the fourth day (Genesis 1:14-18). The second is the separation of the seas from the land masses on the third day of creation (Genesis 1:9, 10). Because of God's intervention, it is not true to say that the universe has always been like it is today.

Peter accuses these scoffers of being somewhat dishonest in their criticisms. He says that they *willingly are ignorant* of the implications of God's creative activity. After all, the scoffers introduced the concept of creation in their challenge (verse 4), but they pretend not to see how it actually weakens their argument. Compare this thought to Paul's teaching in Romans 1:18-20 that all people know from observing nature that there is a God. Those who reject this truth do so willfully and are thus without excuse before God's judgment.

6. Whereby the world that then was, being overflowed with water, perished.

Another example of a radical, supernatural event in history is the universal flood of Noah's day (Genesis 6-9). This was an event that had never happened before, and, as the rainbow continues to remind us, will never happen again with water (Genesis 9:11-17). But it does establish a clear precedent for the idea of a universal destruction of the earth, albeit by a different agent (fire, not water).

7. But the heavens and the earth, which are now, by the same word are kept in store, reserved unto fire against the day of judgment and perdition of ungodly men.

The existence of the universe is maintained on a daily basis *by the same word,* that is, by God's ability (referred to in verse 5) to speak a universe into existence. It is by the power of God that all of nature operates smoothly, and if that divine providence were ever withdrawn, creation would cease to exist. Such will be the case on the final *day* when God speaks a word of *fire* and of *judgment.* This will be the occasion for Him to bring *perdition,* or condemnation, upon all who have lived *ungodly* lives.

Thus Peter has offered a powerful refutation of the scoffers' argument that a universal destruction by fire is impossible because it is without precedent. There is a clear precedent for supernatural activity on a universal scale. It remains for Peter now to respond to the argument that the long delay in Christ's return implies a promise forgotten.

B. God's Amazing Grace (vv. 8, 9)

8. But, beloved, be not ignorant of this one thing, that one day is with the Lord as a thousand years, and a thousand years as one day.

The psalmist declares that "a thousand years in thy sight are but as yesterday when it is past" (Psalm 90:4). Peter echoes this description of God, affirming that God does not measure the passage of time in the same way we do. While we do not fully comprehend how God relates to time, we know that He sees it from a broader perspective than does man. Thus when Christ promises, "Behold, I come quickly" (Revelation 22:7, 12, 20), we should not doubt His promise as the years pass by, but should assume that He speaks from His divine perspective. Perhaps it would be consistent with Peter's thought to say that the last two thousand years of waiting have been for God "just a couple of days."

A word of caution is in order concerning this verse. Peter's statement should not be understood as a prophetic key for determining the timing of Christ's return. Many people have tried to use a "day equals one thousand years" formula to calculate the date of the second coming, but thus far all attempts have proven futile (and ultimately embarrassing). Reading this verse in its context tells us that Peter has no interest in prophetic speculation. His focus is upon the reality of Christ's promise and our appropriate response to that promise.

9. The Lord is not slack concerning his promise, as some men count slackness; but is long-suffering to us-ward, not willing that any

should perish, but that all should come to repentance.

With God there is no *slackness* as though He were "dragging His feet" or forgetting His responsibilities. God is being *long-suffering*; He is exercising patience. Every day God waits means another opportunity for His people to rescue sinners from Hell. Each day that passes is actually a testimony to God's patience and grace.

It is this attitude of grace that stands behind one of the classic statements of Scripture: God is *not willing that any should perish, but that all should come to repentance.* We Christians should not allow our faith to be disturbed by the years of waiting for our Lord to return. We should be grateful that God is giving us this much time to try to help others get ready for that day before it is too late.

III. What We Must Do
(2 Peter 3:10-13)

A. Our Present Challenge
(vv. 10, 11)

10. But the day of the Lord will come as a thief in the night; in the which the heavens shall pass away with a great noise, and the elements shall melt with fervent heat, the earth also and the works that are therein shall be burned up.

Peter echoes the words of Christ in Matthew 24:43 when he says that Christ will return *as a thief in the night.* Of course, nothing criminal or evil is intended by this analogy. The point of comparison is that there will be no advance warning before Christ appears. For the Christian who stays ready, this presents no difficulty. For everyone else, the thief imagery should be seen as an urgent warning.

Peter's description of the destruction of the universe on the final day is a sobering one. There will be the sound of a *great noise,* or as the Greek word specifies, something like the roar of a huge fire. The sun, moon, stars, and planets will melt in the *fervent,* or intense, *heat.* Closer to home, *the earth also and the works that are therein*—every physical element of life on earth—will be consumed by the fire.

A THIEF IN THE NIGHT

When the Bible makes comparisons between two items, the items may actually have only one or two qualities in common. We know that, although the return of Jesus will be "as a thief in the night" (2 Peter 3:10), Jesus is not like a thief in most respects. In fact, there is only one way that Jesus resembles a thief. The thief does not give any warning. He does not send a note: "If it

is convenient, I will break into your house and steal your valuables about 2:00 A.M. next Tuesday." No, the thief comes without advance notice. He comes when we do not expect him. He makes use of the element of surprise.

The same is true of the second coming of the Lord Jesus Christ. It is not that He has not warned us; He most certainly has. It is rather that He will give no advance notice. This is why "date setters" are wasting their time. It is not the case that a few are "in the know" about the signs of the second coming, while the rest of us must live in ignorance. Jesus comes unexpectedly. He comes like the thief. This is necessary if our Lord is to be fair and just. If some get advance notice and others do not, then the judgment cannot be just nor impartial. We must conclude that everything necessary for our Lord's return has already happened. He can return at any time. We must be ready today and every day.

—R. C. S.

11. Seeing then that all these things shall be dissolved, what manner of persons ought ye to be in all holy conversation and godliness.

Having affirmed the fiery dissolution of every aspect of the material universe, Peter points to one obvious implication. We need to invest more of our time in building that which will survive the fire. There is a place for the pursuit of items such as food, clothing, and pleasure, but we need to recognize that these are temporal and will not last. We must give priority to things eternal.

It is here that Peter links his primary theme of godliness with the doctrine of the second coming. The heavenly fire will not only strip away the material universe, but all of our earthly accomplishments with it. We will not be able to stand before the Judge and show Him the jobs we have completed, the structures we have built, the books we have written, or the degrees we have earned. At the judgment, the only thing that will matter is whether or not we have lived a life of faith, expressed outwardly by *holy conversation* (conduct) *and godliness.*

B. Our Future Hope (vv. 12, 13)

12. Looking for and hasting unto the coming of the day of God, wherein the heavens being on fire shall be dissolved, and the elements shall melt with fervent heat?

The *fire* on the day Christ returns should not be viewed with fear by the saints, for it cannot harm us. It simply marks the culmination of our earthly trek and the beginning of an eternity of blessedness. Our hearts should be filled with eagerness and anticipation as we think about the return of Christ. There is even a sense in which we can be *hasting* (hastening) the return of Christ. What does this mean? It is not likely that our actions can actually change God's divine timetable. Perhaps what Peter has in mind is how an expectant attitude can make the delay seem shorter. We should develop the spirit of the apostle John in Revelation 22:20, when, upon hearing Christ say, "Surely I come quickly," he responded with the prayer, "Amen. Even so, come, Lord Jesus" (v. 21).

13. Nevertheless we, according to his promise, look for new heavens and a new earth, wherein dwelleth righteousness.

The present universe will indeed be destroyed by fire, but God promises *new heavens and a new earth.* The traditional view has been that the fire on the last day will annihilate the old creation, and that God will once again create out of nothing a brand new creation. This concept seems to follow naturally from the Biblical imagery of fire destroying the physical elements, and may well describe what will happen.

But there is another possibility worth considering. It may be that this fire would be a refining fire, designed for purging unsuitable elements from the old creation so that it can be restored to something comparable to its original goodness. The heavens and earth would be new in the sense that they would be renewed to a state of perfection. This interpretation develops the parallel in 2 Peter 3 between the great flood (verse 6) and the fire on the last day. When Peter says that the world perished in the flood, he does not mean that everything was annihilated, but that the sinful element was purged away. The fire at the end is said to accomplish a similar purpose and result.

The Biblical descriptions of the end are not precise enough to determine for certain the manner in which God will create new heavens and a new earth. But either method will be a blessing for the saints, for the end result will be an existence *wherein dwelleth righteousness* and nothing else. This is the essence of our hope for the future. The scoffer may ridicule, but we who are faithful to the word of the Lord continue to believe His promise.

Conclusion

A. "Ready or Not, Here I Come!"

Is there anyone among us who cannot remember the classic phrase from childhood, "Ready or not, here I come"? The game was "Hide and Seek." As one child covered his eyes and counted to a set number, the other children ran and hid. In the spirit of fair play, the child who was to find the hiding children was expected to announce aloud when the hunt was underway.

The second coming of Christ is surely no game. There will be the unearthly roar of a heavenly fire. Judgment proceedings will begin. Eternal destinies will be on the line. And yet it would be appropriate for that day to begin with the words, "Ready or not, here I come." Time and time again, through persuasion and warnings, the Bible seeks to motivate us to get our lives ready for facing our coming Judge. We know the kind of faith He requires and the godly lives He expects. What a shame that so many of us put off a genuine response to God's warnings, waiting for a "convenient season" (Acts 24:25). For death can come suddenly, and Christ's return will be without warning. It will make no difference what we have intended to do, for "ready or not," Christ will come at the appointed time. We will then have to answer for the choices we made during the time we were given.

Let us not live like the five foolish virgins of Matthew 25:1-13, who were unprepared for the return of their master. Let us, like the five wise virgins, keep our lamps of godly living burning brightly until the day Christ comes again.

B. Prayer

Father, keep ever before our minds the word of promise that says that Your Son is coming soon. May the certainty of His promise prompt us to make ourselves ready for His return. In Jesus' name, amen.

C. Thought to Remember

"Since everything will be destroyed in this way, what kind of people ought you to be? You ought to live holy and godly lives" (2 Peter 3:11, *New International Version*).

Home Daily Bible Readings

Monday, Feb. 9—Day of the Lord Will Come (2 Peter 3:1-10)
Tuesday, Feb. 10—Where Righteousness Is at Home (2 Peter 3:11-18)
Wednesday, Feb. 11—Heaven and Earth Created New (Isaiah 65:17-25)
Thursday, Feb. 12—Home of God Is Among Mortals (Revelation 21:1-14)
Friday, Feb. 13—Year of the Lord's Favor (Isaiah 61:1-8)
Saturday, Feb. 14—Wealth and the Kingdom of God (Luke 18:18-27)
Sunday, Feb. 15—Believe the Promise (Jeremiah 17:5-10)

Learning by Doing

This page contains an alternate lesson plan emphasizing learning activities.
Classes desiring such student involvement will find these suggestions helpful.

Learning Goals

After this lesson, students should be able to:

1. Tell what Peter says will happen when the Lord returns and what the scoffers say about His coming.

2. Tell how the Lord's patience is an opportunity for believers to serve Christ and for unbelievers to accept Him, though the scoffers see it as a delay.

3. Suggest some specific ways to pursue holiness and to answer modern scoffers as one looks forward to the Lord's return.

Into the Lesson

Before class, write this open-ended statement on the chalkboard: "I believe Jesus is coming again because . . ." Then introduce this lesson on the promise of Christ's return by asking your students to complete this statement. What is the basis for their belief in His return?

Jesus promised that He will return (Matthew 24:44; John 14:3). The angels at Jesus' ascension promised that He will return (Acts 1:10, 11). The New Testament writers, guided by divine inspiration, promised that He will return (1 Corinthians 15:23; 1 Thessalonians 2:19; 5:23; James 5:7, 8; 2 Peter 3:12; 1 John 2:28). The church, acting under such authority, thus believes and teaches that Jesus will return.

Into the Word

The Bible study activities below also appear in the student book. Give your students a few minutes to read today's lesson text and to write out personal responses to the statements and questions. Then use these as a guide to develop your study of the passage. Encourage students to share their responses.

1. I believe this is the most important idea in this passage:

2. This is the key verse of this passage:

3. To me, this is the most personal practical application of this passage:

4. Why did Peter include this passage in his letter?

5. This is one question I would like to ask Peter about this passage:

Next ask, "What were the 'scoffers' in 2 Peter 3:3 criticizing?" (Basically, they were saying that Christ's delay in returning proves that He isn't coming back at all.)

Briefly outline Peter's response to the scoffers. Can your students explain how each item proves that Christ's promise to return is still valid?

1. Creation (v. 5): proves that God is capable of doing the miraculous.

2. The flood (v. 6): proves that God can intervene suddenly and unexpectedly in history.

3. The sustaining power of God (v. 7): proves that God is in control of the universe.

4. The delay (vv. 8, 9): proves that God is merciful, not that He is untrustworthy.

We tend to be so time-oriented that we are frustrated by delays. Challenge your students to see the delay in Christ's return as an opportunity. Ask, "What are some positive, creative, and constructive things that you can be doing while you wait for Christ to return?"

Into Life

Tell the students to suppose that their husband or wife leaves on a trip. He or she promises to return but does not say exactly when. The following questions about this situation can help your students develop a positive perspective on Christ's promise to return and His apparent delay in keeping that promise.

•What will you do as you wait for your husband or wife to return?

•What will you do to keep your love for your husband or wife alive and vibrant?

•Suppose your husband or wife delays returning for an extended period of time. At what point will you begin to lose faith in his or her promise to return?

•All your friends say that if your spouse were really coming back, he or she would have returned by now. How will you answer them?

•How will you feel when your spouse finally returns?

•Suppose you give up hope in your spouse's promise to return and are unfaithful. How will that make you feel when he or she does return?

The lesson writer points out that the theme of both 1 Peter and 2 Peter is *godliness*. Living lives of practical godliness is the best way that we can prepare for Christ's return (2 Peter 3:11).

In closing, challenge your students to keep 2 Peter 3:11 before them throughout the week. Suggest that they write out the verse on an index card and attach it to the refrigerator, so they can read it every day.

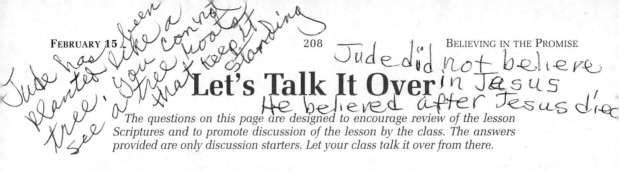

(handwritten annotations) Jude has been planted like a tree; you can see a tree that keep standing — Jude did not believe in Jesus; He believed after Jesus die

Let's Talk It Over

The questions on this page are designed to encourage review of the lesson Scriptures and to promote discussion of the lesson by the class. The answers provided are only discussion starters. Let your class talk it over from there.

1. Peter assumes that his readers have a prior knowledge of the words of the prophets and the apostles, which they can recall. What measures have you taken for learning the Bible? Which have been the most effective?

Today we have many advantages over first-century Christians in learning God's truth. Bibles are readily available and at modest cost. Bible teaching goes on in Sunday worship, Sunday Bible classes, small groups, and in midweek Bible studies. Instructional audio tapes and videotapes are available, as well as many kinds of printed helps for understanding the Bible. In spite of all these tools, however, many believers are woefully ignorant of spiritual truth. Because you are reading this guide for teaching the Bible, you must be trying to gain greater knowledge and understanding of God's Word. Hopefully you are not alone. Compare your experience with that of others in your group, and agree together on some objectives for personal growth and how to fulfill them.

2. Do you believe that those who scoff at the gospel have really examined the evidence, or is there more to their rejection? Explain.

Most believers find the evidence concerning Jesus to be convincing. Obviously not everyone agrees that He is the divine Son of God, worked miracles, or arose from the dead. Upon further discussion with the scoffers, however, we often find that they have given no serious consideration to the testimony and evidence regarding Jesus. What they do know, deep down, is that if Jesus is all that He claimed to be, this fact will require a response of submission and surrender from them. They have closed their minds to that possibility, not so much because it is absurd, and not even because they can discredit the evidence, but because they prefer not to be answerable to a personal Creator and Lord.

3. Should we be glad or sad that Jesus has not yet returned as He promised? Explain.

For Christians the day of Jesus' return will be a time when promises are fulfilled. That day will usher in a "new heavens and a new earth" (2 Peter 3:13) and the indisputable reign of Christ over His eternal kingdom. We look forward to that day as a release from the infirmities and trials of this fallen world. For those reasons, we may want to hasten the day of Christ's appearing, and we may express some regret that He has not already come. On the other hand, when Jesus returns all opportunity for repentance will be over. It will be a day of judgment for the unbelieving. Thus we may be glad (for the sake of unsaved friends and loved ones) that Jesus has not returned. We should pray and work all the harder to share our faith, so that others will also be prepared for that day.

4. If you knew the day that Christ will return, would it change the way you live? Why is it important that no one knows?

Procrastination is a common sin. If we knew exactly when Jesus will return, we would be tempted to put off cultivating our relationship with Him until the last week or the last day. We would plan to cram all of our worship and acts of devotion into a few brief hours prior to His coming. It is important that we do not know when Jesus will return, so that we may live with a sense of urgency every day about obeying Christ and serving Him. I have a problem with those who promote elaborate schemes of events that they claim must occur before Jesus returns, since that diminishes our sense of urgency and watchfulness. We do not know when He will return, and we do not know when He will not return. We do know that it could be any time, and that the passing of each day brings us closer to His coming.

5. How should the expectation that everything in this world will one day be destroyed affect the way we now live?

In our culture personal worth is measured, in large degree, by the possessions one has amassed. We work very hard and make many sacrifices in order to own a larger house, a better car, a summer cottage, a boat, fine clothes, and other luxuries. It is very easy to be consumed by the quest for things, to the detriment of our family, friendships, and personal welfare spiritually, physically, and emotionally. Being reminded that one day it will all go up in smoke helps us regain perspective. If we believe that the material things of this world are passing away, then we should become more focused on eternal values.

Jude was Jesus' half brother
James was Jude's brother

Keeping the Faith

You need strong faith

DEVOTIONAL READING: Isaiah 55:6-13.

LESSON SCRIPTURE: Jude.

PRINTED TEXT: Jude 3, 4, 17-25.

Jude 3, 4, 17-25

3 Beloved, when I gave all diligence to write unto you of the common salvation, it was needful for me to write unto you, and exhort you that ye should earnestly contend for the faith which was once delivered unto the saints.

4 For there are certain men crept in unawares, who were before of old ordained to this condemnation, ungodly men, turning the grace of our God into lasciviousness, and denying the only Lord God, and our Lord Jesus Christ.

. . . .

17 But, beloved, remember ye the words which were spoken before of the apostles of our Lord Jesus Christ;

18 How that they told you there should be mockers in the last time, who should walk after their own ungodly lusts.

19 These be they who separate themselves, sensual, having not the Spirit.

20 But ye, beloved, building up yourselves on your most holy faith, praying in the Holy Ghost,

21 Keep yourselves in the love of God, looking for the mercy of our Lord Jesus Christ unto eternal life.

22 And of some have compassion, making a difference:

23 And others save with fear, pulling them out of the fire; hating even the garment spotted by the flesh.

24 Now unto him that is able to keep you from falling, and to present you faultless before the presence of his glory with exceeding joy,

25 To the only wise God our Saviour, be glory and majesty, dominion and power, both now and ever. Amen.

Feb 22

GOLDEN TEXT: I . . . exhort you that ye should earnestly contend for the faith which was once delivered unto the saints.—Jude 3.

God's People in a Troubled World
Unit 3: Endurance of God's People
(Lessons 9-12)

Lesson Aims

After this lesson, students should be able to:
1. Summarize Jude's call to persevere in the faith.
2. Describe the false teachers and compare their way of life with that of those who keep the faith.
3. Suggest practical ways to contend for the faith and to help others to do so.

Lesson Outline

INTRODUCTION
    A. Veterans Day
    B. Lesson Background
  I. LET US DEFEND THE FAITH (Jude 3, 4, 17-19)
    A. With Sound Doctrine (v. 3)
    B. With Godly Living (vv. 4, 17-19)
  II. LET US PRACTICE OUR CALLING (Jude 20-23)
    A. Through a Growing Faith (v. 20)
    B. Through a Diligent Love (v. 21a)
    C. Through an Enthusiastic Hope (vv. 21b-23)
      Looking for Eternal Life
  III. LET US PRAISE OUR GOD (Jude 24, 25)
    A. For His Abundant Mercy (v. 24)
    B. For His Infinite Glory (v. 25)
      The Only Wise God
CONCLUSION
    A. Carved in Stone
    B. Prayer
    C. Thought to Remember

The visual for Lesson 12 in the visuals packet focuses on the benediction found in Jude 24, 25. It is shown on page 213.

Introduction
A. Veterans Day

People love to celebrate holidays for various reasons. They enjoy time off from work and school. They like to get together with family and friends for fun activities and cookouts. And they like to be reminded of the ideas that holidays commemorate. In the United States this is particularly evident in the way military holidays, such as the Fourth of July, Memorial Day, and Veterans Day, are celebrated. Veterans from past wars, though aged, are still proud to march in parades and demonstrate loyalty to their country. We feel a great sense of patriotism and pride as we honor the people who fought and died on our behalf. At the same time, we are reminded that freedom won in the past brings with it a responsibility for the future. Each generation must be prepared to fight the fight of their forefathers, or risk losing the freedoms we have inherited from them.

Perhaps the church also needs a "Veterans Day" tradition in which we honor the Christian soldiers of old. It can fill our hearts with godly pride to reflect upon the dedicated lives of the faithful men and women who have preceded us, whether they be Bible characters, church history figures, or departed saints who raised us in the faith. Such reflection can also serve to remind us of our duty to "fight the good fight" of our spiritual forefathers and faithfully pass along the apostolic faith to the next generation. There is no greater way to honor the veterans of the faith than to maintain with diligence the faith they have given to us.

B. Lesson Background

The epistle from Jude was apparently written by a brother of the James who wrote the epistle of James. Both men were brothers of Jesus (Matthew 13:55), who were originally quite skeptical of Jesus and His claims. John 7:5 notes, "Neither did his brethren believe in him." We are told, however, that they joined with His disciples after the resurrection (Acts 1:14). Eventually they became noteworthy leaders in the early church on a level somewhat comparable to the apostles (1 Corinthians 9:5).

The epistle of Jude is very similar in content to 2 Peter, with parallels in theme, development of thought, and language. Modern readers are often confused at why one Bible writer would resemble so closely the work of another Bible writer (regardless of who wrote first—Peter or Jude). But both men were confronting the same issue: the rising threat of false teachers to the body of Christ. We should expect that similarities in addressing this problem will be present. In the case of Peter and Jude, each has taken a common message and, under the guidance of God's Spirit, has crafted his epistle so that it expresses his own distinctive style and emphasis. Both speak of God's judgment against false teachers, but Peter emphasizes a call to godliness (as noted in earlier lessons), while Jude issues a call for the defense of the apostolic faith. Despite the similarities, Jude's epistle stands on its own as a portion of Scripture just as worthy of study as 2 Peter.

I. Let Us Defend the Faith
(Jude 3, 4, 17-19)

A. With Sound Doctrine (v. 3)

3. Beloved, when I gave all diligence to write unto you of the common salvation, it was needful for me to write unto you, and exhort you that ye should earnestly contend for the faith which was once delivered unto the saints.

This brief epistle poses several unanswered questions. For example, we do not know to whom it was written. The recipients were apparently a group of Christians who were loved by Jude and who respected his authority, but their identity is not given. We also do not know what Jude originally intended to tell his readers. He says that he had intended to write about their *common salvation*. This would have been a doctrinal treatise that could have covered any number of important New Testament themes. But Jude's attention was diverted by a new problem—the rise of false teachers within the church. Thus Jude considered it more *needful* at this time to write about his readers' need to *contend for the faith*.

Jude refers to the teaching of the early leaders of the church, such as he and the apostles, as *the faith which was once delivered unto the saints*. The unchanging permanence of apostolic teaching is especially emphasized by other translations that speak of the faith as having been delivered "once for all" (*New International Version, New American Standard Bible*). It is the nature of false teachers to try to change God's Word to fit their new ideas. Believers who are committed to sound doctrine will follow the pattern of Acts 2:42 and continue "steadfastly in the apostles' doctrine" as it was originally given.

B. With Godly Living (vv. 4, 17-19)

4. For there are certain men crept in unawares, who were before of old ordained to this condemnation, ungodly men, turning the grace of our God into lasciviousness, and denying the only Lord God, and our Lord Jesus Christ.

In this one verse, Jude summarizes much of what he will say later about false teachers in the church. To put it in a helpful outline form, Jude speaks of their method, their message, and their madness.

The method of these teachers is to have *crept in unawares*. They do not announce themselves to be evil; rather, they portray themselves as spokesmen for God. They can appear to be very zealous in their spirituality, and genuine in their ministry for others. But if what they teach does not harmonize with the Word of God, they are to be rejected as false.

The message of false teachers is found in the phrase *turning the grace of our God into lasciviousness. Lasciviousness* means the freedom to think and do whatever one wants, regardless of what he has been told. There have been hundreds of heretical ideas promoted within the church throughout its history. What they all share in common is an attitude that challenges the teachings of Scripture and entertains ideas that are more personally satisfying. For many, the idea of the Biblical author's intent is irrelevant. What really matters is, "I feel good about what I am thinking and doing." All of this is a perversion of *the grace of our God*, about which Paul warns in Romans 6:15.

The madness of false teachers is seen in the incomprehensible way in which they treat the one who saved them from sin and death. By all rights, Jesus should be regarded as the dominant authority in our lives—*our Lord*. But those who teach and practice false doctrine are in effect *denying* the authority of Christ and His Word, and establishing their own personal feelings as lord. Truly they deserve the judgment that was *before of old ordained* for them by God.

17, 18. But, beloved, remember ye the words which were spoken before of the apostles of our Lord Jesus Christ; how that they told you there should be mockers in the last time, who should walk after their own ungodly lusts.

Jude's call to *remember* the warning of the coming of *mockers* is similar to that of 2 Peter 3:2, 3, but with some different emphases. Whereas Peter attributes the words of warning to both the Old Testament prophets and the apostles, Jude simply focuses upon the *apostles*. In 2 Peter the mocking is directed toward a specific doctrine: the belief that Christ will return one day (despite His apparent delay). But in Jude the mocking is viewed in a more general sense, in which all false ideas are a "mocking" of God's Word.

Jude also notes once again the self-serving attitude of those who would put their own ideas ahead of the teaching of God's Word. They *walk after their own ungodly lusts*.

19. These be they who separate themselves, sensual, having not the Spirit.

Three common characteristics of false teachers are noted. First, they *separate themselves*. The Greek wording is actually stronger than this. It is not that false teachers withdraw themselves from the fellowship of the church, for that is where they find their audience. The idea is that their teaching fosters separation or division among God's people. This is one of the reasons that false doctrine must be aggressively answered, and not simply tolerated as harmless.

Second, false teachers tend to be *sensual*. This English word brings to mind someone who pursues fleshly pleasures such as illicit sexual practices, which is true of some heretics, and leaders and members of cults. But the Greek word actually conveys the idea of someone who thinks and acts on the basis of personal feelings and desires. This is the self-serving attitude Jude alluded to earlier.

Third, false teachers are described as *having not the Spirit*. They may talk about the importance of the Holy Spirit, but their devotion to personal feelings indicates that they are not following the leading of the Spirit, neither through the Word He has inspired nor through the inner power He provides to help Christians develop the "fruit of the Spirit." These false teachers are devoted to self and empowered by self, and thus cannot be pleasing to God.

II. Let Us Practice Our Calling (Jude 20-23)

A. Through a Growing Faith (v. 20)

20. But ye, beloved, building up yourselves on your most holy faith, praying in the Holy Ghost.

Having begun his letter with the negative theme of false teachers, Jude now concludes with a positive message of what his readers can do to keep themselves strong. His description of them as *beloved* reflects his closeness to them and his concern for their spiritual well-being. He presents a brief summary of the Christian's calling by using Paul's familiar trilogy of faith, hope, and love.

Jude begins by calling attention to our *most holy faith*. In the context of this chapter, the word *faith* could refer to the original teachings of the apostles, as in our lesson title, "Keeping the Faith." Thus Jude's admonition in this verse would be that his readers devote themselves to sound doctrine—a theme consistent with his earlier challenge to "contend for the faith" (v. 3). But in the immediate context of the emphasis on faith, hope, and love, it is more likely that Jude is now referring to our commitment of faith to the will of God and His Son. By faith we deny self and say "yes" to God. We believe whatever His Word teaches, and we try to do whatever He commands. Such faith is the fundamental condition for salvation—a basic characteristic of all who are saved by the grace of God.

But note that Jude's picture of faith is not one that is static. Christians should be *building up*

themselves in faith. We are to grow from spiritual infants to mature believers by ceasing our old sinful habits, practicing new godly attitudes and actions, developing our spiritual gifts, increasing our Christian service, and learning how to trust God and not quit during difficult times.

One of the keys to maturing in faith is an active prayer life. Jude does not explain what he means by *praying in the Holy Ghost*, but perhaps he means praying to God the Father, by the name and authority of Jesus Christ, and with the assistance of the Holy Spirit. The Holy Spirit aids our prayers by taking our words and presenting them to God in a manner that is both appropriate and effective (Romans 8:26, 27).

B. Through a Diligent Love (v. 21a)

21a. Keep yourselves in the love of God.

What does it mean to *keep yourselves in the love of God*? The immediate context of the faith, hope, and love theme suggests an interpretation that focuses upon *our* love rather than God's love. What Jude may have in mind is that we diligently practice the love we have learned from God. This could encompass our worshipful expressions of love for God and our loving service in behalf of God toward the people of this world and the saints within the church.

C. Through an Enthusiastic Hope (vv. 21b-23)

21b. Looking for the mercy of our Lord Jesus Christ unto eternal life.

While the word "hope" is not explicitly used in this verse, the concept is clearly evident. Jude speaks of our anticipation of the return of Christ and of our admission into the *eternal life* that awaits us in Heaven. The *New American Standard Bible* tries to bring out the intensity of this hope by rendering the word *looking* as "waiting anxiously."

Jude presents an interesting twist on this familiar concept. He refers to the second coming as a day of *mercy*. We typically think of Christ's return in terms of fulfillment and blessings for the saints, and of justice and condemnation for the wicked. But consider how that day also represents God's *mercy*. Our entrance into *eternal life* will be based not upon our own merit but upon the grace of God. And it appears that the judgment proceedings will in some way remind us of this truth.

LOOKING FOR ETERNAL LIFE

Christians in Communist-dominated Eastern Europe lived in tiny, dingy apartments, with little food and little beauty around them. From time to time some of them were able to come to

Vienna, Austria, to a mission called Haus Edelweiss (House *A*-del-vice). The mission was housed in a lovely old guest house with beautiful gardens, a waterfall, and a goldfish pond. It was so lovely that one couple drove right past it, thinking it could not be the place to which they had been invited. Another said, "Don't ever sell this place. I may never get to come back, but it is a comfort to me just to know that it is here."

As Christians we expect to go to Heaven. It may be a while until we arrive, but it's a comfort just knowing it is there. We are able to endure whatever earth holds for us, knowing that Heaven awaits us. Skeptics may criticize us for that perspective, but the criticism is unjust. Contemplating Heaven has never made believers neglect their work on earth, nor has it made them neglect the needs of others on earth. It is just the opposite. We know that eternal rest awaits us, so we are not afraid to work until we are weary. We know that eternal peace awaits us, so we are not afraid to engage the world about us. We know eternal life awaits us, so we make the most of this life.   —R. C. S.

22, 23. And of some have compassion, making a difference: and others save with fear, pulling them out of the fire; hating even the garment spotted by the flesh.

Thinking about the mercy that awaits us at Christ's return should prompt us to share that mercy and *compassion* with others. This is Jude's brief reference to the evangelistic mission of the church. Jude seems to envision two categories of people who need to hear the truth of the gospel. The first group is described in the *King James Version* with the phrase *making a difference*. Other translations more accurately render the Greek wording by speaking of those "who are doubting" (*New American Standard Bible*). This is an appropriate way to describe people outside the church who have not yet been persuaded of the truth of the gospel.

Verse 23 refers to *others* for whom Christians should feel both caution (*fear*) and disgust (*hating even the garment spotted by the flesh*). This apparently refers to the false teachers who have been the focus of criticism throughout this epistle. It is wise for Christians to exercise caution when trying to correct a false teacher and bring him to the truth, for at the same time he will be trying to bring believers around to his point of view. Some in the church today may not be ready for taking on false teachers, but they should be challenged by Jude's exhortation to maintain a steady pattern of growth. In the meantime, they should show compassion toward the people with whom they can work

visual for
lesson 12

more effectively: those "who are doubting" among their family and friends.

Jude notes the feelings of disgust that naturally arise when we think about the ungodly principles that are being taught by some who claim to be Christians. The reference to *hating the garment* calls to mind some of the Old Testament laws concerning the contaminating impact of sin and disease. Like the leper whose clothing was polluted by his affliction (Leviticus 13:47-52), those contaminated by false teaching are to be seen as a source of corruption.

This does not mean, however, that such individuals should be shunned altogether. We might be inclined to simply ignore the false teachers and cults around us and let them get what they deserve. But as we try to imitate the boundless grace of God, we are obligated to make an effort to pull *out of the fire* even the worst of heretics. We should sentence no one to Hell as long as there is still time for repentance and salvation.

III. Let Us Praise Our God (Jude 24, 25)

A. For His Abundant Mercy (v. 24)

24. Now unto him that is able to keep you from falling, and to present you faultless before the presence of his glory with exceeding joy.

Jude closes his epistle in a manner that is similar to Paul's letters. He ends with a benediction, which is a prayer of praise to God. The focus of praise is first upon the mercy to be revealed at the second coming of Christ, when we will stand *before the presence of his glory* at the judgment. What an amazing thing will then occur! In the splendor of God's perfect holiness, our sins will stand out in sharp contrast. But Jesus Christ our Savior has covered our sins with His blood, and they will not show. By the boundless mercy of our God, we will stand there as if we were *faultless*.

Standing on the precipice of eternity, experiencing the ultimate bestowal of grace, it is an understatement to say that we will be filled with *exceeding joy*. We can experience some measure of that joy in this life, for our present walk with

Christ is one of "joy unspeakable and full of glory" (1 Peter 1:8). How much greater will be the thrill of walking with Him, not by faith, but by sight!

B. For His Infinite Glory (v. 25)

25. To the only wise God our Saviour, be glory and majesty, dominion and power, both now and ever. Amen.

Time did not permit Jude to expound upon the infinite greatness of God. He could mention only briefly how *wise* God is, using His infinite knowledge in ways that have always sought to bless mankind. Jude also speaks of God's *glory and majesty*. These terms can refer both to the radiance that emanates from God's presence, and to the worship and service that He naturally draws forth from His creatures. Jude praises God for His *dominion* over creation, and for the mighty *power* He uses to accomplish His will. He reminds us of God's eternal nature, as He lives and reigns *both now and ever. Amen!*

THE ONLY WISE GOD

Many years ago the Chicago Symphony Orchestra and the Swedish Choral Club combined to present a performance of Handel's Messiah. But the printer made an error when he printed the lyrics for the program. Instead of the word *Reigneth*, the program read, "Hallelujah! The Lord God Omnipotent *Resigneth!*"

It is important to think of our God as described in Jude's stirring doxology (vv. 24, 25): a God of wisdom, glory, and majesty. But what if the Lord God did in fact resign? Certainly He has reason enough to do it. One thinks of man's condition prior to the flood: "Every imagination of the thoughts of his heart was only evil continually" (Genesis 6:5). But the Lord has not resigned. On the contrary, it is still true that He *reigns*, in spite of all that happens in this world. He is still wise, even though humans think themselves wiser, and try to improve on His laws. He still has glory and majesty, even when those made in His image mar that image beyond belief.

One of the most neglected doctrines today is the doctrine of God. He has been scaled down to human proportions. He is referred to (even by some Christians) as "the Man upstairs," in a kind of chummy familiarity that is far removed from the reverence found in the Bible. As the title of one of J. B. Phillips' books puts it, *Your God Is Too Small*. We are to conform to God's image; we must not try to make God in our image.

—R. C. S.

Conclusion

A. Carved in Stone

In our modern age of paper and ink and word processors, we still use an expression that harkens back to the past. When an idea is subject to change we say, "It is not carved in stone." By this we mean that we can be flexible and make a revision if necessary. On the other hand, for something to be "carved in stone" is to imply that it has a permanent nature and is not subject to change.

The Law of Moses was literally carved in stone. This was done because at that time such was the common method of recording something that was to be preserved for generations to come. Perhaps the stone also had a symbolic significance, conveying a message that the Mosaic regulations were to be seen as having an abiding permanence for the nation of Israel.

The teachings of Christ's apostles as recorded in the New Testament should likewise be viewed as being fixed and stable for our present age. We are not to conform our faith to the popular ideas and morality of modern society, but we should daily build our faith upon the foundation that the church was given in the beginning. The church should be a people whose faith is "carved in stone."

B. Prayer

Our Father in Heaven, we thank You for revealing divine truth through the writings of Your servants the apostles. Help us to remain eager students of Your written Word, the Bible, and loyal disciples of the living Word, Jesus Christ, in whose name we pray, amen.

C. Thought to Remember

"Other foundation can no man lay than that is laid, which is Jesus Christ" (1 Corinthians 3:11).

Home Daily Bible Readings

Monday, Feb. 16—False Guides Abuse God's Grace (Jude 1-13)

Tuesday, Feb. 17—Build Yourselves Up in the Faith (Jude 14-25)

Wednesday, Feb. 18—Jesus Christ Is Our Foundation (1 Corinthians 3:1-11)

Thursday, Feb. 19—A Prayer Without Empty Phrases (Matthew 6:7-13)

Friday, Feb. 20—Be Holy as God Is Holy (Leviticus 19:1, 2, 9-18)

Saturday, Feb. 21—They Desired a Better Country (Hebrews 11:8-16)

Sunday, Feb. 22—Names on Palms of God's Hands (Isaiah 49:13-18)

Learning by Doing

This page contains an alternate lesson plan emphasizing learning activities.
Classes desiring such student involvement will find these suggestions helpful.

Learning Goals

After completing this lesson, each student should be able to:

1. Summarize Jude's call to persevere in the faith.

2. Describe the false teachers and compare their way of life with that of those who keep the faith.

3. Suggest practical ways to contend for the faith and to help others to do so.

Into the Lesson

In advance, collect a variety of objects that are or can be used as warning devices, such as a whistle, a bell, a flare, a smoke alarm, a flashlight, or a red flag. These objects can assist you in introducing the idea of warnings.

The Bible is filled with warnings—things we are to avoid and/or not do. Ask your students to suggest some of these warnings. For example, the Ten Commandments contain many warnings. The prophets repeatedly warned the Israelites to change their evil ways (Jeremiah 7:3-15). Jesus warned us to beware of false prophets (Matthew 7:15). The apostles warned first-century converts to avoid their old habits (Colossians 3:5-11).

In today's lesson, Jude has a warning for Christians. Use information from the lesson Introduction to acquaint students with Jude and his short letter.

Into the Word

Tell your students to read Jude 3 and 4, then ask, "What do these verses say about the believers to whom Jude wrote his letter? What was the main problem they were experiencing?"

These believers had been infiltrated by servants of Satan and apparently were unaware of it. Also, it appears that they were taking a passive attitude toward their faith, which is probably what made the infiltration so successful. Jude's letter contains both an exhortation and a warning. First, he exhorts his readers to "contend for the faith" (v. 3). Ask your students to "translate" this phrase into today's language. What was Jude exhorting his readers to do?

Second, Jude also warns his readers. Ask, "What were these first-century Christians to beware of?" This question is answered in detail in verse 4.

Verses 4, 18, and 19 give us a profile of the servants of Satan. Divide the class into groups of three, and ask them to look for characteristics of these dangerous teachers (this exercise is also found in the student book). For example:

• deceptive (v. 4): "crept in unawares." Satan has a special interest in infiltrating the church with malicious hypocrites.

• profane, impious, and godless (v. 4): "ungodly." The unrighteous have no interest in anything that has to do with God or with truth.

• immoral and intent on corrupting others (vv. 4, 18): "turning the grace of our God into lasciviousness"; "walk after their own ungodly lusts." Immoral people want others to join them in their sinful activities (see Romans 1:32).

• anti-Christ and anti-Christian (vv. 4, 18): "denying . . . our Lord Jesus Christ"; "mockers." Any person who denies Christ is an enemy of Christ and the church.

• divisive troublemakers (v. 19): "they who separate themselves," or "the men who divide you" (*New International Version*).

• cater to selfish desires rather than depend on the Holy Spirit (v. 19): "sensual, having not the Spirit."

It seems that people who fit this profile would stick out in a church like the proverbial "sore thumb." Ask, "Why did Jude's readers need to be warned to beware of these people? Why couldn't they recognize and resist them on their own?" Apparently these believers lacked spiritual maturity, which Jude encourages in verses 20 and 21. Also, they needed to be instructed on how to deal with problems within the fellowship (vv. 22, 23).

Into Life

The challenge for us today is to contend for the faith without being contentious. We must stand firmly for what we believe without being offensive.

Jude closes his letter with a stirring doxology—a hymn of praise to God. Ask your students to write their own doxology. Depending on your class, have each student create his own, have several students get together and collaborate, or create one doxology from the whole class. Whether one or several doxologies are created, take time to have the students' efforts read aloud as part of your closing.

Let's Talk It Over

The questions on this page are designed to encourage review of the lesson Scriptures and to promote discussion of the lesson by the class. The answers provided are only discussion starters. Let your class talk it over from there.

1. In today's church, who is responsible to "contend for the faith" (Jude 3)?

Generally we look to ordained ministers to be the experts in the Word of God and all matters of faith. After all, they are the ones who have had college or seminary training and should be the most knowledgeable. Ministers, however, have been known to be honestly mistaken on occasion, to have a personal bias on an issue, or to hold a view that is contrary to historic Christian doctrine. For that reason, it is important to have elders or other mature and capable leaders who are able to evaluate the teaching that goes on. Ultimately, however, every Christian must take responsibility for being familiar enough with the Word of God to test every teaching by its standards.

2. In a culture that rejects the idea of absolute truth, how do we defend a faith that claims to present the only way to God?

Our children today grow up being taught that truth is relative. The "truth" in which you believe and which works for you is your truth, but it may not match the "truth" in which I believe and which works for me. This tolerance for varying truth claims is especially evident in the realms of values, moral judgments, and religion. One may believe that the highest order of human relationships is marriage between one man and one woman, but among those who believe that truth is relative, it is equally valid to hold that polygamy, same-sex marriage, or even incestuous relationships are desirable. Our text maintains that the faith was "once delivered" (Jude 3). It thus applies to every age and every circumstance. Our God is the same yesterday, today, and forever. His principles are universal and absolute. Their veracity does not depend upon who believes them or who agrees with them. They cannot be changed by popular vote or cultural consensus.

3. How does Jude's description of false teachers and "mockers" of the Christian message help us identify them today?

Jude 18 and 19 give us some telltale trademarks of those whom Jude calls "mockers," even though we may not immediately detect a problem with their teaching. First, they walk after "ungodly lusts." The presence of pride, self-promotion, or self-indulgence in any teacher or leader should be a warning. Second, such mockers cause dissension, especially by gathering followers who endorse their strange ideas. This is the meaning of the phrase "they who separate themselves" in verse 19. Third, they are "sensual." They may place an improper emphasis upon sexuality, other appetites, emotions, or experience. Finally, they lack the Holy Spirit. This lack will be discernible by a noticeable absence of the fruit of the Spirit in their character (Galatians 5:22, 23).

4. How can Christians hate "even the garment spotted by the flesh" (Jude 23) and not come across as judgmental and condemning?

Jude prefaces this remark by reminding his readers that Christians depend upon the mercy of our Lord for eternal life. He instructs us to have compassion for the lost, "pulling them out of the fire." In so doing, we must be careful that we hate the sin and care for the sinner, and then be just as careful that we communicate this by our actions. Could you reach out in love to a young woman who has had an abortion? Could you let a homosexual know that you care for him, even though you cannot approve the practice of homosexuality? Remember: Sin is the enemy, not the sinner.

TEACHER: PLEASE NOTE

Normally, each three-month period has thirteen Sundays and our lesson manual thirteen lessons, a lesson for each Sunday. However, the current quarter (December, 1997, January, February, 1998) has only twelve Sundays, and the Spring quarter (March, April, May, 1998) has fourteen. In order to have thirteen lessons in each manual, we have taken the first lesson of the Spring quarter (the lesson for March 1) and included it in the Winter quarter as lesson 13. Therefore, lesson 13 is the first lesson of the Spring quarter's study entitled, "The Gospel of Action (Mark)." The first lesson in the Spring quarterly will be for March 8, the second Sunday in March.

Jesus' Ministry Begins

DEVOTIONAL READING: Acts 10:34-43.

LESSON SCRIPTURE: Mark 1:1-20.

PRINTED TEXT: Mark 1:1, 4, 7-20.

Mark 1:1, 4, 7-20

1 The beginning of the gospel of Jesus Christ, the Son of God.

. . . .

4 John did baptize in the wilderness, and preach the baptism of repentance for the remission of sins.

. . . .

7 And preached, saying, There cometh one mightier than I after me, the latchet of whose shoes I am not worthy to stoop down and unloose.

8 I indeed have baptized you with water: but he shall baptize you with the Holy Ghost.

9 And it came to pass in those days, that Jesus came from Nazareth of Galilee, and was baptized of John in Jordan.

10 And straightway coming up out of the water, he saw the heavens opened, and the Spirit like a dove descending upon him:

11 And there came a voice from heaven, saying, Thou art my beloved Son, in whom I am well pleased.

12 And immediately the Spirit driveth him into the wilderness.

13 And he was there in the wilderness forty days tempted of Satan; and was with the wild beasts; and the angels ministered unto him.

14 Now after that John was put in prison, Jesus came into Galilee, preaching the gospel of the kingdom of God,

15 And saying, The time is fulfilled, and the kingdom of God is at hand: repent ye, and believe the gospel.

16 Now as he walked by the sea of Galilee, he saw Simon and Andrew his brother casting a net into the sea: for they were fishers.

17 And Jesus said unto them, Come ye after me, and I will make you to become fishers of men.

18 And straightway they forsook their nets, and followed him.

19 And when he had gone a little further thence, he saw James the son of Zebedee, and John his brother, who also were in the ship mending their nets.

20 And straightway he called them: and they left their father Zebedee in the ship with the hired servants, and went after him.

GOLDEN TEXT: There came a voice from heaven, saying, Thou art my beloved Son, in whom I am well pleased.—Mark 1:11.

**Mar
1**

Lesson Aims

After this lesson, students should be able to:

1. Relate the key events surrounding the beginning of the ministry of Jesus.

2. Tell how Jesus' baptism and temptation prepared Him for His public ministry.

3. Suggest one way in which to accept Jesus' challenge to become "fishers of men."

Lesson Outline

INTRODUCTION
  A. "There Is No Second"
  B. Lesson Background
 I. JOHN THE BAPTIST'S MINISTRY (Mark 1:1, 4, 7, 8)
  A. The Beginning of the Gospel (v. 1)
  B. The Preaching of John the Baptist (vv. 4, 7, 8)
 II. JESUS' PREPARATION (Mark 1:9-13)
  A. His Baptism (vv. 9-11)
  B. His Temptation (vv. 12, 13)
   Wild Animals and Angels
 III. JESUS' MINISTRY (Mark 1:14-20)
  A. His Mission (vv. 14, 15)
  B. His Calling of Disciples (vv. 16-20)
   Heed the Call
CONCLUSION
  A. Baptism
  B. Fishers of Men
  C. Prayer
  D. Thought to Remember

The visual for Lesson 13 uses Bible art to highlight those events in Jesus' life that are covered in today's lesson. It is shown on page 221.

Introduction

A. "There Is No Second"

In the days of Queen Victoria of England, an international yacht race was held in the English Channel. So that she could stay informed about the progress of the race, the queen stationed men along the shore to send reports. At one point in the race, the queen, growing impatient for information, sent word to the farthest man down shore, asking for a report on the race. He scanned the waters and told the queen that no

yachts were in sight. Not long afterward, the queen again sent for a report. This time the man replied that the American yacht was in sight. Hoping that the English yacht might at least be second, the queen asked which yacht was second. Again the man scanned the sea and sent back this message: "There is no second."

This same assessment could be made concerning Jesus Christ. When God declared at Jesus' baptism, "Thou art my beloved Son, in whom I am well pleased" (Mark 1:11), He was affirming Jesus' uniqueness and superiority for all time. Compared with Him, all other religious leaders and spokesmen must vanish in the distance. Jesus stands alone: "There is no second."

B. Lesson Background

The author of the Gospel of Mark is not named in the book itself, but the most ancient traditions ascribe it to John Mark—the young man who accompanied Barnabas and Saul on a portion of their first missionary journey (Acts 12:25; 13:5, 13). Many scholars believe that the Gospel of Mark was the first written account of the life of Jesus. In the strict sense it is not a biography, for it makes no attempt to cover all the details of Jesus' life. Mark does not even mention Jesus' birth. Beginning with Peter's good confession in chapter 8 (vv. 27-29), he concentrates on Jesus' death, burial, and resurrection, which is the essence of the gospel (1 Corinthians 15:1-4). Many point to the presence of Mark with Peter in Peter's later years (1 Peter 5:13) as evidence that Mark may have consulted Peter in the process of writing his Gospel.

Unlike Matthew's Gospel, Mark does not tend to focus on incidents in Jesus' life that fulfill Old Testament prophecies. He takes the time to explain Jewish customs (7:2-4; 15:42) and to translate Aramaic words (3:17; 5:41; 7:11, 34; 15:22). There is also a sense of urgency in Mark's Gospel. He often introduces an event with expressions usually translated "immediately," "at once," or "straightway." These pieces of evidence lead us to believe that Mark was writing for Roman readers, not Jewish readers. (The Romans were a people of action.)

The date of writing is difficult to determine with any certainty. There seems to be a special interest in persecution in this Gospel (8:34-38; 10:29, 30; 13:9-13), which some believe points to a time close to A.D. 64, when the persecution of Christians by the Roman emperor Nero was about to intensify. This would also fit with the idea of Mark being directed to the Romans, and with the urgent, straightforward style of the book. Such a style is equally appropriate for our busy, pressure-packed culture.

I. John the Baptist's Ministry
(Mark 1:1, 4, 7, 8)

A. The Beginning of the Gospel (v. 1)

1. The beginning of the gospel of Jesus Christ, the Son of God.

Each of the Gospel writers begins his work in a different way. Matthew, reflecting his Jewish heritage and his desire to communicate to Jewish readers, begins with the genealogy of Jesus. Luke begins with the account of John the Baptist's birth, while John transcends time by telling us of Christ's preexistence. Mark passes by all of this and starts with the ministry of John the Baptist, which he treats as a brief prologue to Jesus' own ministry.

B. The Preaching of John the Baptist
(vv. 4, 7, 8)

4. John did baptize in the wilderness, and preach the baptism of repentance for the remission of sins.

The Old Testament closes with the prophecy that before the "coming of the great and dreadful day of the Lord," God would send the prophet Elijah (Malachi 4:5). Now, after some four hundred years, that prophecy was being fulfilled in the person of *John* (Matthew 11:11-14; Mark 9:11-13). Like Elijah of old, John was a powerful preacher whose message touched the hearts of men and women. Word of his preaching spread across the land, and crowds went out to hear him, even though he carried out his ministry *in the wilderness* near the Jordan River.

The content of John's preaching is summarized as *the baptism of repentance*. All who heard John were asked to turn away from their sins and turn back to God. Then they were immersed in the Jordan River *for the remission of sins*. Scholars speculate about the origin of John's baptism. Some believe that it had its origins in the Jewish practice of ceremonial washing that initiated proselytes into the Jewish faith. Others propose that it came from the Jewish sect (thought by some to be the Essenes) whose settlement, Qumran, was located near where John was baptizing. (Qumran is the area where the famous Dead Sea Scrolls were discovered.) Regardless of its origin, John gave baptism a new meaning. This is the reason he came to be called "the Baptist," or "the Baptizer."

7, 8. And preached, saying, There cometh one mightier than I after me, the latchet of whose shoes I am not worthy to stoop down and unloose. I indeed have baptized you with water: but he shall baptize you with the Holy Ghost.

John preached a message of repentance, as had many of the Old Testament prophets, but John's message had an added dimension. The repentance John preached was to prepare the people to receive the promised Messiah. In John's day it was a common practice for a person's *shoes,* or sandals, to be removed when he entered the home of another person. This task was expected to be done by the lowliest of the servants. John saw himself as fulfilling a similar task for the Messiah. His attitude of humility is a model for all today who would serve Jesus.

John further announced that the coming Messiah's ministry would be unique in another respect: the *Holy Ghost* would be actively involved in it. The Holy Spirit had been involved in God's plan for mankind throughout history (see, for example, Nehemiah 9:30), but now the Spirit's participation would be much more direct. Just as those coming to John's baptism were immersed in water, so those who followed the Christ were to be immersed in the Holy Spirit. We see dramatic examples of this on the Day of Pentecost (Acts 2:1-4) and in the house of Cornelius (Acts 10:44-47). The apostle Paul applies similar language to all Christians in 1 Corinthians 12:13.

II. Jesus' Preparation
(Mark 1:9-13)

A. His Baptism (vv. 9-11)

9. And it came to pass in those days, that Jesus came from Nazareth of Galilee, and was baptized of John in Jordan.

After the death of Herod the Great, Joseph had taken Mary and Jesus back to the town of *Nazareth of Galilee.* There Jesus had lived in obscurity until He came to *John* to be *baptized.*

Matthew provides additional details about Jesus' baptism (Matthew 3:13-15). His account gives the impression that John knew Jesus prior to the baptism, or at least was aware of His distinctly righteous character, since John realized he was not worthy to baptize Jesus. The mothers of John and Jesus were related (Luke 1:36), and the two families may have traveled together to Jerusalem for the annual feasts.

Jesus' baptism was not for the remission of sins, because He was sinless. Jesus submitted to baptism as an act of obedience "to fulfil all righteousness" (Matthew 3:15).

10, 11. And straightway coming up out of the water, he saw the heavens opened, and the Spirit like a dove descending upon him: and there came a voice from heaven, saying, Thou art my beloved Son, in whom I am well pleased.

With Jesus' baptism, the thirty years of obscurity and quiet preparation in Nazareth ended. We do not know how many people witnessed His baptism—perhaps several, including some who later became His disciples. Did all these see the dove descend upon Jesus and hear the voice of God? Many believe that only John the Baptist and Jesus saw the dove and heard the voice. The Gospel of John seems to confirm this (John 1:29-34), indicating that the baptism of Jesus was primarily for John the Baptist's benefit, confirming Jesus' messiahship to him.

Jesus' baptism marked the beginning of His public ministry. In the same way, one's baptism today marks the beginning of that person's Christian life and ministry. Jesus' baptism was also an act of humble obedience to God—an example for every person who is baptized. Today a person who is baptized does not expect to see the Spirit descending as a dove or to hear God's assuring voice. But we do not need such dramatic signs. Jesus' example and the further revelation of God's will in the book of Acts and the New Testament epistles give us the assurance that this action has God's approval.

B. His Temptation (vv. 12, 13)

12, 13. And immediately the Spirit driveth him into the wilderness. And he was there in the wilderness forty days tempted of Satan; and was with the wild beasts; and the angels ministered unto him.

Satan knew very well that Jesus' ministry posed a threat to his wicked domain, and so it should not surprise us that he immediately set about to destroy Jesus. At the same time, it is interesting to read that *the Spirit* (who had just descended upon Jesus) led Him to be tempted.

The Gospel writers make no attempt to deal with the theological implications of Jesus' temptation. In the letter to the Hebrews, we receive insights into some of these issues. We are told that "though he were a Son, yet learned he obedience by the things which he suffered" (5:8), and that He "was in all points tempted like as we are, yet without sin" (4:15). He could not serve as our High Priest, able to "succor," or help us, without personally experiencing temptation (2:18).

Mark uses a very strong term to describe the Spirit's action in sending Jesus out into the wilderness: he *driveth him*. The word literally means "to throw out." Matthew and Luke in describing this event express the action in less violent terms. The *wilderness* mentioned was located south and west of the site of Jesus' baptism. The area was a barren desert, resembling Death Valley in southern California. Only Mark adds the interesting detail that the *wild beasts* were with Jesus.

At the conclusion of Jesus' forty-day ordeal in the wilderness, *the angels ministered unto him.* We are reminded of Jesus' experience in Gethsemane where, as He prayed, "there appeared an angel unto him from heaven, strengthening him" (Luke 22:43).

Wild Animals and Angels

New converts often report particularly trying experiences immediately following their baptism. Jesus' personal experience is instructive in this regard. Mark's record says that "the Spirit driveth him into the wilderness" (Mark 1:12), where He was tempted. Though God does not tempt us (James 1:13), He does allow us to be tested and tried to refine our Christian character (James 1:2-4).

Mark also mentions that "wild beasts" were in the desert with Jesus (Mark 1:13). Jesus had to be prepared for the attack of predatory animals. All Christians must be self-controlled and alert against our enemy, the devil, who prowls about like a roaring lion, looking for someone to devour (1 Peter 5:8).

Notice also that angels accompanied Jesus in the wilderness (Mark 1:13). God is present with His people in a special way when they are tempted. Resisting temptation teaches us that "greater is he that is in you, than he that is in the world" (1 John 4:4).

Temptation never stops with just one episode. It may subside at times, but it is an ever-present danger. The good news is that Christ was victorious in every instance of temptation, and thus we too can resist the schemes and seductions of Satan. Remember this word of assurance: "God is faithful; he will not let you be tempted beyond what you can bear . . . he will also provide a way out" (1 Corinthians 10:13, *New International Version*). —R. W. B.

III. Jesus' Ministry
(Mark 1:14-20)

A. His Mission (vv. 14, 15)

14, 15. Now after that John was put in prison, Jesus came into Galilee, preaching the gospel of the kingdom of God, and saying, The time is fulfilled, and the kingdom of God is at hand: repent ye, and believe the gospel.

Some time after Jesus' baptism (the exact time is uncertain), *John was put in prison*. Later Mark records that this was done by Herod Antipas "for Herodias' sake, his brother Philip's wife; for he had married her. For John had said unto Herod, It is not lawful for thee to have thy brother's wife" (Mark 6:17, 18). Apparently Jesus did not begin His public ministry in earnest until John's public ministry was thus ended.

Returning to *Galilee*, Jesus began to preach the *gospel of the kingdom of God*. Of course, the message He preached was not the complete good news, for that had to await His death and resurrection. But it was good news in the sense that the long-awaited *kingdom of God* was *at hand*. Like John, Jesus preached a message of repentance in preparation for the coming kingdom.

B. His Calling of Disciples
(vv. 16-20)

16-18. Now as he walked by the sea of Galilee, he saw Simon and Andrew his brother casting a net into the sea: for they were fishers. And Jesus said unto them, Come ye after me, and I will make you to become fishers of men. And straightway they forsook their nets, and followed him.

After His baptism, Jesus remained in the area of Judea, where He was acclaimed by John as the "Lamb of God" (John 1:36). Some of John's followers were thus introduced to Jesus. One of these, Andrew, sought his brother Simon and brought him to Jesus (John 1:40-42). Others who were later to become Jesus' disciples, including Philip and Nathanael, also met Him at this time (vv. 43-51).

As noted in the previous verse, upon John's imprisonment Jesus returned to Galilee. On the occasion mentioned in these verses, He was walking along the shore of the *sea of Galilee*. There He saw *Simon and Andrew* fishing with a *net*. His words to them were brief and to the point: *Come ye after me, and I will make you to become fishers of men*. They *straightway* left *their nets* and *followed him*. Their immediately positive response to Jesus' invitation was likely a product of their earlier meeting with Him in Judea.

19, 20. And when he had gone a little further thence, he saw James the son of Zebedee, and John his brother, who also were in the ship mending their nets. And straightway he called them: and they left their father Zebedee in the ship with the hired servants, and went after him.

As Jesus walked a little farther along the shore, He came upon *James and John*, who, along with *their father Zebedee* and his *hired servants*, were busy *mending their nets*. Jesus then repeated His challenge to them, and they responded just as had Simon and Andrew.

When these men answered the call of Jesus, they had no idea where it would lead them, nor did they ask. Only later as they matured in their faith did they begin to learn what following Jesus would cost them. The same is true with us: We can never know where the decision to follow Jesus will take us as we place our lives in His service. It is, however, not only a matter of what this may cost us; we must also remember that following Jesus will bless us in ways we never could have imagined.

HEED THE CALL

The Imperials quartet used to sing a song entitled, "Heed the Call." Its message is that God calls us to discipleship by His Spirit through His Word, and He promises to "make good every chance we take."

I was five years old when my father quit his job in an auto plant to enter Bible college where he trained for the ministry. Dad and Mom had heard God's call to Christian service. Relatives and friends thought them foolish to sell most of their possessions, desert a comfortable home, and move their family to a Kentucky log cabin for what seemed to be an uncertain future. They were taking chances in order to "heed the call."

Following Christ can be risky business. Peter, Andrew, James, and John surely must have sensed that. They were burning bridges of both family and vocation, surrendering security for lives of sacrificial service. Their fathers may have thought that these were foolish and irresponsible decisions.

visual for
Lesson 13

God, however, will always "make good every chance we take." My parents, like the apostles, had the promise of Jesus: "Every one that hath forsaken houses, or brethren, or sisters, or father, or mother, or wife, or children, or lands, for my name's sake, shall receive a hundredfold, and shall inherit everlasting life" (Matthew 19:29).

So "everybody, one and all, heed the call."

—R. W. B.

Conclusion
A. Baptism

Jesus' baptism sets an example for all who would be His followers. However, we need to realize that in certain important respects, His baptism was different from ours. First of all, a prerequisite for Christian baptism is faith in God whom we have never seen. This prerequisite was meaningless for Jesus, because He was God's own Son and Himself divine. Second, our baptism is to be preceded by repentance: a sorrow for the sins that we have committed, and a turning away from them and to God. Since Jesus was sinless (a fact that John the Baptist appears to have recognized), repentance was unnecessary for Him. Third, the Holy Spirit descended upon Jesus in the form of a dove following His baptism (Matthew 3:16). While a sinner who is baptized is promised the gift of the Holy Spirit (Acts 2:38), the Spirit does not come to him in the form of a dove. The Christian accepts His presence on the basis of what God has promised in His Word. Fourth, the baptized believer is then added to the church (Acts 2:47), becoming a part of that sacred fellowship of saints. Again, this was not involved in Jesus' baptism, because He was to become the Head of the church (Ephesians 1:22).

Home Daily Bible Readings

Monday, Feb. 23—One More Powerful (Mark 1:1-11)
Tuesday, Feb. 24—God's Kingdom Is at Hand (Mark 1:12-20)
Wednesday, Feb. 25—Revealing God's Glory (Isaiah 40:1-11)
Thursday, Feb. 26—The Anointed One (Psalm 2)
Friday, Feb. 27—Ordained by God as Judge (Acts 10:34-43)
Saturday, Feb. 28—Nations Tremble at the Presence (Isaiah 64:1-7)
Sunday, Mar. 1—Servant Bringing Justice (Isaiah 42:1-9)

Yet in spite of these differences, the baptism of Christ and our baptism are alike in one very important respect: Jesus' baptism required a humble submission to the will of God. And if He, although sinless, humbled Himself to be baptized, how much more should we who are sinners!

B. Fishers of Men

Many years ago I noticed a man wearing a gold-plated emblem of a fish on his lapel. I supposed that he had won some kind of award or was a member of some kind of fishing club, and so I asked him, "Are you a member of a fishing club?"

"Yes," he replied, "and it is the largest fishing club in the world!"

"What club is it?" I asked. "I don't think I have ever heard of it."

"You mean you have never read the first chapter of Mark?" he responded. Then it dawned on me that the fish symbolized being a fisher of men.

Whether we wear a fish pin or not, as Christians we are members of the largest fishing club in the world. Jesus' call to those early disciples to leave their nets and become fishers of men applies to us just as much as it did to them. To be a soul winner, to carry the gospel to lost sinners, is not an option Christians can choose or reject. It comes with our calling.

To be an effective fisher, one must first of all be willing to leave his or her "nets." Anything that keeps us from seeking the lost is a net that traps us and prevents our effective discipleship. This might be a job, wealth or poverty, or friends or family. Regardless of how attractive the item may be, we must be willing to leave it and follow Jesus.

This does not mean that every one of us must become a minister or a missionary. Indeed, in many situations our job, our wealth, or our friends give us unique opportunities for evangelism that others may not have. We need to recognize these opportunities and pray for wisdom to use them to become successful fishers of men.

C. Prayer

Gracious God, we give You thanks for sending Your Son into the world to save us. We also thank You that Jesus was willing to humble Himself and come to us in the form of a servant. May we, like the fishermen by the sea, respond to His call to discipleship and give ourselves in loving service. In His name we pray. Amen.

D. Thought to Remember

"I will make you to become fishers of men."

Learning by Doing

This page contains an alternate lesson plan emphasizing learning activities.
Classes desiring such student involvement will find these suggestions helpful.

Learning Goals

After this lesson, students should be able to:

1. Relate the key events surrounding the beginning of the ministry of Jesus.

2. Tell how Jesus' baptism and temptation prepared Him for His public ministry.

3. Suggest one way in which to accept Jesus' challenge to become "fishers of men."

Into the Lesson

Explain how we often respond in certain prescribed ways to different people, based upon who they are or what they have accomplished. For example, suppose you are at a baseball game. What response would you give your favorite player as he hits a grand slam home run? Answer: stand, applaud, or shout. Why? Because of the excitement of the moment, or perhaps because the winning runs have scored.

What is the prescribed response of an audience when the President of the United States enters a room? Answer: standing. Why? To demonstrate respect for the office.

Suppose Jesus entered this room. What might we do in response to His presence? Answer: fall to our knees, or bow down. Why? Because He is God, the Lord.

Remind the class that God made it very clear that Jesus was more than a mere man when He announced at Jesus' baptism, "Thou art my beloved Son" (Mark 1:11). He is also deity.

Today we will examine the significance of two events that happened before Jesus launched His public ministry: His baptism and His temptation. We will also hear the challenge that Jesus gave to His first disciples. He offers a similar challenge to His followers today.

Into the Word

First, read the Scripture text. Then break into discussion groups or use the following tasks and questions for class discussion.

Group 1: Jesus' Baptism (Mark 1:4-11)

1. Explain why John would claim he was unworthy to untie Jesus' shoes.

2. Why do you think John was reluctant to baptize Jesus?

3. What do you think was the significance of the announcement from Heaven?

After the discussion of the above questions is completed, explain that while our baptism is different from Jesus' (Jesus had no sins of which to repent), it is still like His in one important respect: it requires a humble submission to the will of God.

Group 2: Jesus' Temptation (Mark 1:12, 13)

1. Review for the class the three temptations placed before Jesus, using Matthew's account (Matthew 4:1-11).

2. Why did God allow His Son to suffer this ordeal? Read Hebrews 4:15; 5:8.

3. What model do you find here for avoiding temptation in your own lives?

Group 3: The Calling of the First Disciples (Mark 1:16-20; John 1:35-42)

1. It would be difficult for us to understand the immediate response of these first disciples without knowing about an earlier meeting that they had with Jesus. Read about that meeting in John 1:35-42.

2. When Jesus called the disciples by the Sea of Galilee, what might have been some of the obstacles and uncertainties that would have prevented them from following Him?

3. Explain the significance of Jesus' call to be "fishers of men" for the disciples and for us.

Into Life

Ask three or four members of the class to report on this topic: "My Story—How My Relationship With God Began." (It would probably be better to assign this a few days prior to class.) Who were the principle people involved? What were the key events? Did you respond immediately or did the process take time?

After these testimonies, remind the class that people are called or challenged to follow Jesus in a variety of ways. This was true in Jesus' day and it is true today. Then discuss the following questions:

1. Jesus calls us to follow Him. What do you think it means to "follow Jesus"?

2. Jesus not only calls us to follow Him, but He also calls us to be "fishers of men." What are some practical ways to accomplish this challenge in today's culture? What are some methods that have helped you become a more effective "fisher of men"? What methods for doing this have you observed in other Christians?

Close with a prayer for greater wisdom and effectiveness in fulfilling Jesus' call to follow Him and become "fishers of men."

Let's Talk It Over

The questions on this page are designed to encourage review of the lesson Scriptures and to promote discussion of the lesson by the class. The answers provided are only discussion starters. Let your class talk it over from there.

1. John the Baptist provides us with a beautiful example of humble service on behalf of Jesus Christ. What are some aspects of this humble service that we should imitate?

John was hesitant to baptize Jesus, knowing of Jesus' superior character. Yet when Jesus made it clear that He wanted John to baptize Him, John promptly obeyed. We also may hesitate at times to perform certain tasks that we do not fully understand. For example, we may be asked to accept a job in the church for which we feel poorly qualified. But if God's leading seems to indicate that He wants us to do it, we must humbly obey. Another aspect of John's humble service was his willingness to let all the attention and glory be focused on Jesus. John declared, "He must increase, but I must decrease" (John 3:30). We likewise must be willing to forgo any glory for our spiritual labors, so that attention may be fully focused on Jesus.

2. Why did Satan choose the very beginning of Jesus' ministry as the time to launch such a barrage of temptations at Him?

We should notice that the temptations occurred immediately after Jesus' baptism. Satan loves to assault us when we are fresh from a spiritual victory, for it is a time when pride and self-satisfaction can make us vulnerable. Another possibility is that these temptations constituted merely the opening salvos of a relentless attack that lasted throughout Jesus' ministry. Luke 4:13 tells us that after this series of temptations, the devil "departed from him for a season," or "left him until an opportune time" (*New International Version*). It was surely not long afterward that Satan launched his next attack. We know that he later influenced both Peter (Matthew 16:21-23) and Judas Iscariot (John 13:2) to thwart the ministry of Jesus.

3. How does the incident of Jesus' calling Peter, Andrew, James, and John illustrate the way the Gospels fit together?

The Gospel of John describes Jesus' first encounter with Andrew and then Peter (John 1:35-42). It is likely that He met James and John on the same occasion. (John may have been the other disciple besides Andrew referred to in verse 35.) Jesus made a strong impression on them, but He did not yet call them to leave their fishing and follow Him. Today's text records a somewhat later occasion. The earlier impression Jesus made on these men explains how they so readily responded to His invitation to become "fishers of men." This illustration shows that the Gospels are accounts that complement, rather than contradict, one another.

4. Baptism requires a humble submission to the will of God. How can Jesus' example of submission to baptism be an encouragement to people who hesitate to be baptized today?

The Son of God, pure and sinless, submitted to baptism. He who had created man and water allowed a man's hands to lower Him under the water of the Jordan River. The One whose death, burial, and resurrection give significance to baptism humbly demonstrated the importance of obedience in baptism. Many today who hesitate to be baptized view it as a matter of inconvenience and embarrassment. They find the prospect of matted hair and wet, clinging robes unappealing. Some may fear getting water in their nose and mouth and coming up gasping and sputtering. We should remember that Jesus had far more legitimate reasons than these for not being baptized. Yet He came to John at the Jordan and quietly submitted to this act. People today should be willing to do likewise.

5. We all have unique opportunities for personal evangelism. How can we put this in terms of "fishing for men"?

We need to realize that there are "fishing holes" to which only we have access. There are "fish" for which we alone know the right "bait" to use. In our place of employment, for example, we may come into contact with people who quite possibly have no other Christian acquaintances. Because we work with them, we have the opportunity that no other believer does to develop a friendship with them. Other possible "fishing holes" are our neighborhood, community service group, recreational group, and our circle of friends. When we contemplate all the exclusive "fishing holes" to which we have access, it can be a bit overwhelming. It should drive us to our knees to seek God's guidance and strength for our "fishing" efforts.

Spring Quarter, 1998

The Gospel of Action (Mark)

Special Features

Lessons

Unit 1: Early Ministry of Jesus

Unit 2: Death and Resurrection of Jesus

Unit 3: The Teachings of Jesus

About these lessons

This quarter's lessons are taken from the Gospel of Mark. Mark's record is referred to as "the Gospel of Action," because he places greater emphasis upon what Jesus did than upon what He said. Mark moves rapidly from one incident to another, often using the word "straightway" or "immediately." He challenges us with a Christ who is active, but never too busy to show compassion toward those in need.

Mar 8

Mar 15

Mar 22

Mar 29

Apr 5

Apr 12

Apr 19

Apr 26

May 3

May 10

May 17

May 24

May 31

Quarterly Quiz

The questions on this page may be used in several ways: as a pretest at the beginning of the quarter; as a review at the end of the quarter; or as a review after each lesson. The questions are based on the Scripture text of each lesson (King James Version). **The answers are on page 230.**

Lesson 1

1. In what city did Jesus cast out a demon on the Sabbath? *Mark 1:21*
2. Jesus told the man whom He healed of leprosy to show himself to the (Pharisees, priest, disciples). *Mark 1:44*

Lesson 2

1. How did the four men in Capernaum get their sick friend to Jesus? *Mark 2:4*
2. What were Jesus' first words to the sick man? *Mark 2:5*

Lesson 3

1. What important position did Jairus hold? *Mark 5:22*
2. Name the three disciples who accompanied Jesus to Jairus's house. *Mark 5:37*
3. How old was Jairus's daughter at the time of this miracle? *Mark 5:42*

Lesson 4

1. Near what city did Jesus question His disciples concerning who He is? *Mark 8:27*
2. Fill in these blanks: "What shall it _____ a man, if he shall _____ the whole _____, and lose his own _____?" *Mark 8:36*

Lesson 5

1. How many disciples did Jesus send to get a colt? *Mark 11:1, 2*
2. The people shouted, "Blessed be the kingdom of our father _____." *Mark 11:10*
3. Jesus spoke of God's house as the house of (joy, worship, prayer). *Mark 11:17*

Lesson 6

1. At the crucifixion, who said, "Truly this man was the Son of God"? *Mark 15:39*
2. What question were the women asking themselves as they approached Jesus' tomb? *Mark 16:3*

Lesson 7

1. In Jesus' parable of the husbandmen, the husbandmen mistreated every servant that the owner sent. T/F *Mark 12:2-5*
2. Jesus quoted this Scripture: "The _____ which the builders rejected is become the _____ of the _____." *Mark 12:10*

Lesson 8

1. In the upper room, Jesus pronounced woe upon the man by whom the Son of man is _____. *Mark 14:21*
2. Jesus told the disciples concerning the cup, "This is my _____ of the new _____." *Mark 14:24*

Lesson 9

1. Name the four main types of soils into which the sower's seed fell. *Mark 4:3-8*
2. Name the three levels of yield produced by the good soil. *Mark 4:8*
3. Which seed did Jesus describe as "less than all the seeds"? *Mark 4:31*

Lesson 10

1. Whom did the scribes and Pharisees see eating with unwashed hands? *Mark 7:2*
2. Jesus said that the scribes and Pharisees had rejected the _____ of God in order to keep their _____. *Mark 7:9*
3. According to Jesus, what prophet prophesied of the scribes and Pharisees' hypocrisy? *Mark 7:6*

Lesson 11

1. The (disciples, Pharisees, Sadducees) asked Jesus, "Is it lawful for a man to put away his wife?" *Mark 10:2*
2. Jesus said that Moses' precept concerning divorce was given because of the "_____ of your _____." *Mark 10:5*

Lesson 12

1. Which two disciples asked Jesus about the chief seats in His kingdom? *Mark 10:35, 37*
2. The other ten disciples were unaware of James and John's request. T/F *Mark 10:41*
3. According to Jesus, the chiefest shall be _____ of all. *Mark 10:44*

Lesson 13

1. Name the four disciples who questioned Jesus concerning future events. *Mark 13:3*
2. Jesus said that when the Son of man comes, He will send His _____ and gather His _____ from the four winds. *Mark 13:27*
3. What did Jesus describe as that which "shall not pass away"? *Mark 13:31*

Prepare for Action!

by John W. Wade

FOR THE FIRST TIME IN SEVERAL YEARS, an entire quarter's lessons will be based on "the Gospel of Action"—Mark. The second Gospel is sometimes neglected because it is the shortest, and because much of its contents are found in Matthew and Luke. Some evidence indicates that Mark was written prior to the destruction of Jerusalem in A.D. 70. Tradition holds that Mark wrote his Gospel while in Rome or at least with Roman Christians in mind. This is believed to be one reason why Mark's Gospel is one of action (frequently showing Jesus engaged in doing works and miracles), since the Romans were a busy, active people. Mark's Gospel does not include any material concerning the birth of Christ; instead, Mark emphasizes the final week of Jesus' ministry, which fills more than a third of his Gospel (six of the sixteen chapters).

Unit 1. Early Ministry of Jesus

Our study of Mark, which contains fourteen lessons,* is divided into three units, each emphasizing a different aspect of Jesus' life and ministry. Five lessons, dealing with the early ministry of Jesus, comprise Unit 1. **Lesson 13** of the previous quarter (the March 1 lesson) told of Jesus' baptism and His calling of the first disciples. A highlight of the lesson was the message of affirmation spoken by God at Jesus' baptism: "Thou art my beloved Son, in whom I am well pleased" (Mark 1:11).

Lesson 1 of our Spring Quarter informs us about Jesus' early Galilean ministry, during which He performed several miracles of healing. The ones included in this study are the casting out of an unclean spirit in the synagogue at Capernaum, the healing of many after sunset, and the cleansing of a leper. As a result of these miracles, Jesus received the enthusiastic support of the people, "insomuch that [He] could no more openly enter into the city" (Mark 1:45).

Lesson 2 mentions some of the opposition that began to arise from the Jewish religious leaders. Before healing a paralytic, Jesus forgave the man his sins, arousing the ire of the scribes who witnessed the incident. This opposition was intensified when Jesus healed a man on the Sabbath. Jesus' critics were so angered by this miracle that the Pharisees and Herodians (who were normally bitter enemies) began plotting how they might get rid of Him.

Lesson 3 relates how Jairus, one of the rulers of the synagogue, came to Jesus on behalf of his dying daughter. The account of Jesus' raising her from the dead is one of the most precious stories in the Gospel of Mark.

Lesson 4, the final lesson in Unit 1, tells of Peter's Good Confession that Jesus is the Christ. Immediately after this, Jesus began to tell His disciples in the clearest language that He must "suffer many things" and be killed by the religious leaders (Mark 8:31). We also read of Jesus' challenge to deny self, take up the cross, and follow Him. The urgency of His call has not diminished with the passing of time. In the present hour, it is more crucial than ever that followers of Jesus "glory . . . in the cross" as did Paul (Galatians 6:14).

Unit 2. Death and Resurrection of Jesus

Unit 2 selects those passages from Mark that carry the story of the last week of Jesus' life from the triumphal entry to His resurrection.

Lesson 5 tells of Jesus' triumphal entry on what we have come to call Palm Sunday, and His return to Jerusalem the next day to cleanse the temple.

The subject of **Lesson 6** is the glorious Easter story, highlighting the familiar account of Jesus' death and resurrection—a message of hope that never grows old.

The final two lessons in this unit give us some important insights into the meaning of Jesus' death. **Lesson 7** is based on the parable of the wicked husbandmen. The religious leaders recognized that its contents were aimed squarely at them. The parable intensified their determination to get rid of Jesus.

Lesson 8 tells of the institution of the Lord's Supper, and of Jesus' announcement of the New Covenant.

Unit 3. The Teachings of Jesus

The last five lessons of the quarter give us samples of Jesus' teachings from Mark. **Lesson 9** includes the parable of the sower and two shorter parables, all of which highlight important truths about Jesus' kingdom. They provide examples of Jesus' effective use of parables.

Lesson 10 tells how certain Pharisees and scribes came to Jesus, complaining that His disciples had failed to observe some of the Jewish dietary laws by eating with unwashed hands.

Jesus used this complaint as an opportunity to expose the hypocrisy of His critics.

Lesson 11 deals with Jesus' teaching on marriage and divorce. This was a controversial issue in Jesus' day, and may be so in your class. Be sure to stress, as Jesus did, God's plan for marriage "from the beginning."

Every society has certain standards by which it measures greatness. In **Lesson 12** Jesus sets forth the principle by which greatness in His kingdom is defined: service to others. The disciples of Jesus had difficulty grasping this concept, for it was so different from the thinking of the culture around them. His standard of greatness still contrasts sharply with those by which our society is often guided. As Christians we must resolve to be guided by our Savior, not by our surroundings.

The final lesson of the quarter deals with eschatology—a word meaning "the study of last things." In this lesson Jesus deals with two issues: one is the immediate future, which includes the destruction of Jerusalem and its magnificent temple; the second looks to the end of history, when Jesus will come to claim His own. Since some hold certain views about this subject rather strongly, you will need to handle this lesson diplomatically. Be sure that both the certainty of Christ's return and the need for Christians to be prepared daily for it are stressed.

Mark's "Gospel of Action" is quite appropriate for the busy, hectic, nonstop world in which many live. Make sure your students appreciate that Jesus is more than able to keep pace with our schedules. The key issue is whether we are keeping pace with what He expects of His followers.

---

*Teachers should note the special arrangement of the lessons for both the Winter and Spring Quarters. Normally, each three-month period has thirteen Sundays, and our lesson manual thus has thirteen lessons, a lesson for each Sunday. However, the Winter Quarter (December, January, February, 1997) had only twelve Sundays, and the Spring Quarter (March, April, May, 1998) has fourteen. In order to have thirteen lessons in each quarter, we took the first lesson of the Spring Quarter (the March 1 lesson) and included it in the Winter Quarter as Lesson 13. Therefore, Lesson 13 was the first lesson of the study on "The Gospel of Action (Mark)." The first lesson in the Spring Quarter is for March 8.

OUTLINE OF MARK
(noting where this quarter's lessons fit in
Jesus' ministry)

INTRODUCTION (Mark 1:1-13)

I. THE FULL TIDE OF CHRIST'S POPULARITY IN GALILEE (Mark 1:14—6:56)

Lesson 1—Jesus' Words and Works
Lesson 2—Jesus' Authority Established
Lesson 3—Jesus' Power Demonstrated
Lesson 9—Teaching in Parables

II. JESUS SEEKS RELIEF FROM THE EXCITEMENT OF GALILEE, AND CONTINUES THE SPECIAL TRAINING OF THE TWELVE (Mark 7:1—9:50)

Lesson 4—Jesus' Identity and Mission
Lesson 10—Traditions or God?
Lesson 12—True Greatness

III. THE LORD GOES TO MEET HIS DESTINY IN JERUSALEM (Mark 10:1-52)

Lesson 11—Marriage and Divorce
Lesson 12—True Greatness

IV. THE CHALLENGE TO JERUSALEM AND THE GREAT CONFLICT WITH THE ENEMIES OF CHRIST (Mark 11:1—12:44)

Lesson 5—Jesus Enters Jerusalem
Lesson 7—Jesus is Rejected

V. THE DOOM OF JERUSALEM AND OF THE WORLD FORETOLD (Mark 13:1-37)

Lesson 13—Help for the Future

VI. THE TRIUMPH OF THE ENEMIES OF CHRIST (Mark 14:1—15:47)

Lesson 6—Jesus Died and Lives Again!
Lesson 8—Jesus Gives the New Covenant

VII. THE TRIUMPH OF JESUS OVER HIS ENEMIES AND THE COMMISSION TO TAKE THE WORLD FOR HIM (Mark 16:1-20)

Lesson 6—Jesus Died and Lives Again!

Outline taken from Mark in the *Standard Bible Commentary* series (Cincinnati: Standard Publishing, 1968)

A Foundation for Life

by Carl Bridges, Jr.

ARK'S GOSPEL STANDS OUT from the other three in several ways. To begin with, it is the shortest; an average reader can read the English version of it in a couple of hours. Contrary to what one might expect, though, Mark does not write in an abbreviated or sketchy style. Mark's account often appears more detailed and full of local color when compared with the other Gospels.

In the record of the feeding of the five thousand, for example, only Mark records that Jesus had His disciples seat the people "upon the *green grass*" (6:39). For another example, Matthew uses (in the Greek text) 135 words to tell the story of the Gadarene demoniac, Luke, 293, and Mark, 328. The brevity of Mark's Gospel comes from the writer's selection of material, not from any effort to condense or abbreviate.

A Christ of Action

Mark's Gospel stands apart from the others in another way: Mark portrays Jesus as a doer more than a talker, as a miracle worker more than a teacher. This is not to say that Mark's Jesus does not teach; the collection of parables in chapter four should put that idea to rest. But Matthew structures his Gospel around five long collections of Jesus' teachings; Luke scatters large amounts of teaching throughout his Gospel; and John contains several long discourses of Jesus. Compared with these, Jesus, as Mark presents Him, does not say as much.

Mark clearly presents Jesus as a Christ of action, moving quickly from one deed of power to another. He uses a word meaning "immediately" (often rendered "straightway" in the *King James Version*) in all but three chapters of the Gospel, and more than forty times in all.

Structure of the Gospel

Scholars disagree on the best way to outline Mark's Gospel. This is a sure sign that the Gospel does not easily lend itself to any attempt to analyze its structure. One way to outline the book regards Peter's confession in 8:27-30 as the key turning point. Up to that time, Jesus had done signs and wonders, not neglecting to teach the crowds and His followers, but mainly demonstrating who He is by displaying God's power at work in Him. In Caesarea Philippi, He asked the disciples who they thought He was, and Peter answered, "Thou art the Christ."

"And he began," Mark writes at this crucial point, "to teach them, that the Son of man must suffer many things, and be rejected of the elders, and of the chief priests, and scribes, and be killed, and after three days rise again" (8:31). He then notes (v. 32) that Jesus "spake that saying openly" (or "plainly," in the *New International Version*). Although the disciples did not immediately understand that both Jesus and His followers cannot obtain glory except through suffering, Jesus kept trying to convince them. In chapters fourteen and fifteen, Mark describes the betrayal, arrest, trial, and crucifixion of Jesus—the very suffering that He predicted.

Thus Peter's Good Confession serves to emphasize the purpose for which Jesus came into the world. "Thou art the Christ" could indeed be considered the theme of the Gospel of Mark.

Although Peter's confession of Jesus as Messiah is a crucial point in Mark's account, the title "Son of God" is also important. Three times in the book, an individual solemnly declares that Jesus is God's Son. First, at His baptism the Father declared, "Thou art my beloved Son" (1:11). Then, not long after Peter's confession, the Father uttered similar words on the mountain of transfiguration: "This is my beloved Son: hear him" (9:7). And finally, when Jesus breathed His last, a pagan centurion said, "Truly this man was the Son of God" (15:39). The theme of Jesus' sonship appears at key points in Mark's Gospel; even the demons acknowledged Him as God's Son (3:11; 5:7).

Authorship

Bringing up the question of who wrote the second Gospel may appear foolish, since we have known it as the Gospel of Mark for centuries. It is important to note, however, that evidence for Mark's authorship is abundant in writings from early church history. The earliest evidence we have comes from the church historian Eusebius, who wrote in the fourth century. Using material written by a second-century scholar named Papias, Eusebius passed on to his readers the tradition that the Gospel contained Peter's preaching as recorded by Mark. In Peter's later years, Eusebius says, Peter lived and worked in Rome, and used Mark as a secretary and interpreter. After Peter's death, Mark wrote an accurate account, "though not in order," of what Peter used to say about Jesus when he preached or taught. Later writers claimed that Mark wrote his Gospel while Peter was still alive. Other early church Fathers, including Justin Martyr, Irenaeus, Clement of Alexandria, Tertullian, Origen, and Jerome all attest to Mark's authorship of this Gospel.

Mark is mentioned nine times in the New Testament. His name appears in different forms, sometimes as "Mark" or "Marcus," sometimes as "John," and also as "John, whose surname was Mark" (Acts 12:12, 25; 13:5, 13; 15:37-39; Colossians 4:10; 2 Timothy 4:11; Philemon 24; 1 Peter 5:13). John was his Jewish name; Mark was his Roman name.

There is a lot more one could say on this issue, but for now we can state that the evidence for Mark's authorship of the second Gospel is sound. We have in his Gospel a record, written under the inspiration of the Holy Spirit, of the life and ministry of Jesus, with particular emphasis upon His works of power and upon His crucifixion and resurrection. The purpose of this record is to lead men and women to believe and obey the gospel, through which they can be saved from condemnation (Mark 16:15, 16).

Gospel, Not Biography

For a long time, many Bible students have emphasized the fact that the Gospels are not strictly biographies. By this they imply that the ordinary details that we expect to find in a biography do not appear in the Gospels. For example, we know little about Jesus' early years. Although we know His brothers' names (Mark 6:3), we do not know the name of any one of His sisters (that He had sisters is clear from Mark 6:3). Did Joseph die young, as some have inferred from the fact that he no longer appears in the record after the incident recorded in Luke 2:41-52? However much we would like to know these facts, the Gospel writers do not tell us. This is because these men have not written merely to satisfy our curiosity. What matters to them is Jesus' identity as the Son of God and what He did to verify that identity: working miracles, teaching, dying, and conquering death.

Here is where Mark's Gospel shows the essence of what a Gospel is. Someone has called Mark's Gospel "a passion narrative [that is, a description of Jesus' suffering and death] with an extended introduction." Even if that remark overstates the case, it emphasizes the point that for Mark, the death and resurrection of Jesus stand as the most pivotal events. Everything in the Gospel record leads up to Jesus' death, and everything in the Christian life flows from His resurrection. In Mark's Gospel we see the strong

Son of God coming into the world, healing and teaching, suffering and dying, and then rising to life and leaving an empty tomb. These facts, told in a simple, unadorned style, give us the firmest of foundations on which to build our lives.

The Use of a Gospel

Apparently the Gospels were composed as the first generation of Christians grew older and realized that their firsthand testimony would not be available much longer. They sought to preserve the testimony of the people whom Luke calls "eyewitnesses, and ministers of the word" (Luke 1:2) by committing their words to writing for all time.

Today the Gospels represent the best way to get acquainted with Jesus. Our faith does not consist of opinions, guesses, or philosophical ideas. We have placed our faith in a Person—the Son of God who lived among us, died for our sins, and rose again. What better way to understand Him than to read the books that His earliest followers wrote about Him?

When people express interest in the Christian faith to me, the first thing I do is recommend that they read a Gospel, usually the Gospel of Mark. Here they will find a clear, brief, factual statement of who Jesus is. This Gospel of action will give them a foundation for life.

Mark's Portrait of Jesus

by Marion W. Henderson

IT IS GENERALLY CONCEDED that Matthew wrote to convince the Jews that Jesus was the long-awaited Messiah. This is indicated by his emphasis upon the fulfillment of prophecy, and by his consistent use of Jewish terminology (phrases such as "kingdom of heaven" and "son of David") in his narration of the ministry of Jesus. Luke wrote with an appeal to Gentile readers, as seen in his tracing of Jesus' genealogy back to Adam. John's Gospel is generally considered a "universal Gospel," presenting Jesus as the Savior for all people. Mark wrote to appeal to the practical Roman mind, which measured achievements in terms of deeds rather than words. Thus Mark sought to establish the lordship of Jesus by focusing on what He did rather than what He said.

This is not to say that Jesus' words and His claims concerning Himself are not important in Mark's Gospel. Mark includes Jesus' seaside parables (4:1-34) and His discourse on future events (13:1-37). The divinity of Jesus is also clearly set forth in Mark's identification of Jesus as the "Son of God" (1:1, 11; 3:11; 5:7; 9:7; 14:61, 62; 15:39) and as the "Son of man." This latter title appears most often in Mark (fourteen times) as the one used by Jesus to identify Himself. It calls attention both to Jesus' humanity and His deity.

However, Mark's portrait of Jesus can best be seen through the miracles Jesus performed and in the key events of His ministry that Mark records. In the eighteen specific miracles mentioned by Mark, Jesus demonstrated power over evil spirits, the elements of nature, and a variety of diseases and physical afflictions.

Divinity in Miracles

Jesus' power over sickness was first manifested in His healing of Peter's mother-in-law (1:29-31). Her fever left her when Jesus took her by the hand. The healing of many sick and demon-possessed in Capernaum (1:32-34), and of those who came from the regions around Palestine (3:7, 8), also demonstrated His power over many kinds of illnesses. In reaching out to these people, Jesus risked the criticism of the religious leaders, who considered such individuals as the leper (1:40-42), the paralytic (2:1-12), and the deaf and dumb (7:31-37) as unclean or as guilty of sin. To show that He did not intend to ignore the Law, Jesus instructed the cleansed leper to show himself to the priest (1:44).

Jesus' mastery over demons also clearly set Him forth as One more powerful than the demon world. On one occasion, the teachers of the Law accused Jesus of casting out demons by Satanic power (3:22). Jesus refuted this charge with the parable of a divided kingdom, and affirmed that He had come to "bind" Satan and "spoil his house" (v. 27).

Divinity and Nature

Jesus' control of nature provided further confirmation of His divinity. He stilled the storm on the Sea of Galilee (4:35-41). He fed five thousand men with five loaves and two fish (6:30-44), and later fed four thousand with seven loaves and a few small fish (8:1-10). He came to His disciples walking on the water during a fierce storm on the Sea of Galilee, and calmed the winds and the waves, to the complete amazement of the twelve (6:45-52). He cursed a fig tree and it withered away (11:12-14, 20, 21).

Divinity in Key Events

Equally significant to Mark's portrait of Jesus are the events that occurred at crucial points in His ministry. The first one recorded by Mark is the baptism of Jesus, when the Father declared, "Thou art my beloved Son, in whom I am well pleased" (1:11).

Following the call of four fishermen to follow Him, Mark records the beginning of Jesus' public ministry in Galilee. His teachings were so fresh and challenging that great crowds were drawn to Him. Jesus' first serious encounter with the Jewish religious leaders occurred when He healed the paralytic who had been let down through the roof by his friends (2:1-12). The teachers of the Law charged Jesus with blasphemy when He forgave the paralytic's sins. Jesus then demonstrated His authority and ability to forgive sins by having the man take up his mat and walk. Since both the forgiveness of sins and the healing of a paralytic required divine power, for Jesus to do one implied that He could do the other (vv. 8-11).

In the region of Caesarea Philippi, Jesus asked His disciples the most important question a person can be asked: "Whom say ye that I am?" The response of Peter, "Thou art the Christ," was precise, and revealed an understanding of Jesus that could come only from the Father in Heaven. Such an insight is crucial in addressing man's relationship with God. Every person who has become a child of God has had to recognize and accept Jesus as the Christ, the Son of God. There can be no compromise on this issue. One either accepts Jesus as the Christ, and as God's only means of saving mankind from sin, or he does not. There has never been any middle ground.

The disciples, however, did not understand all the implications of Jesus' messiahship, particularly His suffering. After Peter's Good Confession, Jesus began to speak "openly" concerning His future suffering, death, and resurrection (8:31, 32). Peter proceeded to rebuke Jesus for having uttered such language, which did not fit with the popular concept of the Messiah. Jesus rebuked Peter, charging that he was no longer looking at the matter from God's point of view, but from man's. Jesus then issued the fundamental principle of cross-bearing. Each disciple is to "take up his cross" and follow Jesus (v. 34). This means the denial of self—of one's hopes and aspirations—and the submission of them all to the will of God.

Six days later, Jesus took Peter, James, and John with Him up a high mountain, and was transfigured before them (9:2-8). Moses and Elijah, representing the Law and the Prophets (respectively), appeared and talked with Jesus. Peter suggested that three tabernacles be built: one for Jesus, one for Moses, and one for Elijah. He wanted to prolong this magnificent, mountaintop experience. However, a cloud overshadowed them all, and the voice of the Father declared, "This is my beloved Son: hear him" (9:7). The message was clear: The Law and the Prophets have had their day; now Jesus stands alone as the Father's final word.

Divinity in Jerusalem

As do the other Gospels, Mark's Gospel records the triumphal entry of Jesus into Jerusalem on the Sunday preceding His death. This was clearly a Messianic demonstration, and was probably designed in part as a final appeal to the people to accept Him as the Messiah on His terms, not theirs. His riding on a donkey seems to have been in keeping with the practice in that day of kings riding on donkeys when they were on a mission of peace, and on horses when they were going to war. Two points should be noted here. First, Jesus was indeed on a mission of peace, for He was to die that man might have peace with God. Second, He was assuming a position of humility as pictured by passages such as those in Isaiah's description of the Suffering Servant. That the people took Jesus' entry to be a Messianic demonstration is indicated by their reference to Psalm 118:25, 26.

One last pivotal event prior to Jesus' crucifixion occurred in the Garden of Gethsemane. It was here that Jesus wrestled with the conflict between His human desires and His divine commitment. His humanity cried out against His becoming sin for mankind, as seen in His desire to have the Father "take away this cup," if possible. Three times Jesus sought the Father's intervention, and three times His commitment to doing the will of the Father prevailed (14:32-39). The divine Son of God, who became flesh and dwelt among us (John 1:14), committed Himself without reservation to go to the cross.

Divinity on the Cross

Mark's account of the arrest, trials, and crucifixion does not differ to any great degree from that of Matthew and Luke. Jesus was arrested in Gethsemane, and taken to the chief priests and elders where He was hurriedly condemned. After being shamefully treated, He was then brought before Pilate, where the Jews urged the Roman governor to condemn Him to death. This was necessary, since the Romans had taken away from the Jews the authority to put a prisoner to death. After some futile and half-hearted attempts to release Jesus, Pilate finally gave in to the Jews' demands to crucify Him.

Mark closes His Gospel with the triumphant message of the resurrection and the final commission of Jesus to His disciples to preach the gospel (16:15, 16). Mark leaves no doubt that Jesus had indeed arisen and that His messiahship was confirmed by His resurrection.

Who Do You Say He Is?

This is the question each of us must address, just as surely as Jesus' own disciples had to address it. Was Jesus simply the son of a carpenter in an obscure village called Nazareth, a town usually referred to with disdain, or was He the divine Son of God? When we look at the portrait of Jesus so beautifully drawn by Mark, we see the most wonderful person who has ever graced this planet. As John put it, "No man hath seen God at any time; the only begotten Son, which is in the bosom of the Father, he hath declared him" (John 1:18). That is to say, one of the purposes of Christ's coming into the world was to reveal God to mankind on the level of human experience, so that we could understand what God is like and what He requires of us to become His sons and daughters.

Jesus is worthy of our praise and adoration. He is the fulfillment of our fondest hopes and dreams. The invitation for us to share in His glory is the underlying message of Mark's Gospel. Thanks be to God for Mark's portrait of Jesus!

Jesus' Works and Words

DEVOTIONAL READING: Acts 9:32-42.

LESSON SCRIPTURE: Mark 1:21-45.

PRINTED TEXT: Mark 1:21-27, 32-34, 40-45.

Mark 1:21-27, 32-34, 40-45

21 And they went into Capernaum; and straightway on the sabbath day he entered into the synagogue, and taught.

22 And they were astonished at his doctrine: for he taught them as one that had authority, and not as the scribes.

23 And there was in their synagogue a man with an unclean spirit; and he cried out,

24 Saying, Let us alone; what have we to do with thee, thou Jesus of Nazareth? art thou come to destroy us? I know thee who thou art, the Holy One of God.

25 And Jesus rebuked him, saying, Hold thy peace, and come out of him.

26 And when the unclean spirit had torn him, and cried with a loud voice, he came out of him.

27 And they were all amazed, insomuch that they questioned among themselves, saying, What thing is this? what new doctrine is this? for with authority commandeth he even the unclean spirits, and they do obey him.

. . . .

32 And at even, when the sun did set, they brought unto him all that were diseased, and them that were possessed with devils.

33 And all the city was gathered together at the door.

34 And he healed many that were sick of divers diseases, and cast out many devils; and suffered not the devils to speak, because they knew him.

. . . .

40 And there came a leper to him, beseeching him, and kneeling down to him, and saying unto him, If thou wilt, thou canst make me clean.

41 And Jesus, moved with compassion, put forth his hand, and touched him, and saith unto him, I will; be thou clean.

42 And as soon as he had spoken, immediately the leprosy departed from him, and he was cleansed.

43 And he straitly charged him, and forthwith sent him away;

44 And saith unto him, See thou say nothing to any man: but go thy way, show thyself to the priest, and offer for thy cleansing those things which Moses commanded, for a testimony unto them.

45 But he went out, and began to publish it much, and to blaze abroad the matter, insomuch that Jesus could no more openly enter into the city, but was without in desert places: and they came to him from every quarter.

GOLDEN TEXT: Jesus, moved with compassion, put forth his hand, and touched him, and saith unto him, . . . be thou clean.—Mark 1:41.

The Gospel of Action (Mark)
Unit 1: Early Ministry of Jesus
(Lessons 1-4)

Lesson Aims

After this lesson, students should be able to:

1. Describe the kinds of miracles that Jesus performed in today's text.

2. Explain what made Jesus' words and works unique.

3. Select a way to show the love of Christ, through both words and works, to a specific individual this week.

Lesson Outline

INTRODUCTION
  A. Hiding or Seeking the Afflicted?
  B. Lesson Background
  I. JESUS IN CAPERNAUM (Mark 1:21-27)
    A. Jesus Teaches (vv. 21, 22)
    B. Jesus Casts Out a Demon (vv. 23-26)
    C. The People's Response (v. 27)
      Communication and "Clout"
 II. JESUS' GROWING POPULARITY (Mark 1:32-34)
    A. Afflicted Brought to Jesus (vv. 32, 33)
    B. Afflicted Healed by Jesus (v. 34)
III. JESUS HEALS A LEPER (Mark 1:40-45)
    A. The Leper Approaches Jesus (v. 40)
    B. Jesus Heals the Leper (vv. 41, 42)
    C. Jesus Instructs the Leper (vv. 43-45)
      "It's Bubbling!"
CONCLUSION
  A. Divine Healing
  B. The Needs Around Us
  C. Prayer
  D. Thought to Remember

Use the visual for Lesson 1 in the visuals packet (map of Palestine) to display throughout the quarter. It is shown on page 236.

Introduction

A. Hiding or Seeking the Afflicted?

When Marie Antoinette traveled across France to be crowned queen, word was sent out that all the handicapped, the beggars, and other unsightly persons were to be removed from the travel route. She did not wish to be distressed by signs of suffering along the way.

Hundreds of years before this, another Ruler came who, from the very beginning of His min-

istry, sought out the lame, the blind, the lepers, and the demon-possessed. To these He brought healing, new life, and hope.

Both rulers were eventually executed, she by the guillotine and He on a cross. History remembers Marie Antoinette only as a foolish and arrogant queen. Jesus, on the other hand, lives on in the hearts of men and women as their divine Savior and King.

B. Lesson Background

Last week's lesson text covered the baptism and temptation of Jesus, and concluded with His return to Galilee and the calling of Peter, Andrew, James, and John to follow Him. It is likely that during this period He also called the others who would become part of the twelve apostles. After this, Jesus began His public ministry, using Capernaum as His headquarters. During the early part of this period, His ministry was relatively free of controversy, and His teaching and miracles led to a growing popularity among the people.

I. Jesus in Capernaum
(Mark 1:21-27)

A. Jesus Teaches (vv. 21, 22)

21, 22. And they went into Capernaum; and straightway on the sabbath day he entered into the synagogue, and taught. And they were astonished at his doctrine: for he taught them as one that had authority, and not as the scribes.

Jesus chose *Capernaum* as the headquarters for His ministry in Galilee, not only because several of His disciples were from this vicinity, but also because it was the center of a sizable population and would thus provide a large audience for His teaching. As was Jesus' usual practice, He attended the worship at the local *synagogue* on the *sabbath day*. Ordinarily a synagogue did not have a permanent teacher, or rabbi, and so it was a common custom to ask a visiting teacher to speak to the congregation. Jesus received such an invitation to address those present.

Mark notes that the people were *astonished* at Jesus' *doctrine*, or teaching. Jesus' teaching was so very different from what the people normally heard in the synagogue. This applied not only to the content of His teaching, but also to His manner of teaching. Many knew Jesus as the son of a carpenter and as someone who lacked any formal theological training. Yet He spoke with *authority*, not as a typical rabbi or scribe, who based his teachings on tradition and on the teachings of other scribes. Jesus had no need to cite human authorities to support His teaching; it came directly from the mind of God.

B. Jesus Casts Out a Demon

(vv. 23-26)

23. And there was in their synagogue a man with an unclean spirit; and he cried out.

Demon possession is one of the more controversial subjects in Jesus' ministry. Many people in Jesus' day believed that they were surrounded by a host of evil beings. We are told of a number of encounters between Jesus and these forces of evil. These encounters often led to strange behavior on the part of the person who was demon-possessed. It would appear that this man in the synagogue was at first acting "normally," or else he would not have been permitted to enter the synagogue. Only now did the *unclean spirit* choose to reveal his presence by suddenly crying out.

Some ancient cultures believed demons to be responsible for most illnesses. They devised numerous and elaborate rituals to ward off the demons or appease them. The Gospel writers, however, make a clear distinction between demon possession and illness. Mark 1:34, which is part of our printed text, is one example.

Some Bible students believe that demon possession existed only in Jesus' day, because of the singular threat that Jesus posed to Satan's evil dominion. Realizing what was at stake, Satan launched an all-out attack on Jesus, hoping to counter and destroy His ministry. Others hold that demon possession existed not only in Jesus' day but still exists, especially among primitive peoples. Many missionaries who are introducing the gospel to these people for the first time relate experiences that appear unexplainable except by some manifestation of demon possession.

The presence of both the Son of God and a demon-possessed man in the Capernaum synagogue brought Heaven and Hell in direct conflict. Confronted by Jesus, the demon, speaking through its victim, *cried out* in desperation.

24. Saying, Let us alone; what have we to do with thee, thou Jesus of Nazareth? art thou come to destroy us? I know thee who thou art, the Holy One of God.

The use of *us* and *we* indicates that the demon spoke for his evil cohorts. That many demons could possess someone is clear from the case of the Gadarene demoniac (Mark 5:6-9). The demon understood, better than did Jesus' audience, that the nature of His kingdom threatened the very existence of the evil realm and its demonic citizens. Similar responses of demon-possessed persons to Jesus are recorded elsewhere in the Gospel accounts (see Mark 3:11; 5:7; Luke 4:41).

How to Say It

CAPERNAUM. Kuh-*per*-nay-um.
GADARENE. *Gad*-uh-reen.
SYNAGOGUE. *Sin*-uh-gog.

25, 26. And Jesus rebuked him, saying, Hold thy peace, and come out of him. And when the unclean spirit had torn him, and cried with a loud voice, he came out of him.

Jesus' initial response to the demon was to say, *Hold thy peace.* One reason Jesus silenced the demon was that He had a timetable for announcing His deity, and the demon's statement was premature. Also, receiving such testimony might have been taken as a sign that Jesus was willing to accept the testimony of demons. As it was, Jesus' enemies accused Him of being in league with the devil (Matthew 12:24).

This incident clearly demonstrated Jesus' power over the forces of darkness. Beginning with His temptations, Jesus was involved in a series of confrontations with Satan or some of his cohorts. In each of these situations, Jesus emerged as the clear winner. (This much must be said for Satan: he is persistent! This should be a word of caution to us when we seem to have won a victory over Satan.)

The *unclean spirit* did not leave the man without one last struggle. The man was *torn*, or made to go into violent convulsions. The *New International Version* translates this, "The evil spirit shook the man violently." Such a ferocious reaction was not unusual when an evil spirit left a person. The most dramatic demonic response to Jesus' authority occurred when the evil spirits controlling the Gadarene demoniac entered into a herd of swine and plunged into the Sea of Galilee (Mark 5:13).

C. The People's Response (v. 27)

27. And they were all amazed, insomuch that they questioned among themselves, saying, What thing is this? what new doctrine is this? for with authority commandeth he even the unclean spirits, and they do obey him.

VISUALS FOR THESE LESSONS

The *Adult Visuals* packet contains classroom-size visuals designed for use with the lessons in the Spring Quarter. The packet is available from your supplier. Order No. 392.

The people who witnessed this miracle were *amazed*. Some of them may have been familiar with the practice of exorcism (for this was practiced in many ancient cultures), but those exorcists used all kinds of rituals and incantations. In addition, the rituals were often long and drawn out, and frequently ended in failure. Jesus, in bold contrast, cast out a demon instantly, and with complete and indisputable success. No wonder the people began to talk about a *new doctrine* and about the *authority* Jesus had demonstrated over the demons! Even without all the devices of modern media to publicize this miracle, word quickly spread throughout Galilee (v. 28).

COMMUNICATION AND "CLOUT"

We arrived home from work one evening to find water three inches deep all over our basement floor. I immediately reported this to workers in the street outside who were lining the sewer system with a core of "indestructible" material that had temporarily blocked the drain line from our house. In just minutes, the friendly foreman of the job was offering us a fair settlement for the clean-up expense we would incur. (Nothing was damaged, just wet.)

A conversation ensued with this foreman that was most informative and pleasant. I was impressed with his communication skills, as well as with his congeniality. Reflecting on the experience now, I realize why my impression was so favorable. This foreman spoke with authority. He had "clout"—both the position and the authorization to compensate immediately anyone who had a grievance. I respected that power. He "taught" me with confidence, because he knew what he was talking about. Training and experience qualified him, but he also possessed the right kind of personality. He was believable and not arrogant. He conveyed a spirit of humility and respect.

Jesus' hearers were impressed with His authority (Mark 1:27). His "clout" included

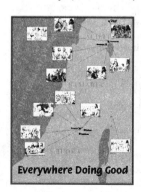

Everywhere Doing Good

visual for
lesson 1

power over unclean spirits. His confidence resulted from His divine origin and His supernatural knowledge. Yet Jesus was not arrogant or "showy"—the boldness of His convictions was coupled with His unassuming demeanor. Such communication was eloquent, but also clear and irresistible. Would that Christians today could communicate in such a manner!   —R. W. B.

II. Jesus' Growing Popularity (Mark 1:32-34)

A. Afflicted Brought to Jesus (vv. 32, 33)

32, 33. And at even, when the sun did set, they brought unto him all that were diseased, and them that were possessed with devils. And all the city was gathered together at the door.

After casting out the demon from the man in the synagogue, Jesus went to the home of Simon Peter. There He healed Peter's mother-in-law of a fever (vv. 29-31).

Word of Jesus' whereabouts spread rapidly, and the house was quickly surrounded by people bringing others in great need. Some were *diseased,* or suffering from various illnesses; others were *possessed with devils.* The people waited until *the sun did set,* in order to avoid breaking any Sabbath regulations (a day was reckoned from sundown to sundown).

B. Afflicted Healed by Jesus (v. 34)

34. And he healed many that were sick of divers diseases, and cast out many devils; and suffered not the devils to speak, because they knew him.

Both this verse and the preceding verse make a distinction between treating *divers*, or different, *diseases* and casting out *devils.* Just as Jesus silenced the unclean spirit in the synagogue, here He *suffered not the devils to speak.*

III. Jesus Heals a Leper (Mark 1:40-45)

In the midst of these busy activities, Jesus arose early one morning and went to a spot where He could be away from the crowd. There He engaged in a period of prayer. Before long, Peter and some others found Jesus and told Him, "All men seek for thee" (v. 37). Jesus then announced His intention to travel into the "next towns" and minister there (v. 38).

A. The Leper Approaches Jesus (v. 40)

40. And there came a leper to him, beseeching him, and kneeling down to him, and saying unto him, If thou wilt, thou canst make me clean.

As the Galilean ministry of Jesus continues, Mark now records an encounter of Jesus with a *leper*. Leprosy was a most dreaded disease, perhaps the AIDS of the ancient world. Its symptoms were chronic and debilitating, and there was no known cure for it. Victims were socially isolated, forced to live apart from the rest of the population. In spite of this fact, word of Jesus' healing power somehow reached the leper in our text. Getting to Jesus, however, would cause some problems, since lepers were required to keep away from other people. Apparently this leper either ignored the taboos that restricted him or was able to avoid the crowds.

This man came before Jesus with a notably mature request: *If thou wilt, thou canst make me clean.* He knew that Jesus had the power to heal him, but he did not know whether Jesus willed to heal him. This is an important principle to keep in mind when requesting God for healing today. Though we recognize that God can heal people, we cannot always be sure that this is His will. We must pray *if thou wilt,* submitting the situation to whatever outcome He deems best. Sometimes the testimony of a Christian in the midst of illness possesses a greater impact than one of a healed Christian.

B. Jesus Heals the Leper (vv. 41, 42)

41, 42. And Jesus, moved with compassion, put forth his hand, and touched him, and saith unto him, I will; be thou clean. And as soon as he had spoken, immediately the leprosy departed from him, and he was cleansed.

Jesus did not always physically touch a person whom He was healing. In this case He did, perhaps as a way of visualizing His *compassion*. The Son of God was not reluctant to touch a man considered an "untouchable" in Jewish society. It is noteworthy that touching a leper brought ceremonial uncleanness upon oneself. Perhaps Jesus was not only demonstrating His compassion for the leper; He was identifying with his position as an outcast, for Jesus was also "despised and rejected of men" (Isaiah 53:3).

As with the man possessed by an unclean spirit, Jesus' words produced immediate and visible results. Just *as soon as* He touched the leper and *had spoken* the words *be thou clean,* the *leprosy* was gone.

C. Jesus Instructs the Leper (vv. 43-45)

43, 44. And he straitly charged him, and forthwith sent him away; and saith unto him, See thou say nothing to any man: but go thy way, show thyself to the priest, and offer for thy cleansing those things which Moses commanded, for a testimony unto them.

Jesus did not intend for the man to try to hide the fact that he had been cleansed. His very appearance would have made it quite obvious that he was no longer a leper. All Jesus wanted the man to do was to delay his public announcement of his cure until he had taken the appropriate steps required under the Law of *Moses.* While it is true that Jesus came to teach principles that transcend the Law, He had no intention of setting aside those provisions that protected the health and welfare of the people. Jesus asked the former leper to *show* himself to the *priest* and make the offering required by the Law (Leviticus 14:1-32). This was a reasonable requirement that guarded the health of the populace, and at the same time showed that Jesus was not an irresponsible rebel out to destroy the Mosaic Law.

45. But he went out, and began to publish it much, and to blaze abroad the matter, insomuch that Jesus could no more openly enter into the city, but was without in desert places: and they came to him from every quarter.

The leper came to Jesus in humble faith, yet he immediately proceeded to disobey Him. We can understand his joy at being saved from a virtual death sentence. His disobedience, however, cannot be endorsed. His actions may have seemed minor or even commendable to him, but they soon created problems for Jesus. The excitement created by the leper's story became so great that Jesus had to cut short His ministry in the cities and towns, and retire to *desert places.* This meant that many were denied the blessings of His teaching and His healing, even though people *from every quarter* continued to search for Him. We too need to realize that disobedience, even when well-intentioned, can have undesirable consequences.

"IT'S BUBBLING!"

Remember this old Sunday school chorus from years ago:

It's bubbling; it's bubbling;
  It's bubbling in my soul!
There's singing and laughing
  Since Jesus made me whole.
Folks don't understand it;
  Nor can I keep it quiet.
It's bubbling, bubbling, bubbling, bubbling,
  Bubbling day and night!

The leper in today's text could have sung a song like that when he realized what Jesus had done for him. Though instructed by Jesus to keep his healing quiet, he could not. He had to tell others of his wonderful news.

Does the joy of the Lord bubble up from your heart and soul? Are you singing and laughing in

Christ who makes you whole? Or have you been keeping your good news quiet among folks who don't understand it? The leper spoke though commanded not to; are we silent though we have been commanded to speak?

Remember: "Do not put out the Spirit's fire" (1 Thessalonians 5:19, *New International Version*). Good news is for sharing; let yours bubble over! —R. W. B.

Conclusion
A. Divine Healing

Some religious groups practice faith healing as a part of their doctrine and worship. Others strongly oppose these activities and are accused by the faith healers of lacking faith in God to heal. The truth is that all Christians believe in divine healing. The real issue is how God answers prayer for healing. Some say He does it in a dramatic, public fashion. Others say He works quietly through the skills of medical professionals—doctors, nurses, and technicians. A Christian physician I know expresses it this way: "I treat patients, but God heals them." It is through God's grace that these people are able to develop their healing skills. God has created the potential for the vast array of pharmaceuticals and special equipment that helps expedite healing. Furthermore, He has given men and women the intelligence and the diligence to spend years in developing these tools that are so effective in fighting illnesses.

Those of us who have devoted time and energy in debating whether God heals through dramatic processes or through natural and scientific medicine might be well advised to spend more time caring for the sick. We also need to realize that although Jesus had compassion for the afflicted, His main concern was not over healing physical bodies. His greatest concern was for people's souls. His healing was but one step in the process of bringing lost sinners to God through Him. This also ought to be our great concern. The healing of the souls of men and women is truly divine healing.

B. The Needs Around Us

The example of Jesus' compassion for those with physical ills has inspired Christians across the centuries to be concerned about such persons. Christianity, more than any other major religion, has sought to find ways to comfort and heal the sick. Probably every major city in our country has one or more hospitals or other medical facilities that were started and are still supported by Christians working either in their churches or in independent organizations.

Millions of dollars are contributed by Christians each year to maintain these facilities.

Christians ought to recognize the significant ministry that they can have in one of these facilities. Hospitals, retirement homes, children's homes, and hospice programs can always use volunteers in a variety of ways. Even teenage volunteers are welcome in many facilities.

Needs are often especially great in nursing homes and homes for the aging. Many of the aging are very lonely people. Most of their friends have passed on, and in many cases their families have either moved far away or have practically abandoned them. These people do not demand much and do not expect much. A few minutes visiting with them, running an errand for them, or having a prayer with them "makes their day."

These kinds of service bring an individual a sense of satisfaction in knowing that he or she has helped another fellow human being. But there is a deeper satisfaction that comes from knowing that one has followed the example of the Great Physician.

C. Prayer

Our Father, we rejoice that You have compassion on us, both in our physical afflictions and in our sinful state. We thank You for providing help both for our physical bodies and for our souls. Teach us to turn to Your Son, who gave His life to save us from the wages of sin. Give us wisdom and enthusiasm to share this saving message with others. In Jesus' precious name we pray. Amen.

D. Thought to Remember

Jesus ministered through both words and works. Let us do the same.

Home Daily Bible Readings

Monday, Mar. 2—Compassion in Action (Mark 1:21-34)
Tuesday, Mar. 3—Jesus Helps and Heals People (Mark 1:35-45)
Wednesday, Mar. 4—Lay Hands on the Sick (Mark 16:14-20)
Thursday, Mar. 5—Peter Heals the Sick (Acts 9:32-42)
Friday, Mar. 6—Faith to Be Made Well (Acts 14:8-18)
Saturday, Mar. 7—Prayer Will Save the Sick (James 5:13-18)
Sunday, Mar. 8—Leaves for Healing the Nations (Revelation 22:1-7)

Learning by Doing

This page contains an alternate lesson plan emphasizing learning activities.
Classes desiring such student involvement will find these suggestions helpful.

Learning Goals

After this lesson, students should be able to:

1. Describe the kinds of miracles that Jesus performed in today's text.

2. Explain what made Jesus' words and works unique.

3. Select a way to show the love of Christ, through both words and works, to a specific individual this week.

Into the Lesson

Early in the week, ask two class members to prepare assignments for this lesson. One should put together an overview of the subject of demon possession. The other person should prepare a description of leprosy. Provide each student with a photocopy of the portion of the lesson commentary covering his subject, and a Bible dictionary that treats the subject.

On a chalkboard, list the following statements as you discuss each: "Authority is given," "Authority comes by training and experience," and "Authority is earned." Ask the class to illustrate each statement (see the notes below). Add their suggestions to the appropriate statement.

Sometimes *authority is given.* Example: a person is hired as a police officer and is given "authority." Sometimes a person receives *authority by training and experience.* Have the class illustrate (nurses, doctors, lawyers, etc.). Sometimes people *earn authority* by demonstrating skills, knowledge, or power. Ask the class to illustrate (wood-carvers, mechanics, hobbyists, etc.). Tell the class that Jesus was recognized as one with "authority" (Mark 1:27). In a sense, Jesus received His authority from all three sources listed above. Ask the class to give illustrations of how this is true.

In today's study, we will examine three encounters that helped establish Jesus' authority as the Son of God. In demonstrating His authority, He also models a compassion for those who are ill that we would do well to imitate.

Into the Word

1. Read Mark 1:21-27, 32-34. Tell the class, "Sometimes Bible students are puzzled about the subject of demon possession. I've asked (name of the class member) to give us a brief report on this perplexing subject." Have the student share his report.

Following the report, use these discussion questions: (1) What words or actions in the text express or indicate how people felt about Jesus' miracles? (2) Why did the people describe Jesus' teaching as "new" (v. 27)? See the discussion in the lesson commentary under this verse. (3) Why, in this context, would the people describe Jesus as one "with authority" (v. 27)? (4) What indications do you find of the respect or fear that the demons had for Jesus (vv. 24, 34)?

Tell the class, "It is clear that the demons were powerless before the authority of Jesus. Let's look at another miracle that demonstrates Jesus' authority—the healing of a leper."

2. Begin this section of the Bible study with the report describing leprosy. After the report, emphasize that it is easy to see why Jesus would be moved with compassion for anyone suffering with this horrible disease. Also point out the risks that Jesus took in approaching such a man, given the teachings of the Law (see the discussion in the lesson commentary under Mark 1:41, 42). Next, ask a student to read Mark 1:40-45. Raise and discuss these questions: "What do this leper's words (v. 40) tell us about his attitude toward Jesus? What indicates his desperation? Why did Jesus tell the man to report to the priest (v. 44)? What indications are there of the respect that people gained for Jesus' authority (v. 45)?"

Into Life

Make two headings on the chalkboard: "Opportunities to Volunteer" and "Personal Assistance for Individuals." Ask students to share ideas of places to volunteer their services (examples are retirement homes, hospitals, support groups, organizations that serve the handicapped), and of ways to be of personal assistance to individuals who are ill (meals, financial help, home or automobile maintenance, to name a few).

Ask the class to discuss the major obstacles to responding to these opportunities. Then remind them that Jesus' heart was "moved with compassion" toward those who were ill. Ask each student to identify at least one way that he or she can imitate Jesus' model by responding to the needs of the ill. (This activity is included in the student book.) As you conclude, ask the class members to form groups of three or four people, share their responses, and pray for each other's commitments.

Let's Talk It Over

*The questions on this page are designed to encourage review of the lesson
Scriptures and to promote discussion of the lesson by the class. The answers
provided are only discussion starters. Let your class talk it over from there.*

1. Why did Jesus command the demon-possessed man, "Hold thy peace," or "Be quiet!" (*New International Version*)?

The demon was identifying Jesus as "the Holy One of God." That was the kind of testimony Jesus did not need. Later, Jesus' enemies would assert that He was in league with the devil, and performed His miracles by the devil's power (Mark 3:22). For Jesus to accept any kind of demonic testimony would seem to support such a charge. Also, we see frequently in the Gospels that Jesus was wary of encouraging anyone to testify publicly concerning His divine character. For example, following Peter's Good Confession we are told that Jesus "charged . . . his disciples that they should tell no man that he was Jesus the Christ" (Matthew 16:20). The popular expectation regarding a political Messiah made such public testimony dangerous. We see in John 6 how the political atmosphere affected Jesus' ministry. After His feeding of the five thousand, some observers were insistent on making Him a king (John 6:15).

2. The people who witnessed Jesus' casting out the evil spirit were amazed at His authority. How can we cultivate a greater sense of wonder at Jesus' authority?

We can experience a very profitable Bible study by examining the occasions on which Jesus performed miracles by means of a brief, authoritative command. One of the most impressive occasions was His calming of the storm on the Sea of Galilee with a simple "Peace, be still." This miracle amazed the disciples (Mark 4:35-41). The cursing of the fig tree required only the words, "No man eat fruit of thee hereafter for ever" (Mark 11:14). Once again the disciples' amazement is recorded (Matthew 21:20). Another dramatic example is the raising of Lazarus. Once the stone was moved away from the entrance of the tomb, all Jesus had to do was cry out, "Lazarus, come forth" (John 11:43).

3. At the leper's request for healing, Jesus was "moved with compassion" (Mark 1:41). How should this statement affect us?

It should touch us deeply to know that physical suffering and human desperation moved Jesus to compassion. On another occasion He was moved with compassion toward a multitude of people "because they were as sheep not having a shepherd" (Mark 6:34). Human hunger for moral guidance and spiritual assurance also stirred His compassionate heart. We have every reason to believe that Jesus looks upon suffering, confused, and lonely people today with the same compassion.

4. The healed leper disobeyed Jesus' command to avoid a public revelation of the facts of his healing. What shall we say about this?

We may feel a tendency to defend the leper's actions. The accounts in the Gospels of Matthew, Mark, and Luke do not tell us how long he had suffered from leprosy. Luke 5:12 tells us that he was "full of leprosy," which indicates an advanced case. Therefore we can imagine the profound sense of relief and the surge of rejoicing that he must have felt upon being healed. It would have been extremely difficult to remain quiet about it. Nevertheless, it is true that he disobeyed Jesus. Mark shows us how such disobedience hindered Jesus' ministry, making it difficult for Him to "openly enter into the city" (Mark 1:45). This account is a reminder to us that we dare not let our emotions, whether they be disappointment, anger, pride, or elation, influence us to disobey the Lord.

5. What are some important principles to keep in mind when we pray for physical healing for ourselves and others?

The New Testament demonstrates that it is not always God's will to heal physical afflictions. Paul's experience with his "thorn in the flesh" makes this clear (2 Corinthians 12:7-10). When we pray for the sick, it is also wise to ask for spiritual benefits—deeper faith, greater patience, a more effective witness—to result from the experience. Another important principle is that God often heals by means of medical treatments, surgeries, and drugs. We should undergird the efforts of physicians, surgeons, and nurses with our prayers. One more principle is the importance of overcoming unhealthy habits and attitudes. We can pray for the sick to eliminate smoking, drinking, poor eating habits, excessive worry, and other such hindrances to health.

Jesus' Authority Established

March 15
Lesson 2

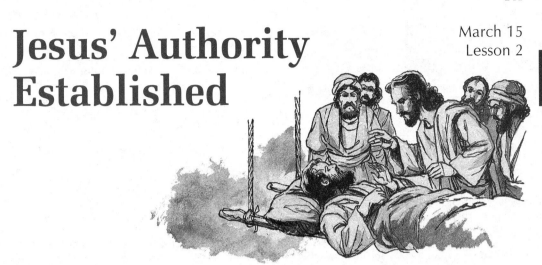

DEVOTIONAL READING: Acts 2:22-36.

LESSON SCRIPTURE: Mark 2:1—3:6.

PRINTED TEXT: Mark 2:3-12; 3:1-5.

Mark 2:3-12

3 And they come unto him, bringing one sick of the palsy, which was borne of four.

4 And when they could not come nigh unto him for the press, they uncovered the roof where he was: and when they had broken it up, they let down the bed wherein the sick of the palsy lay.

5 When Jesus saw their faith, he said unto the sick of the palsy, Son, thy sins be forgiven thee.

6 But there were certain of the scribes sitting there, and reasoning in their hearts,

7 Why doth this man thus speak blasphemies? who can forgive sins but God only?

8 And immediately, when Jesus perceived in his spirit that they so reasoned within themselves, he said unto them, Why reason ye these things in your hearts?

9 Whether is it easier to say to the sick of the palsy, Thy sins be forgiven thee; or to say, Arise, and take up thy bed, and walk?

10 But that ye may know that the Son of man hath power on earth to forgive sins, (he saith to the sick of the palsy,)

11 I say unto thee, Arise, and take up thy bed, and go thy way into thine house.

12 And immediately he arose, took up the bed, and went forth before them all; insomuch that they were all amazed, and glorified God, saying, We never saw it on this fashion.

Mark 3:1-5

1 And he entered again into the synagogue; and there was a man there which had a withered hand.

2 And they watched him, whether he would heal him on the sabbath day; that they might accuse him.

3 And he saith unto the man which had the withered hand, Stand forth.

4 And he saith unto them, Is it lawful to do good on the sabbath days, or to do evil? to save life, or to kill? But they held their peace.

5 And when he had looked round about on them with anger, being grieved for the hardness of their hearts, he saith unto the man, Stretch forth thine hand. And he stretched it out: and his hand was restored whole as the other.

GOLDEN TEXT: That ye may know that the Son of man hath power on earth to forgive sins, (he saith to the sick of the palsy,) I say unto thee, Arise, and take up thy bed, and go thy way into thine house.—Mark 2:10, 11.

The Gospel of Action (Mark)
Unit 1: Early Ministry of Jesus
(Lessons 1-4)

Lesson Aims

After studying this lesson, each student should:

1. Explain how Jesus demonstrated His authority over disease and over the Sabbath.

2. Recognize that being faithful to God sometimes requires one to challenge man-made customs.

3. Demonstrate a bold loyalty to the authority of Jesus (rather than man's traditions or expectations) in a particular circumstance this week.

Lesson Outline

INTRODUCTION
    A. Guarding a Weed Patch
    B. Lesson Background
I. CHRIST'S AUTHORITY OVER SIN (Mark 2:3-12)
    A. The Situation (vv. 3-5)
      Worth Every Effort
    B. The Scribes' Reaction (vv. 6, 7)
      Life by Whose Book?
    C. Jesus' Response (vv. 8-10)
    D. The Result (vv. 11, 12)
II. CHRIST'S AUTHORITY OVER THE SABBATH (Mark 3:1-5)
    A. The Situation (vv. 1, 2)
    B. Jesus' Response (vv. 3-5)
CONCLUSION
    A. Who's in Charge?
    B. The Basis of Authority
    C. Prayer
    D. Thought to Remember

The visual for Lesson 2 in the visuals packet focuses on how Jesus established His authority in today's lesson. It is shown on page 245.

Introduction

A. Guarding a Weed Patch

A Russian czar was once walking through his vast gardens when he came upon a sentry standing guard over what appeared to be a clump of weeds. When asked what he was doing there, the guard replied that he was just carrying out orders. The czar then called the captain of the guard and asked him the same question. The answer was the same. Finally the commanding general for the entire area was called in. When asked about the guard, he replied that when he had assumed command of the area, the orders were on the books, and so he continued to have them carried out.

By this time the curiosity of the czar was aroused, and he ordered that the records be searched until the answer was found. Finally the archives yielded the answer. A hundred years before, Catherine the Great had imported a rare rose from England, and to make sure that no one bothered it, she ordered a guard posted over it. Of course, the rose had long since died, and only a clump of weeds marked the spot where it had grown. However, the guard had been maintained all those years.

This is somewhat like the Jewish leaders who had devised their own interpretations of the Law, which they carefully guarded. Over the years, while maintaining their traditions, they lost sight of the real purpose of the Law.

B. Lesson Background

In the previous lesson we saw how Jesus began His ministry in Galilee. His miracles of healing quickly began to attract attention, and He soon had a large popular following. In fact, His following became so large that for a time He could no longer conduct a public ministry effectively (Mark 1:45).

Jesus' popularity soon began to attract the attention of other people—the religious leaders of the Jews. Undoubtedly some of them had witnessed some of His miracles. Jesus had made no effort to hide this aspect of His ministry, and when He healed the leper (Mark 1:40-44), He requested that he present himself to the priest just as the Law required. Yet His enormous popularity made Him suspect among the scribes and Pharisees, who considered themselves the custodians of orthodoxy. In their thinking, anyone who gained such popularity had to be doing something unorthodox. One cannot escape the feeling that there was some measure of jealousy involved in their suspicions.

Jesus did not attempt to hide from His critics. Eventually the time came for Him to assert His divine authority in their presence. In today's lesson He confronts them in the midst of performing one of His most dramatic miracles.

I. Christ's Authority Over Sin (Mark 2:3-12)

The healing of the leper had caused so much excitement that Jesus had to avoid the bigger towns of Galilee lest the crowds get out of hand. In today's lesson He returns to Capernaum. His presence quickly became known throughout the town, and the house where He was discovered was soon filled to capacity. Faced with such a large audience, Jesus took advantage of the opportunity and "preached the word unto them" (Mark 2:2).

A. The Situation (vv. 3-5)

3, 4. And they come unto him, bringing one sick of the palsy, which was borne of four. And when they could not come nigh unto him for the press, they uncovered the roof where he was: and when they had broken it up, they let down the bed wherein the sick of the palsy lay.

In some situations, people had to be brought to Jesus for healing because of the seriousness of their condition. Here a man had to be *borne*, or carried, for he was *sick of the palsy*; that is, he was paralyzed. We are not told whether his paralysis was the result of an accident or a disease. All we know is that he could not walk, and was brought to Jesus by *four* other persons. Luke tells us that these four were men (Luke 5:18), but we do not know if they were relatives or friends of the sick man.

The four carried the paralytic on his *bed*, which was probably a mat or a pallet carried with ropes or poles (like a stretcher). When the four neared the house where Jesus was teaching, they saw that they had a problem. The *press* of the crowd was so great that they could not get the man into the house, and the crowd was so intent on hearing Jesus that they were apparently unwilling to let them in.

But these four men were not easily discouraged. Apparently they were quite desperate for the help that they knew only Jesus could give their friend. We would be shocked if someone tried to enter a modern house the way they did. We need to understand, however, that houses were constructed differently in ancient Palestine. Many houses had flat roofs that could be reached by an outside stairway. Here was the four friends' opportunity. Carrying the man up the stairs, they reached the *roof* and began to open a hole in it. This was possible because these roofs were constructed of beams over which a thick layer of branches had been placed. Then on top of this a layer of mud had been packed down, forming a roof that may not have been completely waterproof, but at least kept out most of the rain. By digging a hole through this material, the four men could then lower the paralytic into the house. No doubt debris falling from the ceiling above alerted the people below that something was happening. Under such circumstances, some of them may have given the four a helping hand.

How to Say It

CAPERNAUM. Kuh-*per*-nay-um.
HERODIANS. Heh-*roe*-dee-unz.
PHARISEES. *Fair*-ih-seez.

---

5. When Jesus saw their faith, he said unto the sick of the palsy, Son, thy sins be forgiven thee.

Jesus was moved by the *faith* of the paralytic and of those who brought him to go to such efforts. But instead of saying, "Arise and walk" (which might have been expected), He said, *Son, thy sins be forgiven thee*. Jesus was not suggesting that the man's affliction was the result of his sin, although this belief was popularly held, and the man himself may have believed it. It seems that Jesus intended to begin to reveal some of the divine authority that God had vested in Him.

WORTH EVERY EFFORT

The husband of a lady in one of the churches I served was dying with a brain tumor. He was not a Christian. From his hospital bed, he expressed a desire to be "buried with Christ" in baptism. I talked to his doctor and to the hospital administrator. With their permission, and with the cooperation of nurses and orderlies, we secured a portable tub, used for bathing immobile patients, and filled it with enough water to immerse the candidate. He was brought to the bathing room on a gurney, and carefully lifted into the tub. Several of the hospital staff joined his wife and me to witness the baptism. After brief Scripture and prayer, I lowered my friend's head and shoulders beneath the water, then raised him up—a "new creature" in Christ (2 Corinthians 5:17).

A month or so later, I officiated at this new Christian's funeral. I did not regret any of the unusual efforts that had been made to assist him in obeying the Gospel. It was all more than worthwhile.

The four who went to extraordinary lengths to get their sick friend to Jesus knew it was worth the effort. Have you known the joy and satisfaction of putting forth the extra effort to bring someone to Christ? —R. W. B.

B. The Scribes' Reaction (vv. 6, 7)

6, 7. But there were certain of the scribes sitting there, and reasoning in their hearts, Why doth this man thus speak blasphemies? who can forgive sins but God only?

The *scribes*, sometimes referred to as "lawyers," were students and defenders of the

Law. They considered it their duty to make sure that people kept every jot and tittle of the Law. They now appeared on the scene as critics of Jesus. While they did not actually speak out, *in their hearts* they found fault with what He had just said. They were quite right in their reasoning: Only God *can forgive sins.* Any human being who claimed this privilege was guilty of blasphemy. Since these scribes looked upon Jesus as a mere man, He was, by their reasoning, guilty of blasphemy, and they had every reason to expose Him. As "God with us," however, Jesus indeed had the authority to forgive sins.

LIFE BY WHOSE BOOK?

Bob Russell, in his book *Messages for a Growing Church,* relates an incredible episode in the life of John Y. Brown, the former governor of Kentucky. Brown was vacationing in Florida when he experienced some severe chest pains. He drove himself to the emergency entrance of the nearest hospital, and told the admitting nurse he thought he was having a heart attack. The nurse advised him that his car was parked in a "No Parking" zone, and it would have to be moved. Brown reiterated his symptoms, yet she insisted that his car would have to be moved. The former governor then told her who he was, and repeated that he thought he was suffering a heart attack, but the nurse still would not admit him. Finally, Brown went out and moved his car, then came back in to be examined.

That nurse is not the only person who ever had scrambled priorities. She was doing her job "by the book," following regulations despite extenuating circumstances. The world actually is full of such inflexible policy guardians—like the scribes, for example. Jesus' concern, however, was with *people.*

Life by the book is fine, as long as it's God's book. "What does the Lord require of you? To act justly and to love mercy and to walk humbly with your God" (Micah 6:8, *New International Version*).   —R. W. B.

C. Jesus' Response (vv. 8-10)

8, 9. And immediately, when Jesus perceived in his spirit that they so reasoned within themselves, he said unto them, Why reason ye these things in your hearts? whether is it easier to say to the sick of the palsy, Thy sins be forgiven thee; or to say, Arise, and take up thy bed, and walk?

By their gestures and facial expressions, Jesus may have realized what the scribes were thinking. But He also knew their thoughts by divine insight. There are situations involving criticism when the best tactic is simply to ignore the crit-

ics. But this was not one of those times. Jesus knew that if He ignored the scribes and their accusations, they would continue to attempt to neutralize His ministry.

Jesus brought the negative thoughts of the scribes out in the open by asking them a question. Clearly, it is just as easy to say, *Take up thy bed, and walk* as it is to say, *Thy sins be forgiven thee.* But proof is another matter. If a paralytic did take up his bed and walk, that would be such undeniable proof of Jesus' power that it would be hard to challenge Him. But the forgiveness of sin is a very subjective matter, not readily evident to observers. Thus Jesus needed to do more to convince His critics.

10. But that ye may know that the Son of man hath power on earth to forgive sins, (he saith to the sick of the palsy,).

Jesus did not wait for a response to His question. Instead, He proceeded to provide an indisputable demonstration of His power. Here Mark reports Jesus' first use of the expression *Son of man.* This term highlighted Jesus' identification with man, but also carried significant Messianic implications. Daniel saw in a vision "one like the Son of man" who "came with the clouds of heaven, and came to the Ancient of days, and they brought him near before him" (Daniel 7:13, 14). Mark 8:29, 31 shows the close relationship between the terms *Son of man* and *Christ.*

D. The Result (vv. 11, 12)

11, 12. I say unto thee, Arise, and take up thy bed, and go thy way into thine house. And immediately he arose, took up the bed, and went forth before them all; insomuch that they were all amazed, and glorified God, saying, We never saw it on this fashion.

With just a few words, Jesus answered the question He had raised. The instantaneous healing of this helpless man gave dramatic proof of Jesus' authority. Such a miracle should have convinced everyone present of Jesus' power. And indeed it did convince the vast majority of the witnesses, who were all *amazed, and glorified God, saying, We never saw it on this fashion.* This favorable response of the people only further antagonized Jesus' critics.

The scribes, who had been bested in this confrontation, went out and began to seek other ways to undermine Jesus' influence with the people. Their next challenge was to question His piety. They, along with the Pharisees, pointed out that He ate with "publicans and sinners"— people whom pious Jews looked upon with scorn (Mark 2:15, 16). In their thinking, "Birds of a feather flock together," so if Jesus associated with such outcasts, then He must be one of them. Jesus' reply, which highlighted His foes' self-righteousness, was, "I came not to call the righteous, but sinners to repentance" (v. 17). The scribes and Pharisees also accused Jesus and His disciples of not fasting (v. 18) and of violating the Sabbath by picking grain from a field and then eating it (vv. 23, 24). In answering these charges, Jesus again asserted His authority as the Son of man.

II. Christ's Authority Over the Sabbath (Mark 3:1-5)

A. The Situation (vv. 1, 2)

1, 2. And he entered again into the synagogue; and there was a man there which had a withered hand. And they watched him, whether he would heal him on the sabbath day; that they might accuse him.

By this time it seems that Jesus' enemies had formed a kind of committee that followed Him about, seeking to find anything that they could to use as a basis for criticism. The next event in this running battle occurred in a *synagogue*. This might have been any synagogue in Galilee, but since the text says *he entered again*, most likely this was the synagogue in Capernaum (which he had entered in 1:21).

While the text does not indicate it, it is altogether possible that Jesus' foes arranged for the man with the *withered hand* to be in the synagogue on this occasion. They saw in the presence of this man another opportunity to *accuse* Jesus of breaking the Law. While the Law as interpreted by the Pharisees allowed medical treatment *on the sabbath day* in a life-threatening situation, this situation clearly did not qualify as an exception.

B. Jesus' Response (vv. 3-5)

3, 4. And he saith unto the man which had the withered hand, Stand forth. And he saith unto them, Is it lawful to do good on the sabbath days, or to do evil? to save life, or to kill? But they held their peace.

Again, as in the incident involving the paralytic, Jesus understood the hearts of His critics and knew what they were thinking. He might have postponed this confrontation by waiting until the next day to heal the man, but once again He chose to meet the opposition "head on." This situation gave Jesus an opportunity to expose the legalistic hypocrisy of the Jewish leaders before the people. His question whether it was *lawful to do good on the sabbath days, or to do evil* presented the critics with a dilemma that they dared not answer. If they said it was lawful to do good, then Jesus would be justified

visual for lesson 2

in healing the man. If they said it was evil, then their whole legalistic system would be undermined in the eyes of the people. Thus trapped, they *held their peace.*

5. And when he had looked round about on them with anger, being grieved for the hardness of their hearts, he saith unto the man, Stretch forth thine hand. And he stretched it out: and his hand was restored whole as the other.

Mark notes that Jesus *looked . . . on them with anger.* We see this same righteous indignation displayed when He drove the moneychangers out of the temple. For a person caught in the throes of sin, Jesus had mercy and forgiveness. But these religious leaders were characterized by *the hardness of their hearts*—a condition that made it impossible for them to receive His mercy. Jesus then proceeded to heal the man, which publicly exposed His critics for the hypocrites they were. In healing the man on the sabbath day, Jesus illustrated His earlier teaching that "the sabbath was made for man, and not man for the sabbath" (Mark 2:27).

Even though Jesus felt indignation toward the religious leaders, He *grieved* over their sad condition. Verse 6 (not in the printed text) reveals just how hardened the hearts of these people were and how intense their hatred for Jesus had become. They immediately went out and began to plot with their bitter political enemies, the Herodians (who supported the rule of Rome), as to how they might destroy Jesus.

Conclusion

A. Who's in Charge?

When Jesus began His ministry, He quickly gained popularity among the people. Two factors led to His wide acclaim: His miracles, especially miracles of healing and the casting out of demons, and His teaching, which He proclaimed with such unparalleled authority. But not everyone was so favorably impressed. The religious leaders began to have some serious reservations about His teaching, and before long they established a regular surveillance of His whereabouts. In today's lesson we see illustrations of this hostile attitude.

We need to recognize that this opposition was the result of two quite different impulses. Much of the opposition to Jesus arose among the Pharisees. The Pharisees were keen students of the Law. Their movement grew out of an effort to protect and purify the Jewish religion that had fallen on hard times in the period between the Old and New Testaments. While the term *Pharisee* usually conjures up an image of a legalistic, hypocritical person, certainly not all Pharisees or their followers fit this image. The apostle Paul, for instance, belonged to this party, and while at one time in his career he may have been legalistic, no one could ever rightly accuse him of hypocrisy.

The Pharisees who began to oppose Jesus saw in Him a serious threat to their efforts to maintain the purity of the Jewish faith. And they were quite right in their understanding of Jesus' teaching. His emphasis on mercy and grace stood in stark contrast to their emphasis on observing the trivial matters of the Law, or at least of their interpretation of the Law. They recognized that either Jesus' emphasis was right or theirs was right. Both could not be right at the same time. Thus, to defend the principles in which they believed, they had to do everything they could to undermine Jesus' influence with the people. Even though we cannot accept their interpretation of the Law, we can at least respect their commitment to defend what they believed to be right.

The other reason for the Pharisees' opposition to Jesus was not nearly as commendable. It sprang from jealousy. As often happens with a group dedicated to reform, the Pharisees enjoyed some success in their efforts. As a result, they had gained considerable respect and support from the people, including financial gain and prestigious positions. Jesus' ministry challenged the comfortable status quo that they had come to enjoy. For many of them, this became more important than the Law they professed to love and uphold. Clearly, if they were to maintain this preferred status, Jesus had to go. Thus they turned to some of their staunchest enemies, the Herodians, in an effort to silence Him.

B. The Basis of Authority

Religious disputes cannot be settled by using the scientific method. Science deals with physical matters, not spiritual matters. Ultimately, every religious dispute comes down to a question of authority. Unless disputants can estab-lish the basis for their beliefs, then religious debates become nothing more than words.

The religious leaders who opposed Jesus had a valid authority: the Law of Moses and the other Scriptures that we call the Old Testament. These were authoritative because God had given them to the Israelites. But there was a problem: these leaders had substituted their own interpretations and traditions for the revelation that God had given. Their interpretations became more important than God's Word.

Now the leaders were faced with a superior source of authority in Jesus Christ, God's own Son. His authority, however, was unacceptable to them, and so they sought to silence Him. The authority of Jesus is still a crucial issue for us today. The most important question we must answer is, "What think ye of Christ? whose son is he?" (Matthew 22:42). If He is only the son of Mary and Joseph (as some say) and a wonderful teacher, but no more than that, then we may respect Him and love Him; but we are under no compulsion to obey Him. If, however, He is the divine Son of God (as the Scriptures teach), we will respect Him and love Him. More than that, we will obey Him.

C. Prayer

Almighty God, source of all authority in the universe, help us to understand and appreciate what that authority means to us. Lead us to love and obey Your Son, Jesus Christ, to whom You have given all authority. In His precious name we pray. Amen.

D. Thought to Remember

"All authority in heaven and on earth has been given to me" (Matthew 28:18, *New International Version*).

Home Daily Bible Readings

Monday, Mar. 9—Authority to Help People (Mark 2:1-12)

Tuesday, Mar. 10—Come to Call Sinners (Mark 2:13-22)

Wednesday, Mar. 11—Grieved by Hardness of Heart (Mark 2:23—3:6)

Thursday, Mar. 12—Authority to Judge (John 5:19-29)

Friday, Mar. 13—Authority Over All People (John 17:1-11)

Saturday, Mar. 14—Authority in Heaven and Earth (Matthew 28:16-20)

Sunday, Mar. 15—Named Lord and Messiah (Acts 2:22-36)

Learning by Doing

This page contains an alternate lesson plan emphasizing learning activities.
Classes desiring such student involvement will find these suggestions helpful.

Learning Goals

After this lesson, the student should:

1. Explain how Jesus demonstrated His authority over disease and over the Sabbath.

2. Recognize that being faithful to God sometimes requires one to challenge man-made customs.

3. Demonstrate a bold loyalty to the authority of Jesus (rather than man's traditions or expectations) in a particular circumstance this week.

Into the Lesson

Prepare a visual with the following questions:

Who is in Charge
Of you at your job?
Of your mortgage or car loan?
Of the local high school?
Of the school basketball team?
Of the United States?

Write down the answers as students give them (*your boss, your lender, the principal, the coach, the President*). Next, tell students that these persons are given their authority because of their expertise in their field. But not all persons are willing to submit to authority. Ask class members to tell what happens when people refuse to submit to some of the above authorities. Afterward, point out to the class that our Scripture text for today tells of some individuals who would not accept the authority of Jesus, in spite of the fact that people were being wonderfully blessed by it.

Into the Word

Begin the Bible study with a brief lecture using the Lesson Background. Note that Jesus' popularity with the people of Galilee had increased dramatically at this point. However, Jesus also had His critics, who could not accept nor submit to His authority. They were the scribes and the Pharisees in today's text.

Ask a couple of class members to read today's text for the class. Have one read Mark 2:3-12, and the other, Mark 3:1-5. Then use these discussion questions with the class:

1. Jesus' popularity made Him suspect among the scribes and Pharisees. Why do you suppose they were so upset with Jesus? (*He disregarded their traditions and their interpretations of Moses' Law. Also, they were jealous of His popularity with the people.*)

2. Why would the scribes think Jesus was speaking blasphemies when He forgave the sins of the sick man? (*See Mark 2:7.*)

3. In our first passage (Mark 2:3-12), what kind of authority did Jesus demonstrate that is so wonderful to us? (*The authority to pardon sins. Explain the concept of a "pardon," using a courtroom as an illustration. We have broken the law—God's Law. Jesus has the authority to grant a pardon.*)

4. What was wrong with the thinking of the scribes and Pharisees? (*They missed the spirit of the Law. They also missed the spirit of God's love for mankind.*)

5. Were the Sabbath laws that the Pharisees tried to enforce man-made regulations or God's laws? (*Man-made regulations*)

6. Who really honored the Sabbath Day—the Pharisees or Jesus? Why? (*Jesus, because He performed an act of kindness that glorified God*)

Into Life

There are several reasons why there are so many fragments of Christianity today. One of those reasons lies in the authority that people choose to follow. Some follow the tradition of their church or denomination, while others find their source of authority in God's Word.

Make four columns on a chalkboard or on poster board. Write a large heading across the poster: *Man's Traditions vs. God's Authority.* Write smaller headings designating the following columns: Column 1: *Church or Denominational Traditions.* Column 2: *Resolutions.* Column 3: *Local Church Traditions.* Column 4: *Resolutions.* Ask the students to list issues, rooted in tradition or man's authority, that divide churches or denominations. Place these in Column 1. Then ask them to share ideas on how to resolve these issues, and record them in Column 2. Keep steering the discussion back to God's Word as the source of authority.

Next, make the exercise even more personal by asking what issues, which may be rooted in traditions more than the authority of Scripture, cause tension in the local church. Enter suggestions in Column 3, and the resolutions that the students propose in Column 4. (This exercise is in the student book.)

Close the session with prayer, asking God to keep us sensitive to His authority and will.

Let's Talk It Over

The questions on this page are designed to encourage review of the lesson Scriptures and to promote discussion of the lesson by the class. The answers provided are only discussion starters. Let your class talk it over from there.

1. What were some factors that made the healing of the paralytic particularly impressive?

It seems possible that this man was what we today refer to as a "quadriplegic." Not only were his legs paralyzed, but the fact that he was carried on a pallet suggests that his arms also may have been afflicted by paralysis. Otherwise we assume he could have approached the house in an upright position, his arms supported by two of his friends. If his arms were paralyzed, Jesus' command to him to pick up and carry his bed would have been even more significant. Of course, Jesus made this healing especially dramatic by demonstrating through the physical healing His authority to forgive sins.

2. Jesus healed on the Sabbath, in spite of the Jewish leaders' objections. What does this say to us concerning doing good on Sunday, the Lord's Day?

Some Christians think of Sunday as the "Christian Sabbath." They insist that it should be observed as a day of worship and rest. The New Testament, however, never uses the term "Christian Sabbath," and never does it imply that the Lord's Day is merely for rest. We are wise to avoid Sunday employment, if possible. It is also best to leave most personal household duties, such as washing clothes, mowing grass, painting, and repairing, for other days. But it is appropriate to serve others on the Lord's Day. Elderly persons or shut-ins may need help with repairs or cleaning in their homes. Perhaps they must have food carried in, if they are to enjoy a healthy diet. People who are ill at home may require assistance in taking medicine, having dressings changed, getting their bedding washed, or accomplishing other necessary tasks around the house. Such chores often have to be done on Sunday.

3. The healing of the man with the withered hand is the only occasion in the Gospels when Jesus' anger is specifically mentioned. There are other occasions, however, when His anger is implied. The cleansing of the temple is one, and the indictment of the scribes and Pharisees in Matthew 23 is another. How can we contrast Jesus' anger with our own?

Jesus' anger was stirred by others' opposition to God and oppression of man. Our anger is frequently the result of what we regard as attacks against our intelligence, honesty, ability, and the like. We tend to be more concerned with our own reputation than with God's glory. Jesus' anger was righteous, and it was also redemptive. That is, He exhibited His anger with the aim of awakening the sinful to repentance.

4. Jealousy was in part the motive for the Pharisees' opposition to Jesus. Jealousy toward others may also mar our spiritual growth. How can we overcome such jealousy?

The Pharisees' problem with jealousy would have vanished if they had acknowledged Jesus as God's Son, worthy of all glory and honor. Many of our temptations to jealousy spring from a concern for personal glory. By learning to focus on giving glory to Jesus Christ, we can gain victory over these temptations. Other petty jealousies arise from the fact that other people are more physically attractive than we are, have more talents, enjoy a higher standard of living, and possess other advantages. Paul's advice in Philippians 2:3 offers a solution to such jealousies: "Let nothing be done through strife or vainglory; but in lowliness of mind let each esteem other better than themselves." Verses 5-11 of that chapter describe Jesus' own demonstration of the principle Paul had just set forth.

5. Some believers today tend to pit the authority of Jesus Christ against the authority of the Bible. How do they do this, and how must we respond?

We occasionally hear someone declare, "The Lord told me to do such and such." Perhaps we have even heard someone claim the Lord's authority for doing something contrary to Biblical principles. This is a characteristic of our times, in which feelings are often substituted for Scriptural standards. We must respond to this by declaring that Jesus Christ will not contradict Himself. He will not grant to a modern believer the permission to lie, steal, commit adultery, or commit other wrongs. He has made it clear in the Bible that such practices are sinful. No amount of personal feelings, however vivid or intense, can alter that fact.

Jesus' Power Demonstrated

March 22
Lesson 3

DEVOTIONAL READING: 1 Corinthians 1:18-31.

LESSON SCRIPTURE: Mark 5:21-43.

PRINTED TEXT: Mark 5:21-24, 35-43.

Mark 5:21-24, 35-43

21 And when Jesus was passed over again by ship unto the other side, much people gathered unto him: and he was nigh unto the sea.

22 And, behold, there cometh one of the rulers of the synagogue, Jairus by name; and when he saw him, he fell at his feet,

23 And besought him greatly, saying, My little daughter lieth at the point of death: I pray thee, come and lay thy hands on her, that she may be healed; and she shall live.

24 And Jesus went with him. And much people followed him, and thronged him.

· · · · · · · · · · · ·

35 While he yet spake, there came from the ruler of the synagogue's house certain which said, Thy daughter is dead: why troublest thou the Master any further?

36 As soon as Jesus heard the word that was spoken, he saith unto the ruler of the synagogue, Be not afraid, only believe.

37 And he suffered no man to follow him, save Peter, and James, and John the brother of James.

38 And he cometh to the house of the ruler of the synagogue, and seeth the tumult, and them that wept and wailed greatly.

39 And when he was come in, he saith unto them, Why make ye this ado, and weep? the damsel is not dead, but sleepeth.

40 And they laughed him to scorn. But when he had put them all out, he taketh the father and the mother of the damsel, and them that were with him, and entereth in where the damsel was lying.

41 And he took the damsel by the hand, and said unto her, Talitha cumi; which is, being interpreted, Damsel, (I say unto thee,) arise.

42 And straightway the damsel arose, and walked; for she was of the age of twelve years. And they were astonished with a great astonishment.

43 And he charged them straitly that no man should know it; and commanded that something should be given her to eat.

GOLDEN TEXT: As soon as Jesus heard the word that was spoken, he saith unto the ruler of the synagogue, Be not afraid, only believe.—Mark 5:36.

The Gospel of Action (Mark)
Unit 1: Early Ministry of Jesus
(Lessons 1-4)

Lesson Aims

After completing this lesson, students should be able to:

1. Relate the specific ways in which Jesus manifested His power in ministering to Jairus and his daughter.

2. Recognize the difference that Jesus' power can make in dealing with death.

3. Suggest a circumstance (perhaps of a friend or loved one) in which they will be able to bear witness to Jesus' power over death.

Lesson Outline

INTRODUCTION
  A. The Master
  B. Lesson Background
I. JAIRUS APPEALS TO JESUS (Mark 5:21-24)
  A. The Situation (v. 21)
  B. Jairus's Request (vv. 22, 23)
    Capernaum 911
  C. Jesus' Response (v. 24)
II. JESUS GOES TO JAIRUS'S HOME (Mark 5:35-43)
  A. Sad News (v. 35)
  B. Jesus' Reassurance (v. 36)
    Fear vs. Faith
  C. Jesus' Arrival (vv. 37, 38)
  D. Jesus' Miracle (vv. 39-43)
    Laughing at God
CONCLUSION
  A. Only Believe
  B. Silencing the Skeptics
  C. Prayer
  D. Thought to Remember

The visual for Lesson 3 in the visuals packet is a photo of a synagogue that archaeologists discovered in Capernaum. It is shown on page 252.

Introduction

A. The Master

Suppose a cat happened to land on the keys of a piano. She noticed that each time she took a step a different sound came from the instrument. She might then begin to run back and forth on the keys, apparently enjoying the dissonant notes that she heard. Suppose that her owner then tried to teach the cat to play the piano. After hours and hours of training, the cat might be able to play a simple tune or two.

Suppose then that a musician sat down at the piano and began to play from Bach or Beethoven. The cat, if she were able to think about it at all, would not be able to understand it, and certainly would be incapable of playing Bach or Beethoven. Everything in her experience would tell her that such music was impossible.

The cat's response would be like that of the mourners in the house of Jairus. They knew his daughter was dead, and experience had taught them that there was no resurrection of the physical body. Then Jesus entered the house. The mourners laughed in scornful unbelief when He suggested that the girl was not dead but sleeping. Little did they know that in the presence of the Master Physician, death loses its power.

B. Lesson Background

At the time during which the incident in today's lesson occurred, Jesus' popularity in Galilee was reaching its peak. In preparation for the rest of His ministry, He had selected the twelve who would later be called apostles (Mark 3:13-19). In the period between last week's lesson and today's lesson (recorded in Mark 3:6—5:20), Jesus' ministry was highlighted by His teaching in parables and by some of His most notable miracles, including the stilling of the storm and the healing of the Gadarene demoniac.

Jesus' ministry among the Gadarenes was cut short when the people asked Him to leave (Mark 5:17), probably because of the loss of their swine (which had plunged into the water once the demons entered them). As a result of this rejection, Jesus and His disciples returned to the area near Capernaum, where they were once again greeted by large crowds. As the occasion recorded in today's lesson begins, Jesus is teaching the people near the Sea of Galilee.

I. Jairus Appeals to Jesus (Mark 5:21-24)

A. The Situation (v. 21)

21. And when Jesus was passed over again by ship unto the other side, much people gathered unto him; and he was nigh unto the sea.

Since at least four of Jesus' disciples were fishermen, it was natural that they would travel by boat whenever possible. On this occasion Jesus did not do His teaching in the local synagogue, probably because the synagogue could no longer accommodate the crowds that were flocking to hear Him. The level areas along the northwestern shore of the Sea of Galilee provided an excellent place for *much people* to gather.

How to Say It

CAPERNAUM. Kuh-*per*-nay-um.
GADARENES. *Gad*-uh-reens.
JAIRUS. *Jye*-rus or *Jay*-ih-rus.
SYNAGOGUE. *sin*-uh-gog.
TALITHA CUMI (Aramaic). *Tal*-ih-thuh *koo*-me.

B. Jairus's Request (vv. 22, 23)

22, 23. And, behold, there cometh one of the rulers of the synagogue, Jairus by name; and when he saw him, he fell at his feet, and besought him greatly, saying, My little daughter lieth at the point of death: I pray thee, come and lay thy hands on her, that she may be healed; and she shall live.

As the people pressed around Jesus, *Jairus* made his way through the crowd to get to Him. Since he was *one of the rulers of the synagogue* and would be recognized by most of the people, they evidently gave way so that he could reach the Lord. Some of Jesus' most severe critics had confronted Him in the synagogue, but there is nothing to indicate that Jairus was numbered among these critics. Apparently he had seen some of Jesus' miracles and had come to believe in Him. Faced by the serious illness of his daughter, Jairus probably gave little thought about what the critics might say about Jesus or about himself. Desperate need has a way of neutralizing rigid dogmas.

Although his daughter was twelve years old at the time (as v. 42 indicates), Jairus, in typical fatherly fashion, spoke of her as *My little daughter*. Aware that Jesus often touched the person being healed, Jairus requested that Jesus *lay* His *hands* upon her.

It may seem presumptuous for Jairus to have pushed to the front to see Jesus, when others were there to hear His teaching and receive healing. But desperation, combined with the love of a father, compelled Jairus to lay aside the conventional practices of polite society and to bring his need to Jesus. Others coming for healing were probably not facing such an emergency. In addition, up to this point Jesus had not raised anyone from the dead. Perhaps the distraught father felt that he had to act quickly or it would be too late.

CAPERNAUM 911

In a relatively short period of time, emergency medical attention has become universally identified with its easy-to-dial phone number, 911. Is there anyone who doesn't know how to get emergency help? Nearly every fire and police department has an emergency ambulance and a squad of emergency medical technicians (EMTs).

Jairus had no phone, no 911 number to call, and no emergency squad to assist in his family's crisis. But he found a better solution: Jesus, the Great Physician, was available. And He was willing to make a house call! Not only could Jesus heal the synagogue ruler's daughter, He could (and did) bring her back to life. Whatever "miracles" modern EMTs are able to perform, they still fall short of the power demonstrated by Him who is "the resurrection, and the life" (John 11:25) and the conqueror of death (1 Corinthians 15:55-57).

God continues to work life-saving miracles through the efforts and treatments of emergency medical personnel. People in life-threatening situations are wise to call 911. Christians, however, have a decided advantage in such crises—we can also call upon the Lord, "our refuge and strength, a very present help in trouble" (Psalm 46:1). —R. W. B.

C. Jesus' Response (v. 24)

24. And Jesus went with him. And much people followed him, and thronged him.

Knowing that the father came in faith, Jesus did not hesitate to honor his request. Even though it meant that a large and eager crowd would be denied His teaching for a time, Jesus knew that He would be able to teach far more important lessons at Jairus's house. Perhaps most of the people in the crowd were not aware of the situation involving Jairus's daughter. Yet they were willing to follow Jesus, hoping to learn more regardless of the inconvenience of having to move.

II. Jesus Goes to Jairus's Home (Mark 5:35-43)

As Jesus, along with the crowd, made His way to the house of Jairus, the opportunity arose to perform another miracle. "A certain woman, which had an issue of blood twelve years" (v. 25) had found no relief from physicians, and so she came to Jesus for help. Because of the nature of her affliction, she may have sought anonymity by seeking to touch His garment in the hopes of receiving a cure. Her actions, however, did not escape the notice of Jesus. In a crowd such as this, Jesus was being touched by many persons; but only one hoped to receive healing by touching Him, and Jesus knew this. When Jesus asked "Who touched my clothes?" (v. 30), the disciples thought the question absurd, for to them Jesus had no way of distinguishing one touch from another. But they were wrong. They had seen Jesus perform several miracles, but it had not occurred to them that He had special omniscient (all-knowing) powers.

The woman, with considerable apprehension, came forward and fell down before Jesus, acknowledging that she had indeed touched Him. Her fears were needless, however, for Jesus commended her for her faith and sent her away in peace.

A. Sad News (v. 35)

35. While he yet spake, there came from the ruler of the synagogue's house certain which said, Thy daughter is dead; why troublest thou the Master any further?

Jairus, believing that any delay might be fatal to his daughter, may have been quite upset that Jesus stopped to heal the woman. His worst fears were realized when messengers came from his house with the tragic news: *Thy daughter is dead.* A barrage of speculations may have raced through Jairus's mind: if only I had come to Jesus sooner, He could have helped me; if only Jesus had not stopped to cure the woman, He would have come to my daughter in time. Now apparently it was too late; all was lost.

B. Jesus' Reassurance (v. 36)

36. As soon as Jesus heard the word that was spoken, he saith unto the ruler of the synagogue, Be not afraid, only believe.

It is important to remember that until this time, Jesus had not raised anyone from the dead (at least the Gospel writers do not record His doing so). There is nothing to indicate that Jairus believed that such a miracle was possible. Jesus knew that Jairus had faith, but did he have enough faith to see him through this new crisis? Jesus' words brought comfort and reassurance to help Jairus through this most difficult moment.

FEAR VS. FAITH

Our son-in-law was flying home from a seminar in Colorado Springs, with a stopover in St. Louis. The airliner had just taken off when a loud "thump" was heard. Flight attendants

visual for
lesson 3

Capernaum Synagogue

began to scurry about, going in and out of the captain's cabin. Shortly an announcement was made: "We have 'lost' one of our engines; we will be returning immediately to St. Louis."

The damaged plane soon landed safely, but not before passengers developed considerable anxiety and seriously reflected on the meaning of their lives. As soon as the crisis was past, our daughter's husband called to tell us what had happened. "I've never been so frightened in my life," he said. "I found out I wasn't quite as ready to die as I thought. I just prayed that I would see my wife and my little boy again."

Fear is the enemy of faith. Jairus despaired of seeing his daughter alive again. He could not presume that even Jesus would bring her back to life. He dared not believe in such a miracle. At that moment, his fear was greater than his faith. That's why Christ comforted him: "Be not afraid, only believe." His followers today need that encouragement too.

"Fear knocked at the door; Faith answered;
No one was there!"   —Author unknown
—R. W. B.

C. Jesus' Arrival (vv. 37, 38)

37. And he suffered no man to follow him, save Peter, and James, and John the brother of James.

As Jesus neared Jairus's house, He asked the crowd, along with nine of the twelve disciples, to remain behind (*suffered* is used with its older meaning of "permitted" or "allowed"). The presence of so many people in the narrow streets around the house, added to the mourners who were already there, could very well have created additional problems. Furthermore, there likely would not have been room for even the twelve in the house, which must have been quite small by modern standards. The three disciples whom Jesus took with Him—*Peter, James, and John*—seem to have formed an inner circle of followers who accompanied Jesus in other situations: the transfiguration (Mark 9:2) and His agony in the garden (Mark 14:32, 33).

38. And he cometh to the house of the ruler of the synagogue, and seeth the tumult, and them that wept and wailed greatly.

The family, along with friends and mourners, had assembled in and around *the house.* Since it was the practice to conduct the burial very shortly after the death of a person, these people needed to be present almost immediately. Although Capernaum lacked any of the modern media that is a part of our daily lives, word spread rapidly about the town, especially since the family of one of the *synagogue* leaders was involved.

Modern funerals are quite sedate and brief compared with the practices in Jesus' day. As soon as death occurred, the lamenting began. Mark tells us that the people *wept and wailed greatly*. Besides the weeping and wailing of family and friends, professional mourners were likely present, as was the custom, along with flute players who performed plaintive dirges on their instruments. No wonder Mark speaks of *the tumult*, or, as the *New International Version* reads, a "commotion."

D. Jesus' Miracle (vv. 39-43)

39. And when he was come in, he saith unto them, Why make ye this ado, and weep? the damsel is not dead, but sleepeth.

Jesus silenced those creating the tumult long enough to ask why they were making so much *ado*, or noise. What may have been accepted or expected behavior in the case of a death was inappropriate now, because this girl was *not dead*. Some have used Jesus' statement to argue that Jairus's daughter was in an unconscious state and not really dead. This position rejects the view that a miracle actually took place, challenging the truth that Jesus has power even over death. The word "sleep" was used to indicate that death held only a temporary control over the girl, as Jesus was about to demonstrate.

40. And they laughed him to scorn. But when he had put them all out, he taketh the father and the mother of the damsel, and them that were with him, and entereth in where the damsel was lying.

Here we see evidence of the mourners' strictly professional status. They were able to change immediately from mourners to mockers when they heard what Jesus said.

Before entering the room where the girl lay, Jesus ordered everyone but the parents and the three disciples to leave. She was probably *lying* on the bed or pallet where she had died, because there had hardly been time to prepare her for burial. With these witnesses present when He raised the girl, Jesus insured that there would be no misunderstanding about what happened.

LAUGHING AT GOD

Modern media sometimes sneer in contempt at what they call "the religious right." Comics often tell jokes to generate laughs about the faith and convictions of Christians. Nonbelievers of all kinds in all ages have made fun of the tenets and practices of Christianity. Sometimes such laughter borders on blasphemy and sacrilege. Most certainly it is a sign of disrespect for God.

The mourners at the house of Jairus were unbelievers. They mocked what they perceived

as ignorance and arrogance in Jesus. They were skeptics and cynics. Dead is dead, they thought, and no euphemism can change that. They laughed in ridicule of what they considered to be pure nonsense. Later, they were "astonished with a great astonishment" to see the girl walking around.

Abraham's wife Sarah believed in God but not in miracles. So she laughed at the divine announcement that she would give birth in her old age (Genesis 18:12). God's thoughts and ways were higher than hers, as much "as the heavens are higher than the earth" (Isaiah 55:9).

Some may be tempted to laugh in disbelief at some of God's declarations and promises. But at funerals, we want to take seriously Christ's beatitude: "Blessed are ye that weep now: for ye shall laugh" (Luke 6:21). There are no tears in Heaven.
—R. W. B.

41. And he took the damsel by the hand, and said unto her, Talitha cumi; which is, being interpreted, Damsel, (I say unto thee,) arise.

As a tender gesture, Jesus not only touched the girl as her father had requested, but took her *by the hand*. He spoke to her in Aramaic, her native language: *Talitha cumi*. Mark, whose writing was meant for a Roman (non-Jewish) audience, translates the words for his readers: *Damsel, (I say unto thee,) arise*. These were no "magic words" to bring healing, but a direct command for the girl to live again.

42, 43. And straightway the damsel arose, and walked; for she was of the age of twelve years. And they were astonished with a great astonishment. And he charged them straitly that no man should know it; and commanded that something should be given her to eat.

The miracle was instantaneous. The girl *straightway* obeyed Jesus and *arose*. Since Jesus apparently had raised no one from the dead until now, the reaction of those present is understandable: *they were astonished with a great astonishment*, or "completely astonished" (*New International Version*).

Then Jesus gave the witnesses some odd instructions: they were not to tell anyone what they had just seen. Of course, the miracle could not be hidden, for as soon as the girl left the room, people would know that she had been raised from the dead and that Jesus was responsible. But Jesus constantly sought to keep the public's enthusiasm under some restraint, lest it get out of hand and bring His ministry to a premature climax.

Mark concludes his account with Jesus' continuing concern for the welfare of the girl. He *commanded that something should be given her to eat.* During her illness the girl had probably eaten very little if anything, and she naturally would have been hungry. Why didn't Jesus perform another miracle and feed her? We need to keep in mind that God never does for us what we can do for ourselves. Jesus knew that the girl's parents were quite capable of taking care of their daughter's physical needs, and, in fact, would rejoice at the opportunity to do so.

Conclusion

A. Only Believe

Not long ago, as I was looking over my calendar for the past couple of years, I discovered that I had attended more funerals than weddings. Time is beginning to take its toll. Although I have made many new friends over the years, the circle of my old friends has grown smaller. When death comes, there is always a sense of sadness and loss, but when the friend is a Christian, that sadness is mingled with joy. On those occasions, we have an opportunity to share our faith and offer words of reassurance, because we know that even those with a firm Christian faith are tempted to waver.

When the news arrived that Jairus's daughter was dead, all hope must have been drained from him. The pride and joy of his life had been taken, just as she stood at the entrance to young womanhood. Even though Jairus had great faith in Jesus' power to work miracles, he had never seen or heard of His raising the dead. Jesus knew exactly how he felt, and His first response was a message of comfort and assurance: "Be not afraid, only believe."

When we attempt to console a person who has lost a loved one, we cannot speak with the same authority as Jesus did. We lack the power to bring the dead back to life. But we can bring words of hope for a better resurrection—the resurrection into eternal life. We can share this hope with the firm authority of Jesus' words and the words of the New Testament writers. Let us use every opportunity to share in this important ministry.

B. Silencing the Skeptics

Skepticism is nothing new. Jesus experienced it in His ministry, as we have seen in today's lesson. When Jesus informed the mourners that Jairus's daughter was not dead, these skeptics "laughed him to scorn." We do not know exactly how Jesus' miracle affected their attitude toward Him. Some may have persisted in their skepticism, insisting that Jesus had just performed a clever trick, that the girl was not really dead at all. She had simply fainted, and then revived when Jesus entered the room. Others may have left perplexed by what they had seen. They did not want to believe that Jesus had wrought a miracle, but they were unable to find a better explanation for what had happened. We can hope that some of the mourners were impressed by the miracle and, at some point in time, came to believe in Jesus.

While we have no way of knowing how the mourners responded, we should ask the question, "What would have made the difference?" What we need to understand is that belief or unbelief is not based so much on the evidence as it is on the attitude of the witness. Some hearts are cold and skeptical. Others are warm and accepting. When we present the claims of Christ, we should always pray that the hearts of our listeners will be receptive.

Many of us live in an environment full of skeptics, in which our faith is regularly challenged by family members, friends, and fellow workers. While we cannot respond as Jesus did and perform a miracle, we can live daily the kind of life that will win the respect of our critics. Of course, this takes time and patience, but over time a godly life will earn the respect of skeptics, even if begrudgingly.

C. Prayer

Almighty God, Master over both life and death, help us apply today's lesson to our own lives. Lead us to live each day, not for the moment, but for eternity. Teach us to respond with wisdom and with the power of a godly life to the critics who would undermine our faith. In Jesus' name we pray. Amen.

D. Thought to Remember

In the presence of Jesus, death is a beaten foe.

Home Daily Bible Readings

Monday, Mar. 16—After Twelve Years of Bleeding (Mark 5:21-34)
Tuesday, Mar. 17—Dealing With Death (Mark 5:35-43)
Wednesday, Mar. 18—Power of God to Save (1 Corinthians 1:26-31)
Thursday, Mar. 19—Prophet Mighty in Deed and Word (Luke 10:16-24)
Friday, Mar. 20—Power Over the Enemy (Luke 24:13-27)
Saturday, Mar. 21—Power Made Perfect in Weakness (2 Corinthians 12:1-10)
Sunday, Mar. 22—Power at Work Within (Ephesians 3:14-21)

Learning by Doing

This page contains an alternate lesson plan emphasizing learning activities.
Classes desiring such student involvement will find these suggestions helpful.

Learning Goals

After this lesson, students should be able to:

1. Relate the specific ways in which Jesus manifested His power in ministering to Jairus and his daughter.

2. Recognize the difference that Jesus' power can make in dealing with death.

3. Suggest a circumstance (perhaps of a friend or loved one) in which they will be able to bear witness to Jesus' power over death.

Into the Lesson

Today's lesson deals with the very sensitive subject of death. Call attention at the beginning of class to the distinctive difference that Christian faith makes in dealing with death. Ask, "What is the basis for our victory over death?" The answer is the resurrection of Jesus from the dead. Then ask, "What are some of Jesus' statements that focus on His power over death?" Responses may include, "I am the resurrection, and the life" (John 11:25); "Because I live, ye shall live also" (John 14:19); or, "I go to prepare a place for you" (John 14:2). Others may be cited.

Note that we today are richly blessed to live with the knowledge of the empty tomb and the risen Christ. Today's Scripture from Mark tells of a man who did not enjoy this privilege. In fact, according to the Gospel records, our text records the first time that Jesus raised someone from the dead.

Into the Word

Read the printed text (Mark 5:21-24, 35-43) for the class. Then ask the class to complete the following *True-False* quiz as a way to reinforce the details of this miracle, and as a basis for comments about it. Print the quiz and give a copy to each student (unless they have a copy of the student book, where it is found).

____1. Jairus, as an official of the synagogue, was another skeptic and critic of Jesus' healing ministry. (*False. He approached Jesus as a believer. Not all rulers of the synagogue resisted Jesus' authority. There were Jewish religious leaders who were followers of Jesus.*)

____2. Jairus was just one person in a huge crowd pressing to see Jesus. (*True*)

____3. Jairus's fifteen-year-old daughter was dead when he pleaded with Jesus to come to his house. (*False, on two counts. The girl was twelve years old and was "at the point of death" when Jairus first approached Jesus.*)

____4. Responding to Jairus's desperate plea, Jesus went directly to his home. (*False. He stopped to heal another woman on the way.*)

____5. Jairus learned about his daughter's death while on the way to his house. (*True*)

____6. Jesus said the girl was not dead, but was sleeping. (*True. Explain the significance of this statement, using the lesson commentary.*)

____7. Jesus raised the daughter in the presence of her mother and father. (*True*)

____8. Jesus fed the girl after raising her from the dead. (*False. He asked others to feed her.*)

____9. Jesus asked the people not to tell others about this miracle. (*True. Ask the class why Jesus would request this. See the lesson commentary for help.*)

____10. Jesus spoke to the dead girl in Aramaic, and Mark translated Jesus' command for his non-Jewish readers. (*True*)

Into Life

Ask class members to describe Jairus's emotions when he first came to Jesus to request help for his dying daughter. Then ask how he would have felt upon hearing that she had died. Draw an outline of a child's hand on the chalkboard, and write inside the hand the emotions that class members mention.

Beside the first hand on the chalkboard, draw another large hand. Label this hand, "Helping Hand." Jesus is a wonderful model of compassion for those who have lost family members or friends. Explain that we can learn lessons about how to comfort from Him and from those who have gone through this experience. First, ask class members what we learn from Jesus about ministry to the bereaved. Then ask them to relate experiences they have had in trying to minister to the bereaved. What advice do they have on what to do or to say? Write these responses inside the "Helping Hand." If you have time, you may also wish to ask what *not* to do or say to people at their time of grief.

Summarize today's lesson by emphasizing that our comfort and confidence are rooted in Jesus' power over death. While we will not be able to see a family member or friend come back from the dead, we will have a joyous time of reunion with our Christian family in Heaven.

Let's Talk It Over

The questions on this page are designed to encourage review of the lesson Scriptures and to promote discussion of the lesson by the class. The answers provided are only discussion starters. Let your class talk it over from there.

1. The serious illness of Jairus's daughter led him to come humbly to Jesus. Does the illness and death of a family member often lead people to turn to Jesus today? If not, why?

People often react to a death in their family as they do to other forms of tribulation. Some experience a softening of the heart, leading to a trust in and surrender to Jesus Christ. Others become bitter and hardened toward God and Christ. When we ponder such a tragedy as the death of a spouse or parent or child, it seems natural that the bereaved would turn to God. The sense of loss, the feeling of helplessness, the bitterness of sorrow—all would surely cause a person to surrender to a God who loves and cares and promises victory over death. And yet many unbelievers, in the face of such experiences, will cling to godless pride and rebellion.

2. Jesus told the mourners that Jairus's daughter was not dead, but sleeping. Why did He tell them this?

The mourners did not understand that for Jesus, death was like a sleep from which one could be awakened. We remember the confusion of Jesus' disciples when He told them that Lazarus was sleeping, and that He was going to Judea to awaken him (John 11:7, 11-15). They knew by that time that He had awakened the daughter of Jairus from "sleep," but they still had difficulty understanding the full ramifications of Jesus' power. The rest of the New Testament echoes Jesus' terminology, and, in the light of His resurrection, boldly proclaims that "them also which sleep in Jesus will God bring with him" (1 Thessalonians 4:14).

3. It is interesting to note that after raising the little girl, Jesus commanded that she be given something to eat. What could His reasons have been for doing that?

The miracle restored the girl to life, but it apparently did not restore her to perfect health. She was perhaps weak from the effects of the illness. We can imagine that she may have had very little food during the hours or days preceding her death. Jesus had performed an extraordinary act to reverse the effects of death. Now it was time for her parents to resume their normal responsibilities of providing for her health. This command of Jesus serves as a reminder of the truth that God will not do for us what we are capable of doing for ourselves.

4. The daughter of Jairus is one of the three persons whose resurrection from the dead by Jesus is described in the Gospels. What unique insights into Jesus' power over death does each of these descriptions give us?

In the case of Jairus's daughter, we are reminded of the tragedy of death's coming to the very young. Many parents today experience such a devastating tragedy. Jesus' miracle can help them focus their gaze beyond the present tragedy to the ultimate triumph when "death is swallowed up in victory" (1 Corinthians 15:54). The raising of the son of the widow in Nain (Luke 7:11-17) was a victory over the desolation produced by death. The young man was the widow's only son, so Jesus rescued her, not only from sorrow, but from loneliness as well. This miracle illustrates the grand heavenly reunion that will transcend the separations wrought by death. When Jesus raised Lazarus (John 11:43, 44), the man had been dead four days. Jesus called him forth from the grave, and someday Jesus will call forth from the grave those who have been dead hundreds and thousands of years (John 5:25, 28, 29).

5. How do we answer those people who insist that "when you're dead, you're dead"?

Skeptics are fond of belittling those who believe in victory over death as practitioners of wishful thinking. The skeptics declare that there is no credible evidence for life after death. They further suggest that people would be much better off striving for a happier here and now, instead of being preoccupied with "pie in the sky, by and by." We can answer that there is indeed evidence for life beyond the grave. The historical fact of Jesus' resurrection from the dead can hardly be dismissed as wishful thinking. In spite of eras of persecution and the rantings and writings of countless scoffers, Jesus' death and resurrection are still proclaimed two thousand years after they happened. The Lord's Day, the Lord's Supper, and Christian baptism regularly testify to the victory over death that Jesus won.

Jesus' Identity and Mission

Mar 29

DEVOTIONAL READING: Isaiah 43:10-21.

LESSON SCRIPTURE: Mark 8:27—9:13.

PRINTED TEXT: Mark 8:27—9:1.

Mark 8:27-38

27 And Jesus went out, and his disciples, into the towns of Caesarea Philippi: and by the way he asked his disciples, saying unto them, Whom do men say that I am?

28 And they answered, John the Baptist: but some say, Elijah; and others, One of the prophets.

29 And he saith unto them, But whom say ye that I am? And Peter answereth and saith unto him, Thou art the Christ.

30 And he charged them that they should tell no man of him.

31 And he began to teach them, that the Son of man must suffer many things, and be rejected of the elders, and of the chief priests, and scribes, and be killed, and after three days rise again.

32 And he spake that saying openly. And Peter took him, and began to rebuke him.

33 But when he had turned about and looked on his disciples, he rebuked Peter, saying, Get thee behind me, Satan: for thou savorest not the things that be of God, but the things that be of men.

34 And when he had called the people unto him with his disciples also, he said unto them, Whosoever will come after me, let him deny himself, and take up his cross, and follow me.

35 For whosoever will save his life shall lose it; but whosoever shall lose his life for my sake and the gospel's, the same shall save it.

36 For what shall it profit a man, if he shall gain the whole world, and lose his own soul?

37 Or what shall a man give in exchange for his soul?

38 Whosoever therefore shall be ashamed of me and of my words, in this adulterous and sinful generation, of him also shall the Son of man be ashamed, when he cometh in the glory of his Father with the holy angels.

Mark 9:1

1 And he said unto them, Verily I say unto you, That there be some of them that stand here, which shall not taste of death, till they have seen the kingdom of God come with power.

GOLDEN TEXT: Whosoever will come after me, let him deny himself, and take up his cross, and follow me.—Mark 8:34.

The Gospel of Action (Mark)
Unit 1: Early Ministry of Jesus
(Lessons 1-4)

Lesson Aims

After completing today's lesson, students should:

1. Summarize Jesus' teaching in this passage concerning discipleship.

2. Describe what the Good Confession requires both in word and in lifestyle.

3. Suggest one area of their lives where they will determine to serve Jesus sacrificially.

Lesson Outline

INTRODUCTION
    A. No Easy Retirement
    B. Lesson Background
  I. PETER'S GOOD CONFESSION (Mark 8:27-30)
    A. Jesus' First Question (vv. 27, 28)
    B. Jesus' Second Question (v. 29)
    C. Jesus' Charge (v. 30)
  II. JESUS' FUTURE SUFFERING (Mark 8:31-33)
    A. Jesus' Prediction (v. 31)
    B. Peter's Response (v. 32)
    C. Jesus' Rebuke of Peter (v. 33)
  III. THE COST OF DISCIPLESHIP (Mark 8:34—9:1)
    A. Challenge of Self-Denial (vv. 34, 35)
      A Revolutionary Idea
    B. Value of a Soul (vv. 36, 37)
    C. Final Judgment (vv. 38—9:1)
      "I Am Not Ashamed"
CONCLUSION
    A. On This Rock
    B. Prayer
    C. Thought to Remember

Use the visual for Lesson 4 in the visuals packet to highlight Jesus' call to discipleship. It is shown on page 261.

Introduction

A. No Easy Retirement

A personnel officer of a large corporation had done an excellent job recruiting college graduates for his company. Because of his success, he was asked to speak to a large gathering of personnel directors.

"Gentlemen," he began, "there is no secret to what little success I have had. It's really quite simple. We all go to the same colleges and we talk to the same graduating seniors. Like you, I look over their college records. But if I have any secret, it is this: The first thing I do is ask them what they expect from our company. If a candidate is more concerned about an easy retirement program than he is about the challenge of the job, I don't hire him."

In the same way, Jesus seeks those who are more interested in accepting the hard work and the sacrifices involved in following Him than in enjoying an easy retirement program. "Whosoever will come after me, let him deny himself, and take up his cross, and follow me."

B. Lesson Background

By now several months had elapsed since the raising of Jairus's daughter (the subject of last week's lesson). Many exciting events had occurred between that miracle and the incident to be studied in today's lesson. Some of these included disappointments and conflicts. For example, Jesus was rejected in Nazareth, His hometown, leading Him to observe, "A prophet is not without honor, but in his own country" (Mark 6:4). In addition, the Pharisees had not given up trying to discredit Jesus before the people, although their efforts continued to fail. In the midst of all this, word came that John the Baptist, who had been imprisoned by Herod Antipas, had been executed.

But there had been some high points as well. One of these was the feeding of the five thousand (Mark 6:30-44). The people were so impressed by this that immediately they wanted to make Jesus their king. The enthusiasm of the people became so intense that Jesus found it necessary to withdraw to the area around Tyre and Sidon, located on the Mediterranean coast, north and west of Galilee. Even there word had spread concerning Jesus' ministry, and He was met by a Syrophoenician woman, who asked Him to cast a demon out of her daughter. From there He visited again the area of Decapolis, where He had encountered the Gadarene demoniac. The people welcomed Him on this occasion (they had asked Him to leave the first time), realizing the blessings He had brought to them. Returning to Galilee, Jesus once again provided food for the multitude who followed Him, feeding a crowd of four thousand (Mark 8:1-9).

Today's lesson finds Jesus nearing the end of His Galilean ministry. In spite of the various disappointments and setbacks during these months, Jesus' popularity remained strong. However, today's lesson brings us to a turning point in His ministry. Jesus will begin to speak "openly" about His eventual suffering and death and what this will mean for His followers. They too, if they want to "come after" Jesus, will have to take up the cross. We will see that such a demand was as hard for disciples back then to grasp as it is for disciples today.

I. Peter's Good Confession (Mark 8:27-30)

A. Jesus' First Question (v. 27)

27. And Jesus went out, and his disciples, into the towns of Caesarea Philippi: and by the way he asked his disciples, saying unto them, Whom do men say that I am?

Just prior to this, Jesus had been teaching at Bethsaida, a town on the northern shore of the Sea of Galilee, where He had healed a blind man (Mark 8:22-26). The town of *Caesarea Philippi* was located about twenty-five miles north of Bethsaida, near the headwaters of the Jordan River. It had been a center for the worship of the Canaanite god Baal and the Greek god Pan. Herod Philip (a son of King Herod the Great) had honored Caesar Augustus by naming the town *Caesarea*. He then added his own name to distinguish it from the Caesarea located on the Mediterranean coast. The *towns* refer to the small villages that were sometimes grouped around a larger city.

For several months Jesus had been conducting a kind of training school for His disciples. Now, as they made their way to Caesarea Philippi, it was exam time. The test consisted of only two questions, and the first one was easy: *Whom do men say that I am?*

28. And they answered, John the Baptist: but some say, Elijah; and others, One of the prophets.

Of course, Jesus already knew the answer to His question, but He wanted to start the disciples thinking in preparation for His second question. As the disciples traveled with Jesus and mingled among the crowds, they undoubtedly heard many comments about Jesus. Some believed that *John the Baptist* had come back to life. Herod Antipas, who had John executed, held this view (Mark 6:14). Others identified Jesus as *one of the prophets* who had returned. *Elijah* was considered a likely candidate, primarily because of the prophecy in Malachi 4:5, 6.

B. Jesus' Second Question (v. 29)

29. And he saith unto them, But whom say ye that I am? And Peter answereth and saith unto him, Thou art the Christ.

The disciples were able to give several right answers to the first question. It was easy to relate what others thought of Jesus. Now came the tough question: *Whom say ye that I am?* This

one involved them personally, and ultimately it required a personal commitment. Although Jesus addressed the question to all the disciples, it was Peter, who tended to be the spokesman for the group, who answered. Peter was usually rather impetuous, often "sticking his foot in his mouth" when he spoke. But this time his answer was flawless. Without any hesitation he declared, *Thou art the Christ.*

The term *Christ* is the Greek translation of the Hebrew word *Messiah*, which means "an anointed one." In ancient Israel it was a common practice to anoint prophets, priests, and kings as a public symbol of initiation into their office. In later Judaism many looked to a coming Messiah who would free the people from foreign bondage and allow Israel once more to be independent. Many Old Testament passages were quoted to support this view. Some passages do indeed portray the coming Messiah as a conquering King who will lead His people to victory over all their enemies. Other passages, however, see the Messiah as a suffering servant, ready to die for His people. These were often overlooked by those in Jesus' day who saw deliverance from Roman rule as Israel's most pressing need.

It is clear that Peter did not grasp all the implications of his Good Confession. In the next few verses we learn that he did not understand how the Messiah could allow Himself to suffer and die at the hands of others. Peter's understanding of Jesus had to mature, as it must for all of us. In many churches, persons coming to Christ are asked publicly to express their commitment to Him by speaking the words of Peter's Good Confession. This is certainly very appropriate. But what should follow—a total commitment to learn more of Christ and live for Him—is even more important.

C. Jesus' Charge (v. 30)

30. And he charged them that they should tell no man of him.

At first glance, this command of Jesus may seem strange. After all, His mission was to bring the good news that He is the Christ. No doubt, the disciples would have been eager to carry such a message. But at this point, broadcasting such information in this territory could be dangerous. In Galilee the Zealots, a party committed to Jewish independence from Rome, were quite numerous. Had Jesus' messiahship been broadcast widely, it could have led to uprisings that Rome would have put down with a tragic amount of bloodshed and loss of life. Jesus wanted to spare the people these horrors. In His own time and in His own way, He would make the announcement to the larger public.

II. Jesus' Future Suffering
(Mark 8:31-33)

A. Jesus' Prediction (v. 31)

31. And he began to teach them, that the Son of man must suffer many things, and be rejected of the elders, and of the chief priests, and scribes, and be killed, and after three days rise again.

Peter's Good Confession had scarcely been uttered before Jesus introduced a sobering note—one that did not square with the common understanding of the Messiah. He would *suffer many things* at the hands of the religious leaders. This should not have been a great shock to the disciples, for they had already seen Jesus under attack by the scribes and Pharisees. But these earlier confrontations had consisted only of verbal battles that were not physically threatening. Now, Jesus was telling the disciples that His enemies would actually kill Him. This did not sound at all like the conquering king that they anticipated the Messiah to be. In addition, Jesus added that *after three days* He would *rise again*. The disciples, however, were so taken aback by Jesus' talk of suffering and death that they disregarded completely His promise of resurrection. Even after it happened, they were slow to believe it.

B. Peter's Response (v. 32)

32. And he spake that saying openly. And Peter took him, and began to rebuke him.

In the past, Jesus on occasion had presented His teaching in veiled language, challenging His followers to think carefully to the full implica-

tions of His words. Here he began to speak *openly*; His language was plain and unambiguous. Peter had no trouble understanding exactly what Jesus was saying. This disturbed him so much that he began to reprimand Jesus. Matthew gives his statement: "Lord: this shall not be unto thee" (Matthew 16:22).

C. Jesus' Rebuke of Peter (v. 33)

33. But when he had turned about and looked on his disciples, he rebuked Peter, saying, Get thee behind me, Satan: for thou savorest not the things that be of God, but the things that be of men.

Peter had taken Jesus aside when he rebuked Him. Apparently the other disciples were not a part of this discussion, but now Jesus *turned about* to them, including them in His rebuke of Peter and indicating that they shared Peter's views. Jesus did not mince words with Peter: *Get thee behind me, Satan.* Jesus acted quickly and forcefully to correct this serious misunderstanding among His followers.

When Jesus at the beginning of His ministry triumphed over Satan and his three temptations, Satan left Him, but only "for a season" (Luke 4:13). This implies that Satan tempted Jesus at other times during His ministry. In this case the evil one used Peter as an unwitting pawn in an attempt to sabotage Jesus' mission. This incident should serve as a warning to us that Satan may use close friends and even members of our own family to cause us to stumble by persuading us to realign our priorities. This was Peter's primary problem: he was "savoring" (or drawing more satisfaction from) *the things that be of men* rather than *the things that be of God.*

We all face similar temptations to do this daily. Living in a physical body in a physical world all too often entices us to think of physical and material needs first rather than eternal matters. In our increasingly secular society, these temptations are not only more numerous, but more subtle. We need the help of the Lord if we are to resist them successfully. To try to handle them alone is a formula for certain disaster.

III. The Cost of Discipleship
(Mark 8:34—9:1)

A. Challenge of Self-Denial (vv. 34, 35)

34, 35. And when he had called the people unto him with his disciples also, he said unto them, Whosoever will come after me, let him deny himself, and take up his cross, and follow me. For whosoever will save his life shall lose it; but whosoever shall lose his life for my sake and the gospel's, the same shall save it.

How to Say It

ANTIPAS. *An*-tih-pus.
AUGUSTUS. Aw-*gust*-us.
BAAL. *Bay*-ul.
BETHSAIDA. Beth-*say*-uh-duh.
CAESAREA PHILIPPI. Sess-uh-*ree*-uh
   Fuh-*lip*-pie or *Fill*-uh-pie.
CANAANITE. *Kay*-nuh-nite.
DECAPOLIS. Dee-*cap*-uh-lis.
GOLGOTHA. *Gahl*-guh-thuh.
MEDITERRANEAN. *Med*-uh-tuh-*ray*-nee-un
   (strong accent on *ray*).
SIDON. *Sigh*-dun.
SYROPHOENICIAN. *Sigh*-roe-fih-*nish*-un
   (strong accent on *nish*).
TYRE. Tire.
ZEALOTS. *Zel*-uts.

After the discussion *with his disciples* about the future of His ministry, Jesus then turned to *the people* who apparently were not far away. In very pointed language He laid before them the cost of discipleship—a cost that must have seemed frighteningly high.

The first step was self-denial. This was not a popular theme in Jesus' day, nor is it in ours. Jesus meant this in a most radical sense. He demands our wills, our minds, our bodies, our talents, and our wealth. As has often been stated, "If Christ is not Lord *of* all, He is not Lord *at* all."

Next, Jesus called upon the prospective disciple to *take up his cross.* No doubt this expression created images of pain and torture in the minds of His listeners. Many had likely witnessed a Roman execution by crucifixion. The common practice was to force the victim to carry his own cross to the place of execution. Such a demand by Jesus would thoroughly discourage the fainthearted and even cause the bravest to think twice about following Him.

The final step of discipleship was to *follow* Jesus wherever He might lead. This could require one to leave behind his goods, his fame, and in some cases even his family and friends. Jesus' requirements remind us of one of Winston Churchill's speeches during World War II. As Britain stood on the verge of being taken over by the Nazis, he asserted that all he had to offer the British people was "blood, toil, tears, and sweat."

Jesus followed His challenge with two paradoxes (statements that seem contradictory but actually convey great truths). Whoever wishes to *save* his life is certain to *lose* it. On the other hand, if one is willing to *lose* his life for Christ and the gospel, he will in the end *save* it. This makes no sense at all to our modern culture, which often lives by the motto: "The one who dies with the most toys wins." Yet many across the centuries have found truth in Jesus' words: a David Livingstone, who spent his life carrying the gospel to the heart of Africa, a Mother Teresa, whose loving service in India is admired by all, and countless others who have spent their lives without fame or fanfare in faithful service to the Lord. As Jim Elliot, who was martyred for Christ in Ecuador, said, "He is no fool who loses what he cannot keep to gain what he cannot lose."

A REVOLUTIONARY IDEA

Current culture seems dedicated to self-gratification. The messages are mostly the same: indulge yourself, pamper yourself, enjoy yourself, treat yourself, because "You deserve a break

visual for
lesson 4

today!" Celebrities in television commercials tell us that they use expensive personal care products, because "I'm worth it!"

Probably no society has been less inclined than ours to embrace the disciplines of self-denial—not even to achieve worthy goals of self-improvement or social betterment. Many want to lose weight, but not enough to modify food intake or to exercise regularly. Many profess a desire for a personal devotional life, but few give up sleep time or leisure activities to read the Bible and pray. Many acknowledge the importance of weekly worship, yet they will not sacrifice ball games, overtime income, socializing, or other personal pleasures to make it a priority.

Jesus' teaching about the self-denial required of His disciples is not popular. Yet it is a basic principle of Christian "followship." Christianity at its best is lived out in the lives of those who willingly give in, give up and give out—imitating the surrender, sacrifice, and service of the Master.   —R. W. B.

B. Value of a Soul (vv. 36, 37)

36, 37. For what shall it profit a man, if he shall gain the whole world, and lose his own soul? Or what shall a man give in exchange for his soul?

Every day we see examples of people who have never considered the answer to these questions, or, knowing the answer, have rejected it. Politicians sell their votes to the highest bidder, businessmen sell their integrity to make a profit, entertainers sink to any depths to please an audience, and athletes cheat to win a game. All of these gain from a worldly perspective, but in the spiritual realm they are losers.

C. Final Judgment (vv. 38—9:1)

38. Whosoever therefore shall be ashamed of me and of my words, in this adulterous and sinful generation, of him also shall the Son of man be ashamed, when he cometh in the glory of his Father with the holy angels.

To be *ashamed* of Jesus means not only to reject Him and His teachings openly or even vehemently; it also includes claiming to follow

Him, yet "cutting corners" spiritually, or interpreting His teachings in such a way that they have no impact on daily living. There will be a heavy penalty for those who conduct themselves in this manner: When the *Son of man* comes at the final judgment, He will be *ashamed* of them. Peter, when he tried to persuade Jesus not to accept suffering and death, and later when he denied Him three times in one night, was guilty of being ashamed of Jesus. Later, Peter repented of his sins and became a bold, unashamed ambassador for Christ (Acts 5:29).

"I AM NOT ASHAMED"

Jesus was up-front with His recruiting tactics. He spoke of hardships as well as of blessings and benefits. The call to bear a cross was never designed to result in throngs of willing volunteers. Carrying a cross was part of the typical Roman execution process. Jesus was forced to comply with this as He struggled toward Golgotha. When we who follow Him take up our crosses, we symbolize our willingness to lose our lives for Jesus and for the gospel.

Our society needs this kind of bold witness to the gospel. It needs to hear the testimony of those who, like Paul, are willing to declare, "I am not ashamed of the gospel of Christ" (Romans 1:16). Some will be led to Christ through such a witness; others will prove cynical and resistant. Jesus' viewpoint, however, is unmistakably clear: "Whosoever therefore shall confess me before men, him will I confess also before my Father which is in heaven" (Matthew 10:32).

—R. W. B.

1. And he said unto them, Verily I say unto you, That there be some of them that stand here, which shall not taste of death, till they have seen the kingdom of God come with power.

This verse has been the source of much discussion among Bible scholars. It is quite obvious that Jesus did not return with His angels to bring final judgment before those who were present at this time had died. It is better to understand the fulfillment of this prophecy as occurring on the Day of Pentecost when the *kingdom of God*, or the church (Colossians 1:13) was founded. This means that the "coming" referred to in verse 38 is different from the "coming" mentioned in this verse. God began the church with a dramatic display of *power*, and it has continued through the centuries to preach the gospel as "the power of God unto salvation" (Romans 1:16).

Conclusion
A. On This Rock

Matthew notes that after Peter's Good Confession (Matthew 16:16), Jesus turned to him and told him, "Thou art Peter, and upon this rock I will build my church" (v. 18). For centuries theologians have debated the meaning of this passage. Clearly, the rock was not Peter, for within a few moments he was rebuking Jesus for saying that He must die. Peter was not solid enough material upon which to build the church. The rock is the deity of Jesus Christ, which Peter proclaimed in his Good Confession. This is the solid rock that will withstand whatever storms assault the church.

Some today would deny that Jesus Christ is the divine Son of God. For example, the Jesus Seminar, which in recent years has garnered a great deal of publicity, assembled a collection of "scholars" to determine which statements of Jesus in the Gospels can actually be attributed to Him. Its efforts have reduced the "historic Jesus" to a rather pathetic figure about whom we can know very little. The Christ, the divine Son of God, was a myth, they tell us.

It is not a myth, however, but the divine Son of God Himself who has sustained the church over the years. Should He tarry, He will still sustain the church long after the Jesus Seminar has become an obscure footnote in history.

B. Prayer

Strengthen in our hearts, dear God, the conviction that Jesus Christ is Your divine Son. May our convictions be strong enough that we will take up our crosses and follow wherever He leads. In His name we pray. Amen.

C. Thought to Remember
"Thou art the Christ" (Mark 8:29).

Home Daily Bible Readings

Monday, Mar. 23—Pain Awaits the Messiah (Mark 8:27-33)
Tuesday, Mar. 24—Self-Denial for Disciples (Mark 8:34—9:1)
Wednesday, Mar. 25—Seeing Jesus in a New Light (Mark 9:2-13)
Thursday, Mar. 26—God Is Doing a New Thing (Isaiah 43:10-21)
Friday, Mar. 27—Blessing in Midst of the Earth (Isaiah 19:18-25)
Saturday, Mar. 28—Together We Will Be Saved (Acts 15:6-11)
Sunday, Mar. 29—Declare His Glory to All People (Psalm 9:1-13)

Learning by Doing

This page contains an alternate lesson plan emphasizing learning activities.
Classes desiring such student involvement will find these suggestions helpful.

Learning Goals

After this lesson, the student will be able to:

1. Summarize Jesus' teaching in this passage concerning discipleship.

2. Describe what the Good Confession requires both in word and in lifestyle.

3. Suggest one area of their lives where they will determine to serve Jesus sacrificially.

Into the Lesson

Divide class members into two teams. Write the letters of the word D-I-S-C-I-P-L-E vertically on two sheets of paper. Give a sheet to each team, and have someone from each team serve as "secretary." For each letter in the word "disciple," team members are to think of two words that describe a disciple or follower of Jesus. (Thus they will need to come up with four words that begin with "i.") See which team can finish this assignment first. Then call attention to the fact that today's lesson text is one of the most important passages in all of Scripture on the subject of discipleship.

Into the Word

1. Read Mark 8:27-30. Using the lesson commentary, give a brief lecture on the background and content of these verses. Conclude the lecture by explaining the various ways in which people in Jesus' day understood the Messiah's mission. Use material in the lesson commentary under verses 29 and 30.

2. Read Mark 8:31-33. This passage contains two perplexing scenes. One is Peter rebuking Jesus. The other is Jesus rebuking Peter. Ask the following discussion questions: (1) Why would Peter rebuke Jesus? What was the issue? (2) Explain Jesus' rebuke to Peter: "Get thee behind me, Satan." Clarify what Jesus was saying.

Next, explain the wonder of Peter's moving so quickly from the "Good Confession" to being rebuked by Jesus. It seems that Peter still did not understand all of the implications of his confession. However, Peter's commitment to Jesus was apparent. Later, his words and beliefs were demonstrated through his leadership and preaching after Jesus returned to Heaven. The lesson here is encouraging. Even if we don't understand everything about Jesus, we still can confess Him as our Lord and grow in our knowledge and our service.

3. Read Mark 8:34—9:1. Prepare a poster with two columns. Place the heading "Scripture" at the top of Column 1 and "Qualities of a Good Disciple" at the top of the other column. In Column 1 list the following items: Deny yourself; Take up your cross; Follow me; Verse 35; Verses 36, 37; and Verses 38—9:1. Ask class members to tell what quality of a good disciple of Jesus is found in each of the sayings of Jesus or of the verses cited. Ideas for each response are shown below.

Scripture	Qualities of a Good Disciple
Deny yourself	Selflessness
Take up your cross	Service
Follow me	Imitation
Verse 35	Sacrifice
Verses 36, 37	Eternal Investment
Verses 38—9:1	Witnessing

Into Life

As a means of applying the principles in today's lesson, make a copy of the *Personal Reflection Sheet* below for each student. Ask each to take a few moments to evaluate his or her life as a disciple, based solely on today's text. Softly play a tape of a song such as, "Take My Life and Let It Be" or "I Surrender All" as they do this.

Personal Reflection Sheet

1. I am sacrificing portions of my life in order to be a follower of Jesus.

Always   Usually   Seldom

2. I am finding ways to serve the Lord and His church effectively.

Always   Usually   Seldom

3. I strive to imitate the values and lifestyle of the Lord Jesus.

Always   Usually   Seldom

4. My life is transparent enough for people to see my faith. My life is a witness to the lordship of Jesus.

Always   Usually   Seldom

5. My decision: As a result of this lesson and my personal reflection, I have decided to . . .

Close with prayer, asking God to bless the decisions made on the personal reflection sheets.

Let's Talk It Over

*The questions on this page are designed to encourage review of the lesson
Scriptures and to promote discussion of the lesson by the class. The answers
provided are only discussion starters. Let your class talk it over from there.*

**1. Jesus asked His disciples, "Whom do men
say that I am?" (Mark 8:27). What value is
there in raising this question today?**

We must admit that people in our time hold
many incomplete or erroneous views regarding
Jesus Christ. It is important to have some knowledge of these views, so that we can correct them.
For example, we may learn that someone holds
the view that Jesus was no more than a great
moral teacher. We must show that Jesus' moral
teaching cannot be separated from His divine
authority (Matthew 7:28, 29). Other people
regard Jesus as an ordinary, fallible human
being. They deny the reality of His miracles, and
they explain away the fact of His bodily resurrection. We must demonstrate to them that the
Gospel writers are credible, dependable eyewitnesses. We can trust the writers when they
describe Jesus' healing the sick, raising the dead,
and exercising power over nature. We can
accept their testimony that they saw and heard
Jesus after His death and resurrection.

**2. Jesus called His disciples to a life of self-
denial. How can this call be harmonized with
the various New Testament passages that speak
of Christians' experiencing joy?**

Paul wrote that part of "the fruit of the Spirit"
is joy (Galatians 5:22). He exhorted the
Philippians, "Rejoice in the Lord always: and
again I say, Rejoice" (Philippians 4:4). Peter said
of the believers to whom he wrote, "Ye rejoice
with joy unspeakable and full of glory" (1 Peter
1:8). In spite of such exhortations, Paul and
Peter practiced and advocated self-denial. There
is obviously no contradiction between joy and
self-denial. When we think about it, we recognize that careless indulgence in many kinds of
behavior (some of them permissible in themselves) can harm body and mind. Damaged
health and impaired thinking negate the joy that
such indulgence promises. When we exercise
self-denial, we preserve physical, mental, and
spiritual health. That frees us to experience joy
at a high level.

**3. Jesus called His disciples to a life of suffer-
ing. How can this call be harmonized with the
various New Testament passages that speak of
Christians' experiencing peace?**

The "fruit of the Spirit" also includes peace
(Galatians 5:22). Jesus spoke of giving His peace
to His disciples, and contrasted it with the peace
that the world promises (John 14:27; 16:33).
Paul also spoke of believers' possessing "the
peace of God, which passeth all understanding"
(Philippians 4:7). Yet the book of Acts and the
epistles describe constant persecutions and trials suffered by the early disciples. The secret of
their peace in the midst of all this was their
knowledge of ultimate victory through the resurrection. We have the same source of peace today
when we suffer.

**4. Jesus called His disciples to follow Him
wherever He leads. How can we discern where
He is leading us?**

Many of the commands and exhortations that
Jesus gave to His disciples are also directed to
us. In a previous lesson we focused on the command, "Come ye after me, and I will make you
to become fishers of men" (Mark 1:17). When
there is an opportunity to "fish" for the souls of
others, we can be sure that Christ leads us to do
it. Our present lesson deals with the Good
Confession. When we have a chance to speak up
for Jesus as the Christ, we know that He leads us
in making that confession. Jesus also instructed
His disciples to minister to the needy and the
poor. We often encounter situations that challenge us to do the same. When that happens, we
can be certain that Jesus is leading us through
those circumstances.

**5. In what ways do Christians sometimes
show that they are ashamed of Jesus and His
words?**

Someone has said that silence is not always
golden; at times it is just plain yellow! Remaining silent about Jesus when He is being attacked
is one example. Holding our tongue when we
could be mocked or rejected for acknowledging
Him as our Savior and Lord is another. How
about those people who attend church and give
to the church, but deny Jesus by the way they
live outside the church? Also, how about those
who replace the Biblical Jesus with a watered-
down version requiring little faith and personal
commitment? These are tragic demonstrations of
being ashamed of Jesus.

Jesus Enters Jerusalem

DEVOTIONAL READING: Psalm 118:19-29.

LESSON SCRIPTURE: Mark 11.

PRINTED TEXT: Mark 11:1-10, 15-18.

Mark 11:1-10, 15-18

1 And when they came nigh to Jerusalem, unto Bethphage and Bethany, at the mount of Olives, he sendeth forth two of his disciples,

2 And saith unto them, Go your way into the village over against you: and as soon as ye be entered into it, ye shall find a colt tied, whereon never man sat; loose him, and bring him.

3 And if any man say unto you, Why do ye this? say ye that the Lord hath need of him; and straightway he will send him hither.

4 And they went their way, and found the colt tied by the door without in a place where two ways met; and they loose him.

5 And certain of them that stood there said unto them, What do ye, loosing the colt?

6 And they said unto them even as Jesus had commanded: and they let them go.

7 And they brought the colt to Jesus, and cast their garments on him; and he sat upon him.

8 And many spread their garments in the way; and others cut down branches off the trees, and strewed them in the way.

9 And they that went before, and they that followed, cried, saying, Hosanna; Blessed is he that cometh in the name of the Lord:

10 Blessed be the kingdom of our father David, that cometh in the name of the Lord: Hosanna in the highest.

. . . .

15 And they come to Jerusalem: and Jesus went into the temple, and began to cast out them that sold and bought in the temple, and overthrew the tables of the money changers, and the seats of them that sold doves;

16 And would not suffer that any man should carry any vessel through the temple.

17 And he taught, saying unto them, Is it not written, My house shall be called of all nations the house of prayer? but ye have made it a den of thieves.

18 And the scribes and chief priests heard it, and sought how they might destroy him: for they feared him, because all the people was astonished at his doctrine.

GOLDEN TEXT: They that went before, and they that followed, cried, saying, Hosanna; Blessed is he that cometh in the name of the Lord.—Mark 11:9.

Lesson Aims

After completing this lesson, students should:
1. Describe the reactions to Jesus' entry into Jerusalem and His cleansing of the temple.
2. Explain the significance of Jesus' triumphal entry.
3. Take specific steps to eliminate something from their lives that keeps Jesus from ruling triumphantly.

Lesson Outline

INTRODUCTION
  A. Watching the Parade
  B. Lesson Background
  I. PREPARING TO ENTER JERUSALEM (Mark 11:1-7)
  A. Sending for the Colt (vv. 1-3)
  B. Bringing the Colt (vv. 4-7)
  II. JESUS ENTERS THE CITY (Mark 11:8-10)
  A. The Crowd's Actions (v. 8)
  B. The Crowd's Words (vv. 9, 10)
    We Love a Parade
  III. JESUS CLEANSES THE TEMPLE (Mark 11:15-18)
  A. Jesus Drives Out the Money Changers (vv. 15, 16)
  B. Jesus Explains His Actions (v. 17)
    Church Work
  C. The Religious Leaders React (v. 18)
CONCLUSION
  A. "Hail to the Chief"
  B. A House of Prayer?
  C. Prayer
  D. Thought to Remember

The visual for Lesson 5 challenges us to consider the two kinds of crowds that Jesus faced in Jerusalem. It is shown on page 269.

Introduction

A. Watching the Parade

A country boy once learned that a circus was coming to a nearby town. He had never seen a circus before, and day by day as he saw the posters, he became more excited. He worked and saved his money, looking forward to the day when the circus would arrive. When the day came, some neighbors took him into the town and found him a spot along the street where he

could watch the parade. How thrilled he was when the parade came by, with elephants, caged lions, clowns, jugglers, acrobats, and all sorts of things that the boy had never seen before.

When the last member of the parade had passed, the boy ran out and gave the surprised ringmaster the money he had saved for the circus. Then he went back to the place where his neighbors were waiting for him. He was ready to go home. He thought that when he had seen the parade, he had seen the circus.

Many who cried, "Hosanna!" when Jesus rode into Jerusalem on a donkey were like that boy. They thought that when they saw Jesus enter Jerusalem, they had seen everything. Many of them went home and missed the real reason for His coming. No doubt some of them were among those who later cried, "Crucify him!"

B. Lesson Background

Last week's lesson focused on Peter's Good Confession: "Thou art the Christ" (Mark 8:29). Shortly after this, Jesus took Peter, James, and John with Him up a high mountain. There He was transfigured with Moses and Elijah. As the disciples recovered from this experience, the voice of God came from a cloud and declared, "This is my beloved Son: hear him" (Mark 9:7).

The weeks that followed were busy ones. The Gospel of John indicates that Jesus made a hurried trip to Jerusalem for the Feast of Tabernacles, where He became involved in conflict with the religious leaders (John 7–9). Jesus then retired to Perea, the region east of the Jordan River, where He carried on a short ministry. He then returned to Judea and to Bethany, where Lazarus was raised from the dead. Today's lesson finds Jesus coming to Jerusalem for His final confrontation with the Jewish leaders—the confrontation that led to His death.

I. Preparing to Enter Jerusalem (Mark 11:1-7)

A. Sending for the Colt (vv. 1-3)

1. And when they came nigh to Jerusalem, unto Bethphage and Bethany, at the mount of Olives, he sendeth forth two of his disciples.

Prior to this, Jesus had been in Jericho, where He healed blind Bartimeus (Mark 10:46-52). The town of *Bethany* was on the eastern slope of the *mount of Olives*, about two miles from Jerusalem. We do not know the exact location of *Bethphage*, but apparently it was near Bethany. The walk from Jericho to Bethany, an uphill climb of about sixteen miles, would have taken most of a day. It seems likely that Jesus and His disciples left Jericho on Friday morning and arrived in Bethany before sunset, which marked the beginning of the Sabbath.

Bethany was the home of Mary, Martha, Lazarus, and Simon the leper, who may have been related to them. Perhaps Jesus stayed in the home of Simon while He was in Bethany. We do know that "six days before the passover" (John 12:1), which was presumably the Saturday evening prior to the day of the triumphal entry, Jesus was present at a banquet in Simon's home. Here He was anointed with precious ointment by Mary (Mark 14:3; John 12:3).

2, 3. And saith unto them, Go your way into the village over against you: and as soon as ye be entered into it, ye shall find a colt tied, whereon never man sat; loose him, and bring him. And if any man say unto you, Why do ye this? say ye that the Lord hath need of him; and straightway he will send him hither.

After spending the Sabbath in Bethany, on the next day (our Sunday) Jesus was ready to enter Jerusalem. Prior to this, He sent two of the disciples *into the village over against* them (probably Bethphage) to bring back a *colt*, which they would find near the edge of the village. None of the Gospel writers identifies the two disciples that were sent.

Although we normally think of a colt as a young horse, it is clear from Matthew's account, and from the prophecy Jesus fulfilled, that this was "the foal of an ass" (Matthew 21:2, 5). The disciples were instructed to speak to someone, only if they were challenged about why they were taking the animal. At first glance, the taking of another person's property seems wrong. It is quite likely, however, that Jesus had made prior arrangements to borrow the animal for this occasion.

B. Bringing the Colt (vv. 4-7)

4-6. And they went their way, and found the colt tied by the door without in a place where two ways met; and they loose him. And certain of them that stood there said unto them, What do ye, loosing the colt? And they said unto them even as Jesus had commanded: and they let them go.

Matthew tells us that there were two animals: "an ass tied, and a colt with her" (Matthew 21:2). This may have been the reason that Jesus sent two disciples on this assignment. A *colt* that had never been ridden would be more manageable if it were accompanied by its mother. Matthew also sees in this act a fulfillment of the prophecy found in Zechariah 9:9: "Behold, thy King cometh unto thee, meek, and sitting upon an ass, and a colt the foal of an ass" (Matthew 21:5).

When the two disciples untied the donkey and prepared to take it, some of them that *stood* nearby saw at once that they were strangers and stopped them. The villagers acted properly in protecting their property or that of their neighbor. (Their behavior was different from many today, who, not wanting to get involved, would probably have ignored the disciples.) "What are you doing untying that animal?" they asked.

The disciples replied *as Jesus had commanded*; and that settled the matter. Perhaps this reply was a prearranged password that identified the men as Jesus' disciples. In addition to the twelve and His close friends, Jesus had additional followers who provided Him with food, lodging, and other necessities. The owner of the donkey was apparently one of these disciples who served "behind the scenes."

7. And they brought the colt to Jesus, and cast their garments on him; and he sat upon him.

Some writers think it significant that Jesus chose to ride a donkey rather than a horse. Horses were ridden by military leaders and worldly kings. By choosing to ride a donkey (the beast of burden of the common people), Jesus was making a statement that His kingdom was not built on military might or human traditions. His kingdom was "not of this world" (John 18:36). The donkey was also a symbol of peace and humility. It was a fitting animal for the Prince of Peace to use as He entered Jerusalem to fulfill His Father's plan for bringing peace to sinful humanity through His death.

Jesus rode the colt without a bridle or saddle. The disciples did lay some of their *garments* across the back of the colt, thus making the ride more comfortable for Jesus. It was a minor miracle that the colt placidly accepted Jesus as a rider rather than reacting violently to Him. Perhaps the same quality of gentleness that endeared Jesus to children also calmed the fears of animals.

II. Jesus Enters the City (Mark 11:8-10)

A. The Crowd's Actions (v. 8)

8. And many spread their garments in the way; and others cut down branches off the trees, and strewed them in the way.

The response of the crowd to Jesus' arrival was spontaneous. At least there is no indication that the disciples had gone ahead and announced His coming, trying to stir up the people. Many of those who had traveled to Jerusalem for the Passover had seen or heard of Jesus previously, and they responded enthusiastically without

How to Say It

BARTIMEUS. Bar-tih-*me*-us.
BETHPHAGE. *Beth*-fuh-jee.
PEREA. Peh-*ree*-uh.
ZECHARIAH. Zek-uh-*rye*-uh.

any advance promotion. Some of them certainly knew that Jesus was running a risk by entering the city in the face of the bitter opposition of the religious leaders. Knowing this may have intensified the tumultuous greeting that they gave Him.

The emotions of the crowd caused them to throw down their *garments* in Jesus' path as a gesture of their support for Him. Others cut small *branches* from trees and *strewed*, or spread, these in the road. Today there are few trees along the route from Bethany to Jerusalem, but at one time they grew much more plentifully on the slopes of the Mount of Olives. John informs us that some of the people went out to meet Jesus with palm branches (John 12:13). For this reason, we refer to the Sunday before Easter as "Palm Sunday."

B. The Crowd's Words (vv. 9, 10)

9, 10. And they that went before, and they that followed, cried, saying, Hosanna; Blessed is he that cometh in the name of the Lord: Blessed be the kingdom of our father David, that cometh in the name of the Lord: Hosanna in the highest.

All four Gospel writers record the triumphal entry, although there are differences in the accounts, especially in what the crowd shouted. This should not surprise us because this was a spontaneous outpouring of joyous praise, not a carefully planned and orchestrated gathering. Some of the people went *before* Jesus while others *followed*. This is an indication that there may have been two crowds. One was made up of those who had come with Jesus from Jericho and others who had gathered in Bethany when they learned that He was there. They followed Jesus when He started toward Jerusalem. The other crowd, already in Jerusalem, heard the shouts of those with Jesus, and came out of the city and up the slope of the Mount of Olives to meet Him. Once they reached the procession, they turned around and led the way back into the city.

Hosanna is the Greek form of a Hebrew expression that meant something like, "Save us, we pray." As such, it was the form of a prayer, but it came to be used as a shout of praise or acclamation. The shouts that Mark records

reflect Psalm 118, especially verses 25 and 26. Blessings were called upon the one *that cometh in the name of the Lord*, that is, upon Jesus as the promised Messiah. The people also cried out for *the kingdom of our father David*, thus identifying the Messiah as a descendant of David and the one who would fulfill God's promise to David of an everlasting kingdom (2 Samuel 7:16). Many in the crowd, however, saw this kingdom in political rather than spiritual terms.

Luke records that the crowd shouted, "Blessed be the King that cometh in the name of the Lord," and then added, "Peace in heaven, and glory in the highest" (Luke 19:38). In John's account the crowd hailed Jesus as "King of Israel" (John 12:13). Luke also tells us that some of the Pharisees requested that Jesus silence the crowd. Jesus' response was, "If these should hold their peace, the stones would immediately cry out" (Luke 19:40). In addition, Luke speaks of Jesus weeping over Jerusalem as He neared it (v. 41). His heart was heavy, because looking into the future, He saw an enemy coming against the city and leveling it, not leaving "one stone upon another" (v. 44).

Mark then notes that Jesus entered the temple and "looked round about upon all things" (v. 11). He was probably disturbed by the presence of the money changers and those selling sacrificial animals. But since it was evening, Jesus took no actions against these evils. That would come the following day. For now Jesus, along with the twelve, returned to Bethany for the night.

WE LOVE A PARADE

My two-year-old grandson had just come in from watching an Independence Day parade with his grandmother. He gave an excited report of bands, fire trucks and floats. He's an "all-American boy"; he loves parades.

Human nature longs for something to celebrate. Parades are often a way to honor people and their achievements with songs and cheers, clapping and dancing, and waving and yelling. Vicariously, we bask in the glory of celebrities, rejoicing with those who rejoice. There's something about the atmosphere of a parade that makes us feel especially good.

The crowd that accompanied Jesus into Jerusalem was no different. The excitement of leading the way for one who claimed to be a King seized their emotions. They were thrilled to see Jesus enter the city in triumph. Many believed that this signaled the soon-to-come overthrow of Rome, which would result in the freedom of God's people from the tyranny of heathens.

When Jesus' parade turned into His passion, however, the crowds, and even Jesus' closest followers, forsook Him. It's easy to ride the Christian "bandwagon"—until it turns toward Calvary.

Are you a Good Friday disciple, or only a Palm Sunday Christian? Whether you can truly celebrate Easter depends upon your answer!

—R. W. B.

III. Jesus Cleanses the Temple
(Mark 11:15-18)

A. Jesus Drives Out the Money Changers
(vv. 15, 16)

15, 16. And they come to Jerusalem: and Jesus went into the temple, and began to cast out them that sold and bought in the temple, and overthrew the tables of the money changers, and the seats of them that sold doves; and would not suffer that any man should carry any vessel through the temple.

The following day Jesus returned to the *temple*, this time to rid it of those who were desecrating it. At the beginning of His ministry He had purged the temple of those who were defiling it (John 2:13-16). But that was nearly three years ago, and it had been conveniently forgotten by those who were enjoying large profits from their business.

The *money changers* refers to those who exchanged currency so that worshipers visiting Jerusalem from other lands could contribute to the offerings. Those who *sold doves* (as well as animals such as sheep and oxen) provided animals for sacrifices to those who came from a distance for the feasts and were not able to bring animals with them.

The changing of money and the selling of animals were not wrong in and of themselves. Had these services been carried on outside the temple area and conducted fairly and honestly, they would not have been objectionable. But the Jewish religious leaders held a strict monopoly

on these activities, refusing to sacrifice animals not purchased from the temple merchants and charging high prices for those that were. Temple worship had degenerated into nothing more than a business.

We may wonder how Jesus was able to take the drastic action that He did without resistance from anyone. Perhaps the merchants were intimidated by the crowd that accompanied Jesus. However, this may have been one of those situations in which Jesus' divinity shone through His humanity in such a way that His opponents dared not resist Him. (See Luke 4:28-30 and John 18:4-6 for similar circumstances.) Jesus did use physical intimidation to the extent that He *overthrew the tables* of the dishonest merchants.

After driving out the merchants, Jesus then dealt with those who were violating the sanctity of the temple by casually using it as a shortcut as they ran errands. He did not *suffer*, or permit, anyone to *carry any vessel through the temple.* The temple area covered much of the eastern half of Jerusalem, and formed an obstacle in the minds of many who needed to travel across the city. Their sin, like that of the merchants, was that they treated as secular something that had been sanctified to the glory of God.

B. Jesus Explains His Actions (v. 17)

17. And he taught, saying unto them, Is it not written, My house shall be called of all nations the house of prayer? but ye have made it a den of thieves.

Jesus made it quite clear that His actions were not just a whim or a passing fit of anger. They stemmed from a righteous indignation that was based on Scripture (Isaiah 56:6, 7). Jesus' charge that the merchants had made the temple a *den of thieves* was based on their practice of charging exorbitant rates for changing money or for selling animals to be sacrificed. They had been granted a monopoly by the religious leaders, and so they were free to charge whatever they could get away with.

CHURCH WORK

I've written the following rhyme to describe how the idea of "church work" is sometimes misunderstood:

Many a soul is so busy at church,
  They simply don't have a prayer;
The church work they do takes up so much time,
  The work of the church done is rare.
Many's the church where members will ask,
  "Must Christians e'er be in a tizzy?
Is what we're about the work of the church,
  Or is the church work just busy?"

visual for
lesson 5

This poem is not meant to trivialize the problem of misplaced purpose in the Lord's church. It is all too true, however, that busyness among members does not necessarily indicate that the mission of the church is being fulfilled.

Though the temple courts were bustling with activity, the true business of the "house of prayer" was not being conducted. Sometimes the church of today loses its focus as well, and becomes sidetracked with works of lesser importance.

Some congregations wisely have drafted "mission statements" that guide every decision, project, and activity. At the very least, every local body of the church should remind themselves of this twofold purpose:

(1) To win souls *to* Christ, and
(2) To nurture souls *in* Christ.   —R. W. B.

C. The Religious Leaders React (v. 18)

18. And the scribes and chief priests heard it, and sought how they might destroy him: for they feared him, because all the people was astonished at his doctrine.

In Galilee and other places outside Jerusalem, Jesus was most often challenged by the Pharisees, but here the opposition came from the *scribes and chief priests*. They were quite correct in seeing Jesus as a threat to their profitable business in the temple. They clearly saw that His teachings were turning the people against them and their corrupt practices. The high priest and his followers had already begun to make plans to get rid of Jesus (John 11:47-53). His cleansing of the temple must have been the proverbial "last straw" for any who might have had reservations about killing Him.

Conclusion

A. "Hail to the Chief"

Whenever the President of the United States makes a public appearance, it is expected that a nearby band will strike up the familiar melody of "Hail to the Chief." When Jesus approached Jerusalem, He was given an acclamation appropriate to His status. "Hosanna!" the enthusiastic crowd cried out, recognizing that He had come to usher in the kingdom of David. They did not understand all of the implications of their words, but they knew enough to give Jesus the honor He deserved. God's kingdom was at hand and they wanted to be part of it.

Popularity, however, is often very short-lived. A person may win an election in a landslide, and yet be defeated in the next election. It is entirely possible that by the end of this week, some of the same crowd that hailed Jesus so enthusiastically were crying, "Crucify Him!" We may find it difficult to understand such shallow, fickle attitudes until we examine our own hearts. We ourselves are sometimes guilty of betraying our Lord under similar circumstances. We sing songs of praise to Him with fellow believers on Sunday, but during the week we may be with an altogether different crowd. Do we allow Christ to be ridiculed without saying a word to defend Him?

B. A House of Prayer?

Today no building or spot is sacred in the sense that the Jewish temple was sacred. We may respect a church building and behave reverently while we are in it, but we also recognize that a building is not really the church. The church is a spiritual entity.

Have we ever been guilty of behaving casually toward the church or of making it a "den of thieves" by allowing it to conform to secular standards rather than divine standards? When we make financial decisions about the church budget, are we more concerned about doing the job God has called us to do, or are we more concerned about the "bottom line," as though we were handling a business corporation? Would Jesus view us with the same contempt as He did the money changers?

C. Prayer

May our hearts ring with Hosannas, dear Father, as we look to Your Son, our Lord and Savior. Prepare us on earth to be able to sing His praises in Heaven. In His name we pray. Amen.

D. Thought to Remember

If Jesus entered our city today, would we hail Him as King, ignore Him, or crucify Him?

Home Daily Bible Readings

Monday, Mar. 30—Earth's Hosannas Rise to Heaven (Mark 11:1-11)

Tuesday, Mar. 31—A Temple for All Nations (Mark 11:12-19)

Wednesday, Apr. 1—Faith Finds God's Will (Mark 11:20-23)

Thursday, Apr. 2—Obedient to the Cross (Philippians 2:1-11)

Friday, Apr. 3—The Suffering Servant (Isaiah 50:4-11)

Saturday, Apr. 4—One Who Heals the Brokenhearted (Psalm 147:1-11)

Sunday, Apr. 5—Blessed Be He Who Comes (Psalm 118:19-29)

Learning by Doing

This page contains an alternate lesson plan emphasizing learning activities.
Classes desiring such student involvement will find these suggestions helpful.

Learning Goals

After completing this lesson, students should:

1. Describe the reactions to Jesus' entry into Jerusalem and His cleansing of the temple.

2. Explain the significance of Jesus' triumphal entry.

3. Take specific steps to eliminate something from their lives that keeps Jesus from ruling triumphantly.

Into the Lesson

Prepare six cards from poster board. Attach a piece of yarn to each, so that they can be worn around the necks of six students. Each card will have a word or words from Mark 11:9. When all of the cards are together and in order, they will read, "Hosanna/Blessed/is he/that cometh/in the name/of the Lord." Give them to six students as they enter, and ask them to sit scattered among the rest of the class.

Begin by asking the class to share the names of their favorite hymns or choruses expressing praise. List these. Next, ask the students to share the names of songs or lines that speak of the triumphal entry. There will likely be no answer. Show them that there are very few songs listed under the topic "triumphal entry" in your church hymnbook, and those listed may not be familiar. Then tell the class, "People who were there for that occasion were very excited about Jesus' presence. Part of what they said is being worn around the necks of our classmates." Ask those wearing the cards to stand, and let the class arrange the students (and thus the words) in proper order.

Into the Word

Display a large poster with these Scripture references on it: Mark 11:1-10; Matthew 21:1-11; Luke 19:28-40; John 12:12-19. Explain that these texts are the records of the triumphal entry, according to each of the Gospel writers. Divide the class into three groups of two to five students each. Give each group a copy of one of the following assignments.

Group 1: *The Colt.* This group should focus on Mark 11:1-7. (1) Do you think that there was any wrongdoing in the taking of the colt without speaking to anyone ahead of time? Why or why not? (2) Read the four Gospel accounts about this event. How many colts or asses are mentioned in each account? Can you explain the differences? (Use the lesson commentary under Mark 11:2-6. Apparently those accounts that mention only one animal refer only to the animal that Jesus rode.) (3) Read the paragraph in the lesson commentary (under Mark 11:7) about why Jesus may have chosen to ride a donkey rather than a horse. Share this perspective with the entire class. (Teacher: please provide this group with a photocopy of the lesson commentary on Mark 11:1-7.)

Group 2: *The Response of the Crowd.* Study Mark 11:8-10. (1) What do you think was the significance of the spreading of clothing and branches before Jesus? (2) As you compare the four Gospel records, list on the chalkboard or on poster board all the accolades of the crowd as they poured out their joyous praise. Display this for the remainder of the class. (3) Define the word "Hosanna." (Teacher: provide this group with one sheet of poster board, a marker, and a photocopy of the lesson commentary on Mark 11:8-10.)

Group 3: *Jesus in the Temple.* Read Mark 11:15-18. (1) What was the function of the money changers in the temple? Why would Jesus be upset with them? (2) Why were birds and livestock sold in the temple? Why was Jesus upset about this activity? (3) Bible students often overlook another group that Jesus confronted in the temple. Who were they, and why were they driven from the premises (v. 16)? (Teacher: provide this group with a photocopy of the lesson commentary on Mark 11:15-18.)

Allow each group to report. If you do not wish to use small groups, the tasks or questions above may be used with the entire class.

Into Life

Ask the class if the Jewish temple still exists today. (Answer: no, it has been destroyed.) What does God consider His temple today? (Answer: our bodies, according to 1 Corinthians 6:19.) If Jesus were to examine you as His temple, what would He want to drive out? What would He want to change in you?

Tell the class to conduct a "housecleaning." Give them a few moments to reflect and decide what the Lord would like to change in them. Then ask them to pray and tell the Lord what they want Him to change in their lives.

Let's Talk It Over

The questions on this page are designed to encourage review of the lesson Scriptures and to promote discussion of the lesson by the class. The answers provided are only discussion starters. Let your class talk it over from there.

1. Jesus rode a donkey rather than a horse into Jerusalem. Why is this significant?

Jesus did not enter Jerusalem as a conquering hero, but as one who came to serve. Perhaps His selection of a donkey instead of a horse somewhat dampened the enthusiasm of those followers who wanted Him to be a political type of king, and hoped He would lead a military uprising against Rome. Had Jesus ridden in on a horse in regal splendor, His enemies may have become much more upset than they did. In addition, the Roman officials would probably have been inclined to act against one who was so openly publicizing His kingly claims. By riding on a donkey, Jesus helped to establish the timing for His death and resurrection. His enemies did not act as hastily as they may have acted if His entry had seemed more aggressive. Of course, Revelation 19:11-16 tells us that ultimately Jesus will ride the white horse of conquest.

2. The multitudes who witnessed Jesus' triumphal entry into Jerusalem were carried away with emotion. And yet many of them seemed to have become silent during Jesus' trials and crucifixion. What does this suggest about religion that is purely emotional?

The emphasis here is on "purely emotional." Certainly true worship and discipleship should involve the emotions as well as the intellect and will. It is obvious that among the multitudes were many whose allegiance to Jesus had nothing to do with the intellect or will. They were caught up in the excitement of the moment, but when the excitement was over, their discipleship vanished. In a similar manner, today it is possible to worship God with an emotional fervor, but fall short of genuine discipleship.

3. It seems amazing that one man could enter the temple and expel the evil merchandisers from it. How did Jesus accomplish this?

Jesus likely used the same power by which He thwarted the deadly aims of the crowd in Nazareth. Luke 4:28, 29 describes how that furious mob drove Him out of town and toward a nearby precipice. Then we are told in verse 30 that "he, passing through the midst of them, went his way." We can only imagine the display of His divine authority that caused the mob to

refrain from seizing Him. It seems likely that a similar display of authority enabled Jesus to cleanse the temple. The buyers, sellers, and money changers may have become quite angry; the priests may have raised their voices in protest; the temple guards may have rushed to the scene; but no one was brave enough to interfere with the actions of the Son of God.

4. Could we refer to our church building as a "house of prayer"? Why would it be helpful to do so?

For some, the church building could be a "house of rest" or a "house of fellowship" or a "house of boredom." To think of it as a "house of prayer" implies that we will be active worshipers in it. Instead of sleeping or daydreaming, we will pray for the growth of God's kingdom and for the health of our own congregation. If our church building is truly a house of prayer, we will not want to bring into it any attitudes that hinder prayer. Excessive pride, jealousy, anger, thoughts of revenge—all these must be banished from our minds. If our church building is to be a house of prayer, we will undergird with prayer every activity that takes place in it: the preaching, the music, the Lord's Supper, the offering, and other areas of church life.

5. The temple in Jesus' time was corrupted by the human quest for financial gain. This should not surprise us, because many human beings and enterprises are similarly corrupted today. How can we protect ourselves from that form of corruption?

"The love of money is the root of all evil" (1 Timothy 6:10). That perilous love can entrap people of both sexes, all ages, various social levels, and even Christians. We should not consider ourselves immune to it. It is easy for us to imagine ourselves being very wise and generous if we were to accumulate or receive a sizable amount of money. But we must ask ourselves, "Are we wise and generous in our use of the relatively small amount we presently have?" Jesus observed, "He that is faithful in that which is least is faithful also in much: and he that is unjust in the least is unjust also in much" (Luke 16:10). We need to begin now to exercise a godly stewardship of what we have.

Jesus Died and Lives Again!

April 12
Lesson 6

DEVOTIONAL READING: 1 Corinthians 15:19-26.

LESSON SCRIPTURE: Mark 15:21—16:8.

PRINTED TEXT: Mark 15:33-39; 16:1-8.

Mark 15:33-39

33 And when the sixth hour was come, there was darkness over the whole land until the ninth hour.

34 And at the ninth hour Jesus cried with a loud voice, saying, Eloi, Eloi, lama sabachthani? which is, being interpreted, My God, my God, why hast thou forsaken me?

35 And some of them that stood by, when they heard it, said, Behold, he calleth Elijah.

36 And one ran and filled a sponge full of vinegar, and put it on a reed, and gave him to drink, saying, Let alone; let us see whether Elijah will come to take him down.

37 And Jesus cried with a loud voice, and gave up the ghost.

38 And the veil of the temple was rent in twain from the top to the bottom.

39 And when the centurion, which stood over against him, saw that he so cried out, and gave up the ghost, he said, Truly this man was the Son of God.

Mark 16:1-8

1 And when the sabbath was past, Mary Magdalene, and Mary the mother of James, and Salome, had bought sweet spices, that they might come and anoint him.

2 And very early in the morning, the first day of the week, they came unto the sepulchre at the rising of the sun.

3 And they said among themselves, Who shall roll us away the stone from the door of the sepulchre?

4 And when they looked, they saw that the stone was rolled away: for it was very great.

5 And entering into the sepulchre, they saw a young man sitting on the right side, clothed in a long white garment; and they were affrighted.

6 And he saith unto them, Be not affrighted: ye seek Jesus of Nazareth, which was crucified: he is risen; he is not here: behold the place where they laid him.

7 But go your way, tell his disciples and Peter that he goeth before you into Galilee: there shall ye see him, as he said unto you.

8 And they went out quickly, and fled from the sepulchre; for they trembled and were amazed: neither said they any thing to any man; for they were afraid.

GOLDEN TEXT: Be not affrighted: ye seek Jesus of Nazareth, which was crucified: he is risen; he is not here: behold the place where they laid him.—Mark 16:6.

Lesson Aims

After this lesson, students should be able to:

1. Relate the significant details of Jesus' crucifixion and resurrection.

2. Tell what makes Jesus' crucifixion and resurrection such pivotal events.

3. Tell the message of Jesus' crucifixion and resurrection to someone who needs His good news.

Lesson Outline

INTRODUCTION
    A. Celebrate Easter
    B. Lesson Background
 I. AT THE CROSS (Mark 15:33-39)
    A. Jesus' Words of Agony (vv. 33-36)
      Last Words
    B. Jesus' Death (vv. 37, 38)
    C. The Centurion's Response (v. 39)
      Seeds of Faith
II. AT THE TOMB (Mark 16:1-8)
    A. Arrival of the Women (vv. 1, 2)
    B. Amazing Discovery (vv. 3-5)
    C. Angelic Instructions (vv. 6-8)
CONCLUSION
    A. Just Suppose
    B. Prayer
    C. Thought to Remember

The visual for Lesson 6 in the visuals packet encourages us to proclaim the message of the risen Christ today. It is shown on page 276.

Introduction

A. Celebrate Easter

On Easter Sunday morning in 1799, one of Napoleon's armies appeared on the heights surrounding the town of Feldkirk, located on the Austrian border. When the town council became aware of the situation, they met hastily to try to decide a course of action. Should they resist, or should they send a delegation to surrender the town to the French?

In the midst of the debate, an elderly minister stood up and said, "This is Easter Day. This day of all days should remind us that to trust in our own strength is but to fail. Let us ring the church bells, have our service, and trust the matter to God."

The tolling of the bells broke the stillness of the early morning. The French, hearing them, concluded that they signaled the arrival of an Austrian army. Unwilling to do battle at that site, they withdrew, and the town was spared.

The bells on that Easter morning rang a message of deliverance to that Austrian town. Today we are surrounded by forces more powerful and more insidious than those facing the Austrians. Should we not then rejoice and trust in God to deliver us through the power of Christ's resurrection?

B. Lesson Background

During the days preceding His death, Jesus engaged in a series of controversies with the religious leaders in Jerusalem. On Thursday evening, the evening before His death, He gathered the twelve with Him to celebrate the Passover and to institute the Lord's Supper.

Following this, Jesus led the disciples to the Garden of Gethsemane. There He drew apart and agonized in prayer over His coming death. Afterward, the authorities, led by Judas, seized Him and took Him back into the city. Following a series of trials before the Sanhedrin, Pilate, and Herod Antipas, Jesus was condemned to the cross.

Two thieves were also crucified, one on each side of Jesus, by the Roman soldiers who carried out Pilate's orders. As Jesus hung in agony, His enemies stood jeering at Him. To them it must have appeared that they had finally succeeded in ridding themselves of their most hated enemy. They were relishing their moment of triumph.

I. At the Cross
(Mark 15:33-39)

A. Jesus' Words of Agony (vv. 33-36)

33. And when the sixth hour was come, there was darkness over the whole land until the ninth hour.

Since a day, as reckoned by the Jews, began at six o'clock in the morning, *the sixth hour* would have been noon, and the *ninth hour* would have been three o'clock in the afternoon. Some have suggested that this *darkness* was caused by a solar eclipse. However, this would have been impossible, for this was the middle of the lunar month and the moon would have been in its full phase. Matthew, Mark, and Luke all report this unusual phenomenon without further comment. The obvious conclusion is that this was a miracle—one of many surrounding the crucifixion and the resurrection of Jesus.

In the Scriptures, darkness is often used as a symbol of God's displeasure or judgment (as in Isaiah 5:30; Amos 5:18, 20; Zephaniah 1:15). It was certainly most appropriate that God should show His displeasure at this most dastardly of all deeds by shrouding it in darkness.

34. And at the ninth hour Jesus cried with a loud voice, saying, Eloi, Eloi, lama sabachthani? which is, being interpreted, My God, my God, why hast thou forsaken me?

At the end of the three-hour period of darkness, Jesus raised His *voice* in a *loud* cry. The actual words of Jesus were in Aramaic, which Mark translated into Greek for the benefit of his readers. Jesus was quoting Psalm 22:1, a psalm rich in Messianic prophecy. Some scholars have been troubled by these words, feeling that they cast a shadow over Christ's absolute deity. Although our human minds cannot fully grasp what was involved in Christ's divine-human nature at this point, we must acknowledge that there was far more to these words than when David (author of Psalm 22) uttered them. Since God cannot look upon sin (Habakkuk 1:13), He hid His face when the sins of mankind were placed upon His Son. Jesus was forsaken of God that we might not be forsaken, but forgiven. This cry of Jesus from the cross gives us a sense of how terrible the burden of the world's sins were, and what a staggering price was paid that we might be saved.

LAST WORDS

You may have heard of the delicatessen owner whose family was gathered around his deathbed. When the oldest son leaned close to hear his father's final words, the dying man whispered, "Slice the ham thin!"

Last words can be revealing of character and priorities. This is particularly true of the seven final utterances of Jesus on the cross. Mark's Gospel records only one of these: "My God, my God, why hast thou forsaken me?" The others provide just as many insights into Jesus' matchless character: "Father, forgive them; for they know not know what they do" (Luke 23:34); "Verily I say unto thee, Today shalt thou be with me in paradise" (Luke 23:43); "Father, into thy hands I commend my spirit" (Luke 23:46); "Woman, behold thy son! . . . Behold thy mother!" (John 19:26, 27); "I thirst" (John 19:28); and, "It is finished" (John 19:30).

Jesus died as He had lived—with grace, forgiveness, compassion, sensitivity, commitment to God's will, and a firm grasp of His divine purpose and mission.

Have you considered what your last words should be? What epitaph would be appropriate

How to Say It
ANTIPAS. *An*-tih-pus.
ARAMAIC. Air-uh-*may*-ick.
ARIMATHEA. *Air*-uh-muh-*thee*-uh (strong accent on *thee*).
ELOI (Aramaic). E-*lo*-eye.
GETHSEMANE. Geth-*sem*-uh-nee.
HABAKKUK. Huh-*back*-kuk.
LAMA (Aramaic). *lah*-muh.
MAGDALENE. *Mag*-duh-leen or Mag-duh-*lee*-nee.
SABACHTHANI (Aramaic). suh-*back*-thuh-nee.
SANHEDRIN. San-*heed*-run or *San*-huh-drin.
SEPULCHRE. *sep*-ull-kur.

for your headstone? Final statements on deathbeds will be meaningless, if the life you have lived is not an enduring tribute to the truth you profess.

—R. W. B.

35, 36. And some of them that stood by, when they heard it, said, Behold, he calleth Elijah. And one ran and filled a sponge full of vinegar, and put it on a reed, and gave him to drink, saying, Let alone; let us see whether Elijah will come to take him down.

Because Jesus' body was racked with pain, and because His mouth and lips were parched and dry, some of the bystanders misunderstood what He was saying. They thought that He was calling for the prophet *Elijah* to come and *take him down* from the cross. This reflected a popular belief that Elijah would come to the rescue of people in desperate situations.

In response to Jesus' outcry, one of the bystanders (perhaps one of the soldiers) *filled a sponge full of vinegar*. Putting it on a *reed*, or stalk, he lifted it to Jesus' mouth. John's account tells us that this was done in response to Jesus' words, "I thirst" (John 19:28, 29). The *vinegar* was a sour wine (not vinegar as we think of it), and it was often consumed by the common people because it was cheaper. This would have been a soothing drink to one in Jesus' condition. The moisture from it probably allowed Jesus to utter His final cry.

B. Jesus' Death (vv. 37, 38)

37. And Jesus cried with a loud voice, and gave up the ghost.

It is amazing that Jesus remained conscious to the very end, drinking the cup of suffering to its dregs. Ordinarily one who had suffered as much as Jesus had even before He was nailed to the cross, would have gone into shock and lost consciousness, relieving some of the pain at the end. Mark gives us an abbreviated account of the last words of Jesus. Luke tells us that Jesus said, "Father, into thy hands I commend my spirit" (Luke 23:46). This indicates that at the end Jesus did not feel forsaken by God (in contrast to His earlier words in v. 34). The agony of bearing the sins of humanity was now tempered with the assurance that Jesus had fulfilled the Father's plan. John 19:30 reports Jesus' words as "It is finished," which may have been what he *cried with a loud voice.*

38. And the veil of the temple was rent in twain from the top to the bottom.

That *the veil of the temple was rent,* or torn, possessed special significance. Actually there were two veils, or curtains—one separating the outer court from the Holy Place, and the other separating the Holy Place from the Holy of Holies. In the light of Hebrews 6:19, 20; 9:3; and 10:19, 20, it appears that the inner veil was the one that was torn. The symbolism is striking. Under the Old Covenant, only the high priest could enter the Holy of Holies, and he could do so only once a year on the Day of Atonement. The tearing of this veil, coming as it did just as Jesus died, suggests that the Holy of Holies has now been opened to all Christians, who are a "holy priesthood" under the New Covenant (1 Peter 2:5).

C. The Centurion's Response (v. 39)

39. And when the centurion, which stood over against him, saw that he so cried out, and gave up the ghost, he said, Truly this man was the Son of God.

The Roman *centurion* who had supervised Jesus' execution was in a position to observe all that had gone on; and he readily noted that Jesus had not conducted Himself in the usual manner, especially in His final words. Jesus' actions, along with the accompanying darkness and earthquake (Matthew 27:51), convinced him that this was no ordinary man. Thus he proclaimed Jesus as *the Son of God.*

Probably the only knowledge this centurion had of Jesus was what he had observed at His trial and execution, and so we should not try to read too much into his remarks. After all, he was speaking from a pagan background in which many gods, including the emperor, were worshiped. There is an old tradition that the centurion later became a Christian, but there is no solid basis for supposing that at the time of the crucifixion he really understood what the Son of God had just accomplished.

visual for lesson 6

SEEDS OF FAITH

Faith often arises and is nurtured by life's experiences. In some cases, crises and hardships, such as accidents, illnesses, lost jobs, and broken relationships, cause people to begin to believe. Sometimes auspicious occasions mark the conception of faith—graduations, weddings, the birth of a child, and personal achievements or awards. Experiences of danger and "close calls" (real or perceived) can also heighten one's awareness of a need or desire to trust and obey God. By a variety of happenings almost as numerous as those to whom they happen, faith can begin to come alive in the human heart.

One of the soldiers who watched Jesus die began to believe that day, as evidenced by his confession: "Truly this man was the Son of God." We can only hope that his "mustard seed" faith ultimately blossomed into full-fledged conviction and commitment. The soldier had probably seen hundreds or even thousands of men die; Jesus' death convinced him that He was different.

Ironically, the crucifixion caused the faith of Christ's followers to waver and falter. For them, it was the *resurrection* that bolstered their belief and renewed their hope.

Today your convictions can be doubly reassured. The crucifixion and resurrection of Christ are both part of the good news of salvation. Whether by His death or by His living again, we can believe His truth, walk His way, and live His life "abundantly."   —R. W. B.

II. At the Tomb
(Mark 16:1-8)

A. Arrival of the Women (vv. 1, 2)

1, 2. And when the sabbath was past, Mary Magdalene, and Mary the mother of James, and Salome, had bought sweet spices, that they might come and anoint him. And very early in the morning, the first day of the week, they came unto the sepulchre at the rising of the sun.

Late Friday afternoon, Jesus' body had been placed in the tomb of Joseph of Arimathea (Matthew 27:57-60). Since the Sabbath began at sundown on Friday evening, the body had not been completely prepared for its final burial. To arrive at the *sepulchre at the rising of the sun*, the women must have left the place where they were staying while it was still dark. The Jews did not practice mummification of dead bodies as did the Egyptians, and so the *sweet spices* were meant not to embalm Jesus' body, but to cover the odor of decomposition as the body decayed. Joseph had included myrrh and aloes when he wrapped the body and laid it in the tomb (John 19:39, 40). But the women wanted to do more while they still had an opportunity to do so.

B. Amazing Discovery (vv. 3-5)

3, 4. And they said among themselves, Who shall roll us away the stone from the door of the sepulchre? And when they looked, they saw that the stone was rolled away: for it was very great.

When Jesus' body had been placed in the tomb, a large *stone* had been rolled in front of it to seal it and protect it from either grave robbers or predatory animals. To further protect the tomb, Pilate had ordered a seal placed on it and guards assigned to watch it (Matthew 27:65, 66). The women were probably not aware of these arrangements. Their problem was how to roll away the massive stone that had been placed before the *door of the sepulchre*.

Visitors to Jerusalem today are likely to visit the "Garden Tomb" where many believe Jesus was buried. Beside the opening is a large, round stone, shaped something like an oversized millstone. Cut in the rock beneath the opening is a channel in which the stone could be rolled. It is not likely that this is the original stone, but the original stone must have been something like this. If so, it is quite unlikely that the women could have moved it unless they had long, sturdy poles that could have been used as levers.

However, when the women arrived at the tomb, they found that the problem already was solved. From Matthew we learn that prior to their arrival an earthquake had occurred, and that an angel of the Lord had descended and rolled back the stone. The guards at the tomb were so frightened that they had fainted (Matthew 28:2-4). All of this must have occurred as the women made their way to the tomb in the early morning darkness.

5. And entering into the sepulchre, they saw a young man sitting on the right side, clothed in a long white garment; and they were affrighted.

Since the stone had been removed, the women were able to enter the *sepulchre* without any problem. If this tomb was like most of that period, the opening was lower than the inside of the tomb. Thus the women would have had to stoop as they entered. The tomb was probably large enough to accommodate several bodies, which were placed on shelves or niches along the wall. Since this was a new tomb (Matthew 27:60) and Jesus' body was the first to be placed in it, there would have been room for all of the women inside.

What the women saw, once their eyes became accustomed to the darker surroundings, was a *young man* dressed in a *long white garment* and sitting on one of the shelves or benches along the *right side* of the chamber. While Mark does not call this young man an angel, Matthew does (Matthew 28:2-5). Like the guards who had been overwhelmed with fear, the women were also terribly *affrighted* (frightened). But at least they did not faint as the guards did!

C. Angelic Instructions (vv. 6-8)

6. And he saith unto them, Be not affrighted: ye seek Jesus of Nazareth, which was crucified: he is risen; he is not here: behold the place where they laid him.

It is not surprising that the women were shocked and unsettled at what they saw in the tomb; thus the first words of the angel were reassuring: "Don't be afraid!" For a fleeting moment the women may have supposed that they had entered the wrong tomb. They had watched when Jesus was placed in the tomb (Mark 15:47), and so it was quite unlikely that they had made a mistake. Still, in their troubled frame of mind they may have considered the possibility. The angel settled the matter at once: *Ye seek Jesus of Nazareth . . . he is risen; he is not here*. If that was not enough to convince them, he continued, *Behold the place where they laid him*. No one was there!

7. But go your way, tell his disciples and Peter that he goeth before you into Galilee: there shall ye see him, as he said unto you.

Once the women recovered from their initial shock, they were ready for further instructions. Their first orders were to go and *tell* Jesus' *disciples* what they had witnessed. This incident lends credibility to the resurrection account. A writer making up the story would never have chosen women to convey the first news of the empty tomb. In that culture women were not considered reliable witnesses, and men would not have been inclined to believe them. In fact, this is exactly what happened. When the women reported their discovery to the disciples, their story was dismissed as impossible: "their words seemed to them as idle tales, and they believed them not" (Luke 24:11).

The words *and Peter* seem to convey a special delicate touch. Three days earlier Peter had vehemently affirmed his faithfulness to Jesus, and then within hours had just as vehemently denied Him. Peter was overwhelmed with remorse. Through the angel, Jesus was now saying to Peter, "I understand. It's all right. All is forgiven."

The disciples were instructed to return *into Galilee*, where they would *see* Jesus. Exactly how many days passed until this happened is difficult to determine. John tells us that Jesus appeared to seven of the disciples on the shore of the Sea of Galilee (John 21:1-14). Other appearances are recorded in 1 Corinthians 15:5-7, but we do not know how many of these occurred in Galilee.

8. And they went out quickly, and fled from the sepulchre; for they trembled and were amazed: neither said they any thing to any man; for they were afraid.

After the women *went out* of the tomb, the realization began to sink in of how wondrous their experience had been. Matthew records their feelings as a combination of "fear and great joy" (Matthew 28:8). For a time they were unable to talk to anyone about what they had seen. As they hurried along their way, Jesus appeared to them, giving them further assurance (Matthew 28:9, 10). Mark records the special appearance of Jesus to Mary Magdalene (Mark 16:9-11), which is recounted in greater detail by John (John 20:10-18). As noted earlier, Luke informs us that the women faithfully carried out their assignment to tell the disciples what they had witnessed, even though the disciples did not believe them.

Home Daily Bible Readings

Monday, Apr. 6—Crucified Between Two Thieves (Mark 15:21-32)
Tuesday, Apr. 7—Became Like a Broken Vessel (Psalm 31:9-16)
Wednesday, Apr. 8—Single Offering for All Time (Hebrews 10:11-25)
Thursday, Apr. 9—Body Wrapped in Linen Cloth (Mark 15:33-47)
Friday, Apr. 10—Last Enemy Is Death (1 Corinthians 15:21-28)
Saturday, Apr. 11—Going Before Them to Galilee (Mark 16:1-8)
Sunday, Apr. 12—Mary Magdalene Sees the Lord (John 20:11-18)

Conclusion

A. Just Suppose

Just suppose that when the women reached the tomb, the stone was still in front of the door and was guarded by Roman soldiers. Just suppose that they had been able to persuade the soldiers to roll the stone away, allowing them to enter the tomb. Just suppose that they found Jesus' body, cold and lifeless, lying just where Joseph of Arimathea had placed it. Just suppose that no angel greeted the women, who then proceeded to anoint the body with the spices just as they had planned, and then left the tomb. The soldiers would have rolled the stone back in place and sealed it again.

Everything that has happened since would be drastically different. The women would not have bothered to find the disciples and deliver the angelic message, for there was no angel, and thus no message to deliver. Without the women's message, the disciples would not have visited the tomb. The smartest thing for them to have done under those conditions would have been to get out of town as quietly and as quickly as they could. With Jesus dead, they themselves might very well be the next targets of the religious leaders.

A dead Jesus would never have given His followers the Great Commission to carry the good news to the whole world, because with Jesus dead there was no good news. Without the gospel the sophisticated unbelievers of the Roman world would never have been converted, nor would there have been a message to tame the savage barbarians outside the empire. Without the good news there would have been no churches in which to worship the risen Lord, no schools to teach His saving message to the next generation, no hospitals to care for the sick, no orphanages to shelter those without parents, and no concern for the hungry and homeless.

Without a risen Christ we would have to face life without hope and without Heaven. Or as Paul so eloquently stated it, "If Christ be not raised . . . we are of all men most miserable" (1 Corinthians 15:17, 19).

B. Prayer

Father, we give You thanks for sending Your Son into the world. We especially thank You that He died for us, and conquered the grave that we might have the hope of eternal life. Teach us how to share our faith with others. In the name of our risen Lord we pray. Amen.

C. Thought to Remember

"Because I live, ye shall live also."

Learning by Doing

This page contains an alternate lesson plan emphasizing learning activities.
Classes desiring such student involvement will find these suggestions helpful.

Learning Goals

After this lesson, the student will be able to:

1. Retell the significant details of Jesus' crucifixion and resurrection.

2. Tell what makes Jesus' crucifixion and resurrection such pivotal events.

3. Tell the message of Jesus' crucifixion and resurrection to someone who needs His good news.

Into the Lesson

Tell the class that the death and resurrection of Jesus are the pivotal points of history. Here is where man and God are reconciled. Here is where we lose our fear of death.

Tell the following story: A Christian physician specializing in allergy treatment told of a young child who nearly died from an insect sting. He was warned that another such sting could be fatal. One day, when the child was riding with his father in the car, a bee flew inside. The child became hysterical.

The quick-thinking father pulled the car off the road and caught the bee in his hand. Then the child relaxed. But after a moment, his dad let the bee go. The little boy became upset again, screaming and jumping into the back seat.

"Don't worry, Son. You don't have to be afraid anymore," said his father tenderly. He pointed to his hand: "See, the stinger is in my palm. This is what could have hurt you. I have taken the sting of death away." So did Jesus (*Christian Standard*, April 19, 1992, p. 3).

Into the Word

Write on a large visual (chalkboard, transparency, poster board, etc.) this heading: "Significant Sayings." Then make three subheadings: "Who," "What," and "Why." Read the account of Jesus' crucifixion from today's text in Mark 15:33-39. Ask the students to complete the chart using this text. The "Who" column should have these entries: Jesus (v. 34), those standing by the cross (v. 35), the individual who gave Jesus something to drink (v. 36), and the centurion (v. 39). The "What" column should include the words uttered by Jesus (v. 34), the bystanders (v. 35), the one who gave Jesus vinegar to drink (v. 36), and the centurion (v. 39). For the "Why" column, focus especially on the words of Jesus and of the centurion. Use the lesson commentary for information about the significance of these statements. After completing this exercise, ask these questions about the crucifixion: (1) Why was there darkness at three o'clock in the afternoon ("the ninth hour")? (2) Why would Jesus feel as if God had forsaken Him? (3) What is the significance of the temple veil being torn in two?

Next, read Mark 16:1-8 and continue the "Significant Sayings" exercise. The "Who" column should have these entries: the women (v. 3) and the young man or angel (v. 6). Under "What," place the question of the women (v. 3) and the words of the angel (vv. 6, 7). Use the "Why" column to point out how the concerns expressed by the women's words were addressed by the angel's words. Then ask, "Why does the resurrection of Jesus stand as the pivotal event of human history?" See the section entitled "Just Suppose" under the lesson Conclusion for insights into this question.

Into Life

Choose one or more activities from these three options to apply today's lesson.

Option 1. For a devotional closing, show a video that portrays the crucifixion and resurrection. Visual Bible International has an excellent two-part presentation called "The Gospel According to Matthew." Follow this with a closing prayer time in small groups.

Option 2. Prepare a short lecture on the importance of telling the good news of the resurrection. Ask the class to list ways to use today's technology to accomplish this task. Then ask if using technology is enough. What is still the best method to share the good news? (Answer: personal testimony.) Have class members complete the following statement: "I will let the joy of the resurrection shine through my life by . . ." Have students share their answers with the class.

Option 3. Consider the following imaginary situation: The twenty-year-old son of your friend has been killed in a car accident. While this young man was a Christian, your friend (the boy's father) is not a Christian. He attends church about once a month. List the important points of a letter you might write to your friend, using this opportunity to share the significance of Christ's death and resurrection.

Let's Talk It Over

The questions on this page are designed to encourage review of the lesson Scriptures and to promote discussion of the lesson by the class. The answers provided are only discussion starters. Let your class talk it over from there.

1. On the cross Jesus cried out, "My God, my God, why hast thou forsaken me?" What are some valuable truths that these words teach us?

It is a reminder of the extent to which Jesus' mind was immersed in Scripture, even in the midst of His intense suffering. The words come from the first verse of Psalm 22. We should aim to fill our minds in the same way with Biblical statements, principles, and facts. The outcry also reminds us of the way Jesus fulfilled Old Testament prophecy. We would gain much benefit from a thorough study of Psalm 22 and its fulfillment in various aspects of the crucifixion. Another truth this outcry teaches is the extent to which the Father and the Son were willing to go to effect our atonement from sin. One more truth that is underscored by this outcry is the horribleness of sin. It required nothing less than the Father's temporary forsaking of His Son.

2. The temple veil was ripped from the top to the bottom at the instant of Jesus' death. This should have stirred the Jewish leaders to reconsider who Jesus was. Their reaction is not recorded, but what could it have been?

Perhaps some of them saw it as mere coincidence. An earthquake happened to take place as Jesus died; to them this may have caused the ripping. Others may have reasoned that it signified God's judgment against this man whom they regarded as a blasphemer. They may have concluded that the damage within the temple illustrated God's displeasure with such blasphemy. It is interesting to note, however, that Acts 6:7 mentions the conversion of many priests to the Christian faith. Did the tearing of the temple veil play a significant role in their finally coming to Christ?

3. When Jesus died, the Roman centurion declared, "Truly this man was the Son of God." What aspects of Jesus' behavior during the crucifixion may have led him to say that ?

We assume the centurion had participated in many previous crucifixions. He was probably accustomed to hearing the condemned men shouting curses at their accusers and executioners. But from Jesus he heard this prayer: "Father, forgive them; for they know not what they do"

(Luke 23:34). Unless the man was hopelessly hardened, he must have been touched by Jesus' regard for His mother (John 19:25-27). Other victims of crucifixion were likely to be too preoccupied with their own sufferings to be concerned about family or friends. But what seems especially to have impressed the centurion was the exact manner of Jesus' death. When Jesus "cried with a loud voice" and committed His spirit to God (Luke 23:46), the centurion was moved to acknowledge Jesus as different from anyone whom He had ever seen.

4. Why should we be thankful for the stone that was placed at the entrance to Jesus' tomb?

The presence of that stone negates certain alternative explanations for the resurrection set forth by unbelievers. Some unbelievers, for example, have concocted the absurd claim that Jesus was not actually dead when His body was placed in the tomb. According to this view, He revived in the coolness of the tomb and escaped it. The presence of the heavy stone is one of several reasons why this claim can be dismissed. Another false claim is the one made by the Jewish leaders: that the disciples stole Jesus' body (Matthew 28:11-15). To accept this, one must believe that the disciples were able to remove the heavy stone without disturbing the supposedly sleeping Roman soldiers who were guarding the tomb—soldiers who faced punishment by death if they fell asleep at their post.

5. The lesson writer points out that in New Testament times, women were not generally regarded as credible witnesses. Why, then, did Jesus make His first resurrection appearances to women?

The women were the followers of Jesus who had been most supportive of Him during His crucifixion and after His burial. When you add to this the fact that the women were the ones concerned enough to go to the tomb as soon as the Sabbath was past, it is quite understandable that Jesus appeared first to them. The eleven disciples, on the other hand, were apparently absent from the cross, with the exception of John. When they received the women's testimony regarding the resurrection, their first reaction was to dismiss it.

Jesus Is Rejected

DEVOTIONAL READING: Isaiah 5:1-7.

LESSON SCRIPTURE: Mark 12:1-12.

PRINTED TEXT: Mark 12:1-12.

Mark 12:1-12

1 And he began to speak unto them by parables. A certain man planted a vineyard, and set a hedge about it, and digged a place for the winefat, and built a tower, and let it out to husbandmen, and went into a far country.

2 And at the season he sent to the husbandmen a servant, that he might receive from the husbandmen of the fruit of the vineyard.

3 And they caught him, and beat him, and sent him away empty.

4 And again he sent unto them another servant; and at him they cast stones, and wounded him in the head, and sent him away shamefully handled.

5 And again he sent another; and him they killed, and many others; beating some, and killing some.

6 Having yet therefore one son, his well-beloved, he sent him also last unto them, saying, They will reverence my son.

7 But those husbandmen said among themselves, This is the heir; come, let us kill him, and the inheritance shall be ours.

8 And they took him, and killed him, and cast him out of the vineyard.

9 What shall therefore the lord of the vineyard do? he will come and destroy the husbandmen, and will give the vineyard unto others.

10 And have ye not read this Scripture; The stone which the builders rejected is become the head of the corner:

11 This was the Lord's doing, and it is marvelous in our eyes?

12 And they sought to lay hold on him, but feared the people; for they knew that he had spoken the parable against them: and they left him, and went their way.

GOLDEN TEXT: The stone which the builders rejected is become the head of the corner: this was the Lord's doing, and it is marvelous in our eyes.—Mark 12:10, 11.

The Gospel of Action (Mark)
Unit 2: Death and Resurrection of Jesus
(Lessons 5-8)

Lesson Aims

After completing this lesson, students should be able to:

1. Summarize the parable of the wicked husbandmen.

2. Recognize what a tragic decision one makes when he or she rejects Jesus.

3. Confront a specific area of life where they are rejecting the lordship of Jesus.

Lesson Outline

INTRODUCTION
   A. Patient to a Point
   B. Lesson Background
 I. PROVISION FOR THE TENANTS (Mark 12:1, 2)
   A. The Owner's Goodness (v. 1)
   B. The Owner's Expectations (v. 2)
 II. REBELLION AGAINST THE OWNER (Mark 12:3-8)
   A. Rejecting His Messengers (vv. 3-5)
   B. Killing His Son (vv. 6-8)
 III. RESPONSE TO THE REBELLION (Mark 12:9-12)
   A. Severe Punishment (v. 9)
     Ownership and Stewardship
   B. Application of the Parable (vv. 10, 11)
   C. Response of the Religious Leaders (v. 12)
     Day of Reckoning
CONCLUSION
   A. God's Delayed Judgment
   B. The Inevitable
   C. Prayer
   D. Thought to Remember

Introduction

A. Patient to a Point

I knew a family that once had a large Saint Bernard. His very size made him appear ferocious, but he was really a gentle giant. He allowed small children to ride on his back, pull his tail, and tug on his ears. One day a strange dog, a much smaller terrier, appeared in the yard. He came up behind the big dog, barking and nipping at his heels, but the Saint Bernard walked slowly away, paying no attention to him.

Then the little dog turned and began to bark and snarl at one of the children. With one bound the Saint Bernard was upon him, and with one swipe of his huge paw he sent the little

dog sprawling. Yelping in pain and fear, the terrier quickly scurried out of the yard.

In Jesus' parable of the wicked husbandmen, the owner of the vineyard was somewhat like the Saint Bernard. He patiently tolerated the wicked husbandmen for a long time, but finally, when they killed his son, he acted swiftly and forcefully. It did not take the Jewish leaders long to get the point of this parable. As a result they were more determined than ever to do away with Jesus.

B. Lesson Background

Last week's Easter Sunday lesson focused on Jesus' death and resurrection. These pivotal events constitute the very heart of the gospel—the good news that Christ came to die for our sins that we might have the hope of eternal life (1 Corinthians 15:1-4).

The lessons for today and next Sunday are concerned with the significance of Jesus' death. Today's study examines this by calling our attention to Jesus' parable of the wicked husbandmen (also referred to as the parable of the vineyard). Most likely this parable was given on Tuesday of Passion Week. This day was one of intense debate, involving a series of challenging questions from the Pharisees, Herodians, and Sadducees. As Jesus turned back their assaults one by one, thereby gaining additional favor with the people, these men realized that they had to find some way to get rid of Jesus. In this parable, told only a few days before His crucifixion, Jesus both predicted His death and indicted the religious leaders for their rejection of Him.

I. Provision for the Tenants (Mark 12:1, 2)

A. The Owner's Goodness (v. 1)

1. And he began to speak unto them by parables. A certain man planted a vineyard, and set a hedge about it, and digged a place for the winevat, and built a tower, and let it out to husbandmen, and went into a far country.

In many important respects, this parable resembles the "Song of the Vineyard," found in Isaiah 5:1-7. This song tells of how God planted a vineyard and did everything necessary to make it fruitful, yet it yielded only bitter fruit. Finally, God destroyed it. The religious leaders, who would have been quite familiar with Isaiah's parable, no doubt became increasingly apprehensive as Jesus began to tell His parable of the vineyard. They may very well have realized where He was leading.

In the same way, the *certain man* in Jesus' parable had done everything possible to make his *vineyard* fruitful. He undoubtedly had selected the vines with care. Then, to protect his vineyard, he had *set a hedge* around it. The hedge commonly used was some variety of cactus or thorny plant that grows in Palestine. This protected the vineyard from thieves who might steal the fruit, or animals that could damage it.

Within the vineyard or near it a *winevat*, or winepress, was built. This usually consisted of two basins hollowed out of limestone. In the upper basin the ripe grapes were placed, and the juice was pressed out by trampling on them barefooted. The juice then flowed into the lower basin where it was collected and stored in wineskins or large jars. In addition, a *tower* was constructed, perhaps out of the stones cleared from the land when the vines were set out. The person in the tower was able to spot from a distance any threat of robbers or animals.

Finally, the vineyard was leased out to *husbandmen*, or farmers, who were to take care of it during the absence of the owner. This arrangement was common in ancient Palestine. Since it took several years before a vineyard would reach full production, only a rich person had the resources to set out a vineyard and wait for it to become productive. Many of these owners were absentee owners who lived some distance away from their vineyard. Jesus' listeners would have been familiar with the arrangement that allowed the owner to go into *a far country.*

Obviously, the owner in this parable is God. The ample preparation the owner made represents the bountiful provisions God made for His people.

B. The Owner's Expectations (v. 2)

2. And at the season he sent to the husbandmen a servant, that he might receive from the husbandmen of the fruit of the vineyard.

At the season, that is, when the grapes had ripened and were harvested (which is in late summer), the owner sent one of his servants to *receive . . . the fruit* that was due him. Usually this was a portion of the crop that had previously been agreed upon. Perhaps, since the owner was not living nearby, the servant planned to sell that portion of the crop and take the money back to his master.

In similar fashion, God had a right to expect a proper return from His "investment" in Israel. This involved much more than tithes and offerings; more important, it included penitent hearts and obedient lives.

II. Rebellion Against the Owner (Mark 12:3-8)

A. Rejecting His Messengers (vv. 3-5)

3-5. And they caught him, and beat him, and sent him away empty. And again he sent unto them another servant; and at him they cast stones, and wounded him in the head, and sent him away shamefully handled. And again he sent another; and him they killed, and many others; beating some, and killing some.

The behavior of the husbandmen was shocking. The owner of the vineyard (through his *servant*) had asked only what was due him, and in response they had beaten the servant and sent him away with nothing. One wonders how the owner could have chosen so many wicked husbandmen. Were all of them so cruel, heartless, and irresponsible? Wasn't there even one decent person among them who could have prevented such behavior? However, a study of the history of Israel shows how the behavior of the husbandmen accurately reflected the Israelites' response to God and His messengers.

The second servant suffered even more severe treatment. He was stoned, and was fortunate to escape with only a wound *in the head.* The third servant was actually *killed,* and those who came afterward were either treated with violence or killed. How much longer was the owner's patience going to last? Why didn't he summon the officials of the country or the courts to take care of these rascals?

Again this parable accurately reflects the history of God's dealings with His people and His extraordinary patience with them. Second Chronicles 36:15, 16 provides this tragic summation of God's repeated attempts to reach His wayward people: "And the Lord God of their fathers sent to them by his messengers, rising up betimes, and sending; because he had compassion on his people, and on his dwelling place: but they mocked the messengers of God, and despised his words, and misused his prophets, until the wrath of the Lord arose against his people, till there was no remedy." Time and again, God had sent His prophets, and, like the servants in Jesus' parable, they had been *shamefully handled.*

As we study the Old Testament, we see that part of the problem was the leaders of Israel, who frequently were guilty of abusing God's

Law and mistreating His spokesmen (1 Samuel 2:12-17; Jeremiah 2:8; 5:31; 36:20-26; Ezekiel 34:1-10). Through this parable, Jesus was exposing the same problem with the leaders of His day.

B. Killing His Son (vv. 6-8)

6. Having yet therefore one son, his well-beloved, he sent him also last unto them, saying, They will reverence my son.

The willingness of the owner to send his *one son, his well-beloved* brings us to a critical point in the parable. The owner hopes that this appeal will soften the hard hearts of his husbandmen. The reference is clearly to God's final attempt to reach lost humanity by sending His Son. A word of caution is in order: While this parable does illustrate God's actions, we must not try to make every detail of the parable fit. It may have been normal to expect that the husbandmen would honor the owner's son. But if we try to attribute to God the statement that *they will reverence my son*, we run into problems. As it stands, the statement suggests that the owner was naive about how the husbandmen would respond to his son. God was certainly not naive. He knew exactly how the religious leaders were going to treat His Son; yet He sent Him anyway, because His death was essential to redeem the world from its sins.

7. But those husbandmen said among themselves, This is the heir; come, let us kill him, and the inheritance shall be ours.

The *husbandmen* saw in the appearance of the son an opportunity for further profit. They may have interpreted his arrival as an indication that the owner was dead, and since he had only one son, the death of the son would mean that the land had no heir. Perhaps the husbandmen could legally claim the *inheritance* as their own. In addition, with both the owner and his son dead, who would be left to punish them for their act? They had gotten away with mistreating and even killing some of the owner's servants, so why worry about being caught and punished for this greater crime?

8. And they took him, and killed him, and cast him out of the vineyard.

The husbandmen immediately seized the son and carried out their wicked scheme. They did not even attempt to conceal their crime. In their contempt for the owner and the law, they did not try to hide the son's body but threw it *out of the vineyard*, where someone was almost certain to discover it and begin to ask questions.

Up to this point, the parable illustrated how the Israelites had treated God and His messengers. In speaking of the owner's son, Jesus now brought the parable to its intended application.

He was predicting how the religious leaders would treat Him—the Son of God. He knew full well what lay ahead, yet remained firmly committed to His Father's purpose. Luke describes how Jesus "steadfastly set his face to go to Jerusalem" (Luke 9:51). Speaking of giving His life, Jesus said, "No man taketh it from me, but I lay it down of myself" (John 10:18). Jesus' enemies did not take His life; He *gave* His life.

III. Response to the Rebellion (Mark 12:9-12)

A. Severe Punishment (v. 9)

9. What shall therefore the lord of the vineyard do? he will come and destroy the husbandmen, and will give the vineyard unto others.

In Matthew's account of this parable, Jesus' enemies answered the question that He asked: "He will miserably destroy those wicked men, and will let out his vineyard unto other husbandmen" (Matthew 21:40, 41). As Mark's Gospel reads, apparently Jesus repeated their answer to them for emphasis. Their own words convicted them, and Jesus wanted to make sure that they did not miss this point.

Jesus' statement that the owner would *give the vineyard unto others* carried with it an ominous warning. It appears to mean that the wicked *husbandmen* (the religious leaders) would be punished and replaced by others. However, Matthew adds these words of Jesus at the conclusion of the parable: "The kingdom of God shall be taken from you, and given to a nation bringing forth the fruits thereof" (Matthew 21:43). Thus the parable also foretells God's rejection of the Jewish people and the giving of His blessings to the Gentiles.

Home Daily Bible Readings

Monday, Apr. 13—Wild Grapes in God's Vineyard (Isaiah 5:1-7)

Tuesday, Apr. 14—Rejected One Becomes Cornerstone (Mark 12:1-12)

Wednesday, Apr. 15—Forsaken by Everyone (Psalm 22:1-15)

Thursday, Apr. 16—Prophets and Sages Rejected (Matthew 23:34-39)

Friday, Apr. 17—He Knows Our Weaknesses (Hebrews 4:12-16)

Saturday, Apr. 18—Obedient and Suffering (Hebrews 5:5-10)

Sunday, Apr. 19—"Wounded for Our Transgressions" (Isaiah 52:13—53:12)

OWNERSHIP AND STEWARDSHIP

Thomas Magnum, the character played by Tom Selleck in the once-popular TV series *Magnum, P. I.,* was a good illustration of a steward. He lived in someone else's house on someone else's property and drove someone else's car. With his sidekick, Higgins, he was an executive caretaker of another's possessions. Sometimes Magnum acted responsibly, sometimes not. But Higgins usually kept him honest. Together they enjoyed an ideal arrangement—rent-free luxurious living on a Hawaiian estate. And mysteriously the owner was always absent! Magnum had to remember that all he possessed was really owned by someone else.

The husbandmen in Jesus' parable also were privileged to possess property owned by someone else. Their sin was in presuming that possession gave them all of the rights of ownership, including one hundred percent of the profits from the harvest. They were condemned and replaced, because they refused to acknowledge their role and responsibilities as stewards.

Each of us is a steward of the portion of God's property that He allows us to possess. We acknowledge this stewardship by investing ourselves and our possessions in kingdom enterprises, and by rendering to God what belongs to God. We owe it all to Him. —R. W. B.

B. Application of the Parable
(vv. 10, 11)

10, 11. And have ye not read this Scripture; The stone which the builders rejected is become the head of the corner: this was the Lord's doing, and it is marvelous in our eyes?

The passage Jesus quotes came from Psalm 118:22, 23. The Jewish leaders had certainly read these verses many times, but they had missed their Messianic implications. The language of the psalm suggests that the *builders* (the leaders) had carefully examined this stone and then deliberately *rejected* it. In spite of such treatment, it would now become the *head of the corner*. Peter quotes part of this same passage in 1 Peter 2:7, and Paul uses the same terminology in Ephesians 2:20, where he calls Jesus the "chief corner stone."

C. Response of the Religious Leaders
(v. 12)

12. And they sought to lay hold on him, but feared the people; for they knew that he had spoken the parable against them: and they left him, and went their way.

On some occasions Jesus taught through parables in order to hide His message from the crowd and reveal it to only a few. Here He did not attempt to hide anything from His critics, nor did He have to give them a detailed, word-by-word explanation of the parable. They *knew that he had spoken the parable against them*, and they were infuriated. They were so angry that they would have seized Him right there and disposed of Him. What restrained them was the presence of *the people*, who still held Jesus in high esteem. The leaders did not abandon their sinister plans; they only delayed them until a more appropriate time.

DAY OF RECKONING

Sinners in Noah's day finally provoked their own destruction in the great flood. The northern kingdom's unfaithfulness ultimately resulted in its defeat and capture by Assyria. The southern kingdom rebelled against God and rejected His prophets, until His judgment fell and the people were taken into exile by Babylon. These are examples of God's law of sin and retribution at work. Disobedience is punished; evil empires fall; unrepentant sinners are condemned.

The enemies of Jesus recognized their own history in His story. Everyone knew the implied answer to His rhetorical question: "What shall therefore the lord of the vineyard do?" Most certainly there will be a day of reckoning, a settlement of accounts. The kind of irresponsible and wicked stewardship demonstrated by the husbandmen cannot be tolerated. There is a price to pay for lawlessness. Sooner or later, God's judgment will be carried out.

Will we learn from the record of those who through the centuries have rejected God's absolutes and His ambassadors? Will our personal experience profit from the prophets? Are we wise enough to apply Christ's teaching to our own relationship with Him?

The lesson is clear: For wickedness there is a literal Hell to pay. "The Judge of all the earth" will do right (Genesis 18:25), including punishing those who do wrong. —R. W. B.

Conclusion

A. God's Delayed Judgment

Israel's relationship with God had followed a tragic cycle for hundreds of years. At the beginning of each cycle God blessed the people. Then after a time, they would rebel against Him and fall into sin. This would bring God's judgment upon them. After enduring oppression by their enemies, the people would then repent. The cycle was completed when God in His mercy restored Israel's lost blessings. However, this state of blessing never existed very long before the people once again yielded to temptation. The long and dismal history of Israel provides adequate documentation for the well-known statement that "those who do not remember the past are condemned to repeat it."

In the book of Judges this cycle was often repeated within a generation or two. During the period of the kings of Israel and Judah, the cycle was sometimes slowed or delayed, because a faithful prophet or king provided righteous leadership. But judgment, though delayed, always came. For about four hundred years after King David, Judah survived a series of cycles, but always repented in time to escape a devastating judgment. In 586 B.C., however, judgment finally arrived. God's patience with His people was exhausted, and He allowed the Babylonians to destroy Jerusalem and the temple, and carry the people into captivity. In 538 B.C. they were allowed to return; and during the more than five hundred years that elapsed between their return and the time of Christ, the cycle was repeated many times. The Biblical record does not cover all of this period, but there are other records that chronicled what took place.

The Israelites were not ignorant about events in their past. Perhaps more frequently than any other ancient people, they referred to these events and celebrated their significance. However, even though they knew about them, they did not really understand the lessons that God was trying to teach. In relating the parable that we have studied today, Jesus gave the religious leaders a sobering view of the past. But they refused to accept the truths He offered them, because it meant that they would have to repent and change their lives.

What does all of this mean to us today? In one important respect we are not like these ancient Jews. They knew about their history even if they did not always know what it meant. What is frightening today is that most Americans are almost totally ignorant of their past. They do not know or appreciate the sacrifices that were made by our forefathers in order for us to enjoy our abundance of freedoms and blessings. We have come to take what we have for granted, always demanding more and complaining if we do not get it. We rarely pause to give thanks to God who is the giver of "every good gift and every perfect gift" (James 1:17).

If God did not spare His chosen people, but eventually allowed judgment to fall upon them, how much longer can we escape His wrath? Peter reminds us that "the Lord is not slack concerning his promise" (2 Peter 3:9). The time may not be far off when "the day of the Lord will come as a thief in the night" (v. 10).

B. The Inevitable

We sometimes speak of an event or a series of events as being inevitable. But as long as men and women have the freedom to make decisions, then what happens to them is not absolutely inevitable. For many weeks prior to the events studied in today's lesson, Jesus had been moving toward a final confrontation with the religious leaders in Jerusalem. Earlier confrontations had been avoided when Jesus withdrew from or avoided Jerusalem because His time had "not yet come" (John 7:6).

The day of Passion Week on which the events in today's lesson took place was one of bitter conflict between Jesus and His enemies. They were furious because they could not discover a way to answer Him or to turn the people from Him. They recognized that the parable that we have studied was aimed directly at them. They may have also understood that Jesus had identified Himself as the son of the owner of the vineyard. In other words, He was God's Son. To them this was an inexcusable act of blasphemy.

Yet these men still had a choice; they did not have to carry out their plot to kill Jesus. In fact, it seems that this parable was designed as one last appeal on Jesus' part to reach them before it was too late. It was not inevitable that they crucify Him. That action came as the result of conscious decisions that they made. Even at this late date, they could have repented.

Of course, Jesus' death was a part of God's plan to provide an atonement for our sins. But this does not mean that the men who carried it out were not responsible for their actions. Joseph of Arimathea and Nicodemus, who were a part of the ruling clique, supported Jesus and chose not to be a part of the plot against Him.

Some may think that they are caught in a web of circumstances that make their sinful actions inevitable. But this is not so. Each one of us has the freedom to make choices, though they may be extremely difficult at times. The good news of the gospel is twofold: We can be forgiven of the bad choices in our past, and we can receive strength to make right choices in the future.

C. Prayer

Loving Father, we pray that our hearts will not be hardened against You and Your will for us. May we open our ears and our hearts, so that we can hear Your Word and obey it. In Jesus' name we pray. Amen.

D. Thought to Remember

God requires that we be good and faithful stewards, whether of a vineyard or of our lives.

Learning by Doing

This page contains an alternate lesson plan emphasizing learning activities.
Classes desiring such student involvement will find these suggestions helpful.

Learning Goals

After completing this lesson, students should be able to:

1. Summarize the parable of the wicked husbandmen.

2. Recognize what a tragic decision one makes when he or she rejects Jesus.

3. Confront a specific area of life where they are rejecting the lordship of Jesus.

Into the Lesson

Begin this lesson by asking the class to "brainstorm," listing all the things they would need to do to start a vineyard. Assume they are fairly wealthy and will hire someone to run the vineyard. Begin with the selection of the location. Discuss preparation of the land, the buildings and equipment needed, personnel, security, rent agreements, etc. Ask another student to record answers while you guide the discussion. After the brainstorming is completed, ask class members how they would handle the renter or manager if he missed his payments. What if the renter were habitually late, or hostile toward you? What if you sent a bill collector and the renter ran him off the property?

Next, summarize the detailed preparation that is mentioned in today's lesson text (the parable of the wicked husbandmen). See the notes under Mark 12:1 in the commentary for assistance with this. Mention that this parable is about a landowner who was patient with his renters—up to a point. Then he took action.

Into the Word

Ask the class to work in three or more small groups of four or five people. If more than three groups are needed, have some groups doing the same tasks. Give the group leader the instructions shown below, a piece of poster board, and a marker. (If you prefer not to use small groups, you may use the group tasks with the entire class.)

Group 1. In Isaiah 5:1-7 you will find a parable very similar to the parable found in today's text. Read the Isaiah passage. Appoint a group member to retell it to the class, using an outline that your group will develop. Have someone write this outline on the poster board, so it can be seen by all the class. Emphasize the careful preparation given the vineyard, its fruitlessness,

and what God did to it. What was the point of Isaiah's parable?

After this report, mention that this parable was probably very familiar to the religious leaders who were listening to Jesus' parable. Jesus used the same setting with a slightly different twist to make a powerful and painful point.

Group 2. Read the parable in Mark 12:1-12. Select a group member to summarize it for the class, using the outline that the group prepares on its poster board. Be sure to emphasize the treatment of the owner's son (verse 7) and the reaction this brought from the owner.

After Group 2 reports, mention the shocking behavior of the tenants. This is a very accurate picture of how the Israelites had responded to God. Then remind the class of the application of the parable: Jesus was predicting how the religious leaders would treat Him. Group 3 will offer a glimpse of this mistreatment.

Group 3. The picture Jesus painted in His parable depicts how the religious leaders would treat Him, the Son of God. You do not need to read the parable at this time (since Group 2 is outlining it). Instead, scan John 18 and 19, and list every word or phrase indicating the rejection or suffering that Jesus experienced.

Into Life

The religious leaders of Jesus' day were not the only ones rejecting Him. Ask the students to list other more current illustrations of a blatant, complete rejection of Jesus as God's Son. They may cite groups, philosophies, or personal illustrations. Next, point out that people can accept Jesus as God's Son, yet not yield themselves entirely to His lordship. This too amounts to a rejection of Jesus.

To conclude, give each class member a three-by-five card. What areas of their lives would they confess that they have not really or fully surrendered to the Lord? With what areas are they struggling to completely surrender to Him? Ask them to jot down on the card any area or areas of incomplete surrender. Remind them that no one, other than the Lord, will know what they have identified. Also remind them that this "confession" may be the first step to significant spiritual growth. Then ask them to circle an area that they are willing to begin addressing immediately. Close with prayer.

Let's Talk It Over

The questions on this page are designed to encourage review of the lesson Scriptures and to promote discussion of the lesson by the class. The answers provided are only discussion starters. Let your class talk it over from there.

1. Jesus' parable of the wicked husbandmen has much in common with the "Song of the Vineyard" in Isaiah 5:1-7. This raises the question of how much we need to know the Old Testament in order to appreciate Jesus' teachings. What shall we say about this?

Jesus' frequent references to the Old Testament demonstrate how thoroughly His mind was steeped in it. It often provided the backdrop for His teaching. In the Sermon on the Mount, for example, He referred several times to what "was said by them of old time" (Matthew 5:21, 27, 31, 33, 38, 43). His discourse on being "the good shepherd" (John 10:1-18) directs us back to Psalm 23 and other Old Testament passages that speak of God as a shepherd. Both Jesus and the Gospel writers often cited prophecies from the Old Testament that He fulfilled.

2. The owner of the vineyard sent his son with the hope that the husbandmen would respect him. But the heavenly Father knew that His Son would be rejected, abused, and slain. Why did Jesus include in His parable this element that contrasted with the literal truth?

Either way, the tragedy of the son's death is obvious. When we ponder the naive confidence of the vineyard owner that his son would be received with respect, the outcome of his decision seems painfully tragic. God's sending His Son to certain suffering and unavoidable death is even more tragic. Also, we need change only one word in the vineyard owner's statement to make it applicable to the heavenly Father. The owner said, "They *will* reverence my son." The heavenly Father could have said, "They *should* reverence my Son." The people of Israel and their leaders in Jesus' day should have respected, accepted, and heeded God's Son. Tragically they did not.

3. "They took him, and killed him, and cast him out of the vineyard." This description of the husbandmen's treatment of the owner's son is brutal and shocking. How does this help us see Jesus' crucifixion in a clearer light?

It gives us insight into the reason for the Jewish leaders' anger with Jesus. Jesus represented a threat to their power and prestige. He also represented a threat in another way:

His claims, or at least the claims His followers were making about Him, carried the danger of provoking a deadly conflict with the ruling Romans. John 11:47-57 records the Jewish leaders' fear that Jesus' popularity would lead to the destruction of their nation. They plotted Jesus' death as a means of saving their nation. The parable of the wicked husbandmen, however, strips away any excuses we might make for the Jewish leaders. Their killing of Jesus was a selfish, heartless act of rebellion against God.

4. Jesus is "the stone which the builders rejected," but He has "become the head of the corner." How is this description helpful to us in connection with our evangelistic efforts?

This description indicates that even if someone rejects Jesus, He remains Lord and Savior. The "builders" were the Jewish leaders. Had they humbly compared Jesus' ministry with Old Testament prophecies, had they investigated His miracles with an open mind, and had they pondered the deeper meanings in His teachings, they would have realized that He was the long-promised Messiah. They stubbornly refused to do any of this. People to whom we bear witness today may also harden themselves against the gospel truth. Nevertheless, we can be confident that the weight of the evidence is on our side.

5. When we observe the wickedness in our present society, we may feel it is inevitable that God's judgment will soon fall upon us. How can we avoid this seemingly inevitable judgment?

As long as we believe in the power of the Holy Spirit, the power of the Word of God, and the power of prayer, we can still hope for a reversal of the present moral and spiritual decline. We serve a Christ who declared to His followers, "I have overcome the world" (John 16:33). When we are most discouraged, we must keep on praying, evangelizing, and standing up for Christ and the principles of His Word. It is not inevitable that Satan will triumph on earth. It need not be inevitable that our society will come crashing down under the weight of its sins. It *is* inevitable that Christ and His followers will prevail; if not in history, then when history comes to its climax.

Jesus Gives the New Covenant

April 26
Lesson 8

DEVOTIONAL READING: 1 Corinthians 11:17-26.

LESSON SCRIPTURE: Mark 14:12-25.

PRINTED TEXT: Mark 14:12-25.

Mark 14:12-25

12 And the first day of unleavened bread, when they killed the passover, his disciples said unto him, Where wilt thou that we go and prepare that thou mayest eat the passover?

13 And he sendeth forth two of his disciples, and saith unto them, Go ye into the city, and there shall meet you a man bearing a pitcher of water: follow him.

14 And wheresoever he shall go in, say ye to the goodman of the house, The Master saith, Where is the guest chamber, where I shall eat the passover with my disciples?

15 And he will show you a large upper room furnished and prepared: there make ready for us.

16 And his disciples went forth, and came into the city, and found as he had said unto them: and they made ready the passover.

17 And in the evening he cometh with the twelve.

18 And as they sat and did eat, Jesus said, Verily I say unto you, One of you which eateth with me shall betray me.

19 And they began to be sorrowful, and to say unto him one by one, Is it I? and another said, Is it I?

20 And he answered and said unto them, It is one of the twelve, that dippeth with me in the dish.

21 The Son of man indeed goeth, as it is written of him: but woe to that man by whom the Son of man is betrayed! good were it for that man if he had never been born.

22 And as they did eat, Jesus took bread, and blessed, and brake it, and gave to them, and said, Take, eat; this is my body.

23 And he took the cup, and when he had given thanks, he gave it to them: and they all drank of it.

24 And he said unto them, This is my blood of the new testament, which is shed for many.

25 Verily I say unto you, I will drink no more of the fruit of the vine, until that day that I drink it new in the kingdom of God.

Apr 26

GOLDEN TEXT: As they did eat, Jesus took bread, and blessed, and brake it, and gave to them, and said, Take, eat; this is my body. And he took the cup, and when he had given thanks, he gave it to them: and they all drank of it. And he said unto them, This is my blood of the new testament, which is shed for many.—Mark 14:22-24.

only ~~Women~~ Carried Water

The Gospel of Action (Mark)
Unit 2: Death and Resurrection of Jesus
(Lessons 5-8)

They went in twas

Lesson Aims

After completing this lesson, each student should:

1. Relate the circumstances under which Jesus instituted the Lord's Supper.

2. Explain the significance of the Lord's Supper for Christians today.

3. Determine to maintain or increase faithfulness in observing the Lord's Supper.

Lesson Outline

INTRODUCTION
 A. Eating Jesus
 B. Lesson Background
 I. PREPARING FOR THE PASSOVER (Mark 14:12-16)
  A. The Disciples' Question (v. 12)
  B. Two Disciples' Task (vv. 13-16)
   Celebration?
 II. OBSERVING THE PASSOVER (Mark 14:17-21)
  A. The Meal Begins (v. 17)
  B. A Traitor in the Midst (vv. 18-21)
 III. THE LORD'S SUPPER INSTITUTED (Mark 14:22-25)
  A. Elements of the Supper (vv. 22, 23)
  B. The New Covenant (vv. 24, 25)
   A New Contract
CONCLUSION
 A. Uniting at the Lord's Table
 B. Five Looks at the Lord's Supper
 C. Prayer
 D. Thought to Remember

Use the visual for Lesson 8 in the visuals packet to focus on Jesus' institution of the Lord's Supper. It is shown on page 293.

Introduction

A. Eating Jesus

Some years ago a missionary in Africa had to make a long trip through the jungle to another station. Since he had never been there before, one of the villagers agreed to serve as his guide for the trip. At noon the two stopped to eat the lunch that each had brought with him. The missionary, eager to be on his way, quickly ate his meal, but the villager ate slowly and quietly. Finally, the impatient missionary urged the man to hurry up and finish. The villager solemnly replied, "Sir, do not ask me to hurry, for I am eating my wife."

The missionary, aware that the people in the area had formerly been cannibals, was shocked and quickly asked, "What do you mean?"

"What I mean," answered the villager, "is that my wife took her precious time to prepare my lunch. In a sense I am eating some of her very life."

In a way this is what we do when we partake of the Lord's Supper. This spiritual meal that Christians celebrate together has been made possible because Christ gave His precious life to prepare it for us.

B. Lesson Background

The events narrated in today's lesson occurred on Thursday of Passion Week, as the Jews prepared to observe the Passover. The Passover was one of the most important Jewish holy days. It commemorated the last meal that the Hebrew slaves ate in Egypt just before they were led to freedom by Moses. The seven days following the Passover were called the Feast of Unleavened Bread, although sometimes the latter term covered the entire eight-day observance.

The Passover centered around the eating of the Passover lamb. This was an animal that had been specially selected (without blemish, as commanded in Exodus 12:5) and prepared for the meal. Ordinarily the meal was shared by members of a family, but sometimes small families would come together and observe the meal. While Jesus and His disciples did not constitute an actual family, it was not uncommon for such groups to eat the Passover together.

The days prior to Passover had been characterized by the increasing hostility of the Jewish leaders toward Jesus. In last week's lesson, we saw how this hostility grew following Jesus' parable of the wicked husbandmen. The religious leaders "sought to lay hold on him, but feared the people" (Mark 12:12). In the two verses preceding today's printed text, Mark tells us of Judas's plot with the chief priests to betray Jesus. A tense and ominous atmosphere was present in the upper room when Jesus shared the Passover there with His disciples.

I. Preparing the Passover (Mark 14:12-16)

A. The Disciples' Question (v. 12)

12. And the first day of unleavened bread, when they killed the passover, his disciples said unto him, Where wilt thou that we go and prepare that thou mayest eat the passover?

How to Say It

SINAI. *Sye*-nye or *Sye*-nay-eye.

The *first day of unleavened bread* began on Thursday at sunset (as we count time). The preparation of the lamb would have begun earlier in the day. The disciples were concerned about where they might hold this sacred meal. Such concern was well-grounded, for thousands of visitors would be in Jerusalem for the *passover*. Unlike today, Jerusalem at that time did not boast numerous large hotels to accommodate visitors. Since houses back then were small compared with our modern houses, finding a room large enough that was not already reserved would be no easy matter at such a late date.

B. Two Disciples' Task (vv. 13-16)

13. And he sendeth forth two of his disciples, and saith unto them, Go ye into the city, and there shall meet you a man bearing a pitcher of water: follow him.

The disciples had no need to worry about a room. Jesus had already made arrangements for it (as He had for the donkey that He rode into Jerusalem). And just as Jesus had sent two disciples for the donkey, He now sent *two of his disciples . . . into the city* (Luke 22:8 identifies them as Peter and John). They were to look for *a man bearing a pitcher of water*. Carrying water jugs was ordinarily done by women, and so a man carrying a jug would stand out. The disciples were to *follow him* to the house where he was taking the water.

14, 15. And wheresoever he shall go in, say ye to the goodman of the house, The Master saith, Where is the guest chamber, where I shall eat the passover with my disciples? And he will show you a large upper room furnished and prepared: there make ready for us.

It is quite obvious that Jesus, without conferring with the disciples, had made arrangements with the *goodman*, or owner, to reserve the *upper room* for this occasion. Jesus, of course, knew that Judas was making plans to betray Him. Had Judas known of the arrangement for the room, he could have directed the chief priests there before Jesus had an opportunity to observe the Passover or institute the Lord's Supper. Through His foreknowledge, Jesus knew when the man would be carrying the water jar, and sent Peter and John at just the right time to see him. Thus Judas had no way of knowing the location until he, along with Jesus and the rest of the disciples, arrived there.

16. And his disciples went forth, and came into the city, and found as he had said unto them: and they made ready the passover.

Peter and John followed Jesus' instructions and went *into the city* as He had told them. He may have sent them on their mission early in the day, for the preparations for *the passover* were rather elaborate. One of the first items to take care of was to search for leaven in the house where they would meet. This is reminiscent of the Exodus, when the Israelites were commanded to eat unleavened bread (Exodus 12:8). Any leaven found had to be removed. Then they had to kill the lamb. This ordinarily occurred in the temple under the supervision of the priests. After this, the lamb had to be cooked. It could not be boiled, but had to be roasted on a spit over an open fire. Furthermore, they had to secure the bitter herbs and the other food and drink that were a part of the feast. No doubt there were shops where these items could be purchased; but this would take some time, given the large number of people who had come to Jerusalem for the feast.

CELEBRATION?

One month from now, we will celebrate Memorial Day. Millions will enjoy the holiday aspects of the occasion: a three-day weekend, the reopening of swimming pools, warm weather sports, parades, and other activities. For some, emotions will be mixed. On the one hand, they will participate in the fun, yet there will also be a sense of sadness, as graves of loved ones are decorated and as dead soldiers are remembered.

Can solemn observances rightly be called *celebrations*? Actually, "to have a good time" is only one definition of *celebrate* in the dictionary. Others include: "to perform a ritual," "to commemorate with festivity," and "to honor publicly." To limit its meaning to mere fun and laughter is to understand *celebration* in a very limited sense.

Sober rituals can be celebrations too. A primary case in point is Passover. Orthodox Jews have celebrated this memorial for centuries. The meal is designed to remind participants of the bitter oppression of Hebrew slaves in Egypt, the slaying of lambs, the marking of doorways with blood, and the hasty evacuation led by Moses. It is a serious ritual, yet celebrated by people who rejoice in God's deliverance.

The Lord's Supper is also a bittersweet observance. We remember with remorse the crucifixion of Christ, yet we rejoice that by His death we have been freed from bondage. It is the primary act of celebration in our worship.   —R. W. B.

II. Observing the Passover
(Mark 14:17-21)

A. The Meal Begins (v. 17)

17. And in the evening he cometh with the twelve.

When *evening* approached, Jesus led the rest of His disciples into the city and to the upper room. As we count time this would have been Thursday evening, but since the Jewish day began at sundown, this was now Friday.

B. A Traitor in the Midst
(vv. 18-21)

18, 19. And as they sat and did eat, Jesus said, Verily I say unto you, One of you which eateth with me shall betray me. And they began to be sorrowful, and to say unto him one by one, Is it I? and another said, Is it I?

The Greek word rendered *sat* really means "reclined" and is so rendered in several more recent versions of the Bible. Many of us think of Leonardo da Vinci's famous painting *The Last Supper*, which depicts Jesus sitting at the table with the twelve apostles. However, the practice in the first century was to recline on low benches while eating.

None of the Gospel accounts reports all the events that occurred in the upper room. For example, John 13:3-11 tells us that after the meal, Jesus took a basin of water and a towel and proceeded to wash the disciples' feet. In this act, Jesus attempted to teach the disciples the importance of humility and service among those who would seek greatness in the kingdom of God. The disciples needed this lesson, for even in the upper room they had been quarreling among themselves about who would be greatest (Luke 22:24-30).

At some point in the evening, Jesus revealed that one of the group would *betray* Him. The disciples replied with surprise and shock: *Is it I?* With the exception of Judas, the disciples all knew that they would never intentionally commit such an act. Their concern seems to have been that in some unintentional way they would betray Jesus. Even Judas, hypocrite that he was, asked the same question (he likely felt obliged to do as the others had done). Then Peter urged the disciple "whom Jesus loved" to ask Jesus who the traitor was (John 13:23, 24).

20. And he answered and said unto them, It is one of the twelve, that dippeth with me in the dish.

Jesus did not answer directly, but indicated that the traitor was the one *that dippeth with me in the dish.* Apparently the disciples missed this clue; perhaps they were too distracted by Jesus' disturbing announcement of a traitor among them.

21. The Son of man indeed goeth, as it is written of him: but woe to that man by whom the Son of man is betrayed! good were it for that man if he had never been born.

Jesus never stopped loving Judas. With these words He seems to have been reaching out to the betrayer, giving him one last chance to repent. But Judas rejected this final opportunity, for at this point "Satan entered into him" (John 13:27), closing his heart to any possibility of repentance. The judgment that Judas brought upon himself was so tragic that it would have been better for him *if he had never been born.* Notice that although Jesus came to fulfill what was *written of him,* this did not excuse Judas from doing what he did.

III. The Lord's Supper Instituted
(Mark 14:22-25)

A. Elements of the Supper (vv. 22, 23)

22. And as they did eat, Jesus took bread, and blessed, and brake it, and gave to them, and said, Take, eat; this is my body.

In these few verses Mark tells us of Jesus' instituting what we call the Lord's Supper, or Communion. It became the center of worship in the early church and has remained so in many churches today. Sadly, it has also become the center of a great deal of controversy. Scholars have debated over who is eligible to receive Communion, when and how often it should be offered, and what it means. It is beyond the scope of this lesson to go into these matters, but they should be addressed in light of what the Scriptures teach.

As they did eat, Jesus took a dramatic departure from the usual Passover observance. He had often used object lessons or symbolic language in His teaching, and the institution of the Lord's Supper is another example of this.

When *Jesus took bread,* this was not bread that had been specially prepared for the occasion; it was unleavened bread that had been left over from the Passover meal. The fact that this bread was unleavened is the reason that unleavened bread should be used in the observance of Communion today.

After blessing the bread, Jesus *brake it, and gave it to* the disciples, saying, *Take, eat; this is my body.* His words must have been somewhat puzzling to His followers. But they had been accustomed to Jesus' use of figurative language on many occasions before. They would not be likely to take His words literally, any more than when He said, "I am the light of the world," or "I am the door." Obviously Jesus did not give them a piece of His flesh to eat; such an idea would have been utterly abhorrent to them.

23. And he took the cup, and when he had given thanks, he gave it to them: and they all drank of it.

As with the bread, this *cup* must have been left over from the Passover meal. Its contents, the "fruit of the vine" (v. 25), represented Jesus' blood that would soon be shed on the cross. In eating the bread and drinking of the cup, the disciples were, in a spiritual sense, uniting with Jesus in the mission for which He came into the world.

B. The New Covenant (vv. 24, 25)

24, 25. And he said unto them, This is my blood of the new testament, which is shed for many. Verily I say unto you, I will drink no more of the fruit of the vine, until that day that I drink it new in the kingdom of God.

The phrase *new testament* is translated "new covenant" in many of the more recent translations. This seems to convey more accurately the idea intended here. The Jewish people were quite familiar with the idea of a covenant. They knew of the covenant that God had made with Abraham and had renewed with Isaac and Jacob. They knew of the covenant that He had made with His people through Moses at Mount Sinai. They were aware that this covenant was sealed by blood. Moses sprinkled sacrificial blood on the people, saying, "Behold the blood of the covenant, which the Lord hath made with you" (Exodus 24:8).

To the phrase *which is shed for many*, Matthew adds "for the remission of sins" (Matthew 26:28). The Jewish people understood the connection between the shedding of blood and the remission of sins (Leviticus 17:11). However, the animal blood that was offered under the Old Covenant sacrificial system was inadequate to provide complete forgiveness. Hebrews 10:4 states, "It is not possible that the blood of bulls and of goats should take away sins." A perfect sacrifice was necessary in order for our sins to be forgiven, and Jesus came to provide that sacrifice.

When Jesus said that He would not drink of *the fruit of the vine* until He drank it *new in the kingdom of God*, He was implying His impending death. His concluding reference to the kingdom of God is taken by some to mean that He will not share in this feast again until the saints join with Him in the triumphant "marriage supper of the Lamb" in Heaven (Revelation 19:9). Others hold that Jesus was referring to the spiri-

visual for lesson 8

"Take, eat; this is my body."
Mark 14:22

tual union that Christians enjoy with Him when they celebrate the Lord's Supper. If this is the meaning, then that union was experienced only a few weeks later when the church began on the Day of Pentecost and began to observe the "breaking of bread" (Acts 2:42).

A NEW CONTRACT

1994 was a momentous year in American politics. The midterm elections resulted in a Republican majority in Congress for the first time in several decades. Newt Gingrich and his conservative Congressmen framed what they called "A Republican Contract With the American People." The contract promised legislation and changes in government that most of the voting public had been demanding.

Contract is one meaning of the term *covenant*. Others are *testament* or *agreement*. Biblical history, and the Bible itself, is divided into the "Old Covenant" period and the "New Covenant" period. The Old Testament was received from God through Moses; the New Testament was established by God through Jesus Christ. When Jesus initiated the memorial of Communion, He spoke of the new "contract" between God and man. The next day He signed it with His blood, and on the Day of Pentecost, fifty days later, He sealed it with His Spirit.

Christians can rejoice in their New Covenant with God—a contract based on grace, not law. Truth, forgiveness, and freedom are blessings of divine providence that we enjoy because of Calvary. God is always faithful to the promises of His agreement; we must be faithful to what His contract demands of us.   —R. W. B.

Conclusion

A. Uniting at the Lord's Table

Almost all persons who claim to be Christians participate in what we call Communion, or the Lord's Supper. But in different cultures across the centuries, the manner in which this act of worship is observed has differed widely. It is tragic that this ordinance, which ought to bring unity, has instead been the source of much strife and bitterness. Many feel that the only way to overcome these differences is to return to the New Testament and attempt to duplicate in our services exactly what Jesus and His apostles did in the upper room.

But even this does not solve the problem. We immediately have to decide what items in the upper room were essential and what items were only incidental. Obviously, we ought to comply with whatever is essential and not argue too much about the incidentals. Some things clearly are incidental. For example, I have never known anyone who insisted that Communion was valid only if it was observed in the upper room of a dwelling place. Nor have I ever known anyone who felt that the Communion ought to be preceded by eating a Passover meal.

Several years ago I worshiped in a church behind the former Iron Curtain. Since Jesus offered only one cup to His disciples, these Christians believed that they should do the same, and so in a congregation of a hundred, we passed the cup from person to person. I worshiped in another church in Europe where we were called forward, twelve at a time, to kneel around a table where we were served. Because twelve persons were present around the first Communion table, these believers thought it important to follow that precedent.

What if someone does not have access to unleavened bread and grape juice? I knew a family that often vacationed in remote areas far from any church. For their family Communion they used crackers and grape Kool-Aid. On one occasion I worshiped in a village in the jungles of Papua, New Guinea, where neither grain for making bread nor grapevines grow. The villagers used coconut milk and flakes of coconut in their Communion service. Some groups practice footwashing as a part of the Communion service. While this can be a loving symbol of humility, is it a necessary part of observing the Lord's Supper? Some insist that only an ordained minister or priest may preside at the Communion. Others insist that an elder do this. This list of different ways in which people observe the Lord's Supper could be expanded by several paragraphs.

Is there any way that we can lay aside our cultural differences and our personal preferences, and come together as one in Christ about His table? Let us work and pray toward finding that way.

B. Five Looks at the Lord's Supper

The Lord's Supper is first of all a look *backward*. As we participate in it, we do so in remembrance of what happened in the past—our Lord's suffering and death for us.

The Lord's Supper is a look *inward*. "Let a man examine himself," Paul wrote (1 Corinthians 11:28). This inward look forces us to examine our hearts, repenting of any sins that keep us from true communion with God.

The Lord's Supper is a look *outward*. Paul wrote that in partaking of Communion we "show the Lord's death" (1 Corinthians 11:26). As we gather about the Lord's table, we are saying to the world that we are different, that we are members of His family.

The Lord's Supper is a look *forward*. We are told to share in this memorial meal "till he come" (1 Corinthians 11:26). As we meet about this table week by week, we are witnessing to our belief that someday Jesus is coming back to claim His own.

Finally, the Lord's Supper is a look *upward*. Jesus promised His disciples that someday He would drink "the fruit of the vine" with them again in the kingdom of God (Mark 14:25). This promise is also ours if we are willing to claim it.

C. Prayer

Father, help us come to a richer, deeper understanding of the meaning of communing with You through the Lord's Supper that Your Son gave us. May we commit ourselves to assemble regularly about the Communion table. Teach us to examine ourselves as we partake, so that we do not partake carelessly or casually. In the name of our Savior we pray. Amen.

D. Thought to Remember

"This do in remembrance of me."

Home Daily Bible Readings

Monday, Apr. 20—Keep the Passover As a Sign (Exodus 12:1-14)

Tuesday, Apr. 21—Lift Up the Cup of Salvation (Psalm 116:12-19)

Wednesday, Apr. 22—Blood Poured Out for Many (Mark 14:12-25)

Thursday, Apr. 23—New Covenant With God's People (Jeremiah 31:27-34)

Friday, Apr. 24—Sharing in the Blood and Body (1 Corinthians 10:14-22)

Saturday, Apr. 25—Love As Christ Loved (John 13:3-15)

Sunday, Apr. 26—New Covenant in Christ's Blood (1 Corinthians 11:17-26)

Learning by Doing

This page contains an alternate lesson plan emphasizing learning activities.
Classes desiring such student involvement will find these suggestions helpful.

Learning Goals

After completing this lesson, students should be able to:

1. Relate the circumstances under which Jesus instituted the Lord's Supper.

2. Explain the significance of the Lord's Supper for Christians today.

3. Determine to maintain or increase faithfulness in observing the Lord's Supper.

Into the Lesson

Begin this lesson by referring to the story found in the lesson commentary Introduction under "Eating Jesus." Then explain that there are many different traditions surrounding the Lord's Supper, and many ways in which people observe it. Practices are affected by culture, experience, theology, and other factors. Ask class members to relate the different practices they know of or have observed regarding this special meal. Ask someone to list these on the chalkboard or on poster board.

Point out to the class that we must be careful not to allow these differences to cloud the Lord's purpose for the Lord's Supper. Today's lesson will focus on the origin and the significance of this precious meal.

Into the Word

Early in the week, ask a student to prepare a brief five-minute report on the background and practice of the Passover feast in Jesus' day. Give him or her a Bible dictionary as a resource.

Tell the class that today's study of the Lord's Supper will include a glimpse of three meals. The first meal is the Passover feast, which is the setting for today's text. Allow your guest speaker to give his or her report.

Next, ask a class member to read Mark 14:12-21. Explain that the events in verses 18-21 occurred during the eating of the Passover meal. Give a brief lecture about these events, using the notes in the lesson commentary.

Then explain that the second meal is our central focus—the Lord's Supper (verses 22-25). Ask the following series of questions:

1. What are some names that are used in various churches for this meal? (The Last Supper; the Lord's Supper; Communion, or, in some cases, Holy Communion; the Eucharist, which means "thanksgiving"; the Mass)

2. Verses 22 and 23 describe the elements of the Lord's Supper. When Jesus took the bread, it was the unleavened bread that had been left over from the Passover meal. What is the significance of unleavened bread? (Be sure to tie this in with the significance of the original Passover in the Old Testament.) What is the significance of the fruit of the vine? (Some draw a parallel between the crushing of grapes to produce juice and the piercing of Jesus' body to produce blood.)

3. Why does Jesus ask us to share in this meal? What is it intended to do for us?

4. What is the "new testament" Jesus mentions in verse 24? Note the discussion of the phrase in the lesson commentary.

5. For whom is the Lord's Supper? Who should partake of it? Who should not?

Finally, introduce the third meal. Ask what Jesus meant by His comment in verse 25 concerning "the kingdom of God." You will probably need to use the discussion found in the lesson commentary, which lists two possible answers. Either answer means a wonderful time of fellowship for Christians to anticipate!

Into Life

To conclude this lesson, deal with two practical issues of the Lord's Supper. Ask class members to work in pairs or threes. They may choose either of the following tasks: (1) Make a list of a few ideas of appropriate things to think about or do during the quiet time of Communion. (2) Make a list of a few reasons to participate in the Lord's Supper faithfully. Be prepared to share these with the class.

Before asking the teams to share their ideas with the class, appoint a person to list them on the chalkboard or on poster board. Also appoint someone to copy the list of things to think about or do during the Communion time. Tell the class that you will have this list printed and mailed to them this week. Class members can use the list as a helpful resource during worship. Suggest that they keep it in their Bibles and refer to it as Communion time approaches during worship.

After the teams have shared their ideas, close the class on a devotional note by reading the words of an appropriate hymn, such as "Here, O My Lord, I See Thee Face to Face," or "When I Survey the Wondrous Cross."

Let's Talk It Over

The questions on this page are designed to encourage review of the lesson Scriptures and to promote discussion of the lesson by the class. The answers provided are only discussion starters. Let your class talk it over from there.

1. Why did Jesus choose such an unusual way to identify the place where He and His disciples would share the Passover meal? How is this significant?

As the lesson writer points out, Jesus must have aimed at delaying Judas's betrayal of Him. If Judas had known the location of the meal beforehand, he could have arranged for Jesus to be arrested in the upper room. Jesus obviously did not want this occasion with His disciples to be interrupted. Therefore, He arranged for Passover preparations to be made without revealing the location. This intent on Jesus' part is not spelled out in any of the Gospels, but it is an obvious explanation.

2. Preparations for the Passover meal were detailed and time-consuming. How can we compare this with our preparations for the Lord's Supper?

It may require a substantial amount of time for a member of a large church to prepare the Communion trays. But whether in a large or small congregation, the persons who perform this unheralded task do a valuable service. Our focus here, however, is on the kind of readiness of heart that the worshipers make. We often declare that the Lord's Supper is the center of Sunday worship. If that is so, then each worshiper should devote significant time to preparing his or her heart for partaking. Perhaps we should think of Communion preparation as a week-long activity.

3. Even though Jesus told the disciples, "This is my body . . . This is my blood" when He instituted the Lord's Supper, it is clear that He never intended for anyone to regard the emblems as His literal body and blood. How is this so?

This is one of the many examples of Jesus' use of figurative language. His enemies refused to accept or understand this. When He spoke of the destruction and rebuilding of the temple of His body, they concluded that He was speaking of Herod's temple (John 2:18-22). His disciples also struggled with such terminology. However, when He spoke of being "the door of the sheep" (John 10:7), they knew that He was not claiming to be a literal door. And in the upper room they surely understood that He was not referring to the emblems as His literal body and blood. He was, after all, physically present with them. His body was intact; His blood was not yet shed. The disciples were partaking of bread and the fruit of the vine, and these were what believers were to partake of ever afterward.

4. When Jesus instituted the Lord's Supper, He spoke of "that day that I drink it new in the kingdom of God." This may refer to a grand observance of Communion in Heaven. How can contemplation of this Communion to come help us in our earthly observance?

Our present Communion should be characterized by a keen anticipation of that heavenly celebration. When we commune now, we may struggle with distractions. Troubling experiences from the previous week or problems likely to emerge in the coming week make it difficult to focus on our Savior. What a joy to envision a Communion service where earth's irritations will no longer exist! When we commune now, it may bother us that fellow believers are absent from the Lord's table. No genuine believer will be absent from that Communion to come.

5. The Lord's Supper should contribute to a spirit of unity among Christians. How can we make it so in our congregation?

Frequent sermons and lessons pertaining to the Lord's Supper are one key. Church members may feel that they understand what the Lord's Supper involves, but there is always much more to learn. How do we prepare ourselves? What can we do to put distractions from our minds? What must our attitude be toward our fellow partakers? Why is it important to be present regularly at the Lord's table? These are some questions that must be answered from the pulpit and in the classroom. When we are united in our understanding of the Lord's Supper, we take a giant step toward unity in general. Also, the persons who present Communion meditations must recognize that they have a grave responsibility. They must remind worshipers of the importance of putting away conflicts, grudges, bitterness, and the like before communing. They must help make the Lord's Supper a healing time within the congregation.

Teaching in Parables

DEVOTIONAL READING: 2 Corinthians 5:6-17.

LESSON SCRIPTURE: Mark 4:1-34.

PRINTED TEXT: Mark 4:1-9, 26-34.

Mark 4:1-9, 26-34

1 And he began again to teach by the sea side: and there was gathered unto him a great multitude, so that he entered into a ship, and sat in the sea; and the whole multitude was by the sea on the land.

2 And he taught them many things by parables, and said unto them in his doctrine,

3 Hearken; Behold, there went out a sower to sow:

4 And it came to pass, as he sowed, some fell by the way side, and the fowls of the air came and devoured it up.

5 And some fell on stony ground, where it had not much earth; and immediately it sprang up, because it had no depth of earth:

6 But when the sun was up, it was scorched; and because it had no root, it withered away.

7 And some fell among thorns, and the thorns grew up, and choked it, and it yielded no fruit.

8 And other fell on good ground, and did yield fruit that sprang up and increased; and brought forth, some thirty, and some sixty, and some a hundred.

9 And he said unto them, He that hath ears to hear, let him hear.

. . . .

26 And he said, So is the kingdom of God, as if a man should cast seed into the ground;

27 And should sleep, and rise night and day, and the seed should spring and grow up, he knoweth not how.

28 For the earth bringeth forth fruit of herself; first the blade, then the ear, after that the full corn in the ear.

29 But when the fruit is brought forth, immediately he putteth in the sickle, because the harvest is come.

30 And he said, Whereunto shall we liken the kingdom of God? or with what comparison shall we compare it?

31 It is like a grain of mustard seed, which, when it is sown in the earth, is less than all the seeds that be in the earth:

32 But when it is sown, it groweth up, and becometh greater than all herbs, and shooteth out great branches; so that the fowls of the air may lodge under the shadow of it.

33 And with many such parables spake he the word unto them, as they were able to hear it.

34 But without a parable spake he not unto them: and when they were alone, he expounded all things to his disciples.

GOLDEN TEXT: With many such parables spake he the word unto them, as they were able to hear it.—Mark 4:33.

The Gospel of Action (Mark)
Unit 3: The Teachings of Jesus
(Lessons 9-13)

Lesson Aims

After completing this lesson, students should be able to:

1. Summarize the messages of the parables found in today's text.

2. Explain the principles of how God's Word works and how His kingdom grows.

3. Determine to spend more time in the Scriptures, so that God's Word can bear fruit through them.

Lesson Outline

The visual for Lesson 9 in the visuals packet highlights one of the parables in today's lesson. It is shown on page 299.

Introduction

A. The Kingdom of God Is Like . . .

There is an old fable from India that tells about six blind men who had heard about the elephant, and decided to find out for themselves just what this animal was like. One of the blind men seized the elephant's trunk and said, "The elephant is like a large snake."

Another, upon feeling the elephant's tusks, insisted that the elephant was like a spear. A third felt its ear and argued that it was like a large fan. The fourth man ran into the animal's leg and was certain that the elephant was like a tree. Another felt the elephant's massive body and was sure that it was like a wall. The sixth man happened to grab the tail and insisted that the elephant was like a rope. In a way, all the men were right; yet they were also wrong when they insisted that the elephant was *only* this or *only* that.

The fictitious experiences of these blind men can be applied to understanding the parables that Jesus told about the kingdom of God. Each parable is a true reflection of the kingdom in the particular aspect that it highlights; but if we insist that any one aspect is a complete description of the kingdom, then, like the blind men, we make a serious error.

B. Lesson Background

With today's lesson, we begin the final unit of studies from Mark: "The Teachings of Jesus." Jesus was the Master Teacher. As such, He used various methods to get His message across to His students. One of the methods He used was telling parables. A parable, according to the classic Sunday school definition, is an earthly story with a heavenly meaning. If we keep in mind this simple definition, it will help us understand the teachings of Jesus in today's lesson.

These parables, sometimes referred to as the "parables by the sea," were presented approximately halfway through Jesus' Galilean ministry. During this same period Jesus had called the twelve, to whom He gave special responsibilities and powers (Mark 3:14, 15). At this point Jesus' popularity was growing, but so was the antagonism of the religious leaders. Some may have even closed their synagogues to Him. This fact, along with the growing crowds, led Jesus to do more of His teaching outdoors.

The truths revealed in some of Jesus' parables were quite obvious. In others, the truths seemed deliberately obscured in order to encourage the listeners to think for themselves or to ask questions of Jesus at a later time (Mark 4:10). Several of the parables Jesus used during this period in His ministry dealt with the kingdom of Heaven, or the kingdom of God (see the terms used interchangeably in Matthew 13:11 and Mark 4:11). Through these parables, Jesus began to open the eyes of the multitudes to the true nature of His kingdom. They needed to realize that His was not the earthly kingdom that many anticipated.

I. Parable of the Sower
(Mark 4:1-9)

A. Setting of the Parable (vv. 1, 2)

1, 2. And he began again to teach by the sea side: and there was gathered unto him a great multitude, so that he entered into a ship, and sat in the sea; and the whole multitude was by the sea on the land. And he taught them many things by parables, and said unto them in his doctrine.

In the events narrated prior to this verse, Jesus had been teaching in a house, perhaps the house of a follower. However, because of the growing crowds, meeting in a house became impractical; and so Jesus moved His classroom to the *sea side.* We do not know the exact location where this incident occurred, but it was at some spot on the western shore of the Sea of Galilee. A number of locations along the shore would have been close to several towns, from which the people came to hear Jesus.

The press of the *great multitude* eventually made it necessary for Jesus to get into a boat and push out a few feet into the water. Though this may have constituted a temporary inconvenience, a *ship* would have provided an excellent "pulpit" from which Jesus could be seen as He *taught* the people. (Many of us may remember similar situations where a boat was used in a "Galilean" service in Christian service camp.) Jesus had used *parables* before in His teaching (Matthew 7:24-27), but on this occasion His teaching was exclusively in this form.

B. Seed by the Wayside (vv. 3, 4)

3, 4. Hearken; Behold, there went out a sower to sow: and it came to pass, as he sowed, some fell by the wayside, and the fowls of the air came and devoured it up.

Hearken. Listen! Jesus was not necessarily trying to quiet the crowd; He was trying to impress upon them that what He had to say was important. Jesus frequently used common, everyday objects as a basis for His parables. It is entirely possible that even as He spoke, the

visual for
lesson 9

crowd could see in the distance a farmer sowing his crop. Even if one was not visible, the people would be familiar with how seeds were broadcast by hand.

Although there were no paved roads in farming areas, there were paths along side of and between the individual parcels of land. Through the years, these paths became packed down and almost as hard as pavement. Any seed that fell on them was not covered and would quickly be *devoured* by *the fowls of the air.*

C. Seed on Stony Ground (vv. 5, 6)

5, 6. And some fell on stony ground, where it had not much earth; and immediately it sprang up, because it had no depth of earth: but when the sun was up, it was scorched; and because it had no root, it withered away.

In many places in Palestine, the limestone bedrock is covered by only a thin layer of soil. Such soil heats up more quickly than does the soil with greater depth, causing the seed to sprout quickly. But under the intense heat of the *sun,* these plants quickly wither and die. Their *root* system has not developed enough to provide them with the necessary nourishment to survive.

D. Seed Among Thorns (v. 7)

7. And some fell among thorns, and the thorns grew up, and choked it, and it yielded no fruit.

Every gardener knows what happens when he fails to keep the weeds out of his garden. The good seeds may sprout and even start to grow, but the weeds always seem more aggressive. Soon they overtake the desirable crops.

E. Seed on Good Soil (v. 8)

8. And other fell on good ground, and did yield fruit that sprang up and increased, and brought forth, some thirty, and some sixty, and some a hundred.

Some seed *fell on good ground* and produced a bountiful harvest. Different grains produce in different quantities, but in this parable the seeds are all the same. The difference in yields reflects the variety of soils.

F. Jesus' Admonition (v. 9)

9. And he said unto them, He that hath ears to hear, let him hear.

Jesus frequently used this admonition (Matthew 11:15; 13:43; Mark 7:16; Luke 14:35; and to each of the seven churches in Revelation 2 and 3). Of course, He had in mind much more than just physical hearing. He wanted the people to hear His teachings with understanding.

This saying was especially appropriate in regard to this parable, for even the twelve did not understand it until Jesus explained it (v. 10).

Jesus' interpretation of this parable is found in verses 14-20 (not in our printed text). The seed is the Word, or God's message for man. The sower is not specifically identified, but it is fair to assume that he is Jesus, and by extension, anyone else who proclaims His good news. The different soils represent people who hear the Word and respond in different ways.

It is important to note what Jesus says concerning the good ground, which receives the Word and becomes productive. The fact that Jesus describes three different kinds of soils producing at different rates (thirty, sixty, a hundred) may suggest that sincere Christians have different levels of productivity in His kingdom. Jesus is in no way critical of those who produce less, for He recognizes that one's productivity is often quite dependent upon circumstances beyond the individual's control.

II. Parable of the Growing Seed (Mark 4:26-29)

A. The Seed Planted (vv. 26, 27)

26, 27. And he said, So is the kingdom of God, as if a man should cast seed into the ground; and should sleep, and rise night and day, and the seed should spring and grow up, he knoweth not how.

According to the previous verses, Jesus presented another parable, that of the candle, or lamp (vv. 21-25). In the verses before us now, Jesus turned again to agriculture as the basis of another parable on *the kingdom of God*. Anyone who has given just a passing thought to gardening stands amazed at the mystery of how seeds grow. The farmer can prepare the soil, fertilize it, water it, and then trust that the seed will grow; but he really cannot make the seed grow or explain what happens to it.

PHOTOSYNTHESIS

My dictionary (*Webster's New World Dictionary of the American Language*) defines *photosynthesis* as "the production of organic substances, especially sugars, from carbon dioxide and water by the action of light on the chlorophyll in green plant cells." Would that description have helped the farmer in Jesus' parable understand the process of seed growth? Even though we know that plants grow in combination with the elements of air, light, and moisture, the actual ways and means of this happening remain one of the wonders in God's creation.

Farmers today, more so than in the Middle East two thousand years ago, know what happens when good seeds are buried in good soil. Germination, sprouts, stems, leaves, buds, blossoms, and fruit all come in predictable sequence to produce a bountiful harvest. Still, no one has been able to demystify totally the miracle of life. The Creator alone fully understands. As poet Joyce Kilmer once wrote, "Only God can make a tree."

In the realm of the Spirit, life is even more inscrutable. Gospel seeds are sown, faith germinates, trust sprouts upward, obedience follows —all in sequence. A new creature is born; and as he matures, love, joy, peace, and other spiritual fruit are produced. Describing it doesn't explain it; it is a miracle!   —R. W. B.

B. The Crop Harvested (vv. 28, 29)

28, 29. For the earth bringeth forth fruit of herself; first the blade, then the ear, after that the full corn in the ear. But when the fruit is brought forth, immediately he putteth in the sickle, because the harvest is come.

The word *corn* is used in the *King James Version* to describe grain in general (as in the phrase "corn of wheat" in John 12:24). Thus *full corn in the ear* is better translated as "full kernel in the head," as in the *New International Version*. A plant grows at a rate characteristic of its strain, and a farmer can do little to change this rate of growth. When the plant has reached maturity and its crop has ripened, then it is time for the *harvest*.

This parable suggests that the growth of the kingdom of God is on a time schedule established by God Himself. When we work hard for the kingdom of God and still it does not grow as rapidly or in the way that we want it to, we need to remember that God is still in control. He is the "Lord of the harvest" (Matthew 9:38) and the One who gives the increase to our efforts to sow the good seed and to build His kingdom (1 Corinthians 3:7). The harvest may also refer to what will take place when Jesus returns to judge the world (Matthew 13:39).

III. Parable of the Mustard Seed (Mark 4:30-34)

A. A Tiny Seed Grows (vv. 30-32)

30-32. And he said, Whereunto shall we liken the kingdom of God? or with what comparison shall we compare it? It is like a grain of mustard seed, which, when it is sown in the earth, is less than all the seeds that be in the earth: but when it is sown, it groweth up, and becometh greater than all the herbs, and

shooteth out great branches; so that the fowls of the air may lodge under the shadow of it.

Once again Jesus compared the kingdom of God to a seed; however, the lesson He drew from this parable is quite different from that of the previous one. The *mustard seed* to which Jesus referred is not the plant from which the familiar seasoning comes. The plant Jesus mentioned grew wild in Palestine. The leaves were used as "greens," and the seeds were made into either powder or paste. While the seed may not have been the smallest seed in the world, it was the smallest of which Jesus' audience would have been aware. This tiny seed, when carefully cultivated, could grow to heights of twelve to fifteen feet—taller than any other garden plants. It grew so large that birds could *lodge under the shadow of it.*

The point that Jesus was making in this parable is that the kingdom of God would have a small, even insignificant, beginning, but would then grow mightily. So it was that the church began on Pentecost in A.D. 30 with only twelve men. These simple, uneducated men pitted against the might of the Roman Empire whose population numbered into the millions seemed like insurmountable odds. Yet today Christ's church numbers hundreds of millions around the world, while the Roman Empire lies buried in the musty pages of history.

CONSIDER THE BANANA

Have you heard of the person who complained that eating bananas is a waste of time? He said, "When you peel it and throw the core away, there's nothing left!"

Jesus might have enjoyed that joke. In any case, if He were teaching today, He might illustrate His kingdom with banana seeds instead of mustard seeds. But the comparisons and applications would be the same.

Banana seeds are among the smallest of which we are aware. (Often they are not found in commercially grown varieties.) Yet the growth and reproduction potential of banana seeds is truly amazing. Banana stalks become trees that are ten or fifteen feet tall. Leaves are huge, some as large as ten feet long and two feet wide. Harvesting one hundred and fifty bananas from one plant is not unusual. Bananas are one of the most prolific food crops in the world. And all of this from a seed the size of a pinhead!

Kingdom growth is incredible too. The church of Jesus Christ thrives and expands, often in adversity. She persists and perseveres according to God's purpose and promise.

Sometimes the growth in a local church seems imperceptible. But global growth continues as God's will is done more and more on earth as it is in Heaven. Christians must simply continue sowing seeds of faithfulness. Our labor will not be in vain.   —R. W. B.

B. Jesus' Use of Parables (vv. 33, 34)

33. And with many such parables spake he the word unto them, as they were able to hear it.

Although Jesus possessed wisdom far superior to anyone, He never sought to overwhelm His listeners with His knowledge. His pace was guided by the ability of His students to grasp what He said; He taught the truth *as they were able to hear it.*

34. But without a parable spake he not unto them: and when they were alone, he expounded all things to his disciples.

This statement summarizes the teaching of Jesus on this particular day, since at other times Jesus spoke plainly and did not use parables. Those of *his disciples* who desired greater understanding of the parables met with Jesus later to receive additional insights. The parables thus served to distinguish between the curious bystanders and the sincere seekers of truth.

Conclusion

A. Cracks in the Hardened Soil

Some years ago I was reseeding a section of my lawn. Since the area was not large, I did not bother to rent a seeder, but broadcast the seed by hand. A puff of wind blew some of the seed onto a walk that bordered the lawn. Before long some birds spotted the seed, landed on the walk, and began to make a meal of my grass seed. I allowed the birds to finish their meal, thinking to myself how this incident resembled a portion of Jesus' parable of the sower.

Well, not quite. A couple of weeks later I noticed some blades of grass sprouting from a crack in the walk. Some of the seed had fallen there, out of the reach of the birds. With sufficient warmth and moisture, they had begun to sprout just like the seed in the lawn. This is not to suggest that Jesus' parable was inaccurate. But we need to recognize that He was speaking in general terms. Many of us probably have known people to whom we have presented the Word, only to see them reject it without any serious consideration. Even when the Word was presented repeatedly the result was still rejection, indicating that the hearts of some persons can become so hardened that they will not receive our message. When this happens, the limits on our time and resources require that we turn our efforts to someone who is likely to be more receptive.

However, we should never completely close the door on any person. The Word may lodge in a crack in the hardened heart that we did not see. Like my grass seed on the walk, it will germinate and begin to sprout. Sometimes the Word may take root in a hardened heart when someone else presents it. Sometimes a friend, a loved one, or even a child can succeed when others fail. In other situations, a person with a hardened heart may go through a devastating experience, producing cracks where the Word will lodge and take root. A serious illness, an accident, the loss of a loved one, or financial reverses can afford opportunities for the Word to find an opening. And when all else appears to fail, we can continue to pray for the person.

B. Church Growth

In recent years we have heard much about the "church growth movement." Those involved in this take seriously the parable of the mustard seed, and stress the Biblical truth that God wants His church to grow. Leaders in this movement have emphasized a scientific approach to church planting and church growth. By using findings from psychology, sociology, and demographics, they seek to make more effective use of resources in seeking the lost.

Some reject church growth principles, insisting that when we turn to a cold scientific approach to evangelism and edification, we eliminate or bypass the work of the Holy Spirit in spreading the Word. When we make these criticisms, we must take care that we do not limit the power of the Holy Spirit. Is it possible that the Spirit can use even science to advance the cause of the kingdom?

We understand the parable of the mustard seed to teach that the kingdom of God will grow mightily from a tiny beginning. On the other hand, the parable of the growing seed ought to serve as a warning that we do not always have all the answers about how churches grow. Even as we employ all the modern techniques we can to promote the expansion of God's kingdom, we should salt our efforts with a bit of humility, lest we come to believe that any one set of methods (especially our own) is superior to all others. Regardless of the approach we may take in carrying out the Great Commission, let us rejoice when lost souls are brought to the Lord.

C. Six Soils

In the parable of the sower, we are accustomed to speak of four soils—the hard soil, the stony soil, the thorny soil, and the good soil. But a farmer would look at it differently. Perhaps he would see in the soil that produced thirtyfold a clay hilltop that failed to produce very well. In the soil that yielded sixtyfold, he would see a good field. In the field that produced a hundredfold, he would see some rich bottomland.

Some students feel that the mention of the differing yields of the good soil is merely a series of details that Jesus used to enhance the story, but not necessarily to convey any meaning. It is true that Jesus in His explanation of the parable does not attach any special significance to these differences. Yet they do suggest an important truth about persons who receive the Word and become obedient to it.

It is quite obvious that all Christians are not equally productive. Some are naturally more talented than others, and, other things being equal, a highly talented Christian is likely to be more productive than one not so talented. Where one happens to live or work can have an effect on his or her fruitfulness. Family circumstances beyond one's control may also have an impact on that person's opportunity to bear fruit.

It is worth noting that Jesus did not attach any blame to the less fruitful seed. We must be careful not to judge the work of other Christians. After all, God does not require us to be successful; He requires us to be faithful.

D. Prayer

Dear Father, may we be like the good soils, receiving the Word and bringing forth a bountiful harvest for Your kingdom. May all of our efforts help Your kingdom grow as does the tiny mustard seed. Help us to keep sowing faithfully, even when our efforts meet with resistance. In Jesus' name we pray. Amen.

E. Thought to Remember

"He that hath ears to hear, let him hear."

Home Daily Bible Readings

Monday, Apr. 27—Learning From Sowing Seeds (Mark 4:1-9)
Tuesday, Apr. 28—Secrets of God's Kingdom (Mark 4:10-20)
Wednesday, Apr. 29—Heed What You Hear (Mark 4:21-34)
Thursday, Apr. 30—Live for the Risen One (2 Corinthians 5:6-15)
Friday, May 1—Sowing and Reaping Bountifully (2 Corinthians 9:6-15)
Saturday, May 2—Sow the Spirit and Reap Eternity (Galatians 6:1-10)
Sunday, May 3—Reap With Shouts of Joy! (Psalm 126)

Learning by Doing

This page contains an alternate lesson plan emphasizing learning activities.
Classes desiring such student involvement will find these suggestions helpful.

Learning Goals

As a result of this lesson, students should be able to:

1. Summarize the messages of the parables found in today's text.

2. Explain the principles of how God's Word works and how His kingdom grows.

3. Determine to spend more time in the Scriptures, so that God's Word can bear fruit through them.

Into the Lesson

Begin the class session by asking volunteers to tell about a time when they tried to grow something in their garden and could not get it to grow, no matter how hard they tried. These stories will help you make a transition into Jesus' parable. Note: As students tell their stories, be sure to draw out the reasons that their plants did not grow (such as bad soil, neglect, or animals eating the plants).

Make a transition to today's text by pointing out that Jesus often taught by telling stories (parables) about common activities, such as farming, to illustrate some truth about the kingdom of God. This method of teaching forced His listeners to think more deeply. It concealed the truth about His kingdom from those whose hearts were not open to what was being taught. On the other hand, anyone who desired to know more could approach Jesus later in a more private setting (as Mark 4:34 indicates).

In today's text, Jesus tells us about a farmer who planted his field with mixed results. As you move from the opening activity into Jesus' parable, lead your class in a time of prayer, asking God to open your hearts and minds to the truth that this story contains.

Into the Word

Write the following words across the top of a chalkboard: Wayside, Stony, Thorny, Good.

Ask the class members to pay special attention to what happens to the seed that falls on each kind of soil in Jesus' parable. Then lead the class through Mark 4:1-9, section by section, stopping to allow them to discuss the different types of soil. List the characteristics of each type as the class suggests them.

As an alternative to reading the text together, ask someone in the class with a flair for drama to tell the story from the farmer's perspective. You will need to arrange this well in advance and be certain that the retelling contains all the important facts of the story.

Help your class make an application of this parable by asking them to describe someone they know who is an example of "good soil."

Into Life

Ask your students to prayerfully consider what type of soil they are at this time in their lives. As they do so, point out that most farmers realize that their land changes over time. Good land can become unproductive, and poor land can be improved. This is also true of our attitude toward Jesus and His teachings.

Encourage your students to see in themselves a combination of soils, with some areas more fertile and open to God's truth than others. Also, help them to see that, like a farmer's land, these areas can improve or deteriorate over time.

Ask your students to gather in small groups of three or four and talk about times in their lives when they responded to God as one of the four types of soil. Encourage them to write the four types of soil down one side of a sheet of paper (as you have written them across the top of your chalkboard), and to write next to each one a time in their lives when they were hard (like the wayside), without any roots (like the stony ground), seduced by the cares of the world (like the thorny ground), or productive (like the good soil). (This activity is found in the student book.)

Next, point out to your class that just as certain types of soil are more conducive to raising one particular type of crop, so also we may be good soil concerning one aspect of our Christian walk and stony or thorny soil concerning another. Ask your students to decide what kind of soil they are in the following areas:

Relationship to other members of the body of Christ (fellowship)

Relationship to non-Christian acquaintances (evangelism)

Relationship to possessions (stewardship)

Relationship to God (worship)

Encourage the students in each small group to close the class session praying for one another, that they might become good soil in each of these areas.

Let's Talk It Over

The questions on this page are designed to encourage review of the lesson Scriptures and to promote discussion of the lesson by the class. The answers provided are only discussion starters. Let your class talk it over from there.

1. What comparisons and contrasts can we draw between the time it takes to grow earthly crops and the time it may take to reap a spiritual harvest?

The farmer who plants corn or wheat can have a fairly good idea of when his crop will be ready for harvest. The gardener growing tomatoes, green beans, or potatoes is aware of the time it will take between planting and harvesting. With the seed of God's Word, the time is not so certain. The preacher or teacher may long to see fruit from his sowing of the Word, but it can be long in coming. The parents who have consistently labored to implant God's Word in their children's hearts may be discouraged by an apparent "crop failure." But we are assured of a blessed harvest, if we persist in sowing to the Spirit (Galatians 6:7-9).

2. The parable of the mustard seed depicts the remarkable growing power of God's kingdom. How can this encourage us?

This parable is something of a prophecy of the tremendous expansion of the church. From a seemingly insignificant group of believers in Jerusalem, it grew to embrace millions of people. Today it is a worldwide fellowship including believers from almost all nations, races, and languages. This is exciting, but equally exciting is the fact that the kingdom of God has the power to continue growing. Certain unbelievers delight in thinking of this as a "post-Christian era." They suggest that the time may be near when the human race casts off the "shackles" of religion. But the seed of the kingdom, the Word of God, contains the same potential for growth as it did in the first centuries of Christianity. We simply need to keep on sowing it.

3. Jesus spoke of some hearers as resembling the hard ground of the wayside. And yet we know of hardened unbelievers who have at last yielded to Christ. What should our attitude be toward those who are hardened?

It is certain that Jesus did not mean for us to assume that "human soil" is unchangeable. We are not to say, "That man is wayside soil—we need not bother to try to evangelize him." Sometimes a painful experience, such as illness or financial ruin, will soften a person's heart.

The person who resists the efforts of a preacher to win him may surrender to the witness of an ordinary believer. The individual who reacts against one kind of evangelistic approach may be reachable through another. So we should not be too hasty in giving up on any unbeliever. Instead, we must pray for that individual, for the Christians with whom he has contact, and for ourselves whenever we have the opportunity to demonstrate our faith to him.

4. In describing the good soil, Jesus spoke of three levels of fruitfulness, indicating that Christians will not be equally productive. How should this truth affect us?

Once again it is important that we avoid making too hasty an assumption on the basis of this parable. We should not say, "I am only a thirty-fold hearer. God cannot expect too much from me." Thinking of ourselves as soil can be very helpful at this point. We know that a farmer strives to make his soil as productive as possible. Similarly, we should be determined to make the most out of what we have for the glory of God. We can learn God's Word to the highest extent of our intellectual capacity. We can take advantage of opportunities for training. Never should we be satisfied with minimal fruitfulness where the cause of Christ is involved.

5. The lesson writer leads us in praying, "Dear Father, may we be like the good soils, receiving the Word and bringing forth a bountiful harvest for Your kingdom." How is this an excellent prayer for the teachers and learners of the Word?

It is a God-centered prayer, very much in harmony with the way Jesus taught us to pray: "Thy kingdom come. Thy will be done in earth, as it is in heaven" (Matthew 6:10). It is a prayer that emphasizes openness to God. In terms of the parable of the sower, we could say that it is a prayer that we may become good soil. A teacher's aim should be, not that the lesson will draw compliments from the class members, but that the Word may be sown into willing hearts. A learner's aim should be to clear away "rocks of resistance" and "weeds of worldliness," so that his or her heart may be fully open to the implanted Word.

Traditions or God?

DEVOTIONAL READING: Ephesians 6:10-20.

LESSON SCRIPTURE: Mark 7:1-23.

PRINTED TEXT: Mark 7:1-13.

Mark 7:1-13

1 Then came together unto him the Pharisees, and certain of the scribes, which came from Jerusalem.

2 And when they saw some of his disciples eat bread with defiled, that is to say, with unwashen hands, they found fault.

3 For the Pharisees, and all the Jews, except they wash their hands oft, eat not, holding the tradition of the elders.

4 And when they come from the market, except they wash, they eat not. And many other things there be, which they have received to hold, as the washing of cups, and pots, brazen vessels, and of tables.

5 Then the Pharisees and scribes asked him, Why walk not thy disciples according to the tradition of the elders, but eat bread with unwashen hands?

6 He answered and said unto them, Well hath Isaiah prophesied of you hypocrites, as it is written, This people honoreth me with their lips, but their heart is far from me.

7 Howbeit in vain do they worship me, teaching for doctrines the commandments of men.

8 For laying aside the commandment of God, ye hold the tradition of men, as the washing of pots and cups: and many other such like things ye do.

9 And he said unto them, Full well ye reject the commandment of God, that ye may keep your own tradition.

10 For Moses said, Honor thy father and thy mother; and, Whoso curseth father or mother, let him die the death:

11 But ye say, If a man shall say to his father or mother, It is Corban, that is to say, a gift, by whatsoever thou mightest be profited by me; he shall be free.

12 And ye suffer him no more to do aught for his father or his mother;

13 Making the word of God of none effect through your tradition, which ye have delivered: and many such like things do ye.

GOLDEN TEXT: Laying aside the commandment of God, ye hold the tradition of men.—Mark 7:8.

The Gospel of Action (Mark)
Unit 3: The Teachings of Jesus
(Lessons 9-13)

Lesson Aims

After this lesson, students should be able to:

1. Relate the key points of the confrontation between Jesus and the Pharisees in today's text.

2. Recognize the danger of respecting man's traditions more than God's commandments.

3. Pinpoint an area in their lives where obeying God needs to take priority over following tradition.

Lesson Outline

INTRODUCTION
  A. Who Makes the Rules?
  B. Lesson Background
 I. THE PHARISEES' CHALLENGE (Mark 7:1-5)
  A. Eating With Unwashed Hands (vv. 1, 2)
  B. The Pharisees' Practice (vv. 3, 4)
  C. The Pharisees' Question (v. 5)
II. JESUS' RESPONSE (Mark 7:6-13)
  A. The Pharisees' Hypocrisy (vv. 6, 7)
    Easy for You to Say!
  B. Loyalty to Tradition (vv. 8, 9)
  C. An Example of Hypocrisy (vv. 10-13)
    Designated Offerings
CONCLUSION
  A. Neither Libertine nor Legalist
  B. A "Bread-Side Manner"
  C. Prayer
  D. Thought to Remember

The visual for Lesson 10 in the visuals packet challenges us to place loyalty to God's Word above loyalty to tradition. It is shown on page 309.

Introduction

A. Who Makes the Rules?

I once knew an evangelist whose sermons usually contained a long litany of negatives. "A Christian," he insisted, "doesn't use tobacco or alcohol and doesn't go to places that serve liquor; he doesn't play cards, attend dances, or enter poolrooms; and he doesn't go to movies." (TV hadn't been invented yet, or I'm sure it would have been on the list.)

Later the evangelist met with some of the youth to discuss the sermon. One young person asked, "Sir, I have a dog that doesn't use alco-

hol, smoke, play cards, go to dances, play pool, or attend movies. Does that mean that he is a Christian?"

In every age, religious leaders have devised lists of what others must do or not do to be considered in proper standing. This approach to religion has a couple of advantages for people. First of all, many feel uncomfortable when they do not know exactly where the boundaries for behavior are, and so they prefer to have someone draw precise limits for what is expected of them. Jesus' day was no different. The scribes (those who were students of the Law) along with the Pharisees had drawn up long, detailed lists of both acceptable and prohibited behavior, which they sought to impose on everyone.

Second, by insisting that these traditions of men had to be obeyed, these leaders were able to control the people. In addition, by clever interpretation of these laws, they were able to avoid the responsibility of keeping some of their own obligations. In today's lesson, Jesus points out the hypocrisy of these leaders, and challenges the entire legalistic approach to religion.

B. Lesson Background

Today's lesson finds Jesus' popularity near its peak. Just before the events recorded in our text, He had fed the five thousand (Mark 6:30-44). To escape some of the pressure of the crowds, He and His disciples had then sailed across the northern end of the Sea of Galilee. When they landed, Jesus left the disciples and went up into a mountain to pray. When night came, the disciples, who had gone back out in the boat, found themselves caught in a violent storm. Late in the night, Jesus came walking on the water toward the boat. Peter attempted to walk on water to meet the Lord, but his faith gave way to fear and he began to sink (Matthew 14:28-33). As soon as Jesus entered the boat, the storm ceased, leaving the disciples "amazed in themselves beyond measure" (Mark 6:51).

After the dawning of the new day, the disciples arrived at Gennesaret, a town south of Capernaum on the Sea of Galilee. As soon as

How to Say It

CAPERNAUM. Kuh-*per*-nay-um.
CORBAN. *Kor*-bun.
GENNESARET. Geh-*ness*-uh-ret.
JUDAIZERS. *Joo*-duh-*eyes*-erz (strong accent on *Joo*).
LIBERTINE. *lib*-er-teen.
PHARISEES. *Fair*-ih-seez.

they landed, the people recognized them, and the news quickly spread through the country-side. As a result, the people gathered to hear Jesus, bringing their sick for Him to heal. The incident in today's lesson must have occurred shortly after this.

I. The Pharisees' Challenge (Mark 7:1-5)

A. Eating With Unwashed Hands (vv. 1, 2)

1, 2. **Then came together unto him the Pharisees, and certain of the scribes, which came from Jerusalem. And when they saw some of his disciples eat bread with defiled, that is to say, with unwashen hands, they found fault.**

Early in His ministry, Jesus had traveled to Jerusalem, where He cleansed the temple and was confronted by the Jews (John 2:13-17). However, before the religious leaders could take specific action against Him, He had left for Galilee, where He carried on much of His ministry. From Galilee, word of Jesus' ministry had reached *Jerusalem*. It soon became obvious that His activities posed a serious threat to the religious establishment. It was also obvious that the Pharisees and scribes in Galilee were no match for Jesus. Again and again He rebuffed their attacks.

These factors, along with Jesus' miracles, contributed to His growing popularity. The Jewish leaders feared that this new movement would get out of control, threatening their leadership and raising the possibility of Roman intervention if the people's enthusiasm boiled over. For this reason a delegation of *Pharisees . . . and scribes* came from the "headquarters" in Jerusalem to investigate Jesus and to discredit Him publicly. Some of the Jerusalem scribes had already attempted this (Mark 3:22).

At one point these men noticed that some of Jesus' *disciples* did not wash their *hands* before they ate *bread*. This gave them the opening they sought to find *fault* with Jesus. At first glance, the Pharisees' concern appears valid. Most of us were taught to wash our hands before eating, and we have taught our children to do the same. Our concern has been primarily for health reasons. But the issue here was not personal cleanliness or hygiene, but a ceremonial cleansing that the religious leaders thought important.

B. The Pharisees' Practice (vv. 3, 4)

3, 4. **For the Pharisees, and all the Jews, except they wash their hands oft, eat not, holding the tradition of the elders. And when they come from the market, except they wash, they eat not. And many other things there be, which they have received to hold, as the washing of cups, and pots, brazen vessels, and of tables.**

It is likely that Mark was writing for a Roman (non-Jewish) audience. For this reason, he believed it was necessary to explain why eating with unwashed hands was such a critical issue. The party of the *Pharisees* arose during the period between the Old and New Testaments. During those troubled times, the Jews were under great pressure to compromise their religious convictions. The Pharisees emerged as a group committed to protecting what they considered to be Jewish orthodoxy. Although they were probably always a minority party, they wielded considerable political influence. *All the Jews* is not to be understood in the absolute sense that every Jew observed the teachings of the Pharisees, but as saying that a great many of them did.

The phrase *except they wash their hands oft* literally reads, "unless they wash their hands with the fist." Apparently this referred to washing the hands in an especially careful manner. *Today's English Version* renders the phrase, "unless they wash their hands in the proper way." The fact that this involved *holding the tradition of the elders* holds the key to understanding much of the conflict that occurred between Jesus and the Pharisees. The Pharisees recognized the authority of the Law of Moses. However, its regulations were often rather general; and so the scribes, who were students of the Law, had provided detailed explanations and applications of them. These explanations were not actually a part of the Law, but in the minds of many religious leaders they had come to have an authority equal to the Law. The Pharisees were the champions of these traditions, and when Jesus challenged their rules, He drew their wrath.

Anything the Pharisees would purchase in the *market* was considered ceremonially unclean, because it may have been touched by a Gentile or an unclean person. As with the washing of hands, the washing of food was for ceremonial, not hygienic reasons. A great number of regulations also governed the washing of various *vessels* used in cooking and eating.

C. The Pharisees' Question (v. 5)

5. **Then the Pharisees and scribes asked him, Why walk not thy disciples according to the tradition of the elders, but eat bread with unwashen hands?**

The *Pharisees and scribes* concentrated their attacks on Jesus' *disciples*. While many of the common people tried to observe the strict laws advocated by the Pharisees, their lifestyle often made this impossible or impractical. Those who accompanied Jesus on His travels often had to get by without even the common amenities of life. Frequently they had to camp out without the equipment to carry out the ritual cleansing that the *tradition of the elders* required. The religious leaders certainly knew this. Still, they chose to attack Jesus on this issue, because He had blunted every other weapon they had used against Him. Since the scribes and Pharisees enjoyed the respect of many of the people, they tried to use this leverage to turn the people against Jesus.

II. Jesus' Response
(Mark 7:6-13)

A. The Pharisees' Hypocrisy (vv. 6, 7)

6. He answered and said unto them, Well hath Isaiah prophesied of you hypocrites, as it is written, This people honoureth me with their lips, but their heart is far from me.

Instead of trying to defend the actions of His disciples, Jesus took the offensive against His critics. He knew that any attempt to give a detailed response to their charges would only lead to further wrangling and nit-picking. Instead, he spoke to the very heart of the issue— their hypocrisy. The scribes were regarded as the authorities on the Scriptures, so Jesus turned to the Scriptures to document His charge. His quotation is found in Isaiah 29:13 and offers a perfect definition of what constitutes hypocrisy: the lack of agreement between the claim of the *lips* and the condition of the *heart*.

At the beginning of his ministry, *Isaiah* had been warned that the people would not listen to his message (Isaiah 6:9-12). In the passage that Jesus quoted, Isaiah was seeing the fulfillment of God's warning. Eventually God's judgment fell upon Isaiah's audience. Perhaps Jesus' reference to this passage was a subtle hint that a similar punishment awaited the Jews of His day.

EASY FOR YOU TO SAY!

A good friend died recently; actually, he died a hundred deaths before his heart quit beating. Strokes had left him speechless. Kenny courageously bore the pain and paralysis of his right side, but the loss of speech killed his spirit. He had always been a talker, an eager conversationalist. He knew no strangers, and always had something interesting to say to his friends. Numbness he could endure, but dumbness was hardly bearable.

Vocal communication is a fantastic gift, and, quite literally, an unspeakable loss. The irony is that those of us who retain the capacity of speech take it for granted. The power of speech is so easily abused. Much talk is too glib, too cheap. Sadly, religious people often represent the case in point. Many Pharisees and scribes were chief offenders in this regard, giving only lip service to God. Their professions of faith were insincere, betrayed by their hardened hearts. Their cleverly contrived loopholes regarding the Law demonstrated the superficiality of their commitment.

Christians must beware of such "easy speak." Let our prayers be like those of Frances R. Havergal:

> "Take my voice, and let me sing
> Always, only, for my King; . . .
> Take my lips, and let them be
> Filled with messages for Thee . . ."   —R. W. B.

7. Howbeit in vain do they worship me, teaching for doctrines the commandments of men.

The *doctrines* were the clear teachings of the Scriptures; the *commandments of men* were men's interpretations of or additions to the Scriptures. In the thinking of the Pharisees, these had been given the same authority as the Scriptures. We are frequently tempted to commit this same sin—forcing our own interpretations upon others by insisting that they have the same authority as the Bible. It is obvious that the Pharisees had yielded to this temptation.

B. Loyalty to Tradition (vv. 8, 9)

8. For laying aside the commandment of God, ye hold the tradition of men, as the washing of pots and cups: and many other such like things ye do.

The rabbis had divided the Law of Moses into 613 separate decrees. Of these, 248 were positive commands and 365 were prohibitions. These decrees were interpretations of and additions to the Law. There was nothing wrong with these decrees as such. In fact, many of them were sincere attempts to apply the Law to new and different situations that had arisen in everyday life. We often do the same thing when we try to apply the teachings of Jesus to modern daily living. The problems arose when the scribes and Pharisees made the Law of Moses subordinate to their interpretations. In so doing they were, in effect, playing God.

9. And he said unto them, Full well ye reject the commandment of God, that ye may keep your own tradition.

This verse reaffirms the point made in the previous verse. Since the traditions that the Pharisees defended were the products of fallible human minds, it was dangerous to allow them to overrule the Scriptures. Jesus was not a revolutionary who was bent on destroying the entire Jewish religious system. He actually taught respect for the Law of Moses, which had often been set aside out of deference to the traditions of men. Jesus made it clear that the scribes had gone far beyond a reasonable effort to make the Law more understandable to the people, and had substituted their traditions for the Law.

C. An Example of Hypocrisy
(vv. 10-13)

10-12. For Moses said, Honor thy father and thy mother; and, Whoso curseth father or mother, let him die the death: but ye say, If a man shall say to his father or mother, It is Corban, that is to say, a gift, by whatsoever thou mightest be profited by me; he shall be free. And ye suffer him no more to do aught for his father or his mother.

When Jesus charged the Pharisees with setting aside the Law, He was not using idle words or making reckless statements. Here He proceeded to give a specific example to prove His point. Both Jesus and the Pharisees agreed that the Law required children to honor their parents (Exodus 20:12). Indeed, a severe punishment was to be administered to anyone who spoke harshly against his or her parents (the law Jesus quoted is found in Leviticus 20:9). However, though the Pharisees gave lip service to this command, they cleverly managed to violate its intent.

Honoring one's *father* or *mother* meant much more than just showing respect for them verbally. It included caring for them when they became too old or feeble to care for themselves. However, a person could escape this obligation by use of the term *Corban*. This word comes from a Hebrew word meaning "to draw near," and was used to describe an offering or gift dedicated to God. The money involved in such an offering, however, did not necessarily have to be used for religious or benevolent purposes. An individual could thus declare his wealth or possessions *Corban*, and thereby avoid having to use them to care for his parents. By this disingenuous application of the traditions of men (today we would call this a "loophole"), a person could avoid the responsibilities imposed by the Law, and yet at the same time feel that he had acted "legally." Such practices were the basis of the charge of hypocrisy that Jesus made.

Mark's explanation of *Corban* in this verse provides another indication that he was writing for non-Jewish (likely Roman) readers, who would have been unacquainted with this particular custom.

DESIGNATED OFFERINGS

Sometimes people play games with God's money. Christian stewards should acknowledge that when they determine an amount to drop in the offering plate, they are not deciding how much of their money to give to God, but how much of God's money they will keep for themselves. However, some churchgoers get "creative" in their giving to serve their own selfish interests. If they don't like the preacher, or if they have a conflict with church officers, they may designate their total tithe to missions or to the building fund, often to the detriment of church finances. If they don't approve of a building project, they may funnel all their giving to other funds. If they don't get their way in church elections or in other congregational votes, they may withhold all offerings and disburse the money to non-church charities. They may even quit giving any amount to anyone, claiming that providing for their families comes first, lest they become "worse than an infidel" (1 Timothy 5:8).

Ironically, this last maneuver is just the reverse of the hypocritical contrivance of some of the Pharisees, who dodged their responsibilities for their families by claiming that all available funds were earmarked for God. People still rob God by manipulating Scripture to justify their stinginess, or by designating offerings vindictively. "My brethren, these things ought not so to be" (James 3:10).   —R. W. B.

13. Making the word of God of none effect through your tradition, which ye have delivered: and many such like things do ye.

The scribes and Pharisees were guilty of two wrongs. First of all, by the clever ruse described in verse 11, people were able to cheat their parents out of the support that they rightly deserved under the Law. But worse, the scribes and Pharisees were setting aside the *word of God* in the process. When we ignore the plain teachings of God's Word for the sake of pleasing ourselves, we establish a practice that has far-reaching consequences. If I have the right to set aside the

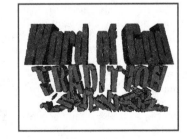

visual for
lesson 10

teachings of God that I don't like and you have the same right, then before long the Word of God is sapped of any real authority. Instead, every person becomes an authority unto himself.

In this exchange with the Pharisees, Jesus used one specific illustration to prove His point. He certainly could have cited other examples had the situation called for it, for the Pharisees did *many such like things* (this was also noted by Jesus in verse 8). One, however, was embarrassing enough for the Pharisees, and proved that Jesus' charge of hypocrisy was accurate.

Conclusion

A. Neither Libertine nor Legalist

Jesus never promised that it would be easy to live the Christian life. For the nearly two thousand years of the church's existence, Christians have had to steer a difficult course between two extremes. On the one hand are the libertines, who refuse to accept any kind of restraints on their behavior. This was a problem even in the first century. The good news of the gospel is that man is saved by grace, not by works. Some misunderstood this doctrine, choosing to sin abundantly that grace might abound. "God forbid," asserted Paul in rejecting this kind of reasoning (Romans 6:1-4). Had not Paul faced this heresy "head-on," the church would have degenerated into a moral and theological free market where anything was permissible.

The other extreme was represented by the Judaizers, who insisted that Gentiles had to become obedient to the Mosaic Law before they could become Christians. The leaders in the early church laid this theology to rest in the Jerusalem conference (Acts 15:1-35). Had they not taken decisive action, Christianity may very well have remained nothing more than another Jewish sect.

Throughout the history of the church, Christians have had to struggle to find a way to avoid either extreme—being a libertine or a legalist. One approach to this problem has been to write creeds, catechisms, or manuals of discipline. While these have often been helpful to Christians, they have sometimes hardened into rigid rules that ended up losing touch with the demands of a changing society, and lessening the church's impact on that society.

The only safe approach to this problem is to encourage every Christian to become a careful student of the Scriptures, which are able to make us "wise unto salvation" (2 Timothy 3:15). We must also keep open minds and humble hearts, so that we may accept and apply Biblical truths when we learn them.

B. A "Bread-Side Manner"

A friend once accepted a ministry in a small rural church. One Sunday morning, when it came time for Communion, there was only one other man present to serve at the table. Not knowing the usual procedure, my friend stepped down and took his place at one side of the table. Later he was informed that he had made a serious mistake. In that congregation, the minister or presiding elder always stood at the end of the table where the tray holding the loaf was placed. My friend later made the wry comment that to serve that congregation, he would have to develop a "bread-side manner."

We may smile at a church that allowed a practice to become frozen into a rigid tradition, the violation of which was considered a serious offense. Yet many congregations have traditions that are just as firmly fixed, and one dares challenge them only at great risk. When a change in some church practice is suggested and it is opposed by the words, "We've always done it this way," we can be sure that we have uncovered a cherished tradition. In a world that is rapidly changing, we need to pray for the courage to affirm what the Bible teaches, the humility to change what needs changing, and the wisdom to tell the difference between the two.

C. Prayer

Help us, Father, to come to a fuller knowledge of Your Word. May we avoid the trap of allowing our traditions to take precedence over Your Word. We pray in Jesus' name. Amen.

D. Thought to Remember

May we honor God with our hearts as well as with our lips.

Home Daily Bible Readings

Monday, May 4—Testing Traditions (Mark 7:1-13)

Tuesday, May 5—Soiled by the Human Heart (Mark 7:14-23)

Wednesday, May 6—Preserve the Ancient Landmark (Proverbs 23:6-11)

Thursday, May 7—Old Has Passed Away (2 Corinthians 5:16-21)

Friday, May 8—Put on the New Nature (Ephesians 4:17-24)

Saturday, May 9—Know Christ's Resurrection (Philippians 3:1-11)

Sunday, May 10—Stand Strong in the Spirit (Ephesians 6:10-20)

Learning by Doing

This page contains an alternate lesson plan emphasizing learning activities.
Classes desiring such student involvement will find these suggestions helpful.

Learning Goals

After completing this lesson, students should be able to:

1. Relate the key points of the confrontation between Jesus and the Pharisees in today's text.

2. Recognize the danger of respecting man's traditions more than God's commandments.

3. Pinpoint an area in their lives where obeying God needs to take priority over following tradition.

Into the Lesson

To prompt your students to begin thinking about the theme of today's lesson, ask them to share one family tradition from their childhood that they will always remember. Be sure they explain what it was about this tradition that made it so memorable. Also, ask if they still carry on this tradition. Why or why not?

After the class has had the opportunity to share some positive experiences with traditions, ask them to think of a tradition that once had a great deal of meaning but has now become routine (or perhaps even harmful). If they have more difficulty with this question, ask them to think about traditions in areas of their lives outside their immediate families, such as the workplace, the school, or the church. Be sure to explore with each of them any reasons they can think of as to why a particular tradition has lost its meaning.

Make your transition into today's lesson by pointing out that Jesus often encountered people who were caught up in observing religious traditions with little concern for their meaning. Such a confrontation is the subject of today's study from the Gospel of Mark.

Into the Word

Prepare a brief lecture (five to ten minutes) outlining the background of the encounter between Jesus and the Pharisees. Focus on the following points.

Set the scene: This confrontation occurred at the peak of Jesus' popularity, shortly after He fed the five thousand and walked on the water to the disciples. Note the threat that Jesus posed to the religious establishment, and the desire of the scribes and Pharisees to embarrass Jesus publicly. Explain that many of the rules and regulations that the scribes and Pharisees had created

to apply the Law had become more important than the Law itself. Tie this idea to the charge that the disciples had not ceremonially washed their hands, and therefore were "unclean."

Next, divide your class into three groups. Give each group five minutes for the following Bible study activities.

Ask the first group to determine the main point Jesus makes in this text and to state it in a single sentence. (For example: "The scribes and Pharisees were focused on outward cleanliness and not inward purity.")

Ask the second group to make a list of characteristics that describe a hypocrite. Possible responses could include: paying more attention to our reputation than to our character; emphasizing our virtues while magnifying others' sins; constant nit-picking and faultfinding.

Ask the third group to list some external standards that we use to judge others. Examples could include: frequency of church attendance, appearance, and forms of worship.

Into Life

While the class is working on these projects, write on the chalkboard or on poster board the following phrases:

• When the Bible speaks, we speak.
• When the Bible is silent, we are silent.

After the aforementioned groups have completed their assignments and reported on them, direct students' attention to these two sentences. Ask them which of the two principles is more difficult to follow. Since there is no right or wrong answer, you may get quite a variety of opinions. Regardless of the position students take, ask them to give the reasons they have chosen one principle to be more difficult than the other.

Lead a directed prayer time to close the class session. Pray: (1) that each member would learn from Jesus' example to be more understanding of those Christians whose traditions or practices in worship are different from ours; (2) that each one would be more focused on inward purity and less on outward appearance; (3) that the Holy Spirit would convict each student of his hypocrisy and bring repentance; and (4) that each student would endeavor to speak only where the Bible speaks, and be silent where there is no clear Biblical instruction.

Let's Talk It Over

The questions on this page are designed to encourage review of the lesson Scriptures and to promote discussion of the lesson by the class. The answers provided are only discussion starters. Let your class talk it over from there.

1. When we realize that the Pharisees were trying to protect God's Law, we can feel a bit of sympathy toward them. How can we combine sympathy with firmness in dealing with believers who exhibit pharisaical attitudes in the church today?

What the Pharisees in Jesus' time failed to see was that they were guilty of protecting their traditions more than the Law. In the church today, we sometimes encounter believers who are victims of the same kind of confusion. They defend a certain practice or procedure in the church as though it were a Biblical principle. We can appreciate their steadfastness and their fervor, even as we lament over the way their rigidity has hindered the church's growth. We must point out to them prayerfully and patiently that their position is not based on Scripture. But we must also be firm with them if they persist in promoting a viewpoint that is divisive.

2. Jesus bluntly charged the Pharisees with being hypocrites. Why must we be careful in applying that term to others?

Jesus could read human hearts—something we are not able to do. Jesus had perfect spiritual discernment—something we do not have. Jesus could call a person a hypocrite out of a loving desire for that person's spiritual awakening. When we call someone else a hypocrite, we are more likely to be venting our displeasure. Of course, there are times when we witness unmistakable hypocrisy and must speak up about it. It is not wise to let such obviously hypocritical behavior go unchecked. Paul's counsel in Galatians 6:1 is applicable: "Brethren, if a man be overtaken in a fault, ye which are spiritual, restore such a one in the spirit of meekness; considering thyself, lest thou also be tempted."

3. Jesus pointed out how the scribes and Pharisees were using tradition to avoid caring for their parents. What are methods people use in our time to avoid taking responsibility for aged parents' care?

Too many people live by the mottoes, "Let the government do it!" or "Let the nursing homes do it!" or "Let some other family members do it!" Possibly some individuals may believe that they are honoring their parents by placing them in a

nursing home and then virtually forgetting about them. Even among Christians, we occasionally hear of family squabbles over who will "get stuck with" Mom and/or Dad. It is clear that honoring aged parents must involve visiting them, encouraging them, sympathizing with their woes, and generally exhibiting love and gratitude toward them. Social Security, Medicare, pensions, retirement accounts, and nursing homes serve an important role; but they must never take the place of our exercising personal care.

4. The Christian life, lived according to Jesus' standards, is often difficult. On the other hand, the libertine and the legalist are looking for an easy life. How is this so?

The libertine assumes that he is free to do what he pleases. He sees no need for restraints. Of course, this does not really lead to an easy life. When one indulges every appetite and obeys every whim, he opens himself to many problems and griefs. The legalist tries to make his life easier by centering it around a personally selected set of rules. As long as he adheres to these rules, he need not be troubled about true holiness and the requirements of Christlike love. But life is not easy for him either, because his legalism can bring him into conflict with those who fall short of his standards.

5. The key to avoiding the pitfalls of the libertine or legalistic viewpoints is to be a careful student of the Scriptures. How is this true?

Perhaps we should emphasize the importance of being a student of *all* the Scriptures. The libertine who has a familiarity with the Bible tends to focus on those passages that speak of God's grace and mercy and our human freedom. To be a student of all the Scriptures, he must give equal attention to passages dealing with obedience, holiness, and service to others. In the case of the legalist, he centers all his attention on the Scriptures that fit his preconceived standards. To be a student of all the Scriptures, he must consider everything God has to say about faith, discipleship, holiness, and service. Every Christian must beware of focusing his or her Bible study too exclusively on certain books, doctrines, commands, promises, or other topics.

Marriage and Divorce

DEVOTIONAL READING: **Genesis 2:18-24.**

LESSON SCRIPTURE: **Mark 10:1-12.**

PRINTED TEXT: **Mark 10:1-12.**

Mark 10:1-12

1 And he arose from thence, and cometh into the coasts of Judea by the farther side of Jordan: and the people resort unto him again; and, as he was wont, he taught them again.

2 And the Pharisees came to him, and asked him, Is it lawful for a man to put away his wife? tempting him.

3 And he answered and said unto them, What did Moses command you?

4 And they said, Moses suffered to write a bill of divorcement, and to put her away.

5 And Jesus answered and said unto them, For the hardness of your heart he wrote you this precept.

6 But from the beginning of the creation God made them male and female.

7 For this cause shall a man leave his father and mother, and cleave to his wife;

8 And they twain shall be one flesh: so then they are no more twain, but one flesh.

9 What therefore God hath joined together, let not man put asunder.

10 And in the house his disciples asked him again of the same matter.

11 And he saith unto them, Whosoever shall put away his wife, and marry another, committeth adultery against her.

12 And if a woman shall put away her husband, and be married to another, she committeth adultery.

May 17

GOLDEN TEXT: What therefore God hath joined together, let not man put asunder.—Mark 10:9.

The Gospel of Action (Mark)
Unit 3: The Teachings of Jesus
(Lessons 9-13)

Lesson Aims

After completing this lesson, students should:

1. Summarize the teaching of Jesus concerning marriage and divorce found in our text.

2. Recognize that Jesus' teachings remain authoritative, regardless of society's attitudes toward marriage and divorce.

3. Determine that Jesus' standards will provide the basis of their personal conduct at home.

Lesson Outline

INTRODUCTION
  A. Divorce or Murder?
  B. Lesson Background
 I. THE PHARISEES TEST JESUS (Mark 10:1, 2)
  A. The Setting (v. 1)
  B. The Question (v. 2)
 II. THE REASON FOR DIVORCE (Mark 10:3-5)
  A. Jesus' Question (v. 3)
  B. The Pharisees' Reply (v. 4)
  C. Jesus' Response (v. 5)
 III. THE SANCTITY OF MARRIAGE (Mark 10:6-9)
  A. Created Male and Female (v. 6)
  B. Leaving and Cleaving (v. 7)
    Reluctant to Leave
  C. Becoming One Flesh (v. 8)
  D. God's Seal on Marriage (v. 9)
    Mock Marriages
 IV. THE CONCERN OF THE DISCIPLES (Mark 10:10-12)
  A. Their Question (v. 10)
  B. Jesus' Additional Teaching (vv. 11, 12)
CONCLUSION
  A. Dealing With Divorce
  B. The Need for Wisdom
  C. Prayer
  D. Thought to Remember

The visual for Lesson 11 highlights today's Golden Text. It is shown on page 318.

Introduction

A. Divorce or Murder?

A wife was complaining about her husband to a friend. "If things are as bad as you say, why don't you divorce him?" the friend asked.

"Oh, no," came the first woman's reply. "My church doesn't approve of divorce."

"So what can you do about your unhappy marriage?"

"Well, I would never consider divorce, but I have to admit that on several occasions I have considered murder!"

This conversation (we hope it was in jest) highlights the confusion in our society concerning the subject of marriage, and how to deal with problems when they arise.

A man and a woman once came to a minister for premarital counseling. After he had explained the Biblical teaching about marriage and divorce, the couple began to object to the high standards he held before them. "If that's what the Bible teaches, then there's no hope for any couple. People would have to be perfect to succeed in marriage."

"No, not perfect," replied the minister, "but they must be very forgiving. You came saying that marriage ought to be a fifty-fifty agreement. But that will never work. Marriage, if it is to succeed, and become all God intended it to be, has to be a 'hundred-hundred' agreement. Each of you must be willing to give yourself completely on behalf of the other."

B. Lesson Background

The incident recorded in today's lesson occurred during the last four months of Christ's ministry. The area where it took place, "the farther side of Jordan" (that is, east of the Jordan River), was called Perea. When Jesus had completed His ministry in Perea, He then crossed the Jordan near Jericho, and headed toward Jerusalem, where the cross awaited.

We have noted that earlier in Galilee, the Pharisees had begun their attempts to challenge Jesus' claims and teachings (Mark 3:22; 7:1, 2; 8:11). Their attacks did not cease just because He moved His ministry east of the Jordan. In fact, Jesus' critics intensified their efforts to discredit Him before the people.

I. The Pharisees Test Jesus (Mark 10:1, 2)

A. The Setting (v. 1)

1. And he arose from thence, and cometh into the coasts of Judea by the farther side of Jordan: and the people resort unto him again; and, as he was wont, he taught them again.

The Gospel of Mark passes over several months of Jesus' ministry in Judea and Jerusalem. This period receives fuller treatment in the Gospels of Luke (9:51—13:21) and John (7:10—10:39). After this, Jesus apparently returned to Galilee, then proceeded toward Jerusalem. However, instead of going directly to

Jerusalem, He crossed to *the farther side of Jordan* (the east side) into Perea. Even here the crowds followed Him, and, *as he was wont,* or accustomed, He used this opportunity to teach them.

B. The Question (v. 2)

2. And the Pharisees came to him, and asked him, Is it lawful for a man to put away his wife? tempting him.

In last week's lesson, we learned that the religious leaders in Jerusalem had become concerned about Jesus' growing popularity, and had sent scribes and Pharisees from Jerusalem to investigate Him (Mark 7:1, 2). It is quite possible that this was another group sent from Jerusalem to try to hinder Jesus' ministry. Mark makes it clear that in asking this question, they were not seeking truth, but were *tempting,* or testing, *him* by raising a particularly sensitive issue.

The answer to the Pharisees' question had numerous implications. One was that it dealt with a practical matter that touched the lives of all married people. If Jesus' reply made divorce difficult or impossible to obtain, He would certainly offend many of the people. On the other hand, if His answer made divorce easy, He would offend those who held marriage in high esteem as part of God's plan.

Furthermore, whatever answer Jesus gave would thrust Him into the midst of an ongoing argument between two opposing schools among the religious leaders. The controversy hinged on the interpretation of Deuteronomy 24:1, which states that if a wife found "no favor" in her husband's eyes or if he "found some uncleanness in her," he was permitted to divorce her. The stricter school, that of a rabbi named Shammai, insisted that this referred only to unchastity, or the committing of adultery. The followers of Rabbi Hillel, on the other hand, interpreted these expressions much more broadly. If the wife burned the bread while preparing it, or if she spoke to a strange man in public, or even if she spoke so loudly that she could be heard in the next house, the husband was considered justified in divorcing his wife.

How to Say It

ANTIPAS. *An*-tih-pus.
HERODIAS. Heh-*roe*-dee-us.
HILLEL. *Hill*-el.
PEREA. Puh-*ree*-uh.
PHARISEES. *Fair*-ih-seez.
SHAMMAI. *Sham*-eye.

There may have been another issue involved. King Herod Antipas had married Herodias, the wife of his half-brother, Philip. John the Baptist had boldly confronted Herod: "It is not lawful for thee to have thy brother's wife" (Mark 6:18). John's words had so infuriated Herodias that she conspired to have him executed. If Jesus took a strict view that limited divorce, then Herodias might be offended and seek His execution as well. Perhaps this possibility lurked in the back of the minds of Jesus' critics.

II. The Reason for Divorce (Mark 10:3-5)

A. Jesus' Question (v. 3)

3. And he answered and said unto them, What did Moses command you?

As He often did, Jesus answered a question with a question of His own. He did not use this ploy as a clever debating tactic. In asking the Pharisees this question, He was able to bring the issue directly to the forefront.

B. The Pharisees' Reply (v. 4)

4. And they said, Moses suffered to write a bill of divorcement, and to put her away.

The Pharisees answered correctly, basing their reply on Deuteronomy 24:1-4. The Law of *Moses* specified that a man must go through a formal process of giving his wife a *bill of divorcement* before the divorce would be recognized. A woman who had been divorced was permitted to marry another man. But if her second husband divorced her or died, she was not permitted to remarry her first husband. The very fact that a kind of "due process" was required prevented the casual dismissal of wives by their husbands.

It should be noted that the Mosaic regulation did not give wives the same right to divorce their husbands. Still, this law represented an effort to provide the new nation of God's people with guidance in a crucial area. As slaves in Egypt, perhaps they had lost all awareness of God's will for marriage.

C. Jesus' Response (v. 5)

5. And Jesus answered and said unto them, For the hardness of your heart he wrote you this precept.

Jesus did not reject the *precept* of Moses, but He did point out that it represented a concession that Moses had made for a particular situation. The fact that a man had to follow "due process" forced him to think seriously about his action, and not behave on mere whim. This certainly must have reduced the number of divorces. Had not Moses made this concession *for the hardness of* the people's *heart*, a man may have resorted to more violent means, even murder, to rid himself of an unwanted wife.

III. The Sanctity of Marriage (Mark 10:6-9)

A. Created Male and Female (v. 6)

6. But from the beginning of the creation God made them male and female.

The Pharisees, lovers of the Law, rested their case on the Mosaic code. But Jesus transcended the Law and went even farther back in time, basing His position on *creation*. The record in Genesis declares that God designed the man and the woman to be together, not separated. It was "not good that the man should be alone" (Genesis 2:18). Adam and Eve were created for each other. Marriage is not something designed by man, and therefore subject to whatever changes he deems necessary. Its origin is divine; and only when we follow the Creator's instructions does marriage become all it was meant to be.

B. Leaving and Cleaving (v. 7)

7. For this cause shall a man leave his father and mother, and cleave to his wife.

Family ties were (and still are) very strong in Jewish society. The loyalty to one's blood relatives normally took precedence over any other human relationship, except marriage. This did not mean that a married couple could ignore the responsibilities they had to their families, but it did mean that their primary loyalty belonged to one another.

RELUCTANT TO LEAVE

Funny incidents can occur at weddings. One ceremony I performed nearly bogged down when the couple lit the unity candle. Each took a taper representing their single lives, and together touched the separate flames to the wick of a large candle representing their married life. So far, so good. When they returned the tapers to their respective holders, however, the groom forgot to extinguish his. When the bride whispered, "Blow out the candle," he misunderstood and nervously blew out the flame of the unity candle. Back to square one! Finally, I personally stepped closer, relighted the large candle, and pinched out the flame of his taper. It seemed as though we were acting in a situation comedy, but most of the audience were oblivious to our dilemma.

Actually, this mistake turned out to be symbolic of a problem that threatened this couple's relationship for several years. The husband was reluctant to "leave and cleave." His parents lived

nearby; he spent inordinate blocks of time with them, and talked to them at length on the phone. He expected most of his and his wife's leisure time and any time off for holidays to be spent with his family.

Only by the grace of God and a considerable amount of time spent in counseling did that couple survive their first few years together. How wise are God's words: "For this cause shall a man leave his father and mother, and cleave to his wife." —R. W. B.

C. Becoming One Flesh (v. 8)

8. And they twain shall be one flesh: so then they are no more twain, but one flesh.

In the eyes of God, marriage is much more than two persons leaving their families and going their own separate ways together. They are *no more twain*, or two, said Jesus; they *shall be one flesh*. Within the marriage bond, a man and a woman unite to create a new life. But the oneness of marriage is much more than a physical joining of two bodies for the purpose of procreation. The divine ideal is that two personalities—two souls—will grow together so that each is enhanced and will become more mature.

D. God's Seal on Marriage (v. 9)

9. What therefore God hath joined together, let not man put asunder.

Even though Moses had permitted divorce because of the "hardness" of the people's hearts, divorce was not God's design in creation. God intended that a man and woman be *joined together* in the bond of marriage for life. He certainly knew that such a high standard would be difficult to maintain. However, we should not immediately reject a standard just because it is difficult. After all, we are challenged to be holy as God is holy (1 Peter 1:15, 16). We should not be satisfied with lesser goals simply because they are easily attainable.

MOCK MARRIAGES

Nowadays, the first question many ministers ask couples who approach them about conducting a wedding ceremony is, "Are you presently living together?" This sad commentary on our times reflects the prevailing complacent attitude toward adultery, and a total disrespect for the sanctity of holy matrimony.

Some ministers refuse to perform weddings for couples who are cohabiting. They contend that a church wedding under those circumstances trivializes the institution and makes a mockery of sacred vows and traditions.

God's intention for marriage from the beginning was that a man and a woman should become one, committing themselves to a lifelong relationship of unity and faithfulness. Not incidentally, statistics reveal that couples who live together before marriage are twice as likely to divorce. Thus their sins are compounded, and Biblical values are eroded to new extremes.

What would Jesus say about marriage and divorce in the nineties? "What therefore God hath joined together, let not man put asunder" (Mark 10:9). He has not changed, and His truth has not changed.   —R. W. B.

IV. The Concern of the Disciples (Mark 10:10-12)

A. Their Question (v. 10)

10. And in the house his disciples asked him again of the same matter.

Apparently Jesus had spoken with such authority that the Pharisees dared not question Him further. The *disciples* were quite perplexed by their Master's words; and when they had an opportunity to speak to Jesus in private, they voiced their concerns.

B. Jesus' Additional Teaching (vv. 11, 12)

11, 12. And he saith unto them, Whosoever shall put away his wife, and marry another, committeth adultery against her. And if a woman shall put away her husband, and be married to another, she committeth adultery.

The disciples had not misunderstood Jesus; He had set up strict standards for marriage, and was now reaffirming those standards in His reply. In fact, to show how serious God considered divorce and remarriage, Jesus labeled such action *adultery*—an offense that was punishable by death under the Mosaic Law.

Home Daily Bible Readings

Monday, May 11—Facing the Fact of Divorce (Mark 10:1-12)

Tuesday, May 12—Two Become One (Genesis 2:18-24)

Wednesday, May 13—Hold Marriage in Honor (Hebrews 13:1-6)

Thursday, May 14—Love As Christ Loves You (Ephesians 5:21-33)

Friday, May 15—Our Bodies Are Members of Christ (1 Corinthians 6:9-20)

Saturday, May 16—Facing Distress in Marriage (1 Corinthians 7:25-28)

Sunday, May 17—God Has Called You to Peace (1 Corinthians 7:10-16)

Jesus also considered the possibility that *a woman* might *put away her husband.* In the society of Jesus' day, women had very few rights. Thus Jesus was probably stating a principle rather than reflecting a common practice of the time. However, the case of Herodias, who left her husband to marry Herod Antipas, has already been noted. Like His forerunner John the Baptist, Jesus did not hesitate to call sin exactly what it was.

We should note Matthew's account of this conversation, which records an exception for which Jesus permits divorce: fornication (Matthew 19:9; see also 5:32). This does not mean that divorce is mandatory following such an act—only that it is allowed. The process of divorce has been likened to an amputation. The amputation of a limb is tragic, but it may be necessary, under some circumstances, to avoid a greater evil—the death of the patient. Still, the amputation is tragic. In the same way, a divorce may be permitted to avoid a worse evil, but it is still an evil.

Let us also keep in mind that divorce is as forgivable as any other sin. We need to treat those who have committed this sin in the same way we should treat other sinners: with compassion and with the desire to show them the path to new life in Jesus.

Conclusion

A. Dealing With Divorce

Marriage and the home are the foundation stones of any stable society. Christians have been appalled at the rapid erosion of these foundations in contemporary society. No one can seriously deny the terrible price we are paying for the sexual promiscuity that has swept across our land like a tidal wave. All of us have been affected by the broken homes, bitterness, crime, and poverty that have resulted.

How can we as Christians bring sanity and hope to this situation? We can, on the one hand, take a rigid, legalistic stance concerning divorce and marriage. Several years ago, a Christian friend was elected a county judge. Among the various types of cases that came before him were cases involving divorce. The minister of the church where he served was quite upset about this, and led the congregation to ask my friend to resign as an elder. When I talked to my friend later, he acknowledged that as a judge he was required by the law to dissolve some marriages when the proper legal requirements had been met. But what his critics did not know was how many marriages he was able to save by giving wise Christian counseling to couples who were considering divorce. Persons taking a hard, legalistic stance would never have been able to save these marriages.

The other extreme is to simply "go with the flow," that is, to accept the standards that the world is setting. What only a generation or two earlier was known as the "Hollywood lifestyle" has now become the norm for all of society. Unfortunately, many religious groups have taken the easy way out and have lost their opportunity to bring a strong Christian witness to a world that so desperately needs it.

If the teachings of Jesus are to make an impact on our world, we must begin in our homes and in our congregations to teach the sanctity of marriage and the home. But teaching alone is not enough. We must give our young people living models of what a Christian home should be like. We must let them see the blessings that flow from a home where Christ is made central and His teachings followed.

At the same time, we must frankly acknowledge that in spite of our best efforts to teach and model, we may not succeed in making every marriage a stable one. We need to realize that even in a healthy marriage, conflicts will arise occasionally. The church should make every effort to provide help in salvaging troubled marriages. In many congregations the minister is capable of providing counseling if needed. We should make certain, however, that professional counseling is available, and that it is presented from a Christian perspective.

Even as we take a strong stand against divorce and remarriage, we must not in the process reject those who have experienced a divorce. These casualties of our modern society need our loving support, not our cold shoulder, as they struggle to put their lives back together. We must be especially sensitive to the children who are the victims of divorce. Some seem to survive amazingly well, but may carry many concealed bruises. Others are severely scarred and never recover. Christians must be prepared to meet the needs of these people.

B. The Need for Wisdom

"I wish I had the wisdom of Solomon," a Christian counselor once remarked to me. He went on to explain the frustrations he had experienced as he tried to salvage marriages that were on the brink of collapse. "I always feel a painful sense of defeat when a couple I have been counseling decides to go ahead and get a divorce, in spite of everything I have done. I take very seriously what Jesus said in Mark 10.

"As a Christian, I grew up believing that when adultery occurred in a marriage, the innocent party was permitted to get a divorce and to remarry. That seemed as simple and clear-cut as could be. But real life is never that simple. Ordinarily, when a couple comes to me for counseling, I arrange to speak to the man and the woman individually. From the two accounts I hear, I could easily be convinced that they weren't talking about the same marriage. I don't talk much anymore about the 'innocent' person and the 'guilty' person. In my experience, both persons share a great deal of the guilt. An important step in bringing about a reconciliation is getting each person to acknowledge his or her guilt."

He further revealed to me that most of the persons he counsels professionally come from Christian backgrounds, which at least gives him a place to start. A surprisingly large number of them come from among those who are leaders in the church—ministers, elders, deacons, and teachers. In a way, this should not surprise us completely. Satan aims his deadliest weapons at Christian leaders, because they are giving his evil kingdom the most trouble. He need not worry about those already under his control.

We need, not just the wisdom of Solomon, but of the One greater than Solomon.

C. Prayer

Dear Father, we come to You deeply concerned about the desperate condition of homes in our land. We pray that You will guide us as we strive to build solid Christian homes where Your name is honored and Your commandments are obeyed. May we hold high the standard You have set for marriage, and at the same time extend loving arms to those who need assistance and encouragement. In Jesus' name we pray. Amen.

D. Thought to Remember

"The sanctity of marriage and the family relation make the cornerstone of our American society and civilization."   —James A. Garfield

visual for
lesson 11

Learning by Doing

This page contains an alternate lesson plan emphasizing learning activities.
Classes desiring such student involvement will find these suggestions helpful.

Learning Goals

As a result of this lesson, students should be able to:

1. Summarize the teaching of Jesus concerning marriage and divorce found in our text.

2. Recognize that Jesus' teachings remain authoritative, regardless of society's attitudes toward marriage and divorce.

3. Determine that Jesus' standards will provide the basis of their personal conduct at home.

Into the Lesson

Use a "neighbor nudge" activity to begin the session today. To do this, ask each student to turn to the person on his or her right and ask the individual, "Who had or has the best marriage you have ever seen?" Allow four to five minutes for them to share examples, and then have them discuss what made (or makes) that marriage so special. When the pairs have finished this activity, ask each pair to share its conclusions with the rest of the class while you record the observations on the chalkboard.

Make the transition into today's Bible study by pointing out that Jesus held marriage in high esteem. This is particularly clear in our lesson text, which records how the Pharisees challenged Jesus on the sensitive issue of divorce.

Into the Word

Set the scene for your class by pointing out that the crowds had followed Jesus over to the east side of the Jordan River, in the area known as Perea. Jesus used this as an opportunity to teach the people. While He was doing so, the Pharisees came to Him with a question about divorce.

At this point, read today's text from Mark 10:1-12 with your class. Then divide the class into three groups, and ask them to work on the following questions:

Group One: Ask this group to read together the account in Mark 6:14-29 of the beheading of John the Baptist. Give them a slip of paper with the following questions to consider: (1) How would Herod and Herodias have responded to Jesus' teaching on divorce? (2) What do you think the Pharisees were trying to accomplish by challenging Jesus on the subject of divorce? (Students should be able to see the negative consequences that Jesus might have faced, had His

teaching about marriage became known to Herod and Herodias. Perhaps this was the motivation of the Pharisees in drawing out Jesus' views in public.)

Group Two: Ask this group to read Deuteronomy 24:1-4, and give them the following questions to consider: (1) What was the intent of this teaching? (2) Did this text approve of divorce? (3) Whom did this law protect? (Students should note that God allowed divorce as a concession to man's sinfulness, or to the "hardness of your heart," as Jesus put it. Divorce was not approved, but it was instituted to protect the injured party from potentially adverse situations.)

Group Three: Ask this group to read Ephesians 5:21-33 and answer these questions: (1) How does the relationship of Christ and the church explain the role of the wife in marriage? (2) How does it explain the role of the husband? (3) Are there any differences between the two roles here? (4) What would you conclude about divorce from these verses?

Allow several minutes for the groups to work together. Afterward lead each group in a time of discussion so that the entire class can get an overall picture of today's text from three important perspectives: the Pharisees' motivations, the Old Testament background, and Paul's teaching concerning marriage.

Into Life

Ask the class to agree or disagree with the following statement: "According to Jesus, marriage is a contract." Ask those who agree to raise their hands, then have those who disagree do the same. Point out to your class that part of the Pharisees' problem was that they saw divorce as strictly a legal problem to be properly litigated, and not as a spiritual problem to be resolved by submission to God. A contract may be declared void when one party breaks it. Marriage as God intended should be viewed not so much as a contract as an unconditional commitment. Lead your class in some discussion of the different types of marriage that these two points of view produce. Perhaps some can draw upon their own experiences during the discussion.

Close this class session in prayer, asking God to forgive our hardness of heart, and to empower us in letting Jesus be the Lord of our marriages and our homes.

Let's Talk It Over

The questions on this page are designed to encourage review of the lesson Scriptures and to promote discussion of the lesson by the class. The answers provided are only discussion starters. Let your class talk it over from there.

1. Many persons enter the marriage relationship with the viewpoint of "What's in it for me?" How can this viewpoint be changed?

Paul's instructions to husbands and wives in Ephesians 5:22-33 have evoked much controversy. But one principle Paul espouses there should catch the attention of every husband and wife: marriage is a means of serving one another. The wife's submission and the husband's sacrifice should lead to the same question: "What can I do to bring my spouse happiness and fulfillment?" When a man and a woman enter a marital relationship and each is preoccupied with his or her own sexual satisfaction, ego, self-fulfillment, and the like, disillusionment and conflict are certain to result. But if each will accept the challenge of serving one another through love, each will find joy in giving and receiving.

2. "What therefore God hath joined together, let not man put asunder." However, many couples seem to go into marriage with the idea, "If this does not work out, we can always get a divorce and marry someone else." What can we do about this attitude?

It seems strange that in a society in which problem-solving plays such an important role, we are unwilling to commit ourselves to solving marital problems. In business and industry, in education, and elsewhere, people are regularly engaged in solving problems. Why aren't people entering marriage with the viewpoint, "Of course we will have problems, but we are determined that we will find solutions to each one"? In Christian marriages we have the extra "problem-solving power" of God's Spirit, His Word, His church, and prayer to help us.

3. What can we do in the church to train children for the day when they will marry and have a family?

It is worth noting that the Bible provides us with both the "how to" and "how not to" regarding marriage and family life. When we teach Bible lessons to children, we can point out, for example, what was good and bad about Abraham as a husband and father, and about Sarah as a wife and mother. When we study Samuel, we can highlight all that distinguished Hannah as a godly mother. It is also a good idea to have pro-

grams in which families in the church can show what works for them. While children in a Christian home have their own parents as role models, it can be helpful to see how other Christian men and women fulfill their roles as godly husbands and wives and parents.

4. Why is it difficult for some congregations to minister to families torn by divorce?

No doubt the leadership in some congregations is concerned about any action that might suggest that they believe divorce is an acceptable practice. However, divorce is but one of many sinful situations in which church people have been involved. Some have been alcoholics; others have been addicted to the use of foul language; still others have suffered from violent tempers; and the list could go on. It has been suggested that the church is a kind of "Sinners Anonymous," in which people who have fallen prey to various sins can experience forgiveness and receive encouragement. Let us also remember that the children of divorced parents often feel guilt, and also need the church's ministry.

5. How should Jesus' words regarding marriage and divorce be applied to the selection of church leadership, especially in light of Paul's teaching that an elder must be "the husband of one wife" (1 Timothy 3:2)?

Paul's words regarding the qualifications of an elder (or "bishop") reinforce Jesus' teaching that marriage is the union of one man with one woman. Paul also stresses that the elder's leadership in his home should reflect the kind of leadership required in the church (1 Timothy 3:4, 5). Any instances involving divorce should be handled on an individual basis. These points should be considered: Divorce is not unpardonable (Matthew 12:31). Sin, however, may carry conseqences that are not removed even by forgiveness. Was the divorce caused by a reason allowed in Scripture? (See Matthew 19:9; 1 Corinthians 7:15.) Will service by the divorced person promote or damage the reputation of the church? (See 1 Timothy 3:7.) Will service by the divorced person cause offense to believers within the church? (See 1 Corinthians 8:9-13.) These are some of the issues that need to be carefully and prayerfully addressed.

True Greatness

DEVOTIONAL READING: John 13:3-17.

LESSON SCRIPTURE: Mark 9:33-37; 10:35-45.

PRINTED TEXT: Mark 9:33-37; 10:35-45.

Mark 9:33-37

33 And he came to Capernaum: and being in the house he asked them, What was it that ye disputed among yourselves by the way?

34 But they held their peace: for by the way they had disputed among themselves, who should be the greatest.

35 And he sat down, and called the twelve, and saith unto them, If any man desire to be first, the same shall be last of all, and servant of all.

36 And he took a child, and set him in the midst of them: and when he had taken him in his arms, he said unto them,

37 Whosoever shall receive one of such children in my name, receiveth me: and whosoever shall receive me, receiveth not me, but him that sent me.

Mark 10:35-45

35 And James and John, the sons of Zebedee, come unto him, saying, Master, we would that thou shouldest do for us whatsoever we shall desire.

36 And he said unto them, What would ye that I should do for you?

37 They said unto him, Grant unto us that we may sit, one on thy right hand, and the other on thy left hand, in thy glory.

38 But Jesus said unto them, Ye know not what ye ask: can ye drink of the cup that I drink of? and be baptized with the baptism that I am baptized with?

39 And they said unto him, We can. And Jesus said unto them, Ye shall indeed drink of the cup that I drink of; and with the baptism that I am baptized withal shall ye be baptized:

40 But to sit on my right hand and on my left hand is not mine to give; but it shall be given to them for whom it is prepared.

41 And when the ten heard it, they began to be much displeased with James and John.

42 But Jesus called them to him, and saith unto them, Ye know that they which are accounted to rule over the Gentiles exercise lordship over them; and their great ones exercise authority upon them.

43 But so shall it not be among you: but whosoever will be great among you, shall be your minister:

44 And whosoever of you will be the chiefest, shall be servant of all.

45 For even the Son of man came not to be ministered unto, but to minister, and to give his life a ransom for many.

GOLDEN TEXT: The Son of man came not to be ministered unto, but to minister, and to give his life a ransom for many.—Mark 10:45.

The Gospel of Action (Mark)
Unit 3: The Teachings of Jesus
(Lessons 9-13)

Lesson Aims

After completing this lesson, students should:

1. Tell how Jesus illustrated and defined true greatness to His disciples.

2. Explain how Jesus' definition of greatness differs from the world's viewpoint.

3. Take a specific step to become more servant-minded in one area of their Christian lives.

Lesson Outline

INTRODUCTION
    A. Ant Theology
    B. Lesson Background
  I. GOD'S STANDARD OF GREATNESS (Mark 9:33-37)
    A. The Disciples' Dispute (vv. 33, 34)
    B. A Child's Example (vv. 35-37)
      Kids and Pets
  II. JAMES AND JOHN'S REQUEST (Mark 10:35-40)
    A. Desiring the Chief Seats (vv. 35-37)
    B. Jesus' Challenge (vv. 38, 39)
    C. Denying the Request (v. 40)
      Running Mates?
 III. A LESSON FOR THE TWELVE (Mark 10:41-45)
    A. Anger of the Ten (v. 41)
    B. Jesus' Response (vv. 42, 43)
    C. Jesus' Example (vv. 44, 45)
CONCLUSION
    A. The Pyramid Climbers
    B. The Order of the Towel
    C. Prayer
    D. Thought to Remember

The visual for Lesson 12 calls attention to Jesus' life of service. It is shown on page 325.

Introduction

A. Ant Theology

Ants have a way of finding picnics, and a picnic that our family enjoyed some years ago was no exception. However, as irritating as ants may be, we ought to follow Solomon's advice about them: "Go to the ant, thou sluggard; consider her ways, and be wise" (Proverbs 6:6).

So I decided to "consider" the ants during our family picnic. I watched as they soon began to discover the crumbs that had fallen from our table. Ants have great strength for their size, and it was amazing to watch them tug and pull and finally move a crumb two or three times their size.

However, this group of ants soon had a problem. As they carried their crumbs back to their home, they came to a crack in the pavement that was too large for them to cross with their crumbs. Soon there was a traffic jam at the edge of the crack. Very shortly they solved the problem. Two or three of the ants lay down in the crack and formed a bridge for the others.

Oh, that we might learn the lesson of subordinating ourselves for the good of others! This is the path to true greatness, which is the primary emphasis of today's Bible study.

B. Lesson Background

Today's lesson is based on two separate passages from the Gospel of Mark. The first of these incidents, found in Mark 9:33-37, took place in Capernaum near the end of Jesus' final travels through Galilee. Just prior to this a man had brought his son, who was possessed by a demon, to be healed by the disciples; but they had been unable to cast out the demon. Jesus immediately healed the boy, which left the disciples perplexed.

After this, Jesus and the disciples quietly passed through Galilee, headed toward Capernaum. As they traveled, Jesus told the disciples that He would be "delivered into the hands of men" and killed (Mark 9:31). This prediction left them even more perplexed, yet they could not bring themselves to ask Jesus what He meant. Perhaps they "were afraid" (v. 32), because they remembered how Jesus had rebuked Peter when he protested Jesus' earlier prediction of His death (Mark 8:31-33). When the group arrived at Capernaum (Mark 9:33), the incident recorded in our first passage took place.

The second incident occurred later as Jesus prepared to leave Perea, located east of the Jordan River (where last week's lesson took place), and head toward Jerusalem. Along the way, James and John approached Jesus, asking that they be granted the seats on His right and His left when He established His kingdom.

I. God's Standard of Greatness (Mark 9:33-37)

A. The Disciples' Dispute (vv. 33, 34)

33, 34. And he came to Capernaum: and being in the house he asked them, What was it that ye disputed among yourselves by the way? But they held their peace: for by the way they

had disputed among themselves, who should be the greatest.

Jesus had made *Capernaum* the headquarters for His preaching and teaching in Galilee. Located on the northwestern shore of the Sea of Galilee, Capernaum was well-populated and readily accessible to much of the province. Several of the disciples made their homes in the vicinity before they began to follow Jesus.

As the disciples traveled with Jesus, they undoubtedly talked about many subjects, and on occasion may have had disagreements among themselves. From other passages, we get the impression that the question of who was the *greatest* among them came up rather frequently. Apparently they preferred to keep this discussion *among themselves*, not wishing to get Jesus involved in it.

However, in spite of their efforts to keep their dispute private, Jesus knew about it. Nothing could be kept from someone who "knew all men" (John 2:24)—a fact that the disciples should have recognized by this time. They seem to have been embarrassed by Jesus' question, for they *held their peace* when He asked it. They knew He would not approve of the content of their conversation. Like the disciples, we sometimes engage in discussions that would prove embarrassing if they became known.

B. A Child's Example (vv. 35-37)

35. And he sat down, and called the twelve, and saith unto them, If any man desire to be first, the same shall be last of all, and servant of all.

The idea of self-denial was nothing new in Jesus' teaching. Earlier He had issued the challenge that if anyone would follow Him, he must deny himself and take up his cross (Mark 8:34). However, difficult truths such as this are usually not accepted the first time they are spoken; thus Jesus found it necessary to repeat His teaching. The disciples likely had not fully understood what Jesus was talking about when He first raised the issue. This is clear from Peter's reaction when Jesus announced His intention to go to the cross (Mark 8:32).

In effect, Jesus was standing the traditional values system on its head. A *servant*, or slave, did not enjoy a very high status in the first century, yet this was what Jesus called His followers to become.

36, 37. And he took a child, and set him in the midst of them: and when he had taken him in his arms, he said unto them, Whosoever shall receive one of such children in my name, receiveth me; and whosoever shall receive me, receiveth not me, but him that sent me.

How to Say It

AGRIPPA. Uh-*grip*-puh.
CAPERNAUM. Kuh-*per*-nay-um.
DIOTREPHES. Dye-*aht*-ruh-feez.
GETHSEMANE. Geth-*sem*-uh-nee.
PATMOS. *Pat*-mus.
SALOME. Suh-*lo*-me.
ZEBEDEE. *Zeb*-uh-dee.

When Jesus, the Master Teacher, sought to teach a difficult or challenging truth, He often turned to an object lesson—in this case a *child*—to get His point across. Since, as verse 33 notes, He and the disciples were in a house (perhaps they were staying in the home of one of His followers), it should come as no surprise that a child was present.

Jesus proceeded to compare one's treatment of *children* with one's treatment of Him, and ultimately of His Father. This is similar to His identification with the hungry, the thirsty, the naked, and others in need (Matthew 25:35-45). That the disciples missed this lesson is seen in a later incident (Mark 10:13-16), where they "rebuked" those who brought children to Jesus. Jesus was "much displeased with the twelve," perhaps as much by their failure to remember His words as by their rudeness. Adults (in some cases Christian adults) who are impatient and abrupt with children need to remember Jesus' words.

KIDS AND PETS

A lady once said to me, "I don't trust anybody who doesn't love animals and children." I didn't say so, but I could agree with only half of her sentiment. I confess: I'm not an animal lover. A Doberman pinscher traumatized me when I was only three years old. A horse kicked me in the face when I was six. A hostile cat intimidated me when I was twenty. A church member's bird "dive-bombed" me when I was forty. I even encountered a South American monkey (and his stench) in one home I visited. House pets are one of the reasons I don't like to make house calls!

On the other hand, I don't hate children. In fact, most of them I can actually love. I try harder with kids, because Jesus taught us to "receive" ("welcome," in the *New International Version*) children in His name, and enjoyed being in their company.

If Jesus came to town, we would certainly welcome Him with open arms—wouldn't we? If God knocked on our door, we wouldn't hesitate to receive Him—would we? Jesus says that our attitude toward children reflects our acceptance or rejection of Him. That makes our relationship with youngsters extremely important.

So the lady was at least half right: People who don't care about kids may be untrustworthy.

—R. W. B.

II. James and John's Request (Mark 10:35-40)

A. Desiring the Chief Seats (vv. 35-37)

35. And James and John, the sons of Zebedee, come unto him, saying, Master, we would that thou shouldest do for us whatsoever we shall desire.

Matthew 20:20 informs us that the mother of *James and John* came to Jesus with this request. Her name, which we learn from comparing Matthew 27:56 with Mark 15:40, was Salome. Many scholars believe that this woman was a sister of Mary, the mother of Jesus. Some mothers tend to be overly ambitious for their children, and they often impart this same attitude to their children.

Together the mother and the sons played a clever game. They tried to get Jesus to agree to their request before He even knew what they wanted. If He did so, then they could insist that He fulfill it, even if He had some reservations when He learned what it was.

36. And he said unto them, What would ye that I should do for you?

Of course, Jesus did not fall for this scheme. He was able to read their hearts, and knew exactly what James and John had in mind. It is little short of amazing that the two disciples thought they could get away with something like this. They had been with Jesus many months, had seen Him perform numerous miracles, and knew of His power; yet they could not apply this knowledge to their own situation. But are we today much different from them?

37. They said unto him, Grant unto us that we may sit, one on thy right hand, and the other on thy left hand, in thy glory.

This request illustrates that James and John still did not understand the nature of the kingdom Jesus had been talking about, nor did they understand the prophecies of His coming suffering and death that He had just uttered (vv. 32-34). In the ancient world, those who occupied the seats on the *right* and *left* side of a ruler were considered next in authority to the ruler himself. Nepotism (the practice of giving special favors to one's kin) was common in the ancient world, and still occurs in our world today. If James and John could indeed claim a physical

relationship to Jesus (assuming that their mother and Jesus' mother were related), perhaps they felt that this entitled them to the special favors they requested.

B. Jesus' Challenge (vv. 38, 39)

38. But Jesus said unto them, Ye know not what ye ask: can ye drink of the cup that I drink of? and be baptized with the baptism that I am baptized with?

The *cup* and the *baptism* were figurative expressions for the suffering and death that Jesus faced in the near future. In Gethsemane Jesus prayed, "Take away this cup from me" (Mark 14:36), referring to the suffering that lay ahead. On another occasion, He used *baptism* to refer to His suffering (Luke 12:50). Jesus was warning James and John that if they desired positions of prominence in His kingdom, they must be willing to pay the price for them.

39. And they said unto him, We can. And Jesus said unto them, Ye shall indeed drink of the cup that I drink of; and with the baptism that I am baptized withal shall ye be baptized.

Without even asking what the *cup* and the *baptism* might involve, James and John answered Jesus' question with confidence. Their ignorance of what lay ahead left their enthusiasm unrestrained. Later, on the night before Jesus' crucifixion, the other disciples displayed a similar false assurance (Mark 14:26-31).

Jesus went on to assure James and John that they would indeed suffer for the sake of the kingdom. James later died at the hands of King Herod (Agrippa I); he was the first of the apostles to be martyred (Acts 12:1, 2). John suffered imprisonment and beatings (Acts 5:17, 18, 40), and near the end of his life he was banished to the barren island of Patmos (Revelation 1:9).

C. Denying the Request (v. 40)

40. But to sit on my right hand and on my left hand is not mine to give; but it shall be given to them for whom it is prepared.

As the divine Son of God, Jesus had been given great authority; yet there were limits to that authority. It was not Jesus' prerogative to render a decision concerning James and John's request. Jesus' words in Matthew 20:23 indicate that this decision rests with His Father.

Even though Jesus could not grant James and John the positions on His right and His left, He did on other occasions promise that they would "sit upon twelve thrones, judging the twelve tribes of Israel" (Matthew 19:28; see also Luke 22:28-30). James and John had to realize that positions of honor would come, but only if they served Jesus on His terms, not theirs.

RUNNING MATES?

One of the most important decisions a candidate for President of the United States makes is his running mate for Vice President. Media speculation and rumors are rampant as to who the candidate will be. The choice is often critical; a candidate is needed who will give the party a winning ticket.

On the surface, it would appear that presidential candidates choose running mates by themselves. In reality, however, dozens of advisors, campaign managers, and party leaders influence, and often mandate, the choice. If someone were presumptuous enough to ask to be chosen, the politician running for President might say, "That decision is not entirely up to me."

Jesus had been given no authority to make a personal choice of "chiefs of staff" in His kingdom. Besides, the shameless request of James and John was misguided and inappropriate. Christ's kingdom is unlike earthly empires; it is spiritual. The church was divinely designed; it is not to pattern itself after secular models of leadership. Elders, deacons, evangelists, preachers, and teachers—in fact, every Christian—*all* are to be servants.

We each have a ministry as a member of the "priesthood of all believers." We should aspire, not to personal greatness or the acclaim of others, but to God's glory.   —R. W. B.

III. A Lesson for the Twelve (Mark 10:41-45)

A. Anger of the Ten (v. 41)

41. And when the ten heard it, they began to be much displeased with James and John.

By its very nature, the conversation that James, John, and Salome had with Jesus must have been in private. Yet the other *ten* disciples soon learned about it. It is not likely that James and John came back and reported their rejection to the others. Perhaps the ten overheard portions of the conversation. Their resentment of James and John reveals the content of their own hearts. Likely the primary reason for their being *displeased* was that they also desired the chief seats in Jesus' kingdom.

B. Jesus' Response (vv. 42, 43)

42, 43. But Jesus called them to him, and saith unto them, Ye know that they which are accounted to rule over the Gentiles exercise lordship over them; and their great ones exercise authority upon them. But so shall it not be among you: but whosoever will be great among you, shall be your minister.

visual for
lesson 12

The ten could not hide their feelings from Jesus, who used their discontent to teach a very important truth about greatness that all the disciples needed to hear. He called their attention to how the *Gentiles*, or the pagans, understood greatness. The disciples had seen and probably resented those in both the sacred and the secular world who gained power, then used their status to control others beneath them. Jesus must have pricked them in their hearts when He compared their ambitions with the behavior of heathens.

So shall it not be among you. With these few words Jesus introduced a totally different concept of greatness in the kingdom He came to create. In His kingdom, the usual social structure, shaped like a pyramid, was to be turned upside down. The broad base of the pyramid, composed of those who *minister*, or serve others, would now be at the top. To remain in this position, an actual pyramid would have to defy the law of gravity. In the same way, the new understanding of greatness that Jesus outlined defies the usual behavior of people. Such a revolutionary concept made Jesus' teaching quite threatening and thus hard to accept. It is still a difficult perspective for many to grasp.

C. Jesus' Example (vv. 44, 45)

44, 45. And whosoever of you will be the chiefest, shall be servant of all. For even the Son of man came not to be ministered unto, but to minister, and to give his life a ransom for many.

Jesus' words seem to be the ultimate paradox, contradicting everything that we observe about us. Those who succeed in the world often do so by pushing and shoving and trampling on anyone who happens to get in their way as they progress to the top. This happens in politics, business, and, tragically, even the church.

With the words *even the Son of man*, Jesus showed that He was willing to do more than just define true greatness. He Himself was the prime example of what He was talking about. He had left His position at the right hand of God, not to add to His prestige or glory, but *to minister*, or serve, the human race. This was no token service of merely going through the motions just to impress people. Jesus came *to give his life a ransom for many*. There is no greater model of servanthood than this.

Once more, however, the disciples failed to grasp what Jesus meant. Again they apparently missed the ominous reference to His own approaching death. Even at the Last Supper, they were still quarreling about who would be the greatest in Jesus' kingdom (Luke 22:24-27).

Conclusion

A. The Pyramid Climbers

Several years ago, Vance Packard wrote a book entitled *The Pyramid Climbers*. It was a sociological study that included graphic descriptions of the activities and antics of persons who scrambled to reach the apex of the social pyramid. These people were usually motivated by pay and by "perks"—the perquisites that went along with their job. Often these perks (such as a reserved parking space in the company parking lot, or a key to the executive rest room) were deemed more important than the pay. These "status symbols," as they came to be called, conferred prestige on those who could display them. The make and model of the car one drove or the brand of suits one wore also became recognized status symbols.

Those who scrambled for the upper echelons of the social pyramid often became ruthless and scheming in their climb to the top. Whether an action or a decision was right or wrong was given little or no consideration. Other people were trampled underfoot, or used and then tossed aside without remorse. Loyalty to friends or the institution meant nothing if they stood in the way of reaching the pinnacle of success.

The studies in Packard's book were confined to the middle of the twentieth century, but similar patterns of thinking and acting could be found in almost any century. Certainly they were present in the first century. Even among the twelve whom Jesus chose—men who had been willing to leave their businesses and their families to follow Jesus—the desire for a higher position distorted their viewpoint. The early church faced the same problem. The apostle John wrote of a certain Diotrephes, "who loveth to have the preeminence" (3 John 9). Paul warned of the danger of someone thinking of himself "more highly than he ought to think" (Romans 12:3). The New Testament contains these and other warnings, because God knows that we are vulnerable to Satan's temptations in this area.

B. The Order of the Towel

It is not enough for us as Christians just to be humble and unassuming. We must also be willing to serve wherever we are needed. To insure that we understand this, God sent His Son into the world to give us a living and dying example of what He wants us to become. No task was too lowly or obscure for Jesus to perform. In the upper room, on the eve of His arrest, He was willing to gird Himself with a towel and wipe the feet of the disciples. He told them, "I have given you an example, that ye should do as I have done to you" (John 13:15).

To remind its students of this example, a Midwestern seminary that prepares people for the ministry awards each graduating student a towel along with his diploma. These students are thus officially initiated into the "Order of the Towel." It may be a good idea to give a towel to everyone who becomes a Christian, for *every* Christian is called to serve as Jesus did. Herein lies the path to true greatness.

C. Prayer

Father, keep us ever mindful of our Savior, who humbled Himself and became a servant, in order that we may know the blessings of eternal salvation. Keep us humble, but more than that, keep us humble *servants*. Help us to understand that true greatness comes only as we serve You and others. In the name of the Master Servant, we pray. Amen.

D. Thought to Remember

"Many that are first shall be last; and the last first" (Mark 10:31).

Home Daily Bible Readings

Monday, May 18—True Greatness (Mark 9:33-37)

Tuesday, May 19—Greatness Through Service (Mark 10:35-45)

Wednesday, May 20—Righteousness Produces Peace (James 3:13-18)

Thursday, May 21—True Treasure in Clay Jars (2 Corinthians 4:1-15)

Friday, May 22—Serving Christ by Serving Others (Matthew 25:31-40)

Saturday, May 23—The Humble Will Be Exalted (Luke 14:7-14)

Sunday, May 24—Christ Exalted in His Ascension (Ephesians 1:15-23)

Learning by Doing

This page contains an alternate lesson plan emphasizing learning activities. Classes desiring such student involvement will find these suggestions helpful.

Learning Goals

After completing this lesson, students should be able to:

1. Tell how Jesus illustrated and defined true greatness to His disciples.

2. Explain how Jesus' definition of greatness differs from the world's viewpoint.

3. Take a specific step to become more servant-minded in one area of their Christian lives.

Into the Lesson

Before the students arrive, write on the chalkboard or on poster board the following popular phrase: "Nice guys finish last." When you begin the lesson, ask the class to give examples of situations in which this evaluation seems accurate. After allowing four or five students to share their stories, ask the class to describe situations in which "nice guys" seem to finish first.

Into the Word

Lead into the study of today's texts from Mark by asking the class to pay close attention to the ways in which Jesus' idea of greatness seemed to differ from that of the disciples. (We will also want to consider if and how it is different from ours.)

Ask two students to read the two incidents dealing with greatness recorded in today's lesson: the first from Mark 9:33-37 and the second from Mark 10:35-45. Next, lead your class in a discussion of the meaning and application of these two incidents by using the following discussion starters:

• What did James and John really want? (They still believed that Jesus had come to set up an earthly, political kingdom for the Jews. They desired positions of authority in this kingdom, which they believed they would receive when Jesus came into power after overthrowing the Roman oppressors.)

• Was their request appropriate? (No. However, Jesus did not ridicule them for having asked. He simply denied their request and used this opportunity to teach all of the disciples about greatness in His kingdom.)

• Why were the other disciples upset when they discovered what James and John had asked? (They probably harbored similar ambitions, along with similar misunderstandings of what Jesus had come to do. Wrong expectations

have prevented many people from seeing Jesus for who He really is.)

• What expectations do we have of Jesus today that prevent us from seeing Him clearly and understanding how He is working in this world? (Most of us have certain expectations about the way Jesus should work, the kind of people He should use to accomplish His purpose, and the way our lives should be blessed as we serve Him—to name just a few.)

Into Life

Various organizations and institutions in our world measure greatness by personal achievements. Jesus, however, indicated that the path of service is the only way to "get ahead" in His kingdom. Rather than seeking to have all our needs met, we should seek ways to meet the needs of others.

Draw two pyramids, on the chalkboard or on poster board, like those shown below. Ask the class to indicate which pyramid seems to illustrate the world's model of leadership and which illustrates Jesus' model. Point out that the "normal" pyramid, representing one person at the top in authority over everyone else, does not illustrate Jesus' teaching. The inverted pyramid, representing many Christians serving others, more accurately reflects Jesus' standard.

Next, ask the class to compare 1 Peter 5:1-4 with 3 John 9. Point out the difference (both in motivation and outcome) between the leadership style that Peter counsels elders to adopt and the leadership style of Diotrephes.

Then ask the class to move into small groups and consider the following questions in light of today's discussion:

• Do you ever find yourself wanting to sit at the right hand of Jesus? Or wanting to be recognized for all you have given for God?

• Describe a time when you felt good about setting your own desires aside and taking the role of a servant.

• What are you trying to control right now that you need to place in God's hands?

• How can you be a servant for the Lord this week?

Ask the groups to close with prayer.

Let's Talk It Over

The questions on this page are designed to encourage review of the lesson Scriptures and to promote discussion of the lesson by the class. The answers provided are only discussion starters. Let your class talk it over from there.

1. James and John were encouraged in their ambition by their mother, as Matthew observes (Matthew 20:20). Many people today who are excessively ambitious were taught to be so by their parents. How can Christian parents avoid this mistake?

Parents will say, "We don't want our children to have it as rough as we did." And so they nudge, or even push, their children toward goals that involve making a tremendous amount of money or gaining a lofty level of power and prestige. At the same time, they discourage their children from careers that are service-oriented and among the lower paying, less prestigious ones: the ministry, nursing, or teaching school, for examples. Christian parents must guide their children in seeking God's will regarding a career. And they must urge their children to pursue that career in harmony with the Christian principles of honesty, diligence, forbearance, and compassion.

2. Jesus asked James and John, "Can ye?" And they immediately responded, "We can." Do we ever answer unthinkingly, "We can," when presented with a challenge for Christian service? Give some examples.

Perhaps we have sung Earl Marlatt's hymn, based on Matthew's wording of the incident in our text. In that hymn the Lord asks us, "Are ye able?" and the chorus leads us to respond, "Lord, we are able." Do we sing those words without any thought as to what we are really claiming? Various examples may come to mind of people we know who said, "We can," too hastily. Individuals and families leave enthusiastically for the mission field and return discouraged sometime later. A zealous young man commits himself to prepare for the ministry and then is unable to discipline himself enough to complete his studies. The experience of James and John reminds us to "count the cost" before we say, "We can." Even then we should pray, "We can, Lord. We are able, as long as You provide the power and wisdom."

3. Jesus declared that He came, not to be ministered unto, but to minister, or serve. Do we live up to His example in the modern church? If not, how can we?

Many church members have developed an attitude quite the opposite of what Jesus expressed. They come to church to be ministered unto, not to minister. Of course, all of us require a certain amount of spiritual feeding, comfort, and encouragement. But if we are always on the receiving end and not giving in ministry to others, we are likely to become stagnant. Perhaps only a few can major in ministry on Sundays. However, during the week there is plenty for every member to do. Some may minister through persistent prayer on behalf of fellow believers. Others may contact the sick or absentees through letters, telephone calls, or personal visits. Others may labor at keeping the church building and grounds clean and in good repair. In any church there is enough work that no one should be merely "ministered unto."

4. Jesus declared that He came to give His life a ransom for many. Do we imitate His example of sacrifice in the modern church? If not, how can we?

First John 3:16 tells us: "We ought to lay down our lives for the brethren." Can we say that we are laying down our lives for our brethren if we fail to rejoice with them at a wedding in their family, or to mourn with them when they are afflicted by a death in their family? Are we laying down our lives for them when we seem unable to find time to visit them in the hospital? The kind of sacrifice Jesus made, the kind John calls us to make, requires our going beyond what is convenient and easy. We must be prepared to spend some significant time and effort in order to demonstrate love to those in need.

5. The church is always in danger of adopting the world's standards of greatness. What are some ways in which we might do this?

The world often equates greatness with bigness. Nations, cities, businesses, and churches are thought to be great because of their impressive size. To build a church that has a membership in the thousands is a worthy goal. We must always remember, however, that the level of servanthood within any congregation is its true measure of greatness. A growing church must take steps to insure that people are not ignored, or opportunities for service missed.

Help for the Future

DEVOTIONAL READING: Joel 2:28-32.

LESSON SCRIPTURE: Mark 13.

PRINTED TEXT: Mark 13:1-7, 24-27, 31-35.

Mark 13:1-7, 24-27, 31-35

1 And as he went out of the temple, one of his disciples saith unto him, Master, see what manner of stones and what buildings are here!

2 And Jesus answering said unto him, Seest thou these great buildings? there shall not be left one stone upon another, that shall not be thrown down.

3 And as he sat upon the mount of Olives, over against the temple, Peter and James and John and Andrew asked him privately,

4 Tell us, when shall these things be? and what shall be the sign when all these things shall be fulfilled?

5 And Jesus answering them began to say, Take heed lest any man deceive you:

6 For many shall come in my name, saying, I am Christ; and shall deceive many.

7 And when ye shall hear of wars and rumors of wars, be ye not troubled: for such things must needs be; but the end shall not be yet.

. . . .

24 But in those days, after that tribulation, the sun shall be darkened, and the moon shall not give her light,

25 And the stars of heaven shall fall, and the powers that are in heaven shall be shaken.

26 And then shall they see the Son of man coming in the clouds with great power and glory.

27 And then shall he send his angels, and shall gather together his elect from the four winds, from the uttermost part of the earth to the uttermost part of heaven.

. . . .

31 Heaven and earth shall pass away: but my words shall not pass away.

32 But of that day and that hour knoweth no man, no, not the angels which are in heaven, neither the Son, but the Father.

33 Take ye heed, watch and pray: for ye know not when the time is.

34 For the Son of man is as a man taking a far journey, who left his house, and gave authority to his servants, and to every man his work, and commanded the porter to watch.

35 Watch ye therefore: for ye know not when the master of the house cometh, at even, or at midnight, or at the cockcrowing, or in the morning.

GOLDEN TEXT: Heaven and earth shall pass away: but my words shall not pass away.—Mark 13:31.

The Gospel of Action (Mark)
Unit 3: The Teachings of Jesus
(Lessons 9-13)

Lesson Aims

After this lesson, students should be able to:

1. Summarize the questions raised by Jesus' disciples in today's text, and His response to those questions.

2. Recognize those truths that are both known and unknown about the return of Christ.

3. List some specific steps one can take to prepare for the return of Christ, regardless of when it takes place.

Lesson Outline

INTRODUCTION
  A. "I Shall Return"
  B. Lesson Background
I. THE TEMPLE'S DEMISE (Mark 13:1-7)
  A. A Disciple's Observation (v. 1)
  B. Jesus' Surprising Response (v. 2)
    Disposability
  C. "When Shall These Things Be?" (vv. 3, 4)
  D. Jesus' Answer (vv. 5-7)
II. OTHER FUTURE EVENTS (Mark 13:24-27)
  A. Celestial Signs (vv. 24, 25)
  B. Coming of the Son of Man (vv. 26, 27)
III. PREPARING FOR CHRIST'S RETURN (Mark 13:31-35)
  A. Only God Knows the Time (vv. 31, 32)
    "Fulness of the Time"
  B. Watch and Pray (vv. 33-35)
CONCLUSION
  A. Too Busy to Watch
  B. Prayer
  C. Thought to Remember

Use the visual for Lesson 13 in the visuals packet to emphasize today's Golden Text from Mark 13:31. It is shown on page 332.

Introduction

A. "I Shall Return"

After the Japanese attacked Pearl Harbor in December of 1941, they quickly moved into the Philippines. The small band of Filipino and American troops there was no match for the superior Japanese forces. The defenders were quickly overrun, and only a handful were able to take refuge in the heavily fortified island of Corregidor in the mouth of Manila Bay. There they held out for several weeks, but as their supply of food and ammunition dwindled, it became obvious that the island would soon fall. Due to these circumstances, General Douglas MacArthur was ordered to leave his post and go to Australia. As he left his troops, his final, memorable words were, "I shall return."

In Australia the Allied forces gathered their strength and made plans to return. But as month after long month passed, the promise remained unfulfilled, and the burden of the Filipino people became heavier under the Japanese occupation. Gradually, however, signs of hope began to appear. The Allies initiated an offensive that brought them closer, island by island, to the Philippines. Supplies were smuggled in to the Filipino freedom fighters, and messages of support were radioed to them. Finally, in October of 1944, more than two and a half years after he had left Corregidor, General MacArthur stepped ashore on the island of Leyte (*Lay*-tee). His first words were, "I have returned."

In a similar way, Jesus left this world, committing His work to just a handful of ordinary, unlearned men. But He also left His followers with hope. "I shall return," He said. Nearly two thousand years have passed since Jesus made that promise, and still He has not returned. However, each day that passes brings us closer to the fulfillment of His promise. We watch and wait, knowing that someday the trumpet of the Lord will sound, and He will triumphantly proclaim, "I have returned!"

B. Lesson Background

Most likely the events discussed in today's lesson occurred on Tuesday of Passion Week. On the previous Sunday, Jesus had entered Jerusalem in triumph. On Monday He had cleansed the temple of the money changers and merchants, arousing the ire of the scribes and chief priests. When He returned to Jerusalem on Tuesday, His critics were waiting for Him. What followed was one of the busiest days in Jesus' entire ministry.

In a furious assault on Jesus, the religious leaders in Jerusalem did everything they could to discredit Him, and thereby turn popular support away from Him. First, they challenged Jesus' authority to cleanse the temple. He turned away this challenge and then told the parable of the wicked husbandmen, which clearly made the religious leaders its target. Next, there came two difficult questions dealing with controversial issues. The Pharisees and Herodians tried to trap Jesus by asking whether it was right to pay tribute to Caesar. The Sadducees raised a question involving life after death. Jesus addressed both subjects, silencing His critics in the process. Later, one of the scribes, apparently an honest seeker after truth, asked what was the greatest commandment. Jesus answered the scribe by stating both the greatest and the second greatest commandments, and then commended him for his understanding.

At the close of this busy day, Jesus and the disciples left the temple. As they did so, one of the disciples commented about the impressive buildings that made up the temple complex. Jesus responded by predicting that all these structures would be destroyed. This sweeping statement led to further questions from the disciples. Jesus answered with a discourse about the fulfillment of "all these things" (Mark 13:4) and about His return.

I. The Temple's Demise
(Mark 13:1-7)

A. A Disciple's Observation (v. 1)

1. And as he went out of the temple, one of his disciples saith unto him, Master, see what manner of stones and what buildings are here!

The second *temple*, built after the Israelites returned from their captivity in Babylon, was a mere shadow of the temple built by Solomon. But King Herod the Great undertook a massive remodeling of it. This was done primarily in an attempt to win the favor of the Jews, most of whom disapproved of his leadership. His efforts resulted in an impressive and magnificent structure, surrounded by other buildings that were impressive not only for their size but for their splendor. Luke mentions that the temple was adorned with "goodly stones" (21:5). In light of this, such a comment as that made by one of Jesus' *disciples* is not surprising. Matthew tells us that all the disciples wanted to show Jesus the temple buildings (Matthew 24:1); apparently they all held the temple in high esteem.

B. Jesus' Surprising Response (v. 2)

2. And Jesus answering said unto him, Seest thou these great buildings? there shall not be left one stone upon another, that shall not be thrown down.

It is likely that the disciples expected Jesus to share in their admiration of the magnificence of the temple, and so they must have been shocked at His reply. For many months Jesus had been trying to teach the disciples that His kingdom was spiritual, not material. Yet their comments at the end of a day in which Jesus had engaged in a bitter battle with the religious leaders indicated that they still had not grasped the truths He was trying to teach them. The *buildings* of

the temple and the massive walls that surrounded the temple area seemed as solid and permanent as anything could be. Yet someday, said Jesus, they would be reduced to a shambles.

DISPOSABILITY

We found ourselves at the hospital on short notice recently, when our son's wife gave birth to our second grandchild. We had forgotten our camera, and were disappointed to think that we would miss those first photo opportunities when the baby was just minutes old. Then my wife discovered a vending machine in the waiting room that dispensed disposable cameras—obviously for proud grandparents like us. The cameras were not inexpensive, but we splurged and bought one for that momentous occasion.

We live in a throw-away culture—disposable cameras, disposable diapers, disposable swimsuits, disposable graduation gowns. Everywhere there are reminders that the material world is temporary. Like the first-century disciples, we often admire man's handiwork, including beautiful edifices not unlike the Jerusalem temple. Some structures are truly awe-inspiring, yet all such buildings one day will become rubble.

The temporary nature of earth's possessions is a hard truth to swallow, but one that ought to refocus our perspective: "Set your affection on things above" (Colossians 3:2). —R. W. B.

C. "When Shall These Things Be?"
(vv. 3, 4)

3, 4. And as he sat upon the mount of Olives, over against the temple, Peter and James and John and Andrew asked him privately, Tell us, when shall these things be? and what shall be the sign when all these things shall be fulfilled?

After leaving the city, Jesus and His disciples climbed the slopes of the *mount of Olives*, directly east of Jerusalem. The spot they selected may have been in or near the Garden of Gethsemane. The Mount of Olives afforded an excellent view of the temple area, since it rises to a height of approximately 2,700 feet.

The disciples had been perplexed about Jesus' prediction of the destruction of the temple, and so *Peter, James, John,* and *Andrew* took Him aside

---

How to Say It

ESCHATOLOGY. ess-kuh-*tah*-luh-gee.
GETHSEMANE. Geth-*sem*-uh-nee.
HERODIANS. Heh-*roe*-dee-unz.
PHARISEES. *Fair*-ih-seez.
SADDUCEES. *Sad*-you-seez.

and began to question Him more thoroughly about His comments. They had two questions. First, they wanted to know when these catastrophic events would take place. Second, they wanted to know what *sign* would indicate that their occurrence was near.

Matthew gives us a more detailed report of this conversation. The disciples first asked Jesus, "When shall these things be?" referring to the destruction of Jerusalem. Then they asked, "What shall be the sign of thy coming, and of the end of the world?" (Matthew 24:3). This makes it clear that Jesus was making predictions about two separate events—the destruction of Jerusalem and His return in glory—that have been separated by many hundreds of years. To understand what Jesus was saying in the verses that follow, we must carefully sort out which predictions belong to which event. If we do not, the result is likely to be confusion.

D. Jesus' Answer (vv. 5-7)

5-7. And Jesus answering them began to say, Take heed lest any man deceive you: for many shall come in my name, saying, I am Christ; and shall deceive many. And when ye shall hear of wars and rumors of wars, be ye not troubled: for such things must needs be; but the end shall not be yet.

Jesus prefaced His remarks with a warning about coming false prophets, who would *deceive many*. Such words were appropriate for the events surrounding the destruction of Jerusalem, which occurred within the lifetime of many of Jesus' followers. In the approximately four-decade period between Jesus' discourse and the fall of Jerusalem, the Jewish people continued to long for their version of a Messiah, who would lead them to victory over the hated Romans and give them their freedom. Many claimed to be this promised Messiah, and led groups to revolt against Rome. In A.D. 70 Rome sought to end these uprisings by capturing and destroying Jerusalem. In this way, the *wars and rumors of wars* of which Jesus spoke came to pass in a devastating fashion.

Verse 8 lists additional calamities, including earthquakes and famines, that would befall the earth. Yet these were only "the beginnings of sorrows"; *the end shall not be yet*. Scholars debate whether *the end* Jesus was talking about was the fall of Jerusalem or His second coming. At this point, it appears He was still addressing the disciples' first question, which concerned the destruction of the temple. The transition point at which Jesus moves from this topic to the topic of His return is verse 24, where the next portion of our printed text begins.

II. Other Future Events
(Mark 13:24-27)

A. Celestial Signs (vv. 24, 25)

24, 25. But in those days, after that tribulation, the sun shall be darkened, and the moon shall not give her light, and the stars of heaven shall fall, and the powers that are in heaven shall be shaken.

The words *but in those days, after that tribulation* show that Jesus has turned from discussing the fall of Jerusalem to discussing His return. These verses give no hint about when He will return. The only thing that we can conclude with certainty is that His return will follow the sorrows that accompanied the destruction of Jerusalem. More than nineteen hundred years have passed since that event, yet we still await Christ's return.

The darkening of the *sun* and *moon* indicate that the return of Jesus will be a worldwide event. These events, along with the falling *stars* and the shaking of the heavenly *powers*, imply the sudden destruction of the old order of creation (similar to what is pictured in 2 Peter 3:10-12). However, we must also note that such language as this is used symbolically in numerous Old Testament passages to describe the pouring out of God's judgment upon people and nations in a sudden, cataclysmic event (see Isaiah 13:9-11; Ezekiel 32:7, 8; Joel 2:10, 11; 3:15; Amos 8:9; Micah 3:5, 6).

B. Coming of the Son of Man
(vv. 26, 27)

26. And then shall they see the Son of man coming in the clouds with great power and glory.

The heavenly disturbances mentioned in the previous verses were not intended to be warning signs that the end is near. When these signs appear, it will be too late to repent and turn to the Lord. The phrase *coming in the clouds* reminds us of Jesus' ascension into Heaven, when He was taken up in a cloud. As the disciples stood watching, they were told that Jesus

visual for
lesson 13

would return "in like manner" (Acts 1:9-11). He will also come *with great power and glory.*

27. And then shall he send his angels, and shall gather together his elect from the four winds, from the uttermost part of the earth to the uttermost part of heaven.

The return of Jesus will be a time of judgment, for He will *send his angels* and *shall gather together his elect,* that is, the ones who have accepted His offer of salvation. No one will be excused from this event. "Every eye shall see him" (Revelation 1:7). At the judgment, "every knee shall bow" to Him and "every tongue shall confess" that He is the divine Son of God (Romans 14:11; Philippians 2:9-11).

III. Preparing for Christ's Return (Mark 13:31-35)

A. Only God Knows the Time (vv. 31, 32)

31. Heaven and earth shall pass away: but my words shall not pass away.

When Jesus returns, *heaven and earth* as we know them will *pass away.* Peter tells us that "the heavens shall pass away with a great noise, and the elements shall melt with fervent heat, the earth also and the works that are therein shall be burned up" (2 Peter 3:10). In their place will be "a new heaven and a new earth" (Revelation 21:1). Yet, in the midst of such sweeping change, the *words* of Christ *shall not pass away.* Often men's interpretations of His words go far astray, but this cannot affect the promise that His words will stand. Their truth will be made especially clear when He returns.

32. But of that day and that hour knoweth no man, no, not the angels which are in heaven, neither the Son, but the Father.

Here is another key transition in Jesus' discourse. In verses 28-30, Jesus told the disciples to watch for indications that the destruction of Jerusalem was near. He gave them certain signs that they could "see," such as the "abomination of desolation" (v. 14), so that they would know that the city's fall was "nigh, even at the doors" (v. 29). He then told them, "Verily I say unto you, that this generation shall not pass, till all these things be done" (v. 30). In keeping with Jesus' words, the destruction of Jerusalem occurred in A.D. 70, within the lifetime of most of His disciples.

With verse 32, Jesus moved from a discussion of "these things" (vv. 29, 30) to a discussion of *that day and that hour,* that is, the time of His return. Note this crucial distinction: Predictions concerning the destruction of Jerusalem were clear enough that Christians could read the signs and escape from the city (vv. 14-16). But the predictions concerning our Lord's return are quite vague and general. Neither the *angels,* nor Jesus Himself at the time He spoke, knew when He would return. The implications of this for every generation of believers is clear: All must live in daily preparation for His return, for they do not know when it will occur. Other Scriptures indicate that the time of Christ's return will be unannounced. Certainly this is the thrust of the phrase "as a thief in the night" (1 Thessalonians 5:2; 2 Peter 3:10).

"FULNESS OF THE TIME"

Were you ever in just the right place at just the right time to witness some special or unusual event? Sometimes those whose hobby is photography are lucky or clever enough to have a camera handy to record the once-in-a-lifetime antics of children or tricks of animals. More serious videographers make it a point always to be prepared to tape events that are immediately newsworthy, such as a dramatic rescue or an approaching tornado.

Sometimes job seekers happen to apply for positions that have opened on that very day. Quite suddenly, they are employed! "Timing is everything," they say.

Often such good timing is merely coincidental. Sometimes, though, it is the result of good planning and insightful preparation. Camera buffs who get the best pictures carry their equipment everywhere, loaded with film, fresh batteries, and clean lenses. Smart applicants exercise strategy in their job search, doing their "homework," investigating prospective companies and employers, learning their operations and special needs, and even discovering little quirks in the boss's personal management style.

Christians are not privy to the exact time of Christ's return. But we do know that God has planned that event to happen when the time is exactly right—just as when He sent the Savior the first time in the "fulness of the time" (Galatians 4:4). He has provided us with the "equipment" we need to keep ourselves in a state of readiness. Our best "end-times" strategy is simply to be prepared.   —R. W. B.

B. Watch and Pray (vv. 33-35)

33. Take ye heed, watch and pray: for ye know not when the time is.

Since we cannot know *the time* of the Lord's return, we have a special need for daily vigilance. God in His own wisdom knows the time, and there is nothing we can do to change that date. But we can so live that it really will not make any difference when Jesus comes. If we are always ready for that time, we need not live in dread and fear, but we can live each day expectantly and triumphantly. This is what is meant by the command to *watch*; it does not imply passive inactivity while waiting for Jesus to return. Even as we watch for Christ's return, we are urged to *pray*. We need to pray that we can become more like Him, and that we can reach as many as possible with the message of salvation before He comes.

34, 35. For the Son of man is as a man taking a far journey, who left his house, and gave authority to his servants, and to every man his work, and commanded the porter to watch. Watch ye therefore: for ye know not when the master of the house cometh, at even, or at midnight, or at the cockcrowing, or in the morning.

Jesus concluded His discussion of His return with a parable. In the parable, a *master* gives responsibilities to *his servants* during his absence. In those days travel was always risky. Success often depended on factors that were beyond the control of the traveler. For this reason, the master could not give an exact time for his return. And lacking our modern means of communication, he could not call ahead and give advance warning. Thus the servants were instructed to *work*, and the *porter* (the doorkeeper) to watch, as if any hour could be the time of the master's return. How tragic if "coming suddenly he find you sleeping" (v. 36)! How tragic if Jesus finds us doing the same!

Conclusion

A. Too Busy to Watch

Eschatology, a word meaning "the study of last things," ought to be a matter of concern for all Christians. As Christians, we believe that history is not an endless stream of events, occurring with no discernible meaning or purpose. As someone has observed, history is "His story." God is in control, and, guided by His Almighty hand, history is moving to a climax: the day when Jesus will return to claim His own and to judge the world. It should not surprise us that in every age persons have spent a great deal of time studying the Scriptures that deal with this event. Many have worked out detailed and elaborate schemes to allow them to predict with some degree of precision just when and how this will happen.

In view of all this, what should the attitude of a Christian be? We are urged to watch, but that watching is not some theological game. The watching is to insure that we will not neglect the work that our Lord has given us to do during the brief span of years we have been granted.

We should live every day so that if it is the final day, then we are ready. But if it turns out not to be that day, then fine—we are still ready.

John Wesley once was asked what he would do if he knew for certain that the next day would be his last day on earth. He took out his journal and began to read: "In the morning I would have breakfast with some friends, and we would discuss some plans for the Lord's kingdom in their village. At nine I would speak to a study group in another village. At noon I would have lunch with another minister, and discuss plans for a study group in his church. I would preach at another church in the afternoon, meet with its members at dinner, and then preach there in the evening. After the worship service, I would go to my room, spend time reading the Bible, and have my evening prayers. Then I would blow out my candle and go to bed." From this kind of schedule, Wesley seemed too busy to spend time watching for the Lord's return. Yet, by his activity on behalf of the Lord's kingdom, he was engaged in the kind of watching that Jesus commended.

B. Prayer

Almighty God, we recognize that You hold the future in Your hands. We do not know when You will choose to mark the end of time and send Your Son to claim His own. But we do know that You want us to be busy laboring for You when He comes. Help us not to become discouraged or distracted by our surroundings. Give us the strength and the courage to labor faithfully until we are called home or until Your Son comes for us. In His name, amen.

C. Thought to Remember

Watch and pray.

Home Daily Bible Readings

Monday, May 25—Tests of Our Faith (Mark 13:1-13)

Tuesday, May 26—Christ Will Come in Power (Mark 13:14-27)

Wednesday, May 27—Day and Hour Are Unknown (Mark 13:28-37)

Thursday, May 28—Jesus Will Come for Us (John 14:22-29)

Friday, May 29—Look for the City to Come (Hebrews 11:7-16)

Saturday, May 30—Come, Lord Jesus (Revelation 22:12-21)

Sunday, May 31—Outpouring of God's Spirit (Joel 2:28-32)

Learning by Doing

This page contains an alternate lesson plan emphasizing learning activities.
Classes desiring such student involvement will find these suggestions helpful.

Learning Goals

After this lesson, students should be able to:

1. Summarize the questions raised by Jesus' disciples in today's text, and His response to those questions.

2. Recognize those truths that are both known and unknown about the return of Christ.

3. List some specific steps one can take to prepare for the return of Christ, regardless of when it takes place.

Into the Lesson

Begin class by asking, "If you knew the world would end sometime this year, what would you do differently?" (If you have a large class, it would be best to ask your students to share their ideas in smaller groups.)

When students have had sufficient time to think about this question, read for them John Wesley's response to a similar question, found in the Conclusion of today's lesson commentary. After reading Wesley's response, ask students why they think he would have answered this way. Is this how Jesus would have responded?

Point out that today's lesson from Mark (the final one in this study) deals with Jesus' teaching about the end of the Jerusalem temple and the end of the world. The key question to consider is this: How did Jesus say we should prepare for "the end"?

Into the Word

Help your students to place the teaching of Jesus in Mark 13 in its proper context by asking them in small groups to make a list of the activities of Jesus during what is often called Passion Week. The Scriptures below are all from the Gospel of Mark. Divide the class into six groups and give each group one of the following references (note that the days are reckoned according to our measurement of time rather than the Jewish calculation of sunset to sunset):

Sunday (Mark 11:1-11)
Monday (Mark 11:12-19)
Tuesday (Mark 11:20—13:37)
Thursday (Mark 14:12-52)
Friday (Mark 14:53—15:47)
Sunday (Mark 16:1-11)

Does understanding how close Jesus' death was when He spoke the words found in today's lesson text add any significance to His teaching

about the second coming? Point out that it shows that Jesus' death did not mean that He had "lost control." He knew that His death was part of the Father's plan.

In this passage, Jesus talks both about the destruction of the temple (and all Jerusalem) and the destruction of all things at the end of the world. It is important to recognize when Jesus moves from one subject to the other. Note the important transition points in the printed text (vv. 24, 25 and v. 32). Use the lesson commentary for assistance in explaining these transitions.

Next, ask the groups to study several other references to Christ's second coming. Distribute one of the following Scripture references to each of the six groups, and ask them to compare the teaching in each reference with Christ's teaching in Mark 13. What additional information do we find in these other passages?

Daniel 7:13, 14
Matthew 25:1-13
Matthew 25:31-46
Mark 14:62
1 Thessalonians 4:15-18
Revelation 6:12-17

Do these passages make you fearful or give you hope? Why?

Into Life

Call attention to the "mini-parable" found in Mark 13:34, 35. What is the key word in this parable? The answer is: *watch* (also found in v. 37). When we look around us at the sin in the world, it is easy to lose hope. But the return of Jesus is intended to encourage and reassure us (read 1 Thessalonians 4:18). Spiritual preparedness should be among our highest priorities.

As you conclude today's lesson, ask each student to "pair up" with another, and answer these two questions:

• What is the most distressing thing for you about the second coming, as Jesus describes it in Mark 13?

• What is the most exciting thing about His coming?

Ask these pairs of students to close the lesson time by praying with each other that they would be encouraged by Jesus' words and not afraid— and that they would be prepared for the day when He comes.

Let's Talk It Over

The questions on this page are designed to encourage review of the lesson Scriptures and to promote discussion of the lesson by the class. The answers provided are only discussion starters. Let your class talk it over from there.

1. The temple impressed the disciples with its appearance of permanence. They were thus quite shocked when Jesus spoke of its impending destruction. What are some present works of men that may impress us with a false sense of permanence?

Among the most impressive edifices of our time are the great athletic stadiums and arenas that hold many thousands of spectators. While we are awed at the view inside them, we know that God's power could quickly reduce them to rubble. Also, major cities cultivate their skylines so as to impress approaching visitors with towering buildings and monuments. But these could be flattened in no time, should God's might be directed toward them. Then there are elaborate church buildings, some of them homes to congregations that have abandoned Biblical teaching for a social agenda. These offer an additional example of counterfeit permanence.

2. The Bible student must be careful of his interpretation of Mark 13, because there Jesus combined predictions about the destruction of Jerusalem with those concerning His ultimate return. Why did He do this?

One reason is that the disciples asked Him about both events at the time. From His standpoint, the two events were connected. Both were occasions when God's judgment was to come upon the wicked, and in both safety was offered to the righteous. Some forty years after Jesus delivered this discourse, the city of Jerusalem was devastated by the Romans. Those early followers of Jesus who were still living could declare that His prophecy had come true, and at the same time they could see more clearly that His prophecy of coming again would also come true. Today we can marvel at the accuracy of Jesus' description of Jerusalem's destruction, and we can thereby be assured of His return.

3. When Jesus returns, there will be no mistaking the fact. How does the Bible make this clear?

His coming again is frequently associated with the clouds. Verse 26 of our text and Acts 1:9-11 are two examples of this. In Revelation 1:7 we have the dramatic announcement: "Behold, he cometh with clouds; and every eye shall see

him . . ." Every human being needs only to look up to see the clouds, and it is there that Jesus will appear. The Bible also associates the sound of a trumpet with Jesus' return (Matthew 24:31; 1 Corinthians 15:52; 1 Thessalonians 4:16). Even people who suffer from hearing problems can hear the blaring of a trumpet. Also, Jesus will be accompanied by multitudes of angels. It will be a coming "with great power and glory" (Mark 13:26), and no one then living will miss what is happening.

4. Jesus promised, "My words shall not pass away." Why do we need to give this promise fresh emphasis today?

The words of Jesus are being subjected to a relentless attack by unbelievers. Certain scholars are insisting that Jesus never spoke most of the words attributed to Him in the Gospels. These scholars claim that the early church put words in Jesus' mouth in order to justify their own theological agenda. Other unbelievers accept the authenticity of Jesus' words, but charge that His words were spoken to deceive, or that He Himself was deluded when He spoke them. Still others twist His words in a misguided attempt at humor, holding Jesus and His claims up to ridicule. We who regard Jesus and His words with reverence and faith know that it is our viewpoint that shall prevail.

5. In what ways can we utilize prayer as a means of preparing for Jesus' return?

We can combine prayer with a study of those Scriptures that describe Jesus' return and our need for preparedness. We can ask, "God, impress this truth of Your Son's return on my mind. Help me not to lose sight of it, but to live my life with a constant awareness of it." When we are tempted to let possessions and pleasures distract us, we can echo 1 John 2:15-17 in our prayers: "God, help me not to love the world or the things in the world. Guide me in doing Your will, that I may abide forever." Prayer can also be a source of strength when sorrow and discouragement cloud our vision of victory: "O Lord, deliver me from preoccupation with present pains and pressures. Focus my eyes afresh on the conquering Christ and the eternal fellowship with Him that I will one day inherit."

Summer Quarter, 1998

Wisdom for Living

Special Features

Lessons

Unit 1: When Human Wisdom Fails

Unit 2: Proverbs on Living a Disciplined Life

Unit 3: Choose the Right Way

About these lessons

The lessons for this quarter come from the "wisdom literature" of the Old Testament. They remind us that the key to wisdom is not what you know but who you know: "The Lord giveth wisdom: out of his mouth cometh knowledge and understanding" (Proverbs 2:6).

Jun 7
Jun 14
Jun 21
Jun 28
Jul 5
Jul 12
Jul 19
Jul 26
Aug 2
Aug 9
Aug 16
Aug 23
Aug 30

Quarterly Quiz

The questions on this page may be used in several ways: as a pretest at the beginning of the quarter; as a review at the end of the quarter; or as a review after each lesson. The questions are based on the Scripture text of each lesson (King James Version). **The answers are on page 344.**

Lesson 1

1. The writer of Ecclesiastes describes himself as the _____, the son of _____, king in _____. *Ecclesiastes 1:1*

2. One of the most commonly used phrases in Ecclesiastes is "under the _____." *Ecclesiastes 1:3; 2:11; 4:1, 3*

3. Solomon concludes Ecclesiastes as follows: "Fear _____, and keep his _____: for this is the whole _____ of man." *Ecclesiastes 12:13*

Lesson 2

1. How many sons and daughters did Job have? *Job 1:2*

2. Satan accused God of building a _____ around Job. *Job 1:10*

Lesson 3

1. Give the names of Job's three friends. *Job 2:11*

2. Bildad said that Job's words were like a _____ _____. *Job 8:2*

3. Job labeled his friends as "_____ of no value." *Job 13:4*

Lesson 4

1. The Lord answered Job out of a (fire, whirlwind, cloud). *Job 38:1*

2. When God restored Job, He gave him _____ as much as he had before. *Job 42:10*

Lesson 5

1. Solomon challenges us to seek wisdom as diligently as we would seek _____. *Proverbs 2:4*

2. The Lord "layeth up sound wisdom" for what kind of person? *Proverbs 2:7*

Lesson 6

1. Solomon tells his son to bind mercy and truth about his (neck, arm, heart). *Proverbs 3:3*

2. "_____ in the Lord with all thine _____; and _____ not unto thine own _____." *Proverbs 3:5*

Lesson 7

1. Solomon tells us, "The wise shall inherit _____: but shame shall be the promotion of _____." *Proverbs 3:35*

2. Solomon declares happiness to the person who has _____ on the poor. *Proverbs 14:21*

Lesson 8

1. For the one who turns his ear from the Law, his _____ shall be abomination. *Proverbs 28:9*

2. "He that covereth his sins shall not _____." *Proverbs 28:13*

Lesson 9

1. In what part of the city does wisdom stand and cry out? *Proverbs 8:3*

2. Wisdom is said to be better than what group of precious stones? *Proverbs 8:11*

3. The one who hates wisdom is said to love _____. *Proverbs 8:36*

Lesson 10

1. The sluggard is advised to go to what creature? *Proverbs 6:6*

2. "The way of the slothful man is as a hedge of _____." *Proverbs 15:19*

3. Solomon tells us of going by the _____ of the slothful and by the _____ of the man without understanding. *Proverbs 24:30*

Lesson 11

1. What word does Solomon use to describe someone who "revealeth secrets"? *Proverbs 11:13*

2. Solomon tells us, "A _____ answer turneth away _____: but _____ words stir up _____." *Proverbs 15:1*

3. "Pleasant words are as (choice silver, a honeycomb, rest for the weary)." *Proverbs 16:24*

Lesson 12

1. "He that is hasty of spirit exalteth _____." *Proverbs 14:29*

2. He who controls his spirit is better than the one who (finds gold, kills a lion, takes a city). *Proverbs 16:32*

3. One with no control over his spirit is like "a _____ that is broken down." *Proverbs 25:28*

Lesson 13

1. "_____ up a _____ in the way he should go: and when he is _____, he will not _____ from it." *Proverbs 22:6*

2. The virtuous woman does not eat the bread of _____. *Proverbs 31:27*

3. The virtuous woman's children call her _____. *Proverbs 31:28*

Lessons for Living

by Edwin V. Hayden

P LEASE, GOD, show me everything You have put into all the plants that grow."

"George, that's too much for a little man."

"Then please show me what You have put into the plants that grow in my beloved Southland."

"That's still too much for you, George."

"Show me, then, what You have put into the peanut to be used for the good of Your people."

"Now, that's getting down to something more nearly your size. So go on to your laboratory and get to work, and I'll be there to help you."

That prayer/conversation, as I recall it after nearly sixty years, is the way Dr. George Washington Carver introduced to our Virginia college chapel service his display and description of some thirty useful products that he had developed out of his research of the simple peanut. We came away with great respect for the devout old botanist and his "goobers."

This small gentleman, born seventy years earlier into slavery, focused his boundless curiosity and energy on two goals—glorifying God and benefiting His people—in proceeding to develop some three hundred peanut products (including baby food, barn paint, and building materials) that could be used to help the people of the South. Dr. Carver did not know how many of these items were being produced and used when he visited our college. They have been enough, however, to earn the gratitude of multitudes who live better because of them. Dr. Carver's wisdom was a wisdom for living.

King Solomon, Too

Solomon's wisdom is even more notable for its source in prayer and in God's provision for His people. Perhaps not more than twenty years old when he succeeded his father David to the throne of Israel, Solomon described himself as "a little child" who did not know "how to go out or come in." He did not pray to know everything, but pleaded only that he might have "an understanding heart to judge" God's people (1 Kings 3:9). God was pleased with Solomon's request and gave the young king more than he asked, including wisdom on a vast scale and scope, and abundant riches and honor. On the condition of Solomon's following his father David in steadfast loyalty to the Almighty, he was also promised a long life (v. 14).

During his forty-year reign, however, Solomon faltered in his faithfulness, led astray through marriages that reflected political strategy rather than spiritual discernment. He seems to have lost sight of the purpose for wisdom—to live in God's way—as he became obsessed with an insatiable curiosity to know all about everything (Ecclesiastes 1:12—2:11). Eventually Solomon confessed to the futility of seeking knowledge for its own sake, and returned to the simpler commitment of his earlier days. At the end of Ecclesiastes (12:13) he wrote, "Let us hear the conclusion of the whole matter: Fear God, and keep his commandments: for this is the whole duty of man." In this statement, Solomon echoed his introduction to the book of Proverbs (1:7): "The fear of the Lord is the beginning of knowledge."

Does Solomon's tragic departure from the principles of wisdom cancel the value of his advice? Not at all. The God-centered wisdom in Proverbs is as valid as if he and every other teacher of that truth had followed it perfectly. The faulty teacher's influence, but not the truth of his teaching, is marred by any personal weakness. That teaching is wisdom for living, and the living is better because of the principles involved, even when they are not perfectly applied.

When Human Wisdom Fails

Not all of wisdom, however, is easily and directly applied. The human mind is continually challenged with difficult questions as to how things came to be as they are, and why prosperity (or difficulty) comes to those who least deserve it. These questions must be addressed from the perspective of eternity, and not merely from our understanding, which is so limited. This is the nature of the studies in the month of June, taken from Ecclesiastes and Job (this is also the first unit in our quarter's studies).

Lesson 1, from Ecclesiastes, presents us with "A Search for Answers." The royal "Preacher" (King Solomon) possessed vast resources and opportunities. He tried everything—from work projects of tremendous scope to extremes of self-indulgent pleasure—to discover life's central purpose. He found himself frustrated at every turn, until he found meaning in reverent obedience to God. This is the wisdom that "excelleth folly" (Ecclesiastes 2:13).

In **Lesson 2,** from the first three chapters of the book of Job, "Job Asks Hard Questions." Not knowing that he was being tested to show that a truly God-fearing person will serve Him without any selfish motivation, Job tried to understand his staggering personal tragedies: loss of possessions, loss of his large family, and loss of his health. All of this happened in spite of his indisputable integrity as a godly man.

In **Lesson 3,** four separate passages demonstrate that "Job's Friends Give Wrong Answers." Armed with easy explanations for hard problems, Job's "comforting" visitors assumed that Job must have sinned greatly to deserve such great punishment. But Job appealed his case to the judgment of God, and sought a hearing with Him.

Lesson 4 presents "God's Questions and Job's Response" from Job 38 and 42. God did not explain Job's predicament, but made it clear that this was only a small part of God's activity in the world that Job did not understand. Job accepted God's self-revelation, acknowledged that he had been presumptuous in his demands, and worshiped God with reverence and submission. After praying for his friends, Job was restored in health and prosperity.

Proverbs on Living a Disciplined Life

The book of Proverbs agrees with the conclusion of Ecclesiastes and the solution of Job's dilemma: God is the source of wisdom, both philosophical and practical. Four lessons for July declare and illustrate this theme.

Lesson 5, from Proverbs 2, urges the inexperienced young man to "Listen to Wisdom"—to give attention, accept, and follow the way of godliness according to the counsels of a wise father. The one who does so will be saved from the difficulties that come from the influence of wicked people, and he will be blessed with health, safety, and a productive life.

Lesson 6, from Proverbs 3, is also entitled with a command: "Trust God," rather than your own limited knowledge and inclinations, if you would walk in the way of life. God is the provider of all that is good for life and character. Keep trusting in His love.

Lesson 7, taken primarily from Proverbs 3, points to a practical part of wisdom in human relationships: "Be a Good Neighbor." Be prompt in helping others. Avoid the way of quarrelsome folk, or of those who would take advantage of a defenseless and unsuspecting neighbor. God takes a special interest in the way one treats the people around him.

Lesson 8, from Proverbs 28, returns to focus on one's relationship with God. "Obey God's Law," it says. Emphasized is the moral law that commands consideration for the poor and the innocent, as contrasted with the wickedness that takes advantage of them by charging exorbitant interest on loans. Followers of bad counsel, whether that of wicked men or that of their own scheming and plotting, dishonor God and their parents.

Choose the Right Way

The five lessons for August, built on passages throughout Proverbs, present the good-versus-bad choices that are typical of the poetic contrasts in this book.

Lesson 9, from Proverbs 8, deals with the fundamental choice, "Wisdom or Foolishness." Wisdom is a quality of God Himself. Here it is presented poetically as a person, speaking truths that must be accepted if one is to enjoy all that is worthwhile in life. It is also described as a supremely valuable treasure. When the choice of wisdom is made, lesser and separate choices fall naturally into place.

Lesson 10 finds its theme, "Hard Work or Laziness," expressed in passages selected from seven different chapters throughout Proverbs. The industrious ant is cited as an example of self-motivated activity. Laziness breeds poverty for the lazy person and is hurtful to others. A positive "work ethic" is established.

Lesson 11 also establishes its theme, "Helpful Speech or Harmful Speech," from various passages within Proverbs. One's speech habits, as well as his work habits, identify him as wise or foolish. Flattery and other forms of lying are condemned, as are thoughtless, harsh, and angry words and the "nonstop" talking associated with folly.

Lesson 12 uses several passages to develop its theme, "Slow to Anger or Quick to Anger." The quick and uncontrolled temper is a source of harmful speech and unneighborly violence. Recommended is the prudent patience that ignores insults and overlooks offenses. The patient, self-controlled person is the real hero.

Lesson 13, "Wisdom for Family Relationships," includes texts from five widely separated chapters of Proverbs. These employ the positive approach in urging children's attention to the wise teaching of both father and mother. The well-directed training of children brings lasting results. The patient, wise, and industrious wife and mother earns praise from her children, her husband, and all who know her.

These lessons provide an excellent opportunity to observe the beauty as well as the helpful content of Hebrew poetry. Passages memorized, especially from the *King James Version*, will linger and be recalled for a lifetime of instructive pleasure, to be shared in turn with others.

The Principal Thing

by W. W. Winter

WISDOM IS THE principal thing." So wrote Solomon, the primary author of Proverbs (Proverbs 4:7).

Human beings do not naturally put wisdom in first place. They may pursue knowledge and make models of philosophers or scholars who were well educated. Often great inventors and scientists with astounding insight are idolized. Such informed and knowledgeable individuals have a kind of wisdom, but it is usually speculative. At best, human wisdom comes from experience and extensive investigation. This wisdom, however, takes a back seat to the wisdom that serves as the focus of the book of Proverbs.

Ancients Who Made Wisdom Supreme

Job and Solomon were two famous men of old who sought to make wisdom "the principal thing." Three of Job's friends and another man named Elihu joined Job in the quest, as they tried to reason their way to a solution to Job's personal agony. Solomon describes his quest as follows: "I gave my heart to seek and search out by wisdom concerning all things that are done under heaven" (Ecclesiastes 1:13). Both Job and Solomon found wisdom as the principal thing, only when their thoughts turned to God.

The stories of Job and Solomon appear in what we call the "wisdom literature" of the Old Testament. Job may have written his own story in poetic form. Many think Moses knew the story and added a prose introduction and conclusion. He then delivered it by divine inspiration to encourage God's people. Others believe that the book was written by Solomon (or during Solomon's time), although it records events that took place many years earlier. In any case, the book of Job can still provide sound guidance in making wisdom the principal thing.

Solomon's quest is the subject of the book of Ecclesiastes. Solomon calls himself a "Preacher" (or "Teacher" in the *New International Version*). Ecclesiastes is the story of his search for meaning in life. In addition, he wrote most of the contents of the book of Proverbs, a collection of wise sayings. This book preserves for us the result of Solomon's efforts to make wisdom first in his life.

Job's Journey of Faith

Job appeared to be a righteous and godly man. He refused to have anything to do with evil ways (Job 1:1). His friends and acquaintances treated him with singular respect (29:7-10). He was known as a man of genuine kindness and compassion (vv. 11-17). His great flocks and herds gave evidence of Job's astute business sense. His family (seven sons and three daughters) testified to both God's blessing and Job's wise parenting. His contemporaries considered him "the greatest of all the men of the east" (1:3).

When these evidences of God's favor suddenly disappeared, Job's three friends (Eliphaz, Bildad, and Zophar) determined that they would go to Job to comfort him in his afflictions and losses. All his flocks and herds were gone. His children were dead. Job himself was in the throes of intense physical and mental anguish.

However, Job's friends seemed to lose sight of their original purpose for coming to see Job. They became convinced that Job had sinned grievously, and that this explained the intensity of Job's afflictions. They acknowledged that his sin may not have been widely known, but still they believed that Job's suffering was punishment for his wrongdoing. In contrast, Job was just as sure that he was innocent of such blatant sin. He was so certain of his integrity that he wished to be allowed to appear before God Himself to plead his case. At one point, Job labeled his "friends" as "miserable comforters" (Job 16:2).

A series of discourses left Job, his three friends, and later Elihu groping for answers. Finally God spoke. He revealed true wisdom to Job and his comforters. God told Job's three friends to offer a burnt offering. He told them that Job would pray for them. Job 42:10 then notes, "And the Lord turned the captivity of Job, when he prayed for his friends: also the Lord gave Job twice as much as he had before." Thus, at the end of his search, Job's condition (particularly his spiritual condition) was better than when he began. He could see plainly his need to trust God's guidance in every circumstance.

Solomon's Search for Meaning

Solomon succeeded his father David as king of Israel. As noted earlier, he was young and in need of guidance. The Lord appeared to him in a dream soon after he began to reign. God told Solomon to ask for whatever he desired.

What was first in Solomon's mind? He did not ask for the Lord to kill his enemies, nor did he ask for great riches. He asked God for wisdom to enable him to rule over the nation of Israel. And God answered the young king's prayer. Solomon ruled with distinction. His subjects were pleased with his fairness and wisdom. Solomon's reputation for being wise and benevolent spread abroad, so that his contemporaries considered him to be "wiser than all men" (1 Kings 4:31).

As he prospered, Solomon began to stray from the wisdom that God had granted him. He sought happiness and satisfaction from a variety of sources, including pleasure, food and drink, building enterprises, wealth, wisdom, music, and a large group of servants. The account of his search is found in Ecclesiastes 2:1-11. Nothing in this life brought Solomon any lasting satisfaction. He discovered all earthly pleasures to be transitory. He learned that nothing "under the sun" can bring contentment.

Solomon finally concluded what he should have known all along: God's wisdom is indeed the principal thing. All should fear God and keep His commandments (Ecclesiastes 12:13). He became convinced that only in this way will any human being find ultimate fulfillment. Only then can an individual become whole.

Making Wisdom Supreme Today

James instructs Christians to ask God for wisdom (James 1:5). He describes the wisdom of this world as "earthly, sensual, devilish" (3:15). True wisdom, he says, is pure, peaceable, gentle, and reasonable. He adds that it is full of mercy and good fruits, impartial, and sincere (v. 17).

Life in this present age demands the best efforts from all followers of Jesus Christ. Making wisdom the principal thing always has been necessary, but perhaps never has it been more so than now. Christians find themselves in the midst of a technologically advanced culture. The mind of man has discerned many secrets of this present world. Human beings have split the atom, once thought to be so small that it was indivisible. Visitors from Earth have walked on the moon and plan to explore other realms of outer space. Computers and television sets constantly become more intricate and advanced. Psychologists have gained greater insights into the ways the human mind works. Talented individuals in the medical profession restore health to diseased bodies.

In spite of the fact that we possess such vast amounts of knowledge in a wide range of disciplines, can it be said that we possess *wisdom*? Even the most cursory glance at the condition of modern society should tell us that we do not. Our homes are breaking up with increasing frequency. As amazing as they are, computers and television sets cannot keep families together. Many are even suggesting that we redefine the family. We must give first place in our lives to true wisdom—the wisdom of God. Only then can we deal adequately and successfully with marital and family problems.

We have an abundance of facts and figures to tell us that living beyond our means leads to bankruptcy. Financial counselors sound the warning. But when we do not make true wisdom the principal thing, we continue to spend more than we make. Our charge accounts quickly reach their limits. Our savings are depleted. Debts pile up. Only too late do we realize that we have allowed our habits to get out of control. Following God's plan for being His stewards provides the perspective that we need to discipline our use of money.

Today's teenagers are disillusioned. Among them, suicide rates are growing faster than among any other segment of our society. They know how to program a video cassette recorder, leaving their grandparents shaking their heads in amazement. They can solve intricate problems in mathematics. They have access to a body of knowledge that is staggering. Without true wisdom, however, they cannot solve their personal problems. When God's true wisdom has become the principal thing in their lives, He will guide them safely through life's most troubled times.

Living in Confidence

Victorious Christian living demands that we make true wisdom our principal thing. God has given us in the Scriptures the examples we need to assure us that making true wisdom supreme brings victory.

God revealed Himself to Job. When Job had a clear vision of God, he repented and made wisdom the principal thing. God heard his prayer and restored him. Thus did God bless Job's "latter end . . . more than his beginning" (Job 42:12).

God heard Solomon's prayer. He gave him wisdom. Although for a time Solomon lost his way, he finally recognized God's true wisdom as the principal thing. To fear God and keep His commandments is "the whole duty of man" (Ecclesiastes 12:13).

Christians must exalt the wisdom of God without fear, shame, or hesitancy. Otherwise we will become double-minded and unsure of our faith. There is no reason for us to question our choice to live by His wisdom. God will guide our steps. To God and His wise followers belong the victory.

Take God at His word: "Wisdom is the principal thing; therefore get wisdom."

How Should We Then Live?

by Earl E. Grice

THE QUESTION, "How Should We Then Live?" was raised by the late Christian thinker and writer, Francis Schaeffer, in a book by this title. In the face of modern secularism, humanism, materialism, and relativism (the belief that there are no absolute standards of conduct), as well as a general lack of civility and respect for God and others, how indeed should the Christian then live? Think of the irony: We live in a world of exploding knowledge, yet increasing numbers of individuals think and act without wisdom.

Who is wise? Ralph Cramden (the character played by Jackie Gleason on the old TV series, "The Honeymooners") used to accuse Alice, his wife, of being a "wisenheimer" when she refused to support his harebrained schemes. It is a taunt many have used when they hated to admit the "wisdom" of one who was not supposed to be very smart. Yet at times, it is not necessarily the Ph.D.'s, scientists, or politicians who are the most wise.

The Biblical proverbs are those capsules of truth and wisdom that have stood the test of time. They were written in a culture when reflection on life was a vocation and not just a "time-out" from rapid-fire living. They were often the result of the keen observation of life; for example, to show the negative consequences of laziness, Solomon notes, "I went by the field of the slothful, and by the vineyard of the man void of understanding; . . . Then I saw, and considered it well: I looked upon it, and received instruction" (Proverbs 24:30, 32). Despite their ancient and agricultural setting, these proverbs serve as moral and ethical principles that are just as relevant to the computerized, high-tech life of this almost-concluded twentieth century.

Wisdom—what is it? According to the Bible, it is not only the best course of action or behavior in a given situation, but it also involves a right relationship to God and one's fellowman. It is inseparable from character. It is that quality which knows and carries out the right response to certain situations that might leave the unwise uneasy. Wisdom may be expressed in a paradoxical saying, such as, "A soft tongue breaketh the bone" (25:15); or, "To the hungry soul every bitter thing is sweet" (27:7). It may use a comparison; to comment on the disaster facing a lazy man, 26:14 says, "As the door turneth upon his hinges, so doth the slothful upon his bed." On other occasions, a contrast serves the purpose. To caution against a hurried response, 15:28 states, "The heart of the righteous studieth to answer: but the mouth of the wicked poureth out evil things." True wisdom means seeing and respecting the order revealed by our Creator. According to His timely directives, "How should we then live?"

According to Experience

Experience can be a great teacher—perhaps the best instructor in life; for it reinforces the moral principles that undergird true wisdom. It teaches us that wisdom lies in acknowledging that we do not have all the answers; thus we must place our lives in the hands of the One who does. We are told, "Trust in the Lord with all thine heart; and lean not unto thine own understanding" (3:5). Solomon had seen disaster written over the poor whose poverty was the consequence of his laziness, as well as over the rich because of his greed: "Better is the poor that walketh in his uprightness, than he that is perverse in his ways, though he be rich" (29:6); and, "The sluggard buries his hand in the dish; he is too lazy to bring it back to his mouth" (26:15, *New International Version*). What a vivid picture! Solomon describes the consequences of one's falling into promiscuous sexual behavior: "Whoso committeth adultery with a woman lacketh understanding: he that doeth it destroyeth his own soul" (6:32).

Experience can teach us the hazards of disobeying the laws of God, whether in marriage, personal relationships, respect for others, personal diligence, or any other realm of life. One needs to learn from this wisdom, so that he can avoid experimenting with evil and thus experiencing for himself its disastrous consequences. The reason a bear does not tangle with a skunk is not because the giant beast could not dispose of this small mammal by one swipe of his paw, but because he knows that the consequences of his victory would not be worth the price!

Consequences of evil acts are the "chickens that come home to roost." Scripture states the principle this way: "Be sure your sin will find you out" (Numbers 32:23); "They have sown the wind, and they shall reap the whirlwind" (Hosea 8:7); and, "Whatsoever a man soweth, that shall he also reap" (Galatians 6:7). Our lack of civility and respect for others, and our generally boorish behavior, are already having their harmful effects in our schools, homes, and communities. Experience is reminding us (daily!) that the path of obedience to God, though sometimes difficult, is always worth the effort.

Experience is a gift of the wise. David wrote, "I have been young, and now am old; yet have I not seen the righteous forsaken, nor his seed begging bread" (Psalm 37:25). Experience had provided an impressive array of confirmation that God can be trusted to care for those who put Him and His will first.

According to the Revelation of God

The Biblical writers knew that real wisdom means knowing how to handle life's problems by consulting the Creator and Source of life. "The fear of the Lord is the beginning of knowledge" (Proverbs 1:7). "Fear God, and keep his commandments: for this is the whole duty of man" (Ecclesiastes 12:13). The kind of wisdom that will lead to peace, security, and goodness is from above, and we need large doses of it today. True wisdom is not only right for certain situations, and wrong or inadequate for others; it is right—period!—with no reservations, exceptions, or qualifications. Such wisdom is anchored in the will and Word of God!

Notice how practical and relevant the capsules of wisdom in Proverbs are. Consider these familiar words on rearing children: "Train up a child in the way he should go: and when he is old, he will not depart from it" (22:6). How timely is this counsel on being faithful to one's spouse: "Let thy fountain be blessed: and rejoice with the wife of thy youth . . . why wilt thou, my son, be ravished with a strange woman, . . . ?" (5:18, 20). How much better would our society function if people hated the seven things that God hates: "a proud look, a lying tongue, and hands that shed innocent blood, a heart that deviseth wicked imaginations, feet that be swift in running to mischief, a false witness that speaketh lies, and he that soweth discord among brethren" (6:16-19). Wisdom is built on a right relationship with Almighty God, and from this flows right relationships with man.

Wisdom—who needs it? The answer includes as many roles and professions in society as there are: judges, presidents, politicians, parents, children, homemakers, farmers, factory workers, church leaders, business entrepreneurs, and all others who would lead a gentle and peaceful life on this planet. We would do well to ponder these truths of Proverbs, for they are as right today as they were some three thousand years ago. Solomon and other sages of his time had observed life in the raw. We would do well to

learn from them, in order that we might recover our sense of dependence upon God, and, in so doing, our stability and sanity as a society! The wise person is willing to fear God—to respect His authority and listen to Him—and then to change his attitudes and conduct in order to fit God's moral order. Actions that reflect true wisdom may be costly, but in the long run they are always worth the effort and commitment.

A man took his car to a big, burly mechanic, and told him that the front end seemed to be out of line. The man looked at the auto, grabbed a huge hammer, and proceeded to beat on a portion of the front axle. When he then tested the car, he found that the problem had been fixed. When the customer received the bill charging him one hundred dollars for the job, it seemed much too high. He confronted the mechanic and asked, "How could you charge such an amount for just a few strikes with a hammer?" The mechanic replied, "I'm charging you five dollars for the work done, and ninety-five dollars for knowing where to hit!" Doesn't this illustrate the value of wisdom? Most of us forget that medical bills are often gauged according to the wisdom of the physician, and not the time it takes to counsel the patient. Wisdom that benefits us is costly. The same is true in our relationship with God. It costs to live by the principle, "Fear God and keep his commandments," but it costs much more not to!

How should we then live? The Biblical proverbs are those capsules of wisdom and truth that will teach us how in our increasingly secular world.

A Search for Answers

June 7
Lesson 1

DEVOTIONAL READING: **1 Corinthians 13.**

LESSON SCRIPTURE: **Ecclesiastes 1:1-3; 2:1-15; 4:1-3; 12:1, 13, 14.**

PRINTED TEXT: **Ecclesiastes 1:1-3; 2:1, 2, 10-13; 4:1-3; 12:1, 13, 14.**

Ecclesiastes 1:1-3

1 The words of the Preacher, the son of David, king in Jerusalem.

2 Vanity of vanities, saith the Preacher, vanity of vanities; all is vanity.

3 What profit hath a man of all his labor which he taketh under the sun?

Ecclesiastes 2:1, 2, 10-13

1 I said in mine heart, Go to now, I will prove thee with mirth; therefore enjoy pleasure: and, behold, this also is vanity.

2 I said of laughter, It is mad: and of mirth, What doeth it?

. . . .

10 And whatsoever mine eyes desired I kept not from them, I withheld not my heart from any joy; for my heart rejoiced in all my labor: and this was my portion of all my labor.

11 Then I looked on all the works that my hands had wrought, and on the labor that I had labored to do: and, behold, all was vanity and vexation of spirit, and there was no profit under the sun.

12 And I turned myself to behold wisdom, and madness, and folly: for what can the man do that cometh after the king? even that which hath been already done.

13 Then I saw that wisdom excelleth folly, as far as light excelleth darkness.

Ecclesiastes 4:1-3

1 So I returned, and considered all the oppressions that are done under the sun: and behold the tears of such as were oppressed, and they had no comforter; and on the side of their oppressors there was power; but they had no comforter.

2 Wherefore I praised the dead which are already dead, more than the living which are yet alive.

3 Yea, better is he than both they, which hath not yet been, who hath not seen the evil work that is done under the sun.

Ecclesiastes 12:1, 13, 14

1 Remember now thy Creator in the days of thy youth, while the evil days come not, nor the years draw nigh, when thou shalt say, I have no pleasure in them.

. . . .

13 Let us hear the conclusion of the whole matter: Fear God, and keep his commandments: for this is the whole duty of man.

14 For God shall bring every work into judgment, with every secret thing, whether it be good, or whether it be evil.

GOLDEN TEXT: Fear God, and keep his commandments: for this is the whole duty of man.
For God shall bring every work into judgment, with every secret thing,
whether it be good, or whether it be evil.—Ecclesiastes 12:13, 14.

Lesson Aims

After this lesson, students should be able to:

1. Describe the variety of means by which Solomon attempted to find fulfillment in life, and the conclusion to which he came.

2. Compare Solomon's search for fulfillment with the ways in which people today seek it.

3. Determine to lead one person to see life's futility apart from a relationship with God.

Lesson Outline

INTRODUCTION
    A. Wisdom That Works
    B. Lesson Background
I. THE AUTHOR AND HIS THEME (Ecclesiastes 1:1-3)
    A. Introducing the Author (v. 1)
    B. The Key Issue (vv. 2, 3)
    Under the Soil
II. THE QUEST FOR FULFILLMENT (Ecclesiastes 2:1, 2, 10-13)
    A. Pleasure Is Meaningless (vv. 1, 2)
    B. Work Is Meaningless (vv. 10, 11)
    C. Wisdom Is Meaningless (vv. 12, 13)
III. THE SORROWS OF LIFE (Ecclesiastes 4:1-3)
    A. Considering the Oppressed (v. 1)
    B. Praising the Dead (v. 2)
    C. To Be or Not To Be (v. 3)
IV. THE CONCLUSION OF THE MATTER (Ecclesiastes 12:1, 13, 14)
    A. Remember Your Creator (v. 1)
    The Journey to Joy
    B. Fear God (vv. 13, 14)
CONCLUSION
    A. The Fear of the Lord
    B. Prayer
    C. Thought to Remember

The visual for Lesson 1 calls us to find life's purpose in serving God. It is shown on page 349.

Introduction

A. Wisdom That Works

In the Scriptures, wisdom is the intensely practical art of being skillful and successful in life. It is equated with the skillful application of God's Word to the daily demands of life. As we immerse ourselves in Scripture, our growth in wisdom is measured, not by intellectual prowess, but by the perfection of character. "Who is a wise man and endued with knowledge among you? let him show out of a good conversation his works with meekness of wisdom. . . . The wisdom that is from above is first pure, then peaceable, gentle, and easy to be entreated, full of mercy and good fruits, without partiality, and without hypocrisy" (James 3:13, 17). May we increase in wisdom as we study God's Word this quarter!

B. Lesson Background

Today's lesson is taken from the book of Ecclesiastes. As we will see, this book records the quest of King Solomon for a solution to the puzzle called *life*. What is its purpose? How does one make sense of it? Solomon, also called "the Preacher" in the opening verse, explores a wide range of possible answers to these questions. He concludes that life without God is barren, and subject to futility, cynicism, and bitterness. God is both good and generous, and He is the source of life's joys. Fearing Him and keeping His commandments is described as "the whole duty of man" (Ecclesiastes 12:13). Only by living from such a perspective does life become coherent and meaningful.

In a sense, the book of Ecclesiastes is actually an essay in apologetics. It contains a defense of faith in God and its superiority to other alleged sources of fulfillment. The book's message is particularly timely in the present day, in which many are sadly (and needlessly) duplicating Solomon's quest.

I. The Author and His Theme (Ecclesiastes 1:1-3)

A. Introducing the Author (v. 1)

1. The words of the Preacher, the son of David, king in Jerusalem.

The name of the author of Ecclesiastes never once appears in this book. However, we can deduce who he was by the clues provided in this opening verse: *the son of David, king in Jerusalem.* Later, in 1:12, he adds, "I the Preacher was king over Israel in Jerusalem." These verses indicate that Solomon wrote Ecclesiastes. In addition, the author refers to his wisdom (1:16), wealth (2:8), impressive building accomplishments (2:4-6), and a huge retinue of servants (2:7), all of which characterized Solomon.

We cannot be certain of the time in Solomon's life when he wrote this book. We know that later in his reign, Solomon tragically turned away from the Lord in order to please his pagan wives

(1 Kings 11:4). As a result, the Lord raised up adversaries against him in order to punish him (1 Kings 11:14-26). If Solomon repented because of the pressure God put upon him through these adversaries, then perhaps the book of Ecclesiastes can be considered as his advice on how to live the best possible kind of life and how to avoid the foolish choices that tarnished his own life. He is writing from the perspective of one whose life is mostly behind him, for the sake of instructing those who have much of their lives before them.

The English title of this book, *Ecclesiastes*, comes from the Septuagint, the translation of the Hebrew Old Testament into Greek. The Hebrew title, *Qohelet* (the word rendered "Preacher"), is believed by some to describe a speaker in a public assembly. Perhaps it is a way of saying that Solomon's experiences have valuable lessons to teach everyone who will listen.

B. The Key Issue (vv. 2, 3)

2. Vanity of vanities, saith the Preacher, vanity of vanities; all is vanity.

This verse, which recurs near the end of Ecclesiastes in 12:8 (before the conclusion), is the "motto" of the book. All earthly experience is subject to *vanity*; no human endeavor will in itself bring permanent satisfaction.

The Hebrew word translated *vanity* (*hevel*) occurs thirty-three times in Ecclesiastes. The basic meaning of this word is "vapor" or "breath." Since breath is fragile and transitory, "vanity," "meaningless," or "futility" are all appropriate translations.

Does this evaluation include godliness—and God? The answer to this question comes in verse three.

3. What profit hath a man of all his labor which he taketh under the sun?

Since the earthly realm is subject to vanity, as just stated in verse two, there is no hope of finding ultimate gain or satisfaction from its resources alone. As a result, the physical toil, financial demands, and mental anguish of human endeavors pay no dividends. In short, there is no true *profit*. The balance sheet shows no credit—only a debit. One is left with a nagging, discouraging emptiness. Jesus addressed the same issue when He asked, "For what shall it profit a man, if he shall gain the whole world, and lose his own soul? Or what shall a man give in exchange for his soul?" (Mark 8:36).

In the Old Testament, the phrase *under the sun* occurs only in Ecclesiastes, appearing twenty-nine times. This term is a key to unlocking the meaning of the book. If our gaze rises no higher than this world, then life is indeed the

---

How to Say It

ECCLESIASTES. Ik-*leez*-e-*as*-teez (strong accent on *as*).
HEVEL (Hebrew). *hehv*-ell.
QOHELET (Hebrew). Koe-*hel*-it.
SEPTUAGINT. Sep-*too*-ih-jent.

"vanity of vanities." If man lives his life apart from God, solely in the context of this world ("under the sun"), he will profit nothing and will reap dissatisfaction.

Eventually Solomon will contend that there is more to this universe than what we can observe under the sun, for "God is in heaven" (5:2). Our perspective must be guided by what is unseen, not by what is seen (read Paul's words in 2 Corinthians 4:18). God alone can bring meaning to life. Solomon affirms, "He has also set eternity in the hearts of men" (3:11, *New International Version*). In other words, we have a capacity for eternal things, and cannot be complete until we come to know the Eternal One.

UNDER THE SOIL

As is pointed out in this lesson, the phrase "under the sun" is used again and again in Ecclesiastes. It epitomizes what is earthbound, pessimistic, and negative. Someone has suggested that this point of view could be illustrated by an imaginary conversation between a mole and a robin. The mole might poke his head out from the earth and say, "How dark and desolate everything is. Most of the time all I can see is dirt, roots, and worms." The robin might reply, "That's not my view of things at all. I see the blue sky and the green earth. I fly through clear air and have branches of beautiful trees on which to sit. Certainly I see worms, too, but I eat them and they do me good."

Just as Solomon saw many things as "vain" or "meaningless" because they were "under the sun," so does the mole when he is "under the soil." There are dark and dismal realities in life, but when we look at the world from Heaven's perspective and through the eyes of the Creator, there are also matters of exquisite beauty, gladness, and delight.

Jesus our Lord took great joy in His Father's world. He said that the lilies of the field are more glorious than Solomon in all his splendor (Matthew 6:28, 29). A sparrow does not fall to the ground without the Father's knowledge. Jesus taught His followers that even when tribulation is their lot in this world, they should "be of good cheer," for He has "overcome the world"

(John 16:33). So it was for Jesus Himself: the darkness of a cross of shame only pointed the way to the triumph of Easter morning.

Life "under the sun" can make sense only when we desire to live it "under the Son."

—J. G. V. B.

II. The Quest for Fulfillment (Ecclesiastes 2:1, 2, 10-13)

A. Pleasure Is Meaningless (vv. 1, 2)

1, 2. I said in mine heart, Go to now, I will prove thee with mirth; therefore enjoy pleasure: and, behold, this also is vanity. I said of laughter, It is mad: and of mirth, What doeth it?

In this section, Solomon suggests that hedonism (the pursuit of *pleasure*) also deserves the verdict of *vanity*. *Laughter* and *mirth*, superficial and thoughtless pleasure, fail to meet the needs of the man whose viewpoint remains limited to what is "under the sun." The merrymaker drowns the reality of life in a sea of frivolity. But when the fun has subsided, *what doeth it?* What does it ultimately achieve? Solomon admits that there is a time for laughter (3:4); but here laughter is vanity, since it arises from self-indulgence and does not contribute to genuine happiness. Laughter is a good medicine, as Proverbs 17:22 teaches. However, laughter does not help those who need something more basic and substantial to deal with life's sorrows.

B. Work Is Meaningless (vv. 10, 11)

10. And whatsoever mine eyes desired I kept not from them, I withheld not my heart from any joy; for my heart rejoiced in all my labor: and this was my portion of all my labor.

Eyes suggests visible entertainment; *heart* denotes inward satisfaction. The *labor* or activity designed to fulfill Solomon's desires seemed to give a temporary burst of satisfaction; with achievement, however, the pleasure began to fade.

11. Then I looked on all the works that my hands had wrought, and on the labor that I had labored to do: and, behold, all was vanity and vexation of spirit, and there was no profit under the sun.

The terms *vanity* and *no profit under the sun* suggest that Solomon's activity (*all the works that my hands had wrought*), which had for a time kept him pleasurably occupied, resulted in bitter disillusionment. His summary of these exploits is found in 2:4-8. One is struck by the frequency of the pronoun "I" in these verses. Solomon had indulged himself with every material pleasure imaginable, yet his soul remained empty.

C. Wisdom Is Meaningless (vv. 12, 13)

12. And I turned myself to behold wisdom, and madness, and folly: for what can the man do that cometh after the king? even that which hath been already done.

Solomon assures the reader that he has experienced the ultimate in wisdom and pleasure, and that there is no need for anyone else to repeat the experiment. What can anyone add to what Solomon has already attempted? How could anyone improve on the experiment of a *king*, especially one who had the means of obtaining anything he wanted?

If the reader accepts the conclusion of Solomon, then he will have no need to prove through his own experience that life "under the sun" is "vanity." The reader can be spared the agony of discovering this to be true (though many will respond with the frequently used argument, "I've got to find out for myself"). If the reader is convinced by Solomon's argument, then he must continue on to the conclusion, where Solomon reaches "the conclusion of the whole matter" and provides the key to real and lasting fulfillment (12:13, 14).

13. Then I saw that wisdom excelleth folly, as far as light excelleth darkness.

Even though human *wisdom* should never become the ultimate source of guidance (1:17), wisdom is still of value. Wisdom is "profitable to direct" (10:10); it preserves and protects life (7:12); it causes one's "face to shine" (8:1); and it is better than brute strength (7:19; 9:16).

Verse 16, however, reminds the reader that wisdom is not adequate to address the ultimate issues of life: "For there is no remembrance of the wise more than of the fool for ever; seeing that which now is in the days to come shall all be forgotten. And how dieth the wise man? as the fool."

III. The Sorrows of Life (Ecclesiastes 4:1-3)

A. Considering the Oppressed (v. 1)

1. So I returned, and considered all the oppressions that are done under the sun: and behold the tears of such as were oppressed, and they had no comforter; and on the side of their oppressors there was power; but they had no comforter.

Here Solomon suggests that injustice characterizes life in every age. Earlier he broached this subject: "And moreover I saw under the sun the place of judgment, that wickedness was there; and the place of righteousness, that iniquity was there" (3:16).

Solomon is not a defeatist; he is a realist. The reign of evil is a reign of cruelties and *oppressions*. To spite the influence of the church as salt and light in a decaying and darkened world, Satan will work even harder to enslave the world in the grip of sin's oppression. He will also seek to corrupt the church, thus negating its impact on the corruption.

The repetition of the phrase *they had no comforter* heightens the sense of helplessness expressed in this verse. David once wrote, "Reproach hath broken my heart; and I am full of heaviness: and I looked for some to take pity, but there was none; and for comforters, but I found none" (Psalm 69:20). On another occasion he wrote, "There was no man that would know me: refuge failed me; no man cared for my soul" (Psalm 142:4).

If this life is all that there is to experience, then there is no enduring consolation to lift us above the anguish of this present age. Contrast this with the consolation that the psalmist found in God: "This is my comfort in my affliction: for thy word hath quickened me" (Psalm 119:50).

B. Praising the Dead (v. 2)

2. Wherefore I praised the dead which are already dead, more than the living which are yet alive.

From the horizontal viewpoint of life—that is, life "under the sun" lived apart from God—*the dead* are truly better off than *the living*. The dead no longer have to endure the misery of oppression.

C. To Be or Not to Be (v. 3)

3. Yea, better is he than both they, which hath not yet been, who hath not seen the evil work that is done under the sun.

Better still is never to have lived, and to have been unaware of life's anguish and frustration. Jeremiah 20:18 echoes this thought: "Wherefore came I forth out of the womb to see labor and sorrow, that my days should be consumed with shame?" (see also Job 3:3-10).

IV. The Conclusion of the Matter (Ecclesiastes 12:1, 13, 14)

A. Remember Your Creator (v. 1)

1. Remember now thy Creator in the days of thy youth, while the evil days come not, nor the years draw nigh, when thou shalt say, I have no pleasure in them.

In light of the brevity of both youth and life, Solomon exhorts his readers to *Remember now thy Creator in the days of thy youth*. Determine to serve God, so that all of life can be lived in

visual for
lesson 1

the awareness of His holiness and in the true enjoyment of His blessings. *Now* is the time to prepare for eternity!

In the context of the following verses, *evil* is a reference to the distressing days of old age, in which mental and physical powers fade, and in which time will no longer signal growth, but decline. Solomon has characterized the life of faith as one of enjoyment (2:24-26; 3:12, 13, 22; 5:18-20; 9:7-10; 11:9, 10). But where God is neglected, man's capacity for joy is lost.

THE JOURNEY TO JOY

The pessimism of "the Preacher" was magnified, because he discovered that there was no permanent satisfaction in pleasure. He says, "Whatsoever mine eyes desired I kept not from them, I withheld not my heart from any joy" (2:10). He found it all "meaningless, a chasing after the wind" (v. 11, *New International Version*). It is certain that when we make it our primary aim in life to "have all the fun we can for as long as we can," the inevitable result is frustration and disillusionment. The novelist, college professor, and preacher Charles Kingsley wrote of this in a powerful poem.

"When all the world is young, lad,
  And all the trees are green;
And every goose a swan, lad,
  And every lass a queen;
Then hey for boot and horse, lad,
  And round the world away;
Young blood must have its course, lad,
  And every dog his day.

"When all the world is old, lad,
  And all the trees are brown;
And all the sport is stale, lad,
  And all the wheels run down;
Creep home and take your place there,
  The spent and maimed among;
God grant you find one face there
  You loved when all was young."

Enjoyment is not our employment. Our job is to do God's will in every aspect of life. When we seek His will first, then joy comes as an added, bountiful, and beautiful by-product. —J. G. V. B.

B. Fear God (vv. 13, 14)

13. Let us hear the conclusion of the whole matter: Fear God, and keep his commandments: for this is the whole duty of man.

Solomon is now prepared to summarize the *conclusion* of his research. He focuses on two areas: the greatness of God and the Word of God. Here we shall find reality. All else is "vanity of vanities."

To *fear God* is the beginning of wisdom (Psalm 111:10; Proverbs 9:10), and the first and controlling principle of wisdom. In fact, one cannot progress in the Christian walk and leave wisdom behind. Many associate the fear of God primarily with the Old Testament. But in the New Testament, Paul writes, "Having therefore these promises, dearly beloved, let us cleanse ourselves from all filthiness of the flesh and spirit, perfecting holiness in the fear of God" (2 Corinthians 7:1).

The order of the two commands (*fear* and *keep*) is instructive. The Christian shows his attitude toward God in the quality of his moral life. This same order is seen in Deuteronomy 13:4: "Ye shall walk after the Lord your God, and fear him, and keep his commandments, and obey his voice, and ye shall serve him, and cleave unto him."

Why should we fear God? Why should we obey His truth? The answer to these questions is found in verse fourteen.

14. For God shall bring every work into judgment, with every secret thing, whether it be good, or whether it be evil.

Earlier Solomon wrote, "I said in mine heart, God shall judge the righteous and the wicked: for there is a time there for every purpose and for every work" (3:17); and again, "Rejoice, O young man, in thy youth; and let thy heart cheer thee in the days of thy youth, and walk in the ways of thine heart, and in the sight of thine eyes: but know thou, that for all these things God will bring thee into judgment" (11:9).

God holds and will hold every person accountable for the life he or she lives. Nothing—no *secret thing*—will be hidden from Him. This should be a sobering truth! How will you live your life in light of it? Let us hear and heed Solomon's counsel: "Fear God, and keep his commandments."

Conclusion

A. The Fear of the Lord

The meaning of the fear of the Lord may be summarized by the following five principles:

(1) **F**aithfulness: "And he charged them, saying, Thus shall ye do in the fear of the Lord, faithfully, and with a perfect heart" (2 Chronicles 19:9). "He was a faithful man, and feared God above many" (Nehemiah 7:2).

(2) **O**bedience: "Fear the Lord, and serve him in truth with all your heart: for consider how great things he hath done for you" (1 Samuel 12:24). "Blessed is every one that feareth the Lord; that walketh in his ways" (Psalm 128:1). "The fear of the Lord is to hate evil: pride, and arrogancy, and the evil way, and the froward mouth, do I hate" (Proverbs 8:13).

(3) **R**everence: "Let all the earth fear the Lord: let all the inhabitants of the world stand in awe of him" (Psalm 33:8). "My flesh trembleth for fear of thee; and I am afraid of thy judgments" (Psalm 119:120).

(4) **T**rust: "Ye that fear the Lord, trust in the Lord: he is their help and their shield" (Psalm 115:11). "Trust in the Lord with all thine heart; and lean not unto thine own understanding" (Proverbs 3:5).

(5) **H**umility: "The meek will he guide in judgment: and the meek will he teach his way" (Psalm 25:9). "By humility and the fear of the Lord are riches, and honor, and life" (Proverbs 22:4).

Go *forth* in the *fear* of the Lord!

B. Prayer

Thank You, Father, for delivering us from the verdict of vanity through the death, burial, and resurrection of Jesus Christ, who is man's only source of meaning, hope, and eternal life. In Jesus' name we pray. Amen.

C. Thought to Remember

Keeping Heaven's perspective in mind is the only way to enjoy life on earth.

Home Daily Bible Readings

Monday, June 1—Solomon Prays for Understanding (1 Kings 3:5-15)
Tuesday, June 2—Nothing New Under the Sun (Ecclesiastes 1:1-11)
Wednesday, June 3—Chasing After Wind (Ecclesiastes 1:12—2:5)
Thursday, June 4—Our Days Are Full of Pain (Ecclesiastes 2:9-23)
Friday, June 5—Life Isn't Fair (Ecclesiastes 4:1-6)
Saturday, June 6—Don't Wait to Know God (Ecclesiastes 12:1-8)
Sunday, June 7—Keep God's Commandments (Ecclesiastes 12:9-14)

Learning by Doing

This page contains an alternate lesson plan emphasizing learning activities.
Classes desiring such student involvement will find these suggestions helpful.

Learning Goals

After today's lesson, students will be able to:

1. Describe the variety of means by which Solomon attempted to find fulfillment in life, and the conclusion to which he came.

2. Compare Solomon's search for fulfillment with the ways in which people today seek it.

3. Determine to lead one person to see the futility of life apart from a relationship with God.

Into the Lesson

Write the phrase "True Confessions" on a chalkboard or poster board, then ask the following questions: What is the silliest thing you ever did? When did you work hard, only to have nothing to show for it? What is the biggest waste of time you can think of? (These questions are included in the student book.) Be ready to share your own answers. Have some fun with the class members as they "confess" and share their responses. Make the transition into today's lesson by stating that Solomon wrote an entire book of the Bible to deal with serious issues related to questions just like these.

Into the Word

Ask someone to read Ecclesiastes 1:1-3; 2:1, 2, 10-13; and 4:1-3. Explain that Ecclesiastes 1:2 contains one of the key phrases in the book, and that "vanity" means futility, meaninglessness, or emptiness. If life "under the sun" is all there is, then life will be meaningless.

Divide the class into two groups. Ask each group to search the Scripture passages and find the ways Solomon attempted to find fulfillment in life: hard work, 1:3 and 2:10; mirth and laughter, 2:1, 2; possessions, 2:4-8; entertainment and joy, 2:10; human wisdom, 2:12; being a victim, 4:1-3; being an oppressor, 4:1-3. (This activity is in the student book.) The first group is to describe why each attempt is meaningless. The second group is to come up with several "convincing arguments" why some people could expect each attempt to bring fulfillment. Alternate between groups: Group One should present an attempt at fulfillment and why it fails, then Group Two should present the argument why "it just might work." Then let Group Two present the next attempt to fulfillment and why "it just might work," followed by Group One's explanation of why it is meaningless. Have some fun with this "debate" while encouraging serious thought. Reinforce the conclusion of Solomon: All is vanity. Stress that life can be very empty if we seek fulfillment only in what is found "under the sun."

Into Life

Ask the class to brainstorm answers to this question: "What are the ways in which people today are seeking fulfillment apart from God?" (This is included in the student book.) Write their responses on a chalkboard or poster board, assembling a variety of answers (big homes, fancy cars, becoming a workaholic, TV and movies, changing jobs, sex, politics, fine arts, athletics, job promotions, membership in civic organizations, drugs, physical fitness, etc.).

Separate the class into several small groups, with each group assigned to create a simple skit that illustrates the pursuit of fulfillment "under the sun" and its vanity. Give them enough time to develop their skits and then perform them. Probe any idea or example that presents itself as particularly insightful.

Now ask, "How have you been caught up in any of these?" Encourage and allow openness here. Ask how class members came to understand the futility of such pursuits. Draw attention to Ecclesiastes 12:1, 13, 14. Ask how fearing God and keeping His commandments would have affected the behavior of the people in each skit. If no one else does so in the discussion, point out that Solomon's ultimate answer to meaningfulness "under the sun" is a relationship with God (Ecclesiastes 5:2).

Remind the class that our society is filled with people who are leading empty lives, and who need to be introduced to meaningfulness in a relationship with God through Jesus Christ. Ask each person to think of one friend or acquaintance who needs to find meaning and purpose in life. As we show our love and respect for God and keep His commandments, hopefully such individuals will see the abundant life that we have in Christ. Ask class members to share, in pairs or small groups, how they can, through their actions and words, lead a friend or acquaintance to see the futility of life apart from God. Have them close with prayer for one another's efforts to accomplish this.

Let's Talk It Over

The questions on this page are designed to encourage review of the lesson Scriptures and to promote discussion of the lesson by the class. The answers provided are only discussion starters. Let your class talk it over from there.

1. Because the Bible is God's Word, given to instruct us in godly wisdom, it is an infallible source of wisdom. However, we cannot simply read it and become wise all in one step. Explain how we can use the Bible to gain true wisdom and to live wisely.

We begin by reading the Bible and learning what it says. Next, we need to meditate upon its words until we understand them and are convinced of their truth within our own hearts. The Word gives us many examples to help us understand its principles. We also can look at our own lives and at the lives of people around us, and compare what happens when we keep the teachings of the Bible with what happens when we disregard them. Wisdom comes when we know what the Bible says, when we believe its truth, when we understand how that truth applies to the situations we face, and when we actually do what we know to be the right and wise thing. The hardest and most crucial step is to discipline ourselves to do the right thing.

2. The basic error of the fool who says in his heart, "There is no God," is that he has the wrong world view. Describe common world views, and show why only the Biblical world view can be the foundation of wisdom.

The Biblical world view is that we were made by the Creator God, who holds us responsible to obey Him and who will reward or punish us eternally. True wisdom, then, consists of knowing and doing whatever pleases God and thus preparing to meet Him. The atheistic, humanistic, and evolutionary world views hold that we are accidents of nature, responsible to no one, and that our existence ends at death. To those holding this view, wisdom is subjective, meaning that each person does what is right in his own eyes. Such people live out of harmony with God and will not be prepared to meet Him.

3. We often say that no one has more fun than Christians, but our text says that mirth and pleasure are "vanity" (Ecclesiastes 2:1). Explain how fun can be either refreshing or frustrating, depending on how it is approached and used.

Evidently Solomon tried everything from comedians to concubines, and found them all unfulfilling. His problem was that he pursued pleasure as an end in itself. A life based on the pursuit of pleasure will prove to be vain in the day when nothing is funny or there is no pleasure to be had. However, when laughter is used as a relief for labor, stress, or even tragedy, it can be refreshing and renewing. Immoral "fun" is always destructive.

4. Solomon encourages us to remember our Creator in the days of our youth (Ecclesiastes 12:1). State some reasons why it is important to remember and fear God in our youth. Why is it hard to do this during one's youth?

One of the most basic principles of life is that we live it only once. As the saying goes, "You're only young once." The temptation of youth is to seek all the pleasure and gratification possible "before it is too late." Solomon tells us that instead, we should use the strength and energy of youth to serve and obey God, before all that we have left to offer Him are the feeble years of old age. Youth devoted to pleasure is spent on that which is vain, and leaves one empty and unfulfilled. Youth devoted to God also offers pleasure, but its end is satisfaction and contentment. Because we live only once, the wise young person will spend this most vital and energetic part of life on that which has true value and which offers permanent reward.

5. Those of us who are older sometimes wish we had understood in our youth what we understand now. How can we use the wisdom and understanding we have gained in life to help youth make wise decisions?

Teens and young adults usually don't like to be told what to do. Advice, even good advice, may be ignored or even resented. Instead of trying to tell them what to do, we can tell them what we have done. This requires us to be vulnerable and to humble ourselves, but the result may be worth it. Young people often reject pious platitudes and holy clichés, but they listen intently when we open up our lives and reveal some of our worst mistakes, some of our toughest decisions, or even some of our best choices. Young people are not stupid; they just lack experience. If we share our experiences with them, we can help them make wise choices

Job Asks Hard Questions

DEVOTIONAL READING: Job 3:11-26.

LESSON SCRIPTURE: Job 1:1-12; 2:1-8; 3:1-4, 20-26.

PRINTED TEXT: Job 1:1-4, 8-11; 2:3-6; 3:1-3.

Job 1:1-4, 8-11

1 There was a man in the land of Uz, whose name was Job; and that man was perfect and upright, and one that feared God, and eschewed evil.

2 And there were born unto him seven sons and three daughters.

3 His substance also was seven thousand sheep, and three thousand camels, and five hundred yoke of oxen, and five hundred she asses, and a very great household; so that this man was the greatest of all the men of the east.

4 And his sons went and feasted in their houses, every one his day; and sent and called for their three sisters to eat and to drink with them.

. . . .

8 And the LORD said unto Satan, Hast thou considered my servant Job, that there is none like him in the earth, a perfect and an upright man, one that feareth God, and escheweth evil?

9 Then Satan answered the LORD, and said, Doth Job fear God for nought?

10 Hast not thou made a hedge about him, and about his house, and about all that he hath on every side? thou hast blessed the work of his hands, and his substance is increased in the land.

11 But put forth thine hand now, and touch all that he hath, and he will curse thee to thy face.

Job 2:3-6

3 And the LORD said unto Satan, Hast thou considered my servant Job, that there is none like him in the earth, a perfect and an upright man, one that feareth God, and escheweth evil? and still he holdeth fast his integrity, although thou movedst me against him, to destroy him without cause.

4 And Satan answered the LORD, and said, Skin for skin, yea, all that a man hath will he give for his life.

5 But put forth thine hand now, and touch his bone and his flesh, and he will curse thee to thy face.

6 And the LORD said unto Satan, Behold, he is in thine hand; but save his life.

Job 3:1-3

1 After this opened Job his mouth, and cursed his day.

2 And Job spake, and said,

3 Let the day perish wherein I was born, and the night in which it was said, There is a man child conceived.

GOLDEN TEXT: The LORD said unto Satan, Hast thou considered my servant Job, that there is none like him in the earth, a perfect and an upright man, one that feareth God, and escheweth evil? and still he holdeth fast his integrity, although thou movedst me against him, to destroy him without cause.—Job 2:3.

Wisdom for Living
Unit 1: When Human Wisdom Fails
(Lessons 1-4)

Lesson Aims

After studying this lesson, each student should:

1. Tell why Job experienced the extreme trials recorded in Job 1 and 2.

2. Explain how trials today can give a person the opportunity to "vindicate God" or yield to Satan.

3. Commit to faithfulness to God in spite of difficulty.

Lesson Outline

INTRODUCTION
    A. The Test of Wisdom
    B. Lesson Background
  I. JOB: A GREAT AND GODLY MAN (Job 1:1-4)
    A. His Place and Piety (v. 1)
    B. His Posterity (v. 2)
    C. His Prosperity (vv. 3, 4)
      Gain and Godliness
  II. SATAN'S FIRST ASSAULT (Job 1:8-11)
    A. God's Honored Servant (v. 8)
    B. Satan's Slander (vv. 9, 10)
    C. Satan's Challenge (v. 11)
      Saints in Satan's Hands
  III. SATAN'S SECOND ASSAULT (Job 2:3-6)
    A. God's Honored Servant (v. 3)
    B. Satan's Slander (v. 4)
    C. Satan's Challenge (vv. 5, 6)
  IV. JOB'S COMPLAINT (Job 3:1-3)
CONCLUSION
    A. Honest to God
    B. Prayer
    C. Thought to Remember

The visual for Lesson 2 shows Job in the midst of his affliction. It is shown on page 357. (Note: This visual should also be used with Lesson 3.)

Introduction

A. The Test of Wisdom

Pain and suffering are an inevitable part of life. We saw this expressed by Solomon in the Scripture that we studied last week (Ecclesiastes 4:1-3).

How we respond to pain and suffering is one of the true tests of our wisdom. In Philippians 4:6, 7 Paul exhorts us to bathe our cares and tears in prayer: "Be careful [anxious] for nothing; but in every thing by prayer and supplication with thanksgiving let your requests be made known unto God. And the peace of God, which passeth all understanding, shall keep your hearts and minds through Christ Jesus."

But Paul was not someone who merely talked about trusting God. He experienced a "thorn in the flesh" and prayed to God three times for its removal. The answer God gave was not physical relief, but spiritual power: "And he said unto me, My grace is sufficient for thee: for my strength is made perfect in weakness" (2 Corinthians 12:9).

Today we will begin a series of three lessons from a book whose focus is suffering. Probably many of us can relate to the "hard questions" asked by Job, for we too have struggled to understand the place of suffering in the plan of God for ourselves and for others.

B. Lesson Background

It is not easy to assign a specific date for when Job lived. Many incline toward a date prior to the time of Moses, because the lifestyle and longevity of Job are most similar to what is described in Genesis. For example, as the head of the family, Job offers sacrifices, rather than having those sacrifices offered by an official priesthood. (The Israelite priesthood was instituted under the leadership of Moses.) The existence of roving bands of Sabeans and Chaldeans (Job 1:15, 17) also suits a time in the early second millennium before Christ.

Many Bible students draw a distinction between the probable date for the life of Job and the time when this record of his life was composed. Some believe that Moses authored the book of Job, and that it was preserved through the course of Israelite history. Others favor the view that the book was composed during the reign of Solomon. This view is suggested, because Solomon lived during a time that exhibited a keen interest in wisdom and wisdom literature, of which Job is a prime example (both Proverbs 8, written by Solomon, and Job 28 exalt godly wisdom). As it stands, we simply do not have enough information from the text to know who wrote Job. Whoever he was, the contents of the book reveal unmistakable evidence of God's Spirit at work. For example, the subject matter of the introductory chapters had to be revealed to the author, since they contain information that only God could know.

The book of Job begins with a prose introduction (chapters 1 and 2), continues with poetic dialogue and discourses (3:1—42:6), and then concludes with a prose epilogue (42:7-17). Today's printed text includes portions of the introductory material in chapters 1 and 2 and the poetic material found in chapter 3.

I. Job: A Great and Godly Man (Job 1:1-4)

A. His Place and Piety (v. 1)

1. There was a man in the land of Uz, whose name was Job; and that man was perfect and upright, and one that feared God, and eschewed evil.

We do not know exactly where *the land of Uz* was located. Lamentations 4:21 appears to associate it with Edom (south and east of Judah); Genesis 10:23 links the name with Aram, or Syria, in the vicinity of the northern Euphrates River. Since Job is given no tribal identification, one cannot be certain if he was an Israelite. Clearly, however, he was a believer in Israel's God! In addition to the book that bears his name, the only other Biblical references to Job are found in Ezekiel 14:14, 20 and James 5:11.

That Job *feared God, and eschewed evil* indicates that he possessed the kind of godly wisdom described in Job 28:28: "Behold, the fear of the Lord, that is wisdom; and to depart from evil is understanding." His character received the approval of both men (4:3, 4) and God (42:8). He describes himself as someone who was "eyes to the blind, and feet . . . to the lame," and "a father to the poor" (29:15, 16). Job was a force for righteousness in his community.

The reference to Job as *perfect* does not mean that he was sinless. The Bible declares that all have sinned (Romans 3:23). Indeed, Job spoke of the sins of his youth (Job 13:26). Words such as perfect, blameless, and just are used in the Scriptures to describe individuals, who, though not sinless, were still considered faithful to the will of God revealed to them. Clearly the Lord was pleased with Job. He said of Job, "There is none like him in the earth" (1:8; 2:3).

B. His Posterity (v. 2)

2. And there were born unto him seven sons and three daughters.

Job had an ideal family. Both numbers (*seven* and *three*) and their sum (ten) are used in the Scriptures to symbolize completeness.

C. His Prosperity (vv. 3, 4)

3. His substance also was seven thousand sheep, and three thousand camels, and five hundred yoke of oxen, and five hundred she asses, and a very great household; so that this man was the greatest of all the men of the east.

Job's *substance*, or possessions, made him *the greatest of all the men of the east.* His wealth is described in terms of his livestock and his *household*, or number of servants. That Job's holdings included land is clear from Job 1:14 and 31:38. *Oxen* were used to plow that land; *asses* carried the produce of the fields. The substantial numbers of animals that Job possessed obviously required a large staff of servants. All told, Job was a very wealthy man, yet one not governed by "the love of money" (1 Timothy 6:10).

GAIN AND GODLINESS

We are told at the very beginning of the book of Job about Job's blessings and his prosperity. He possessed thousands of sheep and camels, hundreds of oxen and donkeys, and "a large number of servants" (Job 1:3, *New International Version*). When Satan was told about Job's godliness and devotion to righteousness, Satan asked scornfully, "Doth Job fear God for nought?" (1:9).

Very often material benefits result from strict attention to spiritual discipline. Honesty, integrity, good work habits, and concern about the needs of others are character traits of those devoted to doing God's will. These also happen to be qualities that promote successful endeavors in business activities. However, when these are exalted as the *reasons* or *ends* for which God is served, they become snares and delusions. To the truly devout person, material prosperity is not his primary goal.

Christians do not follow Jesus and love God because it leads to prosperity, nor do they do so because they are suffering adversity. They do so *whatever their circumstances*, because they belong to One who has bought them with a great price and loves them with an everlasting love.

—J. G. V. B.

4. And his sons went and feasted in their houses, every one his day; and sent and called for their three sisters to eat and to drink with them.

How to Say It

ARAM. *Air*-um.
BILDAD. *Bill*-dad.
CHALDEANS. Kal-*dee*-unz.
EDOM. *E*-dum.
ELIPHAZ. *El*-ih-faz.
ESCHEWETH. ess-*shoe*-ith.
EUPHRATES. You-*fray*-teez.
SABEANS. Suh-*be*-unz.
ZOPHAR. *Zoe*-far.

Job's children shared in the blessings of their father. The *day* of each of *his sons* could refer to either a birthday or simply a special time of celebration. This verse explains how all the children could be together in one place, and thus become victims of the same tragedy (1:18, 19). Presumably the *three sisters* were still living with Job and his wife.

II. Satan's First Assault (Job 1:8-11)
A. God's Honored Servant (v. 8)

8. And the LORD said unto Satan, Hast thou considered my servant Job, that there is none like him in the earth, a perfect and an upright man, one that feareth God, and escheweth evil?

The Lord speaks about *Job* with delight, repeating what is said about him in verse one. *My servant* is a title of honor that is also used of Abraham (Psalm 105:6, 42), Isaac (Exodus 32:13), Jacob (Deuteronomy 9:27), and Moses (Numbers 12:7, 8).

The name *Satan* means "adversary," a fitting description of his activity in the book of Job, and one consistent with his character throughout Scripture. He is engaged in activities against the best interests of both God and those made in His image. In Job he is described as one of the "sons of God" who come to present themselves before the Lord (Job 1:6). This indicates that Satan is accountable before God and must yield to His authority. Notice that it was the Lord, not Satan, who brought up the case of Job.

B. Satan's Slander (vv. 9, 10)

9. Then Satan answered the LORD, and said, Doth Job fear God for nought?

Satan asked a highly cynical question, similar to the one he raised with Eve in the Garden of Eden (Genesis 3:1). He suggested that Job feared God because of what he could get from Him. Job's worship was an act of convenience, not one of conscience. Worship was a means to an end, and that end was material prosperity and social acceptance. According to Satan, Job's religion was guided by sheer self-interest.

10. Hast not thou made a hedge about him, and about his house, and about all that he hath on every side? thou hast blessed the work of his hands, and his substance is increased in the land.

In verse 9 Satan slighted Job's character. In this verse he slighted the character of God. Satan suggested that God had secured Job's devotion through bribery. God had *made a hedge about* Job—that is, He had insulated Job's life and sheltered him from anything harmful.

C. Satan's Challenge (v. 11)

11. But put forth thine hand now, and touch all that he hath, and he will curse thee to thy face.

Satan then suggested a test to prove his claim that neither Job's piety nor God's goodness was impartial. If all of the material benefits that Job has enjoyed are removed, will he still hold on to God? Could Job love God for Himself, not just for His gifts? Is Job's worship genuine, or is it merely self-motivated? Are his piety and prosperity independent of one another?

The succeeding verses tell how God accepted Satan's proposal, with the restriction that he not harm Job himself (v. 12). Thus Job was being given the task of vindicating God's trust in him. Remember that he will face the coming ordeal because of his innocence, not because of some identifiable sin in his life.

Luke 22:31, 32 records these words of Jesus to Peter: "Simon, Simon, behold, Satan hath desired to have you, that he may sift you as wheat: but I have prayed for thee, that thy faith fail not: and when thou art converted, strengthen thy brethren." Apparently Satan had asked for and obtained the right to test Simon's loyalty toward Jesus. Just as in Job's case, God allowed Satan this liberty, but within bounds. The evil one must always submit to the overruling and permissive authority of the Lord.

Thus Satan received permission to test Job. Likewise, he secured approval to test Simon Peter. Perhaps he has had a similar conversation with God concerning me or concerning you. Keep in mind that Job was never told about the conversations that took place between the Lord and Satan.

SAINTS IN SATAN'S HANDS

Job was serving the Lord as best he knew. He was not swerving from God's way or offending Him in any manner. However, in order to prove the sincerity of his devotion, he was delivered into the hands of Satan. Darkness and disaster came upon this faithful man, and finally his body itself was racked with excruciating pain. But though Job was in Satan's power, he was not on Satan's side.

In order to gain victories over the power and pride of the evil one, there are times when God allows dire and dreadful things to happen to His children. Surely no one has ever been more beautiful in character or more pleasing to God than His Son Jesus. Yet, for the sake of saving lost mankind from the tyranny of sin, Jesus had to experience the scorn, rejection, and agony of the cross.

In the moment of His betrayal and arrest in the garden, Jesus said to His enemies, "Every day I was with you in the temple courts, and you did not lay a hand on me. But this is your hour—when darkness reigns" (Luke 22:53, *New International Version*). Jesus was delivered into the hands of malignant and merciless men—agents of Satan. But, as Paul says, He "spoiled principalities and powers" and "made a show of them openly, triumphing over them" at the cross (Colossians 2:15).

Let us also keep trusting in our Father's plan and purpose, whatever "dark nights" our souls may experience.   —J. G. V. B.

visual for
lessons 2 and 3

III. Satan's Second Assault
(Job 2:3-6)

A. God's Honored Servant (v. 3)

3. And the LORD said unto Satan, Hast thou considered my servant Job, that there is none like him in the earth, a perfect and an upright man, one that feareth God, and escheweth evil? and still he holdeth fast his integrity, although thou movedst me against him, to destroy him without cause.

Job 1:13-19 recounts the disasters that took from Job his wealth and prosperity and his sons and daughters. Would his love for God also disappear? Verse 20 provides the answer: "Then Job arose, and rent his mantle, and shaved his head, and fell down upon the ground, and worshipped."

Satan had lost his first challenge. Job's response demonstrated that man can be godly apart from material gain—indeed, that he can be godly in the midst of severe material loss. Job responded to adversity with adoration, to woe with worship. He passed the first test: "In all this Job sinned not, nor charged God foolishly" (1:22).

But Satan did not give up. He again came before the Lord full of fury and accusation. And once again God commended Job, repeating the verdict of 1:8. He reminded Satan that Job had indeed passed the first test, *and still he holdeth fast his integrity.* God was also aware of the real purpose behind Satan's interest in Job: *to destroy him without cause.*

B. Satan's Slander (v. 4)

4. And Satan answered the LORD, and said, Skin for skin, yea, all that a man hath will he give for his life.

Notice how Satan turned God's earlier request (that Satan not harm Job himself) against Job. Satan again implied that Job was being selfish. The phrase *skin for skin* was probably a common

proverb in that day. Here Satan used it to malign Job's integrity: Job was willing to give up the skins of others (his livestock, his servants, and his children) as long as his own skin was protected. He was not genuinely hurt by all of the previous calamities, because all he cared about was himself.

C. Satan's Challenge (vv. 5, 6)

5. But put forth thine hand now, and touch his bone and his flesh, and he will curse thee to thy face.

Satan dared the Lord to cause injury to Job himself. Loss of his material possessions and his children did not shake Job's piety. But suppose that loss includes Job's own health—what then?

6. And the LORD said unto Satan, Behold, he is in thine hand; but save his life.

Satan was again given permission to do what he pleased, short of killing Job. (The death of Job would prove nothing in this challenge.) Verse 7 tells us, "So went Satan forth from the presence of the Lord, and smote Job with sore boils from the sole of his foot unto his crown."

Apparently, judging from these words and others that Job uses to describe his condition, Job was stricken with a horrible skin disease that covered his entire body. The symptoms and complications that accompanied this affliction included: itching (2:8); sleeplessness (7:4); "worms," or maggots, in his sores (7:5); nightmares (7:14); fits of depression (7:16); difficulty in breathing (9:18); darkened eyelids (16:16); foul breath (19:17); loss of weight (19:20; 33:21); constant pain (30:17); and blackened skin (30:30), which was likely a sign of fever.

However, as was the case with Satan's first assault, his second onslaught brought nothing but renewed submission to God from His servant Job: "What? shall we receive good at the hand of God, and shall we not receive evil? In all this did not Job sin with his lips" (2:10). Job proved Satan wrong again and vindicated God's trust in him.

IV. Job's Complaint
(Job 3:1-3)

1-3. After this opened Job his mouth, and cursed his day. And Job spake, and said, Let the day perish wherein I was born, and the night in which it was said, There is a man child conceived.

According to Job 2:11-13, Job's friends—Eliphaz, Bildad, and Zophar—came to comfort him, but "none spake a word unto him: for they saw that his grief was very great." For seven days the friends kept a silent vigil with their suffering companion.

Then Job broke the silence with a curse uttered against *his day*, presumably the day of his birth. He expressed the vain wish that he had never been *born*. Of course, it was clearly too late to do anything about the day of his birth. But in the midst of severe suffering and adversity, people often fail to think rationally. They simply give voice to the anger and the agony that they feel.

Job was in pain. His words expressed the wretchedness of his present existence. He wanted to root his present life out of the world, carrying with it the moments of his conception and birth. He cursed his birth (vv. 3-10), he longed for death (vv. 11-19), and he deplored life (vv. 20-23). His words include a combination of wishes (beginning with "let") and questions (beginning with "why").

Job's despair is not an isolated voice in Scripture. Perhaps Jeremiah's complaint provides the most striking parallel: "Cursed be the day wherein I was born: let not the day wherein my mother bare me be blessed. Cursed be the man who brought tidings to my father, saying, A man child is born unto thee; making him very glad"

Home Daily Bible Readings

Monday, June 8—The Limits of Righteousness (Ezekiel 14:12-23)
Tuesday, June 9—Believing When Things Go Right (Job 1:1-12)
Wednesday, June 10—Believing When Things Go Wrong (Job 1:13-22)
Thursday, June 11—Blameless But on Trial (Job 2:1-8)
Friday, June 12—Job Didn't Sin in Word (Job 2:9-13)
Saturday, June 13—Cursing the Day of His Birth (Job 3:1-10)
Sunday, June 14—When "Why?" Has No Answer (Job 3:11-26)

(Jeremiah 20:14, 15). The psalms are frequently characterized by statements and questions of doubt and despair, directed toward God (13:1; 60:1; 74:1; 88:14-18; 143:7). Jesus used one of the psalms to express His sense of separation from God at the cross: "My God, my God, why hast thou forsaken me?" (Psalm 22:1; Matthew 27:46).

Throughout all the words reflecting Job's despair, nowhere would he come closer to cursing God to His face than here in chapter 3. By cursing the day of his birth, Job was questioning the wisdom of his Creator. At this point the drama is intense, for Job is close to proving Satan right. However, his trust in God has not been destroyed—only overcast by a cloud of doubt. The epilogue to this book suggests that eventually Job triumphed. He spoke "the thing that is right" (42:7, 8).

It is interesting that Satan is never mentioned in the book of Job after the prologue. This absence suggests that he has retired, defeated, from the challenge. In the epilogue, God pours out an abundance of blessings upon Job, indicating to Satan that He will continue to bless the righteous.

Conclusion
A. Honest to God

Job's struggle of faith is a source of support for every sufferer. He teaches us to speak honestly with God, even in our moments of deepest hopelessness. God prefers honesty to religious clichés that are far removed from reality.

We should also remind ourselves that we possess an advantage Job did not: the perspective of the cross, and the knowledge gained from it that our suffering is "light" compared with the glory that awaits (Romans 8:18; 2 Corinthians 4:17). Paul wrote, "Who shall separate us from the love of Christ? shall tribulation, or distress, or persecution, or famine, or nakedness, or peril, or sword?" (Romans 8:35). For Paul, suffering was an occasion to acknowledge God's presence, not curse His absence.

B. Prayer

Father, thank You for Jesus, who embraced and absorbed the undeserved consequences of all evil. He was truly an innocent sufferer. Your suffering, Father, and Your pain, O Lord Jesus, are the final answers to Job and to all the Jobs of humanity. Amen.

C. Thought to Remember

Remember, in the midst of any suffering, that the Lord always has the last word.

Learning by Doing

This page contains an alternate lesson plan emphasizing learning activities.
Classes desiring such student involvement will find these suggestions helpful.

Learning Goals

After this lesson, students will be able to:

1. Tell why Job experienced the extreme trials recorded in Job 1 and 2.

2. Explain how trials today can give a person the opportunity to "vindicate God" or yield to Satan.

3. Commit to faithfulness to God in spite of difficulty.

Into the Lesson

Ask the class to recall Scripture verses that have been comforting to them in times of trouble. Whether they can quote them, summarize their message, or just give a reference, spend a few minutes listening and reading. Some possible passages include: Philippians 4:6, 7; 2 Corinthians 12:9, 10; Psalm 23; and Romans 8:28, 35, 37-39. If no one has mentioned it, call the students' attention to James 5:10, 11. Use these verses as a transition into this lesson, which introduces us to Job.

Into the Word

After giving a brief explanation of the book of Job (use the material provided in the lesson Introduction), point out that most of the book of Job (3:1—42:6) is poetry in the original Hebrew text. Invite the class to write their own poetry to summarize what they know about Job, starting with Job 1:1-5 (use the exercise found in the student book or provide blank sheets of paper). Have class members work together or individually. After several minutes, invite them to share their compositions.

Now use a watch to time a brief contest. Have each person write as many different facts as possible in one minute about Satan. For example: he is a deceiver; he fell from Heaven (this seems to be the event described in Isaiah 14:12-15); he tempted Eve as a serpent; he tempted Jesus; he is a roaring lion (1 Peter 5:8)—just to name a few facts. Find out who has the longest list (offer a prize if you like), and let that person share his or her points. Ask others to add any other facts that they listed.

Next, divide the class into two or more teams. Ask the class members to read Job 1:6-12; 2:1-6; and 3:1-3, and then have them close their Bibles. Use the following questions (which are also in the student book) to engage in some

friendly competition. Award "points" to the team that can best answer each question.

What words are used to describe Job's character? ("Perfect and upright"; he also "feared God, and eschewed evil," according to Job 1:1.) What is Satan saying about Job's reason for fearing God in Job 1:9, 10? (That Job fears God because of the way that God has blessed him.) Of what does Satan accuse God, according to Job 1:10? (That God has "made a hedge about" Job, so that Job will worship Him.) Why does Satan slander Job and God? (Because that is who Satan is and what he does; it is part of his nature.) How does the second round of accusation and testing differ from the first? (The accusation is that all Job really cares about is himself. Job is then tested through intense personal affliction.) After the first round of hardships, Job worshiped God (Job 1:20-22). How would you characterize Job's reaction to the second round (his personal affliction)? (In 3:1-3, he is bitter and angry.)

Then raise this question for discussion by the class: Why do you think God permits Satan to test Job? (God is honoring Job by allowing Him the opportunity to be faithful; God trusts Job's faith. Point out to the class that Job is never told about the conversation between God and Satan.)

Into Life

Lead the class in taking turns "challenging" one another by asking, "How would you respond if . . . ," completing the question with a hypothetical test or trial, such as "if you lost your house in a fire?" Encourage the person being asked to answer honestly. Probe the response carefully with questions like, "How could you respond in a way that brings honor to God?" or, "What would an ideal response be?" After responding, the person gets to ask someone else, specifying a different test or trial. Keep this exercise going for as long as the responses provide thoughtful and thought-provoking discussion. Emphasize the fact that trials and hardships can give a Christian the opportunity to honor God and to show the difference that our faith can make when life seems unfair.

Remind the class of 1 Peter 5:8: "Your adversary the devil, as a roaring lion, walketh about, seeking whom he may devour." We must "be vigilant," be aware of his schemes, and stay faithful to the Lord in every situation.

Let's Talk It Over

The questions on this page are designed to encourage review of the lesson Scriptures and to promote discussion of the lesson by the class. The answers provided are only discussion starters. Let your class talk it over from there.

1. Handling mirth, pleasure, and work wisely, as discussed in Lesson One, is only a part of wisdom. Wisdom also must be able to handle suffering wisely, for suffering is as surely a part of our lives as these other experiences. How does Job's reaction to suffering demonstrate his wisdom in this area?

When Satan took away Job's goods and his loved ones, Job mourned and grieved, just as we do whenever similar tragedies happen to us. When Satan afflicted Job's body, he voiced his pain just as we do. But Job handled these tragedies wisely in the way he responded toward God. He did not hate God, or reject Him, or curse Him to His face as Satan predicted. He continued to worship God as before, and spoke of Him "the thing that is right" (Job 42:7). Some of us today suffer intense tragedies like Job, losing whole families to accidents, or seeing a life's work destroyed in a moment. Some become so angry at God that they reject Him altogether. We handle these events wisely, if we respond by worshiping God even more intensely.

2. The story of Job raises many hard questions. Why did God point out Job to Satan? Why did He allow Satan to afflict him so severely? How can this be reconciled to God's goodness and justice? We cannot answer completely these kinds of questions, but the account of Job does reveal many truths to us. What can we learn?

God was aware of Job as an individual and loved him. He accepted Job's worship and had regard for his righteous manner of living. God had blessed Job very richly for many years. Though God allowed Satan to oppress Job, He set specific limits. Therefore, Satan is not free to do with us whatever he will. We can be assured that God knows each of us individually and intimately. If we strive to live righteously, He takes note of it. Though He blesses each person differently, all of us can count many ways the Lord has blessed us. Though Satan may attack us, God will not allow him to overwhelm and destroy us. These are important truths to keep in mind whenever we experience any kind of affliction. We must not allow the things we cannot understand to overshadow the things we *do* know and understand.

3. Satan's goal is to separate people from God. To this end he uses various strategies and every tool at his disposal. List and discuss some of the ways Satan tries to drive a wedge between us and God. Which have been most successful on you?

Satan uses three basic strategies in his attacks upon us. One is *temptation*: He tries to lure us away from God by promising greater pleasure than we get from obeying God. He surely had tried this with Job, but failed because Job "eschewed evil" (Job 1:1). A second weapon is *doubt*. Satan tries to get us to doubt God's existence, His power, His goodness, His love, or His care. This is what he tried to do with Job; He tried to shake Job's confidence in God. Today Satan has succeeded in convincing multitudes that God does not even exist, that Jesus is not the divine Son of God, and that the Bible is nothing more than a collection of myths. A third weapon is *pressure*: Satan tries to raise the cost of faithfulness so high that we will give up. He uses everything from ridicule to martyrdom. In Job's case, he used the pressure of taking possessions and family away from Job, and then added intense physical and mental suffering, hoping that Job would "crack" and curse God.

4. For a time, the apostle Paul chafed at his suffering, his "thorn in the flesh" (2 Corinthians 12:7). But when the Lord refused to take away his suffering, Paul learned to accept it and even glory in it. How could he (and how can we learn to) have this attitude?

Paul had to begin by accepting the Lord's will and not resenting it or struggling against it. Once he had this attitude, the Lord was able to use Paul's weakness as a tool to make him strong and to increase his ministry. The wife of a missionary became sick, and the couple prayed for a long time for her healing. Finally they began to pray that the Lord would use her in her sick condition. The couple testify that from that time forward, the woman had frequent visitors until she died. During that time, she had a very powerful ministry from her sickbed to those who came to see her. Perhaps we ought to stop devoting all our prayers to relief from suffering, and begin to pray that God would use us in the midst of our weakness and suffering.

Job's Friends Give Wrong Answers

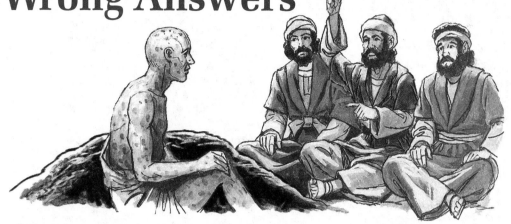

DEVOTIONAL READING: Job 7:1-11.

LESSON SCRIPTURE: Job 2:11; 4:1-7; 8:1-7; 11:1-6; 13:1-4; 23:1-7.

PRINTED TEXT: Job 2:11; 4:1, 6, 7; 8:1-6; 13:1-4.

Job 2:11

11 Now when Job's three friends heard of all this evil that was come upon him, they came every one from his own place; Eliphaz the Temanite, and Bildad the Shuhite, and Zophar the Naamathite: for they had made an appointment together to come to mourn with him, and to comfort him.

Job 4:1, 6, 7

1 Then Eliphaz the Temanite answered and said,

. . . .

6 Is not this thy fear, thy confidence, thy hope, and the uprightness of thy ways?

7 Remember, I pray thee, who ever perished, being innocent? Or where were the righteous cut off?

Job 8:1-6

1 Then answered Bildad the Shuhite, and said,

2 How long wilt thou speak these things? And how long shall the words of thy mouth be like a strong wind?

3 Doth God pervert judgment? Or doth the Almighty pervert justice?

4 If thy children have sinned against him, and he have cast them away for their transgression;

5 If thou wouldest seek unto God betimes, and make thy supplication to the Almighty;

6 If thou wert pure and upright; surely now he would awake for thee, and make the habitation of thy righteousness prosperous.

Job 13:1-4

1 Lo, mine eye hath seen all this, mine ear hath heard and understood it.

2 What ye know, the same do I know also: I am not inferior unto you.

3 Surely I would speak to the Almighty, and I desire to reason with God.

4 But ye are forgers of lies, ye are all physicians of no value.

GOLDEN TEXT: Surely I would speak to the Almighty, and I desire to reason with God.—Job 13:3.

Wisdom for Living
Unit 1: When Human Wisdom Fails
(Lessons 1-4)

Lesson Aims

After completing this lesson, each student should be able to:

1. Summarize the "advice" given by Job's friends.

2. Tell why Job's friends' philosophy of divine retribution alone is not valid for explaining all suffering or all blessing.

3. Seek to minister to a hurting family member or acquaintance with greater understanding.

Lesson Outline

INTRODUCTION
   A. Helping the Hurting
   B. Lesson Background
 I. JOB'S CIRCLE OF COMFORTERS (Job 2:11)
 II. ELIPHAZ SPEAKS (Job 4:1, 6, 7)
   A. Source of Man's Hope (vv. 1, 6)
   B. Security of the Righteous (v. 7)
      Do Bad Things Happen to Good People?
 III. BILDAD SPEAKS (Job 8:1-6)
   A. Job's Words Criticized (vv. 1, 2)
   B. God's Justice Defended (v. 3)
   C. Job's Character Questioned (vv. 4-6)
 IV. JOB'S RESPONSE (Job 13:1-4)
   A. His Self-defense (vv. 1, 2)
   B. His Appeal (v. 3)
   C. His Accusation (v. 4)
      Thoughts on Friends
CONCLUSION
   A. When Silence Is Golden
   B. Prayer
   C. Thought to Remember

Introduction

A. Helping the Hurting

A young ministerial student was doing an internship with a congregation whose preacher had served there for nearly twenty years. Not long after the student began working with the church, he was asked to assist the preacher in arranging a funeral service for one of the members. As they drove to the funeral home to visit the family of the deceased, the student voiced his concerns about how to handle such a delicate situation. "What do I say?" he asked. "I don't want to sit there and seem uninterested."

"Remember," said the preacher, "that no matter what you say at a time like this, the family will probably forget it in a few days. What they won't forget is the fact that you cared enough to be there when they needed help. This is one instance where actions really do speak louder than words."

In another situation, a couple's teenage daughter had been critically injured in an automobile accident. For ten weeks she lay unconscious. She then underwent sixteen surgeries during a nearly six-month stay in the hospital. Consider the parents' thoughts and reflections on what meant the most to them during this agonizing time:

> To us, the presence, not the sage counsel, of visitors was the most meaningful. They chatted with us about various subjects, helping to pass the time. We sensed little value in attempts to "theologize" about the purpose for this trial. We needed encouragement for the immediate moment more than speculation about the past or future. (Roy B. Zuck, "No Cliches, Please," *Kindred Spirit*, Summer 1980, p. 21)

No, words are not that important to someone who is having difficulty expressing his or her sorrow. In fact, words can often confound and confuse rather than comfort. Such was the case with Job's three friends, whose words only poured salt into Job's already agonizing wounds. They provide a classic example of how *not* to help the hurting. Although their initial intentions were quite noble, they soon became more interested in justifying themselves than in ministering to Job. What began as a visit designed to console a friend turned into an angry exchange that generated more heat than light! No wonder Job labeled his friends "miserable comforters" (Job 16:2)!

B. Lesson Background

Last week's lesson introduced us to Job, a man who "was perfect and upright, and one that feared God, and eschewed evil" (Job 1:1). We then saw Satan's twofold assault on Job: first, Job's livestock and family were snatched from him through a series of disasters; and second, he himself was stricken with "sore boils from the sole of his foot unto his crown" (2:7). (For a list of the complications that accompanied Job's affliction, see last week's lesson commentary under Job 2:6.) The man who was renowned as "the greatest of all the men of the east" (1:3) was now relegated to a spot "among the ashes," with only a piece of pottery to scrape his boils (2:8). Despite the magnitude of his loss, Job remained true to his God: "In all this did not Job sin with his lips" (2:10).

Today's lesson introduces us to Job's three friends, who came to him with the intent of comforting him. The printed text highlights a portion of the speeches of two of them, and records their attempts to explain: (1) why Job was suffering, and (2) what he needed to do to restore his lost dignity. The last portion of the printed text includes an excerpt from one of Job's responses to his friends' advice.

I. Job's Circle of Comforters
(Job 2:11)

11. Now when Job's three friends heard of all this evil that was come upon him, they came every one from his own place; Eliphaz the Temanite, and Bildad the Shuhite, and Zophar the Naamathite: for they had made an appointment together to come to mourn with him, and to comfort him.

Eliphaz was a name associated with the Edomites (Genesis 36:9, 10). Teman was the name of one of his sons (v. 11), and was also used in association with Edom (Jeremiah 49:7; Ezekiel 25:13; Amos 1:11, 12; Obadiah 8, 9). The Shuah mentioned in Genesis 25:2 may relate to the tribe or people of *Bildad*. The name *Zophar* is not known outside Job, nor is a land or tribe called Naamath. In short, the homes of *Job's three friends* cannot be identified with any certainty. The possible connection with Edom reflects the reputation of Edom as a place renowned for its wisdom (Jeremiah 49:7; Obadiah 8).

These friends felt it would be helpful to come *together* on behalf of Job. Their original purpose in visiting Job was wholly supportive—"to mourn with him, and to comfort him" (2:11). The Scripture notes that when they were still some distance from the ashes where he sat (v. 8), they "knew him not" (v. 12), or "could hardly recognize him" (*New International Version*), so severe were the effects of his affliction. For seven days the friends remained silent, "for they saw that his grief was very great" (v. 13). They did not speak until after Job had "cursed his day" (3:1) and voiced his frustration.

II. Eliphaz Speaks
(Job 4:1, 6, 7)

A. Source of Man's Hope (vv. 1, 6)

1. Then Eliphaz the Temanite answered and said.

Eliphaz and Bildad address Job on three different occasions; Zophar speaks only twice. The words of Eliphaz are found in chapters 4, 5, 15, and 22; Bildad's in chapters 8, 18, and 25; and Zophar's in chapters 11 and 20. Job's response

to these eight speeches includes chapters 6, 7, 9, 10, 12-14, 16, 17, 19, 21, 23, 24, and 26-31. A fourth comforter, Elihu, who was younger than the other three (32:4), speaks in chapters 32-37. No rebuttal of his words is recorded.

Eliphaz was the first of the friends to speak, perhaps because he was the oldest.

6. Is not this thy fear, thy confidence, thy hope, and the uprightness of thy ways?

Eliphaz suggests that Job's life of godliness gives him resources for facing the present crisis. Job's *fear* (of God) and his godly conduct (*the uprightness of thy ways*) should provide him with a basis for *confidence* and *hope*. Eliphaz is suggesting that God helps those who are good and hinders the wicked.

B. Security of the Righteous (v. 7)

7. Remember, I pray thee, who ever perished, being innocent? Or where were the righteous cut off?

Here Eliphaz implies that Job, as a *righteous* man, can expect a speedy recovery, since the righteous will not die (be *cut off*) prematurely. The Lord will deliver righteous Job from his troubles.

Eliphaz's words need to be studied carefully. They insinuate that a person's premature death is proof of his wickedness. Such an assumption was hardly comforting to Job, for it attributed the death of his seven sons and three daughters to some sinfulness of theirs. This insinuation is clearly mistaken. Having read the prologue to the book, we know the real reason behind Job's suffering. (Remember that neither Job nor his friends are ever told about the discussions between God and Satan.)

Of course, Eliphaz is also hinting at some manner of sinfulness in Job's life. The three friends, who held firmly to the tenets of traditional wisdom, believed that all suffering is punishment for sin. Since Job is presently suffering so greatly, he must be guilty of some heinous sin. But the prologue to the book indicates that Job is suffering because of his innocence. In fact, Job repeatedly maintains his innocence (6:10, 24; 10:7; 13:18; 16:17; 23:11, 12; 27:6). It is the friends who are clearly mistaken. They have overestimated their grasp of the situation; they see only a small part of it, and what they see is distorted through their preconceptions about God and about suffering.

The Scriptures affirm that God will prosper the righteous and punish the wicked. Paul writes, "Tribulation and anguish, upon every soul of man that doeth evil; of the Jew first, and also of the Gentile; but glory, honor, and peace, to every man that worketh good; to the Jew first,

How to Say It

BILDAD. *Bill*-dad.
EDOMITES. *E*-dum-ites.
ELIHU. Ih-*lye*-hew.
ELIPHAZ. *El*-ih-faz.
NAAMATH. *Nay*-uh-muth.
NAAMATHITE. *Nay*-uh-muth-ite.
SHUAH. *Shoe*-uh.
SHUHITE. *Shoe*-hite.
TEMAN. *Tee*-mun.
TEMANITE. *Tee*-mun-ite.
ZOPHAR. *Zoe*-far.

and also to the Gentile" (Romans 2:9, 10). This principle must not be used, however, to jump to conclusions regarding a person's character, based upon his surroundings at a given moment. We must not follow the lead of Job's friends and conclude that those who prosper must be righteous while those who suffer must be wicked. The world is more complex than that. Experience teaches us that the wicked may prosper in this world, while the righteous may suffer (see Psalm 73 for the same observation).

God may have other purposes in a person's suffering that are not immediately apparent. Jesus taught His disciples, in the case of the man born blind, that someone innocent had suffered in order to accomplish God's higher purpose (John 9:3). Certainly the crucifixion of Jesus also bears witness to this truth.

Also noteworthy is the apostle Paul's testimony, recorded in 2 Corinthians 12. After requesting three times that God remove his "thorn in the flesh," Paul learned that God's "no" involved a positive purpose: to make him a more compelling and convincing witness to the power of Christ (v. 9). The apostle came to view his sufferings and persecutions from Heaven's vantage point: "Therefore I take pleasure in infirmities, in reproaches, in necessities, in persecutions, in distresses for Christ's sake: for when I am weak, then I am strong" (v. 10).

Even though the words of Job's friends often represent the truth to some degree, as is evident from the fact that the apostle Paul approvingly quotes Eliphaz (Job 5:13) in 1 Corinthians 3:19 (compare also Job 5:17 with Hebrews 12:5), in the epilogue God charges the three men with folly and slander. "My wrath is kindled against thee [Eliphaz], and against thy two friends: for ye have not spoken of me the thing that is right, as my servant Job hath. Therefore take unto you now seven bullocks and seven rams, and go to my servant Job, and offer up for yourselves a burnt offering; and my servant Job shall pray for you: for him will I accept: lest I deal with you after your folly" (42:7, 8).

Job's friends were claiming to speak with authority in matters that were clearly beyond the scope of their knowledge. God rebuked their arrogance, proving that He values the integrity of the persevering protester—namely Job—and abhors pious hypocrites who would heap accusations on a tormented soul to uphold their theological position.

DO BAD THINGS HAPPEN TO GOOD PEOPLE?

Eliphaz the Temanite asked Job, "Who ever perished, being innocent? Or where were the righteous cut off?" (Job 4:7). This query reveals a view of righteous living that is popular in many circles today. Large numbers of people assert that goodness and steadfast conformity to spiritual principles lead to prosperity, plenty, and personal enhancement. They maintain that service to others—honesty, helpfulness, kindness, and trustworthiness—will secure success in many of our ventures in life.

Of course, there is an element of truth in this. That material abundance is a result of dedication to God is a prominent Old Testament theme. For instance, in Deuteronomy 28:1-14 nearly all of the blessings promised to the children of Israel if they faithfully served and obeyed God are material.

However, this is only a part of the truth. We cannot forget that Jesus our Lord, who was a perfect man—beautiful in goodness, spotless in character, and One who "went about doing good" —was rejected, betrayed, despised, mocked, tortured, and finally nailed on a cross to die. He warned His followers, "If they have persecuted me, they will also persecute you" (John 15:20). Paul wrote, "All that will live godly in Christ Jesus shall suffer persecution" (2 Timothy 3:12).

Eliphaz may not have heard of "bad things" happening to anyone righteous, but the Scriptures, along with our own experiences as followers of Jesus, tell us of many instances. For such individuals, suffering did not negate or diminish their testimony for God; it was part of their testimony to the sustaining presence and power of Christ.   —J. G. V. B.

III. Bildad Speaks
(Job 8:1-6)

A. Job's Words Criticized (vv. 1, 2)

1, 2. Then answered Bildad the Shuhite, and said, How long wilt thou speak these things? And how long shall the words of thy mouth be like a strong wind?

In suggesting that Job's words are a *strong wind*, *Bildad* recognizes them as tempestuous, threatening to assault cherished beliefs. Like Eliphaz, Bildad also believes that the doctrine of retribution (God prospers the righteous and punishes the wicked) provides the primary explanation of human circumstances. Job's defense of his innocence challenged this.

B. God's Justice Defended (v. 3)

3. Doth God pervert judgment? Or doth the Almighty pervert justice?

According to the traditional wisdom espoused by Job's friends, the very foundation of the moral order is the retribution principle. Any exception to this principle amounts to injustice. Job's maintaining of his innocence, therefore, implicitly charges God with injustice. Bildad realizes that his theology is being questioned and undermined; he has forgotten that he and his friends originally came to Job to support him, not their theology.

Later, Elihu follows the same line of thought: "Therefore hearken unto me, ye men of understanding: far be it from God, that he should do wickedness; and from the Almighty, that he should commit iniquity. For the work of a man shall he render unto him, and cause every man to find according to his ways. Yea, surely God will not do wickedly, neither will the Almighty pervert judgment" (Job 34:10-12).

C. Job's Character Questioned (vv. 4-6)

4. If thy children have sinned against him, and he have cast them away for their transgression.

As did Eliphaz, Bildad suggests that if there is premature death, as there was in the case of Job's *children*, then there must be prior *transgression*. Again, this assumption is mistaken. According to the prologue (1:5), Job sought to maintain the righteous standing of his children by offering sacrifices on their behalf. It was unspeakably cruel of Bildad to thus revive the memory of Job's children, without a single expression of sympathy or regret.

5, 6. If thou wouldest seek unto God betimes, and make thy supplication to the Almighty; If thou wert pure and upright; surely now he would awake for thee, and make the habitation of thy righteousness prosperous.

Since Job is still alive, there is no evidence that he has sinned unquestionably against God. Bildad holds out hope for Job if two conditions are met: he must make *supplication to the Almighty* and must live a *pure and upright* life. If these conditions are met, then, according to Bildad's rigid doctrine of retribution, God will respond with signs of favor and make Job *prosperous* as he was before.

Bildad comes across as aloof and superior. He treats Job with heartless indifference. That he did not accept the possibility that Job was innocent made him unwilling to listen and thus "miserable" as a counselor (Job 16:2). Good counselors must be willing to listen, must genuinely care for those who need help, and must bear in mind that they may not fully understand all the details of the case at hand.

IV. Job's Response
(Job 13:1-4)

A. His Self-defense (vv. 1, 2)

1, 2. Lo, mine eye hath seen all this, mine ear hath heard and understood it. What ye know, the same do I know also: I am not inferior unto you.

Clearly irritated at Zophar's remarks about his being "full of talk" (11:2) and one of the "vain men" (11:11), Job claims to be his friends' intellectual equal (12:3). He concedes that they share some common theological ground. But do the truths of conventional wisdom apply in this case?

B. His Appeal (v. 3)

3. Surely I would speak to the Almighty, and I desire to reason with God.

Throughout Job's rebuttals of his friends' accusations, he longs to present his case before *God*. "I will say unto God, Do not condemn me; show me wherefore thou contendest with me" (10:2). "Surely I would speak to the Almighty, and I desire to reason with God" (13:3). "Oh that one might plead for a man with God, as a man pleadeth for his neighbor!" (16:21). "Oh that I knew where I might find him! That I might come even to his seat! I would order my cause before him, and fill my mouth with arguments" (23:3, 4). "Oh that one would hear me! Behold, my desire is, that the Almighty would answer me, and that mine adversary had written a book" (31:35).

What Job wants is an audience with God. He wants desperately to settle this whole matter through rational discussion. His friends have failed to provide a suitable explanation for his suffering. He believes that if he can state his case personally and directly to God, he will be vindicated.

Job's protests may surprise the reader who knows only the "patience" of Job. But the perplexed Job is just as important to study as the patient Job. Job was an intense man of spiritual passion, who wrestled with the mystery of the divine will. At times Job wished that God would leave him alone (7:17-21; 10:20), and even perceived God to be his enemy (10:8, 16, 17; 16:9; 19:6-12). At other times he yearned for God to communicate with him (see the Scriptures cited in the first paragraph of this section). This turmoil is evidence of Job's struggle to understand God's will and purpose for him in the midst of his pain.

C. His Accusation (v. 4)

4. But ye are forgers of lies, ye are all physicians of no value.

Job suggests that his friends' counsel has been incompetent and fraudulent. They are *physicians of no value*—spiritual "quacks." They have diagnosed an imaginary illness—some hidden, but heinous crime; and they have prescribed an irrelevant cure—repentance (5:8; 8:5; 11:13, 14; 22:21-25). Job has reasoned, "Why should I repent? I am not guilty of some identifiable sin. I will not confess to unknown or imaginary sins to appease an angry deity. I will not treat my God as one would treat a pagan god."

THOUGHTS ON FRIENDS

The longest section of the book of Job consists of the speeches of Job's friends and his responses to them. Since friends are so prominent in Job, perhaps some observations about them are in order.

Leonardo da Vinci in his *Notebooks* remarked, "Reprove a friend in secret, but praise him before others." However, Job's friends reproved him openly because they were sure he had committed some evil act or acts, which in turn led to his afflictions.

Writing in 1732, Thomas Fuller made two insightful observations about friends: "If you have one true friend, you have more than your share"; and, "There is no better looking glass than an old friend." Job's friends seem to have been sincere in their desire to help him. They "made an appointment together to come to mourn with him, and to comfort him" (Job 2:11). However, their "comfort" hurt him deeply, because they felt that he must have done some great wrong for which God was punishing him.

It is significant that Jesus called His disciples "friends" in a well-known passage found in John 15:13-15. Jesus loved us enough to die for us. Our responsibility is to love Him enough to live for Him. Job's friends were appalled that so much disaster had befallen him. Often those to whom the early Christians spoke could not understand how a righteous person could have suffered as Jesus did. However, Jesus' friends were more successful in explaining the reason for His suffering than were Job's friends in explaining his. When our suffering does not appear to make sense, let us fix our eyes on Jesus and look to Him for strength. —J. G. V. B.

Conclusion

A. When Silence Is Golden

Job concludes that the words of his friends would have been better left unspoken: "Oh that ye would altogether hold your peace! And it should be your wisdom" (13:5). Proverbs 17:28 suggests that at times there is more wisdom in silence than in speech: "Even a fool, when he holdeth his peace, is counted wise: and he that shutteth his lips is esteemed a man of understanding."

As noted earlier, Eliphaz, Bildad, and Zophar came to Job at first with the best of intentions. Eventually, however, they confused comforting Job with imposing on him their understanding of his circumstances. The truly wise friend knows that just being present is often enough to comfort someone in trouble. Little needs to be said. If any counsel is offered, it must be compassionate to be healing.

B. Prayer

Father, forgive us when we overestimate our grasp of truth, misapply the truth we know, and close our minds to any facts that contradict what we assume. Forgive us when our counsel is neither compassionate nor truthful. In our trials, make known to us Your strength and grace. May You be our rock and refuge. Amen.

C. Thought to Remember

Hurting people do not need our words as much as they need *us*.

Home Daily Bible Readings

Monday, June 15—Eliphaz: Job Innocent (Job 4:1-11)
Tuesday, June 16—Job: Anguish in Spirit (Job 7:1-11)
Wednesday, June 17—Bildad: God Is Just (Job 8:1-10)
Thursday, June 18—Zophar: God Knows More Than You (Job 11:1-12)
Friday, June 19—Job: Laughingstock to My Friends (Job 12:1-12)
Saturday, June 20—God Even Destroys Great Nations (Job 12:13-25)
Sunday, June 21—Friends Repeat Proverbs of Ashes (Job 13:1-12)

Learning by Doing

This page contains an alternate lesson plan emphasizing learning activities.
Classes desiring such student involvement will find these suggestions helpful.

Learning Goals

After the completion of this lesson, students should be able to:

1. Summarize the "advice" given by Job's friends.

2. Tell why Job's friends' philosophy of divine retribution alone is not valid for explaining all suffering or all blessing.

3. Seek to minister to a hurting family member or acquaintance with greater understanding.

Into the Lesson

Begin by asking, "What is the last thing you want to hear your dentist say?" Encourage both serious answers ("I think we have some problems") and humorous ones ("Wow, now I can afford that trip to Hawaii!" or, "Oops!"). Continue with the same basic question, but refer to other professions, such as *your plumber, your counselor, your mechanic*, etc. Make the transition to the lesson by explaining that Job had to listen to "friends" whose words were some of the last things he wanted (and needed) to hear.

Into the Word

Approach the Bible study as if today's passages from Job were the script for a play. Have the class divide into three groups. Assign the first group Job 4:1, 6, 7 as the script for Eliphaz. The second group takes Job 8:1-6 as Bildad's script. The third group uses Job 13:1-4 as Job's script. Make sure the students look at the context of each passage. Each group is to select one person as their "actor," and then coach that person as to how to deliver his or her lines as written. Invite the three actors to the front and begin by reading Job 2:11 as the introduction. The three should then act out the "play" by delivering their lines with some sense of the drama that must have been involved.

Next, ask each group to rewrite its script, using some other Bible versions (provide copies of the *New International Version, New American Standard Bible*, and other versions). After five to ten minutes, invite the three actors back to the front, and "take two" using the newly rewritten scripts.

Point out to the class that Job's friends believed in a philosophy of divine retribution: Good things happen to good people, and bad things happen to bad people. When bad things

happen to a person, then that person must have sinned to deserve such circumstances. See the comments under Job 4:7 for further discussion of the "retribution principle."

Into Life

Ask for examples of "good" people who have experienced "good" consequences. Then ask for several examples of "evil" people who have experienced "bad" consequences. Point out that in a just world a righteous person would receive only blessings, and an evil person would always suffer. Job's friends believed this.

Next, have someone read 1 Peter 3:13-17 and 4:12, 13. Note that becoming a Christian does not imply a trouble-free life. On the contrary, Peter tells believers not to be surprised if they suffer. Ask the class to cite other references that: (1) make it clear that Christians can expect suffering and trials in this life, or (2) state that evil people may experience prosperity (such as Psalm 37:1-3; 73:3-5; Matthew 5:10-12, 44, 45; Romans 8:18, to name a few). Write each reference on a chalkboard or poster board as it is read (this exercise is also in the student book).

Lead a discussion regarding why Job's friends' philosophy of divine retribution is not valid. Ask the class to give examples from real life of righteous people who suffer and evil people who prosper. Point out that Job's friends thought they possessed understanding of his situation, but they did not. As a result, they gave Job bad advice.

Now ask the class to divide into three or more small groups. Each group is to write out a scenario in which a person is suffering or undergoing some type of trial. These are to be as realistic as possible. Each scenario should be passed to another group. Each group should then address the question, "What would you say to the person in the situation that you have read about?" After each group develops a statement of its response, have a spokesperson share its "advice." (This activity is also in the student book.)

In closing, encourage each class member to think of a friend or relative who is in the midst of a difficult time. Ask, "What can you do or say to that person in the name of Christ?" In pairs or as a class, have class members share their responses. End with a time of prayer for their ministry to others who are hurting.

Let's Talk It Over

The questions on this page are designed to encourage review of the lesson Scriptures and to promote discussion of the lesson by the class. The answers provided are only discussion starters. Let your class talk it over from there.

1. This lesson deals with the problem of suffering, or, more exactly, with the problem of explaining suffering while claiming to have faith in God. To help us see the heart of the lesson, state the problem clearly. Identify the premises and the apparent contradiction that make this problem so difficult.

We believe that God is the all-powerful, loving, good Creator of the world and of mankind. We define pain and suffering as being undesirable—a defect in the design or order of the world because of the presence of sin. The apparent contradiction is that a good, loving, powerful God surely would not let an evil such as suffering exist in His world. Suffering, however, is a necessary part of His plan and His will. Remember that God created the world perfect and free of any suffering. He created man with the freedom of choice to obey or to disobey. When man introduced sin into the world, he opened the door to all the suffering that we experience. Also, keep in mind that God sent His Son to suffer the punishment of sin for us that we could be saved, and could someday live with Him in a place perfect and free of any suffering—Heaven.

2. God needs no vindication, but as a matter of fact God is irrefutably vindicated against all accusations of unfairness, cold-heartedness, and the like by the ministry of Jesus Christ. Explain why the atoning sacrifice of the Lord should silence all critics and calm every fear.

It would be one thing if God sat on His throne safe in Heaven, immune from all suffering while He watched us in agony on earth. Some might feel justified in accusing Him of not caring. But that is not the case. For one thing, we must understand that our suffering causes Him grief. We understand this, because we hurt when someone we love hurts. God was so moved by our suffering that He sent His Son to suffer in our place. Do we grieve when innocent children are abused by wicked men? So did God grieve when His innocent Son was abused by wicked men. Yet He knew this suffering was necessary in order to deliver us from eternal suffering. If God Himself and the Lord Jesus Christ are willing to suffer for us, then we ought not complain when God asks us to suffer.

3. Job's friends believed that God watches over the world to protect and bless the righteous while punishing the wicked. This is why Bildad said that Job or his children must have committed some great sin to have been punished so severely (Job 8:4). In what way or to what extent is this true?

It is true that God is the ultimate guarantor of the moral order of the universe. He will punish His enemies and reward those who love, obey, and worship Him. But He does not settle all accounts in this lifetime. Jesus spoke of the suffering endured by God's prophets, who surely were righteous (Matthew 23:29-36). He said that we should not think that those who die tragically are any worse sinners than others (Luke 13:1-5). The story of the rich man and Lazarus (found in Luke 16:19-31) shows us that God administers punishment and reward after we die. We learn from such Scriptures as these that there is no necessary correlation between our sinfulness or righteousness and the amount of suffering and prosperity that we experience.

4. Sometimes, in times of trial, our consciences condemn us, and we begin to wonder if God is punishing us because of our sins. We know all too well that none of us is perfect. Is this a proper reaction? How can we have assurance of God's acceptance even in times of suffering?

It may be that God is seeking to purify us from some specific sin that is keeping us from real fellowship with Him. Read about the process and purpose of His discipline in Hebrews 12:3-11. But we should take heart. In such a case, God is not seeking to destroy us but to perfect us. Therefore, in a time of testing, it is good to examine our hearts and lives to see if we have allowed some sin to overtake us. If so, God has promised to cleanse us and forgive us if we confess our sin to Him (1 John 1:8-10). However, sin may not be the cause of our suffering at all. We may suffer for righteousness' sake (1 Peter 3:14), or we may suffer for some reason that we do not understand at all. Nonetheless, as long as we are God's children, we can be assured of His love and care for us, even in the most difficult times. He has promised us this, and He is faithful. Read Romans 8:31-39.

God's Questions and Job's Response

June 28
Lesson 4

Jun
28

DEVOTIONAL READING: Job 28:20-28.

LESSON SCRIPTURE: Job 38:1-7; 42:1-6, 10.

PRINTED TEXT: Job 38:1-7; 42:1-6, 10.

Job 38:1-7

1 Then the LORD answered Job out of the whirlwind, and said,

2 Who is this that darkeneth counsel by words without knowledge?

3 Gird up now thy loins like a man; for I will demand of thee, and answer thou me.

4 Where wast thou when I laid the foundations of the earth? Declare, if thou hast understanding.

5 Who hath laid the measures thereof, if thou knowest? Or who hath stretched the line upon it?

6 Whereupon are the foundations thereof fastened? Or who laid the corner stone thereof;

7 When the morning stars sang together, and all the sons of God shouted for joy?

Job 42:1-6, 10

1 Then Job answered the LORD, and said,

2 I know that thou canst do every thing, and that no thought can be withholden from thee.

3 Who is he that hideth counsel without knowledge? Therefore have I uttered that I understood not; things too wonderful for me, which I knew not.

4 Hear, I beseech thee, and I will speak: I will demand of thee, and declare thou unto me.

5 I have heard of thee by the hearing of the ear; but now mine eye seeth thee:

6 Wherefore I abhor myself, and repent in dust and ashes.

. . . .

10 And the LORD turned the captivity of Job, when he prayed for his friends: also the LORD gave Job twice as much as he had before.

GOLDEN TEXT: Then Job answered the LORD, and said, I know that thou canst do every thing, and that no thought can be withholden from thee.—Job 42:1, 2.

Lesson Aims

After studying this lesson, each student should:

1. Summarize the message behind the series of questions God asked of Job, and tell how Job responded.

2. Tell how faith in God allows us to see the "big picture," even in the midst of our suffering.

3. Cite an example of someone in need of the reassurance of God's presence, and seek to give that reassurance.

Lesson Outline

INTRODUCTION
    A. Who Is Wise?
    B. Lesson Background
  I. GOD ANSWERS JOB (Job 38:1-7)
    A. Challenge to Job (vv. 1-3)
      A Voice Out of the Storm
    B. Hard Questions (vv. 4-7)
      Singing Stars
 II. JOB CONFESSES TO GOD (Job 42:1-6)
    A. God Is Superior (vv. 1, 2)
    B. "I Did Not Understand" (vv. 3-6)
      Things Too Wonderful
III. GOD RESTORES JOB (Job 42:10)
CONCLUSION
    A. The Last Word
    B. Prayer
    C. Thought to Remember

The visual for Lesson 4 in the visuals packet encourages us to provide a ministry of comfort to those who hurt. It is shown on page 373.

Introduction

A. Who Is Wise?

One of the critical issues at the heart of the book of Job is, "Who is wise?" Who has the correct insight into Job's distress? Job's friends believed that their perspective has the support of years of tradition and experience. Eliphaz declares, "With us are both the grayheaded and very aged men, much elder than thy father" (Job 15:10). Job admits that experience brings wisdom (12:12); however, he is not impressed with the "wisdom" being propounded by his friends.

He scolds his "comforters": "If only you would be altogether silent! For you, that would be wisdom" (Job 13:5, *New International Version*). Later he tells them, "I cannot find one wise man among you" (17:10).

As we noted in last week's lesson, Job's three friends adhered to a rigid, mechanical understanding of the retribution principle. God prospers the righteous, and He punishes the wicked. Since this is true, then if Job is suffering, he must be guilty of some sin. Obviously Job protests this line of reasoning. In chapter 21 he presents evidence that conflicts with the retribution principle. He is aware of many cases where the wicked have prospered and have said to God, "Depart from us; for we desire not the knowledge of thy ways" (v. 14). He concludes this speech with these words: "How then comfort ye me in vain, seeing in your answers there remaineth falsehood?" (v. 34). Later, Elihu grew impatient with the wisdom of the three friends "because they had found no answer" (32:3). He too claimed to be able to impart wisdom to them (33:33), but failed.

So, who is wise? The book of Job proclaims the answer that echoes throughout Scripture: God alone is the source of wisdom. This is especially clear in Job 28, which contains a stirring poem on divine wisdom. Consider verses 12-14, 23, 24: "But where shall wisdom be found? And where is the place of understanding? Man knoweth not the price thereof; neither is it found in the land of the living. The depth saith, It is not in me: and the sea saith, It is not with me. . . . God understandeth the way thereof, and he knoweth the place thereof. For he looketh to the ends of the earth, and seeth under the whole heaven."

In today's lesson, we will see how Job came to understand the proper response to God's wisdom: humility and submission. Since God alone is the source of ultimate wisdom, the wisdom of the world is therefore limited and inadequate. This is emphasized in the New Testament as well. Paul notes the failure of "the wisdom of this world" to know God (1 Corinthians 1:20, 21). Let us devote ourselves to the superior wisdom of God as revealed in His Word, and reject all counterfeits.

B. Lesson Background

Last week's lesson included excerpts from some of the dialogue between Job and his friends. In the book of Job, the speeches of the three friends are presented in three cycles. Each man speaks three times, except for Zophar, who speaks only twice. The second cycle of speeches is shorter than the first (except for Zophar's), and the third cycle is shorter yet (noticeably so with Bildad). The following chart shows the length (in verses) of each speech:

Eliphaz	Bildad	Zophar	Total
48	22	20	90
35	21	29	85
30	6	—	36

In short, the friends ran out of arguments against Job. Their wisdom was powerless to either convince or to console. At the same time, Job could not convince his friends of his innocence. The exchanges between Job and his friends had reached a stalemate. Though the younger Elihu claimed to be able to shed some light on the controversy, he could not. Human wisdom had reached its limits (as indeed it must). It was time for God to speak.

I. God Answers Job
(Job 38:1-7)

A. Challenge to Job (vv. 1-3)

1. Then the LORD answered Job out of the whirlwind, and said.

In Job's final speech (just before Elihu steps forward), he concludes with these words: "Oh that one would hear me! Behold, my desire is, that the Almighty would answer me, and that mine adversary had written a book" (31:35). This was not the first time that Job had expressed his desire for an audience with God (see 10:2; 13:3; 16:21; 23:3, 4; 31:35). Chapters 38-41 record God's response to Job's earnest request. God speaks to Job twice: the first time is recorded in 38:1—40:2; the second, in 40:6—41:34. Job's two responses are found in 40:3-5 and 42:1-6.

According to Job 1:19, a "great wind" killed Job's children. Now God spoke from a *whirlwind*. The Old Testament commonly associates the appearance of God with a mighty storm, accompanied by thunder, lightning, clouds, and wind (Psalms 18:7-15; 29:3; Nahum 1:3; Zechariah 9:14).

A VOICE OUT OF THE STORM

The most powerful and compelling words that Job heard in the midst of his pain and perplexity were the ones that came to him "out of the whirlwind." It was in those words that the Lord's voice was discerned. Job's friends sat and reasoned with him, but to little avail. It was amid the tumult of the elements of nature that Job finally came to an awareness of the attitude he needed to have.

Every year hurricanes blow in from the Atlantic Ocean and lash the southern sections of

How to Say It

BILDAD. *Bill*-dad.
ELIHU. Ih-*lye*-hew.
ELIPHAZ. *El*-ih-faz.
ZOPHAR. *Zoe*-far.

the United States with furious onslaughts of wind and water. Buildings are destroyed, beaches are eroded, highways are flooded, and lives are interrupted.

Is it possible that God speaks to us in these storms as He once spoke to Job? Storms teach us that man is not all-powerful. There are elements he cannot control. Storms teach us how much we need each other. We share warnings, escape routes, and shelters. We realize how much more valuable than property or possessions are our families and our fellow human beings. We learn we can rise up and rebuild, even when many of the necessities and conveniences of life are destroyed.

Through storms we find the meaning of fellowship, the value there is in quiet days, and the need we have for One in whom we can trust when situations are desperate. As skies darken and great winds blow, we often hear the voice of God in the storm. —J. G. V. B.

2. Who is this that darkeneth counsel by words without knowledge?

Job is "in the dark" because he lacks *counsel* and *knowledge*. God will now provide these. Earlier Job had acknowledged, "He reveals the deep things of darkness and brings deep shadows into the light" (Job 12:22, *New International Version*).

3. Gird up now thy loins like a man; for I will demand of thee, and answer thou me.

In ancient times, whenever a man was engaged in strenuous activity such as running or working, he would gather up his robe and tuck it into a sash or belt (Exodus 12:11; 1 Kings 18:46). The command to *gird up now thy loins* became a figure of speech associated with preparing oneself for a difficult task. Job was being commanded to prepare, not for anything physically demanding, but for an experience that would challenge him spiritually and intellectually.

B. Hard Questions (vv. 4-7)

4-6. Where wast thou when I laid the foundations of the earth? Declare, if thou hast understanding. Who hath laid the measures thereof, if thou knowest? Or who hath stretched the line

upon it? Whereupon are the foundations thereof fastened? Or who laid the corner stone thereof?

We should first note that, whereas Job had demanded answers from God, God addresses Job with a series of questions. This first series asked Job to consider the *foundations of the earth*. Who is responsible for all of this? How did it come about? The language used is that of a builder, who conducts all the necessary planning and measuring before putting the *corner stone* in place. Similar terminology is used in Psalm 24:1, 2 and Isaiah 40:12-14.

7. When the morning stars sang together, and all the sons of God shouted for joy?

Biblical poetry often describes the elements of nature as joining in songs of praise to their Creator (Psalms 65:13; 96:12, 13; 98:8, 9; Isaiah 44:23; 55:12). The *sons of God* most likely describes the angels, and is thus rendered in the *New International Version*. Stars and angels are mentioned together in Psalm 148:2, 3: "Praise ye him, all his angels: praise ye him, all his hosts. Praise ye him, sun and moon: praise him, all ye stars of light." God's creation was not only "very good" in His eyes (Genesis 1:31); it also elicited the joyous praise of both stars and angels. They were present to witness the Master Designer's handiwork. But Job had no such personal experience of the creation. His ignorance of the earth's origin disqualified him from governing the earth, or even suggesting that God govern it differently.

In the succeeding verses, God elaborates on the intricacy and complexity of His creation. Job is challenged to consider the oceans (vv. 8-11); the dawn (vv. 12-15); the realm of the dead (vv. 16-18); the source of light and darkness (vv. 19-21); snow, storms, rain, and ice (vv. 22-30); stars (vv. 31-33); clouds and lightning (vv. 34-38); and an impressive array of beasts and birds (38:39—39:30). Following Job's initial response to God's questions (40:3-5), the Lord then calls Job's attention to the "behemoth" (40:15-24) and the "leviathan" (41:1-34). The former is believed by some to describe either an elephant or a hippopotamus; the latter appears to refer to the crocodile. Job becomes overwhelmed with a sense of wonder and reverence at the beauty and order of God's world. At the same time, he begins to sense his own frailty and unworthiness before such a God.

SINGING STARS

Joseph Addison (1672-1719) was a poet, political figure, and essayist. He was a judicious, rather elegant man, who moved in the university and upper cultural circles of his era. He spent many years of his life in Italy and France before becoming an essayist for several London periodicals, including *The Tattler*, *The Spectator*, and *The Guardian*.

One of Addison's most famous poems is based on Psalm 19, which declares how God's glory is manifested through His "handiwork." The poem deals with the creation and with the spiritual meaning of the physical universe. It is significant that in his composition, Addison speaks of the stars "singing" as does God in His series of questions to Job (Job 38:7). This is a most intriguing idea—that there is a lyrical quality about the heavenly bodies. They are not just purposeless, flaming objects, wandering in everlasting happenstance through space. They join all portions of the universe in a hymn of praise to their Creator, joyfully declaring that they owe their existence to Him.

> What though in solemn silence all
> Move round the dark terrestrial ball;
> What though no real voice or sound
> Amidst these radiant orbs be found;
> In reason's eye they all rejoice,
> And utter forth a glorious voice,
> Forever singing as they shine,
> "The Hand that made us is divine."
>
> —J. G. V. B.

II. Job Confesses to God (Job 42:1-6)

A. God Is Superior (vv. 1, 2)

1, 2. Then Job answered the LORD, and said, I know that thou canst do every thing, and that no thought can be withholden from thee.

Job's first response to God (40:3-5) is evasive. He does not admit to any sin, neither does he retract any of his former statements. There is neither confession nor submission.

God's second speech (40:7—41:34) raises issues relevant to God's sovereignty over not only the physical realm, but also the moral realm. God alone puts down evil and brings to pass His holy will. Job had heretofore questioned this truth. Earlier Job had said of God, "He destroyeth the perfect and the wicked" (9:22). Later he declared, "Know now that God hath overthrown me, and hath compassed me with his net" (19:6). Now, in His second speech, God rebukes Job's impertinence: "Would you discredit my justice? Would you condemn me to justify yourself?" (40:8, *New International Version*). Shortly thereafter comes this devastating challenge to Job: "Look on every one that is proud, and bring him low; and tread down the wicked in their place. . . . Then will I also confess unto thee that thine own right hand can

visual for
lesson 4

save thee" (vv. 12, 14). Job has expressed displeasure with God's sense of justice; but can he do better?

Now we are more able to discern the purpose behind the questions God has set before Job. We may have wondered how God's questions regarding the natural world had anything to do with the concerns that Job raised about his suffering. The implication is clear: If Job cannot grasp God's control over the world that he can see, how can he begin to understand deeper, unseen mysteries such as human suffering? Both realms—the seen and the unseen—must be committed to God's sovereignty. Man's responsibility is to trust God.

In Job's second response to God (beginning with the verses before us), he tells God that he understands this message. He freely admits that he is no more able to exercise wisdom and proper judgment in the moral realm than he is in the natural realm. He cannot govern the world more justly than God. These verses express Job's heartfelt admiration for God's power, wisdom, and justice.

B. "I Did Not Understand" (vv. 3-6)

3. Who is he that hideth counsel without knowledge? Therefore have I uttered that I understood not; things too wonderful for me, which I knew not.

Here Job repeats the question that God had raised earlier (38:2). The *New International Version* reads, "You asked, 'Who is this that obscures my counsel without knowledge?'" Job's attempts at self-defense had prevented him from understanding God's true wisdom. His admission of having *uttered* what he *understood not* was actually a vital step toward true understanding, for it drove Job to deeper trust in God.

THINGS TOO WONDERFUL

Job had been questioning God as to why all the tragedies that had occurred in his life happened. His friends believed that these circumstances had to be the result of some sin or shortcoming in Job's life. Job felt this was not so, and continued to maintain his integrity. God finally

spoke to Job, and convinced him that he really knew so little about God's ways in the ordinary functioning of His world that he could not begin to speak of God's ultimate purposes and acts.

In spite of our incredible advances in information and technology, should we not reach the same conclusion as did Job? Who really understands all there is to know about the process of digestion? Who can describe all that is involved with tears, or sleep, or dreams, or with the exercise of the five senses? Who has grasped all there is to know about the actions of the heart, lungs, central nervous system, and especially the human brain? In addition, consider all that is so unusual and fascinating about animal life, whether on land, in the sea, or in the air.

Through the series of questions that God posed to Job (Job 38-41), He called Job's attention to these same areas. Job came to realize that all of these intricate matters encompassed "things too wonderful for me" (Job 42:3). He discovered that if he could not grasp God's purposes and plans regarding what he could see, how could he expect to speak with any knowledge of God's dealings in the realm of the unseen, including the problem of his own suffering? Confronted with "things too wonderful," Job had to walk by faith in the One who is "wonderful in counsel, and excellent in working" (Isaiah 28:29) and whose ways are "past finding out" (Romans 11:33).

And so must we.   —J. G. V. B.

4. Hear, I beseech thee, and I will speak: I will demand of thee, and declare thou unto me.

Again, Job quotes in this verse the words that God had used twice in addressing him (38:3; 40:7).

5, 6. I have heard of thee by the hearing of the ear; but now mine eye seeth thee: wherefore I abhor myself, and repent in dust and ashes.

Repeatedly Job had sought God's presence, but in vain. He had declared, "Lo, he goeth by me, and I see him not: he passeth on also, but I perceive him not" (9:11). "Let him take his rod away from me, and let not his fear terrify me: then would I speak, and not fear him; but it is not so with me" (9:34, 35). "Behold, I go forward, but he is not there; and backward, but I cannot perceive him: on the left hand, where he doth work, but I cannot behold him: he hideth himself on the right hand, that I cannot see him" (23:8, 9).

Job's new awareness of God, compared with his former inferior and uninformed knowledge, was like seeing compared with *hearing*. This seeing refers to spiritual insight, not to optical vision. Paul prayed for the Ephesian Christians that "the eyes of your understanding" may be "enlightened" (Ephesians 1:18). This is similar to what happened to Job.

Having come into the presence of the Almighty, Job withdraws the rash statements that he once uttered in bitterness and frustration. The verb translated, "I abhor myself" could be rendered, "I reject what I said." Job now understands that God was his friend, never his enemy. Job admitted to sinning because he had suffered, not to suffering because he had sinned.

Dust and ashes were signs of grief over sin or a catastrophe. Earlier these were associated with Job's sorrow following the devastating tragedies that befell him (2:8, 12). Now they are a sign of his repentance.

III. God Restores Job
(Job 42:10)

10. And the LORD turned the captivity of Job, when he prayed for his friends: also the LORD gave Job twice as much as he had before.

In the verses immediately preceding this one, God spoke to Eliphaz: "My wrath is kindled against thee, and against thy two friends" (v. 7). God then commanded the three to offer sacrifices for themselves and said that "my servant Job shall pray for you: for him will I accept: lest I deal with you after your folly" (v. 8). Twice in these verses, the Lord affirmed that Job had spoken of Him "the thing that is right." This teaches us an important lesson about our relationship with God during difficult times: It is better to be honest with God (as Job was) than to claim false knowledge about Him (as Job's friends did).

In the course of God's response to Job, He did not publish a list of Job's sins and failures. This was not necessary, since Job had maintained a right relationship with his Creator. Nor did He issue to Job a formal declaration of his innocence. In fact (as we have noted in earlier lessons), none of the events or conversations of the prologue was ever revealed to Job. He was never told all the facts of his case.

That God spoke at all was enough for Job. Job's primary source of anguish was over the thought that he was separated from God. All Job needed to know was that everything was right between himself and God. The Lord's words provided this assurance. Job learned that he was not the target of God's displeasure. God was with him, even in his suffering. The tragedies he had experienced were not evidence of God's abandonment.

The story of Job concludes with God blessing Job by restoring both his posterity and his prosperity. The Lord repays double what he took away (v. 10). Only in the number of children is there no doubling; they are replaced with another seven sons and three daughters, presumably because the first ten children, who perished during the windstorm, were all safe in God's care. Job would see them again someday.

Conclusion
A. The Last Word

Noticeably absent from the concluding verses of the book of Job is Satan—the adversary who had originally sought to destroy Job and to thwart God's purposes. The enemy is now silenced at the end of the book, just as he will be silenced at the end of time.

James reminds us that the story of Job encourages Christians to consider "the end of the Lord" (James 5:11), or "what the Lord finally brought about" (*New International Version*). In watching over His people, God always has the last word.

B. Prayer

Father, we kneel in Your presence, having been reminded of the astonishing complexity of Your creation. We submit to Your moral rule in this universe. Forgive us whenever we question Your goodness and justice. Thank You for Your presence with us. Your Son and Your Holy Spirit bear constant witness to Your love for us. Thank You for the surpassing hope of the resurrection and for Your surpassing power. You have indeed been mighty to save even us. Amen.

C. Thought to Remember

"You have heard of Job's perseverance and have seen what the Lord finally brought about. The Lord is full of compassion and mercy" (James 5:11, *New International Version*).

Home Daily Bible Readings

Monday, June 22—Larger Mystery of God's Creation (Job 38:1-7)

Tuesday, June 23—Job Has Heard and Seen (Job 42:1-10)

Wednesday, June 24—Stand in Awe Before God (Ecclesiastes 3:9-17)

Thursday, June 25—Fear of God Is Wisdom (Job 28:20-28)

Friday, June 26—Full of the Knowledge of God (Isaiah 11:1-9)

Saturday, June 27—God Gives Us Dignity (Psalm 8:1-9)

Sunday, June 28—God's Way (John 14:1-7)

Learning by Doing

This page contains an alternate lesson plan emphasizing learning activities.
Classes desiring such student involvement will find these suggestions helpful.

Learning Goals

As a result of participating in today's lesson, a student will be able to:

1. Summarize the message behind the series of questions God asked of Job, and tell how Job responded.

2. Tell how faith in God allows us to see the "big picture," even in the midst of our suffering.

3. Cite an example of someone in need of the reassurance of God's presence, and seek to give that reassurance.

Into the Lesson

Pass out blank sheets of paper to class members, and ask them to write the answers to these two questions: "With whom would you like to talk if you could?" and, "What would you ask him or her?" Have them sign their sheets and give them back to you. Read their answers, pausing after each to let the class guess who wrote it. Do several of these before making the following transition: As if it were submitted by a class member, read this set of answers: "I want to talk with God. I would ask Him why He contends with me, and whether it pleases Him to oppress me." Hopefully, someone will recognize that these were Job's sentiments. Read Job 10:1-3, and state that Job repeatedly wished for the ability to talk with God. Today's lesson shows how he finally got his opportunity.

Into the Word

Point out that Job had previously affirmed that God alone is wise. Ask for a volunteer to read Job 28:20-28. But Job had also claimed that he had understanding, and considered himself to be righteous. Ask volunteers to read Job 12:3; 27:6; and 31:5, 6. In his anguish, Job was confused as to where he stood with God. Ask volunteers to read Job 10:15 and 23:1-5.

Divide the class into an even number of working groups. Assign half the groups Job 38:1-7 (God's questions to Job), and assign Job 42:1-6, 10 (Job's response) to the other half. Provide paper and pencils for each group to summarize the meaning of what was said by reducing each verse to four or fewer words. (For example, Job 38:2 could be summarized as, "Who darkens my wisdom?" and Job 42:2 could be stated as, "God knows everything.") Ask a spokesperson from each group to report that group's summary.

Now ask class members to summarize all of God's questions into one short question (this activity is also found in the student book). Take individual responses, writing them on a chalkboard or poster board. After several have been offered, blend them into one question that brings out the essence of God's question to Job. Then do the same for Job's response to God.

Into Life

Ask class members to recall times in their lives when suffering, trials, or serious problems caused them to feel confused or alone. Allow two or three to give brief examples. Explain that sometimes we respond to hardships by moving our focus from the "big picture" to the immediate problem. Again, ask for a few people to give examples from their own past experiences of how they have done this.

Point out that Job had forgotten to trust God in the midst of his suffering. Though he did not lose his faith and did not commit the kind of "folly" that his friends did (Job 42:7, 8), he lost sight of the "big picture." Ask class members to define what that "big picture" is. What are the elements of that picture that we tend to forget when we are suffering? Allow this question to begin a discussion. Probe responses for deeper insights. For instance, if someone says that we can forget how God has helped us in past situations, ask the person to give an example. If someone says that immediate difficulties draw our focus away from God's promise to provide a way of escape from temptation (1 Corinthians 10:13), ask why we can so quickly forget His promises. Encourage people to ask questions, and allow other class members to provide answers. Guide the conversation to the positive affirmation of God's faithfulness and wisdom. When we keep our focus on Him and what we know to be true, we can endure hardships and suffering through our faith.

In closing today's lesson (and this study of Job), have someone read James 5:11. This is the only reference in the New Testament to Job. Note the reference to "the end of the Lord" (see how other versions translate the phrase if class members have any others). Emphasize that just as God had the last word with Job and his circumstances, He will have the last word with us in our circumstances.

Let's Talk It Over

The questions on this page are designed to encourage review of the lesson Scriptures and to promote discussion of the lesson by the class. The answers provided are only discussion starters. Let your class talk it over from there.

1. God asked Job to consider how His wisdom and power are revealed in creation. Indeed, the heavens and earth do reveal the glory of God (Psalm 19:1). List some of the marvelous aspects of creation, and explain what they tell us about God. How does this relate to Job's questions?

The universe is so immense that our most powerful telescopes cannot see its edge. Its stars are truly beyond counting. This helps us understand God's infinite power. Our earth is marvelously crafted to promote the nourishment of life. The simplest living creatures are unimaginably complex. The number of species and their variety are staggering. The development of a baby in a mother's womb defies understanding. Such marvels as these show us God's infinite wisdom, knowledge, and imagination. If neither Job nor we can begin to comprehend the natural realm, let alone control it, how can we expect to be competent judges in the moral realm? We are as incapable of showing God to be wrong as we are of creating a new world.

2. God's character and power are revealed in many ways other than creation. Name some of God's works that reveal His power and His control over the world. What lessons can we learn from these actions?

God's power is seen in His control of history. He raises up and destroys nations as He will. For example, the prophet Isaiah predicted the removal of the Assyrian "yoke" from Israel (Isaiah 14:24, 25). He then declared, "This is the purpose that is purposed upon the whole earth: and this is the hand that is stretched out upon all the nations" (v. 26). No man, whether Nebuchadnezzar, Napoleon, or Hitler can thwart His purposes. It should encourage us to know that if God can control history, surely He is able to take care of the problems we face. God's power is also shown in His ability to execute judgment. This assures us that He is quite able and willing to judge the world once and for all at the time of His choosing. In addition, God's power is shown in His ability to overcome sin and death and Hell through the atonement of Christ. He delivers us from the curse of sin and will finally usher us into the glories of Heaven, where all suffering will be banished.

3. When Job responded to God's questioning, he repented of the many words he had spoken when questioning God (Job 42:3-6). All the speeches and protests he had desired to present before God were instantly shown to be foolish at best and blasphemous at worst. How can we "see" God as Job did (v. 5), so that we too can learn not to say something about God that we really don't understand?

Job probably did not expect God to speak to him from a whirlwind, and it is not likely that we will hear God speak to us in such a manner either. Nonetheless, our hearts and minds can see what God is like, so that we will not sin against Him with our words. We must see that He is all-powerful and that we cannot oppose His will. We must see that His perfect plans and purposes are inscrutable to us, because they are beyond our understanding. We must see that God is under no obligation to explain or justify Himself or to ask for our permission or approval before He acts. We are His to do with as He pleases. We must trust Him in every circumstance. We are to be a people who live by faith, not by sight (2 Corinthians 5:7). Only then can we develop the kind of spiritual vision that Job came to possess.

4. Job learned a lot about his relationship to God through his experience of suffering. Surely he was much closer to the Lord after his suffering than he was before. What lessons can we learn from Job about how to live in close harmony with the Lord in our Christian walk?

Job learned to trust God in even the most trying of circumstances, and so must we. We must trust His will, His love, and His promises that He will never forsake or leave us. Job learned humility and submission, and we must learn these same lessons. God cannot be resisted, and so we ought to learn to humbly submit to His will. Rather than sulking and complaining in hard times, we should continue to serve and worship God faithfully. Rather than being puffed up in good times, we should remember that God has given all our blessings, and He can take them away from us. Also, we should learn to seek and be sensitive to God's will. Is He calling us to some area of service? Then let us accept it, even if it will require sacrifice on our part.

Listen to Wisdom

DEVOTIONAL READING: Psalm 53.

LESSON SCRIPTURE: Proverbs 2:1-15.

PRINTED TEXT: Proverbs 2:1-15.

Proverbs 2:1-15

1 My son, if thou wilt receive my words, and hide my commandments with thee;

2 So that thou incline thine ear unto wisdom, and apply thine heart to understanding;

3 Yea, if thou criest after knowledge, and liftest up thy voice for understanding;

4 If thou seekest her as silver, and searchest for her as for hid treasures;

5 Then shalt thou understand the fear of the LORD, and find the knowledge of God.

6 For the LORD giveth wisdom: out of his mouth cometh knowledge and understanding.

7 He layeth up sound wisdom for the righteous: he is a buckler to them that walk uprightly.

8 He keepeth the paths of judgment, and preserveth the way of his saints.

9 Then shalt thou understand righteousness, and judgment, and equity; yea, every good path.

10 When wisdom entereth into thine heart, and knowledge is pleasant unto thy soul;

11 Discretion shall preserve thee, understanding shall keep thee:

12 To deliver thee from the way of the evil man, from the man that speaketh froward things;

13 Who leave the paths of uprightness, to walk in the ways of darkness;

14 Who rejoice to do evil, and delight in the frowardness of the wicked;

15 Whose ways are crooked, and they froward in their paths.

GOLDEN TEXT: The LORD giveth wisdom: out of his mouth cometh knowledge and understanding. —Proverbs 2:6.

Wisdom for Living
Unit 2: Proverbs on Living a Disciplined Life
(Lessons 5-8)

Lesson Aims

This study should prepare the student to:
1. Recall what Proverbs 2 says about the acquisition of wisdom and the result of having it.
2. Contrast wisdom as described in Proverbs 2 with what modern culture calls wisdom.
3. Suggest an area of one's relationship with God where His wisdom needs to be applied more consistently.

Lesson Outline

INTRODUCTION
  A. Can You Wiggle Your Ears?
  B. Hearing Aids
  C. Lesson Background
 I. THE WAY TO KNOW GOD (Proverbs 2:1-5)
  A. The Quest for Wisdom (vv. 1-4)
    The Search for Hidden Treasure
  B. The Reward of Wisdom (v. 5)
II. GOD'S BLESSINGS IN WISDOM (Proverbs 2:6-15)
  A. His Word Conveys Wisdom (v. 6)
    Using Wisdom Wisely
  B. Wisdom Provides Protection (vv. 7, 8)
  C. Wisdom Gives Understanding (vv. 9, 10)
  D. Wisdom Protects From Evil (vv. 11-15)
CONCLUSION
  A. There Is More
  B. Home Schooling
  C. Prayer
  D. Thought to Remember

The visual for Lesson 5 in the visuals packet emphasizes that God is the source of true wisdom. It is shown on page 380.

Introduction
A. Can You Wiggle Your Ears?

Jimmy was the only member of his family who could not wiggle his ears. He could never lift and lower the sides of his scalp enough to produce the desired movement of those appendages. His father, who was himself an accomplished ear wiggler, assured Jimmy that a vastly more important exercising of the ears was still available. That was listening and hearing—a skill not sufficiently appreciated and practiced, but available to almost anyone willing to try it.

Jimmy's father may have learned the importance of this skill from Jesus, who challenged those who came to hear Him, "If any man have ears to hear, let him hear" (Mark 4:23). As the apostle John recorded Jesus' messages to the seven churches in Revelation, he heard Jesus urge each church to practice the same simple ear exercise (Revelation 2, 3).

For more than a thousand years before Christ, however, God's messengers had been exhorting their hearers to be good listeners. This is a key thought in the introduction to the book of Proverbs: "My son, hear the instruction of thy father" (Proverbs 1:8).

B. Hearing Aids

Hearing does not always take place when one person talks in the presence of another. The hearer may be for the moment a nonlistener, preoccupied with something more urgent. Thus he may not really hear the other person at all. A deaf person may be helped by voice amplification, but an inattentive audience may only be irritated by the increased volume.

The Biblical proverbs earn a hearing by what they say and how they say it. They speak with the emphasis and wit of Hebrew poetry, which depends for its interest, not on rhyme and meter, but on a balance of comparisons and/or contrasts, coupled with bold figures of speech and vitality of content. It is never dull.

The poetic pattern found in today's text goes beyond repetition or comparison. It builds one thought upon another in an ascending progression. What begins as a simple idea becomes most impressive and hard to ignore.

C. Lesson Background

The Hebrew word for "proverb" (*mashal*) signifies a comparison—laying one idea alongside another for comparison and instruction. King Solomon, known worldwide for his wisdom (1 Kings 4:29-31) and for being the author of three thousand proverbs (v. 32), is named in Proverbs 1:1; 10:1; and 25:1 as the source of major sections of the book. Agur and King Lemuel (both of whom the Bible says little) are also named as sources (Proverbs 30:1; 31:1), while King Hezekiah is said to have had men who "copied out" some of the proverbs of Solomon (25:1). Thus the material found in Proverbs reflects a process of both writing and compiling.

The first nine chapters of Proverbs contain segments longer and more detailed than the brief maxims found in the rest of the book. These nine chapters provide an excellent introduction to wisdom and what is included within its scope.

How to Say It

AGUR. *A*-gur.
HEZEKIAH. Hez-ih-*kye*-uh.
LEMUEL. *Lem*-you-el.
MASHAL (Hebrew). muh-*shahl*.
REHOBOAM. Ree-huh-*boe*-um.

Proverbs 1:1-7 sets forth the purpose of the book: to convey instruction to one who is addressed as "my son." Either the young man will accept good counsel from his father, or wicked influence from so-called "friends" (1:8-19), who will only drag him into the snares of sin. Proverbs 1:20-33 introduces wisdom, personified as "she," and urges acceptance of her protective counsel. Chapter 2, which provides our text for today's lesson, begins with another plea to heed the father's wise teaching as the way to enjoy the knowledge of God and His protection against the influences of the wicked.

I. The Way to Know God
(Proverbs 2:1-5)

The first five verses of our text are given to one long sentence, stating a condition and a conclusion. If the condition is met in a progressive series of commitments to wisdom, then the promised blessing—an acquaintance with the living God—will occur.

A. The Quest for Wisdom (vv. 1-4)

1. My son, if thou wilt receive my words, and hide my commandments with thee.

The instruction given in Proverbs is cast in the form of a father's serious conversation with his child at home. One may imagine Solomon the father addressing his son Rehoboam; however, this *son* failed to learn and apply the wisdom of his father (1 Kings 12:1-15).

Many commentators on Proverbs are inclined to neglect the family relationship implied in these verses and in the phrase *my son*. Instead, they prefer to speak of wise teachers addressing their disciples as "sons." For grasping the kind of moral and practical teaching found in this book, however, there has never been a satisfactory substitute for a father's patient, insistent, and personified instruction of his own son. Without it, any society suffers.

"My son, hear the instruction of thy father, and forsake not the law of thy mother" (Proverbs 1:8). *Words* are the channels of instruction, but words must be received, accepted, believed, and made a part of the hearer's inner being—inter-

nalized, if you please—before they become effective. For best results, the words need to be enforced by the example of a consistent life.

The *commandments* referred to are God's precepts in general—principles set forth and urged as rules of action. Observe the forward movement, from *words* to *commandments*, and from receiving the truth to hiding, or making it a part of one's innermost being. The way to wisdom does not leave one standing still.

2. So that thou incline thine ear unto wisdom, and apply thine heart to understanding.

Again we have an important thought stated within a poetic pair, with the second element advancing beyond the first. And again the hearer is expected to be active in the learning process. He is to *incline*, or "prick up" his ears, and turn his head to the sound of *wisdom*, much as a pet dog does at the approach of his master. The attentive son is to turn deliberately toward the kind of teaching that will bless and enhance his life. The *heart*, as used in this context, signifies the mental faculties of thinking, reasoning, and determining.

Wisdom is the grand theme of Proverbs, echoing the prayer of Psalm 90:12: "So teach us to number our days, that we may apply our hearts unto wisdom." One word cannot contain all that is included in wisdom, so the book of Proverbs regularly calls up a number of synonyms including *knowledge, insight, judgment, understanding, discretion, instruction, justice,* and *the fear of the Lord.*

3. Yea, if thou criest after knowledge, and liftest up thy voice for understanding.

Here the son is directed to go beyond passive acceptance of wise and godly counsel and to become an activist, demanding it in the manner of militant campaigners for any cause. The words describe an attitude similar to that of a child demanding his favorite food or toy, and refusing to quiet down until he gets it. One is reminded of Jesus' blessing upon those individuals who "hunger and thirst after righteousness" (Matthew 5:6).

4. If thou seekest her as silver, and searchest for her as for hid treasures.

The word rendered "understanding" at the end of the previous verse (a word that is feminine in Hebrew) gives rise to the personification that we find here. Wisdom is frequently described in Proverbs as a woman. The demand for wise teaching and the quest for it are pictured as a laborious search similar to that of a miner digging for *silver*, or of fortune hunters searching for *hid treasures* in faraway lands. These words contain echoes of Job 28, with its own references to mining and to searching after precious stones (Job 28:1-3, 6). The search for wisdom is primarily a spiritual quest: "It cannot be gotten for gold, neither shall silver be weighed for the price thereof" (v . 15).

THE SEARCH FOR HIDDEN TREASURE

The search for hidden treasure has consumed significant human effort for many centuries. Because the pharaohs of Egypt arranged to have jewelry, objects made of gold and silver, and other riches placed in their tombs, these were searched for and robbed over the course of many years. When burial places of ancient Egyptian monarchs are discovered, almost without exception they are found to have been robbed at some time in the past.

In later years, the Spaniards sent ships laden with treasures of silver, jewels, and gold from America back to their native land. Several of these were wrecked in storms and sank. Their hidden treasures have been diligently sought by modern diving expeditions. These efforts have been undertaken with intense concentration, even at the cost of peoples' lives. Several great "treasure ships" have been found, and immense wealth has been brought to the surface.

In addition to these finds, hoards of Roman gold coins, rings, bracelets, and necklaces have been unearthed in Great Britain. Hidden treasures of great value have been discovered in Mexico and Peru, where Aztec and Inca royal grave sites have been located. In the field of literature, we remember that Robert Louis Stevenson's *Treasure Island* involved a search for a buried chest of pirates' plunder.

Just as men have fervently sought for hidden treasure in mountains, on islands, and under the sea—so we should devote ourselves, without reservation, to search for the greater riches of the wisdom of God.   —J. G. V. B.

B. The Reward of Wisdom (v. 5)

When the conditions of listening and receiving, requesting and demanding, and seeking and searching diligently for the words of wisdom have been met, then will come the most precious of rewards.

visual for
lesson 5

5. Then shalt thou understand the fear of the LORD, and find the knowledge of God.

The *fear of the Lord* is reverent awe in the presence of Him who identified himself to Moses as I AM (Exodus 3:14). *Knowledge* is also what one will *find* as a result of his quest. This includes not only information about *God*, but also a personal acquaintance with Him.

The book of Proverbs is a study of practical wisdom rather than religion, but it declares a solid link between the two. "The fear of the Lord is the beginning of knowledge" (Proverbs 1:7). You cannot have one without the other.

II. God's Blessings in Wisdom (Proverbs 2:6-15)

A. His Word Conveys Wisdom (v. 6)

6. For the LORD giveth wisdom: out of his mouth cometh knowledge and understanding.

Early in Solomon's reign, he concluded that he needed understanding and discernment—*wisdom*, that is—that he did not then possess. When the opportunity came one night to ask God for whatever he desired, Solomon requested "an understanding heart" (1 Kings 3:9). God was pleased and granted Solomon's request, giving him far more than he could have gained from any other sources (1 Kings 3:5-14; 10:23, 24).

Words are important, especially those words from the *mouth* of God. A great part of His wisdom is given through His written Word. God's creation demonstrates His power, but His words are needed to convey the *knowledge and understanding* of His will and purpose.

USING WISDOM WISELY

The assurance is given in Proverbs 2:6 that the wisdom that will bless and benefit life is a gift from God. It is a sad commentary on our human condition that certain inventions of very wise men have been perverted for purposes of destruction and desolation.

The work of Galileo in the invention of the telescope is described in a poem by Alfred Noyes (1880-1958). A group of old men are given a telescope, which they are asked to focus on a ship far out to sea. As they look through it, one by one, they exclaim at how clearly they can see what is indistinguishable with their naked eyes. Then they begin to speculate as to its uses. One man says, "This instrument should give us great advantages in time of war." In essence, Noyes comments, "How sad! Dazed with new power, awed by new ability, these old men dreamed of blood."

It is tragic that explosives, which can help build canals and tunnels and assist in mining efforts, are also utilized in bombs that destroy and kill. As Ecclesiastes 7:29 says, "God hath made man upright; but they have sought out many inventions."

Our great challenge is to use the ever-increasing knowledge of humanity for ends that will benefit and bless rather than blast and bereave. Our knowledge must be tempered with wisdom—God's wisdom. —J. G. V. B.

B. Wisdom Provides Protection
(vv. 7, 8)

7. He layeth up sound wisdom for the righteous: he is a buckler to them that walk uprightly.

As a father may establish a fund for his children's education, so God provides a substantial account of wisdom to insure victory for those who follow His direction. They are protected by the *buckler*, or shield, of God's presence before them. They are not defenseless, as are those who seek only ease and pleasure. The self-disciplined wise ones triumph over difficulties that destroy many of the "rich and famous."

8. He keepeth the paths of judgment, and preserveth the way of his saints.

As crossing guards stand watch over the route of children on their way to and from school, so God's wisdom lovingly stands guard over the *paths* laid out for the wise and obedient followers of God.

This figure became clearer to us one winter day when motor failure stranded us on the West Virginia Turnpike. Within minutes a service vehicle provided by the Turnpike authorities arrived to give us just the help we needed. On the route God has laid out for us, help is always available!

C. Wisdom Gives Understanding
(vv. 9, 10)

9. Then shalt thou understand righteousness, and judgment, and equity; yea, every good path.

Many matters previously unclear or downright frustrating will become clear in the light of God's wise counsel. The basic principles of *judgment*, or justice, are often ignored amid the complexities of human experience; and yet these basic principles constitute the foundation upon which all decisions have to be made. They are set forth in the wisdom of God's words. The *path* of life becomes clear to the one who lives by those words.

10. When wisdom entereth into thine heart, and knowledge is pleasant unto thy soul.

The entering of *wisdom* and *knowledge* is followed naturally by a feeling of pleasure—a

sense that one's search for the lastingly sweet and beautiful experiences of life is over. Here is echoed the description of the godly man whose "delight is in the law of the Lord" (Psalm 1:2).

D. Wisdom Protects From Evil
(vv. 11-15)

11. Discretion shall preserve thee, understanding shall keep thee.

Discretion is one of the many aspects of wisdom that *preserve* the one who lives by wisdom. It describes a meditative thoughtfulness that results in a prudent plan of action. It suggests the carefulness of a swimmer who checks to see if the water is deep enough before he goes off the diving board. It also includes the ability to distinguish among choices that are offered, and to separate what is valuable from what is worthless or harmful. As one familiar with plants can distinguish between an edible mushroom and a poisonous toadstool, so the possessor of discretion can, in the words of Hebrews 5:14, "discern both good and evil."

12. To deliver thee from the way of the evil man, from the man that speaketh froward things.

The elements of divinely given wisdom, such as discretion and understanding, will erect a barrier before the wide gate into the broad *way* that leads to destruction (Matthew 7:13). The wicked way is chosen by wrong-minded persons. In many cases it is reflected early in someone's life through wicked speech—the kind of twisted speech that often seems deliberately chosen to offend and defy the authority of both God and man.

The old English word *froward*, found here, is worth noting. As "to" and "fro" are opposites, so "to-ward" (going to an object) and *fro-ward* (going the other way) are opposites. The godly person looks and moves *toward* God; the ungodly person is *froward*, looking and moving away from God. He gravitates toward opposition, rebellion, and disobedience.

13. Who leave the paths of uprightness, to walk in the ways of darkness.

Jesus spoke of those who "loved darkness rather than light, because their deeds were evil" (John 3:19). These individuals prefer the *darkness*, for it provides the covering that they believe will hide their evil deeds from God (Isaiah 29:15). In contrast, Christians have left the paths of darkness to "walk as children of light" (Ephesians 5:8).

14. Who rejoice to do evil, and delight in the frowardness of the wicked.

Here is a striking foreshadowing of the fearsome development of juvenile crime in our country, where acts of robbery, vandalism, brutality, and even murder are committed "just for fun." There has long been a wicked pleasure in flouting the rules of God and men. The apostle Paul found this same perverted sense of pleasure among the pagans of the first-century world, and wrote of it in Romans 1:18-32.

Love, on the other hand, "rejoiceth not in iniquity, but rejoiceth in the truth" (1 Corinthians 13:6). Wisdom will keep one from straying toward the wrong sources of pleasure and falling into their seductive trap.

15. Whose ways are crooked, and they froward in their paths.

In describing the *ways* of a person's chosen behavior, one also describes the person who chooses them. The terms *crooked* and *froward* summarize him who chooses devious ways in speech, action, and entertainment. "Straight," on the other hand, is a good and accurate (though not always popular) description of him who follows God's way of wisdom.

Conclusion

A. There Is More

Verses 16-19, not included in our printed text, promise wisdom's protection against the wiles of wicked women as well as against the ways of wicked men. The "strange" woman (a woman who is not one's wife) is described as being faithless to her vows and as using the deceptions of flattery. Her ways are the ways of death —a truth all too evident in pagan societies, both ancient and modern.

Our chapter concludes with a restatement of affirmative promises for the one who listens attentively and applies faithfully the teachings of wisdom and righteousness. Verses 20-22

Home Daily Bible Readings

Monday, June 29—Wisdom Begins With God (Proverbs 1:1-7)
Tuesday, June 30—Guard Against Sinners (Proverbs 1:8-19)
Wednesday, July 1—Seek Wisdom and You'll Find It (Proverbs 2:1-15)
Thursday, July 2—Wise Persons Look for God (Psalm 53:1-6)
Friday, July 3—Established in the Word (Psalm 119:129-136)
Saturday, July 4—Be Hearers and Doers (James 1:22-27)
Sunday, July 5—Delight in the Law (Psalm 1:1-6)

assure that "the upright shall dwell in the land, and the perfect shall remain in it." Much greater and richer promises, of course, are available through God's Son, "who of God is made unto us wisdom" (1 Corinthians 1:30), and "in whom are hid all the treasures of wisdom and knowledge" (Colossians 2:3).

B. Home Schooling

In the opening chapters of the book of Proverbs, we find what might be called an introductory course in home schooling. The text speaks first to the listening child and then to the teaching parent.

The concept of home schooling was prescribed in detail for the children of Israel (Deuteronomy 6:6-9). Today it is accepted as an alternative to public schools, if the home teacher is adequately prepared and will follow an acceptable program producing acceptable results in the child's learning. Even public schooling without supportive teaching at home is weak and incomplete at best.

The "home schooling" pattern of Proverbs requires a listening learner, using both his two ears and controlling his one tongue. He must respect his parent-teacher (Exodus 20:12; Ephesians 6:1-3). A desire to learn, helped by a habit of careful attention to what is said, is essential to efficient listening.

The pattern of Proverbs also requires a wise parent. Ephesians 6:4 and Colossians 3:21 forbid erecting barriers to learning by building up resentment in the child. The wise parent of Proverbs shapes his teaching by much listening, thinking, and working over of his material, so as to make it easy and pleasant to hear, understand, and remember. It is hoped that those who are thus taught will one day tell their children, "As my parents used to say . . ." The parent who would be remembered for wise counsel will do well to fill his or her mind with God's wisdom from Proverbs.

C. Prayer

Thank You, God, for making Your way known through the wise counsel of the book of Proverbs. Thank You for faithful parents who convey this counsel to their children. Thank You especially for making Yourself known through Jesus, Your Son and our Lord. May we listen to His Word eagerly, and may we speak Your Word faithfully to our children. In Jesus' name we pray. Amen.

D. Thought to Remember

"If any man have ears to hear, let him hear" (Mark 4:23).

Learning by Doing

This page contains an alternate lesson plan emphasizing learning activities.
Classes desiring such student involvement will find these suggestions helpful.

Learning Goals

This study should prepare the student to:

1. Recall what Proverbs 2 says about the acquisition of wisdom and the result of having wisdom.

2. Contrast wisdom as described in Proverbs 2 with what modern culture calls wisdom.

3. Suggest an area of one's relationship with God where His wisdom needs to be applied more consistently.

Into the Lesson

On the chalkboard or on poster board, write two words: *fear* and *wisdom*. Then pose this question: What does the fear of the Lord have to do with wisdom? (It is wise to fear the One who is our Creator, who loves us and knows what is best for us, and who will decide our eternal destiny.)

Next, ask your students to describe the wisest individual they have ever personally known. After several people have been mentioned, ask what made each one wise. (For an alternative introduction, give your students an opportunity to relate the values they hold most dear, and to tell where they got those values.)

Draw your discussion toward the conclusion that God must be our ultimate source of wisdom (or values, if you use the exercise concerning values). The book of Proverbs, from which the remaining lessons of this quarter will be taken, focuses on the wisdom that comes from fearing and obeying God.

Into the Word

Introduce the book of Proverbs. Give the names of those men responsible for either writing or collecting the Proverbs (Solomon, Hezekiah, Agur, Lemuel). Note to whom the Proverbs were written (specifically to the next generation and, in general, to God's people then and now). From the Lesson Background, define a proverb ("laying one idea alongside another for attention, interest, and instruction").

Have a student read Proverbs 2:1-5. Afterward, ask for the conditional statement that is contained within those verses:

If you . . . (verses 1 and 2)
If you . . . (verse 3)
If you . . . (verse 4)
Then . . . (verse 5).

Following this, have each of the Bible passages listed below read and summarized by a member of the class:

1 Corinthians 1:21 (God's wisdom is foolish in the eyes of the world.)

Psalm 90:12 (Living by God's wisdom is the best way to make use of our days.)

James 3:17 (God's wisdom produces many good fruits.)

James 1:5 (God's wisdom is ours for the asking.)

Job 28:20-28 (Wisdom is not found anywhere on earth, but rather in the fear of the Lord.)

Then review with the class the history of the following families:

Eli and his sons, Hophni and Phinehas: 1 Samuel 2:23, 24; 3:12, 13 (disobedient sons)

Samuel and his sons, Joel and Abijah: 1 Samuel 8:3-5 (corrupt sons)

David and his son Absalom: 2 Samuel 15:13, 14 (a rebellious son).

Solomon and his son Rehoboam: 1 Kings 12:12-15 (a willful son, apparently not a good listener). Use these examples as a basis for discussing the need to transmit wisdom and proper values from one generation to the next. Use the last reference to Solomon and Rehoboam to refer back to the printed text in Proverbs 2. Out of this discussion, emphasize that fearing God means acknowledging His authority in every area of our daily lives.

Into Life

Recite this short verse to the class and ask for opinions about what it means:

The high soul takes the high road;
  The low soul takes the low;
And on the misty flats between,
  The rest drift to and fro.

Use the ensuing discussion to focus on the idea that God wants us to have our minds made up (call attention to Joshua's advice: "Choose you this day whom ye will serve"). Ask for suggestions as to how we can encourage each other to have a "made-up mind" regarding God and His wisdom.

To close, form a circle, hold hands, and ask for sentence prayers aimed at seeking God's wisdom with a faith that contains no doubts, and with the courage to transmit what we value to others.

Let's Talk It Over

The questions on this page are designed to encourage review of the lesson Scriptures and to promote discussion of the lesson by the class. The answers provided are only discussion starters. Let your class talk it over from there.

1. Some people are wise, and some are fools. Some people never seem to learn. But wisdom is available to everyone. Why do only some people have it? What must a person do to gain wisdom? Give practical suggestions for becoming wise.

We bemoan the fact that so many of our children come out of high school ignorant and illiterate. One reason for this is that some children have no desire to learn. They do not pay attention or do any homework. A child must invest a great deal of work to achieve an education. In the same way, we must have an intense desire for wisdom and invest a great deal of work to achieve wisdom. We must seek out sources of wisdom. These include God's Word; writings by wise, godly people; sermons and Sunday school lessons; experienced Christians who are filled with wisdom; and God Himself. We must learn all we can from these sources, studying written material and pressing wise people to share their wisdom. And we must do our homework, applying this wisdom to the decisions we face until we understand how it works.

2. Wisdom has many components and facets. Suggest several synonyms for wisdom, briefly explaining each one, as a way to help understand all that is included in wisdom. (Our text provides several synonyms.)

Wisdom is often conveyed through *words*, which are the basic building blocks of thought and reason. The proverbs are words of wisdom. *Knowledge* is the awareness of true facts and principles. (Believing falsehood is not knowledge but ignorance.) *Commandments* of God are truths stated in the imperative. "Thou shalt not kill" is based on the truth that it is wrong to murder. God never commands foolishness. *Understanding* implies that we comprehend what words of knowledge actually mean. *Judgment* is the ability to call to mind relevant truths and commandments, so as to make good, proper, and beneficial decisions. *Discretion* is the wariness that enables us to detect and avoid evil or destructive principles, decisions, and actions.

3. The book of Proverbs affirms that wisdom and righteousness are closely linked. Wisdom always chooses righteousness and acts righteously. Explain this relationship.

Wisdom chooses righteousness, for it knows that this is the best course to follow. It knows that this is true, even if the right choice is hard, expensive, or dangerous. Righteousness is wise, because it is based on obedience to God; and it is always wise to obey the righteous Judge of the universe. Righteousness is wise, because doing right always produces the best possible outcome in any situation. Doing right in one circumstance may mean that we help someone who needs it. In another circumstance, doing right may get us killed. In both cases, we reach the best outcomes, though they are greatly different. Wisdom knows that living righteously keeps us in harmony with God, which means that He will give us His guidance, protection, and blessing, and will always work through our circumstances for good (Romans 8:28).

4. Our lesson text reads as if a father were addressing his son, urging him to seek wisdom and to live wisely. Obviously it is very important that parents teach wisdom to their children. Suggest some specific steps that parents must take to help their children learn and apply God's wisdom.

First, parents must understand that it is their responsibility to teach godly wisdom to their children. They must make a conscious, deliberate, and committed effort to accomplish this. This begins with insuring that the children are thoroughly instructed in God's Word. Such instruction must take place both at home and at church. Parents need to discuss these matters with their children and see that they understand what is at stake. They must not depend on the Sunday school to do the training that God requires of them. Parents can help children make wise decisions by applying godly principles. Parents must insist on godly behavior, whether or not the child understands or agrees. Many times it is helpful, especially with older children, for parents to explain the issues their children are facing and the reasoning behind the decisions they need to make. Perhaps most important, parents must display wisdom in their own lives, if their words are to have any genuine impact.

Trust God

DEVOTIONAL READING: **Psalm 91.**

LESSON SCRIPTURE: **Proverbs 3:1-20.**

PRINTED TEXT: **Proverbs 3:1-8, 11-15.**

Proverbs 3:1-8, 11-15

1 My son, forget not my law; but let thine heart keep my commandments:

2 For length of days, and long life, and peace, shall they add to thee.

3 Let not mercy and truth forsake thee: bind them about thy neck; write them upon the table of thine heart:

4 So shalt thou find favor and good understanding in the sight of God and man.

5 Trust in the LORD with all thine heart; and lean not unto thine own understanding.

6 In all thy ways acknowledge him, and he shall direct thy paths.

7 Be not wise in thine own eyes: fear the LORD, and depart from evil.

8 It shall be health to thy navel, and marrow to thy bones.

. . . .

11 My son, despise not the chastening of the LORD; neither be weary of his correction:

12 For whom the LORD loveth he correcteth; even as a father the son in whom he delighteth.

13 Happy is the man that findeth wisdom, and the man that getteth understanding:

14 For the merchandise of it is better than the merchandise of silver, and the gain thereof than fine gold.

15 She is more precious than rubies: and all the things thou canst desire are not to be compared unto her.

GOLDEN TEXT: Trust in the LORD with all thine heart; and lean not unto thine own understanding. In all thy ways acknowledge him, and he shall direct thy paths.—Proverbs 3:5, 6.

> ## Wisdom for Living
> ### Unit 2: Proverbs on Living a Disciplined Life
> #### (Lessons 5-8)

Lesson Aims

After completion of this lesson, students should be able to:

1. Memorize Proverbs 3:5, 6, and cite some of the benefits of trusting in the Lord mentioned in Proverbs 3.

2. Contrast trusting in God with trusting in self.

3. Think of a circumstance where they need to trust God, rather than depend too much on their own wisdom or cunning.

Lesson Outline

INTRODUCTION
   A. "Who Do You Trust?"
   B. Lesson Background
I. REWARDS FOR REMEMBERING (Proverbs 3:1-4)
   A. Life and Peace (vv. 1, 2)
   B. Favor With God and Man (vv. 3, 4)
II. GOING GOD'S WAY (Proverbs 3:5-8)
   A. Trusting in God (vv. 5, 6)
      The Peril of the Partial
   B. Departing from Evil (vv. 7, 8)
III. ACCEPTING GOD'S CORRECTION (Proverbs 3:11, 12)
      The Desirability of Discipline
IV. BOUNDLESS VALUE OF WISDOM (Proverbs 3:13-15)
CONCLUSION
   A. Help My Lack of Trust!
   B. Prayer
   C. Thought to Remember

Use the visual for Lesson 6 to call attention to today's Golden Text from Proverbs 3:5, 6. It is shown on page 388.

Introduction

A. "Who Do You Trust?"

My fifth grade English teacher would have had us say, "*Whom* do you trust?" However, the producers of a television program that was quite popular several years ago left off the *m*. For each telecast, they brought in married couples to answer questions and win prizes for the right answers. Each question was preceded by asking, "Do you trust your wife (husband) or do you trust yourself?" Whoever was trusted bore the responsibility for answering the question.

Each of the countless decisions made every day by every one of us demands an answer to that same question: "Whom do you trust—in making your decision?" Sometimes I have to depend on myself, unless someone else—God, parent, teacher, or friend—has already provided a principle on which I base my choice. Even then I must decide whether or not to follow that other individual's leading.

Small children usually trust in and depend on their parents or other caregivers for directions, but that condition changes as the youngster develops, gains confidence, and approaches the status of a self-supporting adult. We all know that this process is often rocky and fraught with conflict between parent and teen. "Trust me!" says the self-confident youth. Or, "You don't trust me!" he complains.

Such complaints really indicate the young person's lack of trust in the adults to whom he still looks for daily provision. The trusting teen will respect the parents' wisdom and good intentions as well as their ability to feed him and provide wheels for him.

The same is true of us as children of God. He is the ultimate provider of all that we have, both materially and spiritually. Along with these provisions, He has given a Book of instruction to guide us in their proper use. We are dependent on Him, and it is folly for any of us to say to Him, "Trust me—just hand me the keys to Your world!"

B. Lesson Background

The book of Proverbs has been described as a thesis on practical wisdom. Most of it is made up of brief, poetic maxims, easily remembered for daily application to circumstances and choices that one faces every day. Such single gems will be considered in future lessons. First, we must be convinced that God is the source of all true wisdom, and that "the fear of the Lord is the beginning of knowledge" (Proverbs 1:7). If we trust Him, we will listen to what He says. If we fail to trust Him, it will not make much difference to whom we listen; our path will be marked by failure and frustration.

Today we are looking at a brief poetic essay—one within a nine-chapter treatment of the general subject of wisdom (Proverbs 1-9). A wise father addresses his son with a series of observations, occupying two verses each in our printed text (except for the final section, which consists of three verses). These observations describe blessings to be gained from hearing and heeding the wisdom that comes from God.

I. Rewards for Remembering
(Proverbs 3:1-4)

A. Life and Peace (vv. 1, 2)

1. My son, forget not my law; but let thine heart keep my commandments.

Strong feeling echoes in every word from father to *son*. The son is to *keep* the *commandments*, or teachings, of the father, not only through obedient action, but through storing them up as precious treasure, to be brought out and invested again and again.

Family relationships provide golden opportunities for solid moral teaching. Such teaching can be reinforced through careful wording, repetition, and association with times, places, and material objects related to the occasion of its being spoken. Good words should be associated with good memories.

2. For length of days, and long life, and peace, shall they add to thee.

The second half of this couplet provides the motivation for doing what is urged in the first. Here is echoed the promise of Exodus 20:12, found again in Ephesians 6:2, 3: "Honor thy father and mother; which is the first commandment with promise; that it may be well with thee, and thou mayest live long on the earth." Generally speaking (and understanding that there are exceptions), the life of the obedient child will be longer than that of the rebel. It is unfortunate that some of the more recent translations have rendered the word *peace* as "prosperity." This is the Hebrew word *shalom*, which includes completeness, wholeness, harmony, and fulfillment (much more than the presence of material wealth or the absence of war!). God's wisdom adds days to one's life, but it also adds life to one's days—quality as well as quantity.

We should note that in Christ these blessings take on an added dimension. Long life becomes everlasting life, and peace becomes "peace with God through our Lord Jesus Christ" (Romans 5:1). Added to these are treasures in Heaven, and membership in the boundless family of God. For all of this, wise Christians have elected to give up material and temporal blessings, considering themselves the beneficiaries of a great bargain (Philippians 3:7-11).

B. Favor With God and Man (vv. 3, 4)

3. Let not mercy and truth forsake thee: bind them about thy neck; write them upon the table of thine heart.

Here we see wisdom in action. *Mercy* is expressed in sympathy, generosity, kindness, and forgiveness. For the Christian, mercy is not an occasional exercise, but rather a constant practice, patiently continued because it is a part of one's new personality. Mercy expresses itself in activity such as feeding the hungry, clothing the poor, and visiting the lonely. Jesus referred to such service as service to Him (Matthew 25:31-46).

In order that *mercy and truth* may never be lost, they are to be worn around the *neck*, either as a necklace, or as a collar or yoke. As a necklace, they are a valuable ornament (Proverbs 1:9), held close to one's person for safekeeping. As a collar or yoke, they are used in continual, obedient service. Instructions regarding mercy and truth are to be engraved on the writing *table*, or tablet, of the *heart*, which in this context describes the mind. These words are similar to those found in Deuteronomy 6:6-8, where parents are commanded to be diligent teachers of truth.

4. So shalt thou find favor and good understanding in the sight of God and man.

Here is a step beyond the promise in verses 1 and 2. The rewards named there were physical and material; here they include the realm of personal relationships: *in the sight of God and man*. By showing consistent kindness toward the needy, the wise one will gain the goodwill of those who know him.

The *good understanding* cited here is translated elsewhere as "a good name" (*New International Version*) or "good repute" (*New American Standard Bible*). Those who know the merciful one best will be most inclined to speak well of him. Luke 2:52 says of the boy Jesus that He "increased in . . . favor with God and man." Such growth in Heaven's eyes and earth's eyes should be the aim of every follower of Jesus.

II. Going God's Way
(Proverbs 3:5-8)

At this point the teaching moves to a consideration of our relationship with God.

A. Trusting in God (vv. 5, 6)

5. Trust in the LORD with all thine heart; and lean not unto thine own understanding.

Here is an echo of the theme sounded in Proverbs 1:7 and 2:6. Wisdom comes from God. It leads to God. And along the way it believes in, trusts in, and depends upon God. Just as the pilot looks to his compass and the traffic controller looks to his radar, so the godly person looks to his heavenly Father for the final word on any subject. But there is a difference. God is not a mechanical device; He is the Person who knows and shows the way.

Trust in the Lord with all thine heart; and lean not unto thine own understanding. In all thy ways acknowledge him, and he shall direct thy paths.

Proverbs 3:5, 6

visual for
lesson 6

The necessity of unreserved commitment to God is underscored by the phrase *with all thine heart*. A halfhearted or token commitment produces constant uncertainty, and results in confusion between God's way and that proposed by other "authorities." It results in one's becoming a "double-minded man . . . unstable in all his ways" (James 1:8).

As a weary shepherd might *lean* on his staff or a warrior on his spear, so anyone seeking answers to life's questions will lean on what he considers most dependable. Very often it is his own *understanding*, or intelligence. It is easy to think that one's education or experience qualifies him to deal competently and successfully with any situation. Real wisdom acknowledges the inadequacy of man's understanding. Let us choose God over all other "authorities," and henceforth lean confidently on His Word.

6. In all thy ways acknowledge him, and he shall direct thy paths.

By your choices and actions, let it be known that God is the ultimate authority and determiner of your *paths*. You know that He is the all-powerful, all-knowing, all-loving Creator and Ruler of the universe. Let your choices reflect that knowledge; then He will lay out before you a straight course, not difficult to see nor complicated to follow.

A famous old story tells of an intelligent dog that was carried away to Scotland, far from his master's home in England. Breaking out at last from his captivity, the animal set out on a directly southward course that took him many days and through many obstacles, but finally to his beloved master. Even so, the love of God will lead the Christian to search and find in God's wisdom the course toward home. The one grand decision to follow God and to let Him direct our steps will simplify every decision that has to be made thereafter.

THE PERIL OF THE PARTIAL

Surely Proverbs 3:5, 6 must be considered one of the most helpful and definitive passages in all the Old Testament. It derives much of its power from its use of the word "all." It stresses the

superlative and has no time for the timid and the trivial. One is to trust in the Lord with *all* one's heart. One is to acknowledge Him in *all* one's ways.

This stress on being wholehearted rather than fainthearted or halfhearted is important in many areas. A less than serious swing of a baseball bat results in a pop-up. A halfhearted golf swing usually sends the ball into the rough. A timid swing of the tennis racquet fails to carry the ball across the net.

When trying to cook, one must provide sufficient heat, or the result will be a half-cooked steak or a half-baked cake. When a man and a woman pledge their loyalty and devotion in marriage, it has to be "for better or for worse," not, "I guess I'll try it for a while."

If we want our relationship with God to be firm and fruitful, there must be a commitment with *all* our heart. If we want to be God's children, we must acknowledge Him in *all* our ways. Paul tells us, "God is able to make *all* grace abound to you, so that in *all* things at *all* times, having *all* that you need, you will abound in *every* good work" (2 Corinthians 9:8, *New International Version*). —J. G. V. B.

B. Departing From Evil (vv. 7, 8)

Another poetic pair of verses lends force to the exhortations to walk in God's way.

7. Be not wise in thine own eyes: fear the LORD, and depart from evil.

Isaiah 5:21 warns, "Woe unto them that are wise in their own eyes, and prudent in their own sight!" Romans 12:16 offers this challenge to Christians: "Be not wise in your own conceits." We should avoid the temptation common to students who have come suddenly upon some exciting new information. They may think they have received all there is of it! Consider the eager teenager who absorbs the information contained in the manual supplied with his automobile learner's permit, and then tells his father, "I know all there is to know on that subject." We all need to recognize that in God's world we hold learners' permits, not drivers' licenses.

The second part of this verse (*fear the Lord*) echoes the declaration of Proverbs 1:7. Follow the gracious and upward-leading way of "repentance toward God" (Acts 20:21). That way leads one to *depart from evil*.

8. It shall be health to thy navel, and marrow to thy bones.

There are clear physical benefits to godly living. Here the *navel* is considered as the center of the body, perhaps not only in regard to location, but also because of the fact that the navel (given its connection to the umbilical cord) is linked with the beginning of one's earthly existence. The *marrow* in the bones is essential in the production of blood. The Hebrew word used also suggests nourishing moisture, as reflected in the rendering of the *New American Standard Bible*: "refreshment to your bones."

Frequently we read of "new" discoveries by the medical community suggesting that the godly life is, in general, the healthy life. God's people do have thorns in the flesh, and sometimes their Christian service brings on afflictions and even illnesses. However, the godly person will always have more to give in productive work than will the one who indulges the flesh.

Another couplet (verses 9 and 10, not included in our printed text) promises material blessings to the individual who honors the Lord with appropriate gifts and offerings. Compare this with the Lord's promise in Malachi 3:10.

III. Accepting God's Correction (Proverbs 3:11, 12)

The promises of blessing that accompany the way of wisdom may lead some to expect in it nothing but prosperous ease. That would be wrong. God's people experience other circumstances, but these also come from a loving Father for the good of His children.

11. My son, despise not the chastening of the LORD; neither be weary of his correction.

Do not resent the Lord's disciplinary action as an injustice, or even think of it as unnecessary or unimportant. Be patient with it, and do not complain of it as a tiresome burden. It is essential to your growth and development.

If, like Job, you suffer much for no discernible reason, that too may be part of God's program for your maturity in Him. The testimony of saints who have been enriched rather than embittered through years of physical suffering speaks eloquently on this subject.

12. For whom the LORD loveth he correcteth; even as a father the son in whom he delighteth.

The element of reward found in this pair of verses is the assurance of our heavenly Father's love. We are reminded that our trials are not a sign of God's absence; they contain opportunities to deepen our awareness of His presence.

This link between love and chastening is not always easy to see, as Hebrews 12:5-11 admits in quoting and applying the verse before us to Christians. It concludes, "No chastening for the present seemeth to be joyous, but grievous: nevertheless, afterward it yieldeth the peaceable fruit of righteousness unto them which are exercised thereby." A pertinent illustration is the plight of the young person who has no loving

---

How to Say It
SHALOM (Hebrew). shah-*lome*.

father to admonish him, and so is neglected as though an illegitimate child or an orphan. Such neglect is not "cured" by simply giving a youngster many toys. Firm discipline, no less than the generous provision of needs, is a part of trustworthy fatherhood, on earth and in Heaven.

THE DESIRABILITY OF DISCIPLINE

The writer of Proverbs assures us that discipline is a characteristic of God's dealings with human beings. Discipline is not a signal of the displeasure of God, but is an evidence of His love.

In today's world, the presence and necessity of discipline is perhaps most evident in the area of sports. Whether it is an individual sport such as bowling or golf, or the various team sports such as hockey, volleyball, baseball, football, basketball, or soccer, there has to be a rigid use of discipline if success is to be achieved. This discipline involves countless hours of practice, and a willingness to regiment one's life in terms of diet, exercise, and the mastery of those skills required to excel in one's sport.

All serious sporting activity involves the use of "coaches." These are individuals who outline the particular tasks involved in each activity, and provide counsel and encouragement as needed. Some people are rejected as "uncoachable." These are persons who refuse to submit themselves to the essential disciplines required to obtain excellence in any sport.

God wants us to succeed in the living of a life which is fulfilling, meaningful, and blessed. To this end we must accept the discipline of obedience to His will and way.   —J. G. V. B.

IV. Boundless Value of Wisdom (Proverbs 3:13-15)

Our concluding cluster of verses is expanded to three, with the first verse introducing both a reward and a condition, and the second and third describing how superior wisdom is.

13. Happy is the man that findeth wisdom, and the man that getteth understanding.

The word rendered *happy* is the same Hebrew word that is normally rendered "blessed" (as in Psalm 1:1). Job 5:17, 18 links this blessedness to the discipline noted in our preceding verse: "Behold, happy [again, the same Hebrew word] is the man whom God correcteth: therefore despise not thou the chastening of the Almighty: for he maketh sore, and bindeth up: he woundeth, and his hands make whole."

14. For the merchandise of it is better than the merchandise of silver, and the gain thereof than fine gold.

Merchandise translates a Hebrew word whose root indicates the movement, or going about back and forth, of a tradesman at his business; thus the word is rendered "profit" in the *New American Standard Bible*. Wisdom is described as far more profitable than *silver*, and as yielding a much better return than *fine gold*, or the highest grade of gold. We could probably name several items more prized by us than these precious metals, but the sense would be the same: God's wisdom possesses more lasting value than anything else.

15. She is more precious than rubies: and all the things thou canst desire are not to be compared unto her.

Here and in the next three verses (not included in our printed text) wisdom is personified as a woman. Proverbs 7:4 invites, "Say unto wisdom, Thou art my sister." Fuller development of this feminine personification is found in Proverbs 1:20-33; 8:1-36; and 9:1-6. The present section continues to develop the thought of wisdom's supreme worth.

Rubies were (and are) highly prized. In some cultures, a slave who found and delivered to his master a ruby or diamond of sufficient size and quality could be given his freedom. Could this suggest that God-given wisdom buys our freedom from greater slaveries—bondage to ignorance, wickedness, prejudice, and all manner of destructive habits? Do we find here a link to Jesus' statement: "Ye shall know the truth, and the truth shall make you free" (John 8:32)? This liberating truth is, of course, Jesus Himself (John 8:36; 14:6).

God's wisdom, especially as found in Jesus, is incomparably more valuable than *all the things thou canst desire*. Those *things* are not only the fragile items of material substance—houses, autos, jewelry, electronic gadgetry, and the like—but other objects of man's fervent ambition, such as fame, power, and physical gratification. In comparison with God-given wisdom, they all fall under Solomon's sober judgment: "Vanity of vanities" (Ecclesiastes 1:2).

What will be your—and God's—final judgment about the things you most desire, seek, and obtain?

Conclusion

A. Help My Lack of Trust!

At this point in our study, we may find much in common with the father of a demon-possessed boy whom Jesus encountered immediately after His glorious transfiguration. Frustrated with failure in all his efforts to find relief for his son, the man pleaded with Jesus to help his son. "All things are possible to him that believeth," Jesus assured him (Mark 9:23). In tears the father cried out, "Lord, I believe; help thou mine unbelief" (v. 24).

Trust God! We hear this exhortation, amply enforced with evidence that this is the right and victorious way of wisdom. But how do we go about developing and exercising this trust? An answer may be found in Hebrews 1:1, 2, assuring us that God has spoken, first through the prophets and finally through His Son Jesus. That aptly summarizes the message of the entire Bible. God's Word provides evidence on which to base our trust in God, and it tells us how to act in expressing that trust. If you are not already following a program of daily Bible reading and study, now is the time to start. It is the best way to develop your trust in God, for it is God's way.

B. Prayer

Thank You, our Father in Heaven, for Your Word. Through it we find You abundantly worthy of our trust. Thank you for Your Son Jesus, in whom we find You perfectly revealed and in whom we find true wisdom. Help us, we pray, to learn Your wisdom and to act as Your trusting children in every circumstance. In Jesus' name we pray. Amen.

C. Thought to Remember

"Trust ye in the Lord for ever: for in the Lord Jehovah is everlasting strength" (Isaiah 26:4).

Home Daily Bible Readings

Monday, July 6—Rely on God (Proverbs 3:1-10)
Tuesday, July 7—Wisdom Is a Tree of Life (Proverbs 3:11-20)
Wednesday, July 8—Angels Come to Guard Us (Psalm 91:1-16)
Thursday, July 9—God Will Ransom Us (Psalm 49:1-15)
Friday, July 10—Trust and Be Like Mount Zion (Psalm 125:1-5)
Saturday, July 11—Giving God Credit (Deuteronomy 8:11-18)
Sunday, July 12—God Will Bring Us Home (Zephaniah 3:12-20).

Learning by Doing

This page contains an alternate lesson plan emphasizing learning activities.
Classes desiring such student involvement will find these suggestions helpful.

Learning Goals

This lesson should prepare students to:

1. Memorize Proverbs 3:5, 6, and cite some of the benefits of trusting in the Lord mentioned in Proverbs 3.

2. Contrast trusting in God with trusting in self.

3. Think of a circumstance where they need to trust God, rather than depend too much on their own wisdom or cunning.

Into the Lesson

Have the class briefly discuss trust in each of the following situations:

a soldier in the army

a child with his or her parents

a depositor in a bank

an employee in a big corporation

an investor in a stock company

The students may think of other situations in which trust is required. In each, focus on the basis of one's trust.

Use the chalkboard to create an acrostic with the word *trust*. Ask for a suitable word or phrase beginning with each letter, which illustrates or describes trust. Here is an example:

T—truthful

R—reliable

U—unchanging

S—steadfast

T—thankful

Pose this question: Should children totally trust their parents? (The answer will likely be "yes," unless the parents give reason to do otherwise.) Then raise this additional question: Is trusting parents a way of learning to trust God? Why or why not?

Into the Word

Ask a volunteer to read aloud Proverbs 3:1-8. Then review the following main points taken from these verses:

Remembering the teachings and commands of godly parents

Clinging to kindness and truth

Trusting God completely

Not trusting our own knowledge and understanding

Recognizing God's place in all our everyday activities

Fearing God and turning away from evil

Next, have another person read aloud Proverbs 3:11-15. Stress the main points in this passage:

Accepting God's discipline

Seeking His wisdom above all other goals in life

Conduct a Bible drill. See which student can be the first to find each of the following Scriptures. After a student has found one, have he or she read the passage and give a brief summary of its message.

Daniel 3:16-18 (Trust God, even when you are not sure what He is going to do.)

Habakkuk 3:17, 18 (Rejoice in the Lord, even in the face of disaster.)

1 Peter 4:12-14 (Be glad when you experience suffering for Christ's sake.)

Philippians 4:6 (Be "careful," or anxious, for nothing; instead, *pray*.)

Summarize these Scriptures by emphasizing that our trust in God is not conditional upon good things happening to us as a result of our trust.

End this part of the lesson by having the entire class read aloud in unison the Golden Text from Proverbs 3:5, 6.

Into Life

Ask the class to list the benefits or blessings of trusting in the Lord. The responses may be listed on a chalkboard. Here are a few possibilities, although others will undoubtedly emerge from your discussion:

No stress (peace that passes understanding)

Confidence (courage to share the gospel)

Walking in straight paths (a sense of purpose and direction)

God's watchful care (Proverbs 3:2 promises long life and family, although Jesus put the emphasis on spiritual blessings such as eternal life and a heavenly family.)

Next, ask for illustrations of how to apply trust in God to each of these daily life situations:

In a relationship (family, friend, co-worker)

In a job search

In the words we speak to fellow Christians

In health matters

In conclusion, form a circle, holding hands, and ask for sentence prayers for God's help during the week ahead in growing in our trust in, reliance in, and obedience to Him.

Let's Talk It Over

The questions on this page are designed to encourage review of the lesson Scriptures and to promote discussion of the lesson by the class. The answers provided are only discussion starters. Let your class talk it over from there.

1. Verses 1 and 2 of our text promise long life and peace to us if we remember God's laws and keep His commandments. Discuss how this principle works in life. How is it ultimately true in the context of our Christian faith?

This reminds us of the promise associated with the Fifth Commandment: "Honor thy father and thy mother." Keeping God's laws does put us on a path that minimizes or eliminates many risks to life. For instance, the righteous are not likely to die in gang fights, or from accidents while driving under the influence of drugs or alcohol. The pure are much less likely to catch AIDS and many other diseases. Beyond this, God promises to add His blessing to the obedient life, though we should not understand this to mean that every Christian is promised a long life. In addition, the righteous enjoy the peace that comes from knowing God, and from being free from guilt and from fear of the future. Ultimately this promise of long life will be fulfilled when we as Christians receive eternal life and the joys and security of Heaven.

2. In verse 5 we are admonished to trust in the Lord with all our hearts. How can we put this into practice? What does it mean to trust God rather than our own understanding?

Trust involves obedience, even when obedience appears to be risky or costly. Trust involves believing in God and in His faithfulness, even when circumstances tempt us to question Him. Trust also involves believing what the Lord says, even when it does not make sense. Much of what Jesus taught may seem to go against our deepest instincts, but we must trust that He is right. An example of this is found in the Beatitudes, which link blessing and prosperity to such conditions as meekness, hunger, and persecution. Trust involves believing in the Lord to keep His promises. It involves waiting on Him to do things in His time, although that may not be as quickly as we would like.

3. Verse 6 admonishes us to acknowledge God in all that we do, and He shall direct our paths through life. This is a wonderful promise, because it means that we need never worry about going the wrong way. How can we live in such a way as to allow God to direct our paths?

This principle involves two parts: ours and God's, and several levels of fulfillment. On the first, general level, we must begin by acknowledging God in such ways as believing in Him, confessing our faith daily, and obeying His commands. John calls this walking in the light (1 John 1:7). When we acknowledge God in this way, He watches over us to guide, protect, and bless us. On a more active level, we ought to take God's will into account as we make plans (see James 4:13-16). We can ask God to guide us and to open or close opportunities, expressing our willingness to be subject to His will. Finally, we may desire to serve God in some specific way, such as becoming a teacher, missionary, preacher, elder, or deacon. It is important to seek God's will and acknowledge His sovereignty in this process, asking Him to use us where and how He pleases.

4. No one enjoys being disciplined or corrected, even when it is from God. By its very nature, discipline is hard, unpleasant, and often painful. But the wise person profits from discipline. How does God discipline us? What is His motive? How can we profit from it?

God disciplines us as His children because He loves us. He knows if we are going in a way that will harm or even destroy us, and so He seeks to turn us back. He does this in many ways. The pain of a guilty conscience is a powerful tool. Many of us have experienced a pricked conscience when we read a Scripture or heard a sermon that convicted us of a particular sin, with the result that we repented and turned away from that sin. God may send family members, friends, or church leaders to warn us when we are going astray. Consider Nathan's rebuke of David, found in 2 Samuel 12:1-14, or Paul's instructions about the unrepentant man in 1 Corinthians 5. God may expose a secret sin, bringing it out for all to see, and thus help to drive it from our lives. Sometimes God brings suffering upon us, showing His displeasure and warning us to repent. Though we may hide it, deny it, or try to excuse it, in the depths of our hearts we all know when we are sinning against God. If we are wise, we will rejoice when God sends us these warnings, repent of our sins, and obey Him with renewed dedication.

Be a Good Neighbor

DEVOTIONAL READING: James 2:1-13.

LESSON SCRIPTURE: Proverbs 3:27-35; 14:21.

PRINTED TEXT: Proverbs 3:27-35; 14:21.

Proverbs 3:27-35

27 Withhold not good from them to whom it is due, when it is in the power of thine hand to do it.

28 Say not unto thy neighbor, Go, and come again, and tomorrow I will give; when thou hast it by thee.

29 Devise not evil against thy neighbor, seeing he dwelleth securely by thee.

30 Strive not with a man without cause, if he have done thee no harm.

31 Envy thou not the oppressor, and choose none of his ways.

32 For the froward is abomination to the LORD: but his secret is with the righteous.

33 The curse of the LORD is in the house of the wicked: but he blesseth the habitation of the just.

34 Surely he scorneth the scorners: but he giveth grace unto the lowly.

35 The wise shall inherit glory: but shame shall be the promotion of fools.

Proverbs 14:21

21 He that despiseth his neighbor sinneth: but he that hath mercy on the poor, happy is he.

GOLDEN TEXT: Withhold not good from them to whom it is due, when it is in the power of thine hand to do it.—Proverbs 3:27.

Wisdom for Living
Unit 2: Proverbs on Living a Disciplined Life
(Lessons 5-8)

Lesson Aims

This study should prepare the student to:

1. List the attitudes and behaviors typical of a good neighbor.

2. Contrast the Proverbs-style good neighbor with the selfishness of many neighbors today.

3. Adopt the practice of doing at least one good deed to a "neighbor" each day.

Lesson Outline

INTRODUCTION

    A. Neighborliness: Where and When

    B. Lesson Background

I. ON BEING A GOOD NEIGHBOR (Proverbs 3:27-30)

    A. Do Not Delay Doing Good (vv. 27, 28)

    Good Not Withheld

    B. Do Not Plot Evil (vv. 29, 30)

II. THE PLIGHT OF BAD NEIGHBORS (Proverbs 3:31-35)

    A. Not to Be Envied (v. 31)

    B. An Abomination to God (v. 32)

    C. Curse Versus Blessing (v. 33)

    D. Scorn Versus Grace (v. 34)

    E. Glory Versus Shame (v. 35)

III. HELPING THE POOR NEIGHBOR (Proverbs 14:21)

    From Sneers to Cheers

CONCLUSION

    A. Mr. Christian's Neighborhood

    B. Prayer

    C. Thought to Remember

The visual for Lesson 7 in the visuals packet contrasts the good neighbor with the self-centered neighbor. It is shown on page 396.

Introduction

A. Neighborliness: Where and When

During the Great Depression, a young man from the South moved to a midwestern city and rented a room in an upstairs apartment. For trips downtown, which he made quite regularly, he rode the streetcar. One day, while on the way home, he saw a lady passenger who looked vaguely familiar. Who was she? He had no idea. When the streetcar reached his home, the lady also got off, entered the building where he lived, walked up the same stairs, and went in the door across the hall from his room. So that's where he had seen her!

These were not unfriendly people. It was just that in the preoccupation with their daily routines, they had failed to notice or acknowledge one another. Needless to say, such a scenario is rather common in today's society, where isolation rather than involvement seems to be the accepted practice. Many people live next door to each other for years and never say a word.

Today's lesson from Proverbs challenges us to "be a good neighbor." In the Old Testament, the word *neighbor* appears (in the *King James Version*) as a translation of four different Hebrew words. These words define the neighbor as a fellow human being, as someone nearby, as an inhabitant or resident, or—in the vast majority of cases—as a friend or companion. This last term is the one used most frequently in the book of Proverbs.

What does it mean to be a good neighbor? It simply means to deal uprightly, mercifully, and honorably with other persons wherever and whenever we encounter them. Some people try to avoid neighborly responsibilities by avoiding contact with others. However, Ecclesiastes 4:9-12 spells out the benefit of companionship in life's experiences, with verse 9 reminding us, "Two are better than one."

B. Lesson Background

Our lessons from Proverbs are following a natural progression. They began with an exhortation to listen to and learn of wisdom, which begins with reverence for God. Then we were urged to trust God as the source of wisdom. Now we move to a consideration of our responsibility to the people around us, as an expression of our trust in and willingness to follow God, who is Himself fair, loving, and merciful to all mankind.

One might expect a study of human relationships to require an acquaintance with the cultural setting in which it was given. Were the words in today's text given to farmers and country villagers, or to businessmen and politicians in the city? The principles of Proverbs speak plainly to both groups, and after almost three thousand years they remain amazingly relevant.

Just eleven verses (Proverbs 3:16-26) supply the link between last week's lesson on trusting God and today's lesson on dealing well with the people around us. These verses exalt the blessings of wisdom, essentially telling us, "Hang on to wisdom; it's worth it!" Now we shall see how God-given wisdom is to be translated into our daily contacts with people.

I. On Being a Good Neighbor
(Proverbs 3:27-30)

A popular adage—definitely not in Proverbs—says, "Better late than never," to which today's text would respond, "Better never late!" Timeliness adds value to any virtue, and shows that our deed is motivated by genuine concern rather than by what is convenient for us.

A. Do Not Delay Doing Good
(vv. 27, 28)

27. Withhold not good from them to whom it is due, when it is in the power of thine hand to do it.

Many people in various circumstances have legitimate claims on us for all kinds of good. The apostle Paul names a number of them in Romans 13:7, 8: "Give everyone what you owe him: If you owe taxes, pay taxes; if revenue, then revenue; if respect, then respect; if honor, then honor. Let no debt remain outstanding, except the continuing debt to love one another" (*New International Version*). The apostle acknowledged his own debt to all people everywhere, to give them the gospel that had been entrusted to him for that very purpose (Romans 1:14, 15). The gospel imposes upon those who have received it a debt to communicate it to others in words. This obligation can be extended to include words that we owe to any neighbors who need them: words of appreciation, caring, sympathy, encouragement, cheerful greeting, or petition in prayer. We can pay endlessly on that neighborly debt without depleting either our supply or others' demand.

Poverty-stricken folk—those who are genuinely unable to meet their own material needs—have a special claim on God's people: "Whoso hath this world's good, and seeth his brother have need, and shutteth up his bowels of compassion from him, how dwelleth the love of God in him?" (1 John 3:17). It is easier, of course, to put off the claims of the poor than the claims of the landlord or the tax collector; however, "payment" to the needy is due whenever payment is in any way possible—*when it is in the power of thine hand to do it.* This is really another way of stating the principle in Galatians 6:10: When we "have therefore opportunity," we respond to a neighbor's need.

GOOD NOT WITHHELD

There are five successive "nots" in the selection from Proverbs in today's lesson (Proverbs 3:27-31). The first of these tells us not to withhold good from deserving persons when it is in our power to share with them.

One of the most remarkable instances of such sharing was the case of C. T. Studd and an inheritance that came to him in 1887. Studd had been an outstanding cricket player during his days at Cambridge University. He was deeply moved by Dwight L. Moody's preaching in England and Scotland, and had decided to give his life to Christian service.

At his father's death, Studd received more than twenty-five thousand pounds, worth about $125,000 today. He proceeded to give the entire amount away. Part of it was given to the work of the noted missionary George Müller, and part to the Salvation Army work in India. He also sent nearly $25,000 to Moody, which was used to underwrite the beginning of Moody Bible Institute in Chicago. These checks were all sent out on the same day—January 13, 1887.

Quite often it takes something of heroic proportions such as this to cause us to realize the impact and the implications of Proverbs 3:27: "Withhold not good from them to whom it is due, *when it is in the power of thine hand to do it.*" It is not just the hand that strikes that is harmful, but the hand that fails to reach out to caress and to help.   —J. G. V. B.

28. Say not unto thy neighbor, Go, and come again, and tomorrow I will give; when thou hast it by thee.

Procrastination—putting off until *tomorrow* the good that can and should be done today—is the great evil in view here. As in the previous verse, the failure to meet a clear need when one has the opportunity and the resources to do so is sharply criticized.

The Law of Moses forbade any delay in paying a needy laborer who relied heavily upon his income (Deuteronomy 24:14, 15). Paul states a principle that those who give willingly to others will be blessed with "all sufficiency" and with the increased ability to "abound to every good work" (2 Corinthians 9:7, 8).

A prevalent evil today is the habit of putting off payment for all manner of purchases through burgeoning credit and installment plans. In many situations, the mounting burden of debt can be ruinous. Such a debt can limit or choke off entirely the debtor's opportunity to help a needy neighbor.

How to Say It

HAMAN. *Hay*-mun.
MORDECAI. *Mor*-dih-kye.
SAMARITAN. Suh-*mare*-uh-tun.

B. Do Not Plot Evil (vv. 29, 30)

29. Devise not evil against thy neighbor, seeing he dwelleth securely by thee.

Who among us would deliberately plan to harm his *neighbor*? Surely none of us would commit premeditated murder or robbery, especially against a next-door neighbor so trusting that he never locked his doors or hid his wife's jewelry. Yet there is more than one kind of planned mischief. The language in this verse refers literally to "plowing" *evil*—that is, planning and working toward the hurtful act, as a farmer plans and works toward reaping a harvest. Consider the temptations in modern society to commit "white collar crime," by adjusting account books, tax returns, or expense reports, just as a crooked merchant in Biblical times would adjust his scales to give a false weight (Proverbs 11:1; 20:23).

The world of business, society, and politics is full of temptations to advance oneself at the expense of someone else—to climb up by pushing someone else down. This often involves a deliberately planned, carefully orchestrated agenda. Frequently the victim is an innocent party who has not done his own protective and competitive planning.

Most forms of gambling—whether in casinos, lotteries, race tracks, or other settings—depend on this kind of plotting against one's neighbors, not singly but *en masse*. The intended victim is anyone and everyone else involved in the game. Without losers (and many of them!) there could be no winners. "He that is glad at calamities shall not be unpunished" (Proverbs 17:5).

30. Strive not with a man without cause, if he have done thee no harm.

This verse elaborates on the thought of the previous one. Do not accuse a man for no reason. Do not pick a quarrel. Quarrels are seldom limited to the persons with whom they begin. Generally they reach a point where they involve and injure family members and friends.

Jesus goes far beyond the teaching of Proverbs at this point, urging His followers against initiating a quarrel even when there is a *cause*. Do not resist evil, He says; go two miles with the person who demands one; give more than is required of you (Matthew 5:39-42). Paul picks up his Master's theme: Do not return evil for evil; do not avenge yourselves; feed and refresh even your enemies when they are hungry and thirsty (Romans 12:17-21). Peter echoes these admonitions, citing the example of Jesus, who, when He was attacked, did not retaliate (1 Peter 2:21-23).

We must also note how these words apply to our dealings with friends. Give careful thought to these questions: If a friend has bared his or her soul to you in strict confidence, is the matter forever safe with you? What do you like to hear about someone: the good in which you can rejoice, or the tabloid kind of "news," which you secretly savor? Are you as careful about damaging a reputation as about hurting a physical body? Remember: In God's eyes, hatred is the equivalent of murder (1 John 3:15).

II. The Plight of Bad Neighbors (Proverbs 3:31-35)

It will be easier to help rather than harm those around us, if we are not overly impressed with the apparent prosperity of those folk who are neither helpful nor kind.

At this point, the poetic structure of our text changes from balanced pairs of verses to a pattern of five similar verses developing one complete thought.

A. Not to Be Envied (v. 31)

31. Envy thou not the oppressor, and choose none of his ways.

Proverbs 24:19 warns against falling prey to this kind of discouragement, saying, "Fret not thyself because of evil men, neither be thou envious at the wicked; for there shall be no reward to the evil man; the candle of the wicked shall be put out." Compare these words with those of Psalm 37:1, 2 and Psalm 73.

Two other potentially dangerous consequences result from the envious attention to wealthy wickedness. First, a twisted sense of values arises from the wrong impression that crime pays. That spirit was demonstrated some time ago in a child's answer to the question, "What did you learn from that televised report of a murder trial?" The child replied, "I learned that if you are rich and famous, you can kill anybody you want to."

The second is that envy leads naturally to imitation. The untaught youngster who observes a fat roll of currency in the hands of the drug dealer is all too often on the way to dealing drugs himself.

visual for
lesson 7

Do not withhold good from those who deserve it, when it is in your power to act.
Proverbs 3:27, NIV

B. An Abomination to God (v. 32)

God was not mentioned by name in the earlier part of our text. Now we are encouraged to view the selfish and oppressive neighbor from His perspective.

32. For the froward is abomination to the LORD: but his secret is with the righteous.

The *froward*, or perverse individual, having set his course in opposition to the Word and the ways of God, is called an *abomination*. This is the same word that is used in the Law of Moses concerning the various repulsive practices of the pagan peoples who were to be driven out of the land of Canaan (Deuteronomy 18:9-14). God finds both the practices and those who engage in them abhorrent.

Those who seek to know and serve God, on the other hand, are welcomed into His presence and taken into His confidence. Thus God dealt with Abraham (Genesis 18:17-19), Moses (Numbers 12:6-8), and thus He deals with all who fear Him (Psalm 25:14).

C. Curse Versus Blessing (v. 33)

33. The curse of the LORD is in the house of the wicked: but he blesseth the habitation of the just.

One does not sense the full impact of what God's *curse* and God's blessing mean, until he reads Moses' pronouncement in Deuteronomy 28. There one finds fourteen verses describing the blessings attendant on Israel's obedience to the Law, and fifty-four verses describing the curses that would follow as punishment for disobedience. No aspect of human experience was left out of this inventory. Physical health, family life, household welfare, business affairs, politics, national defense, crops, flocks, and herds were all part of the wholesome results of obedience to God or the disastrous results of disobedience.

The *house of the wicked* may suggest not only a structure, but also a household, with family and servants. In contrast, the Hebrew word rendered *habitation* in *the habitation of the just* usually describes a pasture for grazing, or an enclosed pen for sheep! The permanence of a home is not in its building materials but in God, who is honored by those who are faithful to Him, regardless of the kind of structure where they reside. Such individuals are building for eternity.

D. Scorn Versus Grace (v. 34)

34. Surely he scorneth the scorners: but he giveth grace unto the lowly.

Over the course of history, we have seen the dramatic downfall of infamous tyrants, but not before they claimed uncounted hordes of victims who died with no more than a firm hope of justice to come. Such justice will be administered; the Judge of all the earth will do right (Genesis 18:25). Trust God for the fulfillment of His promises, on His schedule. Meanwhile, we still have riches that the mightiest tyrant can never enjoy—God's fatherly presence, the devoted affection of His family, and the joy of helping those who need help in His name.

E. Glory Versus Shame (v. 35)

35. The wise shall inherit glory: but shame shall be the promotion of fools.

Inheritance comes as a natural benefit of a family relationship. In the same way, to God's children who look to Him for wisdom and depend on Him for whatever rewards or honor may come, recognition is assured. Consider, for examples, Joseph in Egypt and Daniel in Babylon. From prison and captivity, and without self-promotion, each of them rose by God-given wisdom to heights of honor and power within a pagan society.

On the other hand, *fools* whose self-confidence becomes self-*promotion*, draw the Lord's judgment: "Every one that exalteth himself shall be abased; and he that humbleth himself shall be exalted" (Luke 18:14). Consider the classic example of Haman in the book of Esther. Constantly promoting himself and seeking to destroy faithful Mordecai, Haman ends up giving Mordecai the public honors that he had planned for himself (Esther 6:1-11). In the end, Haman is hanged on a high gallows that he had built for Mordecai (Esther 7:1-10). The promotion of a fool!

III. Helping the Poor Neighbor (Proverbs 14:21)

Our printed text now takes us to one more verse from the heart of Proverbs, reemphasizing the essence of good neighborliness—helping those who need help.

21. He that despiseth his neighbor sinneth: but he that hath mercy on the poor, happy is he.

This verse needs to be taken in context with the one immediately before it: "The poor is hated even of his own neighbor: but the rich hath many friends." This simply recognizes an all-too-prevalent condition. The poor cannot return material favors in kind. They do not have the degree of influence needed to help a person up the social or political ladder. They cannot always maintain the kind of appearance that makes for acceptable or impressive company.

The person who follows the self-serving course *despiseth*, or deals contemptuously with, the poor. James 2:1-7 describes the church that welcomes the wealthy visitor, but is cool in its reception of the poor. James tells such a church, "Are ye not then partial in yourselves, and are become judges of evil thoughts? . . . ye have despised the poor" (vv. 4, 6).

To be *happy*, or blessed, translates the same Hebrew word found in last week's lesson, in the promise made to one who finds wisdom (Proverbs 3:13). Here the promise is made to one who is generous to the *poor*. "Blessed are the merciful: for they shall obtain mercy" (Matthew 5:7). He who shares in the nature of God through being merciful will share in the goodness of God, receiving mercy from Him. That's a double blessing!

FROM SNEERS TO CHEERS

Here is a true account of a way in which the wisdom of Proverbs 14:21 was demonstrated. A portion of the north side of a city in upstate New York was terribly undeveloped. For example, while those who dwelt in other areas of the city had running water, those on the north side carried water to their homes from wells, and used outdoor toilets. Their houses were shabby, their yards often unkempt. In most cases they did not even have electricity.

Some of the people who came from this area wanted to forget that they had ever lived there. They very seldom visited relatives there, and when they did, they never stayed longer than they had to.

Some, however, were not too proud or repulsed by their friends or relatives' poverty to visit and maintain ties with those who lived there. One of my relatives continued to visit and maintain a close friendship with those in this area, and came to acquire property there.

In time, the city spread out to this section, and lovely new homes were built there. Later, a new highway came through and this "slum" area eventually became a highly respected place of affluence and charm. The relative I knew became quite well-to-do through real estate sales, and lived in a home on the edge of this once despised area. Truly, "He that despiseth his neighbor sinneth: but he that hath mercy on the poor, happy is he."   —J. G. V. B.

Conclusion
A. Mr. Christian's Neighborhood

Mr. Christian once read a popular book entitled *How to Win Friends and Influence People*. It advised being friendly as the means toward the goal of making friends. Jesus offered counsel that was noticeably different. He said to seek to please God first, and trust Him to provide whatever human relationships and friendships are most needed (Mark 10:29, 30).

Mr. Christian read Jesus' intriguing story about a good neighbor (Luke 10:25-37), and asked himself some questions based on it:

What did the neighborly Samaritan do? He did everything possible to help a stranger in need. Why did he do it? The man was in trouble and required immediate attention.

Was the Samaritan trying to "win friends and influence people"? If so, did it work? Scripture does not consider either of these questions. Apparently the Samaritan was simply a helpful, compassionate man, and did what came naturally to him. Apparently he believed in God, knew what God said about loving others as much as he loved himself, and wanted to please God.

In Mr. Christian's neighborhood, the motivation for doing good to others is to please God and to help those in need. If that wins friends and influences people, fine. But that is not the reason he does these deeds. The real reason is that he is a Christian, and that's what a Christian does.

B. Prayer

Thank You, Father in Heaven, for the means and the opportunities to become like You in helping people who need help. May we be good neighbors for Jesus' sake, and if in the process we come to have good neighbors, we'll thank You for that, too. Amen.

C. Thought to Remember

"Thou shalt love thy neighbor as thyself" (Leviticus 19:18; Matthew 22:39).

Home Daily Bible Readings

Monday, July 13—Be a Good Neighbor (Proverbs 3:27-35)
Tuesday, July 14—Be Kind to the Poor (Proverbs 14:18-22)
Wednesday, July 15—Wisdom Is Better Than Weapons (Ecclesiastes 9:3-18)
Thursday, July 16—Live Together in Unity (Psalm 133:1—134:3)
Friday, July 17—Love One Another (John 13:31-35)
Saturday, July 18—Seek the Welfare of Babylon (Jeremiah 29:1-14)
Sunday, July 19—Show Respect to the Poor (James 2:1-13)

Learning by Doing

This page contains an alternate lesson plan emphasizing learning activities.
Classes desiring such student involvement will find these suggestions helpful.

Learning Goals

After completing this study, students should be able to:

1. List the attitudes and behaviors typical of a good neighbor.

2. Contrast the Proverbs-style good neighbor with the selfishness of many neighbors today.

3. Adopt the practice of doing at least one good deed to a "neighbor" each day.

Into the Lesson

Ask the class members in advance to bring in a newspaper or magazine article about someone who has helped another person. Have each student briefly share the story. As each story is reported, ask the students to identify one quality about the person who helped. Write those qualities on a chalkboard or on poster board for later reference.

Next, take and record a vote by the entire class as to who is a neighbor:

_____ someone living nearby
_____ a long-time friend living far away
_____ a fellow worker
_____ a relative
_____ a stranger in another country
_____ a public official

Discuss the results for about five minutes.

Then pass out 3 by 5 cards, one to each student, and ask for a written answer to these two questions:

Is there anyone to whom a good deed is not due? If there is, what kind of individual would that be?

Return to the qualities of helpers (listed earlier) and decide whether or not each quality agrees with what the Bible teaches us about being a good neighbor.

Into the Word

To begin today's Bible study, review the parable of the good Samaritan (Luke 10:30-37). Emphasize the qualities of the good Samaritan, such as compassion, generosity, tolerance, and forbearance.

Next, have a student read Romans 13:8, stressing the active rather than passive nature of love. Suggest that loving a neighbor is more than feeling good about him or her. Refer to James 2:14-17 and 1 John 3:16-18, which make this

especially clear. Then have another student read Proverbs 25:17, with its emphasis on not being intrusive or a nuisance.

At this point, have another volunteer read Proverbs 3:27-35, and 14:21. Ask the entire class to go back through the passage and extract the main "don'ts" from it:

Don't withhold good.
Don't procrastinate in doing good.
Don't devise mischief against someone.
Don't strive without cause.
Don't envy the oppressor.
Don't wait until it is convenient to do good.
Don't despise your neighbor.

Present this opinion question and try to arrive at a consensus response: Is gambling a way of hurting our neighbor? (See the lesson commentary under Proverbs 3:29.)

Into Life

Refer to the lesson Introduction for a definition of *neighbor*. Ask each student to rate himself or herself, on a scale of 1 to 5, on each quality listed below (one being lowest and five being highest). Tell the students not to put their names on their evaluations.

Helpful	1	2	3	4	5
Friendly	1	2	3	4	5
Considerate	1	2	3	4	5
Sharing	1	2	3	4	5
Encouraging	1	2	3	4	5
Willing to listen	1	2	3	4	5
Not nosy	1	2	3	4	5

Have each student compute an average, then tell a student to take the cards and compute a class average to report later for analysis.

Next, divide the class into groups of three or four, and ask each group to prepare a plan for being a good neighbor to a specific person. Each group should decide how its members will be a blessing to that person during the next week. If there is time, these plans may be shared with the entire class.

To close today's session, announce the results of the *neighbor* poll. Have class members form a circle. Pray for God to help the class raise their average and to guide all of them as they try to apply today's lesson and "be a good neighbor" to someone this week.

Let's Talk It Over

The questions on this page are designed to encourage review of the lesson Scriptures and to promote discussion of the lesson by the class. The answers provided are only discussion starters. Let your class talk it over from there.

1. We are told not to withhold good from those to whom it is due, when we have the means of giving them the needed help (Proverbs 3:27). This is well and good, but it raises the question, "To whom is it due?" Suggest how we can determine to whom we are under obligation. Also, suggest different kinds of good that we can do to one another.

The most obvious good, and probably the one that Solomon had in mind, is to share material assistance with those in need. True, there are "loafers" who squander their goods; and probably the best thing we can do for them is to refuse them help, so that they can learn to work and budget. However, many people have real needs in spite of their hard work and their best efforts to make ends meet. People afflicted by disaster need our help. Senior citizens on fixed incomes sometimes need help, often in the form of assistance with household tasks. In addition, we should pray for the sick and hurting. We ought to say a word of encouragement to the preacher and his wife. Basically, we should help anyone with a genuine need for what we have available to share, whether the individual needs money, work, prayer, time, or words.

2. Solomon also warns us against delaying our help when we have the means to give the needed help (Proverbs 3:28). Why is it important that we not delay our help? What are some of the motives we have for delay?

If a person is really in need, then likely he needs our help *now*. Every day we delay prolongs his suffering. Generally our motives for delay are not good, although it could be that we need time to organize the needed resources or to contact people who can help in addressing the situation. When an individual comes and asks us for help, we may ask him to come back later, hoping that he won't return because we don't really want to help. Sometimes we salve our consciences by saying that we will do good to someone as soon as we get the chance. But somehow the opportunity never comes. The truth is that we don't care enough to make the time and take the trouble to minister to someone else. None of us can do everything for everyone; but all of us can do something for someone, and we can do it today, not sometime.

3. Motivated by greed, selfishness, ambition, and pride, many people regularly plan ways to do evil to their neighbors. This is exactly the opposite of the second greatest commandment—to love others as ourselves. List some ways that people plot against others. Are there ways that even respectable Christians do this?

Some of this can be fairly direct. Some people watch their neighbors carefully, just waiting for the chance to steal someone else's belongings. But many plots are more subtle. A person covets a co-worker's position, so he plots and plans, seeking ways to make the other person look untrustworthy or incompetent. Some people constantly look for opportunities for lawsuits as a way to extort money from others. If we have a grudge against our neighbor, it may be that we never miss an opportunity to spread unflattering gossip about the person, perhaps adding a little "spice" to make it more interesting. Sadly, Christians have been known to engage in unrelenting criticism against preachers, church leaders, or Christian brothers or sisters, even though the criticism is not really deserved.

4. People always seem to gather around to watch "a good fight." However, our text tells us not to quarrel with our neighbor if he has done us no harm (Proverbs 3:30). Why is this wise? How does Jesus carry this principle one step farther?

It is never wise to pick a fight. For one thing, the other person just might prevail and inflict serious and painful injuries on the troublemaker. Also, fights and arguments have a way of escalating, raising the stakes and widening to involve others. Jesus teaches us to go much farther than the principle of Proverbs 3:30. He tells us not to fight or resist even if we are severely provoked or wronged. Fighting back may make the situation worse. Beyond this, the Lord does not want His people known for their fighting abilities. He wants us to have a reputation for patience, forbearance, and meekness. After all, God Himself is patient with His enemies, preferring to win them over by love instead of force. We, too, are much more likely to make a friend of an enemy by exercising patience instead of force. We may even bring that person to know the Lord.

Obey God's Law

DEVOTIONAL READING: Matthew 7:15-27.

LESSON SCRIPTURE: Proverbs 28:1-13.

PRINTED TEXT: Proverbs 28:4-13.

Proverbs 28:4-13

4 They that forsake the law praise the wicked: but such as keep the law contend with them.

5 Evil men understand not judgment: but they that seek the LORD understand all things.

6 Better is the poor that walketh in his uprightness, than he that is perverse in his ways, though he be rich.

7 Whoso keepeth the law is a wise son: but he that is a companion of riotous men shameth his father.

8 He that by usury and unjust gain increaseth his substance, he shall gather it for him that will pity the poor.

9 He that turneth away his ear from hearing the law, even his prayer shall be abomination.

10 Whoso causeth the righteous to go astray in an evil way, he shall fall himself into his own pit: but the upright shall have good things in possession.

11 The rich man is wise in his own conceit; but the poor that hath understanding searcheth him out.

12 When righteous men do rejoice, there is great glory: but when the wicked rise, a man is hidden.

13 He that covereth his sins shall not prosper: but whoso confesseth and forsaketh them shall have mercy.

GOLDEN TEXT: Evil men understand not judgment: but they that seek the LORD understand all things.—Proverbs 28:5.

Wisdom for Living
Unit 2: Proverbs on Living a Disciplined Life
(Lessons 5-8)

Lesson Aims

This study should equip class members to:

1. State the blessings that come through obedience to God, and contrast them with the consequences of the disobedient life.

2. Give illustrations from Scripture of the fruits of both obedient and disobedient living.

3. Pinpoint one area of their lives where their failure to obey God is clear, and take steps to correct this situation.

Lesson Outline

INTRODUCTION
  A. Read the Directions
  B. Lesson Background
  I. THE LIBERATING LAW (Proverbs 28:4-9)
   A. The Good Fight (v. 4)
   B. Understanding and Good Standing
      (vv. 5, 6)
   C. Honoring the Family (v. 7)
   D. Good Business (v. 8)
   E. Prayer Principle (v. 9)
      Pernicious Piety
 II. PAIRS TO PONDER (Proverbs 28:10-12)
   A. The Deceitful and the Upright (v. 10)
   B. The Rich and the Poor (v. 11)
   C. The Righteous and the Wicked (v. 12)
III. COVERING OR CONFESSING? (Proverbs 28:13)
CONCLUSION
  A. You're on Your Own Now
  B. Prayer
  C. Thought to Remember

The visual for Lesson 8 uses words from today's text to contrast living in darkness with living in light. It is shown on page 405.

Introduction

A. Read the Directions

Like the makers of machinery, God our Maker has provided descriptions and directions for His creation. No legislative assembly could do what was necessary in this area, for no man or body of men can know the whole creation of God. And no one man or body of men possesses the perfect love to act for the good of all without any self-interest.

The Old Testament records how God revealed His purpose especially to Abraham and his family. Later, He revealed His directives to Moses for the nation that was composed of the descendants of Abraham. These directives are found in the books of Exodus, Leviticus, Numbers, and Deuteronomy.

God had more to say, however. In applying His Law to later generations of Israelites, He spoke through prophets, singers, and wise teachers among His people. Most notable of the wise teachers was Solomon, who asked God for "an understanding heart" and was given a measure of wisdom far beyond that of other men (1 Kings 3:3-15). The book of Proverbs preserves much of his written sayings. It acknowledges, "The Lord giveth wisdom: out of his mouth cometh knowledge and understanding" (Proverbs 2:6). It also emphasizes the role of the family in passing that wisdom on to the next generation. Proverbs 3:1 urges, "My son, forget not my law," and Proverbs 6:20 adds, "Forsake not the law of thy mother." The teachings in Proverbs echo the moral and practical directives of God's Law. Both contain His guidelines for successful living by persons such as us in a world such as ours.

B. Lesson Background

Our previous lessons from Proverbs were taken from the introductory section of the book —the first nine chapters. There the proverbs are grouped in clusters of verses, developing exhortations to "my son." Today's lesson comes from a later segment of the book—chapters 25-29. Proverbs 25:1 introduces this portion, saying, "These are also proverbs of Solomon, which the men of Hezekiah king of Judah copied out."

The proverbs of Solomon had been known for approximately two centuries before Hezekiah came to the throne in Judah and restored the temple worship, which had become corrupted by pagan elements. Second Chronicles 29:30 recounts that Hezekiah restored the use of "the words of David" in the temple worship. It appears that he also restored interest in the proverbs of David's son, Solomon.

The proverbs in chapters 25-29 follow a different style from those found in the first nine chapters. They are brief, usually presenting a complete thought in one verse of comparison or contrast. They present little or nothing of direct admonition. Instead of urging "my son" to do or not to do something, they set forth observations and evaluations that say, in effect, "Here is the good and here is the bad. Take your pick!" Our lesson title presents the challenge in these words: "Obey God's Law."

I. The Liberating Law
(Proverbs 28:4-9)

The first six verses of our printed text provide a sort of scaffolding for today's study, with three specific references to the *law* as forsaken (v. 4), kept (vv. 4, 7), and avoided (v. 9). The *law* refers to God's Law, whether found in the writings of Moses or received through parental instruction.

A. The Good Fight (v. 4)

4. They that forsake the law praise the wicked: but such as keep the law contend with them.

With the recounting of God's Law through Moses (just before the Israelites crossed the Jordan and entered Canaan) came a solemn warning against forgetting it: "Beware that thou forget not the Lord thy God, in not keeping his commandments, and his judgments, and his statutes, which I command thee this day" (Deuteronomy 8:11). Even worse, however, is the practice of those who deliberately turn away from God's standards. Such are those described in Romans 1:28-32, who are portrayed as not only engaging in abominable practices, but as taking "pleasure in them that do them." Being resentful of any effort to curb their wickedness, they cheer at the apparent progress made by those of their own kind who flaunt their rebellion against God and against Biblical standards. We see them all about us in the entertainment world, the communications media, and some areas of public education.

The idea that the righteous are to *contend with*, or "resist" (*New International Version*), the *wicked* reflects the tension that is bound to occur between these two points of view and those who hold them. Does this contradict other passages of Scripture (in particular, the Sermon on the Mount) that command the righteous to love their enemies, resist not evil, and turn the other cheek? Not at all; the verse before us is simply stating that there will always be a conflict between righteousness and evil.

How to Say It

ARIMATHEA. *Air*-uh-muh-*thee*-uh (strong accent on *thee*).
ATHALIAH. Ath-uh-*lye*-uh.
BATHSHEBA. Bath-*she*-buh.
BOAZ. *Boe*-az.
HEZEKIAH. Hez-ih-*kye*-uh.
JEHOASH. Jeh-*hoe*-ash.
SANHEDRIN. San-*heed*-run or *San*-huh-drin.

"Contention" is inevitable. In certain situations, when personally attacked or ridiculed, we will "contend" with the evildoer by love or by nonresistance. In other settings, where evil principles are being promoted and flaunted in a community, we will "have no fellowship with the unfruitful works of darkness, but rather reprove them" (Ephesians 5:11). Christians are called to challenge evil's presence in their surroundings and to "contend" on behalf of God's perspective, even when (and particularly when) no one else is doing so. This is part of our responsibility to be "salt" and "light" (Matthew 5:13-16).

B. Understanding and Good Standing
(vv. 5, 6)

5. Evil men understand not judgment: but they that seek the LORD understand all things.

A familiar non-Biblical adage says, "The wish is father to the thought"; that is, a person tends to believe what he wants to believe. Having set himself on a course that is contrary to God's Law, the rebellious one finds that divine *judgment*, or justice, does not make sense to him. He concludes that a good God, who must also be a merciful Judge and a loving Father, would never administer painful punishment to someone. He simply refuses to recognize that his willful and defiant ways must bring their own dire consequences, and that God's chastening may be his last and best hope to escape a self-imposed destiny. Thus he joins those whom Isaiah described as "them that call evil good, and good evil" (Isaiah 5:20, 21).

On the other hand, those whose reverence for God leads them to accept His directions for living in His world find no difficulty in accepting His explanations and following as He leads. Thanks to God's guidelines, they *understand* what is good and right and fair. So "he that is spiritual judgeth all things" (1 Corinthians 2:15). God's Word becomes the standard for accurate measurements.

6. Better is the poor that walketh in his uprightness, than he that is perverse in his ways, though he be rich.

The quality of understanding, just mentioned, is enough to overcome the disadvantages of poverty in establishing one's standing before God and men. The *rich* man, if he turns away from God and godliness in both speech and actions, forfeits the respect that his wealth may have gained for him. Deuteronomy 8:11-20 warns against the ever-present temptations of prosperity: to lead the prosperous person to think that he gained his wealth by his own powers and abilities, and that therefore he can get along very well without God.

How, though, is one person *better* than the other? Is he more highly approved by God and men? More useful as a member of the community? More valuable as a friend? Perhaps any or all of the above. Our text makes the evaluation and leaves detailed analysis and application to the reader.

C. Honoring the Family (v. 7)

7. Whoso keepeth the law is a wise son: but he that is a companion of riotous men shameth his father.

This echoes the thought of Proverbs 10:1: "A wise son maketh a glad father: but a foolish son is the heaviness of his mother." Wisdom is demonstrated by works. It accepts authority, whether that authority is a heavenly Father or an earthly father.

The child of a godly family usually does not set foot upon the path of wickedness alone; he or she "falls into bad company." It is likely that the rebellious prodigal son had all kinds of companionship as he ventured into "riotous living" (Luke 15:13). The *riotous men* mentioned in our text are described further in Proverbs 23:20, 21: "Be not among winebibbers; among riotous eaters of flesh: for the drunkard and the glutton shall come to poverty." Among today's urban gang members that may sound like rather tame "riotousness," but it is enough of a start in the wrong way to embarrass a caring parent.

On the other hand, what youthful accomplishments stir the most enthusiastic pride in those of us who are parents? What do we encourage, praise, and brag about in our children? Are we as eager to boast about their spiritual accomplishments as their social, athletic, or academic prowess? Precious to one preacher is the boyhood memory of attending prayer meetings with his father, and feeling the warm and gentle squeeze of the parental hand when the lad participated meaningfully in prayer or Scripture quotation. Who could turn his back on that kind of encouragement?

D. Good Business (v. 8)

8. He that by usury and unjust gain increaseth his substance, he shall gather it for him that will pity the poor.

Here God demonstrates His concern with the practical affairs of men. The Law of Moses forbade the Israelites from charging *usury* (interest) on anything they lent to a fellow Israelite (Exodus 22:25; Deuteronomy 23:19). Deuteronomy 23:20 permitted them to lend to a stranger with interest. In any circumstances where interest might be charged, high rates were forbidden. Thus the *New International Version* reads, "He who increases his wealth by exorbitant interest amasses it for another, who will be kind to the poor."

What does the promise of this verse mean? Will the offender's money be taken from him, as in Jesus' parables of money handled faithfully by some and mishandled by others (Matthew 25:28, 29; Luke 19:24-26)? Will the sinner's amassed wealth be left at his death to someone who will deal with it more generously, as implied in Proverbs 13:22: "The wealth of the sinner is laid up for the just"? In any case, it is abundantly clear that God's favor rests with those who share His spirit of caring for those who cannot care for themselves.

E. Prayer Principle (v. 9)

9. He that turneth away his ear from hearing the law, even his prayer shall be abomination.

For those who simply do not want to hear the instructions of God's *law,* there are many ways to escape. One was used by a radio listener who heard the introduction of a religious program when his favorite talk show ended. "Turn that thing off!" he growled, and silenced the radio. Others change the subject when conversation at home or at work comes dangerously close to introducing God. Multitudes simply stay away from church. As a last resort, anyone can think about something else while the offensive subject is discussed.

How can such a person pray acceptably? Desperate necessity sometimes causes people to turn to God—people who have never given Him a passing thought:

> "Eyes the parson could not school
>   By wayside graves are raised,
> And lips say, 'God be pitiful'
>   That ne'er said, 'God be praised.'"

No hope is held forth for the one who willfully rejects God's directives and then expects to win His favor by suddenly deciding to turn to *prayer.* The word used to describe such an attempt is *abomination*—the same word that describes God's assessment of the sin of idolatry and its accompanying evil practices (Deuteronomy 18:9-12).

PERNICIOUS PIETY

One would think that the very act of praying requires a submission before God, and an awareness of His presence and power. Yet Proverbs 28:9 tells us that when one turns a deaf ear to God's Law, "even his prayer shall be abomination."

Jesus was especially "turned off" by the religious leaders of His day who wanted to impress people by their lengthy prayers, but who took advantage of widows for their own profit. "Beware of the scribes, which love to go in long clothing, . . . which devour widows' houses, and for a pretense make long prayers: these shall receive greater damnation" (Mark 12:38-40).

One of Jesus' most powerful parables involved a prayer that was indeed "abomination." Luke tells us, "He spake this parable unto certain which trusted in themselves that they were righteous, and despised others" (Luke 18:9). Many of us are familiar with this parable about the contrasting prayers of a Pharisee and a publican. The Pharisee was thankful because he was "not as other men are, extortioners, unjust, adulterers, or even as this publican" (v. 11). Because he did not commit certain sins, he felt himself to be very righteous. He seemed especially proud of not being like the publican.

This Pharisee indeed had neglected the weightier matters of the law, such as humility, kindness, and a sense of loving concern for others. He was proud, austere, self-righteous, and contemptuous of those he considered inferior to himself. Therefore, his prayer was "abomination."   —J. G. V. B.

II. Pairs to Ponder
(Proverbs 28:10-12)

Verses 10-12 may be considered as a commentary on the principle stated by Paul in Galatians 6:7: "Be not deceived; God is not mocked: for whatsoever a man soweth, that shall he also reap."

A. The Deceitful and the Upright
(v. 10)

10. Whoso causeth the righteous to go astray in an evil way, he shall fall himself into his own pit: but the upright shall have good things in possession.

Righteous persons frequently find that their less conscientious neighbors feel uncomfortable in their presence. Nothing pleases the worldly one more than to lead his innocent neighbor into behavior more like his own. Jesus was unsparing in His condemnation of such a cal-

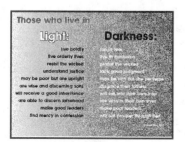

visual for
lesson 8

lous attitude: "Whoso shall offend one of these little ones which believe in me, it were better for him that a millstone were hanged about his neck, and that he were drowned in the depth of the sea" (Matthew 18:6). Similarly, Deuteronomy 27:18 declared, "Cursed be he that maketh the blind to wander out of the way." The sin of tempting another to sin will bring ruin to the tempter. The one who leads others in the wrong direction will be the first to arrive at the wrong destination.

On the other hand, there is a promise of *good things* given to the *upright* or blameless one. In Psalm 84:11 is found this assurance: "No good thing will he [the Lord] withhold from them that walk uprightly." For the faithful in Christ, this includes an everlasting inheritance and an unfading crown of glory (1 Peter 1:3, 4; 5:4).

B. The Rich and the Poor (v. 11)

11. The rich man is wise in his own conceit; but the poor that hath understanding searcheth him out.

Rich and *poor* are usually relative terms. He who possesses significantly more than his neighbors is called rich, and he who possesses significantly less is called poor. But a man's life is far more than the total of his possessions (Luke 12:15). It is what he would be without any possessions at all. First Timothy 6:9, 10, 17-19 warns that the gaining of wealth brings with it a multitude of temptations, which one may significantly reduce when he uses his wealth to serve God and His people.

If a rich person eliminates God from his outlook, he is likely to suppose that his wealth is an indication of his superior wisdom and worth as a person. He may revel in the flattery, the fawning, and the following of those who hope to gain something from him. All this can build within him a dangerous *conceit*. He considers himself a champion in his own realm, and sees no other course worth pursuing. Yet there are godly men, who, despite the temptations of wealth, remained wise and humble. Consider the examples of Boaz of Bethlehem (Ruth 2:1) and Joseph of Arimathea (Matthew 27:57-60).

The *King James* reading of *searcheth him out* seems to say that the poor person looks to the righteous for direction or help. The phrase actually describes the poor person's ability to see through all the pretensions of power and prestige associated with the rich. The *New American Standard Bible* reads, "The poor who has understanding sees through him." While the poor lack the financial means of the wealthy, they usually possess a great deal more in the area of "common sense." They understand truths that the rich and powerful are often too preoccupied to see. Such a one was the man whom Jesus healed of his blindness, and who then stood firm in his testimony against all the pompous threats of the powerful Sanhedrin (John 9:13-17, 24-34).

C. The Righteous and the Wicked
(v. 12)

12. When righteous men do rejoice, there is great glory: but when the wicked rise, a man is hidden.

Here the focus moves from personal considerations to a general observation about the impact of righteousness and wickedness in public life. The *New International Version* renders the verse as follows: "When the righteous triumph, there is great elation; but when the wicked rise to power, men go into hiding."

Second Kings 11 provides an illustration of this truth from the history of God's people. Wicked Queen Athaliah destroyed all the rightful heirs to the throne of Judah, except for young Jehoash, who was successfully hidden for six years while Athaliah reigned in Jerusalem. When at last Athaliah was deposed and Jehoash was established as rightful ruler, a time of national celebration and peace followed. Proverbs 11:10 states the lesson of our verse in this manner: "When it goeth well with the righteous, the city rejoiceth: and when the wicked perish, there is shouting."

May God give us godly rulers!

III. Covering or Confessing?
(Proverbs 28:13)

Our printed text concludes with an important observation that has as much (or more) relevance today than it did when first uttered.

Home Daily Bible Readings

Monday, July 20—Keep the Law Like Wise Children (Proverbs 28:1-7)
Tuesday, July 21—Turn From Sin and Get Mercy (Proverbs 28:8-13)
Wednesday, July 22—Happy Are Those Who Keep the Law (Proverbs 19:14-18)
Thursday, July 23—Spiritual Wisdom for Good Lives (Colossians 1:9-14)
Friday, July 24—Learn Inner Wisdom and Be Clean (Psalm 51:1-14)
Saturday, July 25—Happy to Keep God's Decree (Psalm 119:1-7)
Sunday, July 26—Wise Builders Choose the Rock (Matthew 7:15-27)

13. He that covereth his sins shall not prosper: but whoso confesseth and forsaketh them shall have mercy.

King David learned this truth personally and painfully after his sin with Bathsheba, when he became a deceiver and a murderer in order to hide his adultery. The consequences of his sin threw his family into chaos. His silence (which brought anguish and illness), then his confession (which brought forgiveness and relief) are recounted in Psalm 32:1-5 and Psalm 51. Unconfessed sin, like an infected wound covered over and untreated, will fester and poison one's whole system. It must receive cleansing before it can be healed.

First John 1:8, 9 describes both our problem and God's prescription for it: "If we say that we have no sin, we deceive ourselves, and the truth is not in us. If we confess our sins, he is faithful and just to forgive us our sins, and to cleanse us from all unrighteousness."

Conclusion
A. You're on Your Own Now

It's time to leave home. You're going away to college, or to a job that takes you out of town, or just to an apartment of your own. No one will be with you now to tell you to eat right or to pick up your clothes. But the echo of those admonitions and others like them will always be with you. The directives are replaced with bills, deadlines, and responsibilities, nudging you toward wise decisions of your own.

So it is with today's lesson text from Proverbs 28. It doesn't tell you what to do, but it reminds you of timeless principles for daily living. It makes pointed remarks about the wisdom of one course in contrast with the folly of another. It talks freely about the consequences of your choices. Then it leaves the decision up to you. You're on your own now, but that does not mean that you've outgrown the need for God or His Word. The message in today's lesson title must become your motto for daily living: "Obey God's Law."

B. Prayer

We praise You, dear God, for the law by which You guide us to live in Your world. Forgive, we pray, our foolish inclination to prefer our ways to Yours, and protect us from destroying ourselves by following our own desires. In Jesus' name. Amen.

C. Thought to Remember

"The law of the Lord is perfect, converting the soul" (Psalm 19:7).

Learning by Doing

This page contains an alternate lesson plan emphasizing learning activities.
Classes desiring such student involvement will find these suggestions helpful.

Learning Goals

This study should equip class members to:

1. State the blessings that come through obedience to God, and contrast them with the consequences of the disobedient life.

2. Give illustrations from Scripture of the fruits of both obedient and disobedient living.

3. Pinpoint one area of their lives where their failure to obey God is clear, and take steps to correct this situation.

Into the Lesson

Select two persons in advance (not necessarily class members) to debate the following proposition: "Our environment influences our ability to obey God." Allow three minutes for the affirmative argument and three for the negative argument, plus one minute each for rebuttal. Then ask the entire class to assess the arguments. Note whether the assessment is divided or united.

Write the following three questions, each on a separate 3 by 5 card, and divide the class into three committees. Instruct each committee to answer its question in five minutes and to be prepared to report the results.

1. What is the connection between Bible reading and prayer?

2. What elements in modern society make it particularly challenging or difficult to obey God?

3. How may we tempt others to disobey God?

Ask the class to describe three common ways that children disobey their parents. Do we disobey God in the same ways? (The aim is to illustrate the ways in which we are an example to our children of how they should relate to God.)

Into the Word

Begin this lesson on obedience with a reminder that all of Scripture stresses that God blesses those who are obedient. Ask the class to think of examples from the Bible of persons who obeyed or disobeyed God and what happened. Many illustrations could be given. Disobedient individuals could include Adam and Eve, King Saul, and Jonah. Examples of obedience toward God could be Noah, Abraham, and Mary.

Arrange two columns on a chalkboard with the headings *Obedient* and *Disobedient*. Then begin to read Proverbs 28:4-13, asking the class to stop you each time an example or consequence of obedience or disobedience is mentioned. List their responses in the appropriate column. Possible responses are given here.

Obedient	*Disobedient*
strives with the wicked	praises the wicked
understands all things	misunderstands justice
discerning	humiliates parents
inherits good	leads upright astray
fears God always	prayer an abomination
	hard-hearted

Next, assign the following Scriptures to different students to be read: Exodus 22:25; Leviticus 25:35, 36; Leviticus 26:3, 11, 12, 14; Deuteronomy 24:19-21; 1 Samuel 15:22; Psalm 1:1-3; Isaiah 5:20, 21; Acts 5:29; Galatians 6:7. Have the reader summarize what his or her passage says about obedience and disobedience.

Conclude the Bible study with a reaffirmation of the blessings of obedience. God calls all to a life of obedience. Everyone must make an "Adam" choice or a "Noah" choice. Adam lived in a perfect environment and chose to turn his back on God—that is, to be disobedient. Noah lived in an evil time and environment, yet remained committed to God. Our environment is not the factor that determines the decision we make about obeying God; our personal will is.

Into Life

Pose this statement for class discussion: *Right is right, even if nobody does it; and wrong is wrong, even if everybody does it.* Direct the responses toward God's Word, where we find absolute truth and a declaration of what is right and wrong. Conclude with the assertion that God's truth is right for all persons in all situations throughout all times. Obedience to its standards is especially needed in the present day.

Ask the class to explain what is wrong with rationalizing or justifying an unrighteous act, even if it seems to be leading to something good. (If the act is unrighteous according to God's Word, then we are tampering with His truth and His authority.) See Romans 3:5-8, where Paul states that the claim that an unrighteous act can promote a righteous end is totally invalid.

To conclude the session today, lead the class in a prayer for discipline to be consistent in studying God's Word and for power to be consistent in obeying His Word.

Let's Talk It Over

The questions on this page are designed to encourage review of the lesson Scriptures and to promote discussion of the lesson by the class. The answers provided are only discussion starters. Let your class talk it over from there.

1. Proverbs 28:5 says that the wicked do not understand God's judgment—a possible reference to His laws and His wisdom. Why is this? How may this be a warning to us when we do not understand God's commands?

Believing and understanding are as much a matter of the will as of the intellect. Creation speaks eloquently of its Creator, but many refuse to see, and choose rather to believe in evolution by chance. We do not believe what we do not *want* to believe. Therefore, the commandments of God seem foolish to the wicked. Homosexuals insist that their sin is just as natural and right as the love between a husband and a wife. Religious terrorists slaughter innocent people in God's name. The person who wants to give his appetites and emotions free reign will not listen to laws that speak of self-control. All of this may be a warning to Christians as well. Do we have a difficult time understanding one of God's commandments? It may be that sin is hardening our understanding and making us reluctant to believe or accept His will.

2. Our text's statement that it is better to be poor and upright than rich and wicked (Proverbs 28:6) is a needed warning in our materialistic age. What are the dangers of the allurement of riches?

Riches can excite many feelings in the heart of man, and most of them are bad. The pursuit of wealth can so consume a person that he neglects God, church, family, and even self in its pursuit. Beyond that, the lust for money can lead one to lie, cheat, steal, or do most anything else for the sake of material gain. If we are intent on getting rich, it is likely that our greed will cause us to be selfish and to harden our hearts against helping others. This attitude often leads us to refuse to give our tithes and offerings to the Lord. If we can prosper while avoiding all these pitfalls, well and good. We should thank the Lord. But if riches pervert us to the point that we worship them, then we have given up all that has true value. It is better to be a friend of the Lord, no matter how poor we may be.

3. Why and how does sin work to kill our prayers? How can its effects be overcome? See Proverbs 28:9, 13.

Sin separated Adam and Eve from God in the Garden of Eden, and it separates us from God now. From God's perspective, He will not listen to the prayer of the person who has no regard for His laws, even if that person should be on the church board and be in worship every Sunday. From our perspective, our feelings of guilt separate us from God. Just as a disobedient child is uneasy around his parents, fearing that they have learned of his disobedience, we are uneasy around God when we have been or are being deliberately disobedient. Consider David after he became involved with Bathsheba and arranged for Uriah's death. Perhaps he went to the tabernacle and followed his regular pattern of worship, at least publicly; but how many psalms do you suppose he wrote during this time? How perfunctory were his prayers? David's prayer life was not restored until he was confronted with his sin and confessed his wickedness (see Psalm 51). So with us: When we sin, we cannot ignore it. We must confess it to God and seek His forgiveness. If we are sincere, He will hear our prayers.

4. Our text warns against leading a righteous person astray (Proverbs 28:10). How does this happen? Who would do such a thing, and why? How can we avoid these dangers?

Sometimes godless schoolmates, co-workers, friends, or family members try very hard to persuade the righteous to participate in their sins. They seem to get a perverse pleasure from causing a Christian to fall. Perhaps it helps to quiet their consciences, for few things prick the conscience of the wicked so much as a Christian who quietly and meekly does what is right. At other times the tempters are harder to detect. Christians who lead a more liberal or worldly lifestyle may try to "liberalize" their more conservative, "stuck-in-the-mud" brothers and sisters. False and deceitful teachers seek to lead others astray. As much as possible, we should avoid those who try to press us to sin, especially if we feel that we are weakening. We can look to strong Christian friends for help. We can call on the Lord's strength through prayer. We can also study God's Word more fervently, perhaps memorizing relevant passages and thus strengthening our convictions.

Wisdom or Foolishness

August 2
Lesson 9

DEVOTIONAL READING: Psalm 1.

LESSON SCRIPTURE: Proverbs 8.

PRINTED TEXT: Proverbs 8:1-11, 33-36.

Proverbs 8:1-11, 33-36

1 Doth not wisdom cry? and understanding put forth her voice?

2 She standeth in the top of high places, by the way in the places of the paths.

3 She crieth at the gates, at the entry of the city, at the coming in at the doors:

4 Unto you, O men, I call; and my voice is to the sons of man.

5 O ye simple, understand wisdom: and, ye fools, be ye of an understanding heart.

6 Hear; for I will speak of excellent things; and the opening of my lips shall be right things.

7 For my mouth shall speak truth; and wickedness is an abomination to my lips.

8 All the words of my mouth are in righteousness; there is nothing froward or perverse in them.

9 They are all plain to him that understandeth, and right to them that find knowledge.

10 Receive my instruction, and not silver; and knowledge rather than choice gold.

11 For wisdom is better than rubies; and all the things that may be desired are not to be compared to it.

. . . .

33 Hear instruction, and be wise, and refuse it not.

34 Blessed is the man that heareth me, watching daily at my gates, waiting at the posts of my doors.

35 For whoso findeth me findeth life, and shall obtain favor of the LORD.

36 But he that sinneth against me wrongeth his own soul: all they that hate me love death.

Aug
2

GOLDEN TEXT: Wisdom is better than rubies; and all the things that may be desired are not to be compared to it.—Proverbs 8:11.

Wisdom for Living
Unit 3: Choose the Right Way
(Lessons 9-13)

Lesson Aims

This study should prepare the student to:

1. Describe wisdom as personified in our text from Proverbs 8.

2. Suggest some comparisons between wisdom and Jesus.

3. Commit to the pursuit of wisdom through following Jesus Christ.

Lesson Outline

INTRODUCTION

 A. "Our Speaker for the Day Is . . ."

 B. Wisdom Personified

 C. Lesson Background

 I. WISDOM DEMANDS A HEARING (Proverbs 8:1-5)

  A. Crying Out in Public Places (vv. 1-3)

   Two Ladies

  B. Calling to Men (vv. 4, 5)

 II. WISDOM DESERVES A HEARING (Proverbs 8:6-11)

  A. Her Message Is True (vv. 6, 7)

  B. Her Message Is Right (vv. 8, 9)

  C. Her Message Is of Supreme Value (vv. 10, 11)

 III. WISDOM REWARDS THE HEARER (Proverbs 8:33-36)

  A. With Blessing (vv. 33, 34)

  B. With Life (vv. 35, 36)

   Hating Life, Loving Death

CONCLUSION

 A. When the Word Became Flesh

 B. Prayer

 C. Thought to Remember

Use the visual for Lesson 9 to focus on today's Golden Text from Proverbs 8:11. It is shown on page 411.

Introduction

A. "Our Speaker for the Day Is . . ."

The ladies had gathered for their meeting, and the guest speaker was present. But the presiding officer had no information about him. So the introduction was brief: "You girls have probably never heard of Professor ____ and neither had I until now; but he is here to speak to us today, and that is what he'll do."

Contrast this with a more familiar introduction, brief because the speaker is already well known: "Ladies and gentlemen, the President of the United States!"

How, we wonder, was Jesus introduced to the crowds He addressed? Or was He introduced at all beyond the announcement of John the Baptist: "Behold the Lamb of God, which taketh away the sin of the world!" (John 1:29)? John's entire ministry was, in fact, an introduction to the ministry of Jesus, in keeping with his task to "prepare . . . the way of the Lord" and to "make his paths straight" (Matthew 3:3).

An earlier and more diverse introduction of Jesus occupied the prophetic spokesmen of the Old Testament. Their messages looked ahead to the coming of the Messiah, highlighting His person, mission, and message. A remarkable part of that introduction is found in Proverbs 8 (the source of today's lesson text), where wisdom is declared to be God's companion and agent in creation (vv. 22-31), and cries for our attention (vv. 32-36).

So wisdom is our speaker for today, and she comes without introduction; Solomon, the author of Proverbs, simply relays her powerful, practical message. He could have spoken personally about wisdom as his close friend and most helpful companion, but here his main concern was that she be helpful to "my son."

B. Wisdom Personified

Among the most powerful figures of speech in Hebrew poetry is *personification*. This means representing a principle or quality as though it were a living and active person. (Even today, we speak of Mother Nature or Old Man Winter.) Wisdom is thus personified in Proverbs 1:20-33; 3:13-18; 9:1-12; and especially in chapter 8. Among some folk this personification has become the basis of songs or hymns addressed to a sort of secondary deity called *Sophia* (the Greek word for "wisdom"). This, of course, is a tragic form of idolatry.

Christians, however, have commonly found in Proverbs 8 a foreshadowing of Christ as the eternal Word, who "was made flesh, and dwelt among us" (John 1:14). Solomon personified wisdom in powerful and prophetic words; Jesus, the eternal Word, put on flesh and fulfilled Solomon's words by revealing "all the treasures of wisdom and knowledge" (Colossians 2:3).

C. Lesson Background

An overall theme of wisdom-versus-folly characterizes the book of Proverbs. It is expressed perhaps most vividly in chapters 7 and 8, by a contrast of two feminine characters: the "strange woman [the adulteress], . . . which flattereth with her words" (7:4, 5), and wisdom, whose "words . . . are in righteousness" (8:8).

Proverbs 7:6-27 describes the wiles of the adulteress and concludes with this warning: "Her house is the way to hell, going down to the chambers of death" (v. 27). In direct contrast is chapter 8, announcing the call and the character of wisdom, and leading to the opposite conclusion: "For whoso findeth me findeth life, and shall obtain favor of the Lord" (v. 35).

I. Wisdom Demands a Hearing (Proverbs 8:1-5)

A. Crying Out in Public Places (vv. 1-3)

1, 2. Doth not wisdom cry? and understanding put forth her voice? She standeth in the top of high places, by the way in the places of the paths.

By its form, the opening question assumes an affirmative response. "Doesn't *wisdom cry?*" Of course she does!

The two parts of the question in this verse really cover the same ground, for *wisdom* and *understanding* are parts of the same concept. Only one speaker is present. She calls loudly in order to be heard, and plainly in order to be understood. She stands in visible areas (*the top of high places*) and in a public, well-traveled area—a forum or square at the convergence of the *paths*, where crowds tend to gather. Not for her is the dark corner of a narrow street; this is where the "strange woman" entraps her unwary victim (Proverbs 7:9, 12).

Jesus' ministry was likewise conducted in the open, where many assembled and where secrecy was impossible: "I spake openly to the world; I ever taught in the synagogue, and in the temple, whither the Jews always resort; and in secret have I said nothing" (John 18:20). Later, Paul would tell an audience, "This thing was not done in a corner" (Acts 26:26).

Preachers and teachers of truth do well to reach the largest possible audience; if not in marketplaces or public parks, then through radio and television. Crass publicity-seeking, however—especially by means of stirring up partisan controversy—should have no place in their ministry. Just because Jesus' ministry was conducted openly does not mean that He was brash or obnoxious. Hear His demeanor described in Matthew 12:19, 20: "He shall not strive, nor cry; . . . a bruised reed shall he not break, and smoking flax shall he not quench."

3. She crieth at the gates, at the entry of the city, at the coming in at the doors.

Wisdom delivers her urgent message where the greatest numbers of people may be encountered coming and going. She is in the area at the *gates* of the *city*, where the elders often positioned themselves to discuss matters of public interest (Ruth 4:1; Proverbs 31:23). A choice spot would be by the side of the archway in the city wall. There the local citizenry or strangers from afar could be addressed as they entered or left the city. Wisdom desires and deserves to be heard!

TWO LADIES

Proverbs 8:2, 3 pictures wisdom as a dignified lady who stands "in the places of the paths . . . at the gates, at the entry of the city, at the coming in at the doors." She lifts her voice and utters a message concerning what is right and true.

It is noteworthy that at the "gates" of New York Harbor, at the "entry" to the "new world" of America, a dignified lady also stands. This is Lady Liberty, the great statue given to our nation by France and dedicated by President Grover Cleveland on October 28, 1886. Today the Statue of Liberty remains a symbol of freedom to oppressed people everywhere.

At the base of the Statue of Liberty is a sonnet, cast in bronze, which was written by Emma Lazarus, a Jewish philanthropist who dedicated her life to ministering to displaced and poverty-stricken Jewish people in New York City. Just as Lady Wisdom utters her voice to instruct people in Proverbs 8, so Lady Liberty is pictured as speaking. The last six lines of Emma Lazarus's poem are justly famous:

"Keep, ancient lands, your storied pomp!" cries she,
With silent lips. "Give me your tired, your poor,
Your huddled masses yearning to breathe free,
The wretched refuse of your teeming shore.
Send these, the homeless, tempest-tost to me,
I lift my lamp beside the golden door!"

Lady Wisdom of Proverbs 8 must be heard and heeded if the message of Lady Liberty is to be meaningful. God's wisdom is the source and the sustainer of the only true liberty—liberty of the soul.   —J. G. V. B.

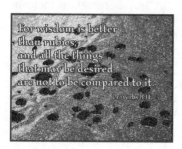

For wisdom is better than rubies; and all the things that may be desired are not to be compared to it. Proverbs 8:11

visual for lesson 9

B. Calling to Men (vv. 4, 5)

4. Unto you, O men, I call; and my voice is to the sons of man.

Wisdom is skillful enough to focus on a selected audience. In this case it is *men*, both old and young. We should consider it as the same audience addressed throughout the book of Proverbs as "my son." Among these men were those who could usually be found in the public areas just described. Note that the *sons of man*, or the "youths," are also the ones whom the seductress seeks to lure into the ultimate folly (Proverbs 7:6-9). This does not mean that women have no need for wisdom, or that they are bypassed by wisdom's call. Men, however, often fall prey to the temptation to appear self-reliant or "self-made," making them more apt to "tune out" the call of wisdom.

5. O ye simple, understand wisdom: and, ye fools, be ye of an understanding heart.

Wisdom addresses her appeal to specific kinds of young men, in order to save them from the "strange woman" (Proverbs 7:4, 5). They are the *simple*—untaught ones who are not yet firm in their convictions, and thus are easily influenced for good or evil. They are also the *fools*—self-confident and headstrong "free thinkers," who think they know it all. Wisdom urges both kinds of men to be receptive and thoughtful, weighing the evidence available to them and coming to well-grounded conclusions.

II. Wisdom Deserves a Hearing (Proverbs 8:6-11)

A. Her Message Is True (vv. 6, 7)

6. Hear; for I will speak of excellent things; and the opening of my lips shall be right things.

Hear! Gather the family around and listen. You will have no reason to be embarrassed by the contents. What a grand slogan for a Christian's conversation: *I will speak of excellent things!* This demands the underlying commitment: "I will *think* of excellent things"; for "out of the abundance of the heart the mouth speaketh" (Matthew 12:34).

The second part of our verse enforces the first. Wisdom accepts the responsibility that the *opening* of the *lips* in speech will promote what is *right*. A New Englander of my acquaintance, known for long silences and short speeches, explained that before he spoke, he wanted to be able to improve on the silence. So wisdom acknowledges the responsibility that goes with the God-given power of speech, and does not attempt to use it in an unworthy or negative manner (see James 3:1-12). How tragic that

today, agencies with the power to multiply words by millions in print, or to distribute their sound worldwide in seconds, should waste that power on trivialities and trash!

7. For my mouth shall speak truth; and wickedness is an abomination to my lips.

Wickedness is described here as the opposite of *truth*. Thus falsehood is wickedness. This is plainly declared in Proverbs 12:22: "Lying lips are abomination to the Lord: but they that deal truly are his delight." In contrast, "flattery" and "subtlety" are the chief stock in trade of the strange woman (Proverbs 7:5, 10, 21).

Truth is an essential ingredient of wisdom, whether it is found in Proverbs or in Jesus Christ, the living Word of God. "I am . . . the truth," He declared (John 14:6), and He made it equally clear that He is the truth that sets men free (John 8:32, 36).

B. Her Message Is Right (vv. 8, 9)

8. All the words of my mouth are in righteousness; there is nothing froward or perverse in them.

Again, as in the previous verse, the way of wisdom is presented by contrasting two opposing perspectives. *Righteousness* speaks of the upright character that meets with God's approval. The opposite qualities of being *froward or perverse* are to be carefully and completely avoided in one's speech. (The meaning of *froward* was explained in Lesson 5 under the discussion of Proverbs 2:12.) Thus is the way of wisdom far removed from the strange woman's devious craftiness, and far removed from the wisdom of the world, which too often depends for its success on keeping the competition from learning the truth.

9. They are all plain to him that understandeth, and right to them that find knowledge.

To the person who considers and accepts the truth of God's Word, following His way makes sense. This individual finds no need to apologize for God's judgments or to second-guess His decisions. Wisdom's *plain* talk is exemplified in Jesus' ministry, during which the common people "heard him gladly" (Mark 12:37). In contrast, the self-congratulating critics complained at one point that he uttered "a hard saying," and asked, "Who can hear it?" (John 6:60).

The believer finds no difficulty in observing that in Christ "all things consist" (Colossians 1:17), or hold together. Jesus draws the diverse elements of creation into a consistent whole. Only by following Him can our lives find contentment and peace, even in the midst of a fragmented world.

C. Her Message Is of Supreme Value
(vv. 10, 11)

10. Receive my instruction, and not silver; and knowledge rather than choice gold.

Receive is an active verb; it reaches out and lays hold on what is offered, as the hearers of Peter's Pentecost sermon "gladly received his word" and responded to his message (Acts 2:41). *Instruction* likewise indicates action, but on the part of the teacher in exercising rigorous discipline. Hebrews 12:5-11 describes discipline as including elements that are less than pleasant at the time they are experienced. Such discipline is to be sought with an eagerness even greater than that of a miner who is intent on searching for *choice gold*.

11. For wisdom is better than rubies; and all the things that may be desired are not to be compared to it.

This repeats the theme of Proverbs 3:14, 15, and foreshadows Jesus' comparison of the kingdom of Heaven to hidden treasure or a "pearl of great price" (Matthew 13:44-46). No direct comparison can be made, of course, between eternal and unchanging values on the one hand and temporary material possessions on the other. They are simply not subject to evaluation in the same category. Jesus acknowledged the need for material things such as food and clothing, but declared a higher value: "Seek ye first the kingdom of God, and his righteousness; and all these things shall be added unto you" (Matthew 6:33). We must treat wisdom as a "required course," not an "elective."

The things that may be desired are not limited to material items. Intense desire may also be attached to fame, power and influence over others, athletic or academic achievements, or the

satisfaction of physical appetites. As matters in which he could have taken great pride, the apostle Paul listed several components of his upbringing and background, together with personal accomplishments that improved that standing. All of these, however, Paul willingly surrendered in order to receive the promise of life in Christ Jesus (Philippians 3:4-9).

Verses 12-21, not included in our printed text, provide a list of advantages offered by wisdom: avoidance of evil; the skill to reign admirably; lasting riches and honor; and guidance in right ways.

Verses 22-31 record the words of personified wisdom, declaring that she was with God at the creation of the world. In this we see one of the clearest foreshadowings of the eternal Word, who is introduced in the opening verses of John's Gospel.

III. Wisdom Rewards the Hearer (Proverbs 8:33-36)

Verse 32, also not in our printed text, introduces the final portion of our printed text, saying, "Now therefore hearken unto me, O ye children: for blessed are they that keep my ways."

A. With Blessing (vv. 33, 34)

33. Hear instruction, and be wise, and refuse it not.

Hear is rendered "listen" or "heed" by other translators. *Instruction* is the discipline that includes chastening. So we hear wisdom saying, "Give attention to what I am trying to convey! If you do, you will act on the teaching I give you, and will become the person I am trying to develop. Don't ignore, reject, or neglect this essential schooling for the sake of pursuing something far inferior. You will do so at your own peril."

Education today is incredibly expensive, and shows no signs of getting cheaper. One has to marvel, then, at how many young people will spend the money for it and then, in many cases, do all they can to reject that for which they are paying. Many will avoid class sessions, or will *attend* without paying *attention*! Jesus addressed this problem in His ministry, saying repeatedly, "Who hath ears to hear, let him hear" (Matthew 13:43; see also the messages to the seven churches in Revelation 2 and 3).

34. Blessed is the man that heareth me, watching daily at my gates, waiting at the posts of my doors.

The person who is eager to receive favors from another will often "camp at the door" (sometimes literally), awaiting the opportunity to appeal to the one he wishes to see. Consider the sales person or the lobbyist seeking out the target of his interests.

Proverbs 9:1 fills in this word picture, saying, "Wisdom hath builded her house," and describing it as a very adequate house, with seven hewn pillars. This may signify wisdom in her completeness (since "seven" often symbolizes completeness or perfection in the Bible).

The lover of wisdom knows where to find her—in the pages of God's Book and in the instruction of godly teachers of the Word. Let him not neglect her invitation, but accept it eagerly.

B. With Life (vv. 35, 36)

35. For whoso findeth me findeth life, and shall obtain favor of the Lord.

The promise of *life* calls to mind the words of Moses: "See, I have set before thee this day life and good, and death and evil; in that I command thee this day to love the Lord thy God, to walk in his ways, and to keep his commandments, . . . that thou mayest live and multiply: and the Lord thy God shall bless thee" (Deuteronomy 30:15, 16). In addition, it compels us to see wisdom's promise as a foreshadowing of Christ and the life He came to bring mankind. Consider these words from John's Gospel: "In him was life; and the life was the light of men" (1:4). "He that believeth on the Son hath everlasting life" (3:36). "Search the Scriptures; for in them ye think ye have eternal life: and they are they which testify of me" (5:39). "I am the resurrection, and the life: he that believeth in me, though he were dead, yet shall he live" (John 11:25).

36. But he that sinneth against me wrongeth his own soul: all they that hate me love death.

Here we see two levels of offense against wisdom. The word rendered *sinneth* means a missing of the mark, or target, toward which one has aimed. Any wandering from the course of wisdom hurts the erring one. Sin also includes willful wickedness, aptly described as an aversion to or hatred of wisdom. According to Solomon, this is charting a certain course toward *death*. It amounts to a kind of suicide.

HATING LIFE, LOVING DEATH

The eighth chapter of Proverbs ends with a terse, dramatic passage about our relationship with wisdom: "All they that hate me love death." It seems inconceivable that anyone could love death—death which is indeed our fiercest enemy. However, one does indeed "love death," if he acts in such a foolish manner that fatal consequences seem inevitable.

How is this done? We can appear to be "hating life" in many ways. For instance, consider the individual who risks driving seventy or eighty miles an hour on a highway replete with curves, or swimming in sea water where signs warn of dangerous undertows. Sometimes people disregard signs that warn of high frequency electric wires. Others ignore warnings about keeping containers of pills away from children. People persist in walking near the edge of mountain trails where signs warn about unpredictable rock slides. Still others take drugs, drink alcoholic beverages, exercise violently when warned that their hearts are vulnerable, or attempt to walk across thin ice over deep water.

Wisdom calls aloud to us to live thoughtfully and carefully, with constant attention to dangers both physical and spiritual. Wisdom helps us to have the proper perspectives—"hating death" and "loving life."   —J. G. V. B.

Conclusion

A. When the Word Became Flesh

Wisdom versus foolishness! The conflict between the two is presented to us in the Bible on different levels. One is the level of *law*. The Bible tells in plain words what God thinks and desires concerning His people, their attitudes, and their behavior. Another level is found in *poetry*, such as we have in Proverbs, with its memorable expressions and figures of speech. It dramatizes the conflict between wisdom and foolishness. Then there is a third level—*revelation* through the Son of God on earth, when "the Word was made flesh, and dwelt among us, (and we beheld his glory, the glory as of the only begotten of the Father,) full of grace and truth" (John 1:14). Jesus' *words* expressed divine wisdom fully; His *life* demonstrated divine wisdom perfectly; His *death and resurrection* brought divine wisdom to bear on the unsolved problems of human sinfulness.

Herein lies the fulfillment of wisdom's promise of life. Wisdom is now found in "Christ the power of God, and the wisdom of God. Because the foolishness of God is wiser than men" (1 Corinthians 1:24, 25).

B. Prayer

Father, cleanse us, we pray, from the folly of being wise in our own opinions. Open our hearts to the wisdom that is available through Your written Word, and especially through Your living Word, Jesus. We pray in His name. Amen.

C. Thought to Remember

"Wisdom is the principal thing; therefore get wisdom: and with all thy getting get understanding" (Proverbs 4:7).

Learning by Doing

This page contains an alternate lesson plan emphasizing learning activities.
Classes desiring such student involvement will find these suggestions helpful.

Learning Goals

After this lesson, students should be able to:

1. Describe wisdom as personified in our text from Proverbs 8.

2. Suggest some comparisons between wisdom and Jesus.

3. Commit to the pursuit of wisdom through following Jesus Christ.

Into the Lesson

Hang large pieces of paper on a classroom wall. As students enter the classroom, ask them to write several definitions of wisdom on the paper. If they are "stuck," suggest that it might be helpful to contrast wisdom with knowledge, understanding, or information. For example, information consists primarily of data and facts, but wisdom is knowing how to use them. Or someone may write, "Information is 'head learning' but wisdom is 'common sense.'"

Have class members read the definitions they have written. Ask the class to vote on the best definition. Move to today's Bible study by noting that today's text from Proverbs 8 deals with the subject of wisdom. Challenge students to clarify or evaluate their definition in the light of what Proverbs 8 says about wisdom.

Into the Word

Option One: Have students look closely at Proverbs 8:22-36. Point out that some see in these verses a prophecy of Jesus Christ. What are some characteristics of wisdom listed in these verses from Proverbs 8 that would appear to describe Jesus? Possible answers include the fact that wisdom is described as present "in the beginning" and as being "from everlasting" (vv. 22, 23). Also, wisdom is depicted as present at the creation of everything (vv. 27-31). Colossians 1:16 and Hebrews 1:2 both teach that Jesus was the main agent of creation. John 1:1-3 teaches that Christ existed "in the beginning" and that "without him was not any thing made that was made." In addition, Colossians 2:3 teaches that in Christ are hidden "all the treasures of wisdom and knowledge." Also call attention to what 1 Corinthians 1:18-31 says about Christ as "the wisdom of God."

Option Two: Make two lists from Proverbs 8:1-21 and 32-36. One should include the benefits and blessings of wisdom. The other should list the qualities and characteristics of wisdom. The two lists could include the following items:

The Benefits and Blessings of Wisdom

Verse 5: The simple gain prudence and understanding.

Verse 15: Rulers rule justly by wisdom.

Verse 18: With wisdom are honor, enduring wealth, and righteousness.

Verse 19: The fruit of wisdom is of more value than material wealth.

Verse 21: Wisdom bestows treasure on those who love her.

Verse 32: Blessed are those who listen to and keep the ways of wisdom.

Verse 35: Wisdom gives life to those who find her.

The Characteristics of Wisdom

Verse 7: Wisdom speaks what is right and true and hates wickedness.

Verse 11: Wisdom is more precious than rubies.

Verse 12: Wisdom dwells with prudence, and possesses knowledge and discretion.

Verse 13: Wisdom hates pride, arrogance, evil behavior, and perverse speech.

Verse 14: Wisdom possesses counsel, sound judgment, understanding, and strength.

Verse 17: Wisdom can be found by those who search for her.

Into Life

Option One: Write a letter to a young person, extolling the virtues of wisdom and of approaching life from God's perspective. Most congregations have young people who are away from home, and who would benefit greatly from a letter from someone at church. The letter could include a list of the benefits of wisdom from Proverbs 8. Or students could make notes from this passage that they could use in a phone call to such a person.

Option Two: Write a personalized response to the invitation of wisdom in Proverbs 8. Use the words of the text in forming your response. Here are some examples:

I admit that I am simple and foolish, and need prudence and understanding (verse 5).

I will choose to pursue wisdom rather than material wealth (verse 10).

I will fear the Lord and hate evil, pride, arrogance, and perverse speech (verse 13).

Let's Talk It Over

The questions on this page are designed to encourage review of the lesson Scriptures and to promote discussion of the lesson by the class. The answers provided are only discussion starters. Let your class talk it over from there.

1. In today's lesson, wisdom is personified as a woman. Describe wisdom's characteristics. What do these characteristics mean literally?

Wisdom is not silent, but goes about imploring men and women to listen to her. She does not prattle, harangue, or jest, for she has a very important message. It is the extreme importance of her message (life and death are in the balance) that motivates her to spread her message to all who will listen or seek her out. When she speaks, wisdom speaks of good and excellent things. She always tells the truth. She speaks of righteousness, and will not even mention anything wicked and filthy. Instruction from her is more valuable than riches. Those who listen to her find life, but those who refuse to heed her message bring destruction on themselves.

2. Personified wisdom bears a striking resemblance to Christ, so much so that many consider the passage from which our text is taken to be a prophecy concerning the incarnate Word. Explore this comparison. What does it illustrate for us concerning the mission and message of Jesus Christ?

Just as wisdom leaves her house to go out into the city streets to proclaim her message, so the Word left His home in Heaven to come to earth and proclaim His message. Wisdom speaks only truth and righteousness. Jesus said, "I am the truth." Without reservation we can believe everything He said. His life was a perfect demonstration of righteousness. Wisdom's instruction is more precious than gold or silver. Jesus said that His kingdom is worth all that a man possesses (Matthew 13:44). Finding wisdom is to find life and favor with God, and to reject her is death. Jesus said that whoever hears and does His words will be building on a rock, but whoever does not receive His words will be building on sand (Matthew 7:24-27). Jesus is life; He is the way to the Father.

3. In many ways, we can compare the gospel with wisdom. Just as wisdom leads us in the way of harmony with God and life, so the gospel brings divine fellowship and eternal life to those who hear and heed its message. What is the role of the church and of Christians in calling out to others with the gospel?

In Proverbs, wisdom is pictured as going out into the public places to proclaim her message. Of course, this is not literally true. Words and truths and messages cannot proclaim themselves. They must be proclaimed by heralds, teachers, and preachers. As the apostle Paul said, how can a person believe the gospel unless he hears, and how can he hear unless someone tells it to him (Romans 10:14)? The church and the individual Christian must proclaim the gospel. Like wisdom, we must leave the comfort of our home (the church building) and take the message throughout the surrounding community or city. Most people will not come seeking the gospel, and so we must go to them, cry out for their attention, and urge them to believe and obey. This, more than anything else, remains the primary task of the church. We must devote a major portion of our planning, our resources, and our efforts to it. How loudly does our congregation shout the gospel? How far do we take it? Do we go out seeking men and women who need to hear it?

4. There are so many kinds of folly in the world, all screaming for attention, and all full of glitz and glamour. Many people listen to their messages. How does this affect the way that the church must proclaim the gospel? What temptations must we avoid?

We must remember never to change the gospel in any way, in the hope that we will win more hearers. We must not mix it with any worldly philosophy or cause in an effort to make it more popular or appealing. The gospel must remain pure. On the other hand, we must proclaim the gospel message in the most effective and attractive way possible. We must never be guilty of making the gospel boring or unintelligible. We should use contemporary equipment and methods of communication, so that we will receive a more ready hearing and be more easily understood. We must use vocabulary and phraseology that are clear to non-Christians. However, we ought not resort to gimmickry, sensationalism, or cheap showmanship, for these methods only trivialize the world's greatest message. The gospel shines bright and clear all on its own. Our task is simply to proclaim it in its beauty and power.

Hard Work or Laziness

DEVOTIONAL READING: 2 Thessalonians 3:6-13.

LESSON SCRIPTURE: Proverbs 6:6-8; 10:4, 5; 13:4; 15:19; 18:9; 20:4; 24:30-34.

PRINTED TEXT: Proverbs 6:6-8; 10:4, 5; 13:4; 15:19; 18:9; 20:4; 24:30-34.

Proverbs 6:6-8

6 Go to the ant, thou sluggard; consider her ways, and be wise:

7 Which having no guide, overseer, or ruler,

8 Provideth her meat in the summer, and gathereth her food in the harvest.

Proverbs 10:4, 5

4 He becometh poor that dealeth with a slack hand: but the hand of the diligent maketh rich.

5 He that gathereth in summer is a wise son: but he that sleepeth in harvest is a son that causeth shame.

Proverbs 13:4

4 The soul of the sluggard desireth, and hath nothing: but the soul of the diligent shall be made fat.

Proverbs 15:19

19 The way of the slothful man is as a hedge of thorns: but the way of the righteous is made plain.

Proverbs 18:9

9 He also that is slothful in his work is brother to him that is a great waster.

Proverbs 20:4

4 The sluggard will not plow by reason of the cold; therefore shall he beg in harvest, and have nothing.

Proverbs 24:30-34

30 I went by the field of the slothful, and by the vineyard of the man void of understanding;

31 And, lo, it was all grown over with thorns, and nettles had covered the face thereof, and the stone wall thereof was broken down.

32 Then I saw, and considered it well: I looked upon it, and received instruction.

33 Yet a little sleep, a little slumber, a little folding of the hands to sleep:

34 So shall thy poverty come as one that traveleth; and thy want as an armed man.

Aug 9

GOLDEN TEXT: The way of the slothful man is as a hedge of thorns: but the way of the righteous is made plain.—Proverbs 15:19.

Wisdom for Living
Unit 3: Choose the Right Way
(Lessons 9-13)

Lesson Aims

This study should enable class members to:

1. Explain the importance of diligence in one's work, and the dangers of neglect.

2. Cite contemporary examples of blessings to the industrious person that are missed by the lazy.

3. Schedule and accomplish some task that he or she has been putting off.

Lesson Outline

INTRODUCTION
    A. The Periodical Section
    B. Lesson Background
  I. CONSIDER THE ANT (Proverbs 6:6-8)
    A. Worthy of Imitation (v. 6)
    B. Orderly and Active (vv. 7, 8)
      A Relev-ant Example
 II. EXPERIENCES GOOD AND BAD (Proverbs 10:4, 5; 13:4; 15:19; 18:9; 20:4)
    A. Poverty or Prosperity (10:4)
    B. Sufficiency or Shame (10:5)
    C. Privation or Plenty (13:4)
    D. Hedge or Highway (15:19)
    E. A Destructive Duo (18:9)
    F. Procrastination and Poverty (20:4)
III. WARNINGS FROM THE WEEDS (Proverbs 24:30-34)
    A. Signs of Neglect (vv. 30, 31)
    B. Looking and Learning (v. 32)
    C. "Lose It Easy" (vv. 33, 34)
      The Deadly Danger of Neglect
CONCLUSION
    A. Where We Work
    B. Prayer
    C. Thought to Remember

Today's visual for Lesson 10 provides a humorous way to illustrate the diligence of the ant (Proverbs 6:6-8). It is shown on page 421.

Introduction

A. The Periodical Section

It may not occupy much space in the public library, but it does serve a lot of visitors. I'm talking about the periodical section, with its daily newspapers and its monthly magazines bringing late-breaking information in compactly written articles. There you will find the reader who wants to know what is currently happening in the field of his own activity or interest. The shelves of hard-bound volumes are left to those looking for more complete treatises on grander themes.

Similarly, in our studies from Proverbs we now find ourselves moving from the more complete prose poems about wisdom and folly to the briefer comments about daily applications of wisdom. Today's subject—exhorting the "couch potato" toward productive labor—is given the kind of treatment that the periodical section of the library offers. Proverbs deals with it in pungent paragraphs, one at a time, then leaves it for a while only to return to it later. Today we bring together a number of brief treatments, not in logical order (for that would be impossible), but with the purpose of doing what Proverbs is designed to do. So may it persuade "my son" to become a mature and productive member in the community of God's people.

B. Lesson Background

For today's study of "Hard Work or Laziness," we must find the background in the experience of the writer and his audience. It is a rural background, speaking of fields and vineyards, of plowing and reaping. This contrasts with a setting such as that of Proverbs 7, with the "strange woman" seducing her unsuspecting prey in more urban surroundings. However, there is a timeless, universal quality about the agricultural lifestyle that fits well with Solomon's wide-ranging observations (1 Kings 4:30-34; Ecclesiastes 2:4-7), as well as with those of Jesus (Matthew 13:1-43). For those who know nothing of working in fields and gardens, some adjustment may be necessary to apply the principles of our text to the setting of a modern factory or office.

Our lesson begins on a positive note, citing a good example and exhorting us to follow it.

I. Consider the Ant
(Proverbs 6:6-8)

A. Worthy of Imitation (v. 6)

6. Go to the ant, thou sluggard; consider her ways, and be wise.

Who of us who has not spent fascinated moments watching an *ant* tirelessly carrying something to its nest? The ceaseless labor of these insects has caught the admiring attention of writers from ancient times, and it continues to captivate our interest.

The inactive *sluggard*, or slothful person, has something important to learn from the ant. *Atsel* is the Hebrew term used in Proverbs and translated either *sluggard* or *slothful man.* These two English words have their own relationship to creatures vastly different from the ant. There is the *slug,* looking and acting like a snail without a shell, and there is the long-legged *sloth* hanging limply from a limb in a tropical forest. Both are very slow!

Consider her ways, and be wise. The ant is referred to as *her,* the gender characteristic of worker ants. Such a statement does nothing for the ego of the young man who has already been asked to learn wisdom from a tiny, ground-crawling insect!

The way to measure the ant's wisdom is by her *ways,* or her behavior. So take a long look at the ant in action, and by the same kind of action demonstrate what you have learned.

B. Orderly and Active (vv. 7, 8)

7, 8. Which having no guide, overseer, or ruler, provideth her meat in the summer, and gathereth her food in the harvest.

The ant is the true self-starter. She works without being compelled or prodded to work (*having no guide, overseer, or ruler*). She works in a timely fashion, providing beforehand for later needs. And she continues to work until a task is completed.

Those who study insect life will note that colonies of ants do include "officers" functioning as guides, commanders, or rulers, but that would be hard for the ordinary observer to discover. The purpose of this illustration is to encourage self-motivation toward purposeful and persistent labor.

The ant engages in the business of gathering *food* (which means the same as *meat* in the *King James Version*) when *summer* makes it available, and stores it up for winter's need. The words *summer* and *harvest* are actually parallel in meaning, for in Bible times, the summer months were the time certain crops were harvested. Though the ant is not aware of it, she lives by the principle: "To every thing there is a season, and a time to every purpose under the heaven" (Ecclesiastes 3:1). A procrastinator fails to respect those seasons and times.

How shall we apply this teaching about the importance of work in the light of Jesus' teach-

ing about "taking no thought" for the necessities of life (Matthew 6:25-34)? Notice that Jesus referred to God's faithful provision for the birds. They do not store up food, but God feeds them —by the means He has ordained. He does not put food into their nests, but makes it available to birds who have to stay as busy as the ants on the ground. A lazy bird will soon become very hungry!

A RELEV-ANT EXAMPLE

The "sluggard," or lazy person, is urged to pay attention to the behavior of the ant (Proverbs 6:6-8). It is apparent to anyone who watches them at work that ants are far from indolent, laying up supplies of food in the summer to use in the winter season.

It is a fact that these tiny insects can serve in several ways as models or challenges to us. A recent encyclopedia article tells us that more than 4,500 known species of ants are found across the whole earth in the temperate and tropical zones.

Ants manifest constant vigor in their actions. They also have defined types of activity. Some are *workers* that gather food material and store it. Some are *soldier ants* that guard the nest and seek to repel intruders. One ant is the *queen,* which constantly lays eggs.

This division of labor is a lesson for us, since we cannot do everything for ourselves. We must depend on each other for many things. From ants we can learn vigorous living, attention to specific duties, and the importance of cooperative endeavor. Pay attention to them, "and be wise!"   —J. G. V. B.

II. Experiences Good and Bad (Proverbs 10:4, 5; 13:4; 15:19; 18:9; 20:4)

All kinds of blessings await the diligent workman, but many evils attend the lazy loafer.

A. Poverty or Prosperity (10:4)

4. He becometh poor that dealeth with a slack hand: but the hand of the diligent maketh rich.

Two different Hebrew words for *hand* appear in this verse. The *slack hand* depicts a limp and open palm. The *hand of the diligent* is the hand braced for vigorous work. *Diligent* translates a Hebrew word that literally means "sharp" (it appears later in our printed text, in 13:4). It speaks of focused attention—sharply pointed and determined to achieve a goal.

Lazy hands produce nothing worthwhile to offset the lazy person's use of what others make available. In contrast, productive hands create wealth to be enjoyed not only by the workman but by others. Thus the apostle Paul urges Christians to do good work with their hands, so they will have something to give their needy neighbors (Ephesians 4:28). Paul himself could say that his own hands had earned a living, not only for himself but for those who accompanied him (Acts 20:34, 35).

B. Sufficiency or Shame (10:5)

5. He that gathereth in summer is a wise son: but he that sleepeth in harvest is a son that causeth shame.

Ruth, who labored throughout the harvest season gleaning barley and wheat to feed her mother-in-law and herself, provides an example encouraging to Bible readers everywhere (Ruth 2:1-7, 23). And she was not even a son!

The opposite and discouraging picture is that of a robust young man, snoring in the shade while the *harvest* goes on without him. What father would point with pride to such a man and say, "That's *my* son"?

We are reminded in statements such as these that our choices and actions do have consequences, often affecting others. On the one hand, there is the young person who honors his parents by following their good example and accepting good advice. On the other hand is the one who flaunts his disregard for his parents, bringing disappointment and *shame* to all who have contributed to his upbringing.

C. Privation or Plenty (13:4)

4. The soul of the sluggard desireth, and hath nothing: but the soul of the diligent shall be made fat.

Here the word *soul* indicates life with its natural appetites. These are similar in both the *sluggard* and the *diligent* person. For the one, there is no fulfillment because there is no productive labor to supply it. For the other, there is abundant satisfaction resulting from intelligent and vigorous application of godly principles. To *be made fat* may seem an undesirable condition to a health-conscious individual; however, it was synonymous in Hebrew thinking with contentment and plenty (see Psalm 92:13, 14; Jeremiah 31:14).

A second application of this verse may also be helpful. Even the lazy person occasionally wishes to do better, but when the time comes for action, he is a "no-show." Perhaps he is ashamed to be so lazy, but he would rather be ashamed than active. The industrious person, on the other hand, enjoys the rewarding fulfillment of his good intentions.

D. Hedge or Highway (15:19)

19. The way of the slothful man is as a hedge of thorns: but the way of the righteous is made plain.

What lies ahead in the way we travel? Is it a barricade of thorns, or is it a smooth, clear path? Proverbs 22:5 echoes this passage: "Thorns and snares are in the way of the froward: he that doth keep his soul shall be far from them."

The *hedge of thorns* may be only a figment of the *slothful* man's imagination, as he looks for excuses to avoid attempting what he has no desire to do. The hedge may also be figurative, referring to social "thorns." The sluggard's reputation may bar him from friendships and opportunities for advancement. No such difficulties face the dependable workman.

Still another possibility is that the verse literally describes the path to the sluggard's house. The ne'er-do-well does not keep his lane clear, and so it becomes a virtual bramble patch. The upright man keeps his roadway clear and open for himself and his neighbors.

Slothful and *righteous* are presented here as opposites. Thus, laziness and industriousness have spiritual significance. The Bible does teach a "work ethic." Let us honor the Lord by keeping our way clear of any unsightly "thorns."

E. A Destructive Duo (18:9)

9. He also that is slothful in his work is brother to him that is a great waster.

Slothful in his work describes the employee who shows up for his job and puts in his time, but is careless in his performance. *Brother* indicates one who is derived from the same source as another, is related to another, and is therefore like him. *Waster* indicates one who corrupts or destroys. Slovenly workmanship and destructive wastefulness are of the same family of evil deeds. Both are born of a selfish desire to have without earning and an unwillingness to accept responsibility.

F. Procrastination and Poverty (20:4)

4. The sluggard will not plow by reason of the cold; therefore shall he beg in harvest, and have nothing.

This verse describes a self-excusing procrastination on the part of *the sluggard*. To avoid an errand he does not want to perform, "The slothful man saith, There is a lion without, I shall be slain in the streets" (Proverbs 22:13). Here he uses *cold* weather as an excuse not to plow in the autumn. He then needs no excuse to avoid the grain *harvest* of the spring, because there is nothing to harvest.

Is farming the only occupation in which timing is vitally important, and a delay at one point in the cycle ruins the entire operation? What about the mathematics student who tries to go on with Algebra 2 after having slept through Algebra 1? Or the news reporter who looks vainly in the morning edition for the story he didn't quite finish by the evening deadline? He who loves to quote, "Better late than never," may find that "Late *is* never!"

III. Warnings From the Weeds (Proverbs 24:30-34)

Having begun the lesson with a positive example and exhortation, we conclude it with a negative example and a warning.

A. Signs of Neglect (vv. 30, 31)

30. I went by the field of the slothful, and by the vineyard of the man void of understanding.

Solomon's observations took him past neglected areas. His comment takes the usual form of Hebrew poetry, emphasizing his report by repetition. The *field* (producing food) and the *vineyard* (producing drink) were of primary importance in farming. The sorry condition of these areas reflects the negligence of one *man*, whose lack of accomplishment shows him to be lazy and/or lacking in good sense. "The sluggard is wiser in his own conceit than seven men that can render a reason" (Proverbs 26:16). He may seek to make up with a glib tongue what he lacks in reason, intelligence, and energy.

31. And, lo, it was all grown over with thorns, and nettles had covered the face thereof, and the stone wall thereof was broken down.

Left untended, a once fertile field will produce wild growth, including *thorns* and *nettles*, or weeds. Even a protective *stone wall* may fall victim at last to weather and vandals. Just a few months of neglect can cancel the accomplishments of many years of labor.

As a modern illustration, we may think of the rundown, graffiti-marred, and trash-littered areas of some inner cities. We may also consider the spiritual condition of nominal church members who have neglected to cultivate the presence of God through worship, study, generosity, and prayer. Is there not a similar growth of worldly weeds?

B. Looking and Learning (v. 32)

32. Then I saw, and considered it well: I looked upon it, and received instruction.

Even if the observer did not spend a lengthy period of time looking at the neglected field, the sight of it lingered in his memory. It became a warning against potential decline in the areas of life for which he was responsible, whether material or spiritual. So the thoughtful observer turned the lazy man's loss into gain for himself. The lesson to be learned is stated in the following two verses, also found in Proverbs 6:10, 11.

C. "Lose It Easy" (vv. 33, 34)

Our oft-heard advice to "take it easy" is revealed here as a way to "lose it easy." We should recall the sounder advice, from the first portion of our printed text, to observe and follow the example of the industrious ant.

33. Yet a little sleep, a little slumber, a little folding of the hands to sleep.

The reluctant riser promises not to *sleep* all day. He has just pushed the "snooze" button on his alarm. He avows that his *slumber* will not last long. Even if the folded *hands* induce genuine sleep, it will be for only *a little* while. So argues the constantly weary one; or perhaps so says someone in defense of the sleepyhead. But a well-established habit of laziness is not so easily dealt with. The resisted signal sounds less stirringly with every resistance, and so at last has no wakening force at all. Such resisting and excusing can become a habit that will yield only to the trumpet blast of Judgment Day.

34. So shall thy poverty come as one that traveleth; and thy want as an armed man.

Laziness, like other kinds of misbehavior, produces tragic consequences. The apostle Paul names this one in 2 Thessalonians 3:10: "If any would not work, neither should he eat." Income for anyone depends on production by someone! Without production there is *poverty*, and poverty becomes *want*. These come swiftly, surely, and violently upon the one who sleeps through the hours when he should be working.

Commentators present more than one explanation of the *one that traveleth*. He is said to be a swift runner who is sure to overtake the lingering sleepyhead. Perhaps he is a highway robber,

visual for
lesson 10

such as those who attacked the man in Jesus' parable of the Good Samaritan. Such a trouble-maker has a long history, including stagecoach bandits in pioneer America and "carjackers" in our own time.

Is the result of habitual laziness really this bad? Isn't the picture exaggerated? To those of us who have never experienced the hunger that comes to a neglected family, it may seem so. Besides, the costs of one person's laziness are usually distributed throughout the community by agencies and programs designed to protect the innocent. So everyone suffers somewhat, and the sluggard feels less guilty. Perhaps we should let the judgment fall where the Bible places it.

The Deadly Danger of Neglect

Proverbs 24:32-34 speaks of the danger of being lazy, careless, and sleepyheaded. The results will not be uncertain or unnoticed. Rather, they will be decisive, dramatic, and destructive.

It is not often recognized, but tragedies occur constantly because of indolence and inattention. We see a farm where once were neat fences, sturdy buildings, and well-tilled fields. Now, however, fences are sagging, buildings look decrepit, and the fields seem to be weedy and worthless. How did this happen? It happened because no one paid attention, no one "kept things up."

The same process affects city apartment houses. Eight- or ten-story apartments are leveled because they no longer can be used. The exterior may not look that bad, but inside paint is peeling, elevators do not work, and halls are dark, with rubbish scattered everywhere. What happened? No one cared, no one was willing to make an effort to maintain a decent appearance.

Hebrews 2:3 asks, "How shall we escape, if we neglect so great salvation?" Apathy and carelessness can result in the deterioration of our spiritual lives. Prayer, fellowship, Bible study, and worship are needed, so that we can maintain a vital, vigorous Christian life.   —J. G. V. B.

Conclusion
A. Where We Work

Not many of us do the kind of farm work described in Proverbs. Does that mean that today's "couch potato" is less rebuked than Solomon's "sluggard"? Not at all.

Jesus placed a high priority on work. He insisted on doing on the Sabbath what the Pharisees angrily called "work," and He told them, "My Father worketh hitherto, and I work" (John 5:17). Jesus' parables honored workmen,

and stressed the importance of a workman's faithful performance in his master's absence (Matthew 24:45-51; 25:14-30).

Paul identified himself as a manual laborer (Acts 20:34), and soundly rebuked those who used their theology as an excuse to get out of work (2 Thessalonians 3:6-15).

Christ began His messages to the seven churches in Asia (Revelation 2 and 3) by saying, "I know thy works," and concluded each message with exhortations to continue working faithfully to the end. But how does all of this apply to our Monday-to-Friday employment?

A great many of us do our work sitting down, and machines do what our muscles cannot. However, we can still resolve to be fully alert and faithful at our place of employment. If we are careless or inattentive on the job, we may ruin a project that involves dozens of other persons. Our actions may destroy machinery and/or merchandise, or even injure or kill other people. Each one should make his or her own checklist, beginning, "If I go to sleep at the switch . . ." Somewhere in the list of consequences should be this one: "I'll be dishonoring the Lord who gave His life to save me."

B. Prayer

Heavenly Father, give us a joy-filled purpose in working for You and with You. If our daily employment does not provide that kind of purpose, then may we find that purpose in the way we use what we earn. So may we labor in love, for Jesus' sake. Amen.

C. Thought to Remember

"I must work the works of him that sent me, while it is day: the night cometh, when no man can work" (John 9:4).

Home Daily Bible Readings

Monday, Aug. 3—Hear This, Lazybones! (Proverbs 6:6-11)
Tuesday, Aug. 4—Slackers Versus Workers (Proverbs 10:4, 5; 13:4; 15:19; 18:9)
Wednesday, Aug. 5—Lazy Ones Lose Control (Proverbs 12:24-28)
Thursday, Aug. 6—Children Known by Their Acts (Proverbs 20:4-11)
Friday, Aug. 7—Overgrown Vineyard (Proverbs 24:30-34)
Saturday, Aug. 8—Warning Against Idleness (2 Thessalonians 3:6-13)
Sunday, Aug. 9—Laborers With God Work With Care (1 Corinthians 3:12-20)

Learning by Doing

This page contains an alternate lesson plan emphasizing learning activities.
Classes desiring such student involvement will find these suggestions helpful.

Learning Goals

After this lesson, students should be able to:

1. Explain the importance of diligence in one's work and the dangers of neglect.

2. Cite contemporary examples of blessings to the industrious person that are missed by the lazy.

3. Schedule and accomplish some task that he or she has been putting off.

Into the Lesson

Option One: Cut pieces of poster board into the size and shape of bumper stickers. As the students enter the class, give them the pieces of poster board along with some felt-tip markers. Have your students create bumper stickers using popular or humorous statements about work. For example, "Whistle while you work"; "Idle hands are the devil's workshop"; "RETIRED: No Job, No Boss, No Work, No Money." Display their finished bumper stickers on a wall at the front of the classroom.

Option Two: Make copies of the following *Agree/Disagree* statements for each student. Or call their attention to the student book, where these statements can be found. The statements are designed to be somewhat debatable, so there may not be an absolutely "correct" answer.

1. *Agree/Disagree*. Most people who are in poverty are poor because they refuse to work.

2. *Agree/Disagree*. Christians have a responsibility to help the poor of the world.

3. *Agree/Disagree*. If a person does not work, he should not eat.

4. *Agree/Disagree*. Most people on welfare would work if they could find a job.

5. *Agree/Disagree*. Many Americans worship their work.

6. *Agree/Disagree*. Laziness is a major problem in the work force today

7. *Agree/Disagree*. I'm looking forward to retirement because I will not have to work anymore.

8. *Agree/Disagree*. Men have a greater tendency toward laziness than women.

9. *Agree/Disagree*. Churches have a hard time getting workers, because people are lazy.

10. *Agree/Disagree*. Being a workaholic is more of a problem to me than being lazy.

Have your class write their answers (when you are finished reading the statements, ask if anyone needs a statement repeated). Then have a different class member read each statement, and ask how many agree and how many disagree. Also ask, "Do you have a Biblical basis for your answer?" With some statements, you may be able to provide such a basis (Statement 3 is almost a direct quotation of 2 Thessalonians 3:10).

Make the transition into today's text by saying, "We have raised many interesting questions about laziness and work. The book of Proverbs has a lot to say about our view of work."

Into the Word

Option One: Many people who study this lesson today will be far removed from the images drawn from the agricultural setting of Proverbs. Have your students try to paraphrase today's verses from Proverbs using images and concerns of their own work place. For example, a student may write, "He who studies regularly during the semester is a wise student who will get good grades; but he who sleeps during class and skips homework assignments will be a disgrace to his family when he flunks out of school." For the same verse, a retailer may write, "He who works extra hours during the inventory will be a valuable employee; he who comes in late or takes a vacation during the Christmas rush will be looking for another job."

Option Two: Distribute several copies of older hymn books to your class members. Make sure the books have songs like "Toiling On", "Work for the Night is Coming", or "There's a Place for Every Worker." Have students do a hymn study. They are to compare ideas within today's lesson text with ideas found in these hymns. For example, the phrase, "Work, for the night is coming, When man's work is done" (from "Work for the Night Is Coming"), is similar to the principles found in Proverbs 10:5 and 20:4.

Into Life

Give each student an index card. Ask them to identify some task or project (perhaps something of a spiritual nature) that they have been putting off until a more appropriate time. Procrastination and laziness are often closely related. As a response to today's lesson, ask them to write the task or project on the card, along with the date by which they plan to have it completed.

Let's Talk It Over

The questions on this page are designed to encourage review of the lesson Scriptures and to promote discussion of the lesson by the class. The answers provided are only discussion starters. Let your class talk it over from there.

1. The lowly ant is set forth as an excellent example for our imitation, and indeed it is. How can an ant display the wisdom that it does? What lessons ought we to learn from it?

Of course, ants are not smart enough to be wise on their own. Their instinctive behavior reveals the wisdom of the Creator who bestowed them with characteristics that are necessary to their survival. When we observe the ways of the ant, we really are looking at God's wisdom. The chief lesson we learn from the ant is industriousness. We must clearly identify the tasks that we need to do and then be busy about doing them. We have many tasks, some at work, some at home and in the family, and others at church. Without being workaholics, we must be industrious just to get the most important tasks done, to say nothing of the jobs that help enrich our own lives and the lives of others. Moreover, we should do this on our own, without the need to be compelled by others.

2. The lazy person is called the brother of the waster (Proverbs 18:9). How is such a person like a thief and a destroyer? How does he rob himself? Are there areas of life in which our laziness has robbed others?

The lazy person steals time that should be devoted to productive labor, using it instead for idleness and slumber. Every person uses a portion of society's resources. If we are lazy, we produce less than we consume and so rob others. Society often is called on to help provide for the lazy person's dependents. Our laziness also destroys the things that we do have because we neglect to care for them. Laziness robs us in other ways. It keeps us from enjoying many of the comforts and pleasures we could easily afford if only we worked conscientiously. It keeps us from promotions. It robs us of self-respect and satisfaction. It robs us of respect from others. It robs us of the joy of helping others. To summarize, the cost of laziness is terribly and tragically high.

3. Work and financial prosperity often go hand in hand, but not always. Sometimes an individual's hard work is not fairly or adequately rewarded. How should we react when this happens to us?

This can happen for various reasons. A farmer can work hard, but see his work wiped out by bad weather or other circumstances. Likewise, a self-employed business person may work hard but be unsuccessful. In these kinds of situations, sometimes persistence is needed. At other times we may need to make drastic changes and channel our work in other directions. Employees are at the mercy of their employers; and some of us have experienced unfair treatment, in spite of being conscientious and industrious. This may tempt us to work halfheartedly, but we ought to give our full efforts for anyone who has employed us. Again, sometimes we may need to have the faith and courage to make a change of employment. No matter the situation, as Christians representing our Lord, we must dedicate all work to Him, giving no one cause to accuse us of laziness.

4. Our lesson text uses agricultural examples to illustrate industriousness, such as plowing and harvesting while the time is right. However, most of us today work in offices, factories, or other business settings rather than on farms. How do we demonstrate conscientious hard work in these settings?

Those of us who work on assembly lines have the speed of work set for us. In these settings, we must be certain to do the best quality of work that we can. If we work at jobs where our time is less structured, then we must be conscientious to work at a steady, reasonable pace, and not waste time daydreaming or in unnecessary visiting. Some workers have designated areas of responsibility, and of course these assignments should be fulfilled faithfully. We show hard work when we prepare adequately for presentations or meetings. We show hard work when we are willing to go beyond the minimum requirements to get the job done in the best way possible. Similarly, we can be alert to ways to improve procedures or designs. Being a hard worker does not require that we work an unreasonable amount of time. It does require that we give our best while we are at work. Such diligence is part of our Christian testimony. Remember Paul's exhortation: "Whatsoever ye do in word or deed, do all in the name of the Lord Jesus" (Colossians 3:17).

Helpful Speech or Harmful Speech

DEVOTIONAL READING: James 3:1-12.

LESSON SCRIPTURE: Proverbs 11:12, 13; 12:18; 13:3; 15:1, 2, 23, 28; 16:24; 17:27, 28; 21:23; 26:21, 28.

PRINTED TEXT: Proverbs 11:12, 13; 12:18; 13:3; 15:1, 2, 23, 28; 16:24; 17:27, 28; 21:23; 26:21, 28.

Proverbs 11:12, 13

12 He that is void of wisdom despiseth his neighbor: but a man of understanding holdeth his peace.

13 A talebearer revealeth secrets: but he that is of a faithful spirit concealeth the matter.

Proverbs 12:18

18 There is that speaketh like the piercings of a sword: but the tongue of the wise is health.

Proverbs 13:3

3 He that keepeth his mouth keepeth his life: but he that openeth wide his lips shall have destruction.

Proverbs 15:1, 2, 23, 28

1 A soft answer turneth away wrath: but grievous words stir up anger.

2 The tongue of the wise useth knowledge aright: but the mouth of fools poureth out foolishness.

23 A man hath joy by the answer of his mouth: and a word spoken in due season, how good is it!

28 The heart of the righteous studieth to answer: but the mouth of the wicked poureth out evil things.

Proverbs 16:24

24 Pleasant words are as a honeycomb, sweet to the soul, and health to the bones.

Proverbs 17:27, 28

27 He that hath knowledge spareth his words: and a man of understanding is of an excellent spirit.

28 Even a fool, when he holdeth his peace, is counted wise: and he that shutteth his lips is esteemed a man of understanding.

Proverbs 21:23

23 Whoso keepeth his mouth and his tongue, keepeth his soul from troubles.

Proverbs 26:21, 28

21 As coals are to burning coals, and wood to fire; so is a contentious man to kindle strife.

28 A lying tongue hateth those that are afflicted by it; and a flattering mouth worketh ruin.

Aug 16

GOLDEN TEXT: A soft answer turneth away wrath: but grievous words stir up anger.—Proverbs 15:1.

Wisdom for Living
Unit 3: Choose the Right Way
(Lessons 9-13)

Lesson Aims

This lesson should help the student to:

1. Summarize the benefits of wise speech and the dangers of foolish speech.

2. Describe the effects of harmful speech.

3. Choose a problem area in his or her own speech, and set about overcoming it.

Lesson Outline

INTRODUCTION
    A. A Great Gift
    B. Lesson Background
I. WORDS AND THE NEIGHBORS: BAD NEWS/GOOD
    NEWS (Proverbs 11:12, 13; 12:18)
    A. Contempt or Concealment (11:12, 13)
    B. Hurt or Healing (12:18)
    Speech That Blasts and Burns
II. WORDS AND THE SPEAKER: GOOD NEWS/BAD
    NEWS (Proverbs 13:3; 15:1, 2, 23, 28)
    A. Self-Control or Self-Destruction (13:3)
    B. Patience or Provocation (15:1, 2)
    Speech That Builds and Blesses
    C. Earned Enjoyment (15:23)
    D. Pondering or Pouring (15:28)
III. WORDS AND WELL-BEING: GOOD NEWS
    (Proverbs 16:24; 17:27, 28; 21:23)
    A. Complete Refreshment (16:24)
    B. Quiet Confidence (17:27, 28)
    C. Safety (21:23)
IV. WORDS AND WARFARE: BAD NEWS (Proverbs
    26:21, 28)
    A. Spreader of Strife (v. 21)
    B. Loveless Liars (v. 28)
CONCLUSION
    A. Words From the Heart
    B. Prayer
    C. Thought to Remember

Today's visual focuses on the good and bad uses of speech. It is shown in the next column.

Introduction

A. A Great Gift

"I just wish he could tell me what he wants!" This remark is often made about the victim of cerebral palsy or of a paralytic stroke, who struggles to say what his mind is thinking. He can make sounds, but the control of lips and tongue, which shape the sounds into understandable phrases, simply is not present. In his acute frustration, the victim yearns for a better share in the precious gift of speech that God bestowed on the creatures whom He made in His own image, so that they could converse freely with one another and with Him.

How thankful we should be for this gift! And how respectful we should be in our use of so great a treasure! To employ it viciously in defiance of God and mankind seems almost unthinkable. To use it carelessly in disregard of God and indifference to the rights and feelings of others is all too common. But God holds His children responsible for their use of this gift. Scripture makes this clear throughout the Law, the prophets, and especially the teachings of Jesus, who said, "By thy words thou shalt be justified, and by thy words thou shalt be condemned" (Matthew 12:37).

B. Lesson Background

Because of its very nature, the book of Proverbs should be expected to include a study in the careful use of words. Its theme is wisdom, and it begins by declaring that God our Creator is the source of wisdom (1:7). The first nine chapters develop that theme. The rest of the book is made up largely of brief statements about wise living. These are constructed in the style of Hebrew poetry—in balanced expressions, sometimes contrasting one thought with another, sometimes comparing similar thoughts, and sometimes repeating or adding one expression to another for emphasis. Picturesque figures of speech abound. It is a kind of teaching easy to hear, remember, and repeat, "tailor-made" for use in a family setting.

Many of the proverbs deal with speech. There are no lengthy discourses on the matter; instead, the subject is addressed in concise, hard-hitting statements. Today's lesson includes several of them. They fall into an interesting pattern.

A gentle answer
turns away wrath,
but a harsh word
stirs up anger.
Proverbs 15:1

visual for
lesson 11

I. Words and the Neighbors:
Bad News/Good News
(Proverbs 11:12, 13; 12:18)

The first three verses in our collection deal with the way that our speech affects those around us. The verses show the dark side (the bad news) first, then the light (the good news).

A. Contempt or Concealment
(11:12, 13)

12. He that is void of wisdom despiseth his neighbor: but a man of understanding holdeth his peace.

The despising referred to here is an attitude of contempt, expressed in words of derision. It may describe a deliberate effort to humiliate someone who is different, or it may represent a thoughtless attempt to appear clever by finding a victim to "put down." Either way, the proverb calls our attention to the fault described by a wise father who told his children, "Fun that is made at someone else's expense is not fun at all; it's just meanness."

The despising may also arise out of lack of *understanding*. It is the kind of problem a hospital once faced among some of its young doctors. The remedy was sought through "role-playing." Some of the interns were required to spend hours blindfolded, others with casts on their limbs, and so on. The physicians' understanding of and respect for the welfare of their patients improved noticeably.

13. A talebearer revealeth secrets: but he that is of a faithful spirit concealeth the matter.

Talebearer is a picturesque word indicating the kind of person who goes from place to place chattering and gossiping. Wise was the woman who sat with a classmate at an anniversary dinner and was asked in confidence about her age. "Can you keep a secret?" she whispered. "Oh, yes!" he responded. To which she answered, "So can I!"

The one who is *of a faithful spirit* respects the feelings of those about him, and would never violate the confidence of any—even if no one said, "Please don't tell." Of such a person it can be said, "Telling her something in private is like dropping it in a well so deep you can't even hear the splash."

B. Hurt or Healing (12:18)

18. There is that speaketh like the piercings of a sword: but the tongue of the wise is health.

This proverb is part of a larger context (vv. 13-20), dealing with the responsible and helpful use of speech—listening to good counsel, keep-

ing prudent silence, maintaining truthfulness, and speaking words that promote peace.

The present verse begins by noting the harm done by reckless words, which enter and wound the inmost being (compare with Proverbs 18:8; 25:18). This gives the lie to the adage that "sticks and stones may break my bones, but words can never hurt me." The bruises wrought by sticks and stones may be forgotten; destructive words will still hurt, long after they have been uttered.

It may be true that thoughtless speech, rather than deliberately harmful speech, does the largest overall damage to people. Exciting and interesting stories and comments are capable of great harm as well as great good. A quick wit and a clever tongue need the control of a kind and gentle spirit.

Fear of offending another must not, of course, cause one to abandon speech altogether. This gift was given for good purposes, among them the healing of the hurts of the wounded. So use generously the healing words of truth, encouragement, comfort, appreciation, good news, and loving exhortation. "A wholesome tongue is a tree of life" (Proverbs 15:4). Paul uses this comparison: "Let your speech be always with grace, seasoned with salt" (Colossians 4:6).

SPEECH THAT BLASTS AND BURNS

The book of Proverbs calls attention, not only to the potential for good in our speech, but also to the immeasurable damage that our words can cause. The book of James (3:3-9) warns us that the tongue is of all things most difficult to bring under control. While man may take great pride in his ability to control various members of the animal kingdom, he still finds himself stymied by the small, but mighty tongue: "the tongue can no man tame" (James 3:8).

In *The First Settler's Story* ("Farm Festivals"), Will Carleton wrote:

Boys flying kites haul in their white-winged birds;
You can't do that way when you're flying words.
"Careful with fire" is good advice, we know;
"Careful with words" is ten times doubly so.

William Cowper wrote, in his poem *Truth*, of a woman who slandered others:

Of temper as envenomed as an asp,
Censorious, and her every word a wasp;
In faithful memory she records the crimes,
Or real or fictitious, of the times;
Laughs at the reputations she has torn,
And holds them dangling at arm's length in scorn.

We never outgrow the need for the advice of the children's chorus: "Oh, be careful, little tongue, what you say."　　　　—J. G. V. B.

II. Words and the Speaker: Good News/Bad News
(Proverbs 13:3; 15:1, 2, 23, 28)

Five verses of our printed text deal with the effect of speech on the speaker. Four of them paint first the positive side of the picture, then the negative.

A. Self-Control or Self-Destruction (13:3)

3. He that keepeth his mouth keepeth his life: but he that openeth wide his lips shall have destruction.

James 3:3-9 warns us that the tongue is of all things most difficult to bring under control. The best policy is the cultivation of a lifelong habit of speaking the truth plainly—so honestly that all you need to remember are the facts, and so clearly as to make it hard for others to misunderstand you. Also remember to think before you speak, which will reduce the occasion to regret what you said, or to say, "Don't quote me!"

The alternative brings difficulty of all kinds, from strained personal relationships to the wartime destruction summarized in the motto: "Loose lips sink ships!" Proverbs 18:21 says, "Death and life are in the power of the tongue." Jesus said the same in terms of eternity: "By thy words thou shalt be justified, and by thy words thou shalt be condemned" (Matthew 12:37).

B. Patience or Provocation (15:1, 2)

1. A soft answer turneth away wrath: but grievous words stir up anger.

An *answer* may be given in response to any of several situations: a thought-provoking silence, a significant event, a question, or a challenge or comment. A *soft* (thoughtful, peaceable) reply works best when it prevents wrath from developing. It may be the first word in a tense situation, as when two cars collide in traffic. If the first word has already been spoken in anger, the *soft answer* becomes more difficult, but also more important. Thus did Gideon overcome the anger of the Ephraimites by gentle words of appreciation (Judges 8:1-3).

On the other hand, where proud arrogance responds harshly in a situation, peace disappears in a flurry of increasingly bitter accusations. Solomon's son Rehoboam lost a kingdom when he rejected the elders' counsel for "good words" and answered harshly to his subjects' plea for leniency (2 Chronicles 10:1-19).

2. The tongue of the wise useth knowledge aright: but the mouth of fools poureth out foolishness.

Not the possession of *knowledge*, but the wise employment of it in what one says, earns compliments here. Satan used his knowledge to entice Eve (Genesis 3:1-6), and he used it again to make trouble for innocent Job (Job 1:6-12). Pagans use their worldly knowledge as an excuse to deny their God and to engage in the vilest behavior (Romans 1:18-32).

Wisdom is shown, not only in what you know, but especially in when and how you present it. Wisdom knows better than to lecture on dieting during dinner in the house of a friend, or to scold a downcast companion immediately after a serious accident. Wise words adorn knowledge, making it attractive and pleasant. This describes what we find in Proverbs, with its powerful and poetic presentation of common truths. The *mouth of fools* does not know any such discipline as this. Having nothing to say and all day in which to say it, the thoughtless one turns on his vocal equipment and leaves it to flow like a constant geyser or to drone on like an untended television.

SPEECH THAT BUILDS AND BLESSES

The passages in today's lesson commend the benefit and blessing of wise and constructive speech. There is speech that soothes and strengthens, undergirds the good, and makes purity attractive.

One of the most famous Puritan preachers and scholars was Richard Baxter (1615-1691). He was a chaplain in the army of Oliver Cromwell during the war that overthrew Charles I of England. In his later years, he was imprisoned for eighteen months because of his faith.

Baxter is one of a great company of people who exemplified the "tongue of the wise" which "useth knowledge aright," not only of temporal but of eternal things. One of his most spiritual works is *The Saints' Everlasting Rest*, first printed in 1650. Here are some of his comments on life in the hereafter:

"We shall then have Rest without sleep and be kept from cold without our clothing . . . For God will be our heat and Christ our clothing . . . The Lord God will be our strength and the light of his Countenance will be health to our souls, and marrow to our bones. We shall then . . . have enlightened understandings without Scripture . . . For the Lord will perfect his law in our hearts, and we shall be all perfectly taught of God; his own will shall be our Law, and his own face shall be our light forever."

In a day when "the mouth of fools poureth out foolishness" with regularity, we need to fill our minds with words that nourish and uplift the soul.   —J. G. V. B.

C. Earned Enjoyment (15:23)

This verse is all positive; no negatives here.

23. A man hath joy by the answer of his mouth: and a word spoken in due season, how good is it!

It is important to note the preceding verse (22), not in our text: "Without counsel purposes are disappointed: but in the multitude of counselors they are established." If one has given good counsel, as Solomon did (1 Kings 3:16-28) and as Jesus did (Luke 20:19-26), he may take *joy* in the result of his words. His *answer* may be given, not in response to a question, but in the midst of an uneasy or uncertain silence, when people are in the throes of a crisis and need to hear supportive words.

A truly appropriate statement, given at exactly the right moment (*in due season*), brings pleasure to both the speaker and the hearer. The hearer will probably enjoy it more if the speaker's pleasure is not too evident. What, after all, was the purpose in the speaker's careful expression: to inform, instruct, comfort, or encourage the hearers? Or was it simply given for the purposes of self-promotion? May we keep the helpful purpose always in mind, and let the approval come as it will. "A word fitly spoken is like apples of gold in pictures of silver" (Proverbs 25:11).

D. Pondering or Pouring (15:28)

28. The heart of the righteous studieth to answer: but the mouth of the wicked poureth out evil things.

Righteous and *wicked* are used here in the same way that the words *wise* and *foolish* appear in other proverbs. Since God is the source of wisdom and the author of wise counsel, these terms do have a religious and moral quality. Think before you speak; it will prevent futile regrets in the future.

An old story tells of the preacher who needed many hours to prepare a five-minute speech, but was "ready right now" with a two-hour sermon. You may have heard that a good carpenter or seamstress will measure at least twice before cutting once. The measurement can be repeated, but the cutting, once done, is permanent. The spoken word, too, has a certain permanence.

How to Say It

EPHRAIMITES. *E*-fray-im-ites.
GIDEON. *Gid*-e-un.
NAOMI. Nay-*o*-me.

Have you ever noticed the degree to which extremists and enemies of Christian values seem to dominate the channels of public communication? The words of the verse before us suggest an explanation: While thoughtful folk consider their words, the open fountains of worldliness *poureth out* their distortions and perversions of the truth. They are not a majority; they just sound like one.

III. Words and Well-Being: Good News (Proverbs 16:24; 17:27, 28; 21:23)

In our next four verses, good speech is described in glowing terms. Nothing negative is present.

A. Complete Refreshment (16:24)

24. Pleasant words are as a honeycomb, sweet to the soul, and health to the bones.

Pleasant translates the Hebrew word from which comes the name *Naomi*. Proverbs 15:26 refers to *pleasant words* as coming from those who are pure. Thus they are *pleasant* to God as well as to those who speak them and hear them. Such words are not to be confused with flattery, which is typically deceitful and designed to trap an unwary victim.

The benefits of pleasant words are both spiritual and physical, affecting both the *soul* and the *bones*. The reference to a *honeycomb* brings to mind the experience of battle-weary Jonathan, who received strength to continue in battle after he found and ate some honey from a honeycomb (1 Samuel 14:27). Christians are urged to "minister grace" by their speech (Ephesians 4:29).

B. Quiet Confidence (17:27, 28)

27. He that hath knowledge spareth his words: and a man of understanding is of an excellent spirit.

The person who really knows his subject does not need to use many *words* in an effort to prove himself. He is not afraid of being shaken in his beliefs, and so can listen to what others have to say without feeling threatened. One thinks of the "strong, silent type," whose words are valuable—not carelessly tossed about, but treated carefully, as if they were costly jewels. So, too, the one who exhibits a genuine *understanding* of the people and circumstances about him is likely to be mild in manner: "swift to hear, slow to speak, slow to wrath" (James 1:19).

28. Even a fool, when he holdeth his peace, is counted wise: and he that shutteth his lips is esteemed a man of understanding.

Frequently the gift of speech is best exercised when not used. Consider Job's friends, who grieved with him in silence for seven days (Job 2:13). Only when they decided to speak did problems arise.

C. Safety (21:23)

23. Whoso keepeth his mouth and his tongue, keepeth his soul from troubles.

We cannot discuss the safety provided by a well-guarded *tongue*, without dwelling on the *troubles* avoided by such diligent guarding. Consider the plight of Peter, whose "mouth guard" failed him (Luke 22:54-62).

The good news is that anyone can turn his tongue to the truth, first in penitent confession, and then in wholehearted acknowledgment of the Savior who brings forgiveness. Such an individual is promised the gift of the Holy Spirit, by whose power one is able to use his speech to glorify God and build up others.

IV. Words and Warfare: Bad News (Proverbs 26:21, 28)

A. Spreader of Strife (v. 21)

21. As coals are to burning coals, and wood to fire; so is a contentious man to kindle strife.

Consider the verse immediately before this: "Where no wood is, there the fire goeth out: so where there is no talebearer, the strife ceaseth." One of the ingredients necessary to build a fire is proper and sufficient fuel. In this verse, two evils are set forth. One is *strife* within any group of people. The second is the *contentious* person, whose bitter tongue keeps the battle fires burning by continually adding fuel. The very presence of a fault-finding complainer or a negative critic is an irritant that makes harmony difficult in any setting. Sadly, such an individual's presence has often wrought havoc in the church, turning a formerly active congregation into a battlefield.

B. Loveless Liars (v. 28)

28. A lying tongue hateth those that are afflicted by it; and a flattering mouth worketh ruin.

Lying may involve slander (the effort to tear down someone's reputation) or flattery (slick, smooth speech used to deceive and manipulate another). Either way it is an expression of ill will—a desire to gain advantage for the liar at the victim's expense. It uses God's gift of speech for selfish purposes.

A person may lie about you because he hates you, or he may come to hate you because he has lied about you. It is common for any of us to resent someone we have injured. If I have lied about you, I tend to despise myself, and so am uncomfortable in your presence. I tend also to be afraid of you as one who may reveal my deceit. The answer to both lying and hatred is available through "speaking the truth in love" (Ephesians 4:15).

Conclusion

A. Words From the Heart

Good and helpful words have come to us from Proverbs, urging that we speak nothing except good and helpful words. We need something more, though, than mere exhortation. Just how are we to accomplish what is advised? At this point, as elsewhere, we must find the answer in Jesus: "How can ye, being evil, speak good things? for out of the abundance of the heart the mouth speaketh" (Matthew 12:34). If the heart is to support a steady flow of such words as Proverbs prescribes, then it must be filled with the proper thoughts. The primary source for these is Christ Himself. A heart in tune with Him will produce both good words and the good deeds to support them.

B. Prayer

What a responsibility You have laid upon us, O God, to use the gift of speech wisely. Equip us with the power to fulfill that responsibility in Christ. Amen.

C. Thought to Remember

"By thy words thou shalt be justified, and by thy words thou shalt be condemned" (Matthew 12:37).

Home Daily Bible Readings

Monday, Aug. 10—An Apt Answer Is Good (Proverbs 11:12, 13; 12:18; 13:3; 15:1, 2, 23, 28)

Tuesday, Aug. 11—Pleasant Words Like a Honeycomb (Proverbs 16:24; 17:27, 28; 21:23; 26:20, 21, 28)

Wednesday, Aug. 12—Do Not Swear At All (Matthew 5:33-37)

Thursday, Aug. 13—Judged According to Our Words (Matthew 12:33-37)

Friday, Aug. 14—Speech Seasoned With Salt (Colossians 4:2-6)

Saturday, Aug. 15—Words Acceptable to God (Psalm 19:7-14)

Sunday, Aug. 16—Fire and Evil Words Spread (James 3:1-12)

Learning by Doing

This page contains an alternate lesson plan emphasizing learning activities.
Classes desiring such student involvement will find these suggestions helpful.

Learning Goals

After this lesson, students should be able to:

1. Summarize the benefits of wise speech and the dangers of foolish speech.

2. Describe the effects of harmful speech.

3. Choose a problem area in his or her own speech, and set about overcoming that weakness.

Into the Lesson

Option One: Bring to class a stack of newspapers (or call some class members on the phone ahead of time and ask them to bring some newspapers with them to class). Distribute the newspapers to class members and ask them to skim the papers, looking for examples of stories where words were harmful and where words were helpful. Have them cut or tear out the stories and make a stack of each kind of story. Make the transition to the Bible study by saying, "Words can be either helpful or harmful. The book of Proverbs has much to say about the use of words and speech. Today's text collects fourteen verses that are found throughout Proverbs to summarize this truth. Let's see what wisdom Proverbs has to give concerning the use of the tongue."

Option Two: Ask two class members earlier in the week to open the class with a skit about two people talking on the telephone. Have them do the skit twice. The first time, they should use words in a harmful way (such as for gossip, lying, flattery, or betraying secrets). The second time, they should use words to help. For example, instead of gossiping, they should pray. Instead of flattery, they should speak truthfully but kindly.

Into the Word

Option One: Give each class member a piece of paper and a pencil. Tell them to divide the paper in half by drawing a line down the center. Have them make the heading, "Helpful or Harmful Speech?" Ask class members to list on one side specific times or occasions that make speech helpful, using today's text. On the other side of the line, list the times or occasions when speech is harmful, according to the text. In both cases, include the chapter and verse number. For example, the left side (Helpful Speech) might list, "Keeping a secret—Proverbs 11:13" or

"Speaking wise words that heal—Proverbs 12:18." The right side (Harmful Speech) could include, "Betraying a confidence—Proverbs 11:13" or "Telling a lie—Proverbs 26:28." (This activity is included in the student book.)

Option Two: Ecclesiastes 3:7 says that there is a time to be silent and a time to speak. This thought is expressed in our text today as well. Have your class members list a specific time to speak, a specific time to be silent, and a specific time to think before speaking. For example, Proverbs 16:24 says that pleasant words are like a "honeycomb." A pleasant greeting or remark can set the tone for a conversation, so it is a proper time to speak. Proverbs 11:13 says that we should not speak when we have something that should remain a secret. Proverbs 15:28 warns against speaking without thinking. A time for such thoughtfulness is when we are asked to do something that will take more time and energy than we can give to it. We need to look carefully at our calendar and our other responsibilities, and kindly but firmly say no.

Into Life

Option One: Ask your class members to list problems of the tongue described in today's printed verses. The list may include gossip (Proverbs 11:13), quarreling (26:21), and lying (26:28). Then from their list, have them mark the three problems that cause them the most trouble. From these three, have them select one that they will work on during this week. Ask them to copy that verse on an index card for ready reference.

Option Two: Ask your class members to write a message of helpful words to someone. Suggest the following: people absent from class, nursing home residents, homebound folks, preachers, elders, and other church workers. Provide stationery or religious greeting cards for this activity. Have stamps available as well to insure that the notes will be sent.

Option Three: Today's text includes a selection of fourteen verses on speech and words from Proverbs. You might think of them as "Fourteen Tongue Tamers." Ask class members to select three that would be most helpful for them in exercising "tongue control." Provide time in class for members to work in pairs, memorizing these "Tongue Tamers."

Let's Talk It Over

The questions on this page are designed to encourage review of the lesson Scriptures and to promote discussion of the lesson by the class. The answers provided are only discussion starters. Let your class talk it over from there.

1. Our lesson contrasts helpful speech and harmful speech. Suggest several examples of ways in which we can use the gift of communication in positive, helpful ways.

Words have a wonderful power to link hearts and minds together. Through the use of words, spoken or written, we reveal our hearts to others or share our knowledge with others. We can use this ability in many positive ways. One important way is to teach others what we have learned. Of course, the most important knowledge we can convey is the gospel. It is with the tongue that we confess Jesus as Lord. At other times we convey emotions with our words rather than knowledge and facts. With our words we encourage one another, showing that we believe in the discouraged person. In times of sorrow we comfort one another with words, telling the hurting person that we love him and share his sorrow. With words we show our approval and pleasure in others. We express appreciation. We pronounce blessings. It is often through speech that we pray to God.

2. Just as words can be helpful, they can be harmful. Suggest several ways in which a person can use speech to harm another.

Every good use of speech has a corresponding evil use. Instead of conveying wisdom and knowledge, the tongue can be used to dispense folly and falsehood. Many times this is done deliberately so as to mislead someone else. The Bible warns against false teachers who misuse the power of speech in this way. The tongue can be used to tell lies. Satan himself is the father of lies (John 8:44). While we can utter words to strengthen and comfort another, it is also possible to use words as weapons. Many a word has been spoken with the intent of hurting another person's feelings, discouraging him, insulting him, beating him down, or wounding him in some other way. Rather than showing acceptance and approval, words can be used to express rejection. Instead of prayer, some use words to accuse or curse God.

3. One of the secrets of being wise in our speech is to know when to talk and when to be silent. Formulate principles that we can use to guide ourselves in making this decision.

Perhaps the first thing we should consider is our motive. Is our motive right? Do we intend good or bad to come as a result of what we say? Needless to say, if our motives are wrong, it is best to keep silent. Assuming our motives are right, we also must consider the likely effect of our words. Will we be able to do good, or are even well-intentioned words likely to have a negative effect? Would it be better to wait until tempers have calmed or people have had time to think? Then keep silent. But if by speaking up we can hope to have a positive result, then by all means we ought to speak. Another question to ask ourselves is whether we actually have anything to contribute. Do we have information, knowledge, or insight that will be useful? Prudence can also guide us. During the Roman persecution of the church, the ancient Christians did not go through the streets shouting, "I'm a Christian." However, if arrested and questioned, they did not hesitate to confess their faith in Christ. It usually serves no good purpose to speak up if the only result will be to bring trouble on our own heads; but when pressed, we must always be ready to stand up for the Lord, no matter the cost.

4. Jesus tells us that our speech flows from our hearts and reveals the contents of our hearts (Matthew 12:33-37). Comment on the importance of listening to our speech and considering what it says about us.

Frequently, someone's speech, even a casual comment, gives us a deep insight into the person's soul. We ought to learn to listen to our own speech in the way that we listen to others. What would we think if someone else said what we just said? When we hear ourselves expressing truth, concern, love, or conviction, well and good. But if we hear ourselves speaking prejudice, anger, slander, lust, envy, pride, and the like, something is wrong. A good practice is to think back over the things we have said in the course of a day and analyze what made us say them. In this way we can identify deep-seated beliefs and attitudes that we may not have been acknowledging to ourselves. Knowing our faults and weaknesses is the first step in overcoming them, and listening carefully to what we say can be the first step in discovering them.

Slow to Anger or Quick to Anger

DEVOTIONAL READING: Matthew 5:21-26.

LESSON SCRIPTURE: Proverbs 12:16; 14:17, 29; 15:18; 16:32; 19:11; 22:24,25; 25:28; 27:4; 29:20, 22.

PRINTED TEXT: Proverbs 12:16; 14:17, 29; 15:18; 16:32; 19:11; 22:24,25; 25:28; 27:4; 29:20, 22.

Proverbs 12:16

16 A fool's wrath is presently known: but a prudent man covereth shame.

Proverbs 14:17, 29

17 He that is soon angry dealeth foolishly: and a man of wicked devices is hated.

. . . .

29 He that is slow to wrath is of great understanding: but he that is hasty of spirit exalteth folly.

Proverbs 15:18

18 A wrathful man stirreth up strife: but he that is slow to anger appeaseth strife.

Proverbs 16:32

32 He that is slow to anger is better than the mighty; and he that ruleth his spirit than he that taketh a city.

Proverbs 19:11

11 The discretion of a man deferreth his anger; and it is his glory to pass over a transgression.

Proverbs 22:24, 25

24 Make no friendship with an angry man; and with a furious man thou shalt not go;

25 Lest thou learn his ways, and get a snare to thy soul.

Proverbs 25:28

28 He that hath no rule over his own spirit is like a city that is broken down, and without walls.

Proverbs 27:4

4 Wrath is cruel, and anger is outrageous; but who is able to stand before envy?

Proverbs 29:20, 22

20 Seest thou a man that is hasty in his words? There is more hope of a fool than of him.

. . . .

22 An angry man stirreth up strife, and a furious man aboundeth in transgression.

Aug 23

GOLDEN TEXT: The discretion of a man deferreth his anger; and it is his glory to pass over a transgression.—Proverbs 19:11.

> *Wisdom for Living*
> Unit 3: Choose the Right Way
> (Lessons 9-13)

Lesson Aims

This study should enable class members to:

1. Explain why a quick temper is foolish and self-control is wise.

2. Suggest some factors that challenge a believer's self-control.

3. Pray about the area in one's life in which self-control is hardest.

Lesson Outline

INTRODUCTION
    A. What Moses Regretted Most
    B. Lesson Background
  I. FOUR FACES OF FOLLY (Proverbs 12:16; 14:17, 29: 15:18)
    A. Advertising Anger (12:16)
      Insult-Anger-Tragedy
    B. Acting in Anger (14:17)
    C. Furthering Foolishness (14:29)
    D. Stirring Up Strife (15:18)
  II. CREDITS OF SELF-CONTROL (Proverbs 16:32; 19:11)
    A. Higher Heroism (16:32)
    B. Disciplined Discretion (19:11)
  III. AVOIDING BAD COMPANY (Proverbs 22:24, 25)
  IV. COST OF LOW SELF-CONTROL (Proverbs 25:28; 27:4; 29:20, 22)
    A. Loss of Protection (25:28)
      Self-Control
    B. Attack From Three Sides (27:4)
    C. Hopelessness (29:20)
    D. Warring and Wickedness (29:22)
CONCLUSION
    A. A+ Anger
    B. Prayer
    C. Thought to Remember

The visual for Lesson 12 in the visuals packet calls attention to the importance of maintaining self-control. It is shown on page 437.

Introduction

A. What Moses Regretted Most

Moses, "the man of God" (Psalm 90:1), includes these words in his prayer recorded in Psalm 90: "Thou hast set our iniquities before thee, our secret sins in the light of thy counte-

nance" (v. 8). Moses knew on a painfully personal level what "secret sins" were. He murdered an Egyptian, then attempted to hide the body in the sand. His act, however, did not go unnoticed by a fellow Hebrew, and certainly not by God.

The Scriptures record other and more public occasions when Moses, noted for his meekness (Numbers 12:3), lost his temper. When he came down from Mount Sinai, carrying the stone tablets engraved with the Ten Commandments, he found the Israelites participating in idol worship. Moses' "anger waxed hot" and he smashed the tablets on the ground (Exodus 32:19).

More tragic was the occasion recounted in Numbers 20:1-13, when the Israelites complained of Moses' having brought them into the desert to die of thirst. God instructed Moses to gather the people before a great rock, to which he was to speak so that water would come forth. But instead, Moses spoke angrily to the people: "Must we [Moses and Aaron] fetch you water out of this rock?" (v. 10). Moses struck the rock twice with his rod, and abundant water came forth. Moses' angry outburst, withholding from God the honor of obedience to Him, cost him the opportunity to enter the promised land (Numbers 27:12-14; Deuteronomy 1:37; 3:23-27). Psalm 106:32, 33 records how Israel provoked Moses, "so that he spake unadvisedly with his lips." Even God's greatest heroes are not exempt from the cost of temper tantrums.

B. Lesson Background

From the collections of brief sayings in Proverbs, today we examine a dozen pungent observations dealing with an important subject: the wisdom of self-control and the folly of yielding to sudden anger. We will see some meaningful overlapping between last week's study of the quick tongue and this week's treatment of the quick temper. Either may stir up the other.

These topics are timeless and universal. They apply where people live with people.

I. Four Faces of Folly
(Proverbs 12:16; 14:17, 29; 15:18)

A. Advertising Anger (12:16)

16. A fool's wrath is presently known: but a prudent man covereth shame.

The kind of *fool* referred to in these verses is the self-confident, headstrong, God-forgetting one represented in the Hebrew word, *evil.*

The preceding verse (15) provides this explanation of a fool's behavior: "The way of a fool is right in his own eyes." Without listening to others, or considering what would be in his own

---

How to Say It

EVIL (Hebrew). *eh*-vill.
KESIL. (Hebrew). *kess*-ill.
NAAMAN. *Nay*-uh-mun.
NABOTH. *Nay*-bawth.

---

best interests, the fool blurts out what comes first to his mind, especially if he has been antagonized in any way. Usually he is eager to broadcast whatever has irritated him. Folk who would never have known of it otherwise will quickly hear his version of what happened!

The reaction of the *prudent man* is quite different. Compare the verse before us with Proverbs 29:11: "A fool uttereth all his mind: but a wise man keepeth it in till afterward." If the victim ignores an insult, he will encourage others to ignore it as well. When you are offended, hold your tongue long enough to rehearse the model prayer of Matthew 6:9-13, particularly, "Forgive us our debts, as we forgive our debtors."

Revenge is not the godly way. Jesus both taught and showed the way to pull the teeth of slander, not only by ignoring it, but also by returning good for evil. Paul gives similar counsel: "Be not overcome of evil, but overcome evil with good" (Romans 12:21).

INSULT-ANGER-TRAGEDY

Alexander Hamilton and Aaron Burr were two of the most outstanding men in the early history of the United States. Hamilton was an important military figure during the Revolutionary War, and played an especially significant role during the siege of Yorktown. After the war, he became a respected lawyer and served as Secretary of the Treasury during George Washington's administration. His efforts in the latter capacity proved particularly valuable.

Aaron Burr's father served as president of Princeton College, and his mother was a daughter of the noted preacher and theologian Jonathan Edwards. Burr served in the army during the Revolutionary War, but was too loose in morals for General Washington, who disapproved of his behavior. However, he enjoyed a successful military career, becoming a lieutenant-colonel. He entered the field of law and was Attorney General of New York State. From 1781 to 1797 he served in the United States Senate. In 1800 Burr ran for President against Thomas Jefferson. The election was so close that the decision was turned over to Congress. On the thirty-sixth ballot, Jefferson won. Burr was made vice-president.

In 1804 Burr was defeated in a bitter campaign for governor of New York. He demanded that Hamilton retract what he considered as slanderous statements that had damaged his hopes of winning. He then challenged Hamilton to a duel with pistols, which took place on July 11, 1804, at Weehawken, New Jersey. As a result of the duel, Hamilton was mortally wounded, and Aaron Burr lived under a cloud ever after.

Truly, "a prudent man covereth shame," or "overlooks an insult" (Proverbs 12:16, *New International Version*). One of the most unsavory incidents in American history resulted from the refusal to heed this wise counsel.   —J. G. V. B.

B. Acting in Anger (14:17)

17. He that is soon angry dealeth foolishly: and a man of wicked devices is hated.

The quick-tempered man not only speaks in haste, but also acts in haste, controlled by the passion of the moment. In our own time, sudden anger all too often erupts in fighting, mayhem, and even murder. As one man observed of another, "The smoke of his anger puts out the light of his judgment." It was so with Naaman the leper, when he was directed to dip seven times in the Jordan to receive healing. He first "went away in a rage" (2 Kings 5:12), and would have missed his blessing entirely if better counsel had not prevailed.

On the other hand, *wicked devices* characterize the crafty man who, instead of committing harmful acts out of sudden rage, deliberately plots mischief against his neighbor. One such crafty plotter was Jezebel, who devised and carried out a plan to have Naboth killed so that his vineyard could become a vegetable garden for her husband Ahab (1 Kings 21:1-16).

Not all *devices* are wicked, though. The Hebrew word used in this verse can indicate planning for good as well as for evil, and is so used in Proverbs (1:4; 2:11; 3:21; 5:2), where it is rendered "discretion." God has given to each of us the gift of creativity; are we using it for good or evil purposes?

C. Furthering Foolishness (14:29)

29. He that is slow to wrath is of great understanding: but he that is hasty of spirit exalteth folly.

Patience (being *slow to wrath*) is a characteristic of our infinitely wise God (Psalm 103:8), and it is to be learned by those who follow Him. Consider Job as a notable example of such patience (James 5:11). Whereas Job's friends exhibited *folly* in their attempts to counsel him, Job himself spoke "the thing which is right" concerning God (Job 42:8). Such a person does not respond rashly to any circumstance. He weighs the evidence before reaching a conclusion and establishing a position.

The "hothead," on the other hand, becomes a promoter of foolishness. He elevates folly to the throne and is ruled by it. His anger has an intoxicating effect like that of alcohol, often readily evident to everyone but himself.

D. Stirring Up Strife (15:18)

18. A wrathful man stirreth up strife: but he that is slow to anger appeaseth strife.

Most of us have known him: the bully on the playground always looking for a fight and seldom disappointed. Some of that kind never outgrow the tendency, and live and die defending their "rights" against all competitors. The sharp edge of antagonism is in their voices, even when it is not so intended. For them, life is one continual battleground.

Jesus blessed persons of a different sort, saying, "Blessed are the peacemakers: for they shall be called the children of God" (Matthew 5:9). Scripture provides a good example in Abram, who became disturbed when competition for pastureland caused contention between his herdsmen and those of his nephew Lot. Abram suggested division of the land, and gave the first choice to Lot. He was then willing to accept what Lot did not want (Genesis 13:2-13). It takes two to make a quarrel, and that is one activity in which God's person should refuse to participate.

II. Credits of Self-Control (Proverbs 16:32; 19:11)

A. Higher Heroism (16:32)

32. He that is slow to anger is better than the mighty; and he that ruleth his spirit than he that taketh a city.

Here is a declaration to ponder, memorize, and follow to its conclusion. Just how is the patient, forbearing person *better* than a heroic warrior or the general who leads his troops to conquest? The comparison is not so much between persons as it is between traits of personality. "Wisdom is better than weapons of war" (Ecclesiastes 9:18); its accomplishments are more lasting. Patience and peaceable self-discipline are virtues useful to any individual in any career and in any stage of life.

B. Disciplined Discretion (19:11)

11. The discretion of a man deferreth his anger; and it is his glory to pass over a transgression.

Verse 12, immediately following, provides a hint for understanding this one. It says, "The king's wrath is as the roaring of a lion; but his favor is as dew upon the grass." The wise attendant of the king knows better than to get all upset at his majesty's morning tirade. He knows that if he rides out the royal storm, there will be a return to normally favorable conditions. If something really serious needs attention, it can be handled better when things have cooled down.

What is true of royal matters can be applied generally to all human relationships. Wisdom manifests itself in patience. Viewed from the Christian's perspective, Jesus provides forgiveness from God to man, and the power for His followers to provide forgiveness to others.

III. Avoiding Bad Company (Proverbs 22:24, 25)

24, 25. Make no friendship with an angry man; and with a furious man thou shalt not go; lest thou learn his ways, and get a snare to thy soul.

Proverbs 1:10-19 warns "my son" against making friends with those who engage in violence and robbery. One may think of the modern gang's appeal to lonely youth, hungry for *friendship* and identification. When that desire leads, however, into more than casual association with *an angry man*, results can be disastrous. Even a brief partnership is ill-advised. Who knows when the fury of such a man will explode, harming the friend who suddenly becomes a foe?

There is, however, a greater danger, as recognized by the saying, "Birds of a feather flock together." Sometimes persons come together because they are already alike; sometimes they become alike through association. Proverbs 13:20 says, "He that walketh with wise men shall be wise: but a companion of fools shall be destroyed." So a second danger of one's association with anger-ridden folk is that their anger may become part of his character as well. Paul warns, "Evil communications corrupt good manners" (1 Corinthians 15:33).

We may always hope, of course, that the patience of the patient person will rub off on Mr. Hothead, and the result will be positive. That may be a little like hoping that a tug-of-war will be won by the team pulling upward on a slope. "The righteous is more excellent than his neighbor: but the way of the wicked seduceth them" (Proverbs 12:26). An angry disposition has been called an infectious and dangerous disease. A diseased person may benefit from observing good health in his neighbors, but for real healing one needs to see a physician. Let's expose Mr. Hothead to massive doses of Jesus!

IV. Cost of Low Self-Control
(Proverbs 25:28; 27:4; 29:20, 22)

Our final four verses remind us of the dangers associated with uncontrolled anger. The harm comes first to the angry one, then gravitates toward his neighbors. No compliments are found in these verses.

A. Loss of Protection (25:28)

28. He that hath no rule over his own spirit is like a city that is broken down, and without walls.

This is the "flip side" of what we found in Proverbs 16:32, which described the patient spirit as more valuable than military skill.

The man with uncontrolled anger would be quick to insist that he is not defenseless at all. He is constantly defending himself, his rights, and his property against attackers, both real and imagined. But in fact he is exposed, always spending his energy and resources on aimless attacks, and holding nothing in reserve for purposeful uses.

The discipline to absorb attacks patiently and to use resources in mounting an effective response is the kind of defense that the hothead does not have. How indeed will the undisciplined spirit ever protect its owner against Satan's arsenal of temptation? To be without discipline is to be without defense.

SELF-CONTROL

During one period of our lives, we lived within walking distance of a major league baseball park. In addition, we were able to secure tickets to many games at greatly reduced prices. We attended quite a number of games and were rather devoted baseball fans.

One becomes increasingly aware of the great importance of self-control and of control in general while watching baseball. The pitcher's greatest success comes when he can so control his pitches that they go where he intends to throw them. Usually when a good game is pitched, the analysis includes the phrase, "He had great control today."

Batting also involves control. One must not swing at pitches that are too high or low, or outside or inside of the strike zone. Often the batter starts to swing and tries to stop. If he cannot, the umpire will call a strike.

One of the most vivid indications of the need for self-control is when "bad calls" are made about whether runners were "safe" or "out" as they crossed first base after hitting the ball and running to the base. Sometimes discussions become quite heated. Bases have been torn up, helmets thrown wildly in the air, dirt kicked over the umpire's shoes, and players ejected from the game for abusive language. How often do we see dire evidences of the problems a man creates for himself, when he "hath no rule over his own spirit."   —J. G. V. B.

B. Attack From Three Sides (27:4)

4. Wrath is cruel, and anger is outrageous; but who is able to stand before envy?

This is the second of two verses, each naming a pair of obstacles, then naming a more serious third one. The previous one reads as follows: "A stone is heavy, and the sand weighty; but a fool's wrath is heavier than them both." The mental and emotional burden of uncontrolled anger is harder to bear than any physically demanding weight.

Then comes the verse before us. The Hebrew word translated *wrath* is somewhat stronger than the word rendered *anger*. Sudden wrath does enormous harm, whether emotional, physical, or both. It is indeed *cruel*. Anger is described as *outrageous*, a word rendered as "overwhelming" in the *New International Version*. Perhaps we should think of this as a sustained anger, or smoldering resentment, that continues harm to another beyond the bounds of reason. Both sudden wrath and resentful anger are used by the obsessive abuser of those about him. And both of these evils are like a two-edged sword, wounding both the user and those against whom they are directed.

All of this is introductory, however, to the purpose of the verse: to declare the greater damage done by a special kind of malice—*envy*, or jealousy. Here Solomon seems to echo what he may have heard from his father David concerning King Saul and the murderous jealousy that poisoned Saul against David. It controlled Saul from the time of David's victory over Goliath (1 Samuel 18:6-9), and destroyed Saul's relationship with his own son Jonathan (1 Samuel

A man's wisdom gives him patience; it is to his glory to overlook an offense.
Proverbs 19:11, NIV

visual for lesson 12

20:30-34). Think of the irony: a king who could not rule himself!

Proverbs 6:34 speaks of the jealous "rage of a man," responding to someone who commits adultery with his wife. At times such jealousy is not so evident. Ordinary anger has been compared to a roaring lion, whose presence is readily known and can be escaped; envy is compared to a scorpion, lurking in hidden places, but always seeking the opportunity to use its venomous sting.

You may not always know the basis of someone's jealousy toward you, thus making it quite difficult for you to defend against it. You can, however, resist the temptation to entertain a vindictive malice in the face of this or any other form of anger. If there is ill-will between you and another, let it be his problem, not yours.

C. Hopelessness (29:20)

20. Seest thou a man that is hasty in his words? There is more hope of a fool than of him.

Being *hasty in . . . words* may be the quick response by which one makes known his irritation (recall Proverbs 12:16, studied earlier). The person so described in that verse is called a *fool* (*evil* in Hebrew). In the verse before us, we are told that *there is more hope* for a *fool* (*kesil* in Hebrew) than for someone who speaks impulsively. The *kesil* appears to be stupid and dull, but to some degree still teachable. And as long as he will listen and learn, there is more hope for his ultimate salvation than there is for the sharper, loud-mouthed *evil*, whose only interest is in justifying himself, his opinions, and his alleged innocence before the whole wide world.

D. Warring and Wickedness (29:22)

22. An angry man stirreth up strife, and a furious man aboundeth in transgression.

This verse relates the kind of detestable harvest associated with the *furious*, quick-tempered, hotheaded man. His record overflows with *transgression*—a word which describes going beyond established standards. He is typical of the rebellious spirit that delights in offending and horrifying the law-abiding citizens around him. The preventive is to "cool it"—in Christ!

Conclusion

A. A+ Anger

"Slow to Anger or Quick to Anger" has been our lesson topic. God becomes angry, but not suddenly: "The Lord is merciful and gracious, *slow to anger*, and plenteous in mercy. He will not always chide: neither will he keep his anger for ever" (Psalm 103:8, 9). Jesus looked "with anger" on those who used a man with a withered hand in an attempt to catch Him breaking the Sabbath law and then refused to answer Jesus' question, "Is it lawful to do good on the sabbath days, or to do evil?" (Mark 3:4, 5).

Jesus earns an A+ grade on controlling His anger in all the circumstances He faced. He did not respond at all when insulted or injured personally (1 Peter 2:23); but He drove out the money changers who dishonored God and His temple (John 2:13-17). Jesus refused to take sides in a family dispute over an estate settlement, but gave teaching to prevent such disputes from occurring (Luke 12:13-21). Two brothers whom Jesus called "sons of thunder" were among His disciples (Mark 3:17), and one of them (John) became known as the apostle of love. If we, like Moses, tend sometimes to be short-tempered, we have access to the Christ whom Moses and Solomon could only anticipate. Let's bring our problems to Jesus for His solution.

B. Prayer

In awe we praise You, our heavenly Father, for the steadfast love that tempers Your wrath against us and forgives us of our sins. Thank You for Jesus, in whom we see that patient love most perfectly revealed. Help us to reflect His patience in dealing with folk around us. In His name. Amen.

C. Thought to Remember

"He that is slow to anger is better than the mighty; and he that ruleth his spirit than he that taketh a city" (Proverbs 16:32).

Home Daily Bible Readings

Learning by Doing

This page contains an alternate lesson plan emphasizing learning activities.
Classes desiring such student involvement will find these suggestions helpful.

Learning Goals

After this lesson, students should be able to:

1. Explain why a quick temper is foolish and self-control is wise.

2. Suggest some factors that challenge a believer's self-control.

3. Pray about the area in one's life in which self-control is hardest.

Into the Lesson

Read the following case studies about anger to your class. Ask them to listen carefully and then give suggestions for the people involved.

Case Study 1. The level of stress in Tom's job just seems to keep climbing. Today his boss came in with more complaints about productivity. Every time Tom's department meets its goal, the goal is simply raised. Everyone is edgy—especially Tom. When his boss started yelling, it was all Tom could do to hold his tongue. When he got home, the stress accelerated. The bicycle was in the driveway. Supper wasn't ready. The kids' music was blaring. The dam finally broke and Tom exploded in anger.

Case Study 2. Ed and Carol were on their way to a dinner party at the home of Ed's boss. They got a late start. Then it began to rain. Before long, they found themselves lost. Carol tried to read the map, but the dome light barely illuminated the page. When a truck came around the curve on their side of the road, Ed completely lost it. Swearing at the driver, he finally pulled to a jerky stop by the side of the road.

Make the transition to today's Bible study by saying, "Anger is perhaps the most difficult emotion to manage. The examples that we have just considered could be episodes from almost any family. What kind of advice would you give these families? What Bible verses or principles would be helpful to them? As we turn to the book of Proverbs this morning, let's look for ways to help these families."

Into the Word

Option One: Make a list contrasting the characteristics of an angry person and a person who is slow to anger. For example, Proverbs 12:16 says that a fool shows his annoyance "presently," or "at once" (*New International Version*). In contrast, a person who is slow to anger overlooks insults rather than overreacting. Proverbs

25:28 tells us that an angry person is as defenseless as a city without walls, while the person who is slow to anger has a wall of protection in his self-control.

Option Two: Make a list of the blessings that come to a person who is slow to anger. In contrast, list the problems that come to a person who is easily angered. For example, Proverbs 22:24, 25 says that just being around a hot-tempered man can ensnare you and make you more apt to be easily angered. In contrast, Proverbs 15:18 says that a person who is slow to anger "appeaseth strife."

Option Three: List the names that Proverbs uses to describe a person who is easily angered. Then make a list of the names used to describe the person who is slow to anger. For instance, Proverbs calls the angry person a "fool" (12:16), one who "dealeth foolishly" (14:1), a "wrathful man" (15:18), and a "furious man" (22:24; 29:22). Proverbs calls the person who is slow to anger "prudent" (12:16), of "great understanding" (14:29), "better than the mighty" (16:32), and an individual of "discretion" (19:11).

Into Life

Option One: Have students write out an action plan for responding to stressful situations, using insights from today's verses. They should focus on how to respond without losing control. For example, one may decide ahead of time to overlook insults rather than let them upset him, based on what Proverbs 19:11 says. Or, using Proverbs 29:20, one might resolve to stop and think before blurting out an answer in anger. Have students, based on today's passages, make up five steps that could be taped inside an appointment book, purse, or wallet.

Option Two: Have class members select three of today's verses to memorize for use in anger management. Pass out cards for class members to use in writing out the verses that they want to memorize. Have them work in small groups of three or four. (Often people who are unable to memorize on their own can do so with the help of others.) Have the group read a specific verse aloud several times. Then go around the group with each person saying just one word. Always say the book, chapter, and verse reference before and after repeating the verse, so that you can remember where it is found.

Let's Talk It Over

*The questions on this page are designed to encourage review of the lesson
Scriptures and to promote discussion of the lesson by the class. The answers
provided are only discussion starters. Let your class talk it over from there.*

1. Proverbs 16:32 says that a person who is slow to anger is better than a mighty man, and a person who rules his own spirit is better than the one who conquers a city. Explain what this means and why it is true.

In this verse the term "better" does not mean complete superiority in every way. Rather, the idea is that when we control our spirits so that we are slow to anger, we have done something that is more important and in some ways harder than being a mighty warrior who conquers a city. It is one thing to overcome an enemy through strength or strategy, but it is quite another to gain control over oneself. It is such a drastic step that Paul referred to it as crucifying self (Galatians 5:24). The goal is to bring all aspects of our personality under such control that we always act in such a way as to obey God.

2. A person with a quick and hot temper often causes strife at home, at work, in church gatherings, or any place else he happens to be. How can cooler heads react so as to keep a situation from getting totally out of control?

Remember that when anger and a quick temper take over, reason is temporarily set aside. With many people, it seems to work best just to remain silent and let them rant and rave until the flare-up has burned itself out. If we control our own tempers and do not add fuel to the fire by persistent argument, it will probably go out more quickly. Sometimes the issue can then be addressed more calmly. At other times, it may be best to drop the disputed issue until a later time. If the angry person is in a position of authority, it may be wisest to agree without argument (except in ethical or moral matters). Family situations are more difficult because of the emotions involved, but the same principle applies: It is better to have one angry person than two. If there is danger of violence, it is best to try to get out of the presence of the enraged person.

3. As our text points out, self-control is very important and beneficial. How can we learn to control anger instead of letting it control us? Suggest practical steps to accomplish this goal.

As with any problem, the first step is to admit that the problem exists. If we find ourselves frequently red-faced or shouting at other people, then we ought to recognize that we have a problem. It is possible, however, to change and to overcome a hot temper. We must begin by confessing our sin to God. We must repent by making a firm resolution to control our anger. When we feel ourselves beginning to get angry about something, we must not speak out. We must keep silent. In some situations, we may want to ask a trusted friend to give us a signal when he feels we are beginning to lose control. It may help to walk away from the situation for a time. Of course, we must pray and seek God's help. We *can* win this battle if we submit to the Lord, call on His help, and imitate His example.

4. Jesus is the perfect example of self-control over anger. Name some occasions when Jesus controlled Himself, and tell the lessons we can learn from these examples.

Several examples of Jesus' exemplary self-control occurred during the final hours prior to His crucifixion. When Jesus was betrayed by Judas, even though He knew full well what was going on, He did not grow angry. In the upper room, Jesus appealed to Judas to stop his treachery before it was too late. When the soldiers came to arrest Him in the garden, He held His peace while Judas kissed Him. When the other apostles deserted Him, or when Peter denied Him, Jesus did not grow angry or become filled with wrath. In the same way, we should learn to be patient and forgiving with our friends, even when they sorely disappoint us or hurt us. After His arrest, Jesus, though innocent, was mistreated in many ways, ending in His crucifixion, yet He held His temper. He could have called legions of angels to destroy His enemies, but instead He prayed for their forgiveness. When we find ourselves persecuted for righteousness' sake, we also must hold our tempers. Perhaps there is hope for our persecutors if we respond as Jesus did. When facing the money changers in the temple, or the hypocritical Pharisees, Jesus rebuked them very severely, but He did not allow His anger to flare out of control. When we face wicked men, false teachers, and the like, whom we must oppose, we also may be incensed by their evil deeds, but we must keep our anger under control.

Wisdom for Family Relationships

DEVOTIONAL READING: Psalm 128.

LESSON SCRIPTURE: Proverbs 4:1-5; 6:20; 10:1; 22:6; 31:26-28.

PRINTED TEXT: Proverbs 4:1-5; 6:20; 10:1; 22:6; 31:26-28.

Proverbs 4:1-5

1 Hear, ye children, the instruction of a father, and attend to know understanding.

2 For I give you good doctrine, forsake ye not my law.

3 For I was my father's son, tender and only beloved in the sight of my mother.

4 He taught me also, and said unto me, Let thine heart retain my words: keep my commandments, and live.

5 Get wisdom, get understanding: forget it not; neither decline from the words of my mouth.

Proverbs 6:20

20 My son, keep thy father's commandment, and forsake not the law of thy mother.

Proverbs 10:1

1 The Proverbs of Solomon. A wise son maketh a glad father: but a foolish son is the heaviness of his mother.

Proverbs 22:6

6 Train up a child in the way he should go: and when he is old, he will not depart from it.

Proverbs 31:26-28

26 She openeth her mouth with wisdom; and in her tongue is the law of kindness.

27 She looketh well to the ways of her household, and eateth not the bread of idleness.

28 Her children arise up, and call her blessed; her husband also, and he praiseth her.

GOLDEN TEXT: Train up a child in the way he should go: and when he is old, he will not depart from it.—Proverbs 22:6.

Lesson Aims

This study should equip class members to:

1. Summarize the instructions in these passages for both parents and children.

2. Cite contemporary challenges that Christian families face.

3. Pinpoint a specific step that can be taken to follow God's guidelines in their family relationships.

Lesson Outline

INTRODUCTION
    A. Back to School
    B. Lesson Background
  I. A FATHER'S TEACHING (Proverbs 4:1-5)
    A. Let Children Receive It (vv. 1, 2)
    B. As Father Received It (vv. 3, 4)
    C. Seize It and Treasure It (v. 5)
 II. TEAM TEACHING (Proverbs 6:20; 10:1; 22:6)
    A. Both Parents' Responsibility (6:20)
      Good Advice—Bad Examples
    B. Both Parents' Reward (10:1)
    C. Lasting Results (22:6)
III. A MOTHER'S MULTIPLE MINISTRY (Proverbs 31:26-28)
    A. She Speaks Wisely (v. 26)
    B. She Works Diligently (v. 27)
    C. She Receives Honor (v. 28)
      Mothers As Models
CONCLUSION
    A. Where Will You Find It?
    B. Prayer
    C. Thought to Remember

The visual for Lesson 13 highlights the importance of setting a godly example in the home. It is shown on page 445.

Introduction

A. Back to School

Are school bells ringing again at your house, marking the end of summer vacations? If so, you may hear some grumbling about the return to schedules, studies, and homework. Less freely expressed may be the anticipation of meeting friends, old and new; teachers, known and unknown; and subjects waiting to be explored.

The young folks' education has been going on all summer, though, in a very significant way. The benefit of additional family time has provided special opportunities for some valuable instruction. If the opportunity was used purposefully, it taught the values most meaningful to Dad and Mom. If not, it conveyed the idea that these values are not a priority. Parents do teach, and if the teaching follows Biblical patterns, it is excellent teaching.

Consider the Biblical pattern found in Deuteronomy 6. God prescribed the Law He gave to Moses as the primary subject matter for the day in, day out family conversation, and for written notices to be displayed where they could not be missed (verses 4-9). Families do talk about something, and they teach by what they talk about (and by what they *don't* talk about!).

Just because the children are headed back to school does not mean that Dad and Mom can quit teaching. It means only that the school-related subjects and activities should become incorporated in what they teach. Lack of contact between home and school indicates indifference, to the disadvantage of both the school and the family. Let prayerful concern go to school with those who go, and let it include the ones with whom they spend their time until they return home.

B. Lesson Background

The Proverbs texts before us today declare the rewards that accompany faithful obedience to God's teaching. They affirm the timeless principles on which sound family life is built—principles designed to prevent the problems that are pointed out elsewhere in Proverbs and throughout Scripture.

If today's lesson is to influence our family relationships, we must see the texts as the words of a father—most naturally Solomon—to his children, including his arrogant son Rehoboam (1 Kings 11:43—12:20). To interpret Proverbs as the words of a wise teacher to various youth whom he addressed figuratively as "sons" removes much of its value and practicality. Let's give the wise king credit for meaning what he said when he addressed "my son."

Today's passages come from the beginning, middle, and end of Proverbs. First studied are texts (4:1-5 and 6:20) from the introductory collection of essays (chapters 1-9). Then we have two verses taken from the very beginning (10:1) and near the end (22:6) of the teachings called, "The Proverbs of Solomon" (10:1—24:34). Our final passage comes from a twenty-two verse poem praising a "virtuous woman." It is the theme with which the book of Proverbs ends.

I. A Father's Teaching
(Proverbs 4:1-5)

Proverbs 4:1-5 deals directly with the young person's responsibility to receive and follow parental instruction. This requires the father's faithful teaching of the appropriate material.

A. Let Children Receive It (vv. 1, 2)

1. Hear, ye children, the instruction of a father, and attend to know understanding.

To *hear* demands more than being quiet while another is talking. Sometimes rendered "hearken," this term includes listening attentively to, accepting, and obeying what is taught. *Instruction* involves the discipline that includes chastening. The *understanding* to be gained refers to much more than just information; it includes perceiving and applying what is learned. Psalm 34:11 records a similar invitation from David: "Come, ye children, hearken unto me: I will teach you the fear of the Lord."

2. For I give you good doctrine, forsake ye not my law.

The father's right to be heard rests on more than his age and paternal authority. There is eternal value in what he is saying. *Doctrine* renders a Hebrew word that literally means, "that which is taken (grasped)." It is *good* in that it comes from a good source (ultimately the revelation of God), it is conveyed with a good spirit, and it leads the practitioner in a good way toward good results.

Law translates the Hebrew word *torah*, and refers to essentially the same material as *doctrine*. Because of its great worth, it is never to be neglected, and certainly not to be cast aside as having no value. One never outgrows the need for study of and devotion to the Word of God.

B. As Father Received It (vv. 3, 4)

3. For I was my father's son, tender and only beloved in the sight of my mother.

The father's authority is enhanced when he can say that he has been where the child is now, and knows something of the road. The child, in contrast, knows nothing yet about being an adult or a parent.

Solomon was certainly not the *only* son of David, and perhaps not the only child of his mother Bathsheba. He was, however, named by the prophet Nathan as "Jedidiah" (meaning, "beloved of the Lord"), giving him a rather special status. The fact that he was the first child of David and Bathsheba (following the child who was conceived out of their adulterous relationship) also marked him as distinctive. First Chronicles 22:9 records a special promise of

God to David concerning Solomon: He was to be a "man of rest," whose reign would be characterized by "peace and quietness." These conditions would give him the opportunity to build the temple of God in Jerusalem. According to 1 Chronicles 22:5, David referred to Solomon as *tender*—receptive, impressionable, teachable, and obedient. For this reason, David made certain that his son was prepared beforehand for such an impressive undertaking as building the temple.

An equally close bond existed between Solomon and his mother, who secured David's promise that Solomon would succeed him to the throne. She protected that promise against those who wanted to challenge Solomon's right to reign (1 Kings 1:5-31).

4. He taught me also, and said unto me, Let thine heart retain my words: keep my commandments, and live.

The *commandments* issued by the loving parent will provide the listening child with the instruction he needs for life and living. *Retain my words*, not simply long enough to give the right answer on the next test so as to receive a good grade and credit toward a diploma, but for recall years later when you will say, "Now I see what he was talking about!" Learning is for life, now and for eternity. It begins and ends with God.

C. Seize It and Treasure It (v. 5)

5. Get wisdom, get understanding: forget it not; neither decline from the words of my mouth.

Wisdom and *understanding* combine to include all the qualities of spirit, mind, and character that Proverbs associates with practical godliness (Proverbs 3:13-18). It deals with *what* is to be done and *how* to do it. More important, it deals with *why* a person should choose one course of action and avoid another.

To *decline* is rendered "swerve" in the *New International Version*. Do not wander from the path of wise teaching. Do not deal carelessly with God's wisdom. It is like a priceless heirloom passed from generation to generation within a royal family. There is one important difference: Wisdom is not to be kept in storage

---

How to Say It

ABSALOM. *Ab*-suh-lum.
BATHSHEBA. Bath-*she*-buh.
JEDIDIAH. Jed-ih-*die*-uh.
TORAH (Hebrew). *tor*-uh.

for bringing out only to display it to a new generation. This treasure gains value only as it is vigorously used and generously shared with family and friends. Then it will become a blessing to an ever-increasing circle of recipients.

II. Team Teaching
(Proverbs 6:20; 10:1; 22:6)

Father and mother are both involved in the family's teaching of wisdom. Responsibilities are shared, as well as rewards.

A. Both Parents' Responsibility (6:20)

20. My son, keep thy father's commandment, and forsake not the law of thy mother.

From the Hebrew words used here, it would be hard to distinguish between the father's *commandment* that the *son* is to *keep* (guard and preserve), and the mother's *law* that he is not to *forsake* (push aside or discard). Keeping also involves obedience, while forsaking also implies disobedience. The language of this verse would indicate equal and parallel roles for the two parents. This does not mean, however, that fathers and mothers must do their teaching in the same way and at the same time. Fatherly strength and motherly tenderness still have their distinctive contributions to a child's upbringing.

The verse before us introduces a passage (6:20-35) that proceeds to deliver a warning against the allurements of the "strange" (adulterous) woman. It is a warning of major importance to family relationships (Exodus 20:14), and it receives strong emphasis in Proverbs (7:1-27, for example). It is also a warning to be sounded equally by fathers and mothers as they convey God's wisdom to their youngsters. The family, whether ancient or modern, lives or dies with the observance or disregard of what God says concerning adultery.

GOOD ADVICE—BAD EXAMPLES

If we think of Solomon as the father giving advice to the "son" who is often addressed in Proverbs, we may find ourselves "turned off" by his example. The Scripture records how Solomon's many wives "turned away his heart after other gods" (1 Kings 11:4). In addition, they must have contributed to the huge expenditures of his kingdom. The oppressive taxes required to maintain such a lifestyle led to the revolt that tore the nation of Israel apart after Solomon's death. Such irresponsible behavior would seem to cast a pall over any advice Solomon might give about married life.

However, we must realize that many times, good advice and wise counsel may be given by people who do not always exemplify their counsel in their own living. To some extent, we all can speak of a higher ideal of conduct than we can always carry out. Paul advises, "Do all things without murmurings and disputings" (Philippians 2:14). Yet he and Barnabas had a disagreement concerning whether to take John Mark with them on a missionary journey. "The contention was so sharp between them, that they departed asunder one from the other" (Acts 15:39).

Sometimes a person's failure to follow the good advice he gives produces results that make his advice look all the more valid and vital.

—J. G. V. B.

B. Both Parents' Reward (10:1)

1. The Proverbs of Solomon. A wise son maketh a glad father: but a foolish son is the heaviness of his mother.

This verse introduces the extensive collection of brief, miscellaneous sayings labeled *The Proverbs of Solomon*. Have you been a good and successful parent? You will know by the results seen in your children. Consider this an application of Jesus' teaching: "Ye shall know them by their fruits" (Matthew 7:16).

Wise and *foolish* are terms with strong moral implications. The wise son responds to good and moral teachings; the foolish does not. The one brings to both of his godly parents a level of satisfaction that cannot be achieved by material wealth, political power, or worldly acclaim. The other brings a feeling of frustration, defeat, and depression, which one senses in the lamentation of David at the death of rebellious Absalom (2 Samuel 18:33).

C. Lasting Results (22:6)

6. Train up a child in the way he should go: and when he is old, he will not depart from it.

To *train* young children means to implant a series of impressions that will establish a lifelong pattern of responses. Again, this is a ministry to which both parents must be committed. A mother's natural association with her children provides many opportunities to direct their conduct. The father's role in training is stressed throughout Proverbs, and is reiterated in Ephesians 6:4: "Ye fathers, provoke not your children to wrath: but bring them up in the nurture and admonition of the Lord."

A more literal translation of the verse before us says, "Start, or initiate, a child in accordance with his way." In order to direct the child successfully in the path he needs to follow, you must consider his capacities at the point where you are dealing with him. No two children are exactly alike at any age, and no one child is exactly like what he was a year ago. The parent can be encouraged by the fact that living by God's standards will benefit the child, no matter what his age or stage of life may be.

The reward for good training in the principles of godliness is partly immediate and partly long-term. If the early impressions have been adequate, and supported by sound reason and a consistent example, they will be recalled to serve as guiding principles in due time. May you see this happen in those you love.

III. A Mother's Multiple Ministry (Proverbs 31:26-28)

An impressive array of womanly virtues, with motherhood idealized, appears in the final chapter of Proverbs (31:10-31). In the three verses that are included in our printed text, we see the godly woman's notable accomplishments on behalf of her family, and the honors given her by her family.

A. She Speaks Wisely (v. 26)

26. She openeth her mouth with wisdom; and in her tongue is the law of kindness.

The *wisdom* with which the godly woman controls her speech has been noted in verses 11 and 12 of this chapter: "The heart of her husband doth safely trust in her, . . . She will do him good and not evil all the days of her life." She will never violate his confidences as one of the city councilmen (v. 23)!

Wisdom provides both the material and the motive for the godly woman's conversation. Therefore she will be a loving and patient instructor to her children and her household personnel, and a respected counselor among her neighbors. There is no gossip, slander, or idle chitchat here, but only orderly, purposeful, and helpful speech.

The *law of kindness* is elsewhere translated as the "teaching of kindness" or "faithful instruction." This woman's words are ruled by truth and by a spirit of goodwill.

B. She Works Diligently (v. 27)

27. She looketh well to the ways of her household, and eateth not the bread of idleness.

Our ideal wife and mother does with her hands what her faithful heart directs and what her helpful speech indicates. In fact, the reader of this passage may be led to wonder how she finds time to do any talking at all. She shops wisely for the best of fabrics, and sews garments and other materials from them (vv. 13, 22, 24). She brings to her table the best of foods from distant markets (v. 14). She gets up before daylight to prepare meals and to direct the day's activities in her household (v. 15). She produces homespun fabrics (v. 19), so that all in her house are clothed in winter with the best and warmest of garments (v. 21). And despite such concerns for her own family, she does not ignore the needy (v. 20).

Nothing, therefore, that affects her family's welfare escapes the attention of this industrious mother. If the *bread of idleness* means lounging in luxury, that is no part of her diet. Whether at home with her family or conducting business on their behalf, she is the hardest working person in the place. And it is clear that the central focus of her hard work is her family. They are the primary reason for her diligence.

If any among us is still tempted to apply terms like "narrow," "dull," and "unfulfilling" to the career of a wife and mother, let him or her read this passage again!

C. She Receives Honor (v. 28)

28. Her children arise up, and call her blessed; her husband also, and he praiseth her.

In the tributes of the godly mother's *children* to her, let us consider two possible applications. Thinking in modern terms, we envision the family observance of Mother's birthdays with noisy demonstrations by all the children still at home. Then comes the time when "arising up" means growing to adult status and becoming productive citizens in their own right. These grateful ones now reach back with warm "thank yous" to the mother who did so much to make them what they have become: "Mother, we owe it all to you!"

Blessed is a term sometimes used to recognize a woman's high fulfillment through her children—especially as applied to Mary of Nazareth, the mother of the Son of God (Luke 1:28, 42). For the children themselves to pronounce such a blessing upon their mother is a high honor indeed. In the praise of our heroine, the children

visual for
lesson 13

are joined by the *husband* and father, who says, "Many women do noble things, but you surpass them all" (Proverbs 31:29, *New International Version*).

To this the inspired writer adds a final word of appreciation: "Favor is deceitful, and beauty is vain: but a woman that feareth the Lord, she shall be praised. Give her of the fruit of her hands; and let her own works praise her in the gates" (Proverbs 31:30, 31).

MOTHERS AS MODELS

Susanna Wesley already was caring for a very large family when the *fifteenth* child was born to her and her husband Samuel, a British clergyman. He was named John and eventually became the founder of what today is known as Methodism.

Susanna was a devout, dedicated woman who reared her family with love and care. Not only did her son John become a great preacher and leader, but her son Charles became the author of many hymns of beauty and power. Among them are, "Hark! the Herald Angels Sing," "O for a Thousand Tongues to Sing," "Christ the Lord Is Risen Today," "Ye Servants of God, Your Master Proclaim," "Jesus, Lover of My Soul," "A Charge to Keep I Have," "Love Divine, All Loves Excelling," and "Soldiers of Christ, Arise." Both John and Charles graduated from Oxford University.

Consider these timely words of Mattie Vose Hall, who writes of two temple builders—one erecting a material building, another working on a child's character:

Gone is the builder's temple,
  Crumbled into the dust;
Low lies each stately pillar,
  Food for consuming rust.
But the temple the mother builded
  Will last while the ages roll,
For that beautiful unseen temple
  Was a child's immortal soul.

—J. G. V. B.

Conclusion

A. Where Will You Find It?

Where in the real world will you find the kind of family relationships depicted in today's texts from Proverbs? Where is the ideal teaching father whom we see reflected in chapters 1-9—the one who was himself an attentive and responsive son, drinking in the godly wisdom of his own father and now conveying it to his equally attentive and responsive children? He would be hard to find in the households of David, Solomon, and their successors in Israel and Judah. David's heart was steadfast in its commitment to God, and Solomon excelled in God-given wisdom; yet each displayed major flaws of character that contradicted some of his own best teaching. The same questions would have to be asked about the husband-wife, father-mother relationships described in the book. As for the ideal wife and mother depicted in chapter 31, the inspired writer raised his own question in verse 10: "Who can find a virtuous woman?" Then he proceeded to describe that elusive ideal.

Where, then, shall we find all of what we are seeking? Only through the power and the provision of God. This is what the New Testament tells us: "All have sinned, and come short of the glory of God; being justified freely by his grace through the redemption that is in Christ Jesus" (Romans 3:23, 24). That justification does produce among us families remarkably close to the ideal depicted in Scripture. We all know some of them. And that justification will continue to produce more and better families—ours among them—as we give it the opportunity.

B. Prayer

Thank You, our heavenly Father, for families. Bless them, as only You can bless them, to be Your kind of people in the world. Help fathers to live and to teach according to Your wisdom, help mothers to bring their special abilities to the family partnership, and help children to obey their parents in the Lord, for Jesus' sake. Amen.

C. Thought to Remember

"Honor thy father and thy mother: that thy days may be long upon the land which the Lord thy God giveth thee" (Exodus 20:12).

Home Daily Bible Readings

Monday, Aug. 24—Pass On Wisdom (Proverbs 4:1-5; 6:20)
Tuesday, Aug. 25—Train Children in the Right Way (Proverbs 10:1; 22:6; 30:17; 31:26-29)
Wednesday, Aug. 26—Home and Family, Gifts of God (Psalm 128:1-6)
Thursday, Aug. 27—Rituals of a Family in Nazareth (Luke 2:39-52)
Friday, Aug. 28—Grandchildren Crown the Aged (Proverbs 17:1-6)
Saturday, Aug. 29—Family Members in the Church (1 Timothy 5:1-8)
Sunday, Aug. 30—The True Family of Jesus (Matthew 12:46-50)

Learning by Doing

This page contains an alternate lesson plan emphasizing learning activities.
Classes desiring such student involvement will find these suggestions helpful.

Learning Goals

As your class members participate in this lesson, they should be able to:

1. Summarize the instructions in these passages for both parents and children.

2. Cite contemporary challenges that Christian families face.

3. Pinpoint a specific step that can be taken to follow God's guidelines in their family relationships.

Into the Lesson

Society exerts tremendous pressure on the family today. While "family values" are popularly affirmed at times, the Biblical model of a family is under attack. Many want to redefine the concept of "family." Even in the church, some speak in favor of family values, but live with little regard for what the Bible teaches.

Option One: Have your class members pretend that they are writing an answer column for a Christian publication. Provide paper and pens for them. (Space is provided for this activity in the student book.) The question they are to answer is found in this letter from a reader: "My wife and I have just become Christians, and we are anxious to reorganize our family according to what the Bible says. Where should we start and what should we do? We have three children—ages six, three, and three months."

Ask several of your class members to read their answers aloud. Affirm any answers that are supported in Scripture. Have students think about how to provide such support if it is needed. For example, if someone says, "Have daily Bible reading," then ask, "Do you have a passage in mind that teaches that idea?" The purpose is to prepare the class to look to the Bible for answers to questions concerning the family.

Option Two: Provide paper and pencils for each member of your class. Ask each to draw his or her family tree. Beside each person, list a practical truth learned from that person. The truth could be positive or negative. (Space is also provided for this activity in the student book.)

When students are finished, ask three volunteers to share their trees with the class. Make the transition to today's Bible study by saying, "Our Scripture for today's class spells out the duties and responsibilities of each member of the family in following the way of wisdom and truth. As we study today, evaluate your own family experience by what we see in the Word."

Into the Word

Option One: Draw a cartoon or stick figure beside each verse in today's text to illustrate how the principle or principles in that verse could be lived out in the family. Some will be delighted to have an art activity. Others will participate if you encourage them to focus on the process of drawing rather than the finished product.

Option Two: Have your class write a song using the melody of a familiar hymn, and words from the ideas in Proverbs that we are examining today. Prepare for this project by listing important concepts from today's text, such as parents' responsibility to teach their children and children's responsibility to listen and obey. To illustrate how this assignment might be carried out, the following ideas could be set to the melody of "'Tis So Sweet to Trust in Jesus," thus creating a song like this:

> 'Tis so sweet to teach our children,
>   Morning, evening, noon and night.
> Show them how to live the Bible,
>   Turn from wrong and choose the right.
> Jesus, help me teach my children
>   Wisdom give me for the task.
> Jesus, help me teach my children
>   Proverbs' wisdom this I ask.

Into Life

Members of your class collectively have a wealth of ideas to help parents pass their faith along to the next generation. It would be a good idea to ask some members in advance to be ready to share ideas that have worked for them.

Another need is for grandparents to develop ways to influence and help their children in training their grandchildren. For example, ask grandparents to share favorite gift items that positively influence both their children and grandchildren, such as compact discs, tapes, and videos.

Also, ask your class members to identify the character qualities that they want to pass on to their children and grandchildren. Your class's list could include love, truth, respect, diligence, and obedience. (Space is provided for this activity in the student book.)

Let's Talk It Over

The questions on this page are designed to encourage review of the lesson Scriptures and to promote discussion of the lesson by the class. The answers provided are only discussion starters. Let your class talk it over from there.

1. Our lesson admonishes parents to teach and train their children, but what is it that parents are to teach? Suggest topics that should be included in this curriculum.

One very important topic is doctrine, for everything that we do is ultimately determined by what we believe. This includes such subjects as God, Jesus, creation, the Bible, the gospel, and other important Biblical topics. Another essential subject is personal ethics, that is, God's commands on how to live. Ethical topics include honesty, sexual purity, respect for others, kindness, faithfulness, and the like. We must be careful not to shy away from sensitive or embarrassing subjects, because our youth will form an opinion whether we talk about such matters or not. It is up to us to teach them God's truth. A third vital area of teaching today is apologetics—the evidences and reasons supporting our faith in God, Jesus Christ, the Bible, and the resurrection and other miracles. We must teach young people apologetics so that their faith will not be destroyed by unbelievers.

2. No matter how good the training offered at home, children must receive it in order for it to guide their lives. How can parents help insure that their children accept their instruction?

The foundation for effective instruction is a relationship of mutual love. Our children may not always like what we make them do or prohibit them from doing, but if they know that our motive is love and not spite, anger, selfishness, or meanness, they are much more likely to comply and learn. It is critical that we live by the same standards we urge upon our children. Paul advises fathers not to frustrate their children through excessive harshness (Ephesians 6:4). This requires that parents have flexibility in applying many of the rules that they establish. After all, rules are a means of teaching God's commands and guiding conduct. They are not ends in themselves. Still, there are times when parents must stand firm regardless of the protests of their children. Parents must be consistent, united, and avoid being arbitrary.

3. Parents are to teach their children the eternal truths of God's Word. But they also convey many traditions and opinions. How insistent should parents be that their children accept their traditions and ideas? How can we distinguish between truths and traditions?

Some facts never change. God will always be the Creator. Theft, murder, and adultery will always be wrong. Jesus will always be the only way of salvation. Such truths are essential matters of faith. We should give every effort to insuring that our children learn and accept these essentials. But many of the things we do and believe are our own traditions and preferences. Examples are styles of church music and worship or of hair and clothing fashions. Such styles vary from place to place and from generation to generation. Which of us does everything exactly like our parents or grandparents? Parents can help avoid tension and a potential "generation gap" by being flexible in such matters. The old saying, "In essentials unity; in opinions liberty; in all things love," is a good goal for which parents and children should aim.

4. Today's text speaks of a virtuous woman. Identify the three characteristics mentioned in the text. How do today's changing husband/wife roles affect these? What is the general principle that guides such a woman?

The three characteristics specifically mentioned in the text are wisdom, kindness, and industry. Of course, all of these are important today as well. The virtuous woman gives no attention to foolishness. Instead, she recognizes what is worthwhile and pursues these things. As a result, she is able to speak with wisdom both to her children and her husband. The virtuous woman also is filled with kindness, freely bestowing her gentle touch, soft words, and tender ministrations to family and stranger alike. Various examples of industry are cited throughout Proverbs 31:10-31. The specific tasks may be different today, but it still takes a lot of hard work to make a household and family function; and much of this work is still the responsibility of the woman. Each couple forms its own "division of labor," which may be more or less traditional, but both must contribute. The general principle upon which the godly woman operates is that she does whatever she can for the welfare and happiness of her family. Blessed are the husband and children of such a woman.